Chapters 1-3

HARCOURT, BRACE & WORLD, INC.

New York | Chicago | San Francisco | Atlanta

John M. Blum

YALE UNIVERSITY

Bruce Catton

EDITOR, *American Heritage*

Edmund S. Morgan

YALE UNIVERSITY

Arthur M. Schlesinger, Jr.

THE CITY UNIVERSITY OF NEW YORK

Kenneth M. Stampp

UNIVERSITY OF CALIFORNIA, BERKELEY

C. Vann Woodward

YALE UNIVERSITY

Part One

The National Experience

SECOND EDITION

A HISTORY OF THE UNITED STATES TO 1877

MAPS BY HARRY SCOTT

ISBN: 0-15-565691-0

Library of Congress Catalog Card Number: 68–11241

Printed in the United States of America

A Note

On the Paperbound Edition

This volume is part of a variant printing, not a new or revised edition, of *The National Experience*, Second Edition. Recently many of the users of that book, which has hitherto appeared only in one-volume form, have requested a two-volume version that would enable them to fit the text into the particular patterns of their teaching and scheduling. To meet that request, the publishers have prepared this printing, consisting of two separate volumes that exactly reproduce the text of the one-volume version of *The National Experience*, Second Edition. The first of these volumes begins with the discovery of America and continues through Reconstruction. The second volume, repeating the chapter on Reconstruction (Chapter 15, "The Aftermath of War"), carries the account forward to the present day. The variant printing, then, is intended as a convenience to those instructors and students who have occasion to use either one part or the other of *The National Experience*. Consequently, the pagination and index of the one-volume version, as well as its illustrations (except for the color plates), maps, and other related materials, are retained in the new printing. The difference between the one-volume and the two-volume versions of the book is a difference only in form.

Preface

Men make history. Their ideas and their hopes, their goals and contrivances for reaching those goals, shape all experience, past and present. The Indians, the first Americans, had to decide, by deliberation or by default, how to use the continent and its extraordinary resources. So have the successors of the Indians and the children of those successors—the early European settlers, the English colonists, the men and women of the new United States, and the generations that have followed them. Each generation has committed the nation to a complex of policies, some the product of thought and debate, others of habit or inadvertence, still others of calculated or undiscerning indifference. As the nation has grown, as its population has diversified, its economy matured, and its responsibilities multiplied, questions of national policy have become more difficult to understand but no more troubling. It took long thought and hard debate to settle the issues of independence, of democratic reform, of expansion, of slavery, of union itself, of control of private economic power, of resistance to totalitarianism across two oceans. All these issues and many more have made up the national experience.

This book endeavors to recount and explain that experience. It examines both the aspirations (often contradictory among themselves) and the achievements (often less grand than the best hopes) of the American people. It examines, too, the ideas, the institutions, and the processes that fed hope and affected achievement. It focuses on the decisions, positive and negative, that reflected national goals and directed national purposes, and consequently it focuses continually on the men who made those decisions, the men who made history. The book emphasizes public policy, but the history of public policy perforce demands continuing discussion of the whole culture that influenced it.

The authors of this book believe that a history emphasizing public policy, so conceived, reveals the fabric and experience of the past more completely than does any other kind of history. They believe, too, that an emphasis on questions of public policy provides the most useful introduction to the history of the United States. In the light of those convictions they have agreed on the focus of this book, on its organization, and on the selection and interpretation of the data it contains. The structure of the separate parts and chapters is now chronological, now topical, depending on the form that seemed most suitable for the explanation of the period or the subject under discussion. The increasing complexity of public issues in the recent past, moreover, has persuaded the authors to devote half of this volume to the period since Reconstruction, indeed more than a third to the twentieth century.

The authors have elected, furthermore, to confine their work to one volume so as to permit instructors to make generous supplementary assignments from the abundance of excellent monographs, biographies, and "problems" books now readily and inexpensively available. Just as there are clear interpretations of the past in those books, so are there in this, for the authors without exception find meaning in history and feel obliged to say what they see; the truth cannot lie halfway between right and wrong. The authors also believe that, especially for the beginning student of history, literature is better read than read about. Consequently, in commenting on belles-lettres and the other arts, they have consciously stressed those expressions and aspects of the arts relevant to an understanding of public policy. Finally, they have arranged to choose the illustrations and the boxed selections from contemporary and other sources in order to enhance and supplement not only the text but its particular focus.

This is a collaborative book in which each of the six contributors has ordinarily written about a period in which he is a specialist. Yet each has also executed the general purpose of the whole book. Each section of the book has been read and criticized by several of the con-tributors. This revision has profited from the careful attention and advice of several friends and from many helpful suggestions from users of the first edition. But not even a collaboration as easy and agreeable as this one has been can erase the individuality of the collaborators. Each section of this book displays the particular intellectual and literary style of its contributor; each contributor has been permitted, indeed urged, to remain himself. The ultimate as well as the original responsibility for prose, for historical accuracy, and for interpretation remains that of the author (in one case the authors) of each section of this book: Edmund S. Morgan, Chapters 1–6; Kenneth M. Stampp, Chapters 7–12; John M. Blum and Bruce Catton, together, Chapters 13–14; C. Vann Woodward, Chapters 16–21; John M. Blum, Chapters 15, 22–27; and Arthur M. Schlesinger, Jr., Chapters 28–33.

JOHN M. BLUM, Editor

New Haven, Connecticut

A Note

On the Suggestions for Additional Readings

The lists of suggested readings that follow the chapters of this book are obviously and intentionally selective. They are obviously so because a reasonably complete bibliography of American history would fill a volume larger than this one. They are intentionally so because the authors of the various chapters have tried to suggest to students only those stimulating and useful works that they might profitably and enjoyably explore while studying this text. Consequently each list of suggested readings points to a relatively few significant and well-written books, and each list attempts to emphasize, in so far as possible, books available in inexpensive, paperback editions—books whose titles are marked by an asterisk.

Use of the suggested readings, then, permits a student to begin to range through the rich literature of American history, but interested and energetic students will want to go beyond the lists. They will profit from the bibliographies in many of the works described briefly in this text, especially from the excellent bibliographies in volumes of the New American Nation Series (Harper & Row), edited by R. Morris and H. Commager. They should also consult the card catalogues in the libraries of their colleges and the invaluable bibliography in the *Harvard Guide to American History* (Belknap). For critical comments about the titles they find, they should go on, when they can, to the reviews in such learned journals as the *American Historical Review*, the *Journal of*

American History, the *Journal of Southern History*, and the *William and Mary Quarterly*.

Those students who want to acquire libraries of their own and who want also to economize by purchasing paperback editions will find the availability of titles in paperbacks at best uncertain. Every few months new titles are published and other titles go out of print. For the most recent information about paperbacks, students should consult the handy guide, *Paperbound Books in Print* (Bowker), which appears quarterly.

The reading lists refer to very few articles, not because articles are unimportant, but because they are often rather inaccessible to undergraduates. There are, however, many useful collections of important selected articles, often available in inexpensive editions. So, too, students will have no difficulty in finding collections of contemporary historical documents that add depth and excitement to the study of history. A growing number of thoughtful books organize both contemporary and scholarly materials in units designed to facilitate the investigation of historical problems.

The problems books, documents books, and collections of articles will whet the appetite of engaged students for further reading in the fields of their interest. They can serve in their way, then, as can the lists of suggested readings in this volume, as avenues leading to the adventures of the mind and the development of the understanding that American history affords.

Contents

15

The Aftermath of War   372

Appendix   i

Maps

The National Experience

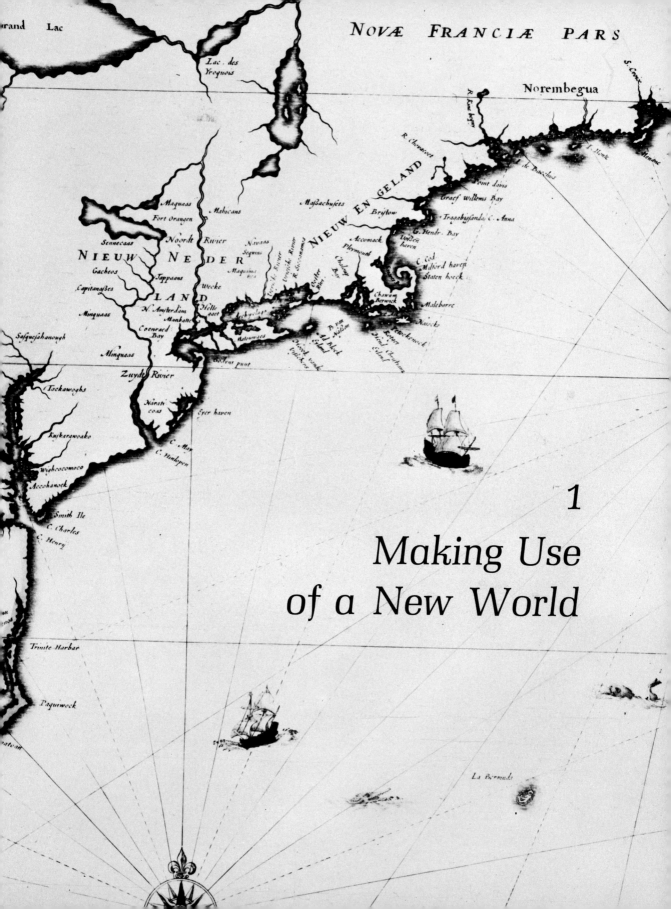

NOVÆ FRANCIÆ PARS

Norembegua

Grand Lac

Lac des Yroquois

NIEUW NEDER LAND

NIEUW ENGELAND

1

Making Use
of a New World

EXPLORATION

The first Americans. The first American was an immigrant. Although anthropologists disagree about where man first appeared on earth, no one claims the honor for the Western Hemisphere, which had probably never been seen by human eyes until twenty or thirty or at most forty thousand years ago. Presumably the earliest immigrant came by way of the Bering Straits and was followed by hundreds, perhaps thousands, more who trickled slowly southward, spreading out across North America and funneling through Mexico into Central and South America, venturing across the water to the Caribbean islands and perhaps much farther to the South Pacific. The immigration may have gone on for centuries, and it probably included people from various parts of Asia, Africa, and Europe.

For these early arrivals America was no melting pot. The people we lump together as Indians, or Amerinds, were divided into hundreds of tribes, enormously varied in physical appearance, language, and civilization. Those who made their homes south of the present United States were unquestionably the most numerous and the most skillful in exploiting their territory. They were the inventors of Indian corn (maize), as efficient a method of transforming earth into food as man has ever devised. Corn is so civilized a plant, so highly bred, that botanists have only recently been able to track down the wild ancestors from which the Indian plant-breeders developed it. The early inhabitants of Mexico and South America were skilled in other ways too. They built great cities of stone, richly carved and ornamented. They knew enough mathematics and astronomy to construct a calendar that required no leap year and to predict eclipses of the sun. And they knew enough political science to construct strong governments under which they worked out an advanced division of labor. In central Mexico their economy supported a population of several million with a city (Tenochtitlan, now Mexico City) that ranked in size with those of Europe.

By contrast, the Indians who lived north of Mexico were primitive. They made less effec-

Dutch Map of 1635.

tive use of the land, and it supported far fewer of them, probably not many more than a million in the present area of the United States. They grew some corn and other vegetables but also relied on nuts and berries, game and fish, and starved when these were unavailable. In parts of the Southeast they organized governments with real authority, the Powhatan Confederacy in Virginia and the Creek Confederacy in the Gulf Plains. But most often they joined together only loosely in tribes or clans under leaders or chiefs whose authority was merely nominal. They had dignity in abundance, self-reliance, and self-control — it was rare for an Indian to show anger or even to raise his voice. Indeed they were so self-reliant, so individualistic, that even in war it was apt to be every man for himself; and in peace they could not achieve the cooperation and organization, the division of labor, needed to make the most of the country's resources or to defend it against strangers better organized than they.

The rise of kings and commerce. Such strangers began to arrive shortly after 1492. There had been earlier visitors in the eleventh century, when some wandering Norsemen from Iceland, led by Leif Ericsson, spent a winter in what they called Vinland, probably somewhere in New England or Nova Scotia. A few years later other Icelanders attempted to establish a settlement. But the Norsemen had no real need for this vast continent and went home, leaving behind only the ruins of their encampments to show that they had been there.

If Columbus had sailed when the Norsemen did, his voyages would probably have had as little effect as theirs on the course of history. By 1492, however, Europeans were ready for new worlds. During the intervening centuries two important historical developments had prepared them. The first was the rise of a large merchant class hungry for foreign trade. Spices, dyestuffs, and textiles from India and the Far East traveled overland by slow, expensive caravan through Asia or partly by sail through the Red Sea or the Persian Gulf, passing from one dealer to another along the way until they finally reached the marketplaces of Europe. The prices people were willing to pay for these exotic imports were enough to send fifteenth-century sailors in search of sea routes to the source of the treasures. A direct sea route would

Christopher Columbus: A man with a mission.

permit importation in greater volume at less expense and would net the importer a huge profit.

Portugal took the lead in maritime exploration with a new type of vessel, the caravel — faster, more maneuverable, more seaworthy than any formerly known. Portuguese explorers, encouraged by their kings and by Prince Henry the Navigator (1394–1460), discovered the Azores and pushed their caravels farther and farther south along the coast of Africa. At first they were probably seeking only new trading opportunities in Africa itself, but by the 1480's they were searching for a way around the continent to the greater riches of the Orient. In 1488 Bartholomeu Diaz rounded the Cape of Good Hope. Ten years later Vasco da Gama reached India.

The rise of kings, supporting and supported by the simultaneous rise of merchants, was the second great development that prepared Europeans to use a new world. At the time of Leif Ericsson's voyage Europe was divided into tiny principalities, usually owing nominal allegiance to a king but actually dominated by local magnates who levied tolls on all trade passing through their territories. Even towns and cities tended to be autonomous, bristling with local regulations that discouraged trade with the outside world. The rise of kings meant the reorganization of society into larger units, into national states more wealthy and more powerful than any one of the towns or cities or principalities of which they were composed. A state organized under a king had the power and resources to cut through the strangling web of local trade barriers, to sponsor exploration for new lands to trade with, and even to seize the lands and their riches when the natives were not strong enough to resist.

During most of the fifteenth century Portugal far outran the rest of Europe in pursuit of foreign trade and of new lands to conquer. Other countries were still too troubled by domestic feuds and foreign wars to offer much competition. The first to emerge as a serious rival was Portugal's neighbor, Spain. And, as luck had it, Spain was also first to find America and first to find a use for it.

Columbus and the Spaniards. Christopher Columbus, the son of a Genoese weaver, was a man with a mission. He wanted to reach the Orient by sailing west, and he was convinced that the distance was no more than three or four thousand miles. Columbus was wrong, and when he tried to sell his idea the experts told him so. The experts had known for centuries that the world was round, but they had a much better notion of its size than Columbus did. The king of Portugal would have none of his scheme, and neither would anyone else until Queen Isabella of Spain, who was not an expert, decided to take a chance. In the very year that the consolidation of the Spanish monarchy was completed by the conquest of Granada from the Moors, she persuaded her husband, Ferdinand II, to pay for an expedition of three ships and to give Columbus authority, under Spain, over any lands he might discover on the way.

Armed with this commission and with a letter to the emperor of China, Columbus made his magnificent mistake. He failed to deliver the letter but found America (so named after his death for a later explorer, Amerigo Vespucci), at the island of San Salvador, on October 12, 1492. From here he threaded his way through the other Bahamas to Cuba and

Voyages of Columbus

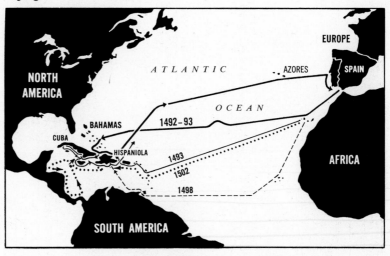

Hispaniola. By March 15, 1493, he was back in Spain. In succeeding years he explored the rest of the Caribbean area, still looking for China and Japan. Though he did not find them, he did find gold; and everyone in Europe knew what to do with that.

But for the gold, Europeans would probably have looked upon America as a mere obstacle on the route to the Orient. Even after Ferdinand Magellan carried out Columbus' original intention by sailing around the tip of South America (1519–22), explorers continued for two centuries to probe hopefully up American rivers in search of the Pacific. But the Spaniards recognized at once that Columbus' substitute for China might have advantages surpassing the original. With approval of Pope Alexander VI they joined the Portuguese in the Treaty of Tordesillas (1494), dividing the world by a line drawn north and south, 370 leagues west of the Cape Verde Islands (between the present forty-sixth and forty-seventh meridians): Spain was authorized to take possession of all the heathen lands she found to the west of the line; Portugal could do the same to the east. Thereafter Spaniards swarmed over the Caribbean islands and onto the mainland of North and South America.

By comparison with the natives the invaders were few in numbers, but they were courageous, unscrupulous, and armed. They wanted gold, and they were ready to take what the

natives had and make them dig for more. The Indians were no match for them. In the West Indies the first Spaniards killed or enslaved wherever they went, and slavery was only a slower form of killing. After working the Caribbean natives to death, they brought in Negro slaves purchased from the Portuguese. The Negroes died too, but the Spaniards got their gold. And when the supply on the islands ran out, they turned to planting sugar, which in the long run proved even more lucrative than digging for gold.

On the mainland, where the Indians were more numerous, small armies led by private adventurers, the conquistadors, subdued whole countries. Hernando Cortez with fifteen hundred men conquered the Aztec rulers of Mexico (1519–21), and Francisco Pizarro with still fewer men conquered the Incas of Peru (1531–35). The extraordinary conquests made by these small forces were possible because Spanish firearms and cavalry seemed irresistible to men who had never seen either guns or horses before — the Indians frequently took a man on horseback to be some superhuman quadruped. But even with this enormous advantage the Spaniards could scarcely have subdued such large and populous areas if the Indians had not been divided among themselves and if most of them had not already been living as subject peoples. To many an Indian the Spaniard was only a more powerful and

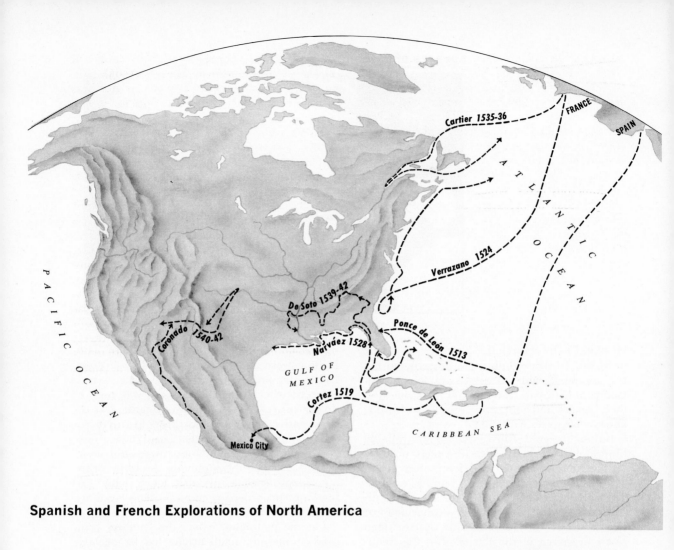

Spanish and French Explorations of North America

exacting master than the Aztec or Inca ruler whom he had served before.

The conquistadors were quick to seize the gold and silver with which the native palaces abounded, but the people themselves were the greatest treasure of Spain's new possessions. Spain in the sixteenth century had a population of about 9 million. The native population of Spanish America probably amounted to many more than that, and they all could be put to work for Spain. In the course of the century thousands of Spaniards came to the new land, most of them to profit from the immense supply of cheap labor that Columbus and the conquistadors had delivered to them.

The Spanish government passed increasingly elaborate legislation to control the exploitation of its Indian subjects, and the Church sent countless priests, friars, and bishops to look after their souls. Devoted Spanish clerics never ceased to denounce the way in which their countrymen relentlessly overworked the Indians. But everyone agreed that they ought to work, and neither church nor state was able to prevent the new lords of the land from exacting the utmost from every Indian who came within their reach.

Indians who resisted the Spanish advance were enslaved. Others, technically free, were parceled out in *encomiendas*, at first to the conquerors but later to nearly every Spaniard who appeared on the scene. From the Indians of his *encomienda* the *encomendero* could demand labor at nominal wages and also an annual tribute. When the government finally brought this form of exploitation under control in the middle of the century, the settlers devised other forms of forced labor.

The Spanish colonists made use of the Indians in mining the great deposits of silver ore that were discovered in both Mexico and Peru and in manning huge ranches and farms (haciendas). While the labor supply lasted, many settlers made fortunes, and the Spanish treasury welcomed the silver that poured in from its numerous taxes, which included a fifth of the proceeds of privately owned mines. But within a century the boom had ended, because overwork, despair, and disease destroyed the Spanish empire's basic resource. In the century after the conquest the native population of Mexico declined from several million (some scholars say 25 million) to little more than a million. A comparable decline is thought to have occurred in Peru.

Of the acknowledged causes for this catastrophic loss, probably the most lethal was the unavoidable introduction of European diseases against which the Indians had no natural resistance. Many of those who did survive were of mixed blood, mestizos as they were called. They, together with the creoles (people of Spanish descent born in America) and with the few remaining Indians, furnished a base from which Spanish America in succeeding centuries was to recover its population and perpetuate the advanced civilization that Spain, at whatever cost, had brought to the New World.

North of Mexico the Spaniards at first found little to interest them. Ponce de León cruised along the shores of the Florida peninsula in 1513, and Panfilo de Narváez and Hernando de Soto both explored the western side of the peninsula and the Gulf Plains before the middle of the sixteenth century. But there was no visible gold or silver about and no extensive population to exploit. Both expeditions marched on across the continent to Mexico without finding anything on the way that made them want to stay. In a futile search for seven legendary cities of gold, Francisco Vásquez de Coronado circled through present Arizona, New Mexico, Texas, Oklahoma, and Kansas (1540–42). He too thought the country not worth taking and returned to Mexico.

During the second half of the sixteenth century the Spaniards began to take a more lasting interest in the northern areas. They established a fort at St. Augustine, Florida (1565), and carried on missionary activities as far north as Port Royal (South Carolina) and for a few years even up to Chesapeake Bay. By the end of the century they were settling into present New Mexico and Arizona, planting missions to benefit the peaceable natives and presidios (military outposts) to hold back hostile ones. The mission was an ambitious undertaking, a nucleus from which Spanish civilization might grow in the borderlands of the empire. The mission gathered Indians (often nomadic in this section) into settled communities where, under supervision of the Church, they were taught Christianity along with techniques of farming and handicrafts. During the seventeenth century Spain sowed missions in Texas and during the eighteenth in California. But long before this the force of the Spanish thrust had spent itself, and other countries were ready to make use of the empty and idle North American continent.

The Europeans in North America. Columbus never saw the shores of North America, nor do we know what European was the first to do so. Perhaps other sailors had happened on it just as the Norsemen had. There may even have been fishermen walking the streets of St. Malo or Bristol or Plymouth who could have told Columbus of a distant coast where pines were tall and codfish plentiful. If so, no chronicler set down their discoveries until in 1497 John Cabot, like Columbus a Genoese, sailed west for the king of England and returned to report a new land. Henry VII gave Cabot £10 and an annuity of £20. Cabot undertook another voyage the next year, but he and other Europeans thought of the new land as a barrier, not an opportunity.

In 1524 the king of France, Francis I, sent a Florentine navigator, Giovanni da Verrazano, along the Atlantic coast from North Carolina to Nova Scotia in search of a passage through the barrier to the Pacific. Ten years later he sent Jacques Cartier on the same errand. Cartier, encouraged by the promisingly large entrance of the St. Lawrence River, sailed inland as far as the first rapids before giving up. He was sufficiently impressed by the surrounding country, however, to attempt a settlement there in 1541. Since Spain had found riches in the southern continent, it seemed reasonable to expect them in the north as well. When Canadian gold proved to be fool's gold, Canadian diamonds quartz, and Canadian winters terrible, the colonists returned home, and France forgot about North America for the rest of the century.

The first people to find a lasting use for the continent were summer people, who liked the fishing there. Every spring in the ports of France, England, Portugal, and Spain fishermen piled aboard their precarious craft and headed for the Grand Banks, where the continental shelf of North America lies submerged at a depth that codfish find congenial. They set up docks and drying stages ashore and assembled knocked-down dories and other small boats carried in the holds of their ships. They killed a few auks or netted some minnows for bait, rowed far out to the deeper waters, and fished all day with hand lines. Each night they brought in their catch to be dried, salted, and packed for sale in the markets of Europe. Caring little for the doings of their remote monarchs, they lived together in little international communities in Newfoundland and Nova Scotia — sleeping aboard their ships or in rough cabins ashore, planting gardens, and visiting one another of an evening — until the approach of winter sent them and the cod to friendlier climates. None of them seems to have contemplated permanent residence.

As the years passed, more and more Europeans sailed west to cruise along the coasts of North America, catching its codfish, prying into bays and rivers, kidnaping an occasional Indian to show off at home. Gradually they became aware that the country had more to offer than fish and pine trees. Behind the coast lay rivers and lakes teeming with beaver, otter, and other fur-bearing animals, which the Indians were adept at trapping. When Indian and European met, the Indian demanded metals, whose superiority to stone he was quick to recognize. The furs he offered in exchange brought a good price in Europe — especially beaver, which was turned into felt for hats.

Early in the seventeenth century the French, the Dutch, and the Swedes all set up permanent fur-trading posts in America. The great French explorer Samuel de Champlain, after reconnoitering the New England coast and the St. Lawrence region, founded Quebec in 1608. Henry Hudson, an Englishman working for a Dutch company, in 1609 sailed up the river he named for himself; the Dutch planted trading posts there in 1624, on the Delaware River in 1623, and on the Connecticut River in 1633. A Swedish company also maintained posts on the Delaware from 1638 until the Dutch seized them in 1655.

The French and the Dutch came to trade with the Indians, not to subjugate them. Neither in New France nor in New Netherland, as their settlements were called, did the Indian become a slave. Instead he lived on in his customary manner, roaming the woods he had roamed before, though trapping beaver in unaccustomed numbers. Contact with the Europeans inevitably meant new things for him: Christianity, comfort, progress, guns, hatchets, deadly drinks, deadlier diseases, sharper rivalry with other tribes, and a weakening of tribal customs. But the continent was still his. In the course of time both the French and the Dutch did try to transform their trading posts into larger settlements of Europeans, who would supplant rather than suppress or exploit the Indian, but this was only after the English had arrived on the continent and begun to fill it with their children.

TUDOR ENGLAND AND THE NEW WORLD

Before England could turn her interests to America at all, before her merchants could support expensive and risky overseas expeditions, she had to experience the same political consolidation under a powerful king that Spain and Portugal had undergone a century earlier. Henry VII, who sent John Cabot to America in 1497, began the job; his son Henry VIII and his granddaughter Elizabeth I finished it. In the process they transformed England from a Catholic country into a Protestant one, a fact that would affect profoundly the land Cabot found.

Henry VIII and the Reformation. Soon after Martin Luther launched the Reformation, which split the monolithic west-European Church into Protestant and Roman Catholic segments, Luther's teachings reached England. Perhaps no Englishman was less receptive to

them than the king, Henry VIII, who demonstrated his devotion to Rome by writing a book against the German heretic. The pope rewarded Henry by conferring on him the title "Defender of the Faith."

Before many years passed Henry found himself, if no friendlier to Luther, a good deal less friendly to the pope. Henry was the most powerful king England had ever known, so powerful that no baron or lesser local potentate could oppose him. Only one set of men in England dared challenge his authority: the priests and bishops, the monks and abbots, who acknowledged a higher power than Henry not only in the heavens but on earth, in Rome. Moreover, the Church owned about one-fourth of England and collected a yearly income of more than £320,000, much of it from the rent of lands owned by monasteries. When Henry needed funds to meet the cost of England's new and growing governmental machinery, the wealth of the monasteries inevitably caught his eye. In 1539 he found an opportunity to lay hold of it.

In 1509 Henry had married Catherine of Aragon, daughter of Ferdinand and Isabella, and in twenty years she bore him no son who lived. Henry desperately wanted an heir, and besides he had grown tired of Catherine. In 1529 he asked the pope for a divorce. When the pope refused, Henry defied him, married Anne Boleyn, severed England's ties with Rome, made himself head of the English Church — and in 1539 confiscated the monastic lands.

The results of Henry's break with Rome. Although Henry never showed the slightest interest in the New World, his divorce and his defiance of the pope had enormous consequences for both England and America.

The first and simplest consequence was that his new wife bore him a daughter, Elizabeth, who was to become England's greatest monarch. Elizabeth became queen in 1558 and ruled for forty-four glorious years — years in which Englishmen triumphed on land, at sea, and in the human spirit. Under her direction England became strong enough to begin the building of a North American empire.

Second, by divorcing his Spanish queen Henry touched off over a hundred years of intermittent hostility with Spain. Spain, the spearhead of Catholicism and the headquarters of the Inquisition, gradually became synonymous in Protestant England with antichrist. Englishmen attacked the Spaniard most successfully at sea not only by outright war but by privateering against Spanish shipping. The English privateers (or sea dogs, as they came to be called) resembled the earlier conquistadors in their daring, toughness, unscrupulousness, and flair for the spectacular and heroic. But the sea dogs operated on water rather than on land, scouring the Atlantic and the Caribbean for Spanish vessels laden with gold and silver from the New World. Under Queen Elizabeth privateering against Spain reached its height and drew England's attention to the riches of America.

Third, Henry's break with Rome gave impetus to a Protestant movement in England that had been covertly under way for some years. Its adherents interpreted Henry's defiance of the pope as a total repudiation of Roman hierarchy, ritual, and doctrine. Henry himself would have been content to serve as England's pope without substantially altering the internal organization or doctrines of the Church. But he could not wholly control the forces he had unleashed. The ideas of Luther and of the French reformer John Calvin became increasingly popular during the next 125 years; and, as their numbers grew, the extreme Calvinists — the Puritans — became increasingly discontent with the incomplete reformation of the English Church. Many of them would come to America with a view to completing the Reformation there.

Finally, Henry's confiscation of the monasteries set off a train of unexpected events that indirectly provided still more Englishmen willing to people a new world. Henry, not content with the income from the lands he had confiscated, began to sell them; succeeding monarchs continued the process, selling other royal lands as well. They were led to do so partly by a steady rise in prices during the sixteenth and seventeenth centuries (the so-called Price Revolution) that was induced or accelerated by the flow of Spanish gold and silver from America. Other people felt the pinch, especially landlords, whose rents were usually fixed by custom and were unalterable. They too began selling land to make ends meet. The turnover of so much real estate had widespread repercussions: in some places rich men got richer and poor men poorer, while in other areas the rich were getting poor and the poor rich. The sale of monastic lands was certainly not wholly responsible for this upheaval, but it was a first step in the chain of events that destroyed the social and economic security of large numbers of Englishmen and helped to make the fortunes of others, especially the merchants. Whoever lost from the rise of prices and the sale of lands, it was not they. As the sixteenth century wore on, they accumulated more and more capital, enough to finance overseas expeditions, while men who lost their homes or fortunes began to think of regaining them, perhaps in another part of the world.

Gilbert finds a use for North America. The historical developments that were set in motion by Henry VIII's break with Rome became significant for America only gradually. After the voyage of John Cabot in 1497, Englishmen showed very little interest in the New World until 1576, when the Cathay Company (Cathay was another name for China) was formed to trade with China by way of North America. The company sent Martin Frobisher to find a way through the continent. He probed the northern waters and found Baffin Land and Frobisher's Bay, where glittering gold-colored rocks diverted his attention from further search. With the usual captive Indian and a case of ore samples, he hurried back to England. The assayers declared that the ore was indeed gold, and he returned to North America for more. When the twelve hundred tons he brought back turned out to be worthless, the Cathay Company folded up. For years thereafter Englishmen with capital to invest were wary of risking it in America.

Although the Cathay Company had planned to establish a small permanent settlement in America, it was intended to serve merely as a supply station for voyages to the Orient. The first Englishman, possibly the first European, to have a glimmering of the northern continent's colonial future was a soldier of fortune named Humphrey Gilbert. Gilbert had served the queen in Ireland, where his skill in exterminating the natives won him a knighthood. While there he concocted a scheme for settling Ireland with Englishmen. But then his interest shifted. North America was a larger Ireland.

Englishmen planted there could exploit the natives (the counterpart of the wild Irish), forestall Spanish settlement, catch codfish, and search for a passage to the Pacific (Gilbert wrote a tract in 1576 to prove that there must be one). When the passage was found, they could supply ships passing through. What was more immediately attractive, an American colony would serve as a base from which sea dogs could raid the Spanish treasure fleets that sailed every year from the Caribbean. In every way America was more attractive than Ireland.

Gilbert, impelled by greed and chauvinism, had great vision: he was the first to see America as a place for Englishmen to live. In 1578 he induced Queen Elizabeth to grant him a charter empowering him to discover and take possession of North American lands not claimed by any other Christian monarch. Within six years he was supposed to settle a colony over which he would exercise absolute authority, provided he made no laws contrary to the Christian faith, and provided he gave the queen one-fifth of the gold and silver he mined (a provision generally inserted by subsequent monarchs in such charters).

Gilbert made two attempts to found his colony. The first attempt, in 1578, is a mystery. No one knows where he went or what he found, but there is a strong suspicion that he went not far and found a number of ships not his own— in short, that piracy, for the moment, proved more attractive than colonization.

Gilbert's second attempt, in 1583, was a larger undertaking, for by this time he had managed to sell his idea to other Englishmen: noblemen who felt the pressure of inflated prices and the loss of lands and power their fathers had had; merchants who scented opportunities for trade in the new land; discontented religious minorities, privateers, pirates, paupers, and fools. Drawing men and money from these divergent sources, Gilbert was able to equip an expedition. One ship he owned himself. Another he stole from a pirate just before departing and took her along, pirate crew and all. Three more ships were contributed by enthusiastic backers. He got under way in June 1583, with 260 prospective settlers, including many craftsmen. Apparently they were ill supplied, and one ship had to turn back

English Explorations of the New World

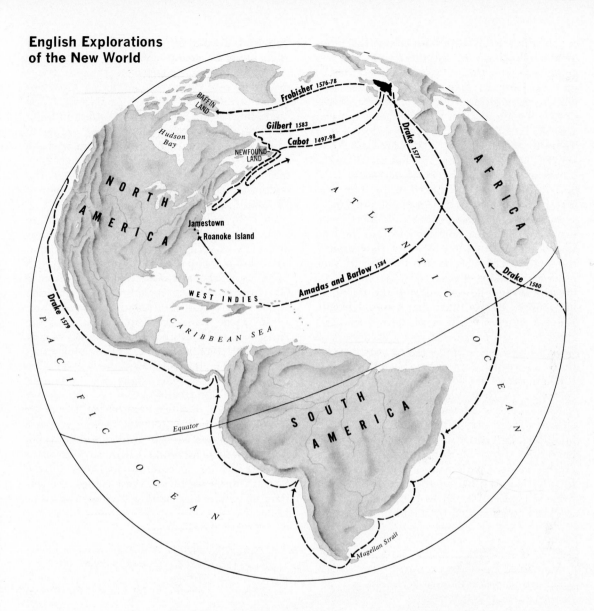

for lack of provisions. The pirate ship had no such trouble: she simply plundered another vessel encountered along the way.

In August the expedition reached Newfoundland, where Gilbert came upon a sizable international community of summer fishermen. He probably did not intend to establish his colony this far north (though it should be remembered that Newfoundland is south of England), but he made a great ceremony of taking possession of the settlement. The fishermen humored him and even agreed to pay rent for their fishing stages. They probably calculated, rightly, that no one would come to collect it.

After two weeks in Newfoundland, the men on one of the ships decided they had had enough of America and sailed for home. Gilbert, with the other three, cruised southward, filled with enthusiasm by the splendor of the uninhabited coast. He lost another ship on a reef, with all the eighty men aboard, and shortly thereafter was obliged to turn the two remaining ships back to England for supplies. But his spirits were still high, and he talked expansively to his comrades about his plans for the following year and the £10,000 he was going to borrow from the queen. In mid-ocean they ran into an alarmingly heavy sea, but Gilbert demonstrated his nonchalance by sitting on the afterdeck of his small vessel reading a book. At one point he shouted across to a friend in the other ship: "We are as near to heaven by sea as by land." That night, as the others watched, the lights of his vessel went out. No more was ever heard of the man who first envisaged England's American empire.

Raleigh and Roanoke. Although Gilbert's ventures accomplished nothing concrete, he had stirred the imagination of other Englishmen: the kind of men who backed him would back other expeditions to the New World. Before his last voyage, he had enlisted the talents of his younger half-brother, Sir Walter Raleigh. Raleigh equaled Gilbert in daring and exceeded him in polish. He was a favorite with Queen Elizabeth, who gave him nearly everything he asked for. After Gilbert's death, Raleigh asked her for a charter to found a colony in the New World.

Raleigh was as interested as Gilbert in piracy against Spanish treasure fleets, but like Gilbert he wanted his colony to be more than a base of operations. From the beginning he planned it as a permanent settlement, and he enlisted his friend Richard Hakluyt to write propaganda persuading Englishmen to emigrate. Hakluyt too became fascinated by the idea of coloniza-

tion and developed into England's greatest advocate of overseas expansion.

Raleigh got his charter in 1584 and immediately sent out a reconnoitering force under Philip Amadas and Arthur Barlow. They made their landfall a couple of thousand miles south of Newfoundland — perhaps in order to be closer to the Spaniards — and explored the coast south of Chesapeake Bay. When they returned with glowing descriptions of the region, Raleigh named it Virginia in honor of Elizabeth, the Virgin Queen.

In 1585 Raleigh fitted out an expedition to settle Roanoke Island, near the present boundary between Virginia and North Carolina. The group, under the command of Ralph Lane, included John White, an artist; Thomas Cavendish, who later sailed round the world; and Thomas Hariot, a noted mathematician. White made some excellent drawings of the American Indians, the best executed during the whole colonial period; Hariot took notes from which he later prepared the first detailed description of any part of the present United States. The settlers themselves, instead of digging in, spent their time searching Virginia's rivers unsuccessfully for the Pacific and her shores unsuccessfully for gold. In June 1586, when Sir Francis Drake called to visit them after searching successfully for gold in the Spanish fortresses of the West Indies, the settlers all climbed aboard with him and went home.

Indians of the Virginia area, as seen by John White.

Arrival in Virginia (the Roanoke colony).

Raleigh tried again the next year, 1587, sending 120 persons under the command of John White. White spent a month getting the new Roanoke settlement started and then returned to England for supplies, leaving his daughter, her husband, and their new-born child with the settlers. A supply fleet commanded by Sir Richard Grenville was prepared, but the Spaniards chose this moment for an all-out attack on England (the great Spanish Armada), and Grenville and his ships were pressed into service for defense. Not until 1590 could White sail back to Roanoke, and when he got there his colonists had completely vanished. Someone had carved the name of a neighboring island, CROATOAN, on a post. But no trace of the colonists was ever found there. Presumably, hostile Indians had overwhelmed them, but to this day no real clue to their fate has been found.

The sixteenth century closed without an English colony in North America. Raleigh turned his attention to South America. Richard Hakluyt sang the praises of England's explorers and published accounts of their great voyages in *The Principal Navigations, Voyages, and Discoveries of the English Nation* (1589). But no one else with the vision of a Gilbert or a Raleigh stepped forward to lead Englishmen to new homes.

Actually Gilbert and Raleigh were as wrong, in their way, as Columbus. He expected to find China and found America. They expected not only to settle North America but to make a profit out of it. They failed, and even if their settlements had succeeded there would almost certainly have been no profit, unless from piracy. But they were not the last to be mistaken. In 1606 another group of Englishmen risked their money, and lost it, in an enterprise from which in the fullness of time grew the United States.

While Elizabeth reigned, men of daring in England enjoyed risking their money and their lives for her by attacking Spain. Her successor, James I, was so different from the great queen that he has always suffered by comparison. Elizabeth knew everything about power and kept her own counsel. James knew everything about everything and told everybody. One of the things he knew was that the war with Spain had gone on long enough. In 1604, the year after his accession, he made a peace that lasted twenty years.

James was probably right in ending the war, but Englishmen did not love him for it, especially after he told them that raids on Spanish shipping must cease. During the sixteenth century the line between legitimate privateering and piracy had been left conveniently thin, and hijacked Spanish bullion had poured into England. Francis Drake alone picked up $200 million worth of loot from Spanish ships he met during his dramatic voyage around the globe (1577–80). Elizabeth knighted Drake for his exploits and cheerfully collected a share of the profits. But James foreswore such profits for his subjects as well as himself. As a result, men with spare lives and money began to think again about getting gold where the Spaniards got it. Efforts to find it in North America had so far been unsuccessful, but no one had tried very hard. Even if no gold was found, the continent might hold other things of value. After the Roanoke venture of 1586, Thomas Hariot had described some promising native commodities, including sassafras, a root that the Spaniards were selling in Europe at high prices as a cure for syphilis. And piracy itself, now that the king had pledged his protection to Spanish shipping, might still be carried on from a base out of royal reach on the other side of the Atlantic. And so the tantalizing possibility of riches from America again lured Englishmen to try to plant a colony there.

Jamestown. In 1606 a number of men joined to petition the king for authority to establish colonies in America. Most of them were merchants, and merchants had discovered a means of undertaking large and dangerous enterprises without risking financial ruin. Their scheme was the joint-stock company, in which participants profited or suffered in proportion to the number of shares they purchased. By investing modestly in a number of companies a man would gain only modest profits from successful ventures, but he would also avoid heavy losses from unsuccessful ones. In this way, through many small contributions, it was possible to accumulate the large amounts of capital necessary for undertakings that were beyond the range of private fortunes. The joint-stock company became the principal instrument of England's overseas expansion.

The men who petitioned the king in 1606 were divided into two groups, one from London, the other from Plymouth; and the king gave them a charter incorporating two companies for the colonization of North America: the Virginia Company of Plymouth was to

Virginia and New England Land Grants

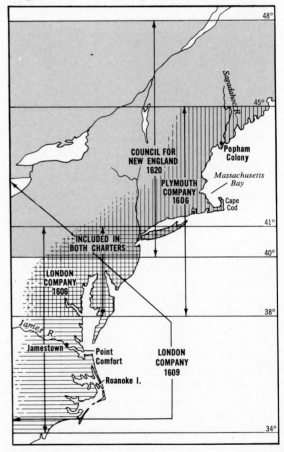

operate in the northern part of the continent, and the Virginia Company of London in the southern part. The companies planned to send out settlers who would agree to relinquish the fruits of their labors to the investors for the first seven years; after that the settlers could enrich themselves. Anyone willing to pay his own passage was free to begin getting rich at once.

Both companies got off to a quick start. The Plymouth group dispatched an exploratory expedition in 1606 and in 1607 founded a colony at the mouth of the Sagadahoc River in Maine. The colony survived only one winter. The Virginia Company of London, in December 1606, sent over its first settlers, a hundred men and four boys crammed aboard three small ships, the *Susan Constant*, the *Godspeed*, and the *Discovery*. In May 1607 they sailed up a river they called the James and landed on a peninsula they called Jamestown. Swampy and forested, the site was well situated for defense but a haven for malaria-carrying mosquitoes. The colonists made almost every possible mistake in their new environment, but they also corrected their mistakes; and they had the vision, the courage, or the foolhardiness to stick it out.

Their first big problem was leadership. In the charter granting authority to settle the colony the king had retained authority to govern the colony himself, and he exercised it through a council sitting in England. This council in turn acted through another sitting in Virginia. The Virginia council consisted of seven men with a president who presided over its meetings but who had no authority to give orders of his own and no power to enforce orders transmitted from the king's council in England. Government by council proved to be no government at all. The members of the council in the colony quarreled with one another, and the colonists, undisciplined and disorganized, neglected the elementary tasks of plowing, planting, and building.

Fortunately one man had the nerve to take command. John Smith, twenty-seven years old, of humble background but no humility, was not popular with the other members of the council, all men of greater age, importance, and indecision. Smith had spent four years fighting the Turks in Hungary, where he had been captured, sold into slavery, and rescued

John Smith had the nerve to take command.

by fair maidens. In Virginia, by his own account, when the other members of the council proved fools, knaves, or cowards he took control of the colony, explored it, mapped it, overawed the Indians (and was again rescued by a maiden, Pocahontas), and obtained from them the corn that kept the settlers from starving. He stopped the disorganized scramble for gold, built fortifications, planted Indian corn, and cut a cargo of cedar wood to send back to the investors as the first tangible evidence of the colony's worth. He later told about it with such relish for his own role that readers ever since have suspected his veracity. Nevertheless, wherever his account can be checked, it holds up. Moreover, he prepared a surprisingly accurate map of the region — a map that could only have been the product of first-hand observation.

In London, however, the armchair colonizers were not pleased. Smith, they heard, was unkind to the Indians. He had failed to find either gold or the Pacific Ocean. And some of the other members of the Virginia council, returning to the mother country, described his leadership as tyranny. The company did recognize, however, that the colony needed stronger direction. In 1609 it obtained a new royal charter establishing a new governing council (resident in London) composed entirely of company members and empowered to appoint an all-powerful governor or governors in the colony. The council decided on a single governor, who should choose a council of Virginians to advise him. To prevent a repetition of the colony's earlier squabbles over leadership and to ensure that the governor's council understood that its function was limited to advice, the London council specified that the Virginia councilors "shall not have, single nor together, anie bindinge or negative voice or power." The post of governor went not to Smith but to a nobleman, Lord De La Warr.

Under the new charter the company launched an elaborate campaign to sell Virginia to the English public. With the proceeds of stock sold at £12 10s. a share, it fitted out a fleet of nine vessels to carry some six hundred emigrants. Some were servants who had agreed to work for the company for seven years in return for their passage. The rest paid their own way (passage was worth about £6) and received a share of stock as a bonus. All would work together until 1616, at which time the servants would be freed, the profits would be divided among the shareholders both in England and in America, and every shareholder would receive at least a hundred acres of land.

The expedition set sail from Plymouth in June 1609. Though one of the ships was wrecked at Bermuda, at least four hundred settlers reached Virginia that summer. Unfortunately Lord De La Warr was not among them. His departure from England had been delayed, and his substitute, Sir Thomas Gates, was on the ship lost at Bermuda. John Smith, injured in a gunpowder explosion, returned to England in the fall of 1609, and from then until the arrival of Governor Thomas Dale in 1611 the colony was without effective government and fell into worse disorder than before. Men starved; fortifications fell to ruins; at one point the entire colony had embarked, prepared to abandon the settlement, when a relief ship arrived. After 1611, Governor Dale and Governor Samuel Argall, who succeeded him, imposed rigorous disciplinary laws and resumed the course set by John Smith. Once again the colonists began to plant corn, erect and repair fortifications, and build houses. The settlement spread up the shores of the James River; women began to arrive; and gradually life in Virginia, though still arduous, became more normal.

But the men who left England for Virginia wanted more than corn bread and a place to lay their heads. To them survival was a means to an end, and they kept looking for a way to wealth, a way to live better in Virginia than they had in England. Since they had found no gold or silver, they had to find some other commodity of high value that they could produce in sufficient quantity and with sufficient ease to make the long voyage to English or European markets worthwhile. They tried cedar. They tried sassafras. But the market for both was quickly satisfied. The directors of the company had high hopes at different times for wines, silk, iron, tar. But in 1612, though they were not at once aware of it, the Virginians discovered their future — in smoke.

Tobacco was native to America. The Indians had taught the Spaniards to use it, and the Spaniards had taught the rest of Europe. At first it was valued only as a medicine, said to cure any disease afflicting a man from the waist up. But by the end of the sixteenth century people were smoking for the fun of it, much to the distress of those who knew better, including King James, and much to the joy of Spanish tobacco merchants. The Indians of Virginia smoked a native variety, coarse and unpalatable. John Rolfe, who later gained greater fame by marrying Pocahontas, in 1612 tried planting the West Indian species, just as other settlers were experimenting with other Spanish products. The West Indian variety grew extraordinarily well in Virginia, but it did not smoke as well as when grown in the tropics and it consequently brought a lower price. It was nevertheless by far the most profitable commodity Virginia had yet been made to yield. The settlers turned enthusiastically to tobacco culture and by 1617 were able to ship twenty thousand pounds to England.

The Virginia Company's great effort. The stockholders of the Virginia Company were pleased to have their faltering confidence in the colony reconfirmed by the promising shipments of tobacco. Hitherto they had received nothing but a few tons of sassafras, cedar, and other trifles in return for an investment of approximately £50,000. In fact, when they sat down to divide up their profits in 1616, they had found nothing to divide except the land itself, and to many of them it hardly seemed worth dividing. Moreover, most of the servants they had sent over to work for the company had served out their time and become free to work for themselves. To hire more men to produce so little would be to throw good money after bad.

Although the colonists' success with tobacco rekindled the expectations of the investors, they did not suppose that the colony could prosper with that product alone. But if Virginia could grow tobacco there must be other things it could produce too. They must keep the settlers experimenting until the right products were found, and then everyone could sit back and reap the profits of perseverance. While this new burst of enthusiasm was upon them, the members of the Virginia Company decided to revitalize and expand their venture by means of a reform program, which they inaugurated in 1618 under the leadership of Sir Edwin Sandys, a prominent figure in the English House of Commons. The program contained four points designed to entice more adventurers (investors), more planters (settlers), and more servants:

1. By overhauling its land policies the company made both investment and emigration more profitable. Henceforth anyone who paid for the passage of a man to Virginia, himself or anyone else, received a "headright" of fifty acres. A wealthy individual investor could send over servants to cultivate headright lands for him as a private plantation. Less wealthy investors could pool their funds and send over servants to cultivate their headright lands as a joint enterprise. The sponsors acquired joint ownership of fifty acres of land for each man sent and received an agreed percentage of the profit from the crops; the servants worked for an agreed number of years in return for their passage and a percentage of the profits. These

People were smoking for fun, to the distress of those who knew better.

joint enterprises were known as "particular plantations." The Virginia Company itself sent over more servants, who worked on company lands for seven years and received half of whatever profit their labor produced. Anyone who owned headright lands paid the company an annual "quitrent" of a shilling per fifty acres. Thus the company, with almost unlimited acreage at its disposal, ensured that it would gain a perpetual income from rents. For the original investors and colonists there was a land bonus. To the hundred acres of land free of rent that had already been given to shareholders (both adventurers and planters), the company added the promise of another hundred acres as soon as the first grant had been "sufficiently peopled." The original servants, who had already served out their terms, were

I tell thee, gold is more plentiful there than copper is with us; and for as much red copper as I can bring, I'll have thrice the weight in gold. Why, man, all their dripping-pans and their chamber-pots are pure gold; and all the chains with which they chain up their streets are massy gold; all the prisoners they take are fettered in gold; and for rubies and diamonds, they go forth on holidays and gather 'hem by the seashore, to hang on their children's coats, and stick in their caps, as commonly as our children wear saffron-gilt brooches, and groats with holes in 'hem.

From John Marston, *Eastward Ho!* 1605.

encouraged to remain in Virginia by the grant of a hundred acres apiece but had to pay the company an annual quitrent of two shillings on it.

2. To make life in Virginia more like life in England the company relaxed the severity of its discipline and assured actual and potential settlers that henceforth the colony would be governed by English law and that the colonists would have the rights of Englishmen.

3. Even more important, the company decided to give the settlers a voice in the management of the colony. The planters were allowed to elect representatives to an assembly, which, along with the governor's appointed council, would have power to make laws for the colony. Both the governor in Virginia and the company in England retained a veto on the assembly's actions. The company could still make laws by itself for the colony, but the assembly was promised an eventual veto on the company's actions.

4. The final point in the new program called for an all-out effort to diversify the colony's activities. The company itself took the responsibility for sending over various craftsmen: vintners, ironworkers, brick-makers, glass-blowers. Somewhere among these skills, it was hoped, would be the right ones to give Virginia a healthy and profitable economy of which tobacco-growing would be only one part.

For five years and more, new settlers streamed into the colony. By the end of 1618 the population, which was only 400 in April of that year, had risen to 1,000. Between 1618 and 1624, about 4,000 more arrived. To judge by the number of ships landing passengers in Virginia, the colony was a success. To judge by the number of graves dug there, it was not. In spite of the heavy immigration the population in 1624 stood at only 1,275. Some of the settlers had doubtless returned to England, but for most of them the colony had been a death trap. Sandys (who never set foot in Virginia) had sent shipload after shipload of men without supplies. Ill fed, ill clothed, and ill housed, they sickened and died. In 1622 the Indians rose up and killed 347.

Sandys was also in trouble in England, for he had managed to antagonize the old leaders of the company by charging them with defalcation and by interfering with a pirate ship in which some of them had invested — piracy was not one of the new occupations Sandys had envisaged for the colonists. In 1624, at the request of the old leaders, James I appointed a commission to investigate the company. The commissioners reported such shocking neglect of the settlers that James dissolved the company and resumed control of the colony himself.

Thus ended the Virginia Company of London. At the cost of several thousand lives and perhaps £100,000 it had established some twelve hundred Englishmen in America. Although the price was high, the colony was there to stay.

In the cultivation of tobacco the Virginians had found a way to use America. And, in spite of all efforts to turn them to other occupations, they persisted in growing tobacco. They demonstrated, indeed, a certain headstrongness that England was to find characteristic of Englishmen living in America. In 1619 (before any other permanent English settlement had even been launched) Virginians met in their first representative assembly and passed their first laws. When James I took control of the colony in 1624 he did not renew the company's request that the colonists furnish advice through a representative assembly; nor did his son Charles I, who became king in 1625. Charles was having enough difficulties with his own Parliament in England. But the governors he appointed found it impossible to rule Virginia without the help of Virginians.

Though Charles refused them recognition until 1639, annual assemblies of representatives began making laws again in 1629 and have been doing so ever since.

THE FOUNDING OF NEW ENGLAND

James I stopped the Virginia Company but not the flow of Englishmen to America. The social, religious, and economic forces that had made their appearance in the time of Henry VIII were still at work, upsetting the lives of an increasing number of people. Prices were still rising; lands were changing hands; and sheep were grazing where men once drove their plows. To make matters worse, a depression settled over the woolens industry in the 1620's and lasted through the next decade. The land seemed "weary of her inhabitants," and the new king made it seem wearier by levying taxes without the consent of Parliament and by repressive measures against religious dissenters. The result was the Great Migration, in which perhaps as many as fifty thousand people left for the New World. The exodus lasted until 1640, when Englishmen began to see a more hopeful future for their own country. By that year Virginia's population had risen to eight thousand; Maryland had been founded and peopled; and so had the Bermudas, Barbados, St. Kitts, and other West Indian islands. About twenty thousand of the emigrants came to that northern part of Virginia now called New England.

After the failure of its Sagadahoc settlement in 1608, the Virginia Company of Plymouth had shown only sporadic interest in its territory. The company's most important action was to send Captain John Smith to explore the country in 1614; Smith named the place New England and first described its attractions. But his backers were not sufficiently impressed or not sufficiently affluent to support him in attempts to colonize it, and in 1620 they surrendered their rights to a more distinguished group of forty men who were impressed with New England but not with Smith.

The new group, made up of a duke, two marquises, six earls, a viscount, three barons, nineteen knights, the dean of a cathedral, and seven esquires, were moved by Humphrey Gilbert's old dream of organizing feudal estates on a grand scale. Led by Sir Ferdinando Gorges, a Devonshire man who had also been the leading spirit of the Plymouth group, they gained from the king a charter establishing them as the Council for New England and granting them proprietary and governmental rights over the whole area from the fortieth to the forty-eighth parallels and from the Atlantic to the Pacific. In addition they were to have a monopoly of fishing in the offshore waters.

Cut up forty ways, the region would have provided each member of the council with a huge estate, a whole new England larger than the old. But the future of New England was to be less grand than gritty. In the very month in which the Council for New England was

---

Another View of Virginia: Maggots and Rats

In those twelve years of Sir Thomas Smythe his government, we aver that the colony for the most part remained in great want and misery under most severe and cruel laws sent over in print, and contrary to the express letter of the king in his most gracious charter, and as mercilessly executed, often times without trial or judgment. The allowance in those times for a man was only eight ounces of meal and half a pint of peas for a day, the one and the other mouldy, rotten, full of cobwebs and maggots, loathsome to man and not fit for beasts, which forced many to flee for relief to the savage enemy, who being taken again were put to sundry deaths as by hanging, shooting and breaking upon the wheel, and others were forced by famine to filch for their bellies, of whom one for stealing 2 or 3 pints of oatmeal had a bodkin thrust through his tongue and was tied with a chain to a tree until he starved.... Many through these extremities, being weary of life, digged holes in the earth and hid themselves till they famished.... So lamentable was our scarcity that we were constrained to eat dogs, cats, rats, snakes, toadstools, horse-hides and what not; one man out of the misery that he endured, killing his wife, powdered her up to eat her, for which he was burned. Many besides fed on the corpses of dead men, and one who had gotten insatiable, out of custom to that food could not be restrained, until such time as he was executed for it.

From "The Tragical Relation of Virginia Assembly," 1624.

created, a band of humble but determined men and women put ashore below Cape Cod and began to use the country in their own way. Their way was called Puritanism.

Puritanism. Puritanism has come to mean prudishness, cruelty, fanaticism, superstition, Philistinism, and hypocrisy. Actually, the Puritans who settled New England had no greater share of these human qualities than did their contemporaries or their descendants. What they did possess in stronger measure than other men was John Calvin's belief that God is omnipotent and good and that men are evil and helpless, predestined before they are born either to salvation or to eternal torment. Critics of this doctrine of predestination have always charged that it leads to moral indifference: if a man's present behavior does not affect his future salvation, why be good? But the facts belie the criticism: those who accept Calvin's doctrine have always outdone their neighbors in efforts to follow God's commandments as given in the Bible. The Puritan, knowing his efforts to be futile, nevertheless took a holy joy in them. They made him feel close to God's transcendent purpose. They also helped to ease his agonizing concern over whether he was headed for heaven or hell. Even though good behavior could not alter a man's predestined fate, it was observable that religious conversion (a personal experience by which God let a saved man know he was saved) often befell those who did try to live godly lives. Moreover, conversion manifested itself outwardly in renewed and intensified efforts to obey God's commands. A man's striving might thus be a sign that he was saved.

Not content with his own striving, the Puritan also felt responsible for his fellow men. Indeed he was certain that any society that failed to honor God by punishing infractions of his commands would meet with his sudden wrath, not in the next world but here and now. Governments, he thought, existed for the purpose of enforcing obedience to God.

The Puritan's ideas of what God required were less rigorous than many people have supposed. God did *not* require that men wear drab clothes, live in drab houses, or drink water when something stronger was available. He *did* require that they refrain from drunkenness, theft, murder, adultery, and breaches of the Sabbath. Puritans were vastly uneasy about the English government's indifference to these evils. They were even more concerned because the Church of England — supported by the government — retained corrupt practices inherited from Rome and not sanctioned by God in the Bible. They thought the Church should abolish bishops and ecclesiastical courts and such other relics of Catholicism as kneeling and the use of priestly vestments and altars.

Puritans all agreed on what was wrong with the English Church, but they disagreed on how to make it right. Though they all relied on the Bible for guidance, they extracted different opinions from it about how God wanted his churches to be run. The group that settled New England were Congregationalists, and they differed from the other principal group of Puritans, the Presbyterians, in two beliefs: first, that there should be no general church organization with authority over individual churches; second, that a church should admit to membership only those who gave visible evidence of their Christian beliefs. Persons who openly flouted the laws of God should be excluded or expelled. Congregationalists wanted to change the structure and practices of the Church to conform with these beliefs.

Their dissatisfaction with the Church of England led them to the problem of all reformers: whether to remain inside a corrupt institution and try to reform it from within or to separate from it and start a pure new one. In 1583 an early Congregational leader, Robert Browne, advocated the latter course in a pamphlet appropriately titled *Reformation without Tarrying for any*. His followers, known as Separatists, deserted the English Church to meet in little churches of their own — of necessity in secret because the government did not acknowledge or permit any church other than the established one. But most Congregationalists were not Separatists. They preferred to stay within the Church of England and await the opportunity for reform.

The Pilgrims. The men and women who began the settlement of New England at Plymouth in 1620 were Separatists, part of a group that originated in 1607 at the village of Scrooby in Nottinghamshire. The English government did not look with favor on Separatists. Under Elizabeth two had been executed and many more imprisoned for long periods. Although the members of the Scrooby group were not seriously molested, they were distressed by the hostility of the government and the contempt of their neighbors. In 1608–09 they made their way, not without many hardships, to Holland, where the Dutch were known to be more tolerant. But as the years passed in Leyden they were still unhappy: their children were turning into Dutchmen; the only work they could get was day labor, poorly paid; and the weak among them were being tempted by the other religions that flourished under Dutch tolerance. They thought of Virginia, a place where they might remain Englishmen and work for themselves, a place isolated from contagious heretical religions and far enough from government control so that they could have a church of their own design.

Since they were poor people, without funds to finance their passage, they proposed to set up a "particular plantation" in Virginia for a group of English merchants. As in other such ventures, they would work together for seven years as a community, and then the profits would be divided between them and their sponsors. They evidently intended to establish themselves some distance north of the other settlements (the claims of the Virginia Company extended as far north as the present site of New York City) and at one point even considered seeking a grant from the Council for New England, which was then being formed. In the end 102 persons boarded the *Mayflower*, bound for Virginia. But after making their landfall at Cape Cod and exploring the coast, they decided to stay. In late December 1620 they began a settlement, which they named Plymouth after the English port from which they had embarked.

These "Pilgrims," as Americans have come to call them, were as poorly equipped in everything but courage as any group that ever landed in America. They had guns but knew little about shooting. They planned to become fishermen but knew nothing about fishing. They expected to settle in Virginia but landed in New England without enough supplies to last the winter. Like their predecessors and contemporaries in Virginia, many of them sickened and died. But the living stuck it out and justified their own estimate of themselves:

three years earlier they had written to the men they hoped would sponsor their emigration, "It is not with us as with other men, whom small things can discourage, or small discontentments cause to wish themselves at home again." Since New England was outside the jurisdiction of Virginia's government, the Pilgrims established a government of their own by the *Mayflower* Compact, which forty-one adult males subscribed before going ashore. For governor they elected John Carver; and upon his death in 1621 they chose William Bradford, who recorded the colony's struggles in an eloquent history and was reelected nearly every year from 1621 to his death in 1657. Under his leadership the Pilgrims liquidated their debt to the English merchants (who had failed to send them the supplies they expected) and established for themselves a self-supporting community.

The Pilgrim settlement was important as a demonstration that men could live in New England. It remained, however, a small and humble community, attracting few immigrants. The great Puritan exodus did not begin until ten years after the landing of the Pilgrims. It engulfed, but did not greatly expand, the Plymouth colony.

The Massachusetts Bay Company. While the Pilgrims went their way outside the Church of England first in Holland and then in America, other Puritans, both Congregational and Presbyterian, continued the struggle to reform the Church from within. While James I reigned, the struggle did not seem hopeless. Although James scolded them, and even married his son to a Catholic princess, he did not "harry them out of the land," as he once threatened to do. If he had tried, they would have had enough strength in Parliament to stop him. But when Charles I became king in 1625, he quarreled incessantly with Parliament and finally announced in 1629 that he intended to rule henceforth without it. At the same time he befriended a group of aspiring churchmen who were as eager to suppress Puritanism as the Puritans were to make it prevail. Under the leadership of William Laud, whom Charles made Bishop of London in 1628 and Archbishop of Canterbury in 1633, these friends of the king deprived Puritan ministers of their pulpits and moved the Church of England ever

Governor of a Puritan republic: John Winthrop.

Massachusetts: A Contented View

I prayse God, we haue many occasions of comfort heer, and doe hope, that our dayes of Affliction will soon haue an ende, and that the Lord will doe vs more goode in the ende, then we could haue expected, that will abundantly recompence for all the trouble we haue endured. yet we may not looke at great things heer, it is enough that we shall haue heaven, though we should passe through hell to it. we heer enjoye God and Jesus Christ, is not this enough? What would we haue more? I thanke God, I like so well to be heer, as I doe not repent my comminge.... I neuer fared better in my life, neuer slept better, neuer had more contente of minde, which comes meerly of the Lordes good hande, for we haue not the like meanes of these comforts heer which we had in England, but the Lord is allsufficient, blessed be his holy name, if he please, he can still vphold vs in this estate, but if he shall see good to make vs partakers with others in more Affliction, his will be doone, he is our God, and may dispose of vs as he sees good.

From John Winthrop, Letter to His Wife, 1630.

closer to Rome in its ceremonies, vestments, and doctrines.

As the prospects of reform grew dim and the sins of the land grew heavy, the Puritans feared that God was preparing England for some great purging catastrophe. In despair and hope they too turned their thoughts to America, where they might escape God's wrath, worship in purity, and gather strength for future victory.

In 1628 a number of prominent congregational Puritans bought their way into a commercial company that was being organized in London. Called the New England Company, it took over the rights of a defunct group, the Dorchester Adventurers, which in 1623 had tried to plant a farming and fishing settlement at Cape Ann. From the Council for New England, the new company obtained a charter authorizing settlement in the area known as Massachusetts Bay, to the north of Plymouth. A year later, on March 4, 1629, the New England Company reorganized as the Massachusetts Bay Company and had its proprietary and governmental rights confirmed by a new charter obtained directly from the king.

In the shuffle the Puritan stockholders gained control of the company, and they had something more than commerce in mind. The royal charter bestowed on the company full authority to govern its own territory and made no mention of where company meetings were to be held. In 1629 the Puritans simply voted to transfer the company to Massachusetts. This meant that if Puritan company members emigrated, they would have full control of the government under which they would live. Thus in one bold stroke the Puritans won for themselves the opportunity to do in Massachusetts what Puritans for nearly a century had been yearning to do in England.

To act as governor, the company elected a solid Puritan squire, John Winthrop of Groton Manor, Suffolk. He and perhaps a dozen other company members, all Puritans, crossed the ocean in 1630, accompanied by a thousand like-minded men and women, who preferred a wilderness governed by Puritans to a civilized land governed by Charles I. Before the year was over they had planted settlements around Massachusetts Bay at Dorchester, Roxbury, Watertown, Newtown (Cambridge), Charlestown, and Boston. During the next ten years, as Charles ruled without Parliament and Laud grew increasingly powerful, fifteen or twenty thousand more followed and their towns stretched out in all directions.

Winthrop and the handful of other company members had authority from the king's charter to govern this whole body of settlers. But Winthrop and his friends wanted a broader base for their government. And so, shortly after their arrival in New England, they transformed the Massachusetts Bay Company from a trading company into a commonwealth. In 1631 they admitted more than a hundred adult males as members, or "freemen," of the company eligible to vote at its meetings. The term "freeman" in seventeenth-century England generally meant a voting member of a business corporation or an incorporated city or borough. In America the word came to mean a man who had the right to vote for representatives to the assembly in his colony. In Massachusetts, when the company and colony were blended, the freemen of the company became the freemen of the colony. The increase in their numbers did not remove the colony from Puritan control, because most of the new freemen (who must have been a majority of the heads of families then in the colony) were probably Puritans; moreover, it was specified that, in the future, members of Puritan congregational churches (and only such) should be eligible to become freemen.

The charter, which had envisaged only a trading company with limited membership, provided that company members assemble as a General Court four times a year to make laws. Between the meetings of the General Court a governor (or his second in command, a deputy governor) and a council of eighteen "assistants," elected annually, were to manage the company. When Winthrop and his associates opened freemanship to all church members, they foresaw that the number of freemen would soon become too large to assemble and work together as a legislature; and they decided to leave lawmaking to the council of assistants, who were still to be elected annually by all the freemen. But in 1634 the freemen insisted that the lawmaking powers assigned to them by the charter be delegated to "deputies" elected from each settlement. Henceforth the

---

Massachusetts: A Hungry View

her cam ouer xxv passeingares and thare cume backe agayn fouer skore and od parsones and as maney more wolld a cume if thay had whare withe all to bringe them hom.... We may liue if we haue suppleyes euerey yere from ould eingland other weyse we can not subeseiste I maye as I will worck hard sete an ackorne of eindey wheat and if we do not set it withe fishe and that will cost xxs and if we set it witheought fishe they shall haue but a por crope so father I pray consedre of my cause for her will be but a uerey por beinge and no beinge withe ought Louinge father youer helpe withe prouisseyones from ould eingland I had thought to a cam home in theis sheipe for my prouisseyones ware all moste all spente but that I humbley thanck you for youer gret loue and kindnes in sendinge me s[o]me prouissyones or elles i sholld and myne a bine halef famiuyshed but now I will if it plese god that I haue my hellthe I will plant what corne I can and if prouisseyones be no cheper betwein theis and mychellmes and that I do not her from you what I wase beste to do I purpose to c[o]me hom at myckellmes

From John Pond, Letter to His Father, 1631.

General Court consisted of the governor, the deputy governor, the executive council of assistants, and a body of deputies, or representatives, all elected annually by the freemen. Since the company had power to govern the colony, this General Court was in reality both the legislature and the supreme court of the colony. Here, in truth, was a self-governing commonwealth, a Puritan republic.

Puritan New England. The freedom to do as they pleased posed many new problems to men who had not hitherto wielded the powers of government. Reformers and idealists are notoriously prone to dissipate their energies wrangling with one another. And there were disagreements in New England, though not so numerous or severe as has sometimes been suggested. The New England Puritans agreed on a great deal. They wanted congregational churches. They did not want bishops, church courts, or hierarchy. They wanted a government that would take seriously its obligation to enforce God's commandments and to support pure religion. Accordingly they confined suffrage to church members and levied taxes to pay ministers' salaries. But, contrary to common assumption, they did not want their clergy to take any hand in government. For a minister to exercise temporal authority of any kind seemed to the Puritans a dangerous step toward Roman Catholicism. Compared to the clergy of England and Europe the New England minister, though highly influential, had little authority even within his own church. He taught, prayed, preached, and admonished; he commanded respect — else he lost his job — but he did not rule his church. Admissions to membership, censures, pardons, and excommunications were all decided by vote of the church members.

Neither the leaders of the Massachusetts Bay Colony nor the great majority of settlers were Separatists. Though they organized their own churches in the congregational manner, they took pains to affirm their love and friendship for the churches of England. Some even thought that the churches of Rome were not beyond redemption. But among the thousands who stepped ashore at Boston every year were substantial numbers of Separatists and other extremists, full of zeal and eloquence, full of impatience with anyone who disagreed with them. John Winthrop, whom the freemen elected governor year after year during most of his life, was good at turning away wrath and directing zeal to constructive ends. But during the three years from 1634 to 1637, when lesser men sat in the governor's chair, Massachusetts all but succumbed to the denunciations of a brilliant, saintlike, intractable man and a brilliant, proud, magnetic woman.

Roger Williams, who arrived in 1631, was a Separatist. He wanted everyone to repudiate the wicked churches of England. Moreover, he insisted that the royal charter of Massachusetts contained a lie (in claiming that England first discovered the region) and that the king had had no right to grant the charter or the people to accept it without first purchasing the land from the natives. If word got back to England that the Massachusetts government allowed the expression of such subversive ideas, the king might be prompted to take control of the colony and end the Puritan republic. Williams also tried to persuade people that no government had authority over religious matters, not even the right to punish breaches of the Sabbath. In a community which believed that the prime purpose of government was to enforce God's commandments, his action was rank sedition.

Williams was a man whom everyone loved on sight; even John Winthrop became his good friend. But he propagated his inflammatory ideas so insistently, first as assistant to the minister and then as minister of the church at Salem, that the unity of the colony was endangered and the government finally felt obliged to banish him in 1636. He went to Rhode Island, where he was joined by those who believed him. There, while retaining his conviction that the state had no authority over religious matters, he reached the conclusion that in the existing phase of human history God authorized no organized churches at all. In spite of this view, which few of his followers could share, he retained the love and respect of his neighbors and lived out a long and useful life as the leading citizen of the new colony.

Scarcely had Williams been banished when a new threat to the civil and religious security of Massachusetts appeared: Anne Hutchinson, the wife of a merchant whom Winthrop described as "a man of a very mild temper and weak parts, and wholly guided by his wife." An amateur theologian, Mrs. Hutchinson took to elucidating her minister's Sunday sermons in informal gatherings of her neighbors. As the circle of her listeners steadily widened, her discourses became more original, for her keen and imaginative mind could not be contained within the standard doctrines of Puritanism. Starting from the accepted principle that God grants salvation without regard to human merit, she denied (what other Puritans affirmed) that good conduct could be a sign of salvation and affirmed (what other Puritans denied) that the Holy Spirit in the hearts of true believers relieved them of responsibility to obey the laws of God. So, at least, her enemies charged, and she gave substance to their accusation by asserting that all the New England ministers except her favorite, John Cotton, and her brother-in-law, John Wheelwright, were preaching unsound doctrines. By emphasizing morality, she said, they were deluding their congregations into the false assumption that good deeds would get them into heaven. The clergymen hotly denied what was virtually a charge of heresy, and Mrs. Hutchinson herself protested that she had intended no insult. Nevertheless, a host of devoted Bostonians hung on every word she uttered and refused to conceal their contempt for her opponents. The colony split into hostile camps, and finally Mrs. Hutchinson was brought before the authorities. After they had cross-examined her for two days, she made the mistake of claiming that she had received an immediate revelation from God. To Puritan ears, this was blasphemy. So Mrs. Hutchinson too was banished and went to Rhode Island, which thus became the refuge for Puritans with too much originality.

After Charles I was forced to resummon Parliament in 1640, Roger Williams applied to that body (which was overwhelmingly Puritan) for a charter for his colony. The charter, granted in 1644, gave the Rhode Islanders a government much like that of the colony from which they had been expelled: they elected annually a representative assembly, a council of assistants, and a governor (at first called a president), but they did not confine suffrage to church members or collect taxes to support the clergy. In 1663 the existing government was confirmed by a royal charter that also guaranteed the "liberty in religious concernments" which had been the colony's distinction from the beginning.

Meanwhile another part of New England was filling up with Puritans who differed from those of Massachusetts primarily in their desire for more elbow room. In 1636 Thomas Hooker, the minister of Newtown (Cambridge), led an exodus overland to the fertile Connecticut Valley, where the small garrison of a Dutch trading post at Fort Hope (Hartford) was unable to prevent them from settling. They formed a government by a simple agreement among themselves (called the Fundamental Orders). The model, once again, was Massachusetts (but suffrage was not confined to church members), and again the existing arrangement was confirmed by royal charter (1662). The charter also joined to Connecticut the colony of New Haven, initiated in 1638 by a group of Londoners who could find no lands in Massachusetts to suit them.

The settlers of New Haven, beginning with a good supply of capital, had been disappointed in their expectations of a thriving commerce; but they had succeeded in establishing a somewhat stricter government than existed elsewhere in New England, and they were not altogether happy about the union with Connecticut.

There was nevertheless no serious difference between New Haven and the rest of New England. In New Haven as in Plymouth, Massachusetts, Rhode Island, and Connecticut, the population was predominantly Puritan. Puritans directed public policy, and the only serious resistance came from other Puritans. Although some of the inhabitants may have been indifferent or hostile to Puritanism, they were never strong enough or discontented enough to challenge Puritan control.

Settlers who wanted nothing more from the New World than an opportunity to make their fortunes or to live more comfortably than in England had little reason to object to Puritan control anyway. The government frowned on private cupidity when it threatened the public welfare, but Puritans saw no virtue in poverty. They had not traveled three thousand miles simply to starve in a holier manner than in England. They were building a society for all the world to copy, a "city upon a hill," and they meant it to be a success, economically as well as religiously.

So long as the Great Migration lasted, the colonists prospered by selling cattle and provisions to the newcomers each year. When the Migration ended in 1640, New England had its first depression. The settlers looked hard for some native product they could sell to the outside world. Fortunately for them, they found no single product such as the Virginians' tobacco, and they consequently developed a more balanced and more prosperous economy. They caught fish, raised corn and wheat, bred cattle, cut lumber, and built ships. Before many years had passed, New England vessels were prowling the Caribbean and the Mediterranean, peddling their assorted wares, transporting other people's, and bringing home the profits to the city on the hill. By the middle of the seventeenth century New England had laid down its economic as well as its religious foundations.

The Colonies in 1650

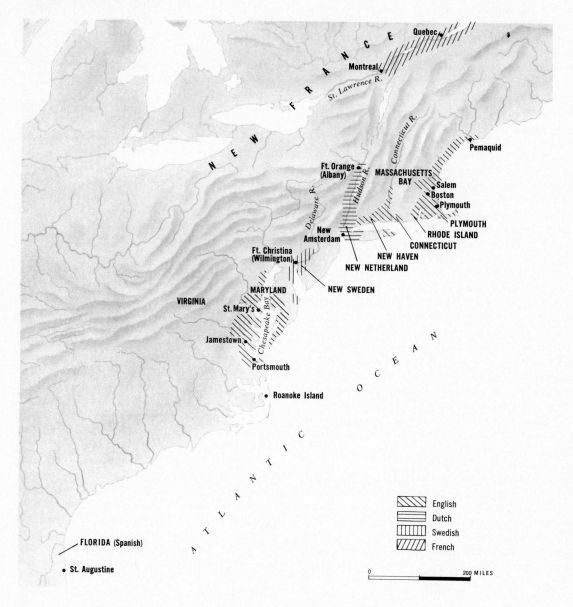

PROPRIETARY VENTURES

During the years that Puritans were building their republics in New England, non-Puritans were trying to establish private domains there and elsewhere. Three years after the Pilgrims landed, Sir Ferdinando Gorges, the most active member of the Council for New England, had backed a settlement at Wessagusset (Weymouth) in the Massachusetts Bay region, but it broke up after a year. Its failure discouraged the rest of the council from further efforts, and they apparently raised no serious objections in 1628 when the Earl of Warwick, president of the council, took it upon himself to grant the Puritans permission to settle the Bay area. In 1637 the Council for New England finally dissolved, leaving behind a host of shadowy claims. Only one claim was perfected: that of Ferdinando Gorges to the region north of the Merrimac River. Gorges divided the area with another would-be New England lord, John Mason, and in 1639 obtained a separate royal charter for his own share. He died in 1647, with no feudal retainers in his New World barony except a few hardy fishermen who pledged allegiance to no one. Massachusetts annexed the whole region in 1651.

The king authorized other ambitious gentlemen to colonize Newfoundland, Nova Scotia, and the Carolinas, but to no effect. The first English nobleman to realize the aristocrat's dream of founding a New World domain for his family was George Calvert, Lord Baltimore. A notable figure in the court of James I, Calvert had become interested in America first as a member of the Virginia Company and later as a member of the Council for New England. In 1620 he purchased rights in southeastern Newfoundland from another noble dreamer and started a settlement there. When he visited the place himself, he found that "from the middle of October to the middst of May there is a sadd face of wynter upon all this land." Deciding to leave Newfoundland to the fishermen, he asked the king for a grant farther south. The charter, which was in the making when Calvert died in 1632, was finally issued to his son Cecilius. It conveyed to him 10 million acres on Chesapeake Bay, where the Calvert family was to have complete powers of government. The colony was to be known as Maryland, in honor of the queen of Charles I.

The name was appropriate, for both the queen and the Calverts were Catholics. Maryland was to be a feudal seigniory and at the same time a religious refuge. As a feudal seigniory it came nearer to success than any other attempted in America. Though the Calverts did not live there, they governed the colony (sometimes through a younger son), owned all the public lands, granted small estates or "manors" to their friends, and collected rents from the settlers. Because Virginia, Plymouth, and Massachusetts lent a hand, the settlers of Maryland were spared the early days of starvation that had been suffered by other colonists. Tobacco grew as readily in Maryland as in Virginia, and the two colonies became identical in their economic pursuits and interests.

As a religious refuge Maryland also succeeded. Although official hostility to Catholicism had relaxed in England under Charles, Catholics were still required by law to take oaths and to attend religious services that conflicted with their beliefs. In Maryland they would be free to worship as they chose, and so would other Christians. As it turned out, more Puritans came to the colony than Catholics. The Calverts welcomed both, and from the time of the first settlement in 1634 tried to prevent either group from oppressing the other. When the Jesuits threatened to become too powerful, Baltimore, in 1641, forbade them to hold land in Maryland. The Puritans were harder to handle, especially after 1640, when their friends gained the upper hand in England, but Baltimore did his best to restrain them. By the terms of his charter he was obliged to obtain the consent of the "freemen" (presumably in this case the term meant all adult males not bound as servants) to all legislation. As the population increased, the freemen deputed a few individuals to act for them in this matter, and thus arose a representative assembly similar to those which developed in the other colonies. This assembly in 1649 consented to the famous Maryland Toleration Act, securing freedom of worship to all Christians, whether Protestant or Catholic, who believed in the Trinity. The Calverts upheld the act through successive generations and thus made their colony, like Rhode Island, a model of what the rest of America was one day to become.

By the middle of the seventeenth century England had seeded North America. Many more immigrants were to come, from England and elsewhere, but the future was already visible on the coasts of New England and of Chesapeake Bay. Englishmen had moved in, and whether they favored toleration, as in Maryland and Rhode Island, or intolerance, as in Massachusetts, whether they caught fish or grew tobacco, the continent was effectively theirs.

SUGGESTIONS FOR READING

A good account of the American Indians before the coming of the white man is Kenneth MacGowan, *Early Man in the New World** (1950). Clark Wissler, *Indians of the United States: Four Centuries of Their History and Culture* (1940), is more comprehensive.

Anyone interested in the age of exploration should give his first attention to S. E. Morison's great biography of Columbus, *Admiral of the Ocean Sea* (1942), and to J. H. Parry, *The Age of Reconnaissance* (1963). J. B. Brebner, *The Explorers of North America, 1492–1806** (1933), is authoritative. A penetrating and succinct study of Spanish exploits and problems is Charles Gibson, *Spain in America* (1966), which contains a good bibliography of the subject. On the English voyages there is no substitute for Richard Hakluyt's collection of first-hand accounts, *The Principall Navigations, Voiages, and Discoveries of the English Nation* (1589, 1599), reprinted in Everyman's Library, *Hakluyt's Voyages,* 8 vols. Hakluyt's work has been carried on in the voluminous publications of the Hakluyt Society. Among these, see especially the volumes edited by D. B. Quinn, *Voyages and Colonising Enterprises of Sir Humphrey Gilbert,* 2 vols. (1940), and *The Roanoke Voyages, 1584–1590,* 2 vols. (1955). A full account of methods of navigation in this period is D. W. Waters, *The Art of Navigation in England in Elizabethan and Early Stuart Times* (1958).

The English Reformation is ably discussed in M. M. Knappen, *Tudor Puritanism** (1939); Maurice Powicke, *The Reformation in England** (1941); and C. H. and Katherine George, *The Protestant Mind of the English Reformation* (1961). For social conditions in sixteenth- and seventeenth-century England, R. H. Tawney, *The Agrarian Problem in the Sixteenth Century* (1912), and *Religion and the Rise of Capitalism** (1926), are both important, as is "The Rise of the Gentry, 1558–1640," *Economic History Review,* XI (1941), 1–38. This article started a lively controversy among historians as to whether the gentry were rising or falling in the sixteenth and early seventeenth centuries. The controversy is summarized and continued in J. H. Hexter, "Storm over the Gentry," *Encounter,* May (1958), 22–34. This and several other penetrating essays by Professor Hexter are reprinted in *Reappraisals in History** (1961). Mildred Campbell, *The English Yeoman under Elizabeth and the Early Stuarts* (1942), is fully documented and has met with no serious challenge. It is matched by Lawrence Stone, *The Crisis of the Aristocracy* (1965). The best account of English political and legal institutions is Wallace Notestein, *The English People on the Eve of Colonization, 1603–1630** (1954).

On the first permanent English settlements in America, the most convenient and the most authoritative account is C. M. Andrews, *The Colonial Period of American History,* Vols. I–III** (1934–37). For the Southern colonies this should be supplemented by W. F. Craven, *The Southern Colonies in the Seventeenth Century* (1949). Captain John Smith tells his own story in *Travels and Works of Captain John Smith,* 2 vols. (1910), ed. by Edward Arber and A. G. Bradley. A sympathetic modern biography is Bradford Smith, *Captain John Smith: His Life and Legend* (1953). The fullest modern study is Philip L. Barbour, *The Three Worlds of Captain John Smith* (1964). W. F. Craven, *The Dissolution of the Virginia Company* (1932), is a masterful study of the internal divisions that impaired the company's efforts in America.

The New England Puritans have been subjected to the scrutiny of historians, sympathetic and unsympathetic, from the time the settlers first stepped ashore. William Bradford, the governor of the Plymouth Colony, told the story of the Pilgrims in *Of Plymouth Plantation,* an American classic that can best be read in S. E. Morison's edition (1952). The most thorough history by a modern scholar is George Langdon, *Pilgrim Colony: A History of New Plymouth, 1620–1691* (1966).

* Available in a paperback edition.

In his *Journal*, Governor John Winthrop did for Massachusetts Bay what Bradford did for Plymouth. The best edition is that of James Savage, 2 vols. (1853), but this is hard to come by. The only edition in print is the modernized and expurgated one of J. K. Hosmer, 2 vols. (1908). For a contrast with Bradford and Winthrop, read Thomas Morton, *New English Canaan* (1637, 1883).

In the nineteenth century J. G. Palfrey, *History of New England*, 5 vols. (1858–90), praised the Puritans excessively, while Brooks Adams, *The Emancipation of Massachusetts** (1886), condemned them excessively. In the twentieth century J. T. Adams again attacked them, in *The Founding of New England** (1921), while S. E. Morison defended them in *Builders of the Bay Colony** (1930), which is by all odds the best introduction to the history of New England. Morison continued his study of the Puritans in his monumental works on Harvard, *The Founding of Harvard College* (1935) and *Harvard in the Seventeenth Century*, 2 vols. (1936), and in a briefer study, *The Puritan Pronaos* (1936), reprinted as *The Intellectual Life of Colonial New England** (1956).

New England Puritanism is also the subject of the most profound study of intellectual history yet written by an American, Perry Miller, *The New England Mind: The Seventeenth Century** (1939) and *The New England Mind: From Colony to Province** (1953). These volumes were preceded by his briefer study, *Orthodoxy in Massachusetts, 1630–1650* (1933), the subject of which falls chronologically between the two. Miller explores other aspects of New England history in a brilliant collection of essays, *Errand into the Wilderness** (1956).

Puritan domestic life and social relations are examined in E. S. Morgan, *The Puritan Family** (1944). The conduct of church affairs is treated in Ola Winslow, *Meetinghouse Hill* (1952); the Puritan conception of the church in E. S. Morgan, *Visible Saints** (1963). The best biography of Roger Williams is Ola Winslow, *Master Roger Williams* (1957). E. S. Morgan, *Roger Williams: the Church and the State* (1967) analyzes Williams' ideas. Emery Battis, *Saints and Sectaries* (1962), gives a provocative psychological interpretation of Anne Hutchinson.

A valuable study of early New England economic history is Bernard Bailyn, *The New England Merchants in the Seventeenth Century** (1955). E. S. Morgan has dealt with some of the political problems faced by the founders of Massachusetts in *The Puritan Dilemma: The Story of John Winthrop** (1958). Later Puritan problems as exemplified in the Winthrop family are treated in R. S. Dunn, *Puritans and Yankees: The Winthrop Dynasty of New England* (1962). G. L. Haskins, *Law and Authority in Early Massachusetts* (1960), describes political and social as well as legal institutions.

* Available in a paperback edition.

2
The Pattern of Empire

The first settlements in America, which cost Englishmen dearly in lives and money, cost the English government nothing. But in authorizing settlement the government did expect to gain something more than an outlet for disgruntled Puritans and adventurous fortune-seekers. Every European government, from the sixteenth century through the eighteenth, followed an economic policy that has been known since 1776, when Adam Smith coined the word, as mercantilism.

MERCANTILISM

Mercantilism meant that the state directed all economic activities within its borders, subordinating private profit to public good. In particular the government sought to increase national wealth by discouraging imports and encouraging exports. The English government let Englishmen go to America because it was persuaded that their presence there would further this end.

Long before the settlement of Jamestown, Richard Hakluyt had explained how the mother country could profit from American colonies: they would furnish England with supplies such as lumber, tar, and hemp, which she was buying from other countries, and they would offer a market for the woolens that were England's principal export. "It behooves this realm," Hakluyt wrote in 1584, "if it mean . . . not negligently and sleepingly to slide into beggary, to foresee and plant [a colony] at Norumbega [a name for northern North America] or some like place, were it not for anything else but for the hope of the sale of our wool." What England wanted from America was what Hakluyt said she would get: a market for her woolen cloth and other manufactures and a source of supply for raw materials that she had to import from other countries.

What England wanted was not incompatible with what the settlers wanted. North America was full of valuable natural resources and short of people. The most profitable activity for the settlers was therefore the extraction of resources that required a minimum of labor — lumber,

New York, 1717.

for example, or iron or furs. It would be unprofitable for them to make things whose value came primarily from the labor that went into them — fine furniture, for example, or clothing or wrought iron. England, on the other hand, was full of people and short of the raw materials that America possessed in such abundance; so her interests lay the other way round. It would be mutually advantageous for the colonies to buy manufactures from the mother country and for the mother country to buy raw materials from the colonies.

The British empire in America was based on this compatibility of interests. But, while the interests were compatible, they required guidance to make them coincide. Left to themselves, the colonies might peddle their produce in France or Holland instead of England and take home French textiles instead of English, or they might produce materials not needed in England. In order to make the system work, it was necessary for the mother country to maintain continuous supervision and control over the economic activities of the settlers just as she did over the activities of Englishmen at home. The English government never doubted its right to exercise such control, but it was slow to develop consistent directives or effective machinery for carrying them out.

England's imperial delay. In the early years, before the colonies began to fulfill Hakluyt's glowing predictions, economic regulation probably did not seem urgent. Although the English government in 1621 ordered all Virginia tobacco to be brought to England, the order was not enforced, perhaps because English authorities considered it a mixed blessing for the nation to have its own private supply of smoke. But other regulations, adopted from time to time, also went unenforced. One reason was distance. Three thousand miles of ocean made a formidable barrier in the seventeenth century. Although it was much faster and easier to travel long distances by water than by land, even over water three thousand miles was space enough in which to lose messages, orders, and interest.

A more serious obstacle to English control than either the distance or the seeming unimportance of the colonies was politics. During the seventeenth century, when most of her American colonies were founded, England was torn by a struggle for power between king and Parliament. In the 1630's Charles I ruled without Parliament, but by 1640 he needed it to pay his bills. He called it, dismissed it, called it again, and then found that he could not dismiss it any more. In 1642 the members raised an army to make war on him; in 1649 they cut off his head, and for eleven years England had no king. In his place from 1649 to 1658 stood Oliver Cromwell, the soldier who had defeated him.

When Charles II, son of the old king, was placed on the throne in 1660, the acts of the preceding eleven years were declared null and void. But Charles had the good sense to realize that English kings henceforth must work with Parliament or not at all. His brother and successor, James II, had no sense, and within three years of his accession in 1685 he had to flee the country. Parliament quietly replaced him with William and Mary in the bloodless Revolution of 1688. After 1688 the king was still no cipher in government, but everyone understood that he was subordinate to Parliament.

All but one (Georgia) of the thirteen colonies that later became the United States were founded before 1688, during the years when the ultimate location of sovereignty in England was uncertain. They were all founded under authority of the king, and their relationship to Parliament remained ambiguous. Parliament sometimes passed legislation affecting them, but even after 1688 it did not do so regularly. Yet if the king had denied the authority of Parliament in the colonies, Parliament would doubtless have brought him up short.

Distance, indifference, and the uncertain location of authority in England conspired to delay the development of a consistent and continuous colonial policy. From the founding of Virginia in 1607 until the middle of the seventeenth century the colonies interested king and Parliament only as a minor prize in the contest for sovereignty. In 1633, when Charles I was trying to rule without Parliament, he appointed a commission headed by Archbishop Laud to govern the colonies. But the commissioners were too busy in England to do anything about America. During the English civil wars of the 1640's, Parliament and king both claimed authority over the colonies, but neither was able to exercise it.

Oliver Cromwell was the first ruler of England sure enough of his position at home to think seriously about fitting the colonies into a general imperial scheme. In 1650 and 1651 he secured legislation to keep foreign shipping out of the colonies. He also planned a great expansion of the empire in the Caribbean and tried to persuade New Englanders to move to the West Indies, where the cultivation of sugar and other tropical products promised rich rewards. But his legislation against foreign shipping led to war with the uncooperative Dutch; his large military and naval expedition to the West Indies in 1655 captured only Jamaica; and his powers of persuasion proved insufficient to lure New Englanders from their rocky soil. They suspected, perhaps, that Puritanism would not work well in the tropics.

The Navigation Acts. When Charles II came to the throne in 1660, the colonies, in spite of Cromwell's failures, had grown enough to require attention. Virginia and Maryland were exporting over 7 million pounds of tobacco yearly, much of which never reached England, and New England harbored a group of merchants whose ships were already familiar in the markets of the world. English merchants, awakened to the potentialities of colonial trade, pressed the government for measures to prevent the profits from leaking into the pockets of foreign rivals. What they wanted was not merely to exclude foreign shipping from the colonies (as Cromwell had attempted in the acts of 1650 and 1651) but to direct colonial trade into channels profitable to the mother country. King and Parliament, in the first flush of Restoration harmony, agreed on two acts to take care of the matter.

These so-called Navigation Acts (1660 and 1663) were modified from time to time during the ensuing century, but their basic principles remained the same: (1) they forbade all trade with the colonies except in ships owned and constructed there or in England and manned by crews of which at least three-quarters were English or colonial; (2) they forbade the transportation *from* the colonies *to* any place except England or another English colony of certain "enumerated commodities," namely sugar, cotton, indigo, dyewoods, ginger, and tobacco; and (3) they forbade the transportation of European goods *to* the colonies *from* any place except England.

Subsequent modification of the Navigation Acts consisted mainly of additions to the list of enumerated commodities (rice in 1704, naval stores in 1705, copper and furs in 1721) or specific limitations on, or encouragement of, colonial products. The act of 1705 that enumerated naval stores (pitch, tar, turpentine, masts, spars) also placed bounties on their production. The Wool Act (1699) forbade export from the colonies of certain textiles manufactured there. The Hat Act (1732) forbade export of colonial-made hats. The Iron Act (1750) removed all duties on English imports of colonial pig and bar iron (thus encouraging their production) but forbade the erection of any new colonial iron mills for manufacturing raw iron into finished products.

The Navigation Acts were ostensibly intended to ensure that the mother country would benefit from the economic activities of the colonies. But, in passing the original acts and in modifying them over the years, Parliament was not immune to the wishes of special groups. Adam Smith, in coining the very name "mercantilism," was charging that English policies were dictated by merchants at the expense of the rest of the community. And indeed particular acts were often opposed by one group as much as they were favored by another. The Iron Act, for example, represented a victory of English iron-manufacturers over English iron-miners and smelters; and in 1733 the Molasses Act, which placed a heavy duty on foreign molasses imported into North America, was a victory for one group of colonists, the West Indian sugar-planters, over another, the rum-distilling colonists of New England.

Besides serving such private interests, and besides subordinating colonial trade to English, the Navigation Acts aimed at increasing the

---

The Use of America: Opportunity

These persons that providence seems to have most fitted for Plantations are,

1st. Industrious Husbandmen and Day-Labourers, that are hardly able ... to maintain their Families....

2dly. Laborous Handicrafts, especially Carpenters, Masons, Smiths, Weavers, Taylors, Tanners, Shoemakers, Shipwrights, etc. where they may be spared or are low in the World....

3dly. A Plantation seems a fit place for those Ingenious Spirits that being low in the World, are much clogged and oppressed about a Livelyhood, for the means of subsisting being easie there, they may have time and opportunity to gratify their inclinations, and thereby improve Science and help Nurseries of people.

4thly. A fourth sort of men to whom a Plantation would be proper, takes in those that are younger Brothers of small Inheritances....

Lastly, There are another sort of persons, not only fit for, but necessary in Plantations, and that is, Men of universal Spirits, that have an eye to the Good of Posterity, and that both understand and delight to promote good Discipline and just Government among a plain and well intending people.

From William Penn, *Some Account of the Province of Pennsylvania*, 1681.

revenue of the English government, at least indirectly. Although the acts of 1660 and 1663 levied no taxes, the government from the beginning had collected duties in England on imports from the colonies. By requiring enumerated commodities to be brought only to England, the government expected to step up the importation of taxable goods. The expectation was not unrealistic. Revenue obtained from duties on tobacco imports alone amounted in the 1660's to £100,000 annually, or as much as the planters themselves made from the crop.

The Navigation Acts transformed the hopeful predictions of Hakluyt into specific legislation that told the colonists what they could and could not make, where and how they could trade. But the colonies were still three thousand miles from the lawmakers. If England was to receive the full benefit of the acts, they had to be enforced against foreign nations on the one hand and against refractory colonists on the other.

The Dutch. The principal foreign threat to England's emerging mercantilist empire in the seventeenth century came from the Dutch. This was their century; they seemed on the way to running the world. After shaking off Spanish domination, they built the largest merchant fleet ever known. Dutch captains nosed out rival vessels everywhere, took over most of the Portuguese empire in the East Indies, opened trade with Japan. Dutch privateers led the pack in raiding Spanish treasure fleets. Dutch merchants controlled the lumber trade from the Baltic and made Amsterdam the sawmill of Europe. Dutch fishermen dominated the North Sea. Dutch textile-workers finished and resold woolen cloth imported raw from England. When England tried to stop the export and save the valuable finishing process for her own workers, the Dutch simply boycotted English cloth, and depression settled over the whole English woolens industry. This was the century of Rembrandt, Vermeer, Hals, Hobbema, DeHooch, the century of Huygens and Spinoza. Man for man, no people has ever matched the seventeenth-century achievement of the Dutch.

In North America the Dutch had not extended themselves with the vigor they showed elsewhere, probably because North America offered fewer prospects of immediate reward. Nevertheless, Dutch ships every year appeared in Virginia's great rivers to carry tobacco to Holland instead of England. Dutch textiles were sold in the shops of Boston. And the region that the Dutch had chosen for their settlements and trading posts in North America was strategically and economically the most important on the continent. The Hudson River commanded access to the interior by the only water-level route through the Appalachian Mountains. From the Hudson, it was possible to reach the Mississippi Valley along the Mohawk River Valley (or with greater difficulty by Lake George, Lake Champlain, and the St. Lawrence). Economically the Hudson River was the principal outlet of the fur trade south of the St. Lawrence; strategically it was an avenue along which an ambitious nation could strike for control of the inner continent. The Dutch were not that ambitious, but they did find New Netherland a convenient base from which to attack the Spaniards, drain off the continent's fur supply, and collect profit from England's settlements to the north and south.

When Charles II set about enforcing the Navigation Acts, he took care of the Dutch problem in North America in the simplest possible way. He made a gift of the Dutch territories to his brother James, the Duke of York. To the seemingly formidable task of delivering the gift he assigned four commissioners, with four frigates and four hundred men. The commissioners arrived in 1664, a time when the Dutch settlers had been demoralized by arbitrary and incompetent governors. To everyone's surprise, the colony surrendered without resistance, and the commissioners took possession for the duke of the entire region from Maryland to Connecticut.

The Dutch in Holland, already at odds with England, declared war and continued to violate the Navigation Acts wherever willing colonists and the absence of the British navy made it possible. In the long run, the problem of enforcement could be solved not by foreign war but only by effective administrative machinery within the colonies themselves. That problem became at once more difficult and more urgent as a new burst of colonizing activity increased the dimensions of the empire.

THE RESTORATION COLONIES

The colonies founded in the second half of the seventeenth century were "proprietary," that is, they were founded by proprietors who exercised government over them and initially owned all the land in them. The proprietors, generally friends or relatives of the king, hoped to grow rich from the sale of their lands and from the annual fees, or quitrents (usually a shilling per fifty acres), that they charged the settlers. They kept the quitrents low enough not to deter prospective immigrants but high enough to guarantee themselves a tidy permanent income when the colony should be fully populated.

The new colonies all resembled Maryland in their proprietary origin (see p. 27); they differed from Maryland and the other old colonies in the sources from which they drew their actual settlers: comparatively few came directly from England. Some were on the spot already, like the Dutch and Swedish settlers in New Netherland. More came from Scotland, Ireland, Wales, France, and Germany. Still more came from America itself, men who had grown discontented for one reason or another with the part of the New World they already occupied and wanted to try a new place.

This search for greener pastures was to become one of the abiding characteristics of American life. Once uprooted, a man might wander long before he found a spot where he could remain content. After a few months or years in a new home, one morning he would turn his back on surroundings that had scarcely become familiar and be off to the promised land beyond the horizon. His children too might never put down the kind of roots that held Europeans to the family farm or village. The Great Migration that ended in England in 1640 never quite ended in America.

From this restless breed of men the new proprietors hoped to draw tenants for their feudal domains. Tenants less likely to pay feudal rents would have been hard to find, but that fact was not immediately apparent.

New York. The most important of the new colonies was New York, whose settlers and problems the Duke of York had inherited from the Dutch. New Netherland had been primarily a series of riverside trading posts, located at Swaanendael (Lewes), Fort Nassau (Newcastle), and Fort Casimir (in Gloucester County, New Jersey) on the Delaware, and at Fort Orange (Albany) and Esopus (Kingston) on the Hudson. But New Amsterdam (New York City) at the mouth of the Hudson and a few other areas had more advanced settlements. The merchants of New Amsterdam were no longer mere Indian traders, and their flourishing overseas business supported a sizable and diversified community. In the Hudson Valley a number of well-to-do Dutchmen had tried to found agricultural settlements, known as patroonships, of the very kind that English proprietors were hoping to establish. One of these, belonging to Kiliaen van Rensselaer, had approached success. Though Rensselaer himself had gained little profit from it, his tenants still occupied the lands. On Manhattan, on the western end of Long Island, and in the lower Hudson Valley there were a few villages of Dutch farmers; and in eastern Long Island a number of New England Puritans had transplanted themselves and their way of life. The Dutch, finding them difficult to cope with, had left them much to themselves.

The Dutch West India Company had governed these sprawling settlements through a director-general. Of the men who held the post, Wouter van Twiller (1633–38) and Willem Kieft (1638–47) had been disastrously foolish; and Peter Stuyvesant (1647–64), who surrendered the colony to the English, was little better. All had governed without benefit of a popular assembly. English rule brought no immediate changes, except in the quality of the governors. The terms of surrender confirmed the old settlers in their property rights. The Duke of York, by the charter that conveyed the area to him, was given full authority to govern as he saw fit. Since the duke had no fondness for representative assemblies, he appointed a governor to rule in the same manner as the old director-general.

Though the Dutch were not happy about rule by Englishmen, they submitted peacefully to the governors James sent: Richard Nicolls (1664–68), Francis Lovelace (1668–73), Edmund Andros (1674–81), and Thomas Dongan (1683–88). The New Englanders on Long Island were less docile. They showed the familiar unfriendliness of Englishmen toward govern-

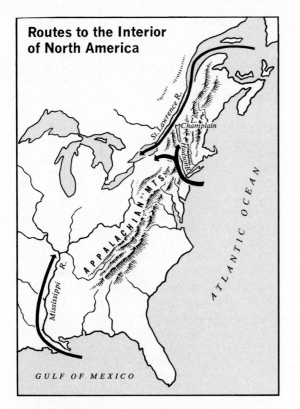

Routes to the Interior of North America

York with eighteen representatives elected from the various areas of the duke's propriety. One of the assembly's first actions was to pass a Charter of Liberties stating the right of the inhabitants to all the traditional political and civil liberties of Englishmen, such as trial by jury and representative government. Though this charter received the duke's assent, he repudiated it in 1686, after New York had been transformed from a proprietary to a royal colony by his accession (1685) to the throne of England as James II.

New Jersey. New York in 1685 was not as large as New Netherland had been. Three and a half months after receiving his grant of the area, James had transferred the part later called New Jersey to two friends: John, Lord Berkeley, a privy councillor much interested in naval affairs, and Sir George Carteret, Vice-Chamberlain of the Royal Household and Treasurer of the Navy (James himself was Lord High Admiral, in charge of the navy). There followed a comedy of errors that was never entirely straightened out.

James' governor in New York, Richard Nicolls, did not learn of the transfer to Berkeley and Carteret until after he had himself granted lands in the New Jersey region to a number of New England Puritans from eastern Long Island. Nicolls, who was anxious to get the land settled and producing revenue, offered the Puritans the right to govern themselves through their own assembly. They in turn agreed to pay quitrents to James. Nicolls actually had no authority to offer such terms, but the Puritans accepted them and moved in.

When Berkeley and Carteret gained possession, they too offered liberal terms to settlers. They too wanted quitrents and promised a representative assembly to make laws. More Puritans, this time from New Haven, accepted the offer and moved in.

James, in transferring New Jersey to Berkeley and Carteret, gave them only property rights over the colony. His own governmental authority was not transferable. Berkeley and Carteret therefore had no authority either to hold a representative assembly or to appoint a governor. Yet they did both, and neither James nor his brother the king objected.

But the cantankerous transplanted New Englanders, who had accepted grants from Nic-

ments in which the governed had no representation. Governor Nicolls tried to appease them at the outset by compiling a special set of laws for them, drawn in part from the New England laws, which they presumably liked. This code, known as the Duke's Laws, was presented to a meeting of representatives from seventeen towns in 1665, but the meeting was not allowed to alter or add to it. The inhabitants accepted it but not gratefully. During the ensuing years they objected continually to paying taxes without representation and, instead of being happy about their rescue from the Dutch, complained that they were now "inslav'd under an Arbitrary Power."

Perhaps because of the noisy discontent of these New Englanders, New York attracted comparatively few new settlers. There was consequently little profit from rents for the Duke of York. His governors told him of the demand for a representative assembly and hinted that the colony might be easier to govern with one than without. In 1683 he gave way, and on October 17 the first assembly was held at New

olls, did object. They held their own assembly and refused to accept the authority of the government established by the proprietors. The vehemence of their protests and their carelessness in paying rents were not diminished by subsequent developments. Berkeley and Carteret divided the province in two in 1674. Berkeley, who had taken the western half, sold it that same year to a Quaker, who resold shares to other Quakers. In 1680, after Carteret died, the eastern half, where both groups of Puritans were located, was sold at auction to another group of Quakers. The fact that the proprietors were now Quakers did not endear them or their government to the Puritan settlers. The Puritans continued to protest until the English government awoke to the fact that the government of New Jersey rested on a false assumption of power by the original proprietors. In 1702 East and West New Jersey were united as a royal colony with a single representative assembly and with the proprietors retaining only their property rights. To this day the public lands of New Jersey belong to two boards of proprietors inheriting their rights from Berkeley and Carteret.

The Carolinas. Before Berkeley and Carteret received the grant of New Jersey, they had already become involved with several highly placed friends in a project for another colony in the region directly south of Virginia, known as Carolina. The moving spirit in this enterprise was probably Sir John Colleton, an old royalist soldier. After Charles I lost his head in 1649, Colleton had gone to Barbados. There he found that the Great Migration had deposited thousands of hopeful immigrants, who had carved the island into small farms. After 1640, however, as sugar gradually became the dominant crop, the land was absorbed into ever larger plantations worked by increasing numbers of imported Negro slaves. Most of the settlers had been squeezed off their farms and were now ready to move to the continent, where land was more plentiful.

When Colleton returned to England in 1660, he realized that this ready-made population for a new colony lay waiting, and he was probably already interested in the Carolina region. In London he met Sir William Berkeley, brother of John and royal governor of Virginia (1641–52 and 1660–77). Berkeley knew that

The Restoration Colonies

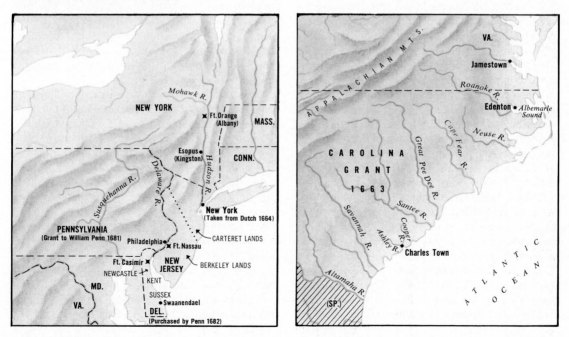

the Virginians had occupied much of their own tidewater land and were ready to expand down the coast into Carolina. Before long, Berkeley and Colleton had assembled a blue-ribbon board of would-be proprietors for the new colony. Besides themselves there were Berkeley's brother John; Sir George Carteret; Anthony Ashley Cooper, later Earl of Shaftesbury; George Monck, Duke of Albemarle (who had engineered Charles II's return to the throne); William, Earl of Craven; and Edward Hyde, Earl of Clarendon. To such men the king could not say no even though they were asking for the whole area extending from the present Atlantic border of the states of North Carolina, South Carolina, and Georgia westward to the Pacific.

The proprietors received the territory by royal charter on March 24, 1663, and they moved at once to fill it with footloose farmers from Virginia, New England, and Barbados. From the beginning they proposed two distinct centers for settlement. The region of Albemarle Sound in the northernmost part of their grant was already sparsely occupied by settlers who had drifted in from Virginia. The proprietors gave them a governor in 1664; a popularly elected assembly met for the first time by June 1665. At the end of the century this colony of North Carolina had a population of four or five thousand engaged in subsistence farming and tobacco culture. They shipped a million pounds of tobacco a year, in shallow-draft vessels sent to Albemarle Sound by enterprising New England merchants.

Farther south, where the Cape Fear River offered a better harbor than did Albemarle Sound, the proprietors intended to plant a second colony. New Englanders had already tried living here without authorization from England but had pulled out after tacking up a sign at the mouth of the river, warning future settlers that the country was not worth occupying. This may have been an early piece of Yankee shrewdness, for the proprietors found a continuing interest in the region among New Englanders — not enough, however, to induce many Puritans to move there and pay quitrents to absentee proprietors (there were no quitrents in New England). The first authorized colonists were mainly Barbadians, who came in 1665 and dispersed in 1667 — to Virginia,

to the Albemarle region, to New England, or back to Barbados. A successful settlement, sponsored primarily by Anthony Ashley Cooper, was finally made farther south. Well equipped with provisions, an expedition set out from England in 1669 and picked up reinforcements at Barbados and other islands en route. The settlers located themselves at first on the south bank of the Ashley River about twenty-five miles from the sea. In 1680 they moved to the present site of Charleston (called Charles Town until 1783), where, as later Carolinians would have it, the Ashley and Cooper rivers join to form the Atlantic Ocean.

The proprietors had provided the settlers with a constitution designed to strike a balance between aristocracy and democracy. Drafted presumably by Cooper's secretary, John Locke, the Fundamental Constitutions of Carolina were based more on the political philosophy of James Harrington than on the philosophy for which Locke himself was to become famous (see p. 69). Harrington believed that the structure of government should match the distribution of property among the governed. The proprietors proposed to people three-fifths of their property with ordinary settlers (who would pay an annual quitrent) and to keep the rest in seigneurial and manorial estates for a hereditary nobility. The government was to consist of a governor appointed by the proprietors and a legislature in which the upper house would represent the nobility, the lower the commoners. The upper house was to have the sole right to initiate legislation (another idea of Harrington's).

The settlers of South Carolina, by accretions of Barbadians, French Huguenots, New Englanders, Englishmen, Scots, and Negro slaves, increased to eight or ten thousand by the end of the century. Having discovered that rice grew well in the area, they cultivated it extensively in plantations around Charles Town. Beyond the plantations, frontiersmen outflanked the Appalachian Mountains, pushed back Spanish missions, and penetrated the interior of the continent to open a brisk trade with the Indians in deerskins and in slaves captured from other tribes. Charles Town grew into a city, the only one in the South. In spite of hurricanes, Indian attacks, and internal quarrels, South Carolina succeeded.

The Fundamental Constitutions did not. As in other colonies, the representative assembly — the lower house of the legislature — was impatient of restrictions: it claimed and took the right to initiate legislation, quarreled with the governor and the upper house, and generally got its way. By 1700 the Fundamental Constitutions were a dead letter, and proprietary rule was faltering. In 1719 a rebellion in Charles Town overthrew the last proprietary governor, and two years later a provisional royal government was organized in the colony. The proprietors finally surrendered their charter in 1729, and royal governments were provided for both North and South Carolina, each with a governor and council appointed by the king and an assembly elected by the land-owners.

William Penn's holy experiment. The last English colony to be founded in the seventeenth century was also the private property of a friend of the king. It would be hard to imagine a more unlikely friend for Charles II than William Penn, Quaker, commoner, and enemy of royal prerogative. The association, a tribute to breadth of character in both men, began in the career of Penn's father, who was no Quaker. William Penn the elder started life as an ordinary seaman and by sheer ability worked his way to the rank of admiral. He was in charge of naval operations in Cromwell's grandiose expedition to the West Indies. When the expedition captured nothing but Jamaica, the admiral retired in disgrace to Ireland, where he remained until Charles II took the throne.

Disgrace under Cromwell was no bar to preferment under Charles. Admiral Penn was on hand to see the new king crowned in 1660 and took the occasion to present his son, then aged sixteen. In the ensuing years, while the father headed the navy office under the Duke of York, young Penn did the things that sons of gentlemen were expected to do. It was conventional that he should attend Oxford and almost conventional that he be expelled after two years and sent on the grand tour of the Continent by a worried father. It was conventional too that he should spend some time at the Inns of Court studying law, but without becoming a barrister. As he reached maturity, Penn had the standard qualifications of a young courtier: high spirits, ready wit, skill as a swordsman. He cut a dashing figure at the court of the king. But he had one quality that was not quite conventional, one that kings, courtiers, and fathers of young gentlemen have often found embarrassing: he took ideas seriously.

What was worse, the ideas he took most seriously were of the most embarrassing kind: radical, lower class, faintly ridiculous. The Quakers (later called Friends) had initially been the lunatic fringe of the Puritan movement. They heard voices; they insulted their betters; they appeared naked in church. One of them, James Nayler, thought he was Jesus Christ and entered the city of Bristol riding on an ass, with his admirers singing holy, holy, holy before him.

The authorities dealt with Nayler: they bored his tongue with a hot iron, cut off his ears, and branded his forehead with the letter *B* for blasphemer — thereby demonstrating what might have happened to Christ if he *had* reappeared. Respectable Englishmen thought that madmen like Nayler were typical of Quakerism. But by the 1660's Quakers had shaken free of these eccentricities and were challenging the world by practicing what they preached.

What they preached was not far different from what other Christians had always preached. What others had variously called conscience, revelation, or saving grace, Quakers called the Inner Light. The Inner Light, they said, glowed in every man. He had only to live by it in order to be saved. Quakers tried to live by it.

All Christians believed that humility is a virtue. But the Quakers studiously, almost fanatically, avoided pride and the institutions that pride erected: they wore conspicuously plain and out-of-date clothes; they refused to honor one another — or anyone else — by bowing or kneeling or taking off their hats, or by using the second person plural when addressing an individual (ultimately they forgot the nominative and used only "thee"). All Christians professed brotherly love; but the Quakers refused to make war. They also refused to give or take oaths, partly because they believed the imposition of an oath implied distrust of one's fellow men.

Samuel Pepys on William Penn

[August 26, 1664] This day my wife tells me Mr. Pen, Sir William's son, is come back from France, and come to visit her. A most modish person, grown, she says, a fine gentleman.

[August 30, 1664] ... after dinner comes Mr. Pen to visit me, and staid an houre talking with me. I perceive something of learning he hath got, but a great deale, if not too much, of the French garbe and affected manner of speech and gait.

[December 29, 1667] At night comes Mrs. Turner to see us; and there, among other talk, she tells me that Mr. William Pen, who is lately come over from Ireland, is a Quaker again, or some very melancholy thing; that he cares for no company, nor comes into any: which is a pleasant thing, after his being abroad so long, and his father such a hypocritical rogue, and at this time an Atheist.

[October 12, 1668] So to supper, and after supper to read a ridiculous nonsensical book set out by Will. Pen, for the Quakers; but so full of nothing but nonsense, I was ashamed to read in it.

From the Diary of Samuel Pepys.

William Penn on William Penn

It is now above Twenty Years, I thank God, that I have not been very sollicitous what the World thought of me. For since I have had the Knowledge of Religion from a Principle in my self, the First and Main Point with me has been, to approve my self in the Sight of God, through Patience and Well-doing: So that the World has not had Weight enough with me, to suffer its good Opinion to raise me, or its ill Opinion to deject me.

He that suffers his Difference with his Neighbour about the other World, to carry him beyond the Line of Moderation in this, is the Worse for his Opinion, even though it be true.... Since all of all Parties profess to believe in God, Christ, the Spirit, and Scripture, that the Soul is immortal, that there are Eternal Rewards and Punishments, and that the Virtuous shall receive the One, and the Wicked suffer the Other: I say, since this is the Common Faith of Christendom, let us all resolve in the Strength of God to live up to what we agree in, before we fall out so miserably about the Rest in which we differ.

From William Penn, Letter to William Popple, October 24, 1688.

William Penn: Enemy of royal prerogative.

Ideas of this kind first attacked William Penn as a student at Oxford and may have been responsible for his expulsion. One reason for the grand tour was to get them out of his head and something more fashionable into it. The tour worked, too, but only until Penn encountered a Quaker named Thomas Loe, whom he may have known earlier. In 1667 Samuel Pepys, a diarist who worked in the navy office, recorded the sad fact that Sir William Penn's son was "a Quaker again, or some very melancholy thing."

From this time forward, Penn was Quakerism's most energetic and effective supporter. He knew enough theology to argue with priests, enough law to argue with judges. He was so friendly with the king that no one dared ignore him, and he had such courage that he never allowed his friendship to weaken his arguments against the king's policies. He fought not only for Quakerism but for the right of all Englishmen to worship as they pleased and to run their own government.

The "golden days of good King Charles" were nevertheless hard times for Quakers. The Anglican Church was doing its best to limit and control dissent. Quakers, because they refused to hold their meetings in secret, spent more time in jail than other Dissenters. Penn joined with other Quakers in the purchase of New Jersey, which for a time served as a Quaker refuge. But eastern New Jersey was full of Puritans, always unfriendly to Quakers, and western New Jersey had poor soil. Penn heard that the land across the Delaware was better and that no one was there but wild Indians, who would be easier to live with than English bishops or New Jersey Puritans. The king owed him £16,000, a debt contracted to his father (who died in 1670) for back pay and loans to the royal exchequer. In 1680 Penn asked the king for the land and, after many protests from the king's advisers, got it. Charles named it Pennsylvania after the admiral. In addition, Penn later bought from the Duke of York the region that is now the state of Delaware, which was already populated by a few Dutch and Swedish settlers.

According to the terms of his charter, issued in March 1681, Penn was specifically required to enforce the Navigation Acts, to submit laws to the king for approval, to allow appeals to the king from Pennsylvania courts, and to provide an Anglican minister whenever twenty or more colonists asked for one. He was also required to obtain the approval of the freeholders (the male owners of land) for any laws that he imposed. Otherwise he had a free hand to govern the colony as he saw fit.

Penn saw fit to govern in a manner that he hoped would demonstrate the virtues of Quakerism and of political and religious liberty. Though, like other proprietors, he hoped to profit from his colony by quitrents on land, his primary purpose was to conduct a holy experiment in popular government and Christian living. He served as governor when in the province and appointed a deputy when absent, but neither for himself nor for his deputy did he retain extensive powers. The people, he made plain in a statement issued a month after he received the charter, "would be allowed to shape their own laws." In the Frame of Government that he worked out to embody this principle, Penn placed the legislative power

Charles II, King of England, 1660–85.

in a council and an assembly, both elected by the freeholders. He probably assumed, however, that the freeholders would choose the more successful and well-to-do among them to the council, while the assembly would be composed of more ordinary men. And Penn, who retained some traditional ideas about the prerogatives of the well-to-do, made the council the more powerful of the two bodies, with the sole right to initiate legislation.

Attracted by the prospect of good land, free government, and religious liberty, English, Irish, Welsh, Dutch, and German Quakers flocked to the colony. It prospered from the start and attracted many non-Quakers as well, partly because Penn advertised its advantages in pamphlets that were circulated widely. Penn himself went to the colony in 1682 but had to return to England in less than two years to defend his southern boundary in a legal dispute with Lord Baltimore. The dispute was not fully settled until the 1760's, when Charles Mason and Jeremiah Dixon surveyed their famous line. Litigation, losses, and revolution kept Penn in England for fifteen years. During that time his friend King Charles died and his friend the Duke of York ascended the throne, only to flee from it in 1688.

In Pennsylvania, Quakerism in power fulfilled many but not all of Penn's anticipations. It brought religious peace (other sects found complete freedom), economic prosperity, and political quarrels. Although the council, where power was concentrated, was elected by the same people as elected the assembly, just as the United States Senate and House of Representatives are today, the assemblymen acted as though their lack of the right to initiate legislation was a denial of popular rights. The council and the assembly joined in attacking the governors whom Penn sent over, even though the executive power in Pennsylvania was weaker than in any other colony. It is true that Penn, who could never believe ill of any man, often sent incompetent, or at least inappropriate, governors, such as the old Cromwellian soldier, John Blackwell. Blackwell left the province saying that Quakers prayed for their neighbors on Sundays and preyed on them the other six days of the week.

After the fall of James II, Penn was for a while suspect in England because of their long-standing friendship. His province was temporarily taken from him and, from 1692 to 1694, was under a royal government, which gave the assembly the right to initiate legislation. Upon recovering the colony, Penn recognized that right, but by then the assembly was in pursuit of still larger powers. In 1699 he finally returned to the province and told the members of the assembly, since they did not like his plan of government, to draft one of their own. They did so, eliminating the legislative authority of the council altogether (it retained only the function of advising the governor), and leaving the proprietor with only the ownership of ungranted land and a veto power over legislation, which was normally exercised through his appointed governor.

The new plan, known as the Charter of Liberties, was established in 1701, with Penn's approval, by an act of the assembly. Pennsylvania thus became the only colony with a unicameral legislature. The same Charter of Liberties gave the counties of Newcastle, Sussex, and Kent (later the state of Delaware) a separate representative assembly, though they retained the same governor as Pennsylvania. In 1701 Penn returned to England, where the brotherly love that had founded Pennsylvania eventually landed him in prison for debts incurred by dishonest agents whom he had trusted. No quitrents arrived from Pennsylvania to extricate him. He died in 1718.

PROBLEMS OF ENFORCEMENT

The settlement of Pennsylvania completed English occupation of the Atlantic coast from Spanish Florida to French Canada. All the

---

Religious Liberty in Pennsylvania

First. Because no people can be truly happy, though under the greatest enjoyment of civil liberties, if abridged of the freedom of their consciences as to their religious profession and worship; and Almighty God being the only Lord of conscience ... I do hereby grant and declare that no person or persons inhabiting in this province or territories, who shall confess and acknowledge one Almighty God, the creator, upholder, and ruler of the world, and profess him or themselves obliged to live quietly under the civil government, shall be in any case molested or prejudiced ... because of his or their conscientious persuasion or practice, nor be compelled to frequent or maintain any religious worship, place, or ministry contrary to his or their mind, or to do or suffer any other act or thing contrary to their religious persuasion. And that all persons who also profess to believe in Jesus Christ the Saviour of the world shall be capable ... to serve this government in any capacity ... he or they solemnly promising, when lawfully required, allegiance to the king as sovereign, and fidelity to the proprietor and governor.

From the Pennsylvania Charter of Liberties, 1701.

colonies had been founded under authority of the king, but without his active participation or financial support. The government of each had been uniquely shaped by the varying purposes of the founders and settlers, not by an overall imperial policy. When, with the Navigation Acts, the king and his Parliament proposed to apply an imperial policy to America, they found that most of the machinery of colonial government by which the acts might have been enforced lay beyond their immediate control. Only in Virginia (through the royally appointed governor and council) did England exercise any voice in colonial government.

Even as the Navigation Acts were passed, Charles II was furthering this dispersion of power. In 1663 he gave Rhode Island a royal charter (to replace a similar parliamentary charter of 1644), authorizing the settlers to choose their own governmental officers. In 1662 he had given the same charter privilege to Connecticut (including New Haven, which would have preferred a separate charter). By these charters and by those granted to the Duke of York, the Carolina proprietors, and William Penn, Charles, perhaps thoughtlessly, distributed authority that might have been used to enforce imperial policies.

At the same time he strengthened another element in colonial government that was to make imperial control difficult. In each of his charters, except the one given to the Duke of York, he required the consent of the settlers to local legislation. The requirement was met by popularly elected representative assemblies such as already existed in the older colonies. Assemblies had demonstrated their usefulness: to operate effectively, a colonial government had to obtain the advice and cooperation of the actual settlers, especially where they were Englishmen, used to having their laws made by their representatives. But the assemblies had also demonstrated a truculence, not unlike that of Parliament in England, which promised trouble for policies imposed from above. Nowhere was the threat greater than in New England.

Recalcitrant colonists. New England, of all the regions in the empire, fitted least well into the mercantilist scheme of supplying needed raw materials to the mother country. She had

Religious Conformity in Massachusetts

Who must have liberty to sit downe in this Commonwealth and enjoy the liberties thereof is not our place to determine, but the Magistrates who are the rulers and governours of the Commonwealth, and of all persons within the same. And as for acknowledging a company to be a sister Church, that shall set up, and practice another forme of Church Discipline, being otherwise in some measure, as you say, approveable, we conceive the companie that shall so doe, shall not be approveable therein. For the Discipline appointed by Jesus Christ for his Churches is not arbitrary, that one Church may set up and practice one forme, and another another forme, as each one shall please, but is one and the same for all Churches.... And if that Discipline which we here practice, be (as we are perswaded of it) the same which Christ hath appointed, and therefore unalterable, we see not how another can be lawfull.

From Richard Mather, *Church Government and Church Covenant,* 1643.

nothing in quantity that the mother country wanted. Since furs from the interior of the continent came out by way of the Hudson or the St. Lawrence, the New England fur trade lasted only until the local animals had been depleted. Lumber and lumber products, such as pitch and tar, were a minor resource. But mostly New England grew rocks, and even these contained no valuable minerals or ores. Because their resources were limited, New Englanders went into the business of distributing what the rest of the world produced. In trading freely wherever the best price was offered, they competed all too successfully with the merchants of the mother country.

They could still have carried on a successful trade in obedience to the Navigation Acts, but disobedience was more profitable. The merchant who bought French silks and laces in France and carried them directly to Boston could undersell one who bought the same goods in England, because English prices included the extra cost of English duties and of transportation from France to England. The same advantage accrued to a merchant or captain who illegally carried enumerated commodities,

New Englanders away from home: John Greenwood's "Sea Captains at Surinam."

such as sugar or tobacco, directly from the colonies to Europe.

New Englanders, therefore, had good economic reasons for resisting or evading directions from England. And, as was often the case in New England, economic interest coincided with religious interest. The New Englanders were Puritans, and they had come to New England to live as Puritans. Charles II, whatever else he may have been, was notoriously not a Puritan. New Englanders consequently looked with suspicion on his government and were wary of any move to bring them under its control. Their fathers had struck this defensive attitude almost as soon as they set foot in New England. According to Governor Winthrop, the Puritans had "hastened" their fortifications in 1633 when they heard that Charles I had appointed a commission under Archbishop Laud to govern them. Fortunately the fortifications did not have to be manned against the archbishop. Thereafter New Englanders had easily withstood the halfhearted efforts at control made by Parliament and by Oliver Cromwell. When Charles II came to the throne, they still had the royal charter of Massachusetts intact and did not hesitate to remind the new king of the privileges granted by his father (even though they were secretly harboring the

men who had passed the death sentence on Charles I).

Charles II knew that New England was full of Puritans, whom he abhorred, and that Massachusetts in particular had passed laws that did not fully satisfy the requirement, stated in her charter (as in other colonial charters), that all laws conform to those of England. In 1662 he sent a letter commanding revisions. The assembly ignored it. And so, in 1664, when Charles sent his commission of four to capture New Netherland from the Dutch, he assigned them the additional task of investigating New England. They were empowered to adjust boundaries, hear appeals from colonial courts, redress grievances against colonial governments, and report to the king on how well New England was obeying the Navigation Acts.

The commissioners, who went to New England fresh from their triumph over the Dutch, made a discovery that was to be repeated often in the history of the British empire: England could govern Dutchmen (and Frenchmen, Spaniards, Egyptians, Indians, and Chinese) more easily than it could govern Englishmen. The commissioners were treated well enough in Rhode Island, Connecticut, and Plymouth, all of which were looking for improvements in their boundaries. Plymouth had no charter and perhaps hoped to get one by good behavior. But when the commissioners appeared in Boston they met with a reception the coolness of which has seldom been matched even in that city. The officers of government referred them to the charter of 1629 and ostentatiously refused to recognize their authority. A herald appeared before the house where the commissioners were staying and, after a blast from his trumpet, in the name of the king formally forbade anyone to appear before them. Frustrated at every turn, they went back to England to report that the Massachusetts government was making no effort to enforce the Navigation Acts. They also recommended to the king that he revoke the Massachusetts charter, a suggestion echoed by every royal official to visit the colony in the next twenty years.

The king could not revoke the charter at will. It was a contract, binding both grantor and grantee. But the terms required that Massachusetts make no laws contrary to those of England. If it could be shown that Massachusetts had done so, a court of law would declare the charter void, and the king would recover all governmental powers.

After the experience of his commissioners, Charles decided to continue the investigation in England and demanded that Massachusetts send agents to account for its behavior. The General Court (as the Massachusetts assembly was called) sent masts for the king's navy, money for the sufferers in the great fire of London, provisions for the fleet, but no agents. The leaders of Massachusetts knew that many of their laws did violate England's, especially their laws about religion. It was precisely these laws that they wished to keep, even more than they wished to escape the Navigation Acts. So they tried every means to avoid a showdown, relying heavily on distance to support them in one delaying action after another. For ten years they got away with it and grew ever more prosperous and powerful.

In England the king paid only sporadic attention to them and made no effective move against them. But Parliament, in 1673, passed an act to make smuggling to foreign countries less profitable. It levied export duties, known as "plantations duties," on any enumerated commodity shipped to another colony instead of to England. Now, if a shipper pretended to be taking tobacco from Virginia to Boston but took it instead to Holland, he would already have paid a tax equivalent to that levied in England, and he would be unable to sell his cargo in Holland at a price much lower than that of tobacco reshipped legitimately from England. The act of 1673 made smuggling more difficult but did not stop it. As before, the most persistent evaders were the New Englanders, and the governors of other colonies complained that the example of Massachusetts undermined their own attempts to enforce the Navigation Acts.

The main reason for Charles II's failure to act decisively against Massachusetts during these years was that he had no administrative body devoted primarily to colonial affairs. At last, in 1675, he appointed a special committee of the Privy Council known as the Lords of Trade, which set about pulling together the strings of empire. The members quickly realized that England could not rely on the colonial governments to enforce her policies. She must have her own means of enforcement in the colonies. The first step, the Lords of Trade decided, was for the king to take a hand in governing them.

The earliest opportunity came in New Hampshire, into which Massachusetts had extended her authority beyond the boundaries set by her charter. Robert Mason, who had inherited a claim to the region from the Council for New England, complained to the king about this encroachment, and in 1679 Charles took New Hampshire away from Massachusetts and gave it a royal government. Massachusetts was in danger of losing Maine as well, after an English court had declared her title to that area invalid. But Massachusetts managed to purchase the title of the counterclaimant, Ferdinando Gorges (who was the heir of the original Ferdinando), before the king could act.

The Lords of Trade took over Charles' fight against the Massachusetts charter by renewing the demand that the colony send agents to London. The General Court finally did so, but it gave them no authority to answer the questions the Lords wanted answered. The Lords insisted that the Massachusetts government enforce the Navigation Acts. The General Court, hardened by thirty years of ignoring and defying orders from England, loftily retorted that

The day after, I went to visit the governour at his house, and among other discourse I told him I tooke notice of severall ships that were arrived at Boston, some since my being there, from Spain, France, Streights, Canaries and other parts of Europe, contrary to your Majesties lawes for encouraging navigation, and regulating the trade of the plantations. He freely declared to me that the lawes made by your Majestie and your parliament obligeth them in nothing but what consists with the interest of that colony, that the legislative power is and abides in them solely to act and make lawes by virtue of a charter from your Majesties royall father, and that all matters in difference are to be concluded by their finall determination, without any appeal to your Majestie, and that your Majestie ought not to retrench their liberties, but may enlarge them if your Majestie please, and said ... that your Majesty could doe no lesse in reason than let them enjoy their liberties and trade, they having upon their own charge and without any contribution from the crown made so large plantation in the wildernesse ... and that notwithstanding the colony had many enemies, yet they did believe your Majestie to be their very good friend, for that your Majestie had by severall letters expressed your kindnesse to them....

From Edward Randolph, Letter to the King of England, 1676.

it was legally endowed by the king's own charter with full powers to govern the province and that therefore Parliament had no authority to pass laws affecting Massachusetts. But, in order to avoid a head-on collision, the General Court formally ordered enforcement of the Navigation Acts. Without waiting to see if Massachusetts would actually carry out the order, the Lords sent an imperial customs officer, Edward Randolph, to do the job; the General Court refused to recognize his commission, set up its own customs office, and imprisoned the deputies appointed by Randolph. The Lords demanded that Massachusetts show cause why its charter should not be revoked; again the General Court sent agents with insufficient powers and inadequate answers. In 1683 legal proceedings were begun, and in 1684 the

charter was revoked. In 1685 the Duke of York became King James II.

The Dominion of New England. The accession of James II, which made New York a royal colony, together with the revocation of the Massachusetts charter, cleared the way for a scheme the Lords of Trade had long had in mind: a reconstruction of the American empire from New Jersey northward. The scheme shows that they had identified clearly the immediate sources of trouble; it also shows that they had learned little about political realities in either England or America. They proposed to place New Jersey, New York, Connecticut, Rhode Island, Plymouth, Massachusetts, New Hampshire, and Maine under one governor. And in this whole area, to be called the Dominion of New England, there would be no troublesome representative assembly. The royally appointed governor would be assisted by a council whose members would also be appointed by the king. It apparently did not occur to their lordships that the people, deprived of any share in their own government, might prove more troublesome than the assemblies had been.

When news reached Boston that the Massachusetts charter had been revoked, men talked of resistance, as their fathers had fifty years

The Dominion of New England

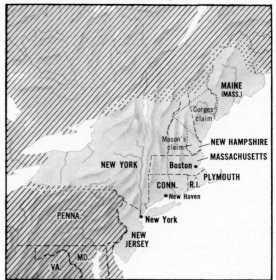

before when threatened with the rule of Archbishop Laud. But their fathers had never been put to the test and had had less to lose in ships, houses, and money than the Bostonians of 1685. Boston was no longer a mere beachhead on an unsettled coast. It was a prosperous city of some 7,000 people with a fleet rivaling that of any English city except London. Most Bostonians held to the faith of their fathers, but they and other New Englanders were perhaps a little more prosperous than Puritan. They allowed their General Court to be dissolved and submitted reluctantly to the interim government of a council appointed by the king. In 1686, when Sir Edmund Andros arrived to establish the Dominion of New England, he faced hard looks and sullen words but no manned fortifications. Although the charters of Rhode Island and Connecticut had not been revoked, Andros extended his government over them without difficulty and in 1688 completed his domain by taking over New York and New Jersey, which he ruled thereafter through a lieutenant-governor. In each colony he dissolved the assembly.

Andros was not a happy choice to inaugurate the new system. An administrator of proved ability, he had already served successfully as governor of New York and would, in the years ahead, serve as governor of Virginia. But the present task called for diplomacy and tact as well as administrative skill. A blunt, outspoken man, Andros made decisions more easily than he made friends. He and the Lords of Trade believed, not without reason, that in order to establish imperial authority in New England the grip of the Puritan leaders must be broken and room made for a party of moderation. But it would have required a man of moderate temper and winning ways to organize and lead such a party.

The Lords of Trade, encouraged by the reports of Edward Randolph, supposed that the Puritans were a minority and that the majority of the population would welcome their fall and gladly step in line behind a royal governor. Nothing could have been further from the truth. Enemies of the old government were few, and Andros, by following the instructions of his superiors in England, succeeded in alienating what few there were. He levied taxes for the support of government, necessarily without the consent of a representative assem-

bly. And when the inhabitants objected and pleaded their rights as Englishmen, he told them they had no rights. Massachusetts had parceled out lands to individuals through the agency of incorporated towns; Andros maintained that the Massachusetts Bay Company had no authority to create corporations and that all titles to land granted by towns were therefore invalid. Anyone who wanted to own the land that he or his fathers had carved out of the wilderness had to ask for a new deed from the governor, pay a fee for it, and agree to pay quitrents ever after.

Andros, with the help of customs officers sent from England, enforced the Navigation Acts, and Randolph later claimed that this was the real cause of opposition to him. But the fact was that the Lords of Trade, in their zeal to establish imperial authority, had assigned Andros an impossible task. They required him to violate long-established rights and privileges and, without the support of an army, a police force, or a political party, to rule arbitrarily over a people who for more than fifty years had ruled themselves. Whether Puritan, non-Puritan, or anti-Puritan they could not be expected to like it. As Andros spelled out the dimensions of his immense authority, they began to have second thoughts about the wisdom of their submission.

The Revolution of 1688. Fortunately for New England, the rule of Andros coincided with the reign of James II. Although James could not dispense with Parliament as he had with the New England assemblies, he made it appear that he would have liked to. By exercising his power of pardon he effectively suspended the operation of many parliamentary enactments. He was, besides, a Catholic and made no secret of it. The political patience of Englishmen was as thin in old as in New England. In 1688 they welcomed William of Orange and chased James out of the country.

In Boston the Puritans did not wait for the fall of James to liquidate the Dominion of New England. After they had heard of William's landing in England, but before they had learned of his success in ousting James, they carried out a tidy, bloodless revolution of their own. Spurred by rumors that Andros and James were plotting to hand New England over to the pope, the inhabitants of Boston seized and imprisoned the governor and his council, restored the old government, and waited to hear how William was faring in England. The colony's most eminent minister, Increase Mather, had gone to London the year before to plead the colony's cause against Andros. Mather did his best to persuade the new monarchs, William and Mary, that the Dominion of New England was part and parcel of James' tyrannical policies in England and that the Glorious Revolution ought to include a glorious restitution of the Massachusetts charter. William gave orders for the recall of Andros and authorized Massachusetts to proceed temporarily under her old government, but he refused to restore the charter until he and his advisers should have time to investigate the situation.

Plymouth, Rhode Island, and Connecticut quietly resumed their old governments, and New Jersey returned to anarchy. But New York had its own revolution, which was not entirely bloodless. Andros' lieutenant-governor there, Francis Nicholson, was left in an anomalous position as the appointee of a deposed officer who was in turn the appointee of a deposed king. Nicholson was, besides, young and inexperienced. When rumors of popish plots alarmed the population, he did nothing to quiet them.

At the end of May 1689 a party of local militia seized the fort that commanded New York harbor and took control of the government. The party was led by Jacob Leisler, a successful German immigrant who had married into a prominent Dutch family. After Nicholson departed for England in June 1689, a meeting of delegates from different parts of the province chose a committee of safety, which in turn named Leisler as commander in chief of the province. Leisler proclaimed the accession of William, and when ambiguously addressed letters arrived from the new king authorizing a continuation of government, Leisler claimed them.

Basing his authority on the letters, Leisler governed the colony arbitrarily but effectively for nearly two years. New York, thinly settled by people of differing nationalities and religions living in widely differing circumstances, was a long way from political maturity. To maintain order, Leisler had to rely heavily on his followers among the militia. When King William finally got around to appointing a regular governor in 1691, Leisler hesitated before surrendering authority to him and thereby gave the new appointee the pretext for an accusation of treason. Leisler and his son-in-law, Jacob Milborne, were convicted and hanged on May 16, 1691. Four years later Parliament reversed the sentence.

The reorganization of 1696. The downfall of the Dominion of New England, together with the revolution in England, brought to a halt the efforts to consolidate the empire. After William mounted the throne, he was kept busy defending England in war against France and trying to shore up what was left of the royal prerogative. The new men he appointed to the Privy Council were unfamiliar with colonial problems, and the Lords of Trade had been turned into a committee of the whole, charged with new and broader functions. Once again nobody in the government devoted himself exclusively to colonial policy. The result was seven years of neglect.

In the colonies merchants and shippers ignored the Navigation Acts, and pirates brazenly pursued their prey in and out of harbors. Edward Randolph, now trying to enforce the acts in Maryland, found himself again thwarted by New Englanders who were buying tobacco from the planters and taking it to Scotland instead of England. Though Scotland had the same king as England, the two countries remained separate until 1707. Under the Navigation Acts, Scotland, like nations on the Continent, was excluded from the benefits of trade with England's colonies.

Scottish competition for the tobacco trade raised such a howl of protest from English merchants that the king and Parliament were driven to act. In 1696, guided by Edward Randolph, Parliament in one extensive enactment constructed machinery for enforcing the Navigation Acts. Henceforth the governors of all colonies, whether royal, proprietary, or corporate (Rhode Island and Connecticut), were to take an oath to enforce the acts. Failure to do so meant forfeiture of office. In place of the occasional peripatetic customs officer, a regular customs service subject to the English Treasury was established in each colony. The customs officers were authorized to take out "writs of assistance" from local courts entitling them to open buildings by force in search of smuggled goods. The officers were also empowered to prosecute violators of the Navigation Acts in admiralty courts, which the Privy Council ordered to be established in the colonies. Admiralty courts operated without juries, and it was hoped that the judges would give short shrift to smugglers.

While Parliament was passing this measure, it also considered, and then rejected, a bill to create a council of trade and plantations to develop and administer colonial policy. The Privy Council, which had already planned a similar body, now swung into action to keep control of colonial policy under the king. In May 1696, by royal order, a new bureau was established to replace the old Lords of Trade. The Lords Commissioners of Trade and Plantations, as it was called, or more simply the

Board of Trade, resembled a national chamber of commerce. It was appointed by the king and was charged to furnish him with information and advice on all colonial matters. Although the board included some members of the Privy Council, ex officio, the eight working members were not councilors and had no authority to issue orders. Their function was purely advisory. But, since they constituted the only body directly concerned with the colonies, their advice was seldom ignored.

Although the king retained control of colonial policy and administration, the circumstances of William's accession affected the kind of control that he and his successors were able to exert in the colonies. After the unhappy experience with James II, Parliament would have looked with suspicion on any move by the king to do away with a representative assembly, even in America. Parliament did not object, however, to the introduction of royal governors in colonies that had not formerly had them. Nor was there serious objection from the settlers, for in almost every case the advent of royal government relieved an intolerable internal situation, just as it had in Virginia in 1624. Maryland was converted to royal government in 1689, after a local rebellion against the proprietor. (It returned to proprietary government in 1715 after the fourth Lord Baltimore turned Anglican.) And, as we have seen, New Jersey became a royal colony in 1702 (see p. 37), South Carolina and North Carolina in 1729 (see p. 39). In the new charter that William granted Massachusetts in 1691 (which incorporated Plymouth and Maine as parts of Massachusetts), the king retained power to appoint the governor. Thus most of the colonies reverted eventually to the king.

Wherever a royal government was introduced, the king gained more direct control over his subjects. He appointed the governor, and he appointed the governor's council (except in Massachusetts). Although in each royal colony a representative assembly of freeholders retained legislative authority, the governor's council served as the upper house of the legislature, and its approval was necessary before any act passed by the lower house became law. Even an act passed by both houses was subject to veto by the governor, and even an act approved by the governor might be disallowed by the king. During the eighteenth century, usually on the advice of the Board of Trade, some 5½ per cent of the acts passed by colonial assemblies were disallowed by the king, though no act of Parliament was ever vetoed after 1708. Moreover, in the eyes of the mother country the king's instructions to his governors were supposed to bind the assembly as well as the governor. But in spite of royal theories the popularly elected lower house of the assembly became in practice the most powerful branch of government in every colony. It enjoyed sole authority to levy taxes, and by threatening to withhold them it was often able to get its own way against both king and governor.

The Old Colonial System. Of the three agencies England now had for enforcement of the Navigation Acts, the admiralty courts proved unable to exercise jurisdiction because of ambiguities in the act of 1696; the customs service was ill paid and susceptible to bribes and could not operate effectively without the support of the local government. England's control of her colonies depended most heavily on the success of her royal governors in working with the colonial assemblies. Since every legislative act required the assent of both the governor and the assembly, the needs of neither the mother country nor the colonies could be satisfied if the two parties were to refuse to cooperate.

Thus in the last analysis the Old Colonial System (embodied in the Navigation Acts and in the act of 1696) rested on the harmony of English and colonial interests. Although occasional discord developed, especially at points of contact between royal governors and assemblies, and, although smugglers often escaped the law, the harmony was real and the system worked. Enriched by her colonies, England grew to be the world's most powerful nation. And, protected by England, the American colonies grew, each in its own style, toward a new way of life.

SUGGESTIONS FOR READING

Eli Heckscher in *Mercantilism*, 2 vols. (1935), sets the economic policies of the seventeenth and eighteenth centuries in historical perspective and thus furnishes the best introduction to an understanding of the Navigation Acts. For the acts themselves and the thinking behind them, the pioneering works of G. L. Beer are still valuable: *The Origins of the British Colonial System* (1908) and *The Old Colonial System*, 2 vols. (1912). On the administration and interpretation of the acts, see L. A. Harper, *The English Navigation Laws* (1939), and C. M. Andrews, *The Colonial Period of American History*,* Vol. IV (1938). Special aspects of British policy are well treated in Curtis Nettels, *The Money Supply of the American Colonies Before 1720* (1934), and A. C. Bining, *British Regulation of the Colonial Iron Industry* (1933).

On New Netherland and on the Restoration colonies the best general work is again C. M. Andrews, *The Colonial Period of American History*,* Vols. II and III. T. J. Wertenbaker, *The Founding of American Civilization: The Middle Colonies* (1938), stresses social and cultural history. J. E. Pomfret has untangled much of New Jersey's early history in *The Province of West New Jersey, 1609–1702* (1956) and *The Province of East New Jersey* (1962). The most important single work on the early history of the Carolinas is Verner Crane, *The Southern Frontier, 1670–1732** (1929, 1956). On the Fundamental Constitutions, see H. F. Russell Smith, *Harrington and His Oceana* (1914).

There is no definitive biography of William Penn, but Bonamy Dobrée, *William Penn, Quaker and Pioneer* (1932), is adequate; and F. B. Tolles and E. G. Alderfer have edited a selection of Penn's writings in *The Witness of William Penn* (1957). M. M. Dunn has made a scholarly study of his political ideas and activities in *William Penn: Politics and Conscience* (1967). Rufus Jones,

* Available in a paperback edition.

*Quakers in the American Colonies** (1911), is a standard work, but see also F. B. Tolles' eloquent essays in *Quakers and the Atlantic Culture* (1960) and his *James Logan and the Culture of Provincial America* (1957).

Efforts of England to enforce the Navigation Acts are dealt with in Michael Hall, *Edward Randolph and the American Colonies* (1960). Viola Barnes, *The Dominion of New England* (1923), is the classic account of that episode, exonerating Andros of blame. Kenneth Murdock, *Increase Mather* (1925), treats fully Mather's role in seeking the overthrow of the dominion and in securing a new charter for Massachusetts. The long-range causes and consequences of Leisler's Rebellion are discussed in J. R. Reich, *Leisler's Rebellion* (1953), and in L. H. Leder, *Robert Livingston, 1654–1728, and the Politics of Colonial New York* (1961). M. G. Hall, L. H. Leder, and M. G. Kammen, eds., *The Glorious Revolution** (1964), is a valuable collection of sources on the revolution in New England, New York, and Maryland.

On the reorganization of colonial administration in 1696, see again C. M. Andrews, *Colonial Period of American History*, Vol. IV,* and Peter Laslett, "John Locke, the Great Recoinage, and the Origins of the Board of Trade: 1695–1698," *William and Mary Quarterly*, 3rd series, XIV (1957), 370–402. The standard works on the Board of Trade are O. M. Dickerson, *American Colonial Government, 1696–1765* (1912), and A. H. Basye, *The Lords Commissioners of Trade and Plantations, 1748–1782* (1925). On the activities of the board in securing the disallowance of colonial acts of legislation, see E. B. Russell, *The Review of American Colonial Legislation by the King in Council* (1915). The role of colonial governors in administering British policy is the subject of L. W. Labaree, *Royal Government in America: A Study of the British Colonial System Before 1783* (1930). Finally, Lawrence Gipson, in a monumental work of which thirteen volumes have appeared, surveys *The British Empire Before the American Revolution* (1936–   ).

* Available in a paperback edition.

3

The First American Way of Life

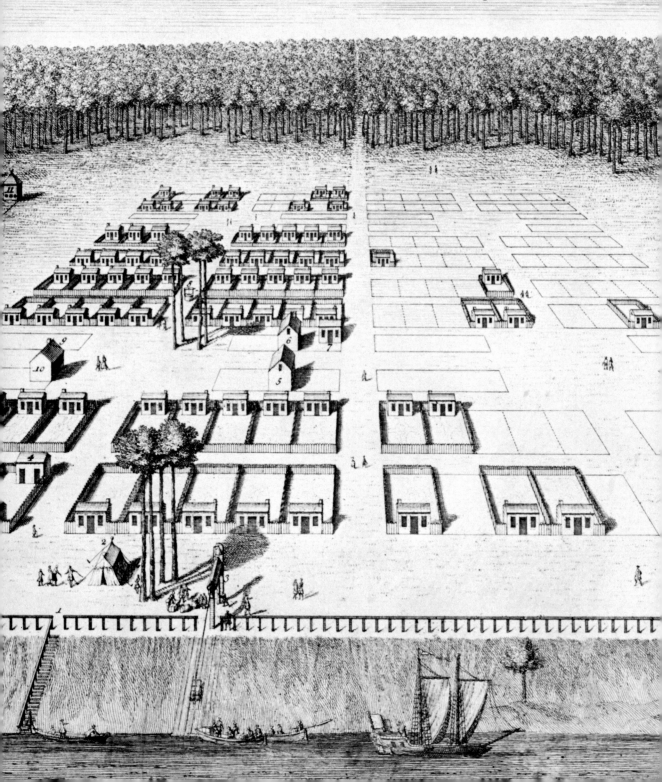

Americans moving across their continent have faced three questions again and again: how to live, how to live with one another, how to live with the outside world. They first learned how to live by tobacco, rice, furs, fish. England told them, in the Navigation Acts, how they must live with the outside world. How did they live with one another?

A few simply did not. When the Puritans explored Boston harbor, they came upon an Englishman at Beacon Hill living alone among the blueberries. William Blackstone was company enough for himself. After the Puritans moved in, he moved out. For nearly three centuries the continent afforded room for men like Blackstone, American hermits who felt crowded when they could see the smoke from their neighbor's campfire.

PATTERNS OF EXISTENCE

Most Americans have been more gregarious. They have asked *how*, rather than whether, to live together, and they have answered partly from the heritage of ideas and institutions carried from Europe, partly from their own ideas evoked by the opportunities and limitations of their strange new environment. Each generation has solved the problem a little differently from the preceding one, but the first settlers, moving from an old established world to an empty new one, had the biggest problem and made the biggest change. Many of them came to America primarily for a chance to live together in a new and, hopefully, a better way. All of them had to adapt ideas made in Europe to existence in America. The results differed from time to time and from place to place. But before the end of the colonial period most Americans were living together in one of four distinct patterns: the Southern plantation, the New England town, the loose collection of individual farms, or the coastal city.

The plantation. Plantations developed in colonies where the majority of the people lived by growing a single crop: tobacco in Virginia and Maryland, rice or indigo in South Carolina, sugar in the West Indies. Originally "planter" meant simply a settler, and "plantation" a set-

Savannah, Georgia, 1734.

The Tidewater and the Piedmont

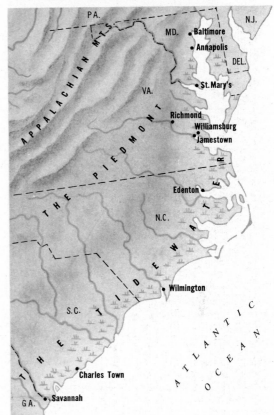

tlement — Jamestown was the London Company's plantation. Gradually the name came to be attached to individual holdings. The size of a plantation in this sense depended on the number of servants the planter brought with him. Under the headright system he got fifty acres per man; if he prospered, he could import more men and get more land. In Virginia, where the system began, fortunes fluctuated rapidly for the first two or three generations, and those who accumulated large tracts were seldom able to retain them. But in the long run free land, low tobacco prices, and a supply of cheap labor favored the development of the large working estate to which we now apply the name "plantation."

At the outset, in 1617, the price of tobacco in Virginia was 3 shillings a pound; it dropped to less than a shilling in the 1630's and thereafter seldom rose above twopence. But the low price of tobacco was balanced by the low cost of labor. Servants (bound by contract or custom to serve without pay for up to seven years) could be bought for £15 to £20 in the seventeenth century; in addition to growing enough corn to feed themselves, they could produce one thousand to two thousand pounds of tobacco in a year, worth £8 to £16. Thus the man who could buy servants (and claim fifty acres of land for each of them) could expect a handsome return on his investment.

Methods of cultivation also favored the large plantation. Since tobacco exhausted the soil in three or four years, the tobacco-grower divided his land into three parts: one where he grew tobacco, one where he had grown it, and one where he would grow it. In order to continue in operation, a plantation had to be much larger than the area under cultivation at any one time.

It had also to be properly located. The tidewater lands of Virginia and Maryland were cut by great rivers and bays up which ocean-going ships made their way as much as a hundred miles inland to collect the tobacco at wharves only a stone's throw from where much of it was grown. The grower who had to pay the cost of carting his crop from the interior to a ship lost much of his profit along the way. Successful planters bought more and more land

Riverside settlement in the South.

adjoining the water, and here the great plantations grew.

They grew slowly in the seventeenth century, when servants arriving each year from England were the main source of labor. As the diminishing supply of unappropriated river land and the falling price of tobacco reduced the ordinary man's prospect of success, fewer and fewer Englishmen were willing to give seven years of their lives, or even a shorter span, in return for passage to Virginia. But by the end of the century a cheaper and more lasting form of labor had become available.

The first Africans reached Virginia in 1619, and during the next half-century a few more were imported from time to time. There is some evidence that they were at first treated like other servants and freed after a term of years. But perpetual slavery, unknown in England, was no novelty in America. The Spaniards had practiced it to the south for more than a century, and in the English colonies Indians who made unsuccessful war on the settlers usually ended up as slaves. The theory was that the lives of captives taken in just wars belonged to the captors, and history records no war acknowledged by the victors to have been unjust. Although Africans may not have grasped the rationale, they knew that slave-traders waited in ships off their coasts, eager to buy the losers in tribal wars.

As time went on, an increasing number of losers became Americans. Traders began bringing them to Virginia and Maryland in quantity toward the end of the seventeenth century. By then the colonists had passed laws differentiating Negroes from other servants. While the courts protected white servants from abuse, they left Negroes almost entirely at the mercy of their masters. Slaves had to serve for life, and so did their children and grandchildren forever.

Slavery is the crudest way that men have devised for living together. Cruelty was essential to it, but cruelty was mitigated by the owner's need to keep his slaves, like his cattle, healthy and by the human intimacy that often grew up between master and slave. What life held for a slave depended on where he lived. On the West Indian sugar plantations slavery meant being worked to death: the life expectancy of a freshly imported field hand was

Indigo drying in South Carolina.

only about seven years. But growing tobacco, rice, or indigo in the mainland colonies was less arduous; here a slave could do his work and raise a family at the same time, so that when he died he left a whole brood of new workers to take his place.

Slavery offered the plantation-owner a permanent solution to his labor problem and a larger profit on his crop. A slave cost more than a servant — from £20 to £30 in the first half of the eighteenth century — but the investment could be recovered by resale, it brought a yearly return, and it appreciated in value by the simple process of human reproduction.

In every American colony slavery was sanctioned by law. And in the colonies with large plantations — Virginia, Maryland, and South Carolina — half or more of the population were enslaved to part of the other half by the middle of the eighteenth century. Slaves who belonged to small farmers often worked side by side with their owners in the fields, but probably the majority lived on plantations where they worked in gangs ranging from ten to a hundred under the direction of the owner or his overseer. Since the largest effective unit of tobacco production was a thousand acres (including uncleared and exhausted land), few colonial plantations outside the West Indies had as many as a hundred slaves. A smaller area, with no more than thirty slaves, was the most efficient unit for rice. If a planter had

more land and men, he divided them into two or more plantations, living on one and hiring overseers to manage the others until he was ready to turn them over to his children.

The large-scale plantation was a community in itself. At the center lay a great house, often facing the river and surrounded by trees and shrubs. Arranged symmetrically around it were attendant buildings: laundry, smokehouse, kitchen, and perhaps a schoolhouse, where a hired tutor taught the planter's children. At some distance lay the barns and the cabins of the slaves, with little plots of ground where they could work evenings and Sundays growing vegetables and raising chickens to piece out their meager rations. They might even be permitted to sell any surplus for pocket money.

In addition to field hands, the community included a small army of household slaves and skilled artisans — carpenter, blacksmith, tailor, cobbler — who might be either indentured white servants (bound by a contract to serve a specific number of years) or slaves educated for the purpose. With its own permanent labor force and with ready access to ocean-going ships, the riverside plantation needed little from its neighbors. What could not be made on the premises was imported directly from London.

And yet the planter and his family were not isolated. The river was a highway to the world by which he kept in touch not only with Lon-

A community in itself: A tidewater plantation.

don but with other planters. His children often went to stay for several weeks at other plantations, and his own home was seldom without guests. Sometimes he gave a ball for friends who came from miles around and stayed for three or four days. Or he might attend the House of Burgesses (the representative assembly) in Williamsburg and take the family with him. Over a glass at the Raleigh Tavern he could arrange to marry his daughter to another planter's son, and the two fathers would haggle over who should give what to set the young couple up on their own plantation. So common was matchmaking of this sort that by the middle of the eighteenth century most Virginia planters could call each other cousin. In South Carolina, young people met and matches were made when planters left their steaming rice fields during the summer months for the sea breezes of Charles Town.

Not all Southerners lived on plantations. Probably the majority of the free population, even in the plantation colonies, consisted of small farmers with holdings well back from the river banks. Here they worked like any slave, but they worked for themselves. It was the great planter, however, who dominated the society, buying and marketing the small farmers' surplus crops, sometimes renting them their lands, lending them money, selling them manufactures, and perhaps commanding their votes. His command of their votes was by no means automatic, however. The deference his neighbors paid him was the voluntary tribute that success has generally exacted in a free society. It took the votes of free men to place him in the House of Burgesses, and votes were withheld often enough to remind him that he represented free men.

By officiating in the House of Burgesses, the county court, and the vestry of his church, and by managing his plantation, the planter learned to deal with men both free and unfree. And the ships that arrived at his wharf brought him regular news of the way men were dealing with one another across the water. Though he lived from the forced labor of slaves, he was no barbarian. When the time came, he showed that slavery had not blinded him to the meaning of freedom.

The New England town. Rivers, tobacco, and slavery made the plantation. Puritanism and past experience made the New England town, an institution that also appeared in the parts of New York and New Jersey settled by New Englanders. The past experience of New Englanders (as of other English colonists) included at least three English types of community: the borough, the village, and the parish.

The English borough was a town that normally possessed a charter of incorporation from the king entitling it to send two members to Parliament and to exercise a degree of local governmental independence. The freemen (or burgesses) of the borough, usually a very small proportion of the population, elected the members of Parliament as well as a mayor or a set of aldermen to handle local affairs. In many boroughs the aldermen had become so powerful that they were bypassing the freemen and were filling vacancies in their ranks by themselves.

The English village was not a formal political institution like the borough. It was simply a cluster of houses inhabited by men and women who cultivated the adjoining lands according to customs prescribed by earlier generations. All the village's arable land was laid out in three or four large fields, and every householder had strips of land scattered through all of them. Each man worked his own strips, but they were not fenced off from those of his neighbors; and everyone worked together at plowing (and subsequently at sowing, tilling, and harvesting) one field before moving on to the next. Thus every man would get part of his crop early, part of it late. By the time the settlers left England, this open-field system was giving way to individual farms, but it still existed in many places.

Every Englishman, whether he lived in a borough or a village, belonged to a parish. Originally the parish was simply the area served by a single church, but it had gradually taken on, outside the boroughs, many of the functions of local government. In most villages a vestry made up of some ten or twenty of the more substantial inhabitants exercised the powers of the parish or chose two or three churchwardens to do so. The churchwardens or vestrymen not only maintained the church and managed its property but provided for the poor, required fathers to support their children, levied taxes, and sometimes acted as a kind of grand jury.

In creating their towns New Englanders drew something from the parish, the village, and the borough; but they also rejected parts of this institutional heritage because of their Puritan ideas about how men ought to live with one another. Puritans generally "gathered" a church before, or about the same time as, they established a town. The two usually

New England town:
Wethersfield, Connecticut.

covered the same territory, as was true of the English village and parish. But in New England the church and its officers were entirely distinct from the town and its officers. The church owned no property, not even a church building. People worshiped in a meetinghouse, which was owned by the town and used for any community meeting. It was not regarded as sacred. Nor did the church exercise any temporal, political powers. There was no vestry and no churchwarden. The church might elect ruling elders to reprimand erring members or to report them to the church, but neither elders nor church enjoyed coercive authority. The church was a spiritual association; its severest penalty was excommunication, which could be pronounced only by unanimous vote of the members. Excommunication deprived a man of his church membership but carried no civil or political disabilities. Once a church assumed temporal powers, Puritans believed, it was on the wicked road to Rome. In New England, therefore, they assigned to the town both the duties of local government, performed in the English borough by the mayor and aldermen, and the secular duties exercised in the English parish by church officers.

New England towns and their governments were created under the authority of the colony's General Court (the legislature). A group of men, perhaps already gathered in a church, approached the court and requested a tract of land, usually adjoining some established town. If the court approved, it had the area surveyed and then named the applicants as proprietors of the town of Concord, Sudbury, or whatever name they chose. The proprietors then moved to their new home and laid out the land in a pattern similar to that of an English village. Every man got a house lot in the center of town, where space was also set aside for a meetinghouse and perhaps for a school. Each man also received one or more parcels of arable land, a parcel of meadow for pasturage, and a parcel of woodland for fuel, all located in different parts of the town. In a few cases there seems to have been an attempt (quickly abandoned) to practice the open-field system. When the land of a town was originally apportioned, most of it was left undivided to meet the anticipated growth in population. The undistributed land, or commons, belonged to the proprietors jointly until they converted it into their private property through subsequent land divisions. A new settler moving into town might buy land from a proprietor's private holdings or might be granted or sold parts of the commons, but he did not become a proprietor: he did not share in the ownership of the remaining commons.

The power of the proprietors was limited to control over the commons; government of the town rested in a town meeting, in which they had no greater voice than other inhabitants. The town meeting acted on matters that intimately concerned the inhabitants: constructing and repairing roads, building a meetinghouse, hiring a schoolmaster, or deciding whether hogs should be fenced into pens or fenced out of gardens. The meeting also elected representatives to the colonial assembly and town officials of all kinds, including selectmen, who administered the rules made by the meeting. There was some attempt in early Massachusetts to confine voting in town meetings to the freemen, who it will be remembered had to be church members. After 1648, however, and probably before then in many towns, all free adult males were allowed to vote on all questions except the choice of representatives. Until 1685, representatives continued to be elected only by the freemen.

In the early years of a town's existence there was no conflict of interest between town meeting and proprietors, because all or most of the free adult males were also proprietors. But from 1676 to 1713, when a series of French and Indian wars dammed up the expanding population inside the existing towns, the proprietors often became a minority, and an extraordinary demand arose for the distribution of the common lands to unpropertied residents. In the resulting conflict between the economic power of the proprietors and the political power of the town meeting, political power usually won.

With the return of peace the frontier began to move again. By this time colonial governments had come to realize that their unoccupied lands were a potential source of public revenue. In creating new towns they did not give the proprietorship to prospective settlers but sold it to groups of investors, assembled for the sole purpose of buying it. These men sold land to settlers, reserving large sections to be divided among themselves as population and land values rose. In western Massachusetts a set of investors known locally as the Connecticut River Gods owned proprietary shares in many different towns and accumulated large private holdings at every division of the commons.

The new towns of the interior were somewhat different in character from the old towns of the coastal areas. For one thing, the houses were set farther apart, frequently strung out along a road instead of grouped together around a green. Each resident, instead of living close to the meetinghouse with his holdings scattered about the countryside, was likely to have all his land in one piece. He rubbed elbows less often with his neighbors and did not know them as intimately as his father had known his.

Still, the New England town remained in the eighteenth century, as in the seventeenth, a closely knit community. On Sunday everyone gathered in the meetinghouse, where the position of a man's pew indicated his place in the community and whether he must be addressed as "Mister," as "Goodman," or by no title at all. In general, the closer he sat to the pulpit, the higher his social rank. But proximity to God's minister was no sign of proximity to God. Though the law required that everyone attend church, only a minority of the town's inhabitants were "members," and membership in itself carried no social prestige. A slave might belong and a gentleman not. During the eighteenth century church membership became increasingly feminine, with women outnumbering men by more than two to one. Members or not, New Englanders went to church, were taxed for the minister's salary, and had a voice in selecting him.

The men of the town met not only at church and town meeting but on training day when the militia exercised. In frontier settlements, under constant threat of Indian attack, this was a serious business; in the older coastal towns it was likely to require more rum than gunpowder. Rum and hard cider lubricated most community activities in New England, whether marrying or burying, raising a meetinghouse or bringing home a harvest. The tavern, originally intended for the convenience of travelers, became another meeting place,

where men of the neighborhood bent an elbow of an evening and where, according to John Adams, "vicious habits, bastards, and legislators" were frequently begotten.

In tavern, school, and church, at town meeting and militia drill, the New Englander measured out the distance between himself and his fellow man. The distance was small, but it was enough to give him an independence of spirit for which he became famous. For those who needed more room, America offered another way of life.

The farm. In the colonies from New England southward, the average American lived a lonely life. He made his living from the land, as his father had done in Europe. But in the great emptiness of the New World, sheer space separated him from his neighbors in a way that few Europeans knew. His farm might run to several hundred acres and might lie miles from any other occupied land, because settlers, whenever they could, chose lands that supported a stand of hardwood. These, they thought, were most fertile.

Hardwood meant hard work in clearing the land, but many farmers simplified the task by girdling trees at the base to kill them, planting crops between the lifeless trunks, and then disposing of the trunks as they rotted away. This technique was probably brought to America by Finnish immigrants who settled along the Delaware River. They had first tried life in the forests of Sweden and had there learned to girdle trees and to build log cabins. The first English settlers, better sawyers than axmen, had built their houses with hand-sawed boards. But succeeding generations copied the Finns. By the eighteenth century an American starting a farm built a log cabin first and put up a frame house only after he had achieved a measure of prosperity.

Though most farmers owned the land they cleared and cultivated, farm tenancy became common in some areas where the soil was fertile enough to support both a landlord and a tenant. In New York's Hudson Valley, for example, landlords exacted high rents and feudal services. In Virginia's tidewater, tenants took farms and even plantations as sharecroppers, paying the owner a proportion of the crop as rent. Even in the uncleared back country it was not always easy for a farmer to obtain title to land in the most fertile areas, because speculators often acquired such lands in advance of actual settlers. By the eighteenth century the headright system (practiced earlier in most of the colonies south of New England) had become a mere form. A speculator could obtain title to as much land as he could afford simply by paying a fee (usually 5 shillings per hundred acres) to the colony's secretary or land office. Later he could rent the land to a bona fide settler or else sell it for a good deal more than he had paid. Not all speculators were rich men. Many farmers, tradesmen, and even parsons invested their small earnings in real estate, for everyone knew that land values would rise as population increased, and everyone could see that population was increasing rapidly.

Most of the increase came from the natural growth of the old stock. In spite of the heavy toll taken by smallpox and diphtheria, scarlet fever and yellow fever, families were large. Then in the eighteenth century a new flood of settlers, mainly from northern Ireland and Germany, entered the colonies. After landing in the New World, usually at Philadelphia, they traveled west to the Appalachian valleys and spilled down into the hinterland of Maryland, Virginia, and the Carolinas. The Scotch-Irish, America's most formidable frontiersmen, led the advance. Germans, in the rear, tidied up the lush valleys into checkerboards of wheat and corn and rye.

At crossroads in the farming areas, storekeepers traded hardware, clothing, and gossip for crops. But there was no real community, no local nucleus of political, social, and religious life. Even the churches responded slowly to the needs of the farmer. In colonies where the Anglican Church was supported by taxation (New York, Maryland, Virginia, and the Carolinas) it organized parishes to keep pace with the westward advance, but they were too large in area to serve the widely scattered farmers, many of whom were not Anglicans anyhow. The parish had been designed for more densely populated areas, where enough people to support a minister lived within Sunday traveling distance of his sermons. By the eighteenth century some denominations, especially Presbyterians and Methodists, were sending itinerant missionaries through the back country. Now the people could hold at least an occasional service, sometimes under a tree, sometimes in a courthouse, sometimes in a church built for the purpose. The circuit-riders, as the missionaries were called, often encountered families whose children had never seen a minister.

In the absence of village or town, colonial farmers relied heavily on a looser and larger community, the county. Every colony was divided into counties, and everywhere the county court was an important arm of government. Even in New England the county judges (appointed as elsewhere by the colonial governments) decided administrative as well as judicial questions, questions as important as where to build new roads. Outside New England, the county court took over the duties of the town and sometimes of the parish. Besides trying cases, both civil and criminal, it might record wills and deeds, take charge of orphans and the poor, register births, marriages, and deaths, collect taxes, license taverns, authorize the establishment of ferries, and pay bounties for wolves' heads. On days when the court was in session, usually once a month, farmers from near and far would gather to sue one another for small sums, to exercise in the militia, to elect a representative to the colony's assembly, or simply to watch the proceedings, learn the news, and share talk and a bottle with distant neighbors.

The thinness of community life put a heavy burden on the family. Everywhere during the colonial period the family fulfilled many more functions than it does today, but among farmers it was everything — factory, church, school, hospital, and tavern. Unless a man held especially rich land and had ready access to a market, his crops went to feed his family, with little left over for sale. He and his wife had to make everything they could not buy, which might be most of their clothing and furniture. Without a school, they had to teach their children to read; without a church, to worship at home; without a tavern, to entertain passing strangers; without a doctor, to care for their sick. Children were plentiful and made more hands to do the endless work. Some might take over the farm as their parents grew old, but most of them would eventually leave to carve new farms out of the empty land.

The farmer, isolated from his neighbors and living a self-sufficient life within his own family, was the typical eighteenth-century American — even the townsman of western New England resembled him. But as farmers spread out through the interior a significant minority of Americans piled up in five cities and several large towns along the coast.

The city. The colonial farmer riding into a city for the first time left a road that was only a ribbon of stumps and mud and came upon streets of gravel or cobblestones, where a bewildering activity surrounded him. Swine roamed everywhere, feeding on the refuse; drovers herded sheep and cattle to the butchers. Elegant carriages rolled impatiently behind lumbering wagons as great packs of barking dogs worried the horses. Sailors reeled out of taverns, and over the roofs of the houses could be seen the swaying masts and spars of their ships. The farmer had been told that the city was a nursery of vice and prodigality. He now saw that it was so. Every shop had wares to catch his eye: exquisite fabrics, delicate chinaware, silver buckles, looking glasses, and other imported luxuries that never reached the crossroads store. Putting up at the tavern, he found himself drinking too much rum. And there were willing girls, he heard, who had lost their virtue and would be glad to help him lose his. Usually he returned to the farm to warn his children as he had been warned. He seldom understood that the vice of the city, if not its prodigality, was mainly for transients like himself. Permanent residents had work to do.

The key men in the community were the merchants, for colonial cities were built on trade. Merchants bought corn, wheat, cattle, and horses from thousands of farms and fish from hundreds of fishermen and shipped them to the West Indies. The planters there could not waste their valuable sugar lands growing corn, but they needed food for their slaves and horses to turn their sugar mills. Colonial merchants supplied them and brought back molasses, a by-product of sugar-making. Distilleries turned it into rum, much of which the merchants shipped off to exchange for slaves on the coast of Africa or to help fishermen fight back the icy winds of the North Atlantic. The merchants also bought beaver and deerskins from Indian traders and huge pine trunks from lumbermen to send to England for masts. From England they brought back woolens and hardware, which the mother country made better and cheaper than the colonists could. Without the merchants there would have been no cities.

Many of the other city-dwellers depended on the merchants for a living. Besides the rum-distillers, there were shipwrights who turned out ships at a lower price than English ones. Workers in ropewalks and sail lofts rigged them. Instrument-makers fitted them with quadrants, telescopes, and clocks. Retail traders helped to distribute the goods imported from abroad. Millers ground wheat and corn into flour, and coopers built barrels to ship it in.

But cities accumulate people by a magic of their own, and many colonists found jobs that had no direct connection with the overseas trade. Schoolmasters were better trained and more plentiful than in the country. Dancing masters taught ladies and gentlemen the newest steps; stay-makers laced them into the newest shapes. Barbers cut their hair; wigmakers put it on again. And dozens of skilled craftsmen offered American-made copies of the latest English fashions in wearing apparel, furniture, and houses.

For all the glamour and excitement of their environment, city-dwellers had problems that other Americans had not yet faced; city opulence bred thieves and vice of all kinds; city filth necessitated sewers and sanitation laws; city traffic required paved streets and lights; and the city's closely packed wooden houses and shops invited fires that might, and repeatedly did, destroy vast areas. To cope with these problems citizens relied both on voluntary associations, such as fire companies, and on their city governments. Boston and Newport were governed by selectmen and town meetings, New York (after 1731) by a popularly elected city corporation. In all three, city officials, under direct control of the citizens, were responsive to their needs. In Philadelphia and Charles Town, on the other hand, the citizens had no voice in their local government. Philadelphia was badly governed by a self-perpetuating closed corporation, and Charles Town just as badly by the South Carolina assembly.

By contemporary standards these were all substantial cities. Though small compared with London, by the middle of the eighteenth century they were larger than most English cities. Boston, which reached seventeen thousand in 1740, was at that time the largest, but it had already begun a decline that lasted for the rest of the colonial period. In the seventeenth century it had served as the shipping center for most of the mainland colonies, and it continued to serve as New England's major port. But other New England towns were cutting into its business, most notably Newport, which grew to urban dimensions in the eighteenth century.

New York City was the natural outlet and supply point for farmers in the Hudson Valley and adjoining regions of Connecticut and New Jersey; Philadelphia served not only Pennsylvania and the Delaware Valley and Bay but also the Southern back country. From the Carolinas, Virginia, and Maryland, farmers drove their wagons and cattle north along the great Appalachian valleys to the Philadelphia market. Although Baltimore began to drain off some of this trade after about 1750, Philadelphia continued to grow so rapidly that by 1776, with forty thousand people, it was probably second only to London in the English-speaking world. South of Baltimore the tobacco-planters dealt directly with London and needed no cities; but in South Carolina the rice- and indigo-planters shipped their produce by way of Charles Town, as did the Indian traders who trekked around the southern limit of the Appalachians and brought deerskins from the lower Mississippi Valley.

Overseas trade gave city-dwellers and plantation-owners communication with the larger world that was denied to most other Americans, and for that matter to most Englishmen and Europeans. Boston and Philadelphia, with hundreds of ships coming and going, were in closer contact with London than many English cities were. The ships carried ideas as well as goods, and colonial cities were as well equipped to distribute one as the other. Every city had at least one newspaper by the middle of the eighteenth century, with every issue devoted largely to news from England and Europe. Through the columns of the newspapers and through the books imported from abroad and sometimes reprinted locally, the city man found his way out of the seventeenth century into the eighteenth. Gradually he learned to make rational-

ity a test of all things, to look upon revealed religion with a degree of skepticism, to cherish tolerance and shun persecution, and to expect from the progress of science (or philosophy, as he called it) what his ancestors had expected only from God. From the city such ideas filtered into the countryside. Although the cities held less than 5 per cent of the colonial population, it was the best informed and most influential 5 per cent.

THE EMERGING AMERICAN MIND

Before the middle of the eighteenth century Americans had little occasion to think of themselves as a distinct people. They had no opportunity at all to act as one. There was no American government, no single political organization in which all the colonies joined to manage their common concerns. There was not even a wish for such an organization except among a few eccentric individuals. America, to the people who lived in it, was still a geographical region, not a frame of mind.

Asked for his nationality, the average American in 1750 would have said English or British. In spite of substantial numbers of Dutch, Germans, and Scotch-Irish, Englishmen and English institutions prevailed in every colony, and most colonists spoke of England as home even though they had never been there. Yet none of their institutions was quite like its English counterpart; the heritage of English ideas that went with the institutions was so rich and varied that Americans were able to select and develop those that best suited their situation and forget others that meanwhile were growing prominent in the mother country. Some of the differences were local: the New England town, for example, and the Puritanism that went with it, set New Englanders off not only from Englishmen but from Virginians. But some ideas, institutions, and attitudes became common in all the colonies and remained uncommon in England. Although American Englishmen were not yet aware that they shared these "Americanisms" with one another or that Englishmen at home did not share them, many of the characteristic ideas and attitudes that later distinguished American nationalism were already present by mid-century.

Responsible representative government. Englishmen brought with them to the New World the political ideas that still give English and American government a close resemblance. But Americans very early developed conceptions of representative government that differed from those prevailing in England during the colonial period. Representative government in England originated in the Middle Ages, when the king called for men to advise him. They were chosen by their neighbors and informed the king of his subjects' wishes. Eventually their advice became so compelling that the king could not reject it, and the representatives of the people, organized as the House of Commons, became the most powerful branch of the English government.

At first the House of Commons consisted of representatives from each county, or shire, and from selected boroughs. Over the centuries many of these boroughs became ghost towns with only a handful of inhabitants, and great towns sprang up where none had existed before. Yet the old boroughs continued to send members to Parliament, and the new towns sent none. Moreover, only a fraction of the English population participated in the election of county representatives. In order to vote, a man had to own property that would, if rented, yield him at least 40 shillings yearly. Few could meet the test. A number of Englishmen thought the situation absurd and said so. But nothing was done to improve it; in fact, a theory was devised to justify it. A member of the House of Commons, it was said, represented not the people who chose him, but the whole country, and he was not responsible to any particular constituency. Not all Englishmen could vote for representatives, but all were "virtually" represented by every member of Commons.

Colonial assemblies were far more representative than the House of Commons. Although every colony had property qualifications for voting, probably the great majority of adult white males owned enough land to meet them. In apportioning representation, New England colonies gave every town the right to send delegates to the assembly. Outside New England, the unit of representation was usually· the county. The political organization of new counties and the extension of representation seldom kept pace with the rapid advance of settlement westward, but nowhere was representation so uneven or irrational as in England.

The American colonist knew nothing of "virtual" representation; to him representation was a means of acquainting the government with his needs and demands and with the amount and method of taxation he could most easily bear. A colonial assemblyman was supposed to be the agent of the people who chose him. In the large counties, of course, it was seldom possible, except on election day, for voters to gather in one place and express their opinions. But elections came every two or three years (annually in New England and Pennsylvania), and a representative was unlikely to stray far from his constituents' wishes in so short a time. In New England, where town meetings could be called any time, people often gathered to tell their delegate how to vote on a particular issue. He was supposed to look after their interests first, those of the colony second.

In America, therefore, representative government meant something different from what it did in England. Government existed to do a job, and it had to be kept responsible to its employers. While "virtual" representatives in Parliament created offices whose only purpose was to enrich the men who filled them, colonial assemblymen, watched closely by their constituents, had comparatively little opportunity to dip into the public purse.

Clergy and laity. Americans looked on their clergymen as they did on their elected representatives. They wanted the clergy to serve, not rule, them. The attitude had its roots in the English Reformation, and most Englishmen were sufficiently Protestant to share it in some degree; English Dissenters shared it wholeheartedly. But the Anglican Church held great powers in England: it was the only church supported by state taxation; during much of the colonial period only its members could hold public office; and its bishops enjoyed an authority that reached far beyond the realm of the spirit. As ex officio members of the House of Lords they voted on every act of Parliament, and as presiding judges in courts with jurisdiction over probate of wills and breaches of morality they could impose sentence of excommunication on offenders. Since excommunication cut a man off from political rights and from intercourse with his neighbors,

The Great Awakening: New Light Conviction

Now it pleased God to send Mr. Whitefield into this land ... I longed to see and hear him, and wished he would come this way ... then on a Sudden, in the morning about 8 or 9 of the Clock there came a messenger and said Mr. Whitefield preached at Hartford and Weathersfield yesterday and is to preach at Middletown this morning at ten of the Clock, I was in my field at Work, I ... ran home to my wife telling her to make ready quickly to go and hear Mr. Whitefield preach at Middletown, then run to my pasture for my horse with all my might.... when we came within about half a mile or a mile of the Road that comes down from Hartford Weathersfield and Stepney to Middletown; on high land I saw before me a Cloud or fogg rising; I first thought it came from the great River, but as I came nearer the Road, I heard a noise something like a low rumbling thunder and presently found it was the noise of Horses feet coming down the Road and this Cloud was a Cloud of dust made by the Horses feet; it arose some Rods into the air over the tops of Hills and trees and when I came within about 20 rods of the Road, I could see men and horses Sliping along in the Cloud like shadows and as I drew nearer it seemed like a steady Stream of horses and their riders, scarcely a horse more than his length behind another, all of a Lather and foam with sweat, their breath rolling out of their nostrils every Jump; every horse seemed to go with all his might to carry his rider to hear news from heaven for the saving of Souls, it made me tremble to see the Sight, how the world was in a Struggle ... and when we got to Middletown old meeting house there was a great Multitude it was said to be 3 or 4000 of people Assembled together.... When I saw Mr. Whitefield come upon the Scaffold he lookt almost Angelical; a young, Slim, slender youth before some thousands of people with a bold undaunted Countenance, and my hearing how God was with him every where as he came along it Solemnized my mind; and put me into a trembling fear before he began to preach; for he looked as if he was Cloathed with Authority from the Great God; and a sweet sollome solemnity sat upon his brow And my hearing him preach, gave me a heart wound; By Gods blessing: my old Foundation was broken up, and I saw that my righteousness would not save me.

From Nathan Cole, "Spiritual Travels," October 23, 1740

it could mean economic ruin as well as social ostracism. An offender could get the sentence lifted only by paying a heavy fee.

In the colonies churchmen had no such powers. Except in Rhode Island, Delaware, Pennsylvania, and New Jersey the assemblies did levy taxes in support of churches, favoring the Congregational churches in New England, the Anglican elsewhere. But this was the only connection between church and state that most Americans would tolerate. The Massachusetts rule that only church members could vote had ended with the revocation of the colony's charter in 1684.

In New England the old Puritan hostility to clerical authority persisted into the eighteenth century. Ministers were influential and highly respected; a few were even elected as representatives to colonial assemblies. But no minister enjoyed temporal authority by virtue of being a minister.

The Anglicans in America also kept their clergymen on short leash. Because England never sent a bishop to the colonies (and without a bishop there could be no ecclesiastical court), the Anglican Church lost most of its temporal powers when it was transplanted to America. In the Northern colonies, Anglicans, who were a small minority of the population, repeatedly asked for a bishop — much to the annoyance of Congregationalists and Presbyterians. In the Southern colonies, where the Anglican Church was the established church, its members were cool to the proposal. The Southerners, acting through their vestries, ran their churches and hired and fired their ministers almost as independently as any New England Puritan congregation. The minister, unless he had been formally inducted into office, could be dismissed at any time. With no bishop at hand to insist on induction, a church could simply omit the ceremony.

Probably one reason for the failure of the Anglican Church to send a bishop was the fear of resistance from non-Anglicans, who multiplied rapidly during the eighteenth century. Besides Congregationalists and Presbyterians, there were Baptists, Quakers, Dutch Reformed, Lutherans, Mennonites, and a host of minor sects. This diversity of religious groups, each growing as population grew, made it increasingly difficult for any one of them to dominate the rest and made the extension of religious authority in America ever more unlikely. Even in New England, where the Congregationalists remained a majority, they ceased after the seventeenth century to persecute Quakers and allowed persons of other denominations to support their own ministers through public taxation.

Religious developments. In the 1740's the number of religious groups was expanded by a rash of schisms that followed a religious revival. The Great Awakening was touched off in 1741 by a traveling English preacher who combined Calvinism and showmanship. George Whitefield, only twenty-seven at the time, was not a gifted theologian. But he had perfected a technique of preaching that brought remarkable results: he frightened his audience by depicting in vivid detail the pain awaiting sinners in Hell. He dramatized the scene for them, playing all the parts himself. Now he was an angry God booming out fearful judgments, now a damned soul weeping in anguish. He strained to bring his audience to the point of hysterical despair. He wanted them to writhe in agony, for he had found that thorough "conviction" — of their own sinfulness, helplessness, and utter dependence on Christ for salvation — was usually followed by "conversion," the feeling that they actually had been saved. As Whitefield journeyed from the Carolinas to New England, preaching indoors and out, Sundays and weekdays, he wrought conversions by the hundreds, among old and young, rich and poor, educated and ignorant.

His technique, requiring only a flair for the dramatic, was not hard to imitate. In his wake other self-appointed messengers of Christ traveled about the country, outdoing him in the sound and fury of their preaching. Gilbert Tennent, a Pennsylvania Presbyterian, made a specialty of laughing loud and long at sinners in the throes of conviction. James Davenport, an itinerant Congregationalist, was at his best at night, when smoking torches revealed him half naked, jumping up and down to stamp on the devil.

In spite of these excesses, the Awakening brought religious experiences to thousands of people in every rank of society. One of its staunchest defenders was Jonathan Edwards, minister of Northampton, Massachusetts, who had himself inspired a local revival in 1735. Edwards was the most talented theologian America ever produced. He preached a stricter

The Great Awakening: Old Light Skepticism

The Question is, whether it be'nt a plain, stubborn Fact, that the Passions have, generally, in these Times, been apply'd to, as though the main Thing in Religion was to throw them into Disturbance? Can it be denied, that the Preachers, who have been the Instruments of the Commotions in the Land, have endeavoured, by all Manner of Arts, and in all Manner of Ways, to raise the Passions of their Hearers to such a Height, as really to unfit them, for the present, for the Exercise of their reasonable Powers? Nay, in order to alarm Men's Fears, has it not been common, among some Sort of Preachers, to speak and act after such a wild Manner, as is adapted to affrighten People out of their Wits, rather than possess their Minds of such a Conviction of Truth, as is proper to Men, who are endow'd with Reason and Understanding? And under the Notion of speaking to the Affections, were the Things of God and another World ever preached with more Confusion of Thought; with greater Incoherence; with the undue Mixture of more rash, crude, unguarded Expressions; or with Conceit to a higher Degree, appearing in fulsome Self-Applauses, as well as unheard of Contempt of others? These are Things of too publick a Nature to be denied: They have been too often practised, and in Places of too great Concourse, to admit of Debate.

From Charles Chauncy, *Seasonable Thoughts on the State of Religion in New England*, 1743.

Calvinism than New England had ever heard, and he recast Calvinist doctrines to give a primary place to the emotions. Although his own manner in the pulpit was an austere contrast to Whitefield's, his doctrines emphasized the emotional impact of an omnipotent God on impotent man. Both conviction and conversion, Edwards insisted, were such overwhelming emotional experiences that the human frame could scarcely contain them. If occasionally a man fell to the ground or cried out in the grip of such powerful experiences, this was no reason to doubt that the spirit of God was the moving cause. Edwards' theology commanded respect in Europe as well as America and furnished the Awakening with an intellectual foundation that Whitefield could not have provided.

But not everyone agreed with Edwards.

George Whitefield: The Great Awakener.

Many ministers thought that the new method of preaching provoked more hysteria than holiness. They were offended by the itinerant preachers who entered their churches unbidden and wrung from a hitherto sane congregation a chorus of shrieks and groans and hallelujahs. After listening to an itinerant, people sometimes decided their own minister was worthless, and the most enthusiastic followers of the Awakening deserted their old churches to form new ones with more rigorous doctrines and standards of admission.

Once the shrieking had subsided, it became apparent that the Awakening had seriously undermined the position of the clergy. In every denomination, but especially in the Calvinist ones, ministers had been forced to take sides in favor of the revival (New Light) or against it (Old Light). The Old Lights were shocked by the sight of ignorant men screaming damnation and of masses of people wallowing in terror or ecstasy. Nor were they comforted by the less exuberant expressions of piety that followed.

"Nay han't it been common," asked the Boston minister Charles Chauncy, "in some Parts of the Land, and among some Sorts of People, to express their religious Joy, by singing through the Streets, and in Ferry Boats?" The Old Lights, having set themselves against such emotional "enthusiasm," prided themselves on a cool rationality. In this mood they reexamined Calvinist dogma and found it wanting. It was absurd, Chauncy decided, that men should suffer eternally by divine predestination: a rational God would allow some merit in human effort. The Old Lights took the road that led ultimately to Unitarianism, Universalism, and deism, to a world in which there was little need either for Christ or for clergymen. Not many Americans went the whole length of that road in the eighteenth century, but many of the best educated traveled it for some distance.

The New Lights undermined the position of the clergy in a more direct manner by teaching congregations to be bold in judging ministers. Itinerant preachers often pronounced local ministers unregenerate and made much of the idea that a minister could not be God's instrument in bringing salvation to others unless he himself was saved. With this principle in mind, the New Lights in a church did not hesitate to interrogate the minister and then declare him saved or damned. The minister's learning, which had once won him respect, suddenly became a handicap, for many itinerants, uneducated and uneducable, dismissed religious erudition as an impediment to saving grace.

Ironically, in the decades that followed the Great Awakening, the New Light clergy of New England involved themselves so deeply in learned pursuit of Edwards' Calvinist theology that they in turn alienated their congregations. Edwards was not easily understood at best, but his disciples drew out his doctrines in subtle elaborations that scarcely anyone understood but themselves. The New Divinity it was called, and among many bright young men of the day it became the prevailing intellectual fashion. Entering the ministry, they uttered its complexities in sermons addressed more to one another than to their audience. The passionate preaching of the Awakening was forgotten, and the New Divinity grew into a recondite game for clergymen.

Congregations reacted with the boldness

they had been taught by deserting the preachers who seemed to have deserted them. By the third quarter of the eighteenth century New England had been infiltrated by Presbyterians, Baptists, Anglicans, Universalists, and other denominations, and a man could shop around for a preacher and a religion that suited him. Samuel Hopkins, leading exponent of the New Divinity, preached away most of his congregation at Great Barrington, Massachusetts. He found another at Newport, Rhode Island, only to see it too dwindle under the impact of his incomprehensible sermons. An American minister was expected to serve his people. When they thought he was failing to do so, they dismissed him or left him.

Education. If the American colonist stood in no awe of his ministers and government officials, it was because the workings of state and church held no mysteries for him. He understood them better than the average European, not only because he had a large share in operating them but because he was better educated. Europeans were fond of picturing Americans as children of nature who learned wisdom from the trees and flowers but not from books. Actually, in spite of their wilderness life, or perhaps because of it, colonial Americans were a bookish lot.

Most of them were Protestants, and Protestants believed that religious truth was incom-

Jonathan Edwards: The most talented theologian America ever produced.

Massachusetts: The Schools

It being one chief project of that old deluder, Satan, to keep men from the knowledge of the Scriptures, as in former times by keeping them in an unknown tongue, so in these latter times by persuading from the use of tongues, that so at least the true sense and meaning of the original might be clouded by false glosses of saint-seeming deceivers, that learning may not be buried in the grave of our fathers in the church and commonwealth, the Lord assisting our endeavors.

It is therefore ordered, that every township in this jurisdiction, after the Lord hath increased them to the number of fifty householders, shall then forthwith appoint one within their town to teach all such children as shall resort to him to write and read, whose wages shall be paid either by the parents or masters of such children, or by the inhabitants in general, by way of supply, as the major part of those that order the prudentials of the town shall appoint; provided those that send their children be not oppressed by paying much more than they can have them taught for in other towns; and it is further ordered that where any town shall increase to the number of 100 families or householders, they shall set up a grammar school, the master thereof being able to instruct youth so far as they may be fitted for the university, provided that if any town neglect the performance hereof above one year, that every such town shall pay £5 to the next school till they shall perform this order.

From the Massachusetts School Law, 1647.

prehensible to the man who did not read the Scriptures for himself. They wanted to read; they wanted their children to read. And their desire was sharpened by the sight of the real children of nature, the Indians, naked, savage, and ignorant. In Massachusetts the law directed every town of fifty families to maintain a schoolmaster, and other New England colonies had similar requirements. The laws were not always enforced, but the rate of literacy (compared to that of England or the rest of Europe) was high throughout the colonies and especially high in New England.

By the middle of the eighteenth century nearly every colony had at least one printing press, and the printer usually produced a weekly newspaper, devoted mainly to news

The Enlightenment: Freedom of Religion

I retain a sincere Affection for my Mother College & wish it in my Power to contribute to her Prosperity and Reputation. The People this Way have conceived a very unhappy Idea of it, as a Nursery of bigotted Presbyterianism, & that all free Inquiry is as much extirpated & kept out of it, as from any of the popish Seminaries.... Different men indeed object from different Motives, some from the Love of Orthodoxy & some from the Hatred of it, & some from the generous sentiments of that generous & equal Liberty for which Protestants & Dissenters have made so noble a stand. It is true with this Liberty Error may be introduced; but turn the Tables the propagation of Truth may be extinguished. Deism has got such Head in this Age of Licentious Liberty, that it would be in vain to try to stop it by hiding the Deistical Writings: and the only Way left to conquer & demolish it, is to come forth into the open Field and dispute the Matter on even Footing. ... *Truth* & this alone being *our* Aim in fact, open, frank & generous we shall avoid the very Appearance of Evil.

From Ezra Stiles, Letter to Thomas Clap, President of Yale, 1759.

from abroad and from other colonies — everybody knew the local news — and to literary and political essays and verse, much of which was culled from English newspapers. The printers also turned out broadsides, almanacs, pamphlets, and books. Though the clergy were the most prolific colonial authors and sermons the most popular reading matter, local political issues were often discussed in print. There were even some efforts at verse. The best of these, the meditative poems of Edward Taylor, minister of Westfield, Massachusetts, were not published until the present century, but colonial readers bought another minister's versified account of the Last Judgment (*The Day of Doom* by Michael Wigglesworth) in such numbers that it went through five editions between 1662 and 1701.

The colonists made early provision for higher education. In 1636, only six years after the Puritans came to Massachusetts, they founded the college that later took the name of its first benefactor, John Harvard. Although the founders' purpose was to furnish the colony with a learned ministry, Harvard was no mere theological seminary. From the beginning its students followed the traditional curriculum of the liberal arts taught in European universities: they studied grammar (Latin, Greek, and Hebrew), rhetoric, logic, mathematics, astronomy, physics, metaphysics, and moral philosophy. Only once a week, on Saturdays, did they turn to theology. Those who intended to become ministers received their professional training after they graduated, not before. But many Harvard graduates, the majority after the seventeenth century, went into professions other than the ministry.

The same was true of most other colonial colleges: William and Mary, chartered in 1693, remained for some years little more than a grammar school, but Yale (1701) offered a program similar to Harvard's, and so did Princeton (1746), Rutgers (1766), Pennsylvania (1755), Columbia (1754), and Brown (1764). It was not simply the children of the well-to-do who attended these colleges. Tuition rates were low, and every class contained boys fresh from the farm. Education even at the college level was widely diffused by comparison with that of England.

The fact that New Englanders fell victim to hysteria over witchcraft has often been cited as evidence of the shallowness of their education. How could educated people be so superstitious? The answer is that educated people everywhere believed in witchcraft. In 1692 twenty persons were hanged as witches in Massachusetts, and hundreds more had been accused when the ministers' objections to the unfairness of the trials induced the government to stop them. No subsequent execution for witchcraft is recorded in America, but in Europe thousands were executed in the seventeenth century, and the executions continued into the eighteenth.

The Enlightenment. The ideas that conquered man's belief in witchcraft were originated, not by Americans, but by a succession of Europeans who had the imagination and daring to take the measure of God's world for themselves. During the sixteenth and seventeenth centuries Copernicus, Galileo, and Kepler had studied the motions of the planets and accumulated evidence to show that they rotated around the sun. Sir Isaac Newton, building on their work, discovered the laws of motion, the "natural laws" by which God governed the movement of the planets. He also studied light and learned to break it into its different colors and to bend it with mirrors and lenses. Newton's success convinced his contemporaries that human reason was capable of exploring the universe and of ascertaining by observation and experiment the principles by which God governed it. Men who had been taught that reason was a feeble instrument, all but destroyed by Adam's original sin, now turned inquiring eyes on the world around them. They wanted to measure everything, to see how the world worked.

In looking so closely at God's world, men formed a new image of God himself. Where he had formerly been an arbitrary monarch, who glorified himself in the damnation of sinners and the salvation of saints, he now became a divine craftsman whose glory lay in his craftsmanship, a celestial watchmaker whose intricate and orderly handiwork lay everywhere visible to the eyes that reason directed toward it. The new God appeared more reasonable than the old, but also more remote and indifferent, a watchmaker who wound up his universe and then left it to run itself. He seemed, in fact, so reasonable that some men decided he was reason itself, or at least that reason was an adequate substitute for him.

Though few went this far, the eighteenth century earned the title of the Age of Reason. And the English philosopher John Locke furnished the century with a theory about reason that gradually won acceptance and further encouraged the pursuit of experiment and observation. In *An Essay concerning Human Understanding* (1690) Locke concluded that the human mind at birth was not the repository of any innate ideas placed there by the Creator. Rather, it was a complete blank and only gradually accumulated knowledge from the experiences of the five senses attached to it. He who would grow in knowledge, therefore, must devote himself not simply to books, perhaps not even to the Bible, nor to abstract contemplation, but to seeing, hearing, feeling, tasting — in a word, to observation and experiment.

Man himself was a fair subject for scrutiny, and Locke turned his attention to the relations of men to one another. He decided that God had provided natural laws to make the human

The Enlightenment: A Free Press

Printers are educated in the Belief, that when Men differ in Opinion, both Sides ought equally to have the Advantage of being heard by the Publick; and that when Truth and Error have fair Play, the former is always an overmatch for the latter: Hence they chearfully serve all contending Writers that pay them well, without regarding on which side they are of the Question in Dispute....

That it is unreasonable to imagine Printers approve of every thing they print, and to censure them on any particular thing accordingly; since in the way of their Business they print such great variety of things opposite and contradictory. It is likewise as unreasonable what some assert, "That Printers ought not to print any Thing but what they approve;" since if all of that Business should make such a Resolution, and abide by it, an End would thereby be put to Free Writing, and the World would afterwards have nothing to read but what happen'd to be the Opinions of Printers.

From Benjamin Franklin, "Apology for Printers," 1731.

world run as smoothly as the physical world; but the enforcement of these natural laws of society God had left to men. In two treatises on civil government (published in 1689 and 1690 but written earlier) Locke explained that men had voluntarily left the free state of nature (in which they were born and originally lived) and had, by mutual agreement, instituted civil government for the purpose of enforcing natural laws. The most important natural law was that no man should take away the life, liberty, or property of another (these were "natural rights" of man). A government that failed to protect life, liberty, and property lost its reason for existence and deserved to be altered or overthrown by the people it governed.

Reason led Locke to condemn absolute government, whether in church or state. It led others to advocate free trade, free speech, free thought. Together, Locke and Newton gave men confidence that all the world's evils as well as its mysteries would yield to the persistent application of human reason.

This confidence in reason, which animated the European philosophers of the eighteenth century, came to be known as the Enlightenment. Although the Enlightenment originated in Europe, its doctrines penetrated society more widely in America. Students in American colleges learned Newton's physics and Locke's psychology. Ministers, whether Old Light or New, adapted their theology to the new ideas and welcomed the discoveries of reason as an aid to revelation, a means to improve their understanding of God's creation. Politicians cited Locke to support their arguments. Gentlemen formed clubs to discuss philosophy. Men awakened to the newness of the New World and turned amateur scientists; they described American plants and animals and made astronomical observations of the American skies to swell the growing body of scientific information that might provide answers to the limitless questions reason could now ask. In Boston the Reverend Cotton Mather and Dr. Zabdiel Boylston demonstrated by experiment the efficacy of inoculation against smallpox. In Philadelphia David Rittenhouse built the first American orrery, a mechanical model that reproduced the motions of the solar system.

Even the common man, who never himself read Locke or Newton, was receptive to their philosophy. To the European peasant, following the footsteps of his ancestors, unable to read or write, with no voice in church or state, the Enlightenment meant little. But the ordinary American colonist had constantly to apply his reason to new situations, whether in field or forest, church or state. The Enlightenment made a virtue of his necessity and encouraged him to lift his voice against unreasonableness wherever he met it.

It is perhaps no accident that the man who best exemplified the Enlightenment both to his countrymen and to foreigners was not only an American but an American who came from the ranks of common men and never lost touch with them. Benjamin Franklin (1706-90) was born in Boston, made his fortune in Philadelphia, and then spent much of the remainder of his life in England and France on political missions for the American people. His genius brought him success in everything he tried, whether it was running a Philadelphia newspaper in his youth or wooing the ladies of Paris in his old age. The Enlightenment sang the praises of intellectual freedom; Franklin as a printer defended his right to publish what he pleased. The Enlightenment called for freedom of trade; Franklin worked as a diplomat to achieve that freedom. The Enlightenment encouraged scientific experiment. Franklin made significant observations on a wide variety of scientific subjects (from ocean currents to the theory of heat); he was a prolific inventor (a stove, a clock, a musical instrument); and, as one of the first experimenters with electricity, he made important contributions to both the theory of the subject (positive and negative current) and to its application (lightning rods).

As a son of the Enlightenment, Franklin was at home anywhere in the world, yet everywhere men recognized him as a typical American. Even without the fur cap he wore to emphasize it, no one could miss his American style, his down-to-earth insistence on doing things his own way and finding out for himself. Franklin's insistence on results in everything he undertook accorded with his countrymen's insistence that their governments and churches perform what was expected of them.

Social mobility. In describing America for Europeans, Franklin advised no one to go there unless he had more to recommend him than high birth, for Americans, he said, "do not inquire concerning a Stranger, *What is he?* but, *What can he do?*" Franklin wrote these words after the period we are considering — probably in 1782. But by mid-century it had already become clear that birth meant less in America than in Europe.

Europeans learned at an early age that God made men unequal. To some he gave riches beyond measure, to others nothing. The land on which European peasants worked was, in a sense, theirs; but it also belonged to their superiors, who did not labor on it but received rents and services from those who did. Riches brought dignity. It might take more than one generation for a wealthy family to climb to the top of the social ladder, but once there its members enjoyed the security of a title — count, duke, earl, marquis — that passed in perpetuity from father to son. Riches and dignity brought power, and men who had neither had to do the bidding of those who had both. In Europe, men of title generally had a voice in government. In England, even though the House of Commons became the dominant branch of Parliament, its members were drawn from the higher ranks of English society, and they could still pass no law without the consent of the highest ranks, assembled in the House of Lords.

Although the eighteenth-century American was taught that God assigned men to different ranks in society, the idea did not have quite the same meaning as in Europe. The American could see plainly that merchants and planters had more wealth and dignity than other men. But the social ladder was both shorter and shakier in America than in Europe. Since huge tracts of land were unclaimed and unsettled, it was not hard for an enterprising man to gain possession of all he needed. Except for slaves, no large class of men worked for other men. And those who did enjoyed a higher status than they would have in England, because labor was scarce, and hired workers were paid accordingly. Everyone knew that the servant bound to his master for a set term would in time be free and might himself become wealthy. At the foot of the ladder, then, free Americans who worked with their hands enjoyed a higher position than European peasants or artisans. At the top of the ladder, the greatest American aristocrats had no titles and would have ranked in England below any member of the House of Lords.

Without the security of a title, American families had difficulty in staying at the top. Hard work and good luck made a man rich; hard work and bad luck made him poor again. And, while wealth brought power, the rich had no place of their own in government. Generally the governor's council, whether popularly elected or appointed by the king, was selected from their number. But no American could claim a seat in the council simply by virtue of his social position. Nor could he expect to retain either government office or social rank indefinitely. Mobility, not nobility, dominated society in America.

In a number of ways, then, the eighteenth-century American differed from the Englishman or the European. He was better educated and therefore less in awe of his superiors, who were in any case not far above him. He had more control over his government and over his clergymen. Unless he was a slave — the exception to most statements about Americans be-

Benjamin Franklin: Arch-American.

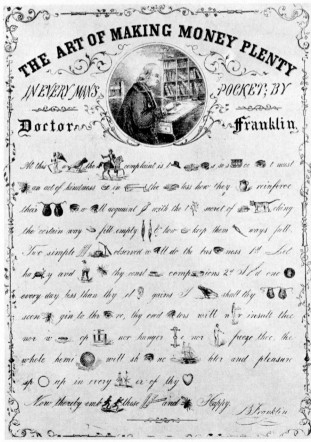

The Extension of Settlement, 1660–1760

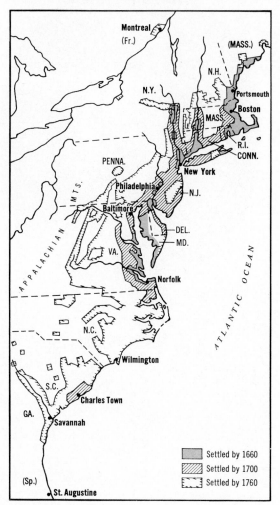

Montreal (Fr.)

(MASS.)

N.H.

N.Y.

Portsmouth

Boston

MASS.

R.I.

CONN.

PENNA.

New York

Philadelphia

N.J.

Baltimore

DEL.

MD.

A P P A L A C H I A N   M T S.

VA.

Norfolk

ATLANTIC OCEAN

N.C.

Wilmington

S.C.

Charles Town

GA.

Savannah

Settled by 1660
Settled by 1700
Settled by 1760

(Sp.)

St. Augustine

fore 1863 — he had a greater opportunity to mold his own life. He used whatever tools might serve him to do it, whether ax, plow, rifle, or vote; and he got results, from governments as well as from forest and field. He did not yet know it, but he was becoming a new kind of man.

THE CONTEST FOR THE CONTINENT

America was the spearhead of European growth. The European population did not begin its own spectacular growth until after the middle of the eighteenth century. Mean-while Europe grew in America, where population doubled every twenty-five years.

American ways of living together had been designed for growth: the plantation with its reserve of unused and uncleared land, the New England town with its undivided commons, the farm surrounded by forest. But population rapidly outgrew existing communities, and Americans thrust steadily westward until they came up against other peoples who were uninterested in sharing American ways of living together. Indians, Frenchmen, and Spaniards preferred their own ways, and the contest with these rivals for the continent was one of the persistent facts of life for colonial Americans.

Indian warfare. The Indians of eastern North America were slow to perceive that their way of life was incompatible with that of the English. They often sold their land or gave it away without realizing that it would no longer be theirs too. They used the land mainly for hunting, and were willing to let the English hunt on it with them. But Englishmen taking possession cut the trees, drove out the game, and evicted the Indians. Before the Indians realized what was happening, they were outnumbered.

They could probably have done nothing to stem the English advance anyhow. They were many peoples, not one, and they made war on one another as often as they did on the white invaders. Indeed they often welcomed the white man for the assistance they hoped he would offer in quarrels with their neighbors. But, except when directed and organized by the French or Spanish, they were not formidable military opponents for the English. Superior woodsmanship gave them some advantage, especially when they were armed with the white man's weapons, and they posed a constant threat to the isolated frontier farmer. But they were too independent, too incorrigibly individualistic, to submit for long to military discipline. They might gather for a surprise assault, but they could not stick together long enough to take advantage of their success.

The colonists, if not more warlike, were better armed, better organized, and more systematic about killing. Indians of the Powhatan Confederacy in Virginia massacred 347 settlers in a surprise attack in 1622 (Indian victories in American history are generally known as

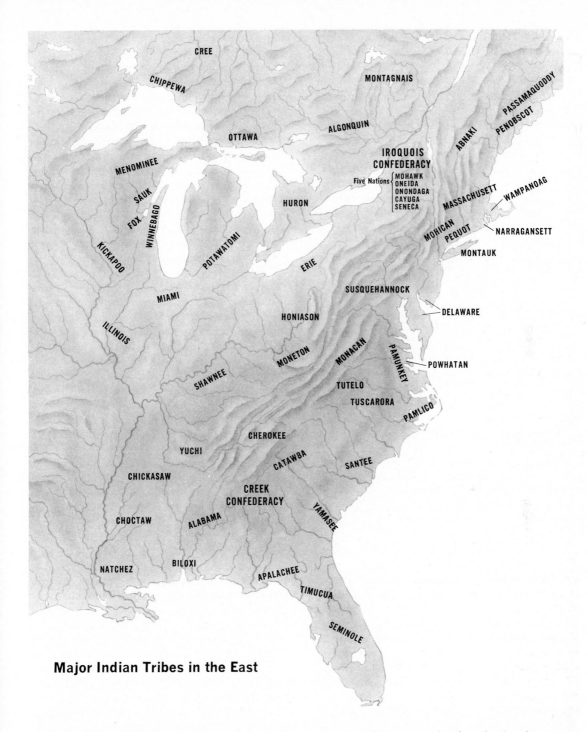

CREE

CHIPPEWA

MONTAGNAIS

OTTAWA

ALGONQUIN

PASSAMAQUODDY

PENOBSCOT

ABNAKI

MENOMINEE

IROQUOIS
CONFEDERACY

Five Nations { MOHAWK
ONEIDA
ONONDAGA
CAYUGA
SENECA }

MASSACHUSETT

WAMPANOAG

SAUK

HURON

FOX

WINNEBAGO

MOHICAN

PEQUOT

NARRAGANSETT

POTAWATOMI

MONTAUK

KICKAPOO

ERIE

MIAMI

SUSQUEHANNOCK

DELAWARE

ILLINOIS

HONIASON

SHAWNEE

MONETON

MONACAN

PAMUNKEY

POWHATAN

TUTELO

TUSCARORA

PAMLICO

CHEROKEE

YUCHI

CATAWBA

SANTEE

CHICKASAW

CREEK
CONFEDERACY

CHOCTAW

ALABAMA

YAMASEE

NATCHEZ

BILOXI

APALACHEE

TIMUCUA

SEMINOLE

Major Indian Tribes in the East

massacres), but from that time on the Virginians pursued a policy of extermination that
gradually eliminated the Indian menace in the
tidewater area. In 1637 the Puritans, acting in
support of a group of tribes, broke the power
of the one most dangerous New England tribe,
the Pequots. An army led by John Mason surprised their main village at night, set fire to

it, and shot men, women, and children as they ran to escape the flames. Thereafter New England suffered no serious Indian attack until 1676, when the Wampanoag chieftain Philip undertook a war that lasted longer than usual but ended with the usual result.

By this time the English had driven most of the seaboard tribes to inland regions already occupied by other Indians, who fought the retreating Indians as well as the advancing English. Virginia, which for many years had been living at peace with the broken remnant of the Powhatan Confederacy, was invaded by displaced Susquehannocks from the north. In September 1675, when a party of Virginia militia on a peace mission murdered the chiefs who had come to negotiate, the Susquehannocks retaliated with a raid that killed thirty-six Virginians.

The new Indian menace caught Virginia at a bad time. Tobacco prices had been low too long, and tobacco farmers were poor and short-tempered. Eastern Virginians had been free of Indians too long, and they did not recognize the danger or know how to meet it. The once-popular governor William Berkeley and the House of Burgesses had been in office too long (Berkeley had not called an election since 1661), and the government had lost touch with the people. When Berkeley and the Burgesses, who were mainly Easterners, proposed to combat the Indian invasion by erecting a series of costly forts, the back country was indignant. Frontiersmen wanted dead Indians now, not more taxes for useless forts next year. In Charles City County a gathering of farmers and planters asked Nathaniel Bacon, a newcomer who had recently been appointed to the governor's council, to lead them in collecting Indian scalps.

During the months that followed, the Virginians battled with one another more often than with the Indians. Bacon, young and headstrong, demanded that the governor commission him to fight the Indians; Berkeley, old and headstrong, declared him a rebel. For six months the two men struggled for mastery of the colony. Initially Bacon attracted a large following among the depressed and discontented of all classes, and for a time he controlled most of Virginia except the Eastern Shore. After he died of a fever in September 1676, his

men carried on without him for a time. But Berkeley had recovered his authority by January 1677, when royal commissioners arrived from England to investigate the conflict and relieve him of office. In the course of the struggle Bacon and his men killed a number of peaceful Pamunkey Indians; the Susquehannocks escaped but ceased to bother the colony.

Rivalry with France and Spain. After 1676 the surviving Indians east of the Appalachians were too few in number to menace the English settlers. But those farther west, led by the French, stood ready to halt English expansion at the mountains. Frenchmen in Canada, from the time of Champlain's founding of Quebec in 1608, had taken an acquisitive interest in the interior of North America. Missionaries in search of souls and *coureurs de bois* in search of furs traveled up and down the Mississippi and through the wilderness of its eastern tributaries. The *coureurs* were as good woodsmen as the Indians and as casual with their lives as the old English sea dogs. One of them, Louis Jolliet, together with the Jesuit Father Marquette, descended the Mississippi to the Arkansas as early as 1673. Robert Cavelier, Sieur de la Salle, reached the mouth of the Mississippi in 1682, and seventeen years later the French took possession of Louisiana by planting a settlement at Biloxi. In 1702 they started another one at Mobile. They also set up forts and trading posts in the Illinois country at Kaskaskia, Cahokia, and Vincennes, way stations between the St. Lawrence and the Mississippi, the two main arteries into the heart of North America.

In the competition for Indian furs, the French worked under a handicap, because French craftsmen could not supply as cheaply as the English did the textiles and hardware that the Indians demanded in exchange. But, in spite of the better bargains offered by the English, the Frenchman did a better job of winning the Indians' friendship. Instead of evicting them from their land, he lived in their wigwams, married their daughters, and taught them to like Catholicism and hate the English.

The French government during the seventeenth century did not appreciate the exploits of its wandering subjects. In 1663 the king had taken New France from a French trading company, and thereafter the colony was governed by royal decrees (executed through a governor

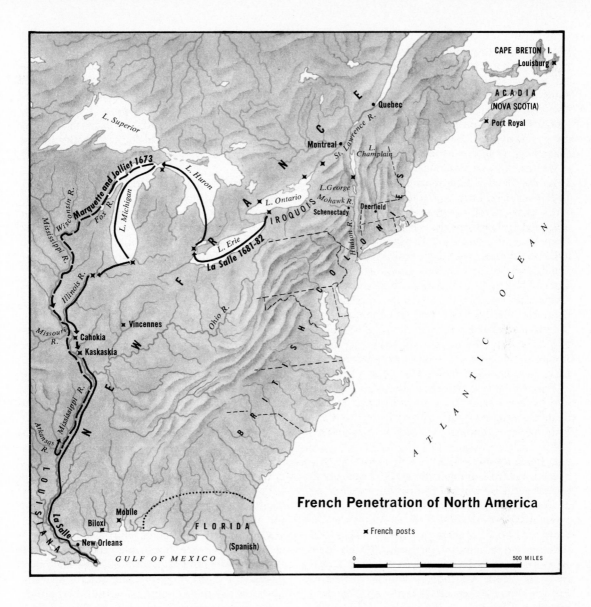

French Penetration of North America

CAPE BRETON I.
Louisburg ✖

A C A D I A
(NOVA SCOTIA)

✖ Port Royal

• Quebec

Montreal •

L. Superior

Marquette and Jolliet 1673

L. Huron

La Salle 1681-82

L. Michigan

Wisconsin R.

Fox R.

Mississippi R.

Illinois R.

Missouri R.

L. Ontario

L. Erie

IROQUOIS

L. George
Mohawk R.
Schenectady

Deerfield

Hudson R.

St. Lawrence R.

L. Champlain

N E W   F R A N C E

B R I T I S H   C O L O N I E S

• Vincennes

Ohio R.

✖ Cahokia
✖ Kaskaskia

Mississippi R.

Arkansas R.

L O U I S I A N A

La Salle

Mobile •
Biloxi ✖ ✖

New Orleans ✖

F L O R I D A
(Spanish)

GULF OF MEXICO

A T L A N T I C   O C E A N

✖ French posts

0   500 MILES

and an intendant, with no representative assembly). The king consistently discouraged the activities of the *coureurs*. He rejected, for example, the scheme of two *coureurs*, Pierre Radisson and Médart Chouart, Sieur de Groseilliers, who proposed a trading company to reach the northern fur supply by sea instead of by land; as a result, in 1672 they formed the Hudson's Bay Company in England instead of France.

Louis XIV was not interested in the wastes of Hudson Bay. Guided by his great minister Colbert, he wanted New France to be populated with hard-working, docile farmers. He sent women to entice the wild *coureurs* into a more settled life; he placed a bounty on large families. He forbade all but a few privileged individuals to engage in the fur trade. He even enlisted the Church in the cause: men who left their farms without permission were liable to excommunication. But all Louis' efforts produced only a meager scattering of agricultural settlements in Nova Scotia, along the St. Lawrence River, and later in Louisiana and in the Illinois country. Immigrants were few, and the total population remained small, no more than fifty or sixty thousand by the middle of the eighteenth century.

That so small and scattered a population could be in any way formidable to the million and a half English colonists was owing to the fact that the government's decrees against the *coureurs* had not been enforced. It is doubtful that they could have been; but some of the governors of Canada, notably Count Frontenac (who governed during most of the period from 1672 to 1698), perceived the strategic importance of what the *coureurs* were doing and disregarded instructions to halt them. Whenever France went to war with England, the *coureurs* led their Indian friends in raids on outlying English settlements in New England and New York. The English protected themselves by an uneasy alliance with the Iroquois. The Iroquois controlled the Mohawk Valley, which, in combination with the Hudson Valley, Lake George, and Lake Champlain, was the only easy invasion route through the mountains that stretched from New England to the Carolinas.

From 1689 to 1713 warfare between England and France was almost continuous, in the War of the League of Augsburg (1689–97) and the War of the Spanish Succession (1702–13), known in the colonies as King William's War and Queen Anne's War. At this time neither France nor England considered America worth the expenditure of royal troops. But the settlers, aware of how much was at stake, carried on their own warfare. The French sent their Indians to raid Schenectady and Deerfield and the thinly populated villages in Maine. The New Englanders in turn captured Port Royal in Nova Scotia in 1690, saw it returned to France at the Peace of Ryswick in 1697, and recaptured it in 1710. The Treaty of Utrecht in 1713, besides recognizing England's claim to Hudson Bay, gave her Nova Scotia with its population of more than a thousand French farmers; it left Cape Breton Island, unpopulated but strategically located at the mouth of the St. Lawrence, to the French.

In the South, where the Appalachian barrier ended, both sides had carried on their warfare largely through Indians. South Carolina furtraders rivaled the French in their skillful handling of Indian tribes. Ranging as far as the Mississippi in search of deerskins, they gradu-

ally gained the allegiance of the Yamasee and of most of the tribes forming the great Creek Confederacy of the Southeast. With Indian assistance they pushed back the Spaniards in Florida and threatened the French in Louisiana. Two years after Queen Anne's War ended, however, the Creeks and Yamasee turned and attacked their allies. But for the loyalty of the Cherokee, South Carolina might have suffered disaster.

After their assault failed, the Creeks moved westward to the Chattahoochee and the Yamasee southward, mostly to the vicinity of the Spanish fort at St. Augustine, thus relieving the English settlers of immediate danger. But the territory vacated by the Indians now offered the French and Spanish an undefended route by which to attack the Carolinians. Spain had always claimed this area as part of Florida, by right of prior discovery and occupation. She now threatened to recover it. The English attempted to forestall Spanish occupation by planting Fort King George on the Altamaha River in 1721. After the fort proved ineffective against Indian raids and had to be abandoned, England turned to a more familiar method of holding the territory. Forts and missions and Indian diplomacy were a Spanish and French specialty. The English way of occupying America had always been to live in it. English settlers had striven not so much to exploit the Indian as to displace him entirely. And in 1732 Englishmen prepared to move their homes into the area deserted by the Creeks and Yamasee.

The founding of Georgia. During the quarter-century of peace following the Treaty of Utrecht, the population of the English colonies passed the million mark. The expansion took place east of the mountains, within the bounds of the old colonies. But one new colony, Georgia, was organized in the exposed region of South Carolina.

Like most of the original colonies, Georgia was founded for two purposes, one worldly and realistic, the other altruistic and hopeful. In order to defend her southern flank in America, England needed settlers. At the same time, an English gentleman with military experience and philanthropic motives wanted to do something for the poor. General James Oglethorpe, while serving on a parliamentary committee, had looked into the appalling condition of debtors jailed by their creditors. Since they could do nothing in jail to work off their debts, they might linger there for years, until they were incapable of working at all.

General Oglethorpe organized other philanthropic gentlemen to seek a charter for a colony in which debtors and other unfortunate but deserving paupers might rehabilitate themselves. The English government was glad to get people out of jail and into the firing line on the southern frontier of the Carolinas, but it did not propose to let them get out of hand. In 1732 the government gave Oglethorpe and his friends a charter granting them authority as trustees for twenty-one years, after which the colony would revert to the king.

The trustees collected enough capital to get the enterprise off to a strong start. The area had been pictured in English tracts as a paradise compared to which the Garden of Eden was "at most but equal," and settlers eager to pay their own way appeared from Scotland, Germany, and New England as well as from England. The trustees gave them their blessing and rounded up deserving debtors to go with them. In Georgia, Oglethorpe himself saw that each man got fifty acres of land (those who paid their own way might get up to five hundred acres), tools to work it with, and enough supplies for the first year.

The trustees did their best to bar sin and temptation from the new paradise. To keep the rehabilitated debtor sober they forbade rum. To keep him industrious they forbade slavery. To ensure his livelihood they forbade land sales without their permission. But the zeal was only on the part of the trustees. Georgia proved after all to be somewhat less attractive than paradise, and the Georgians thought they deserved at least the compensation of sinning like other men. In 1751 the trustees conceded defeat, allowed slavery and rum, and in 1752, a year before their charter expired, turned their fallen colony over to the king.

The colony's more worldly purpose was better realized, for Georgia had begun to serve as a very effective buffer. When England and Spain fought the War of Jenkins' Ear (1739–42) over English infiltration and Spanish atrocities in the Caribbean, Oglethorpe led the Georgians in campaigns against Florida and held off a Spanish invasion.

The Departure of the Creeks and Yamasee and the Founding of Georgia

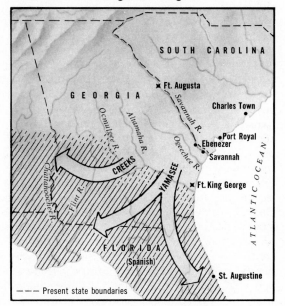

After the European conflict broadened into the War of the Austrian Succession (1740–48), known in the colonies as King George's War, the action shifted to the Northern colonies. There New Englanders got up an expedition under William Pepperell, a merchant from Maine, to attack the French fortress of Louisburg on Cape Breton Island. The colonists' capture of Louisburg was England's only real success on any front during the war, and it enabled her to go to the peace table with a make-weight to set against French conquests in the Austrian Netherlands. Although the Treaty of Aix-la-Chapelle (1748) restored the status quo and thus gave Louisburg back to France, its capture had focused the attention of both countries on the increasing strength and importance of England's American subjects.

They were a million and a half now and growing steadily. The advance guard of settlement — speculators, fur-traders, and explorers — were already probing the mountain passes and eyeing the rich bottom lands of the Ohio. France had no settlers to occupy those lands, but she did have men to fight for them. If the English grew any further, she was prepared to make it hurt as never before. The English grew.

SUGGESTIONS FOR READING

In many ways the most challenging problem of American history has been to discover in colonial America those institutions, attitudes, and events that found fruition in the later American way of life. George Bancroft first made the attempt on a large scale in his *History of the United States*, 10 vols. (1834–74), in which he saw divine providence guiding the colonists toward independence. F. J. Turner searched for the answer along the frontier in *The Frontier in American History** (1920), and V. L. Parrington traced a conflict between the common man and the would-be aristocrat in *The Colonial Mind** (1927). These men were giants, and their works are too lightly dismissed today. More recent attempts to discern the abiding meaning of the colonial past are Max Savelle, *Seeds of Liberty** (1948); Clinton Rossiter, *Seedtime of the Republic* (Part I: *The First American Revolution**) (1953); and D. J. Boorstin, *The Americans: The Colonial Experience** (1958).

The origins of the plantation system in Virginia are traced in T. J. Wertenbaker, *The Planters of Colonial Virginia* (1922), which argues that the seventeenth century was the heyday of the yeoman farmer and that neither slavery nor the large plantation was common before the eighteenth century. The servants who supplied the colonial labor force, both North and South, before the rise of slavery are the subject of A. E. Smith, *Colonists in Bondage* (1947). Oscar and Mary Handlin, "The Origins of the Southern Labor System," *William and Mary Quarterly*, 3rd series, VII (1950), 199 ff., reprinted in Oscar Handlin, *Race and Nationality in American Life** (1957), traces the origin and development of slavery. The Handlins are challenged by Carl Degler in "Slavery and the Genesis of American Race Prejudice," *Comparative Studies in Society and History*, II (1959–60), 49–66.

The best overall account of plantation agriculture is L. C. Gray, *History of Agriculture in the Southern United States to 1860*, 2 vols. (1933). On the Virginia plantation in the mid-eighteenth century, Louis Morton, *Robert Carter of Nomini Hall** (1941), offers a close-up view. L. B. Wright, *The First Gentlemen of Virginia** (1940), does the same for a number of earlier planters. On domestic life in the South see E. S. Morgan, *Virginians at Home** (1952), and Julia Spruill, *Women's Life and Work in the Southern Colonies* (1938). Carl Bridenbaugh, *Myths and Realities: Societies of the Colonial South** (1952), challenges many conventional ideas about Southern society.

The origin of the New England town was a subject of lively discussion among nineteenth-century historians, but the twentieth century has shown little interest in it until recently. The best general discussion of the English institutions from which the town derived will be found in Wallace Notestein, *The English People on the Eve of Colonization** (1954). An important case study of a single town and its English origins is Sumner Powell, *Puritan Village** (1963). R. H. Akagi, *The Town Proprietors of New England* (1924), is still valuable. That it needs revision, however, is evident from Charles Grant's study of a single Connecticut town in *Democracy in the Connecticut Frontier Town of Kent* (1961). Much valuable information about town affairs is contained in Ola Winslow, *Meetinghouse Hill* (1952).

There is no good study of the American farm in the colonial period, but the anonymous *American Husbandry* (1775; reprinted 1939, H. J. Carman, ed.) offers a wealth of information.

On the colonial cities the works of Carl Bridenbaugh are unique and outstanding: *Cities in the Wilderness, 1625–1742** (1938); *Cities in Revolt, 1743–1776** (1955); *The Colonial Craftsman** (1950); and, with Jessica Bridenbaugh, *Rebels and Gentlemen** (1942). The last is a study of Philadelphia in the age of Franklin. An outstanding history of a colonial merchant firm is

* Available in a paperback edition.

J. B. Hedges, *The Browns of Providence Plantation: Colonial Years* (1952). Stuart Bruchey in *The Colonial Merchant** (1966) offers a well-selected collection of source materials.

The rise of American representative government is dealt with in L. W. Labaree, *Royal Government in America* (1930). R. E. Brown, in *Middle-Class Democracy and the Revolution in Massachusetts* (1955), argues convincingly that most adult males in colonial Massachusetts had the right to vote and that all districts of the state were equitably represented. R. E. Brown and B. K. Brown, *Virginia 1705–1786: Democracy or Aristocracy* (1964), offers evidence that Virginia too was more democratic than aristocratic. Charles Sydnor, *Gentlemen Freeholders** (1952), stresses the aristocratic powers that the large planters won by their social prestige. Jack P. Greene, *The Quest for Power* (1963), traces the rising power of the lower houses of assembly in all the Southern colonies. Another general work, Chilton Williamson, *American Suffrage: From Property to Democracy 1760–1860* (1960), shows that the right to vote was enjoyed by the majority of adult males in all the colonies.

The best general survey of colonial social and intellectual history before the Revolution is L. B. Wright, *The Cultural Life of the American Colonies** (1957).

W. W. Sweet, *Religion in Colonial America* (1942), is more concerned with church history than with religion itself. On the Great Awakening, see E. S. Gaustad, *The Great Awakening in New England* (1957); L. J. Trinterud, *The Forming of an American Tradition* (1949); and W. M. Gewehr, *The Great Awakening in Virginia* (1930). Ola Winslow, *Jonathan Edwards** (1940), is the best biography; Perry Miller, *Jonathan Edwards** (1949), is a brilliant interpretation of Edwards' thought. Joseph Haroutunian, *Piety Versus Moralism* (1932), traces the development of Edwards' theology in the New Divinity while Conrad Wright, *The Beginnings of Unitarianism in America** (1955), shows how a liberal theology developed among the opponents of the Awakening. Brooke Hindle, *The Pursuit of Science in Revolutionary America* (1956), concentrates on the organization of scientific investigations from 1735 to 1789. Benjamin Franklin's contributions to science are ably treated in I. B. Cohen, *Benjamin Franklin's Experiments* (1941), and *Franklin and Newton* (1956). The best biographies of Franklin are Carl Van Doren, *Benjamin Franklin** (1941), and V. W. Crane, *Benjamin Franklin and a Rising People** (1954). E. S. Morgan, *The Gentle Puritan: A Life of Ezra Stiles* (1962), shows the influence on a learned New England minister of the various intellectual forces discussed in this chapter.

Bernard Bailyn, *Education in the Forming of American Society** (1960), surveys the scant literature on the subject that has not been fully treated by recent historians. The history of Harvard College through the seventeenth century has been written by a master in S. E. Morison, *The Founding of Harvard College* (1935) and *Harvard College in the Seventeenth Century*, 2 vols. (1936). Robert Middlekauff, *Ancients and Axioms* (1963), is the best study of secondary education.

Francis Parkman made a study of the conflict between England and France in North America his life work, and all his writings are worth careful reading. More recently, George Hunt, *The Wars of the Iroquois** (1940), challenges some of Parkman's views, and A. W. Trelease, *Indian Affairs in Colonial New York: The Seventeenth Century* (1960), offers still another interpretation. Wilcomb Washburn, *The Governor and the Rebel* (1957), sees Bacon's Rebellion as the result of frontiersmen's desire for Indian lands. Alden Vaughan defends the Puritans' treatment of the Indians in *New England Frontier: Puritans and Indians 1620–1675* (1965). Later New England relations with the Indians are treated in Douglas Leach, *Flintlock and Tomahawk** (1958) and *The Northern Colonial Frontier* (1966). A valuable recent study of French institutions in the Mississippi Valley is C. E. O'Neill, *Church and State in French Colonial Louisiana* (1966).

* Available in a paperback edition.

4
The Second Discovery of America

England had joined the War of the Austrian Succession in order to prevent France from gobbling up the Austrian empire and thus destroying the European balance of power. The Peace of Aix-la-Chapelle, which ended the war in 1748, was recognized everywhere in Europe as more a truce than a treaty. It restored the balance but left French ambition unsatisfied and French power unbroken. Having been obliged to give up her conquests in the Austrian Netherlands in order to recover Louisburg, France set about to ensure that her position in America would be stronger in the next war. Not only did she refortify Louisburg, but in a more ominous move she sent her agents along the western slope of the Appalachians to build forts, to cement alliances with the Indians, to claim the region for the king of France.

CONTEST FOR EMPIRE

The Albany Congress. The English Board of Trade and the Privy Council, in order to bolster the loyalty of their own allies, called on the colonies from Virginia northward to send representatives to a meeting with the Iroquois at Albany. Virginia and New Jersey ignored the summons; but in June 1754 nineteen delegates from New Hampshire, Massachusetts, Connecticut, Rhode Island, Pennsylvania, and Maryland, together with the lieutenant-governor of New York and four gentlemen of his council, rode into Albany to confer with Iroquois chieftains who had slipped down the Mohawk Valley in response to a similar summons. As the Iroquois listened, the white men went through the formalities that Indians demanded in all negotiations: the grandiloquent declarations of esteem, the ceremonial presentation of gifts — scarlet coats, silver buttons, axes, scissors, guns. But the Iroquois had just been watching the French at work on fortifications in the interior, and they found English talk and English gifts less impressive than French action. They departed with the gifts but without offering the hoped-for assurance that they would help when the fighting began.

House of Burgesses, Williamsburg, Virginia.

While in Albany the twenty-three colonial delegates discussed a scheme that had been talked of before: the formation of a permanent intercolonial union to conduct Indian relations. Benjamin Franklin, as he rode north from Philadelphia, had thought out a plan, which he presented at the beginning of the congress. By the time the congress ended, the delegates had agreed to propose to the colonial assemblies a grand council with authority over matters of defense, westward expansion, and Indian relations. The council would handle purchases of land from friendly Indians and the planting of new settlements. It would raise armies and build forts and warships. And it would pay its own expenses by levying taxes. Its presiding officer, appointed by the king, would have veto power over all its actions.

When the plan reached the assemblies, their reaction was cool — some rejected it, others ignored it. Experience had shown them that the power to tax was father to every other governmental power. They often used it to get their own way in legislative conflicts with royal governors, and they did not propose to share it with any intercolonial council. Nor did they wish to be deprived of the chance to beat their neighbors in the race for Indian lands.

The assemblies' rejection of the Albany plan spared the English government the embarrassment of having to veto it. England wanted a unified direction of Indian affairs, not a permanent colonial union that might prove more difficult to deal with than the separate assemblies. Failure of the plan suggested that she need not worry about a union: the assemblies were apparently more uncooperative in dealing with one another than with England. No one stopped to think that Indian relations and Western policy had always been the most divisive issues in colonial politics. How to use the unsettled land in the West and how to deal with its Indian inhabitants were questions that divided coast from interior, farmer from fur-trader, merchant from landowner, colony from colony. On other questions the colonists were more united than either they or England knew.

English defeats. As the gentlemen at Albany were conducting their elaborate and unsuccessful courtship of the Iroquois, a younger gentleman was already firing on the French in the Ohio country. Virginia, instead of sending delegates to Albany, had sent a twenty-two-year-old colonel of the militia, George Washington, to help construct a fort at the forks of the Ohio (where the Monongahela and Allegheny rivers join). When Washington arrived in the Ohio country, the French were already in possession of the forks and hard at work on their own Fort Duquesne. He built a crude stockade, which he called Fort Necessity, at Great Meadows, fifty miles south, but was obliged to surrender it to a superior French force on July 3, 1754. Then the French let Washington march his men home to report that the land over the mountains belonged to France.

Washington's defeat was bad news to his fellow Virginians, for many reasons: as Englishmen they disliked Frenchmen; as Protestants they disliked Catholics; as Virginians they disliked anybody who invaded their empire. On the basis of their 1609 charter Virginians claimed all land to the west and northwest of their colony, and they were jealous of encroachments on their territory. Reluctance to admit that other colonies should have any voice in dealing with the great Virginian West may have been behind

The Ohio Country

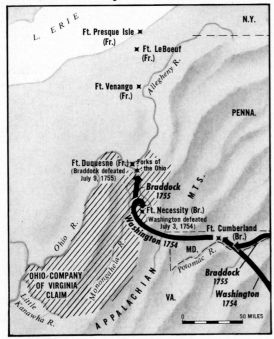

Virginia's absence from the Albany Congress.

One group of Virginians in particular regarded the Ohio country as private property. In 1747 a number of prominent planters, including George Washington's brothers, Lawrence and Augustine, had organized the Ohio Company to trade with the Western Indians and to speculate in Western lands. In 1749, with the approval of the Privy Council, the government of Virginia gave the company 200,000 acres between the Monongahela and the Great Kanawha rivers, and followed this by other grants of Western lands to other speculators. By 1751, when Robert Dinwiddie became governor, many Virginians were looking to the lands of the trans-Appalachian West to make their fortunes, and Dinwiddie himself became a member of the Ohio Company.

Dinwiddie had arranged Washington's expedition in order to hold the Ohio Valley for England, for Virginia, and for the Ohio Company. Upon Washington's return, it was apparent that the job was too big for either the Ohio Company or Virginia, and Dinwiddie signaled for help from England. Although officially England and France remained at peace, the home government recognized that the new war was beginning, and it dispatched General Edward Braddock with two regiments.

Braddock, arriving in Virginia early in 1755, expected to increase his force by a large number of colonists and Indians and then to march on Fort Duquesne and teach the French that the Ohio Valley belonged to England. But Virginia had no wilderness diplomats to furnish the general with Indian braves. South Carolina could have delivered them, but Virginians were wary of letting Carolinians into the affairs of the Ohio country. Some Pennsylvania fur-traders showed up with their own Indian friends, who executed an impressive war dance for the general but disappeared when it came time to march. In the end, Braddock set off with only 8 Indians and about 1,200 colonial militia to supplement his 1,500 regulars. He took them successfully over the mountains, along with enough cannon to pound Fort Duquesne to dust. But as they were approaching the fort on July 9 the French surprised them and turned the march into a disastrous rout. Braddock himself was fatally wounded, and 976 of his men were killed or wounded.

The War in the North, 1758-60

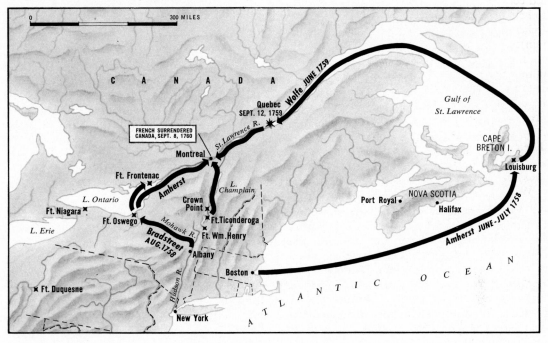

The Indians of the area concluded that the English were finished, and for the next two years it looked as though they were. The colonists, despite their numerical strength, seemed more interested in scoring against one another than in defeating the French; and the English government was occupied with its European involvements. England gave Governor William Shirley of Massachusetts the title of commander in chief but left him to collect most of his men and money from the colonists. Shirley was an able man, the most popular of the royal governors, but his abilities were no match for the jealous intrigues of the other governors, the recalcitrance of the colonial assemblies, or the firepower of the French. While the assemblies dallied over raising troops, Shirley's ill-supported expeditions in 1755 against Fort Niagara and Crown Point both failed, but he did manage to build Fort William Henry at the southern end of Lake George.

Fear that France might try to regain Nova Scotia (or Acadia) led the British government in 1755 to deport several thousand French inhabitants from the province. The Acadians had lived under English rule since 1713, but they had never lost their affection for France and conscientiously passed it on to their children. Governor Shirley, recognizing that in case of a French invasion they were likely to side with the enemy, had suggested their deportation as early as 1747. In 1755 the British dispersed them through the other English colonies instead of sending them off to Canada, where they would have augmented the French forces. The circumstances of the deportations and the treatment of the refugees by the English colonists were unnecessarily cruel. But Nova Scotia was made more secure.

In 1756, after gaining the support of Prussia, England finally resolved on a full-scale conflict and declared war. The declaration did nothing to break her losing streak, for immediately the French defeated the English fleet in the Mediterranean and captured Minorca. In America a new commander in chief, Lord Loudoun, was given military authority over the colonial governors in order to unite the colonies in their own defense. But the colonial assemblies, holding fast the purse strings, regarded Loudoun's authority with suspicion and complied only casually with his requests for men and supplies.

Nor did he achieve success with the troops, regular or colonial, that he did get. Shortly after he assumed command, the French captured Fort Oswego; in the following year they took the new Fort William Henry.

Victory under Pitt. In 1757 the English at last found a statesman to bring their real strength into play. William Pitt had never doubted England's need for him. "I am sure," he said, "that I can save the country, and that no one else can." Pitt's assurance rested on a view of the war and of England's imperial future unlike that of earlier leaders. Hitherto the war in America had been regarded as an incidental part of a traditional European war. The fighting would hopefully facilitate the continued expansion of colonial population, but English statesmen weighed American victories and defeats on a European scale, for their effect on the balance of power. When Pitt took office, English policy underwent a radical change. Pitt's object was not simply to reduce French power in the European balance or to facilitate colonial expansion. He proposed instead to make England master of all North America and perhaps of the rest of the world too.

In Pitt's vision of empire Europe loomed less large than America and India. Accordingly he paid Frederick of Prussia to wage the European war and threw England's weight into a campaign of violent aggression abroad. Territory was his object, and he dipped into the national treasury with a lavish hand to pay the men who would seize it for him. Rather than waste time bickering with colonial assemblies over the cost, he promised them reimbursement for all their expenses in raising troops. The national debt went soaring, but so did colonial enlistments.

To drive France from the New World, Pitt needed not only men and money but military talent. He got it, as statesmen frequently have, by jumping young men over the heads of their elders. His greatest find was a gangly, hollow-chested boy of thirty, with a receding chin and a vile temper. James Wolfe was a prig and a martinet, but Pitt sensed his talent. Pitt also promoted Lieutenant Colonel Jeffrey Amherst, who at the age of forty had been in the army twenty-two years without ever holding an independent command, to the rank of major general and put him in charge of a large-scale expedition against Louisburg. With Wolfe supervising the landing operations, Amherst took the fortress on July 26, 1758, giving England her first great victory of the war.

The capture of Louisburg destroyed French power at the mouth of the St. Lawrence and jeopardized communications between New and old France. A month later Lieutenant Colonel John Bradstreet captured Fort Frontenac, which guarded the other end of the St. Lawrence on the shores of Lake Ontario. Now the French in Canada were cut off from the Mississippi Valley and had to give up Fort Duquesne, which the British renamed Fort Pitt (later Pittsburgh).

At last Pitt was ready for his grand strategy, a pincers move on Quebec and Montreal, with troops approaching from the north by the St. Lawrence and from the south by the Hudson River, Lake George, and Lake Champlain. Amherst was to operate from the south, Wolfe from the north. Wolfe sailed up the St. Lawrence with nine thousand men and on September 12, 1759, made a surprise night attack up one of the steep gullies in the cliffs that protect Quebec. In the battle that then took place on the Plains of Abraham the British were victorious, but both Wolfe and the able French commander, the Marquis de Montcalm, received fatal wounds.

With the capture of Quebec, English victory in North America was only a matter of time. The French immediately laid siege to the city, but, when spring opened the ice-choked river and a British fleet appeared, the French withdrew. During the late summer, the expected troops from the south and a force from Quebec converged on Montreal for the final campaign. On September 8, 1760, the French gave up the city and all Canada with it. The war did not end until 1763, but in its final phases the action shifted from North America to the Caribbean, India, and the Philippines, as England plucked the overseas empires of her European rivals.

George III. Six weeks after the fall of Montreal, King George II died. Between them, George II and his father, George I, had ruled England since 1714, when the latter had been summoned to the throne from the quiet German principality of Hanover. Neither was distinguished in intelligence or character, but George II was the more energetic and enjoyed

The British taking Quebec, September 13, 1759.

leading the army, which knew him affectionately as the Little Captain. Though George II took an active part in selecting his ministers, the English government during his reign and his father's fell more and more into the hands of a powerful group of private families. They called themselves Whigs, in memory of the Revolution of 1688, from which they liked to date their ascendancy. Though they made an occasional bow to the principles of liberty, there was nothing revolutionary about them. Comfortable and wealthy, they entered politics to get wealthier and organized small groups or factions to juggle the spoils of office.

George II outlived his eldest son Frederick (who died in 1751 of a blow from a tennis ball), and George III, who ascended the throne in 1760, was the old king's grandson. At twenty-two George III had a mind, such as it was, of his own and no intention of letting the great Whig families run *his* government. Under the tutelage of a Scottish peer, the Earl of Bute, he had learned to dislike vice, to distrust talent, and to love patriotism, barley water, and the Earl of Bute. As a Scot, Bute had no seat in the House of Lords, and as a lord he was disqualified from the House of Commons. But the new king did not hesitate to give him at once a place in the inner "Cabinet Council," which was taking the place of the larger Privy Council in conducting the executive branch of government. Together, George and the Earl of Bute set about reforming the wicked ways of English politics.

The politicians shared neither the king's aversion to vice nor his fondness for Bute, and they were not interested in reform. Lacking any party organization, they could not present a united front against the king, but he and they both knew that he could not run the government without their help, and they made him pay dearly for it. For ten years George appointed and dismissed members of the council at a bewildering rate. Ministers responsible for colonial affairs came and went and came again as the king sparred with politicians over issues that usually had nothing to do with the colonies. Consequently, English colonial policy in this crucial decade was inconsistent and incoherent, not to say capricious.

George III, King of England, 1760–1820.

The Peace of Paris. With Pitt's resignation in 1761, the king's "dearest friend" became the leading figure in the council and the most unpopular man in England. Bute did not enjoy either role and retired from politics in 1763, but not until he had presided at Paris over the treaty that ended England's most successful war. The momentum of victory generated under Pitt carried the country through the final year of war without him. As he had foreseen, England ultimately had to add Spain to her list of enemies, but after crushing defeats at Manila and Havana Spain was ready to call a halt. When Bute made peace in 1763, he took the whole of North America east of the Mississippi (Florida from Spain, Canada from France), and also took back Minorca, carved up the French possessions in India, and extricated England from her commitments in Germany. But Bute was schooled in the traditional diplomacy of balancing European powers against one another, and he was unmoved by Pitt's imperial ambitions. He gave Cuba and the Philippines back to Spain and let France give Louisiana to Spain. He returned Guadeloupe and Martinique to France and allowed her to keep the two tiny islands of St. Pierre and Miquelon as fishing bases.

When George took the throne, Pitt was running the war and the government. Trouble broke out almost immediately. Tormented by gout, hobbling about on crutches, Pitt snapped at everyone who disagreed with him and did not gladly suffer the many fools he had to deal with. The politicians liked him as little as they liked Bute. With the fall of Canada and the subsequent British successes in the rest of the world, they were ready to make peace with France and rid themselves of the tyranny of this ailing genius.

Pitt was ready for peace too, provided he could strip France of all her overseas possessions. France, however, though defeated abroad, was still a formidable power in Europe and was courting the support of Spain. Pitt, hearing of the negotiations, stopped talking peace and demanded instead that England declare war at once against Spain — Pitt always preferred to attack. No one had dared oppose Pitt while England was underdog in the war with France. But he had made England strong enough to do without him, and now his colleagues would not agree to take on a new enemy. When he could not have his way, Pitt resigned the ministry.

North America in 1763

Pitt was outraged by Bute's liberality toward France and Spain, and some of the colonists shared his view. But most Englishmen, both in England itself and in the colonies, welcomed the treaty even while they denounced its maker and glorified Pitt. For the colonists it meant the end of a threat that had been hanging over them for as long as anyone could remember. Now, as their children grew up and went looking for new homes, they could trek over the mountains into the lush Ohio Valley, into bluegrass lands they would name Kentucky and Tennessee, into the prairies of the Illinois country. The Indians, without the French to organize and direct them, could offer no serious obstacle to the settlement of the interior by Englishmen.

A NEW EMPIRE AND NEW IDEAS

In England men looked with pride at their new territories. America was still the spearhead of European growth, and the conquest of New France conjured up the vision of a Mississippi Valley filled with men who spoke English and talked fondly of a small island across the ocean as "home." Englishmen had been the first to think of North America as a place to live. Now their perception was rewarded with an empire that promised to cover the continent.

The question of imperial authority. With the coming of peace a few men sensed that the government of the empire again needed overhauling, for it was clearly inadequate for a population of 2 million about to advance into the immense interior of North America. Several colonial governors, who had seen America at first hand, wrote urgently on the subject. From Massachusetts, for example, Francis Bernard warned his superiors in England that this was "the proper and critical time to reform the American governments upon a general, constitutional, firm, and durable plan; and if it is not done now, it will probably every day grow more difficult, till at last it becomes impracticable."

Bernard's sense of urgency was justified. Most of the colonies had been founded before the supremacy of Parliament in England had been firmly established. Even after the question of supremacy was settled Parliament concerned itself little with them. But now that America had grown important to England, Parliament would be giving it more attention. That attention (as Bernard foresaw) might not be welcomed by the colonies; for, since the time of their founding, they had regularly dealt with the mother country through the king, his councils, his governors. Before Parliament began making laws for them or levying taxes on them it needed to establish its own authority over them by reorganizing their governments.

Bernard thought that all the colonial governments should be given identical constitutions by act of Parliament, with governors appointed by the king. He recognized that the colonists, like other Englishmen, expected a share in their government, and he suggested that they be represented in Parliament. He did not think that they had any right to such representation, but he felt that it would be good politics to give them a voice in the decisions that Parliament would doubtless be making about them.

Francis Bernard was an ambitious man, and his superiors probably smiled at his advice. They realized that the empire needed repair, but Bernard's far-reaching plans seemed grandiloquent and prompted as much by a desire for promotion as by the actual needs of the situation. At the moment more immediate and pressing problems demanded their attention. For the next thirteen years a succession of short-sighted politicians and an industriously dull king kept their minds on a succession of immediate and pressing problems. By so doing, they inadvertently and unintentionally taught the colonists that Americans had more in common with one another than with Englishmen.

Trouble in the West. After the war England decided to station several thousand troops permanently in America. So much blood and money had been spent winning the continent that it seemed only proper to guard it, and the presence of troops would also help to restrain any possible insubordination on the part of the colonists and discourage France from trying to regain her losses. Almost at once the troops were called into action, not against France but against her former allies, the Indians, for whom the coming of peace presaged another westward surge of English colonists. The Indians of all tribes had been restive ever since the fall of New France, and the contemptuous and shortsighted policies of General Amherst toward them gave them a foretaste of what English rule of the continent would mean. When the Ottawas, led by their chieftain Pontiac, attacked Detroit in the spring of 1763, other tribes, following his lead, fell upon the English forts and settlements from the Great Lakes to the back country of Pennsylvania, Maryland, and Virginia. Since the British troops were not well located to protect the frontiers, the outlying settlers suffered heavily before the attacks could be stopped.

Pontiac's Rebellion had the divisive effect that Western problems usually produced among Americans. Easterners were reluctant to take it seriously. Westerners blamed the Easterners for the loss of farms and the death of wives, husbands, children, and friends. In western Pennsylvania a group of outraged pioneers known as the Paxton boys fell upon a village of peaceful Indians, massacred them, and marched on Philadelphia to get some action out of the government. They were halted by the Philadelphians, who evidently feared other Pennsylvanians more than Indians.

English statesmen could easily conclude that the Americans were a hopelessly uncooperative and cowardly lot, unwilling to help one another and unable to protect themselves against savages. During the preceding French and Indian War British officers had sent back disparaging reports of colonial troops. General Wolfe himself had characterized his four companies of American rangers at Quebec as "the worst soldiers in the Universe." Now, once again, it seemed, the colonists had demonstrated their weakness — and England proceeded to demonstrate hers.

When Bute took the Mississippi Valley from France and returned the islands of Guadeloupe and Martinique, the decision was widely justified on the grounds that the valley was potentially more valuable than the West Indies. But if its potential was to be realized, the area would have to be settled and exploited by Englishmen, not kept as a giant game preserve. British politicians recognized this fact, but most of them saw no need to hurry settlers into the great emptiness beyond the mountains, where they would be less accessible to British control. Moreover, westward expansion would aggravate the most pressing colonial problem

— the Indian resistance. While their troops crushed Pontiac's warriors, the politicians drafted a solution to the problem of Indian warfare: keep the colonists out of Indian territory. They had the king issue a proclamation forbidding settlement beyond the crest of the Appalachian Mountains and advising settlers in search of homes to go to Nova Scotia or Florida, for which England now provided colonial governments.

The proclamation had little effect on American westward expansion, for the colonists took little notice of it. But it showed that the British were incapable of grasping the desperate speed of American growth. They thought they could take their time about developing the West, that they could deflect the expanding population by issuing a proclamation.

George Grenville's search for revenue. While the king was erecting his paper fence along the crest of the Appalachians, one of his ministers was occupied with a matter closer to home, the enormous national debt that England had piled up in acquiring Canada and the Mississippi Valley. George Grenville, First Lord of the Treasury, knew his pounds, shillings, and pence. With the end of the French and Indian War and the retirement of Bute, the king turned to him as the man best qualified to put England's finances in order. Grenville was not impressed with a continent full of naked savages, impecunious Frenchmen, and wild beaver; he was impressed with a national debt that had doubled since 1754; and he was still more impressed with the cost of keeping troops under arms to protect England's new possessions. He did not question the need for the troops. That was beyond his concern. But he had to find the money to pay them, as well as the money to pay the interest on the national debt.

Soon after he took office in April 1763 Grenville came upon a remarkable fact: the American customs service was costing the government nearly £8,000 a year in salaries but was collecting less than £2,000 in duties. Everyone knew that the colonists were importing large quantities of molasses from the French West Indies, on which the Molasses Act of 1733 required them to pay a duty of sixpence a gallon. Obviously they were evading the duty. In October 1763 Grenville issued a sharp directive for its collection and ordered the British navy to patrol American waters for smugglers.

Grenville had another grievance against the colonists: they alleviated their perpetual currency shortage (resulting from their unfavorable balance of trade with the mother country) by issuing paper money. Although the money served an essential purpose and showed little depreciation in most colonies, its value was well below that of silver, and English creditors feared that the colonists might attempt to pay their English debts with it. As a result of complaints by creditors, the New England colonies had been forbidden in 1751 to make their paper money legal tender. By the Currency Act of April 1764, Grenville extended the prohibition to all the colonies.

In the same month Grenville directed through Parliament an act (later known as the Sugar Act) revising American customs duties and regulations. With good reason he reduced the duty on foreign molasses from sixpence a gallon to threepence. The purpose of the original levy had been to induce the colonists to buy their molasses from the British West Indies, where they could get it duty free (though higher priced). But colonial rum-distillers needed far more molasses than the British sugar-planters could supply. More was obtainable from the French islands; but the distillers could not afford to pay the sixpence duty and still sell their rum at a competitive price. So the colonial importers simply bribed the customs officials (from a halfpenny to a penny and a half per gallon) not to collect the duty. Grenville accepted the fact that the sixpence duty was too high, but he believed that the merchants would not be ruined by paying a threepence duty instead of a bribe.

The Sugar Act also imposed new duties on colonial imports of sugar, indigo, coffee, pimento, wine, and textiles. To discourage smuggling, it required that elaborate official papers be filed for every ship entering or leaving a colonial port. Finally, it provided that violators of the customs regulations could be tried in admiralty courts, which operated under royally appointed judges acting without juries (in the common-law courts juries made up of local residents were inclined to sympathize with offenders). The colonists had been subject to such an enactment since 1696, but ambiguities in it had often enabled smugglers to avoid admiralty jurisdiction.

The stated purpose of the Sugar Act was to help defray the expenses England would incur in protecting her new American possessions. Grenville did not expect to raise the whole amount from the colonists, but he did expect more than the new duties were likely to yield; and in introducing the bill for the Sugar Act to Parliament he announced that he might soon levy a stamp tax on the colonies.

There was nothing novel in the idea of stamp taxes. Englishmen at home had been paying them ever since the reign of King William, and there had already been suggestions that Parliament impose such taxes on the colonies. Massachusetts had even tried a stamp tax of her own in 1755. By February 1765 Grenville had completed his study of taxable items being used in the colonies and was ready to introduce his Stamp Act to Parliament. It called for taxes on every type of legal document and on newspapers, almanacs, playing cards, and dice (all of which had to bear a stamp, signifying that the tax was paid). As in the case of the Sugar Act, violators would be prosecuted in admiralty courts. A few members of Parliament raised objections to taxing the colonists. Colonel Isaac Barré, who had served under Wolfe in North America, warned that the Americans would resist. But the act passed both houses and was signed by the king on March 22, 1765, to take effect November 1.

In May 1765 Grenville put through a third measure, the Quartering Act, to help support English troops in America. This act provided that any colony in which troops were stationed must furnish them with living quarters and with fire, candles, vinegar, salt, bedding, and beer, cider, or rum.

Colonial suspicions. The colonists were stunned by Grenville's actions. In 1763 colonial merchants felt sure that his order calling for the strict collection of molasses duties would ruin the rum trade and the whole New England economy with it. Nor did they welcome the reduction in duties provided by the Sugar Act, for they believed that even a threepence duty would drive their rum out of the market. Moreover, the act established customs procedures so strict and complicated that all kinds of trade would be hampered. The currency restriction made matters still worse. With silver in short supply and with paper money no longer legal tender, merchants had no medium of exchange and were sometimes reduced to barter. When economic depression followed the acts, Americans blamed Grenville.

But the most shocking aspect of Grenville's measures was that they seemed to embody a new policy — a deliberate aim to disinherit the colonists by denying them the rights of Englishmen. The Americans believed that it was their right as Englishmen not to be taxed except by their own elected representatives; but Parliament had taxed them directly in the Stamp Act, indirectly in the Sugar Act and the Quartering Act. They believed that it was their right as Englishmen to be tried by juries of their peers; but Parliament had made infringement of the Sugar and Stamp acts punishable in admiralty courts. These courts were objectionable not only because they violated the right to trial by jury but because they put the burden of proof on the defendant, assuming that he was guilty until he proved himself innocent. Furthermore, in England admiralty courts tried only cases arising on the high seas. By giving the courts a wider jurisdiction in the colonies, the Sugar and Stamp acts suggested that England thought Americans not entitled to rights long recognized in the mother country.

Further evidence of some sinister design seemed apparent in the announced purpose of the acts: to support troops in America. Why, the colonists wondered, did England want to keep armed soldiers in their midst? The troops had helped, to be sure, in crushing Pontiac's Rebellion, which the rash actions of their commander, General Amherst, had actually helped to bring on. But protection against Indians was patently not the purpose of keeping troops in America. Before 1754, while the French were sending their Indian allies to attack the colonists from Maine to Carolina, England had maintained scarcely any military garrison in America. Now, with the danger gone, with the French crushed and the Spaniards pushed beyond the Mississippi, she insisted on keeping several thousand men on hand. Why? Perhaps, it was whispered, England intended to use the army not to protect but to suppress the colonists. There is evidence in British documents that such an intention did in fact exist, but the evidence was not known to the colonists. Grenville's acts, however, were sufficient in themselves to prompt suspicions.

Colonial convictions. The British statesmen who started Americans talking of standing armies, taxation without representation, and trials without juries would have done well to consider the origin and history of the colonies. New England and many other parts of America had been founded by Puritans who carried to America the ideas that shortly led to Oliver Cromwell's commonwealth in England. After that commonwealth ended with the restoration of the monarchy in 1660, many more Dissenters joined the exodus to America, and their descendants could talk of Hampden and Pym and other heroes of the struggle against Charles I with a familiarity that might have struck some Englishmen as quaint. Though loyal to the House of Hanover, the colonists admired much in the writings of James Harrington, the advocate of republican government, of Algernon Sidney, and of John Locke.

Locke no Englishman found quaint. In affirming the natural right of a people to alter their government (see p. 69), he had provided his countrymen with an intellectual justification for their long contest to gain ascendancy over their kings. All Englishmen believed that the course of their history had been a struggle to achieve a government that would protect their lives, liberty, and property. They believed that they had at last achieved such a government with the overthrow of James II in 1688 and the establishment of the House of Hanover in 1714. The colonists shared this belief, and they were proud to be members of the nation whose government stood foremost in the world in protecting the natural rights of its subjects.

Like other Englishmen the colonists regarded the representative nature of English government as the most important guarantee of continued protection. They rejoiced in Parliament's supremacy in England and in the supremacy of their own assemblies in America. In each the elected representatives of the people guarded the rights of Englishmen, and the most precious right they guarded was the right of property, without which neither life nor liberty could be secure. Since the power to tax was a power to take away property, no man could call himself free if he was taxed without his own consent, given either personally or by his representative. The right to be taxed in this way, and in no other, was a hard-won principle of the British constitution. In England only the representative branch of Parliament, the House of Commons, could initiate tax bills; and in the colonies the representative assemblies claimed the same exclusive privilege. It therefore seemed monstrous to Americans that, in the Sugar Act and the Stamp Act, Parliament, a body in which they had no representative, had presumed to tax them. If Parliament could levy these taxes it could levy others. Once the precedent was set, the colonists would be as badly off as England had been before the rise of Parliament. They would, ironically, be oppressed by the very body that had rescued England from the same kind of tyranny.

As the colonists measured acts of Parliament against their own ideas of right, they faced the question that Governor Bernard had wished to settle earlier, the question of Parliament's authority in America. Their decision was different from Bernard's. Parliament, they believed, had some right to legislate for them; but it had no right to tax them. It was the central legislative body for matters of common concern to the entire empire, and as such it could regulate their commerce, even by imposing duties to discourage certain kinds of trade that it believed prejudicial to the good of the empire as a whole. But it had no right to levy duties to raise money; such duties were taxes, and Parliament had no right to tax the colonies in any manner. Its members could not grant the property of people whom they did not represent.

The American colonists in 1764 and 1765 were remarkably unanimous in adopting this distinction between taxation and legislation. They began to affirm it in pamphlets and newspaper articles as soon as the Sugar Act was passed. New York and Virginia expressed it officially in petitions to Parliament. By the time the Stamp Act was passed, people in every colony were discussing the limits of Parliament's authority, and during the summer and fall of 1765 colonial assemblies passed resolutions setting forth those limits.

The Stamp Act crisis. The Stamp Act was to go into effect on November 1. In the May session of the Virginia assembly, Patrick Henry, a young lawyer, presented a series of resolutions declaring that only the House of Burgesses had the right to tax Virginians. The Burgesses adopted the resolutions but rejected some additional ones calling for outright resistance if England should try to collect the stamp tax. The other colonial assemblies rapidly followed Virginia's example, modeling their own resolutions on hers. Although the newspapers had printed Henry's rejected resolutions as though they had actually been passed, thus creating the impression that Virginia had acted more radically than was the case, nevertheless most of the other assemblies stopped where Virginia did, with a simple denial of Parliament's right to tax the colonies.

In addition to the resolutions of their individual assemblies, the colonies prepared a joint statement of their position. In June, before the colonial consensus had become apparent, Massachusetts proposed that all the colonies send delegates to a general meeting for the purpose of concerting their opposition to parliamentary taxes. Nine assemblies complied: in October 1765 the Stamp Act Congress met at New York. After avowing "all due subordination" to Parliament, the delegates resolved that colonial subordination did not include acceptance of parliamentary taxation or of admiralty courts operating beyond their traditional limits. They also sent petitions to king and Parliament demanding repeal of the Sugar and Stamp acts.

In objecting to taxation by Parliament, the colonists believed that they had common sense, natural law, and the British constitution all on their side. It was common sense that they already contributed to the wealth of the mother country by submitting to the Navigation Acts. If a more direct contribution was required, it ought to be made by the colonists' own representatives, who alone could know, as the Virginia resolves said, "what Taxes the People are able to bear, or the easiest Method of raising them, and must themselves be affected by every Tax laid on the People." If the members of Parliament could establish their authority to tax the colonies, they would have an all but irresistible motive to shift their own burdens and those of their constituents to America. Every penny collected in the colonies would be a penny less to take from English pockets. It was common sense that such a situation spelled tyranny.

It was also a violation of the British constitution and of the laws of nature by which every free people should be governed. The people's right to be taxed only by their own representatives was "the grand Principle of every free State . . . the natural Right of Mankind," proclaimed the members of the New York assembly. The Massachusetts assembly, in the same vein, announced that "there are certain essential Rights of the British Constitution of Government, which are founded in the Law of God and Nature, and are the common Rights of Mankind." Among those rights was "That no man can justly take the Property of another without his Consent."

Besides informing Parliament and posterity of what was right, the colonists took practical steps to see that right prevailed. Merchants in New York, Philadelphia, and Boston agreed to stop importing British goods, hoping by economic pressure to enlist British merchants and manufacturers against the Stamp Act. Other Americans, too impatient to wait for repeal, were determined to prevent the Stamp Act from taking effect. On the night of August 14, a Boston mob stormed the house of Andrew Oliver, the local stamp-distributor. They broke the doors and windows and roamed through the house calling for the owner's head. Oliver resigned his office the next day. Stamp-distributors in other colonies hastened to follow Oliver's example. Mobs helped those who hesitated to make up their minds. On November 1, when the act was scheduled to go into effect, there was no one to distribute the stamps.

In every colony the violence that forced the resignation of the distributors had been carefully engineered by a group of conspirators. These men now organized under the name of Sons of Liberty and prepared to resist "to the last extremity" any efforts to enforce the Stamp Act. They had learned from John Locke that a people could alter or overthrow a government that exceeded its authority; and they repeated Locke's precepts to their countrymen in resolves, like those adopted at New London on December 10, 1765, declaring that "the People have a Right to reassume the exercise of that Authority which by Nature they had, before they delegated it to Individuals."

The total overthrow of government did not prove necessary. For a few weeks after November 1, people in most colonies simply refrained from doing any business that required stamps. Then newspapers began to appear without them. By threatening mob action, the Sons of Liberty soon persuaded judges to try cases and customs officers to clear ships with unstamped bonds and clearance papers. In less than three months the Stamp Act had been effectively nullified.

English response to colonial defiance was not what it might have been had Grenville remained in power. George III, for reasons that had nothing to do with the colonies, dismissed Grenville in July 1765 and in his place named the Marquis of Rockingham as first minister. Rockingham and the men he brought into the administration with him had opposed the Stamp Act in the first place and wanted nothing more than to escape the embarrassment of trying to enforce it. English merchants, stung by the American boycott, reinforced Rockingham's determination to wipe the act off the books, and he enthusiastically favored a repeal bill in Parliament.

But the spate of resolutions and riots in the colonies made repeal difficult. Most members of Parliament were reluctant to back down, especially after William Pitt, with his usual tactlessness, publicly rejoiced at American resistance and endorsed the colonists' definition of the limits of Parliament's authority. Taxation, he said, was "no part of the governing or legislative power." Other members were baffled by the distinction between taxation and legislation. Grenville declared it absurd. But in March 1766 Parliament repealed the act after first passing a Declaratory Act, which deliberately skirted the distinction and simply affirmed the authority of Parliament to "make laws and statutes of sufficient force and validity to bind the colonies and people of America, . . . in all cases whatsoever." Precisely what that meant Americans were to find out later. For the moment they rejoiced in the end of the contest that had led them to the brink of war with the mother country. Repeal of the Stamp Act seemed to signal a return to the Old Colonial System under which England and her colonies had alike enjoyed freedom, prosperity, and harmony. Now they might take up once again the position of leadership in world trade that they had won together.

Colonial discoveries. Nevertheless, as the colonists joined their English friends in celebrating repeal, they could reflect on their discoveries of the preceding two years. They had already found out more than England could have wished. A decade earlier, when the Albany Congress proposed a union against a danger in the west, they had unanimously declined. This time, when the danger came from the east, they had spontaneously joined to boycott British goods, to prevent the distribution of stamps, to define the limits of Parliament's authority. Indian tomahawks and French guns had revealed nothing but discord; the threat of tyranny had revealed fundamental agreement. The definition of Parliament's authority that the Stamp Act Congress had formulated was no compromise measure reluctantly agreed to under the pressure of circumstance. The congress merely reiterated principles already familiar in newspapers and pamphlets, principles that the colonial assemblies themselves had embodied in their resolutions. It nevertheless surprised the Americans to find themselves agreeing so readily. "The Colonies until now were ever at variance and foolishly jealous of each other," Joseph Warren of Massachusetts wrote to a friend, "they are now . . . united . . . nor will they soon forget the weight which this close union gives them."

In defending their rights the colonists also discovered that the ideas which united them and which they thought inherent in the British constitution were not shared by most Englishmen. Men in England had denied not only the colonists' distinction between taxation and legislation but also their conception of representation. At the outset of the tax controversy Grenville and his backers, admitting that Englishmen had a right to representation in the body that governed them, had claimed that the colonists *were* represented — not actually but virtually. A member of Parliament, Grenville maintained, represented not only the men who elected him, but the whole empire. The concept of virtual representation was widely accepted in England, but it was nonsense to Americans, who thought that a representative should be directly responsible to his constituents. By Grenville's reasoning, they said, Parliament could equally well claim an authority to tax the whole world.

Although a few suggestions had been made, like Governor Bernard's, that England should allow the colonies to send representatives to Parliament, the colonists did not take to the idea. It would be impractical, they thought, because of the great distance. Colonial representatives in London would lose contact with their constituents; it would cost too much to send them back and forth and to pay for their keep; they would be corrupted by the metropolis. But most important, there would be too few of them to have any real effect on the decisions of empire, yet their presence could be used to justify Parliamentary taxation of America.

These objections were serious, but not insuperable had either England or the colonies wanted to resolve them. But the plain fact was that the colonists did not want representation in Parliament. Perhaps they were unconsciously influenced by a new attitude that had been taking shape in the colonial mind but that few men yet recognized. England, by treating the colonists differently from Englishmen at home, was teaching them what she should have done her best to conceal: that they actually *were* different, and perhaps even wanted to be.

Though England had no way of knowing it, the men in whom this attitude first took hold included several of extraordinary ability. In Massachusetts three emerged as leaders of the opposition to Parliamentary taxation: James Otis, Samuel Adams, and John Adams. Otis, a lawyer, was volatile, unpredictable, and unbalanced, but powerful in argument and very influential among the people of Boston. Samuel Adams, a failure at everything else he tried, was a brilliant politician, gifted in organizing popular support for any measure. In the years to come, as Otis became more erratic and finally went insane, Adams would become the virtual dictator of Boston, against whom royal governors would write home in helpless expostulation. John Adams, whose gifts were more those of a statesman than of a politician, was as ardent as his cousin Samuel in hostility to Parliament. He despised everyone who sought political office by royal appointment, and he searched out opportunities to advance the interests of America and Americans.

In Virginia the Stamp Act had alerted another trio of men whose names would likewise become unpleasantly familiar to Englishmen. Patrick Henry, as eloquent and almost as erratic as James Otis, gained instant fame by sponsoring Virginia's resolutions against the Stamp Act. George Washington, known to at least a few outside Virginia for his service in the late war, was more given to actions than to resolutions. He was at the House of Burgesses and may have voted for Henry's resolutions, but his thoughts went more toward home manufactures and new crops as a means of shaking off America's economic dependence on Great Britain. Thomas Jefferson, a twenty-two-year-old law student, was too young for politics in 1765. But he stood at the door of the House of Burgesses and listened to Henry's "torrents of sublime eloquence." Later Jefferson would show a certain eloquence himself.

Townshend's folly. The repeal of the Stamp Act set the bells ringing in England and America. But the Marquis of Rockingham, who had engineered the happy event, found himself unable to please either king or Parliament. In July 1766 he went the way of Grenville, and George III gave the government once again to William Pitt, now Earl of Chatham. Unfortunately, bad health made Pitt a mere figurehead, and the new government fell under the influence of the headstrong and irresponsible Chancellor of the Exchequer, Charles Townshend.

In taking up the search for revenue, Townshend, like Grenville, looked to the colonies. Fastening on their reviving trade as the likeliest source of new income, he persuaded Parliament in 1767 to pass an ill-considered act levying duties on colonial imports of lead, paint, paper, glass, and tea. Since these items could be legally imported only from England, the new taxes would actually discourage purchases from the mother country and encourage the manufacture of taxable goods in the colonies, thus violating every principle that British economic policy had hitherto supported. The taxes also violated the colonists' expressed views on the limits of Parliament's authority.

The colonial assemblies were at this time registering their unabated disapproval of Parliamentary taxes by resisting Grenville's Quartering Act, which they regarded as a form of taxation. To demonstrate their own superior authority, they voted to supply only part of the provisions that the act specified. Townshend nevertheless believed that the colonists were becoming more amenable to taxation, especially to taxes on trade, because they were paying the duty on molasses. In 1766 the duty had been reduced to a penny a gallon, which approximated the cost of a bribe; it had also been extended to include molasses of British production. This new duty was clearly a tax and not a regulation of trade. Encouraged by the colonists' seeming compliance, Townshend decided that, if he but acted boldly, he could now settle the question of Parliament's authority in America for good and all.

To cow the assemblies into obeying the Quartering Act, he made an example of New York, one of the principal offenders: in 1767, at his bidding, Parliament declared all acts of the New York assembly to be void until the colony furnished full supplies for the troops quartered there. To ensure collection of his new taxes on trade and of older regulatory duties as well, Townshend directed a reorganization of the American customs service. Hitherto customs officers throughout the empire had been under the administration of a board of commissioners located in England. From now on a special board of commissioners for America would reside in Boston, the center alike of colonial smuggling and of open resistance to taxation.

Americans did greet the Townshend Acts less violently than they had the Stamp Act, but they soon made it clear that they were just as determined as ever to rid themselves of Parliamentary taxation. The New York assembly was hailed everywhere for its resistance to the Quartering Act. Once again newspapers and pamphlets cited the British constitution and the laws of nature. Once again the representative assemblies, stiffened by a circular letter from Massachusetts, denied the authority of Parliament to tax the colonies. Once again merchants joined in nonimportation agreements, and violators received visits from the Sons of Liberty.

The new customs commissioners were as unpopular as the new duties. They were regarded as superfluous bureaucrats sent by a corrupt ministry to fatten on the toil of Americans. And, it was feared, they were only the first of many to come; soon the colonist would have to support as many functionless officeholders as the taxpayer in England did.

The commissioners lost no time in exceeding everyone's worst expectations. The procedures prescribed by the Sugar Act were immensely complicated, and it was easy for a merchant to make an unintentional mistake in carrying them out. By insisting on technicalities, an unscrupulous commissioner could usually find a pretext for seizing a ship and its cargo of goods. Rather than take the risk, most mer-

Representative Government: An American View

To infer, my lord, that the *British* members [of Parliament] actually represent the colonies, who are not permitted to do the least act towards their appointment, because *Britain* is unequally represented, although every man in the kingdom, who hath certain legal qualifications can vote for some one to represent him, is such a piece of sophistry that I had half a mind to pass by the cobweb without blowing it to pieces. Is there no difference between a country's having a privilege to choose 558 members to represent them in parliament, though in unequal proportions to the several districts, which cannot be avoided, and not having liberty to choose any? To turn the tables, — if the *Americans* only had leave to send members to parliament, could such sophistry ever persuade the people of *Britain* that they were represented and had a share in the national councils?... Suppose none of the 558 members were chosen by the people, but enjoyed the right of sitting in parliament by hereditary descent; could the common people be said to share in the national councils? How trifling then is the supposition, that we in *America* virtually have such share in the national councils, by those members whom we never chose? If we are not their constituents, they are not our representatives.... It is really a piece of mockery to tell us that a country, detached from *Britain*, by an ocean of immense breadth, and which is so extensive and populous, should be represented by the *British* members, or that we can have any interest in the house of commons.

From the Providence *Gazette*, May 11, 1765.

chants were willing to grease the commissioners' palms. Anyone who refused to play the game was likely to have his ship condemned in an admiralty court: unless he could prove that he had fulfilled every provision of the law, the court would order his ship and cargo sold. One-third of the proceeds went to the English Treasury, one-third to the governor of the colony, and one-third to the customs officers prosecuting the case.

The officers had nothing to lose — except perhaps their lives. Even that danger was reduced when the commissioners persuaded the authorities in England to provide special protection against the hazards of their occupation. In September 1768 two companies of troops were sent to Boston.

Samuel Adams: A brilliant politician.

England's readiness to send the troops indicated how far her relations with the colonies had deteriorated and what caliber of men had taken over the empire. In 1768 Lord Hillsborough had just been made Secretary of State for the Colonies, a post created to handle the increasingly complex colonial business. His decision to send the troops to Boston may have sprung from ignorance of the situation there, but it was one of a series of blunders that prompted Benjamin Franklin to characterize his conduct in office as "perverse and senseless."

The English troops landed in Boston without trouble. Samuel Adams had called for resistance. But the Massachusetts assembly was under suspension for refusing to rescind its circular letter against the Townshend Acts, and the extralegal convention that Adams organized in

its place was unwilling to act on his radical demand.

The presence of the soldiers in Boston nevertheless spelled tyranny to Americans everywhere and showed again that England regarded Americans as not quite Englishmen. The soldiers themselves contributed to the impression by their arrogance. Even during the French and Indian War, when British and colonial troops were fighting side by side, the regulars had never disguised their contempt for the Americans. Now the feeling was returned with interest.

For a year and a half the soldiers lived in Boston, suffering icy stares, open taunts, and all the subtle harassments the citizens could devise. Hostility was steadily aggravated by the inflammatory speeches and publications of the indefatigable Samuel Adams on the one side and by the rapacity of the customs commissioners on the other. But there was no real violence until March 5, 1770. On that day a crowd looking for trouble found it in front of the Boston customhouse. They jeered the ten soldiers who stood guard before it, pelted them with oyster shells, snowballs, and sticks of wood, dared them to fire. The soldiers did fire, and so, it was later charged, did some of the customs men from the windows of the building. Eleven of the unarmed rioters were hit, five of them fatally. The massacre, as the Bostonians called it, roused such hostility to the troops that Lieutenant-Governor Thomas Hutchinson ordered them to Castle Island in the harbor. There they sat for the next four years.

Meanwhile a movement to repeal Charles Townshend's taxes was growing in England. Townshend died shortly after his acts were passed, and almost at once Englishmen began to realize that the Townshend duties were a mistake. Even without the pressure of colonial nonimportation agreements, English merchants would have protested against taxes that encouraged colonial manufacturing. Many members of the king's council favored outright repeal of the duties, but once again the government was reluctant to back down in the face of colonial defiance. The new Chancellor of the Exchequer, Lord North, who took office January 31, 1770, suggested that all the duties that encouraged colonial manufactures be repealed and that only the duty on tea, which could not be grown in America, be retained. Since Americans were inordinately fond of tea, they were importing substantial quantities of it in spite of the duty. By keeping the duty in force, England would preserve an annual revenue of ten or twelve thousand pounds and would also sustain her authority.

Parliament adopted North's solution, and the king was pleased. North was the kind of politician George had been looking for — a plodding, dogged, industrious man, neither a fool nor a genius, much like the king himself. For the next twelve years he remained at the head of the government.

TOWARD INDEPENDENCE

North's repeal of all the Townshend duties except the one on tea was well calculated. In England it mollified both the merchants and the Parliamentary critics of the administration. In America it brought a wave of good feeling for the mother country, comparable to that following repeal of the Stamp Act. The Sons of Liberty met defeat when they demanded perseverance in the boycott of British goods until the tax on tea should be repealed. Merchants began importing, and trade boomed. Royal governors reported that only a factious few continued to object to British policies.

Discord and concord. As good will toward the mother country rose, the recent harmony among the colonists themselves gave way to new quarrels, from which England concluded, too hastily, that American unity was a fiction. Anglicans in the Northern colonies petitioned for the appointment of an American bishop; most Anglicans in the Southern colonies opposed such an appointment; Congregationalists and Presbyterians everywhere were horrified at the prospect but were unable to cement an effective union amongst themselves to work against it.

The West was also causing trouble again. In both North and South Carolina settlers in the back country complained that the assembly was dominated by Easterners, that its taxes were too high, that its officials were corrupt, that it had failed to extend county organization in the West. In 1771 a large force of Westerners calling themselves Regulators rose against the tax collectors of North Carolina. An army of Easterners defeated them easily at the Battle of Alamance, but the clash left the back-country men with an enduring hatred of the East.

In other colonies disputes arose over the control of western lands. Connecticut claimed land on the Susquehanna River in northeastern Pennsylvania and even organized a county there. In England Connecticut agents pressed for official recognition of their claim and Pennsylvania agents for its rejection. Meanwhile Pennsylvanians and Virginians were squabbling over lands in the Ohio Valley.

England still adhered to the land policy outlined in the Proclamation of 1763 — namely, that a boundary line should be maintained between settlers and Indians. But now, instead of following the crest of the Appalachians, the line was set farther west by treaties with various Indian tribes (with the Iroquois at Fort Stanwix in 1768, with the Cherokee at Hard Labor in 1768 and at Lochaber in 1770). Americans, however, were still competing vigorously for land beyond the line. A group of speculators from the Middle colonies kept agents in England lobbying for the creation of a colony, to be known as Vandalia, south of the Ohio River. The site of the proposed colony was in territory claimed by Virginia, and the speculators of the Ohio Company angrily protested the scheme. The company was also quarreling with other Virginia speculators. Hillsborough turned a deaf ear on all of them and refused to authorize the new colony.

To British politicians all these disagreements seemed more serious than they were, and colonial good will toward England seemed stronger than it was. The good will, though real, rested on the hope that Parliament was retreating from its new policies. American hostility to those policies was by no means extinguished, nor was it likely to be, so long as customs commissioners sat in Boston, the British navy patrolled American waters, and admiralty courts condemned American vessels without jury trial. Men like Samuel Adams were able to keep the colonists talking about colonial rights and Parliamentary tyranny by seeing to it that every new affront committed by the British was given wide publicity in the

The West: Indian Treaties and Speculative Claims

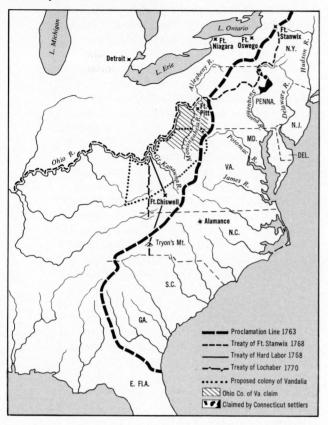

Proclamation Line 1763
Treaty of Ft. Stanwix 1768
Treaty of Hard Labor 1768
Treaty of Lochaber 1770
Proposed colony of Vandalia
Ohio Co. of Va. claim
Claimed by Connecticut settlers

newspapers. And then, in 1772, at Adams' instigation the towns of Massachusetts appointed committees to formulate statements of American rights and grievances and to correspond with one another on the subject. From Massachusetts the idea spread through the rest of New England; and in 1773, as a result of the *Gaspee* affair, it was taken up on an intercolonial basis.

The *Gaspee* was a British naval vessel, which, in 1772, patrolled Narragansett Bay and inflicted daily outrages upon the inhabitants: her commander seized small boats engaged in local traffic; her sailors cut orchards for firewood and helped themselves to livestock. When the *Gaspee* ran aground on one of her missions, the people of Providence came out after dark and burned her. It was a daring action and not the first of its kind. England decided to make an example of the colony. Suspecting that Rhode

Island courts would make no serious effort to uncover the culprits, she appointed a special commission to investigate the incident. But Rhode Islanders would give no helpful testimony, and the commissioners never discovered the guilty parties.

The *Gaspee* commission attracted attention throughout America. Because it bypassed the Rhode Island courts, the colonists regarded it as an infringement of common-law procedures and consequently of the rights of Englishmen. In Virginia the assembly felt incited to establish a committee of correspondence for the whole colony (Patrick Henry was a member) and to propose that each of the other colonies appoint a committee of its own. When the proposal was accepted, Americans gained the machinery for coordinating their views and actions on any question affecting their common interests.

The Intolerable Acts. While men like Adams and Henry were laying the foundations of American union, Lord North was worrying over another immediate and pressing problem. England had left the administration of her empire in the East largely in the hands of a giant trading corporation, the East India Company; and the company was in serious financial trouble. After bringing it under more direct supervision of the British government, Lord North secured legislation to increase the company's profits from tea-drinking Americans.

The Tea Act of May 1773 relieved the company of various taxes in England and empowered it to export tea directly from its English warehouses to America, where it would be distributed by company agents. Hitherto the company had been required to sell its tea only by auction to English wholesale merchants, who sold it to American merchants, who in turn sold it to retailers. By eliminating the middlemen's profits and the company's taxes, North hoped to lower tea prices in America so sharply that the colonists would step up their purchases and put the East India Company back on its feet. The Americans would still have to pay the tax imposed by the Townshend Act, but even so they would be able to buy tea cheaper than ever before. Some members of Parliament urged that the Townshend tax also be removed, but North insisted that this token of English sovereignty be retained.

North, it soon became apparent, had misjudged the colonists. By the Tea Act he lost whatever ground he had won in America by repealing the other Townshend duties. Merchants who had been importing tea themselves resented being shut out of the competitive market by a powerful, privileged company. Even the consumers, who would have benefited by the act, were hostile to it. Political leaders warned that the scheme was a trap to make Americans accept Parliamentary taxation. When the first shipments from London arrived in colonial ports, angry citizens forced the ships to return without unloading or stored the tea in warehouses from which no East India man dared remove it. In Boston, where Governor Hutchinson ruled that the ships could not depart without unloading their cargoes, a well-organized mob boarded the ships and pitched the tea into the harbor.

Lord North, who had had enough trouble with Boston, decided to punish the town with another demonstration of authority. Assisted by a new Secretary of State for the Colonies, Lord Dartmouth (Hillsborough had resigned in August 1772), he drafted the Boston Port Act, which ordered the port closed to shipping until the town made restitution for the tea. Parliament readily passed the act. North and Dartmouth might have been willing to stop there, but their fellow ministers insisted on proving Parliament's authority with three more acts (1774).

The Massachusetts Government Act altered the old constitution established by the charter of 1691 (see p. 49): henceforth the governor's council would be appointed by the king (rather than elected by the assembly) and town meetings would be held only once a year except by express permission of the governor. The Administration of Justice Act provided that any government or customs officer indicted for murder could be tried in England, beyond the control of local juries. A new Quartering Act authorized the quartering of troops within a town (instead of in the barracks provided by a colony) whenever their commanding officer thought it desirable. To underline the meaning of this act the British troops, with heavy reinforcements, were brought back into Boston from the fort in the harbor; and General Thomas Gage, the commander in chief of all

the North American troops, was sent to act also as governor of the colony.

The colonists promptly dubbed these new measures the Intolerable Acts. They were followed by the Quebec Act, which had no punitive intention but which the colonists thought as outrageous as the others. Canada, since its acquisition in 1763, had been provisionally in the hands of a military governor; the Quebec Act gave the province a permanent government with no representative assembly, established French civil law, and offered special protection to the Catholic Church. Although Canada as a French colony had never had a representative assembly, Americans thought it ominous that Parliament had failed to establish one now that it was an English colony. It disturbed them even more that the act ignored colonial territorial claims by annexing the whole region west of the Appalachians and north of the Ohio to the province of Quebec. Now when settlers moved west they would have to live under Canada's autocratic government.

The Quebec Act and the Intolerable Acts were not the result of hasty or capricious decisions. The Quebec Act had been drafted only after lengthy discussions with officials who had been in Canada, and the Intolerable Acts incorporated certain changes that had often been recommended by royal governors and customs officers. The redesigning of the Massachusetts government in particular was a long-awaited assertion of Parliament's authority over colonial governments. It came, however, as Governor Bernard had feared it would, too late. By

The Quebec Act, 1774

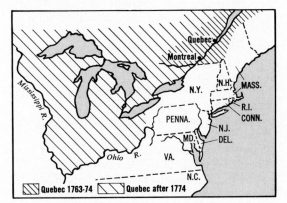

Quebec 1763-74   Quebec after 1774

subjecting Massachusetts to direct Parliamentary control and by backing up that control with an army, Lord North and his colleagues thought they could teach Americans to respect the supremacy of Parliament. But the lesson the colonists learned was that the supremacy of Parliament meant an end to the power of their own representative assemblies and courts, an end to the right to trial by jury, an end to every political principle they held dear.

The committees of correspondence went into action immediately. Boston had once been known, and not loved, throughout the colonies for the hard bargaining of its merchants and the riotous behavior of its inhabitants. Now the town received universal admiration and sympathy. It was deluged with gifts of rice from the Carolinas, flour from Pennsylvania, and pledges of support from everywhere. To help carry out the pledges and to coordinate action against the Intolerable Acts, the committees of correspondence arranged for an intercolonial congress to meet in September.

The First Continental Congress. Fifty-five delegates from twelve colonies (Canada, Florida, and Georgia sent none) assembled at Philadelphia in September 1774. As soon as the sessions began, it became apparent that the Southerners and the New Englanders had more radical ideas about what should be done than did the moderates from Pennsylvania and New York. Samuel Adams of Boston presented a set of resolutions that had just been passed by a convention in Suffolk County, Massachusetts, recommending outright resistance to the Intolerable Acts. The congress adopted these Suffolk Resolves and went on to adopt a nonimportation, nonexportation, and nonconsumption agreement, called "The Association," against trade of any kind with Great Britain, Ireland, and the West Indies.

Joseph Galloway of Pennsylvania, speaking for the moderates, countered with a plan for imperial reorganization, which he wanted the congress to present to the king and Parliament. Galloway's plan called for a grand council of the colonies along the lines projected at the Albany Congress (see p. 81). Enactments of the council would be subject to Parliamentary review and veto; acts of Parliament affecting the colonies would likewise have to receive the approval of the grand council. But Galloway could not quite persuade the delegates to subordinate their union to Parliament. In the years since the Stamp Act crisis they had had time and provocation to think further about their relationship to that body.

In 1765 the colonists had categorically denied that Parliament had the authority to tax them; and they had acquiesced in its general legislative authority over the whole empire, mentioning specifically only trade regulation and amendment of the common law as examples of what kind of legislation they thought acceptable. Apart from an unexpanded stipulation in some of their resolutions that Parliament should not alter their "internal polity" (as it finally did in the Massachusetts Government Act of 1774), they had not defined the limits of Parliament's legislative authority over them.

Since 1765 many of them had decided that Parliament had no more right to make laws concerning them than it did to tax them. This idea had few adherents until the punishment of the New York assembly, the *Gaspee* commission, and the Intolerable Acts clearly demonstrated that Parliament could destroy men's rights as readily by legislation as by taxation. Thereafter the idea spread rapidly. Benjamin Franklin adopted it privately as early as 1766, and Samuel Adams led the Massachusetts assembly in affirming it to Governor Hutchinson in 1773. In the summer of 1774 prospective members of the coming congress could read powerful demonstrations of it in two pamphlets. In *Considerations on the . . . Authority of the British Parliament*, James Wilson, a Pennsylvania lawyer, pointed out that all the familiar arguments against Parliamentary taxation applied equally well against Parliamentary legislation. Jefferson took the same position in *A Summary View of the Rights of British America*.

Neither Jefferson nor Wilson was present at the First Continental Congress, but enough of the delegates agreed with them to defeat Galloway's plan by one vote. The radicals were unable, however, to bring this bloc to repudiate all colonial ties with Parliament. Of those who were no longer willing to admit that Parliament had any authority in the colonies, some still believed that it should be allowed to regulate colonial trade as a just compensation for the British navy's protection of colonial shipping. When the delegates came to framing a statement of colonial rights and grievances, John Adams finally got them to compromise on a series of resolutions that denied that Parliament had any authority over the colonies but agreed — as a matter of fairness and expediency — to submit to its acts for regulation of trade.

The congress was inviting Parliament to return to the same supervisory role it had exercised in the colonies before 1763. Had Parliament been willing to do so, the breach, instead of widening, might have closed. The Earl of Chatham (William Pitt) and Edmund Burke both recognized the opportunity, but neither could muster more than a few votes for proposals to repeal the Intolerable Acts and renounce American taxation. Lord North, however, did secure passage in February 1775 of what he regarded as a conciliatory measure proposing to withhold Parliamentary taxation of any colony whose inhabitants taxed themselves "for contributing their proportion to the common defence." The proposal gave no indication of how much each colony's "propor-

**Colonial Government:
A Representative Assembly's View**

Your Excellency adds, ''for although there may be but one head, the King, yet the two Legislative bodies will make two governments as distinct as the kingdoms of England and Scotland, before the union.'' Very true, may it please your Excellency; and if they interfere not with each other, what hinders, but that being united in one head and common Sovereign, they may live happily in that connection, and mutually support and protect each other? Notwithstanding all the terrors which your Excellency has pictured to us as the effects of a total independence, there is more reason to dread the consequences of absolute uncontroled power, whether of a nation or a monarch, than those of a total independence. It would be a misfortune ''to know by experience, the difference between the liberties of an English colonist and those of the Spanish, French, and Dutch:'' and since the British Parliament has passed an act, which is executed with rigor, though not voluntarily submitted to, for raising a revenue, and appropriating the same, without the consent of the people who pay it, and have claimed a power of making such laws as they please, to order and govern us, your Excellency will excuse us in asking, whether you do not think we already experience too much of such a difference, and have not reason to fear we shall soon be reduced to a worse situation than that of the colonies of France, Spain, or Holland?

From the Answer of the Massachusetts House of Representatives to Governor Hutchinson, 1773.

tion" might be or how large a total contribution would be required, and it was silent on the other issues raised by the Intolerable Acts and by the declarations of the Continental Congress. To Americans it appeared to be only an insidious attempt by the ministry to draw away individual colonies from the new union.

But English statesmen were in no mood for softer measures. Most of them were convinced that Samuel Adams and his tribe were leading the colonists toward independence and that the march could be halted only by more forceful demonstrations of Parliamentary supremacy. The session that passed Lord North's conciliatory resolve also passed an act excluding New Englanders from the Newfoundland fisheries and prohibiting them from all trade except with the mother country and the British West Indies. At the same time the ministry took steps to prevent exportation of arms and ammunition to the colonies. Even the king expected the worst. "The New England Governments are in a State of Rebellion," he had told Lord North in November 1774. "Blows," he added, "must decide whether they are to be subject to this Country or Independent."

England clearly anticipated war, but her leaders had no conception of the size of the enemy. In spite of the increasingly obvious signs of colonial unity, Lord North and his colleagues persisted in regarding the enemy as Massachusetts alone. General Gage, sitting uneasily in the governor's chair in Massachusetts, did his best to disillusion them. The Americans, he reported, were as ready for blows as the English; to enforce Parliament's authority he would need twenty thousand men. Until England was prepared to send that many, he said, it would be well to suspend the Intolerable Acts.

George III thought Gage's dispatches absurd; Lord North turned from them to ask Parliament for a reduction in the size of Britain's armed forces. Gage was allowed about thirty-five hundred.

From Lexington to Bunker Hill. The general knew from his informers that the colonial militia were assembling arms and ammunition at strategic points. In Portsmouth, New Hampshire, they carried off a hundred barrels of powder belonging to the crown. Gage did not dare detach any part of his small force to recover the royal gunpowder, but occasionally he marched sizable columns for a few miles

into the country around Boston, hoping by this show of strength to overawe incipient rebels. On April 14 he received instructions from Lord Dartmouth to take the offensive against the rebellious colonists, and on April 19 he sent seven hundred men to Concord to seize a supply of arms reportedly stored there.

Although the force got started in the dark of early morning, the tolling of alarm bells and the firing of signal guns showed that its errand was no secret. Anticipating trouble, the commanding officer sent back for reinforcements but ordered six companies under Major John Pitcairn to proceed. At Lexington, Pitcairn found colonial militia drawn up on the village green. At his command, they began to disperse. Then suddenly a shot rang out. Whether British or American, musket or pistol, accidental or deliberate, was not apparent; but when they heard the shot, the British soldiers fired a volley into the departing militiamen, killing eight of them and wounding ten.

This episode delayed the troops for only fifteen minutes, and by eight o'clock they were entering Concord. The Americans had already removed most of the military stores they had assembled there, but the British burned a few gun carriages and repulsed a group of militiamen who tried to drive them off. Two colonials and three British were killed in the skirmish. By noon the "battles" of Lexington and Concord were over and the British troops started back to Boston.

Now a real battle began, a battle unlike any the troops had ever seen. Colonial militiamen for miles around had been alerted by a system of riders organized for just such an emergency, and the seven hundred British regulars were obliged to run a gauntlet of fire from three or four thousand Americans. At Lexington the returning troops were joined by nine hundred reinforcements, but still the Americans fired from rock and tree at the massed target of moving redcoats.

The total casualties on both sides were not large: the British lost 73 killed, 174 wounded, and 26 missing; the Americans, 49 killed and 39 wounded. But Gage's worst fears had been justified: his offensive had turned into a rout. That night, as haggard British soldiers dragged themselves into Boston, watch fires dotted the landscape around the city: militia were begin-

Lexington and Concord, April 19, 1775

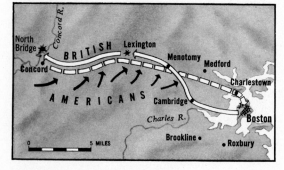

BOSTON

CHARLES TOWN

The assault on Breed's Hill, June 17, 1775.

ning to move in from all over New England. Boston was already under siege by a people who had no proper army, no system of command, no regular government.

On June 17, less than two months later, Gage found how tightly he was held. Reinforced by sea with 1,100 troops and 3 major generals (William Howe, John Burgoyne, and Henry Clinton), he decided to roll back the siege. On the night of June 16, the Americans, forewarned of his plans, marched 1,200 men to Breed's Hill (just south of Bunker Hill, from which the ensuing action, for no good reason, received its name), overlooking Boston from the north. By morning, when 400 more joined them, they had dug a formidable redoubt.

That afternoon General Howe set out with 2,200 men to displace the rebels from their position. Since Breed's Hill was on a peninsula, Howe could have cut the Americans off by landing a force at their rear. Instead, he bombarded nearby Charlestown at the end of

the peninsula and launched a frontal assault. The Americans inside the redoubt held their fire as the enemy, firing regularly and harmlessly, marched coolly up the hill. When the Americans returned the fire, the British went down in rows.

Howe regrouped his forces and tried again, with the same result. But now the Americans were low on ammunition, and the British regulars, reinforced by 600 men, finally forced the redoubt with bayonets. The Americans, clubbing their muskets, retreated slowly, leaving 140 of their men dead, 271 wounded, and 30 captured. Howe's victory had cost him 226 killed and 828 wounded. Another such victory, wrote Clinton ruefully, "would have ruined us." It had now been demonstrated beyond dispute that Americans with guns were dangerous men. The British never again underestimated the men they were fighting.

One people. While 16,000 colonial militia pinned down the British forces in Boston, other

Boston and Charlestown, June 17, 1775

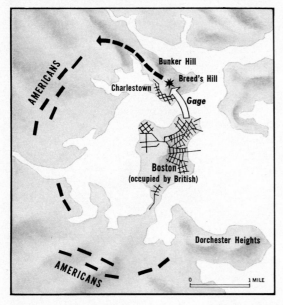

Americans were taking the necessary steps to support the war. Royal governors everywhere watched their authority collapse, as surely as Gage's had collapsed outside Boston. A few tried to organize loyalist support to combat the rebellion, but sooner or later they all gave up and fled to the safety of British warships. The colonial assemblies, which had hitherto met under royal authorization, now gathered as extralegal provincial congresses and began to act as independent governments, raising troops and issuing forbidden paper money to pay them. The transition in government presented no serious difficulty, because the representatives to the provincial congresses were for the most part former assemblymen and they simply carried on with their usual business.

A more extraordinary task faced the delegates who, in May 1775, assembled at Philadelphia for the Second Continental Congress (which had been arranged by the First Congress). Previous intercolonial meetings, the Albany Congress, the Stamp Act Congress, and the First Continental Congress, had devoted themselves to hammering out agreements of principle. But by the time the Second Congress met, the colonists were already deeply committed to common principles and a common cause. Fighting had just begun, and the

delegates, instead of conducting another debating council, found themselves conducting America's first central government: they assumed responsibility for the provincial militia besieging Boston, ordered their transformation into a Continental Army, named George Washington as commander, issued paper money to support the troops, and appointed a committee to negotiate with foreign countries.

Although in taking these actions the congress assumed many of the powers of an independent government, the members still did not intend to establish an independent nation. Repudiation of Parliament was not repudiation of England, and they did not see why Englishmen in America and in England should not retain their brotherhood in loyalty to a common king. In July they laid their cause at the feet of the king with a petition asking him personally to promote repeal of the oppressive measures. Significantly they placed the blame for those measures on the ministry — "those artful and cruel enemies who abuse your royal confidence and authority for the purpose of effecting our destruction." They issued at the same time a "Declaration of the causes and necessity for taking up arms," in which they explained that they were "reduced to the alternative of choosing an unconditional submission to the tyranny of irritated ministers, or resistance by force." In choosing resistance, they said, they had no "ambitious designs of separating from Great Britain, and establishing independent states." As soon as England acknowledged their rights, they would lay down their arms.

Although some Americans had already begun to think of independence, the declarations of the congress were made in good faith. Even at this date the repeal of the Intolerable Acts and the restriction of Parliamentary legislation to the regulation of trade might have kept the colonists in the empire. They still thought of their rights as the rights of Englishmen and of their union as a means of protecting those rights. But George III and Lord North were bent on subjecting the colonists to a Parliament in which they elected no representative. The king did not answer their petition; Parliament did, however, answer their "declaration" — by voting to send twenty-five thousand more troops against them. The addition would bring

British military strength in America to forty thousand. In August the king issued a proclamation declaring the colonies in a state of rebellion, and in December Parliament passed an act outlawing all their trade and subjecting their ships and goods to confiscation.

Each British action weakened the colonists' emotional attachment to England. The principal ingredient in their national feeling had been admiration for the British form of government, which better than any other guaranteed the human rights of its subjects. When their admiration for Parliament crumbled, they had fastened the last shreds of their loyalty on the king alone. But he had enthusiastically supported Parliament against them. If the whole English government was determined to destroy the rights of its subjects, then it was a dubious privilege to be an Englishman.

In January 1776 the new image of George III as a tyrant was presented to the colonists with biting eloquence in a publication called simply *Common Sense*. The author, Thomas Paine, an Englishman who had arrived in America only in 1774, argued that it was foolish for Americans to stake their lives and fortunes simply to obtain a repeal of Parliamentary laws. "The object contended for," he said, "ought always to bear some just proportion to the expence. . . . Dearly, dearly, do we pay for the repeal of the acts, if that is all we fight for." Common sense forbade that Americans should remain loyal to a king who sanctioned the spilling of their blood. In fact monarchy itself was an absurdity, a form of government that had laid the world in blood and ashes. "Of more worth," declared Paine, "is one honest man to society and in the sight of God, than all the crowned ruffians that ever lived." Here Paine struck a responsive chord. Since the days of Cromwell republican government had never ceased to have its devotees both in Great Britain and in America, and the old distrust of kings had never entirely died out. The colonists' very devotion to the House of Hanover was in part an expression of this distrust, an oblique way of denouncing the House of Stuart (which the Hanovers had replaced) and of affirming the right of a people to change kings. By calling on Americans to cast off kings altogether, Thomas Paine kindled a latent enthusiasm for republican government.

In the six months that followed the publication of *Common Sense*, sentiment in favor of independence and republicanism grew rapidly. Many who hoped that George III would save American liberty had been convinced by Paine that no king could help them. Many who had considered independence impossible to attain now began to change their minds. Ever since Lexington, American forces throughout the colonies had been fighting the British with heartening success in one engagement after another. And, as men thought beyond the mere repeal of Parliamentary laws, they began to cut their ties with England and England's king. The provincial congress of South Carolina established a republican constitution in March, and in May the Rhode Island congress repealed the law requiring allegiance to the king. North Carolina in April and Virginia in May instructed their delegates in the Continental Congress to vote for independence.

The Continental Congress, with representatives from thirteen colonies (delegates from Georgia had arrived in September, 1775), was itself behaving more and more like an independent national government. In March it authorized privateering against British ships. In April it forbade the further importation of slaves and declared other trade open to all the world except Great Britain. In May, urged by John Adams, it even recommended that any member colonies who had not already done so should suppress all vestiges of royal authority within their borders and establish governments resting on popular consent.

By this time Adams and many other delegates from New England and the Southern colonies were prepared to make an outright declaration of independence. They were restrained only by the reluctant rebels of the Middle colonies. Although virtually the whole Congress had by now concluded that Parliament had no constitutional authority at all in America, some Americans still felt bound to England by a lingering loyalty to the king and a sentimental attachment to the English people. By the end of June both feelings had worn too thin to sustain the weight of continuing war. On July 2, the Congress finally agreed to a motion that had been introduced by Richard Henry Lee of Virginia nearly a month before: "That these United Colonies are, and of right ought to be free and independent states." Thomas Jefferson, assisted by Franklin and John Adams, expanded the resolution into the famous declaration that was adopted on July 4.

Jefferson's declaration was an eloquent application of the ideas made familiar by John Locke and by a century and a half of American experience. It affirmed the origin of government in the consent of the governed, its obligation to protect natural rights, and the duty of a people to alter or abolish a government that failed to fulfill its obligation. That the British government had failed was demonstrated by a long list of misdeeds. These were attributed not to Parliament, whose authority the colonists had already denied, but to the king, the only remaining link between the colonies and England. Every grievance suffered by Americans since 1763 was laid at his door. The indictment was not altogether realistic, but it effectively expressed the American rejection not only of George III but of monarchy itself. Embedded in the preamble was evidence that the colonists had learned the lesson England had taught: "When in the course of human events, it becomes necessary for one people to dissolve the political bands which have connected them with another. . . ." Englishmen were "another" people; and the colonists, who twenty-two years before had rejected the union proposed at Albany, now spoke of themselves as "one people."

SUGGESTIONS FOR READING

The period covered by this chapter was first treated in the grand manner by George Bancroft in Vols. IV–VII of his *History of the United States*, 10 vols. (1834–74); Bancroft is still grand reading. Although subsequent historians have been able to correct him on many points, few if any have matched him in literary gifts or in comprehensive knowledge of the sources. Where Bancroft saw events with the future of the United States always in mind, G. L. Beer, in *British Colonial Policy, 1754–1765* (1907), viewed the French and Indian War from a British point of view. Lawrence H. Gipson sees events in America in relation to Britain's imperial problems throughout the world in *The British Empire Before the American Revolution* (1936–   ). Vols. V–VIII deal with the French and Indian War, which Professor Gipson has renamed "The Great War for the Empire." Vols. IX–XII cover the years from 1763 to 1776. The first two volumes of Douglas Freeman, *George Washington*, 7 vols. (1949–57), cover Washington's role in the war. Stanley Pargellis, *Lord Loudoun in North America* (1933), is important for its treatment of the problem of command.

The understanding of British politics in the 1760's and 1770's has been considerably altered since Bancroft's time. The older views were well expressed in G. O. Trevelyan's magnificently written *The American Revolution*, 4 vols. (1898–1907), and *The Early History of Charles James Fox* (1901). L. B. Namier, in *The Structure of Politics at the Accession of George III*, 2 vols.* (1929), and *England in the Age of the American Revolution** (1930), has since shown that the party system assumed by Trevelyan did not yet exist and that George III was a better monarch than anyone had supposed. More recently, Herbert Butterfield, *George III and the Historians* (1959), argues that the older views were not quite so mistaken as Namier and his followers thought them to be. A valuable study of the radical political tradition in England is Caroline Robbins, *The Eighteenth-Century Commonwealthman* (1959).

Clarence Alvord, *The Mississippi Valley in British Politics*, 2 vols. (1916), is a classic study of British policy toward the American West. This should be supplemented by T. P. Abernethy, *Western Lands and the American Revolution* (1937), and J. M. Sosin, *Whitehall and the Wilderness: The Middle West in British Colonial Policy, 1760–1775* (1961).

* Available in a paperback edition.

Perhaps the best introduction to the multitude of books on the origins of the Revolution is C. M. Andrews, *The Colonial Background of the American Revolution** (1924). A good one-volume account of the events from 1763 to 1776 is J. C. Miller, *Origins of the American Revolution** (1943). Bernhard Knollenberg, *Origin of the American Revolution, 1759–1766** (1960), stresses the variety of causes that irritated Americans in those years. O. M. Dickerson, *The Navigation Acts and the American Revolution** (1951), argues that the Navigation Acts were not a cause of the Revolution but the creation in 1767 of an American Board of Customs Commissioners resulted in widespread "customs racketeering," which dissolved the cement of empire. A. M. Schlesinger, *The Colonial Merchants and the American Revolution* (1917), shows how the merchants initially took the lead in opposition to England but became wary as popular feeling seemed to threaten their own position. John Shy, *Toward Lexington* (1965), traces the role of the British troops in bringing on the Revolution. B. W. Labaree, *The Boston Tea Party* (1964), shows how this event precipitated the crisis. A contemporary Tory view of the coming of the Revolution, pungently expressed, is Peter Oliver, *Origin and Progress of the American Rebellion*, Douglass Adair and John Schutz, eds. (1961).

Several books discuss the political and constitutional principles developed by the colonists before 1776. E. S. and H. M. Morgan, *The Stamp Act Crisis: Prologue to Revolution** (1953), describes the events and ideas of the years 1764–66; and E. S. Morgan, *Prologue to Revolution: Sources and Documents on the Stamp Act Crisis** (1959), reprints many of the resolutions, petitions, newspaper articles, and pamphlets in which the colonists expressed their views. Later development of colonial opinion is treated in Carl Becker, *The Declaration of Independence** (1922), and R. G. Adams, *The Political Ideas of the American Revolution** (1922). C. H. McIlwain, *The American Revolution** (1923), argues that the colonists' interpretation of the British constitution was well grounded in historical precedent; but R. L. Schuyler, *Parliament and the British Empire* (1929), challenges McIlwain. Bernard Bailyn, ed., *The Pamphlets of the American Revolution* (1965), reprints the most important tracts on the American side, with an introduction analyzing the arguments.

A number of able books describe the internal developments within different colonies in the years preceding independence. Robert Brown, *Middle-Class Democracy and the Revolution in Massachusetts* (1955), stresses the absence of internal class conflict, but R. J. Taylor finds more evidence of such conflict in the West in *Western Massachusetts in the Revolution* (1954). A good close-up of Boston is found in two biographies: J. C. Miller, *Sam Adams: Pioneer in Propaganda* (1936), and Esther Forbes, *Paul Revere and the World He Lived In** (1942). David Lovejoy, *Rhode Island Politics and the American Revolution* (1958), traces political divisions and shows that all sides in Rhode Island were united against the British. Carl Becker, *The History of Political Parties in the Province of New York, 1760–1776** (1909), shows that in New York the Revolution was a contest not only about home rule but also about "who should rule at home." Similar studies for other states are Theodore Thayer, *Pennsylvania Politics and the Growth of Democracy, 1740–1776* (1954); C. A. Barker, *The Background of the Revolution in Maryland* (1940); H. J. Eckenrode, *The Revolution in Virginia* (1916); Carl Bridenbaugh, *Seat of Empire** (1950); and Oscar Zeichner, *Connecticut's Years of Controversy* (1950).

* Available in a paperback edition.

5
An
American
People

Although the colonists had moved slowly and reluctantly toward declaring independence, once the deed was done most of them had no regrets. There were, of course, loyalists, many of whom left for Canada. Of those who remained, some were ready to fight their countrymen for their king — some, but never enough to win. There were also men indifferent to who ruled them and willing to sell supplies to either side, depending on the price offered. But in every colony that joined in the Declaration of Independence, the patriots were sufficiently numerous, vociferous, and aggressive to outweigh the loyalists and the indifferent. Once the royal governments collapsed, it proved impossible to revive British authority except in the immediate vicinity of British guns.

THE WINNING OF INDEPENDENCE

The rebel army. Perhaps because they could overawe the loyalists, the patriots counted too easily on doing the same to the British armies. After the rout on April 19 and the slaughter on June 17 (see pp. 102 and 103), they were inclined to believe that their militia could handle any force the British sent against them. George Washington knew better; the men encamped around Boston did have spirit, courage, and marksmanship, but they were not an army. To make them into one was Washington's first concern after taking command at Cambridge on July 3, 1775.

It was not simply a matter of instruction and training in the art of war. Militia units had to be reorganized under a corps of officers appointed from above. In the process, many of the old officers lost rank and stalked off in a huff. Furthermore, the militia who had come to besiege Boston were used to electing their own officers and were touchy about taking orders from higher up. They were also used to short terms of service (for a local emergency or a particular campaign) and eager to get home to their crops. Wherever the enemy appeared, Americans from miles around would turn out to fight him; but they did not want to join the army. To join the army was to desert one's

Battle of Princeton, January 3, 1777.

family for danger, discomfort, and disease hundreds of miles from home. The pay was low, and no pension system existed to compensate a man or his family for the loss of life or limb. It therefore took all of Washington's diplomacy and tact to persuade ten thousand militiamen to enlist until the end of 1776 as regular soldiers in the Continental Army. In addition the provincial governments supplied him with about seven thousand short-term militiamen.

The total was much smaller than Washington had hoped for. Throughout the war Congress was able to provide him with an ample army of men on paper. But men with arms, legs, heads, and guns remained in short supply. Since Congress had no power either to raise money or to draft men, it was dependent on requisitions to the states for both; and when the states lagged in supplying their assigned quotas, Congress could do nothing to coerce them. Supplies were as hard to come by as men; Washington had to spend much of his time pleading for both, and he had to fight the war with an army that was constantly in danger of dissolution.

The new army's first venture away from Boston began while Boston was still under siege, before independence was declared. In May 1775, militia under Ethan Allen and Benedict Arnold had captured Fort Ticonderoga without resistance and had gone on to take Crown Point (see map inset, p. 113). General Richard Montgomery moved up from Lake Champlain with a small force to capture Montreal on November 13, 1775. He then pushed on toward Quebec to meet Colonel Benedict Arnold, who was bringing more troops through the Maine woods. Congress had invited the people of Canada to join their union, and, though the Canadians had failed to respond, some reports suggested that they would welcome an invading army. In any case, it was desirable to strike at the British in Quebec and Montreal in order to forestall an attack from that direction. After a grueling winter march, the effective forces that converged on Quebec amounted to only a thousand men, and the Canadians showed no disposition to help them. They besieged the city through the winter, but smallpox, hunger, cold, and an unsuccessful assault so thinned their ranks that in the spring they retreated to

Circled numbers ① are keyed to detail maps in the pages which follow. The following symbols are used to designate American and British forces:

⬅ American advance
⬅ ⬅ American retreat
⇦ British advance
⇨ British retreat

Ticonderoga. The colonists made no further military effort to draw Canada into their union.

In the South the Americans fared better when Josiah Martin, the royal governor of North Carolina, tried to hold the colony with the help of loyalists. On February 27, 1776, at Moore's Creek Bridge, 1,100 militia overwhelmingly defeated 1,600 loyalists and captured a welcome £15,000 in cash. Four months later, when Generals Henry Clinton and Charles, Lord Cornwallis, and Admiral Sir Peter Parker arrived off Charles Town, South Carolina, with 50 ships and an army of 3,000 men, few loyalists showed up to greet them. Attempting to enter Charles Town Harbor on June 28, they were met by deadly fire from a seemingly impregnable fort constructed of palmetto logs and dirt. After a ten-hour duel the British withdrew and left Charles Town alone for the next four years.

In Massachusetts Washington had meanwhile built a force strong enough to close in on Boston. He began by occupying and fortifying Dorchester Heights, which overlooked the city on the south as Breed's Hill did on the north. This time the British did not try to storm the hills. Instead, on March 17, 1776, they departed by sea for Halifax, Nova Scotia, taking over a thousand loyalists with them.

A few months after the British evacuation of Boston, when Americans declared their independence, they appeared to be in a strong position. Although they were challenging the world's greatest military and naval power and had failed to win Canada to their cause, they had overpowered the British army in the march from Concord, withstood its assaults at Breed's Hill, forced its withdrawal from Boston, and fought off the British navy at Charles Town. But the British war machine, always a slow starter, was now grinding into action. Parliament had authorized an army of 55,000, and, when recruitment lagged in England, the government hired 30,000 German mercenaries, 17,000 of them from Hesse-Cassel (hence the name Hessians).

The British plan was to split the colonies in two by occupying New York. General William Howe and his brother, Admiral Richard Howe, were given command. They would move on New York City by sea from Halifax; another force would descend from Canada by way of Lake Champlain and the Hudson River. Once they had taken New York and thus cut off communications and reinforcements between the rebels in the North and those in the South, the British could deal with each separately.

The Howes were authorized to end the war as soon as the colonists submitted. Hoping to end it before they began, they addressed a conciliatory letter to "George Washington, Esq." (thus ignoring his military status). But General Washington was not receiving letters for George Washington, Esq., letters that denied American independence even in the address. The Howes therefore proceeded according to plan. On August 12, 1776, they arrived in New York harbor with 32,000 troops and 10,000 seamen (the city's normal population

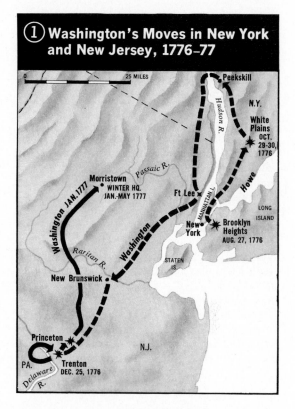

① **Washington's Moves in New York and New Jersey, 1776–77**

was 25,000) aboard 400 transports and 30 warships. Ten days later 20,000 of the troops landed on Long Island near Brooklyn.

Washington had 23,000 men in the New York area, but most of them were inexperienced local militia. When Howe, with plenty of men to spare, launched both frontal and flank attacks, Washington was forced to withdraw to Manhattan with heavy losses. Thinking that this taste of British power might have chastened the Americans, Howe offered to confer about a settlement before any more blows were struck. Congress sent Franklin, John Adams, and Edward Rutledge to deal with him, but the resulting conference broke off when it turned out, as Washington had suspected, that Howe was empowered to negotiate only with submissive colonists, not with the proud representatives of an independent nation. In September the British drove Washington off Manhattan Island; and by November the Continental Army, depleted by captures and desertions, was in full retreat across New Jersey.

Washington crossed the Delaware River into

Pennsylvania on December 7. Now, with the river between him and the enemy, he planned his next move. The outlook was bleak. While pursuing him across New Jersey, the British had been able simultaneously to send a large force to Rhode Island, where on December 8 they occupied Newport. Washington's force was down to fewer than 8,000 effective fighting men, all of them dispirited, exhausted, ready to quit. By the end of the month all but 1,500 would have completed their term of enlistment, and with winter coming on they would sling their packs, head for home, and let someone else fight the war. While he still had them, Washington attacked. On the night of December 25, 1776, in high, freezing winds, he shuttled his men back across the river, marched them nine miles to Trenton, and caught the enemy asleep and befuddled. With a loss of only 4 men he took 900 prisoners. A few days later at Princeton he dealt the British another smashing blow, and they pulled back to New Brunswick for the winter. The brilliant reversal so cheered the troops that Washington was

able to persuade many of them to reenlist. With spirits high again, the army moved into winter quarters at Morristown.

General Howe, contemplating the reverses that Washington had dealt him, had difficulty making up his mind about what to do when spring should come. After changing plans several times he finally decided to storm the rebel capital of Philadelphia, which, like New York, contained a large loyalist population. In July he took 15,000 men by sea from New York to the head of Chesapeake Bay. From there they marched north toward Philadelphia, the Hessians helping themselves to food, furniture, and women along the way. Washington intercepted them at Brandywine Creek; but, as on Long Island, Howe won the pitched battle and entered Philadelphia on September 26, 1777. When Washington challenged him a week later at Germantown, where most of the British troops were quartered, Howe again was victorious.

These defeats discouraged the colonists, but actually Howe's success was hollow. Though

British troops landing in New Jersey, 1776.

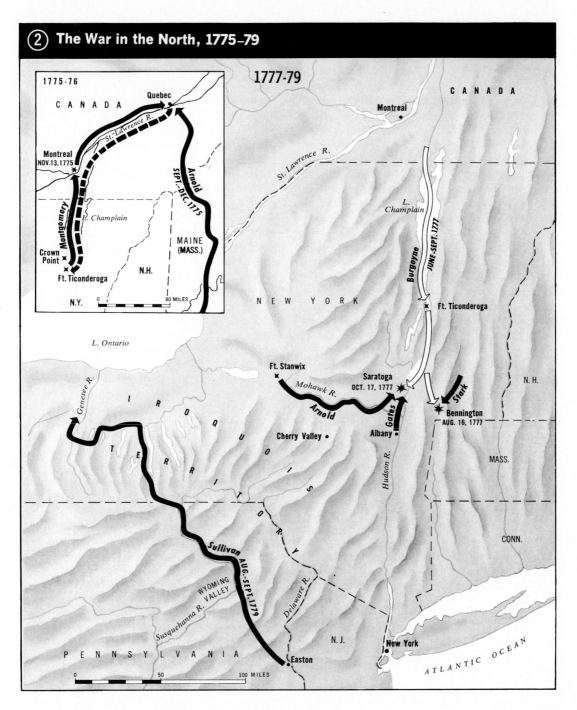

② The War in the North, 1775–79

1777-79

Inset: 1775-76

CANADA

Quebec

St-Lawrence R.

Montreal
NOV. 13, 1775

Montgomery

Arnold SEPT.-DEC. 1775

L. Champlain

Crown Point

Ft. Ticonderoga

MAINE (MASS.)

N.H.

N.Y.

0   80 MILES

Main map

CANADA

Montreal

St. Lawrence R.

L. Champlain

Burgoyne   JUNE-SEPT. 1777

Ft. Ticonderoga

NEW YORK

L. Ontario

Genesee R.

IROQUOIS TERRITORY

Ft. Stanwix

Mohawk R.

Arnold

Cherry Valley

Saratoga OCT. 17, 1777

Gates

Albany

Stark

Bennington AUG. 16, 1777

N.H.

MASS.

Hudson R.

CONN.

Sullivan AUG.-SEPT. 1779

WYOMING VALLEY

Susquehanna R.

Delaware R.

PENNSYLVANIA

Easton

N.J.

New York

ATLANTIC OCEAN

0   50   100 MILES

---

he had captured America's largest cities and repeatedly defeated her generals, he had captured no armies and controlled only a small portion of American territory. And to the north of him disaster was brewing. General

John Burgoyne, a vain, witty, and silly man, had been authorized by the high command in England to mount an expedition for a march south from Canada by the Lake Champlain route. He set out from Fort St. John's in June with 4,000 British, 3,000 Germans, 1,400 Indians, and a pleasing mistress to cheer him along. Everything went swimmingly for a time. But on August 16 a force of New Hampshire militia under John Stark caught a British detachment at Bennington, killed over 200, and took 700 prisoners. As Burgoyne advanced he ran into more traps. His Indians, quick to sense what was coming, quietly left him. American forces, under Horatio Gates and Benedict Arnold, gathered ever stronger before him, and each time they clashed Burgoyne lost several hundred more men. On October 17, 1777, he finally surrendered at Saratoga.

The French alliance. Saratoga was one of the turning points of history, but not because it turned back any threat to the American armies. Burgoyne's march, if successful, would have signified little in a military sense; his surrender did not seriously reduce the British margin of superiority in troops and equipment. Saratoga had its great effect, not in New York or Philadelphia, but in London and Paris.

In London a complacent Parliament began to sense the possibility that England might lose the war. Better make peace, the ministry decided, and it authorized a commission headed by Lord Carlisle to offer the Americans virtually everything they had previously demanded: renunciation of Parliamentary taxation, repeal of the Intolerable Acts, and suspension of every other objectionable act passed since 1763. Two years earlier such concessions would probably have kept the colonies within the empire. But by now the rebels found independence exhilarating. England's eagerness to have them back merely furnished them with the final weapon they needed to make their independence last: the recognition and assistance of France.

From the outset the Americans had been hoping for help from England's traditional enemy, and on November 29, 1775, Congress had appointed a secret committee to seek foreign aid. Louis XVI, delighted by the rebellion of England's colonies, had sent Achard de Bonvouloir to observe the situation in America. With Bonvouloir's encouragement the committee dispatched Silas Deane, a shrewd and sophisticated Yankee, to negotiate with France. Deane arrived in Paris on July 7, 1776, to find that the French foreign minister, the Comte de

Vergennes, had already persuaded the king to help the American rebellion with a million livres' worth of munitions and supplies. Furthermore, Spain had matched the amount. The goods were to be dispensed secretly through a fake trading company run by Pierre Beaumarchais (author of *The Barber of Seville*). They were Deane's for the asking, though whether as a gift or as a loan remained uncertain.

Deane's negotiations took place before news of the Declaration of Independence reached France, when secret assistance was all the Americans dared ask for. Once the declaration had been announced, they hoped that France would recognize their independence and offer open assistance. To help Deane push these more ambitious requests, Congress sent Arthur Lee, a Virginian who had been serving the American cause in London, and Benjamin Franklin, who arrived from Philadelphia in December 1776. The three men constituted a commission with power to make treaties of amity and commerce.

The French at this time envisaged America as an Arcadia peopled by noble savages and almost equally noble farmers, rich in nature's wisdom; Franklin, seeing what was expected, donned his fur cap and played the role to the hilt. Completely enchanted, the Parisians showered the arch-American with favors, but Vergennes and his royal master remained cautious. Besides furnishing supplies to the colonists they sometimes allowed American privateers the use of French harbors. They hesitated, however, to join in open war on England when the British armies, with the capture of New York, appeared to be winning.

As American military fortunes declined, Congress instructed the commissioners to go beyond their request for French assistance and to seek the deeper commitment of an alliance. All Franklin's charm was insufficient to win it. Vergennes wanted Spain by his side before he took on the British lion, and Spain was unwilling. Spain feared even to give open assistance to the Americans lest she encourage her own colonies to revolt.

When news of Saratoga reached Paris on December 3, 1777, Vergennes perceived at once that the American victory might produce a conciliatory temper in England, and the last

Franklin played the role to the hilt.

thing he wanted was to see the rebellious colonies reconciled to the mother country. Franklin played on his fears, and Vergennes sent frantic messages to Spain. When Spain remained immovable, he finally told the commissioners that France was ready to enter into a treaty of commerce and amity and a treaty of alliance with the Americans. He indeed required an alliance before entering the war, in order to prevent the United States from making peace before England was humbled.

The terms of the alliance, signed on February 6, 1778, were all that the United States could have wished for. The stated purpose of both parties was to maintain the independence of the United States. In case of war between France and England (which the signing of the treaty made inevitable), neither France nor the United States was to make peace without the consent of the other. France renounced all future claims to English territory on the conti-

nent of North America and agreed that any such territory captured in the war would go to the United States. These generous terms were less the result of American diplomatic skill than of French determination to weaken England and French distaste for further colonizing in the New World.

Even before the alliance the Americans had depended heavily on aid from France. The victory at Saratoga, for example, would have been impossible without French supplies. And French financial support helped to bolster American credit at a time when Congress, with no authority to tax, was financing the war with money begged from the states or manufactured by the printing presses. With the signing of the alliance the hopes of the Americans soared, for France was the first nation to recognize them as "one people," and she had the military and naval power to make that recognition meaningful.

From Saratoga to Yorktown. After the battle of Saratoga the British fought a cautious war, their dreams of easy victory gone. Howe, snug in Philadelphia during the winter of 1777–78, did not even try to attack Washington's wretched forces, who were starving and freezing in their winter quarters at nearby Valley Forge. In the spring Howe was replaced by Sir Henry Clinton, who was to prove somewhat less languid though no bolder. The spring of 1778 also brought France's entry into the war and American refusal of the Carlisle Commission's peace overtures (see p. 114). Uncertain of where France would throw her weight, the British high command decided to play safe and ordered Clinton to withdraw from Philadelphia to New York. There he should plan a major campaign in the South, where — according to the strategists — loyalists would lend a decisive hand.

At Valley Forge, as mild weather came on, Washington's forces thawed out and were

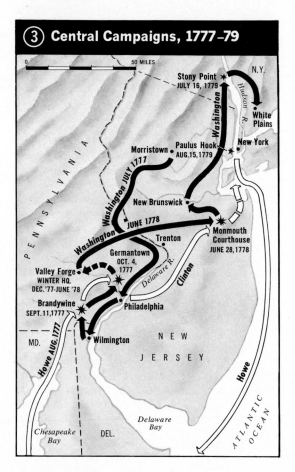

③ Central Campaigns, 1777-79

drilled with Prussian precision by Baron Friedrich von Steuben, an idealist from the Old World who had come to help usher in the independence of the New. By June he and a good supply of provisions had turned the haggard men into a hard and maneuverable army. When Clinton pulled out of Philadelphia to march across New Jersey to New York, Washington kept pace with him on a parallel route and watched for a chance to strike. But the only opportunity that came (the Battle of Monmouth Courthouse on June 28) was badly bungled by General Charles Lee, and the main body of Clinton's troops arrived safely in New York.

While the British and American armies were marching across New Jersey, the first French forces arrived in America — Vice Admiral the Comte d'Estaing with seventeen ships and four thousand troops. Washington proposed to use them in recovering Newport. But in August, just before the American-French assault was to begin, a storm scattered and damaged the French fleet, and the unsupported land forces withdrew when British reinforcements arrived. D'Estaing took his ships to Boston to refit and, in November 1778, sailed south to protect the French West Indies.

The departure of D'Estaing was a serious disappointment to Washington, for the Americans had no means of their own to combat the British navy. It offered deadly support to British land troops along the coast, and it regularly sent raiding parties to devastate towns far from any army. Though the Americans commissioned hundreds of privateers (probably over two thousand in all), which rendered invaluable service in disrupting the merchant shipping, communications, and supply lines of the enemy, the privateers were no more a navy than the militia were an army; they were simply not up to engaging British warships in a sustained action.

The Congress had tried to create a navy, but it could scrape together the money for only a few ships, which were no match for the Royal Navy. Nevertheless, one of them, commanded by the unpopular but unsinkable John Paul Jones, carried the war to the British Isles. Jones raided coastal towns and seized British ships. With French assistance he hoped to do much more. But the French navy preferred to fight its own war. In the only significant engagement in which American and French vessels fought side by side under his command (off Flamborough Head in the North Sea, September 1779) Jones got little help from his supporting force. He lost his flagship, the *Bonhomme Richard*, but not before he had boarded and captured the fifty-gun British *Serapis*.

Unfortunately there were not enough Joneses to divert the British navy from North America; and Clinton kept most of his troops near the coast within reach of naval assistance. Without naval assistance of his own Washington dared not risk an all-out assault on the British army, and after following it from New Jersey to New York he had camped outside the city at White Plains and waited for the French fleet to return or to draw the British ships to other waters. For a year and a half he waited while the fighting was carried on mostly by small forces remote from New York, the strategic center. During the summer and fall of 1778 the British sent a force of loyalists and Iroquois warriors to massacre settlers in the Wyoming Valley of Pennsylvania (July 3 to 6) and in the Cherry Valley of New York (November 11). In December a British expeditionary force landed in Georgia and easily subdued the small population, many of whom were loyalists. Savannah fell on December 29, and the province reverted to British rule. Meanwhile, George Rogers Clark, a twenty-five-year-old Virginian, took a handful of men to the Illinois country and by the end of February 1779 had captured Cahokia, Kaskaskia, and Vincennes for the Americans. When summer came, General Sullivan marched four thousand men against the Iroquois and broke their power forever, while the troops around

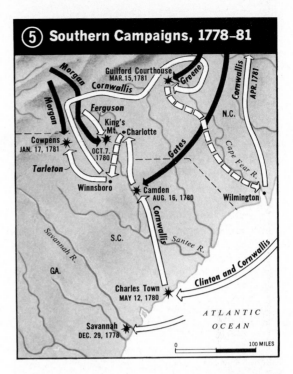

⑤ Southern Campaigns, 1778–81

New York City scored a few minor morale-building victories against local British garrisons (at Stony Point on July 16, 1779, and at Paulus Hook on August 15, 1779). In the fall of 1779 all prospect of French naval support disappeared when D'Estaing took his fleet from the West Indies back to France.

Encouraged by the recapture of Georgia, Clinton now went ahead with the Southern campaign he had been ordered to conduct. Leaving an army equal to Washington's to hold New York, he pulled his troops out of Newport (thus freeing New England of all British troops) and, in December 1779, sailed with an expeditionary force of over eight thousand for Charles Town, South Carolina. He took it on May 12, 1780, along with its defending general, Benjamin Lincoln, and his entire force of fifty-five hundred men. The Carolinas now lay open to a British sweep. But Clinton was still cautious. Departing for New York on June 8, he left Cornwallis in command, with instructions not to fan out beyond South Carolina. If the British forces were spread too thin they might not be able to hold what they had gained. But the British winning streak was not yet over. On August 16, 1780, near

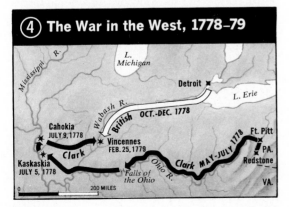

④ The War in the West, 1778–79

Camden, Cornwallis intercepted and routed over three thousand men under General Horatio Gates who were coming to the defense of South Carolina. Washington sent General Nathanael Greene, his ablest commander, to pick up the pieces.

In December, when Greene reached Charlotte, North Carolina, to assume command of the Southern forces, he found less than two thousand men, poorly equipped and without supplies. With the assistance of Daniel Morgan, a Virginia rifleman, Greene built a mobile fighting unit, which owed much to the Southern militiamen who appeared whenever a fight was in the offing. A group of these tough campaigners had already demonstrated their worth before Greene arrived by capturing a British force atop King's Mountain in North Carolina (October 7, 1780). Greene and Morgan lured Cornwallis into trap after trap, chewing off a bit of his force here and a bit there (notably at Hannah's Cowpens on the Broad River, January 17, 1781, and at Guilford Courthouse, March 15).

In April 1781 the two generals turned their backs on each other: Greene headed south to pick off more British outposts in South Carolina and Georgia, while Cornwallis, disregarding his instructions from Clinton, set out to conquer Virginia. By July Greene had pushed the

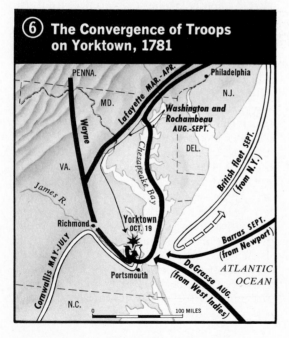

⑥ The Convergence of Troops on Yorktown, 1781

British in Georgia back to Savannah and in South Carolina back to Charles Town; Cornwallis had run through Virginia and had settled at Portsmouth, from which he later moved to Yorktown. Portsmouth and Yorktown both lay on the seacoast, the only safe place for a British army in America; but the coast would remain safe only so long as the British navy commanded the sea. Without naval support Cornwallis could be cut off from his own forces in Charles Town and Savannah and from Clinton's forces in the North.

In New York Clinton still looked out at Washington's waiting army, and Washington still waited for the French navy. The French had sent five thousand land troops under the Comte de Rochambeau to occupy Newport in July 1780, but the eleven warships that accompanied them under the Comte de Barras had been promptly bottled up inside the harbor by a superior British fleet.

In May 1781 Washington's patience was finally rewarded by news that Admiral de Grasse with twenty warships was sailing from France for the West Indies and would detach part of his force to assist a campaign on the mainland. In conference with Rochambeau Washington decided that this was his opportunity to close in on New York. But on August 14 word arrived that De Grasse was heading for the Chesapeake with his whole fleet; he would, however, be able to stay only a short time. Washington immediately decided to give up the planned New York campaign and to dash south for a try at Cornwallis. Leaving behind a part of his New York troops to fool Clinton, he marched the rest to the head of Chesapeake Bay and placed them aboard transports for the last leg of the journey. Additional forces under Anthony Wayne and the French volunteer, Lafayette, were already within marching distance of the target. Barras meanwhile had managed to slip out of Newport and was sailing south loaded with siege guns. When the British naval squadrons discovered what was going on, they hurried to the Chesapeake to drive off Barras and De Grasse but found themselves hopelessly outnumbered and outgunned. French naval power was at last decisive. Back went the British fleet to New York for repairs and reinforcements, and Washington with 5,700 Continentals, 3,100 militia, and 7,000

Washington and his generals at Yorktown.

French began to close in on Yorktown. On October 19, when a relief expedition was already under way from New York, Cornwallis gave up. With the bands playing "The World Turned Upside Down," 7,000 British troops marched out of Yorktown and stacked their arms in surrender.

Peace. Yorktown was as much a French as an American victory. And because the war too was a French war, it could not end at Yorktown. France was ready for peace but encumbered by a commitment to Spain. Vergennes, upon concluding the treaty of alliance with the United States on February 6, 1778, had continued his efforts to bring Spain into the war; he finally succeeded after agreeing not to stop fighting until Spain had won Gibraltar from England. Since the United States had agreed not to make peace without French consent, Americans were indirectly bound to await the capture of Gibraltar also. Spain, on the other hand, refused to recognize the independence of the United States, and after entering the war on June 21, 1779, accorded only a devious and frosty tolerance to the American cause. Once she had seized the thinly held territory of West Florida (a former Spanish posses-

sion) from the British, she confined herself mainly to blockading Gibraltar.

After the defeat at Yorktown, most Englishmen were ready to give up the struggle for the colonies even though George III was bent on continuing it. On March 20, 1782, Lord North was forced from office, and the king was obliged to accept a ministry favorable to peace, which immediately sent agents to get in touch with the American commissioners in France.

Congress had first formulated American war aims in August 1779, when it optimistically sent John Adams to France as minister plenipotentiary. Adams was then forbidden to enter into any peace negotiations with Great Britain unless she first recognized the United States as a sovereign, free, and independent state. After that recognition had been granted, he was to insist on certain boundaries for the new nation: the Mississippi on the west, the thirty-first parallel and the Flint and St. Mary's rivers on the south, and roughly the present boundary on the north.

In June 1781 the French ambassador to the United States, the Chevalier de la Luzerne, persuaded Congress to revise its arrangements for making peace. John Adams was replaced as sole negotiator by a five-man commission consisting of himself, John Jay (minister to Spain), Franklin (minister to France), Henry Laurens (designated as minister to the Netherlands but captured by the British en route and held in the Tower of London), and Thomas Jefferson (who was unable to go and was dropped from the commission). The commissioners' instructions were weak: they were still to insist on British recognition of American independence before undertaking peace negotiations, but they were free to accept any settlement "as circumstances may direct and as the state of the belligerent and the disposition of the mediating powers may direct." What was worse, they must do nothing without the knowledge and concurrence of the French and, indeed, must be governed by their advice and opinion.

These instructions put the commissioners under the direction of Vergennes, a position none of them relished. When secret information reached them that he would not support the American demand for prior recognition of independence, and that his secretary, Rayneval, had secretly encouraged the British to think of a boundary well to the east of the Mississippi, with Spain and England dividing up the territory between, they decided they would do better to negotiate with the British separately rather than to sit down at the peace table under French direction. Violating their instructions, they negotiated with British representatives without insisting on advance recognition of independence, and they did not keep Vergennes informed of what they were doing. Nor did they get all they wanted in the negotiations. Franklin, who had hoped to acquire Canada as a fourteenth state and to secure trading privileges in the empire, got neither.

Nevertheless, by playing on British desires to destroy the American alliance with France, the commissioners were able to secure both recognition of independence and the boundaries prescribed in John Adams' original instructions. In preliminary articles signed on November 30, 1782, they presented this diplomatic triumph to Vergennes as an accomplished fact. Actually there had been no violation of the alliance, for the treaty based on the articles was not to go into effect until France and England had concluded a treaty of their own. The commissioners' coup enabled Vergennes to exert pressure on Spain to give up the fight for Gibraltar, and in the end she settled for East and West Florida and Minorca. The final treaties were signed at Paris on September 3, 1783, and the last British troops left New York on November 25. The Declaration of Independence was at last a statement of fact, not a wish.

THE EXPERIMENTAL PERIOD

At Lexington, Concord, and Bunker Hill Americans had fought against Parliamentary taxation. After July 2, 1776, they had fought for independence, though in the beginning probably few of them had any clear idea of what independence would mean besides the end of British tyranny. Between 1776 and 1789 they explored the possibilities of their new freedom. These thirteen years may be considered the Experimental Period in American history, the time when Americans were trying their wings, discovering their nationality. They formulated ideas and ideals that had been only half articulate before, and they found ways and means to put their ideas and ideals into practice. During this period the Americanisms discussed earlier (see Chapter 3) underwent further development, and some of them were transformed from characteristic attitudes into national principles.

The fruition of Americanisms. American ideas about the separation of church and state and about education advanced less rapidly during the Experimental Period than did political and social concepts. But the assumption that widespread education was desirable did show itself in a revival of schooling, which had lapsed during the war, and in the proliferation of new educational institutions, most of them private. Many academies were founded (especially in New England) to furnish instruction at the secondary level, and sometimes beyond, to both boys and girls. And the number of colleges in the United States doubled: in 1776 there were nine; by 1789 as many more had been opened or chartered; and every state but Delaware had at least one in operation or being organized. Writers in newspapers and pamphlets argued about what kind of education was best suited to Americans. Many demanded that it be made more practical, and new textbooks reoriented traditional subjects like arithmetic and grammar in this direction.

The colonists' wariness of allowing their clergy a hand in government gave rise to a greater separation of church and state. Though most states continued to levy taxes in support of the Protestant religion, the Anglican Church lost the exclusive claims to that support which it had enjoyed in the Southern colonies. Under all the state constitutions a man could at least specify which Protestant church his taxes should support. And in Virginia the principle of complete separation of church and state received its finest expression in an act drafted by Thomas Jefferson and adopted by the Virginia legislature in 1786. Beginning with the assertion that "Almighty God hath created the mind free," the act provided that "no man shall be compelled to frequent or support any religious worship, place, or ministry whatsoever."

Jefferson was also author of the phrase that translated social mobility into an American principle. By declaring on July 4, 1776, that "all men are created equal," the United States committed itself to a doctrine that was to prove the world's most powerful lever for social and political change. The declaration was intended simply to justify the colonists' withdrawal from the mother country, which had refused to treat them as the equals of Englishmen. But no great imagination was required to discern wider implications in Jefferson's axiomatic statement of human equality.

Its relevance to Negro slavery was inescapable. As soon as Americans complained that British taxation would reduce them to slavery, they began to feel uneasy about their own enslavement of Africans; they even foreswore the slave trade in their nonimportation agreements. In the Experimental Period most of the states, Southern as well as Northern, forbade the further importation of slaves, and the Northern states passed laws for the eventual liberation of those already within their borders. Massachusetts seems to have rid herself of the institution by judicial decision: her constitution, echoing the Declaration of Independence, stated that "all men are born free and equal," and her courts interpreted the

North America in 1783

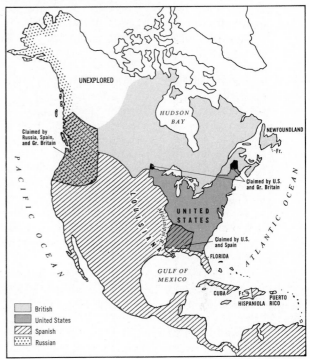

British
United States
Spanish
Russian

phrase literally. With the coming of peace newspaper articles warned that Americans had won only partial freedom; as one writer, who signed himself "Vox Africanorum," put it, "Thousands are yet groaning under their chains; slavery and oppression are not yet banished [from] the land." Though appeals of this kind led many men to free their slaves even in the South, slavery there continued and grew in strength while the doctrine of equality was growing elsewhere, until at last the one could not exist beside the other.

The doctrine of equality was as hostile to aristocracy as to slavery. Having got along without a titled nobility for a century and a half, Americans were determined to continue without one and looked suspiciously at anything that smacked of special privilege. States forbade their citizens to accept titles from foreign nations. And when officers of the Continental Army formed the Society of the Cincinnati in 1783, they met with a storm of protest from critics who feared that the association might become the nucleus of an aristocracy.

In Connecticut even a medical society, seeking to raise the standards of the profession by licensing practitioners, was at first denied a charter because its members were to be chosen for life and might thus become a privileged order.

The Revolutionary War itself had an equalizing effect on property: wealthy merchants had lost heavily from the British blockade of commerce, while many a poor farmer had prospered in selling his produce to the armies. Wartime finance, with its reliance on steadily inflating paper currency, favored debtors (who were most often farmers) at the expense of creditors. The confiscation and sale of loyalists' lands and the abolition of primogeniture (the inheritance of a man's entire estate by his eldest son) by the state governments likewise contributed to a more equal distribution of property by breaking up some of the larger concentrations of wealth. Although in many cases the initial purchasers of loyalist lands were large-scale speculators, the overall effect of the confiscations was probably to increase the number of landowners. By the time the war ended many Americans regarded equality of property as a goal in itself. When economic depression struck in the 1780's, legislators in some states sponsored bills favoring debtors, on the grounds that republican government required a general equality of property.

The emerging doctrine of equality can also be detected in the reform of voting laws. Although property qualifications had disfranchised only a small minority in most colonies (because most Americans owned property) and, though there had been few complaints, every state but Massachusetts reduced the amount of property required for voting. There remained, nevertheless, a strong belief that political rights should be confined to property-holders. Only two states, Georgia and Pennsylvania, opened the franchise to all taxpayers. And in most states there were higher property qualifications for holding office than for voting. In the eighteenth century it was assumed that a man without property had no reason to participate in government either by voting or by holding office. According to Locke the purpose of government was to protect property, so a man without any was thought to have little stake in society. Moreover, only property could free a man from the control of employers or landlords. Without property a man was not a free agent and could not be trusted with authority or even with a voice in the selection of those who were to wield it. Hence the concern already noted for the maintenance of a wide distribution of property. If America were to become like Europe, with a mass of property-less workers and peasants, liberty would fall with equality; and authority, concentrated in the hands of a few, would turn into tyranny.

Authority in the hands of the many, of the people, was the essential characteristic of a republic; and with independence colonial insistence on responsible representative government turned into a conscious pursuit of republicanism. Although nothing in the Declaration of Independence had precluded the possibility of monarchy, Americans took it for granted that the new states would be republics. After severing their ties with England, Connecticut and Rhode Island, which in effect were republics already, simply continued the governments defined by their old charters. In other colonies the provincial congress, which re-

---

Crèvecœur on the American

I wish I could be acquainted with the feelings and thoughts which must agitate the heart and present themselves to the mind of an enlightened Englishman, when he first lands on this continent.... If he travels through our rural districts he views not the hostile castle, and the haughty mansion, contrasted with the clay-built hut and miserable cabin, where cattle and men help to keep each other warm, and dwell in meanness, smoke, and indigence. A pleasing uniformity of decent competence appears throughout our habitations. The meanest of our log-houses is a dry and comfortable habitation. Lawyer or merchant are the fairest titles our towns afford; that of a farmer is the only appellation of the rural inhabitants of our country. It must take some time ere he can reconcile himself to our dictionary, which is but short in words of dignity, and names of honour.... We have no princes, for whom we toil, starve, and bleed: we are the most perfect society now existing in the world.

From Michel Guillaume Jean de Crèvecœur, ''What Is an American?'' *Letters from an American Farmer*, 1782.

placed the representative assembly (often with the same membership), acted without formal authority until independence was declared. Then, sooner or later, it drafted a written constitution establishing and defining a new government, usually similar in structure to the old one but more responsible to the people.

Since the colonial representative assembly (or lower house) had always been the branch of government most directly dependent on the people, the state constitutions gave the greatest powers to the lower houses of the new legislatures. In some states the lower house chose both the upper house and the governor. Only Pennsylvania, which had had a unicameral legislature since 1701, actually did without an upper house or a governor, but everywhere they had less authority than their colonial counterparts.

Determination that the government should be the servant of the people and not their master also prompted the inclusion of bills of rights in most of the state constitutions. The Virginia Bill of Rights began by asserting that "all men are by nature equally free and independent, and have certain inherent rights, of which, when they enter into a state of society, they cannot by any compact deprive or divest their posterity." It then enumerated the rights that lay beyond the reach of government, such as freedom of religion and of the press and the right to trial by jury.

In most states, after the provincial congress had drafted and approved a constitution, it went into effect without being submitted to a popular vote. But Massachusetts (the last state to adopt a constitution) elected a special convention to draft hers and submitted its work to direct vote by the people. Once it had been ratified in 1780, it could be changed only by another popularly elected convention called for that specific purpose. This was a step that other states had groped for but never quite reached. The purpose of writing out a constitution was to set limits to government by a fundamental law embodying the will of the people. British jurists had often maintained that the unwritten British constitution, consisting of traditions and customs, was superior to government, but custom and tradition had failed to protect the colonists from what they regarded as tyranny by the British government. They

wanted something in black and white by which to measure any departure by their own governments from the proper limits of authority. They began to get what they wanted when their provincial congresses wrote and adopted state constitutions. But keen minds soon noted a flaw in this procedure: as the town of Concord pointed out in 1776, a constitution adopted by a legislative body could be altered or abolished by the same body and thus would constitute no protection against legislative tyranny. The device of a special convention and popular ratification elevated the constitution above the legislature and made it easier for the other branches of government to nullify unconstitutional legislation. The courts, for example, could and would refuse to enforce any law that violated the constitution. The Massachusetts invention of the constitutional convention was so widely admired by other Americans that subsequent constitution-making in America followed the Massachusetts method.

Building a national government. The same passion for responsible government that resulted in written constitutions and constitutional conventions prevented for a long time the creation of an effective national government. Americans, like other men of the eighteenth century, believed that republican government was not adaptable to large areas. In a large republic the central legislature must inevitably sit so remote from most of its constituents that it would eventually escape their control and thus cease to be republican. On the other hand, a small republic could never survive in a world of aggressive large nations. There was only one way, it was thought, to overcome these difficulties: a number of small republics might join in a federation and exert their united power for specific purposes.

Americans had formed such a federation in 1774 in the Continental Congress, and after independence the Congress had continued to exercise governmental powers for the whole nation. It was composed of delegates (usually several from each state) appointed annually by the state legislatures. Each state had one vote, which was determined by the majority of its delegates (if they were evenly divided the state's vote was lost).

In the absence of a more effective central organization, Congress served a useful purpose. But it existed only by common consent, and from the beginning the members felt the need for a more binding union. As Americans joined against a common enemy and became aware of their shared principles and beliefs, their feeling of nationality grew stronger. Something more than an unstable succession of congresses was necessary to embody this sentiment and to demonstrate to other nations that the United States too was a nation and not merely a diplomatic alliance of thirteen small republics. Congress accordingly, in the intervals between dealing with the everyday problems of the war, often discussed the formation of a permanent national government. As early as July 12, 1776, a committee had brought in the draft of a constitution, but acceptance had foundered on how expenses and voting power should be apportioned among the states and on the old question of Western policy. This earliest proposal would have given considerable governmental authority to a national legislature; but as the state governments became more firmly entrenched, they grew increasingly reluctant

to surrender any part of their power to a central body.

On November 17, 1777, Congress finally agreed on a constitution to be presented to the state legislatures for approval or rejection. The Articles of Confederation provided for a congress like the existing one. Each state, whatever its size, was still to have only one vote, to be cast, as before, by delegates appointed by the state legislatures; each state (by taxing itself) was to contribute to the common expenses according to the value of its lands; none was to be deprived of its Western lands for the benefit of the United States; and each was to retain its "sovereignty, freedom and independence, and every power, jurisdiction, and right" not expressly delegated to Congress. Congress was permitted to decide on war or peace, appoint military and naval officers, requisition the states for men and money, send and receive ambassadors, enter into treaties and alliances, establish a post office, coin money, borrow money or issue paper money on the credit of the United States, fix weights and measures, regulate Indian affairs, and settle disputes between states.

Although the states found much to object to in the Articles of Confederation, the need to give permanent form to the union moved all but Maryland to accept it by 1779. Maryland's refusal, though probably prompted by narrow, partisan, and pecuniary motives, forced the settlement of a problem that might have wrecked the union — the problem of Western lands.

The West had always been a divisive force, as Bacon's Rebellion, the failure of the Albany Congress, and the Regulator movement all testified. Even more serious trouble lay ahead. Colonial assemblies from Pennsylvania southward had failed to extend full representation to their Western regions as population increased there. Pennsylvania remedied the inequality in her state constitution, but Virginia and the Carolinas did not, and the result was Western resentment against the Eastern-dominated state governments.

Concurrent with these internal disputes the state governments quarreled with one another about the West. The Revolution had dissolved their ties to England but not their territorial boundaries, which had been fixed by royal charters. By their charters, Georgia, the Caro-

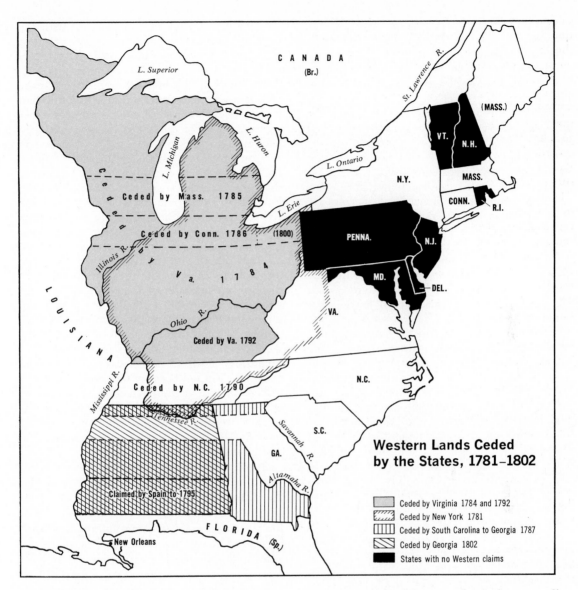

**Western Lands Ceded
by the States, 1781–1802**

- Ceded by Virginia 1784 and 1792
- Ceded by New York 1781
- Ceded by South Carolina to Georgia 1787
- Ceded by Georgia 1802
- States with no Western claims

linas, Virginia, Connecticut, and Massachusetts extended to the Pacific Ocean, while Maryland, Delaware, Pennsylvania, New Jersey, and Rhode Island were limited to a few hundred miles on the seacoast. The "landless" states wanted Congress to take control of unoccupied Western lands and restrict the western boundaries of the "landed" states. The landed states resisted any such proposal and squabbled with one another over their conflicting charters. Virginia, whose charter was the oldest, could claim most of the West all to herself. The people of every state, when they

looked west, found reason for jealousy or distrust of their neighbors.

The problem was aggravated by land speculation. Before the war, speculators from Pennsylvania, Maryland, and New Jersey (all landless states) had purchased land from the Indians and sought authorization from the king to establish a new colony (Vandalia) in the Ohio Valley. Though bitterly opposed by Virginia's Ohio Company, they had been on the verge of success when the Revolution upset their plans. Now they argued that Congress had inherited the king's authority over all unoccupied lands;

and, supported by their state governments, they pressed Congress to recognize their claims. The landed states had fought them off by including in the Articles of Confederation a guarantee that no state should be deprived of territory for the benefit of the United States. But Maryland stubbornly refused to approve the articles as long as the proposed union lacked control over Western lands. Without her the union was stalled, for it was not to go into effect until unanimously approved.

Maryland could produce better arguments than the mere greed of her land-speculators. The landed states, she pointed out, would be able to command such an abundant source of revenue by selling their Western lands that their citizens would pay few or no taxes. People from the landless states would consequently move to the landed ones. Maryland, next door to the leviathan Virginia, would be depopulated.

In Virginia the sentiment for union was strong, and some patriots wanted to give up the state's Western territory, which they thought was too large for a single republican government anyhow. Rather than jeopardize republicanism in Virginia, they preferred to see new states formed in the West and joined to the old ones by the Articles of Confederation. Thomas Jefferson accordingly led Virginia (on January 2, 1781) to offer Congress her claims to all lands north of the Ohio. The transfer was contingent on a number of conditions that in effect canceled speculative claims to the region and required that the land be divided into "distinct republican States," which should ultimately be admitted to the union on equal terms with the old ones. When Virginia's cession was made known, Maryland capitulated (though the speculators still tried to block her) and approved the Articles of Confederation in February 1781. New York had already ceded her shadowy Western claims, and the other landed states eventually followed the example that she and Virginia had set (Georgia held out until 1802).

Congress under the Confederation. In the Articles of Confederation the American people got what most of them at that time wanted. Having just suffered from the power of a distant British government, they were wary of allowing much authority to their own central government. They charged Congress with the responsibility for making decisions about a multitude of their common concerns, but they neglected to give it the powers to carry its decisions into effect. It could pass resolutions, make recommendations, enact ordinances; but it had no courts, no way of enforcing its orders either on individuals or on states. It could not even levy taxes to pay its own expenses but had to rely on the several states to furnish its funds. In fact Congress was allowed less authority than the colonists had once acknowledged in Parliament: Congress did not even have the right to regulate trade. The disadvantages of such a powerless central government soon became apparent.

After the coming of peace diminished the urgency of united action, the states became increasingly enamored of their own power and increasingly casual, even contemptuous, in their relations with Congress, ignoring its resolutions, refusing to fill its requisitions for funds, sending inferior men to represent them or sometimes none at all. Congress was unable to cope with the situation because the Articles of Confederation had provided it with no means to enforce obedience. The weakness of the national government made the years from 1783 to 1789, in the phrase of one historian, the "Critical Period" of American history.

A man elected to Congress during these years might arrive at the meeting place on the appointed day and find a dozen or more delegates like himself eager to proceed to business. But the Articles of Confederation required that each state be represented by at least two delegates and that the representatives of at least seven states be present to make a quorum. Unless more than seven states were represented, every decision had to be unanimous; and the assent of nine states was necessary in most matters having to do with war and peace (including treaties) and with appropriating money. Because the states were often slow about appointing delegates and the delegates themselves slow in taking up their duties, the first arrivals at a session sometimes had to wait several weeks before enough members were present to transact business. Even after a session was organized, it led a precarious existence; for if one or two delegates fell sick, the rest might have to twiddle their thumbs until more arrived or the sick got well.

Each delegate was elected for a one-year term and was prohibited from serving for more than three years in six. As a result, the membership of Congress was constantly shifting. The government was further handicapped by the failure of the Articles of Confederation to provide a regular executive department. Congress exercised executive powers through special commissions and committees and achieved a degree of continuity by appointing three secretaries to manage crucial executive matters. Benjamin Lincoln, the first Secretary of War, served until 1783. After his resignation the office was vacant until Henry Knox was appointed in 1785. Knox served as long as the Articles of Confederation lasted. Robert Morris, the Superintendent of Finance, stayed until 1784; but then his office reverted to a committee of Congress. Robert Livingston, the first Secretary for Foreign Affairs, lasted less than two years; after his resignation the office was vacant until John Jay was appointed in 1784. Jay retained the office until 1789.

These officers struggled to give the United States the appearance of a government. But Congress, pursuing its intermittent existence, belied the appearance. Even when it could scrape together a quorum it had no permanent headquarters or capitol. A mutiny in the Philadelphia barracks frightened it out of that city in 1783, and thereafter the delegates wandered from Princeton to Annapolis to Trenton to New York — talking endlessly about where they should settle permanently. Shortly after they began their travels, Oliver Ellsworth, a congressman from Connecticut, observed dryly, "It will soon be of very little consequence where Congress go, if they are not made respectable as well as responsible, which can never be done without giving them a power to perform engagements as well as make them." Congress, in short, had responsibility without power. It could recommend endlessly but no one either inside or outside the United States paid much attention to what it recommended.

The impotence of Congress made the United States a beggar in the eyes of the world. During the Revolution, Congress had boldly capitalized on popular enthusiasm for the cause of independence by printing paper money, but the money had become worthless before the war's end. Congress had also begged money and supplies from France, but after the peace France preferred to keep her ally poor and humble. Dutch bankers, with more vision than many Americans, did continue to lend. But when Congress turned to the states for funds or for the power to levy a 5 per cent tariff on imports, the states turned the beggar down. The power to levy tariffs would have required the unanimous approval of the states, and each time it was proposed (in 1781 and again in 1783) at least one state refused; and the others insisted on conditions that would have made the power meaningless anyhow.

The one area in which the United States enjoyed at least the appearance of power was the wilderness north of the Ohio River, a region thinly populated by squatters, Indians, and Frenchmen. When Virginia offered to cede the area in 1781, Congress had been prevented from taking any formal action to accept it because of pressure from speculators who objected to the terms attached to the cession. Early in 1784, when Virginia renewed the offer, Congress was stalled for lack of a quorum. But by March 1 enough members were present to act favorably, and the United States gained formal authority over the Northwest.

Now Congress might begin to raise the funds it needed by selling land in the newly acquired territory. On April 23 the delegates passed an ordinance, drafted by Thomas Jefferson, that fulfilled the terms of Virginia's cession. It divided the territory into states, each of which was to be admitted into the Union on equal terms with the existing states as soon as its free population equaled any of theirs. Until then the inhabitants could govern themselves according to the constitution and laws of any of the existing states.

To prepare for the sale of lands to individuals, Congress passed an ordinance in 1785 providing that the Northwest be surveyed into townships six miles square along lines running east-west and north-south. Each township was divided into thirty-six lots one mile square (640 acres). A lot (later called a section) was the smallest unit that could be purchased, and neither a township nor a lot was to be sold for less than a dollar an acre in cash. To speed up the transformation of the national domain into

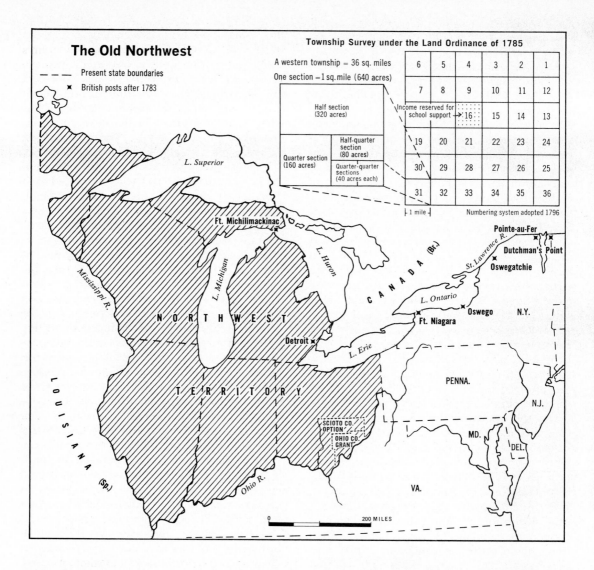

The Old Northwest

- – – – Present state boundaries
- × British posts after 1783

Township Survey under the Land Ordinance of 1785

A western township = 36 sq. miles
One section = 1 sq. mile (640 acres)

Half section (320 acres)		Quarter section (160 acres)	Half-quarter section (80 acres)
			Quarter-quarter sections (40 acres each)

6	5	4	3	2	1
7	8	9	10	11	12
18	17	16	15	14	13
19	20	21	22	23	24
30	29	28	27	26	25
31	32	33	34	35	36

Income reserved for school support → 16

|← 1 mile →| Numbering system adopted 1796

L. Superior

Ft. Michilimackinac

L. Michigan

L. Huron

CANADA (Br.)

St. Lawrence R.

Pointe-au-Fer
Dutchman's Point
Oswegatchie

L. Ontario

Oswego

N.Y.

Mississippi R.

NORTHWEST

Detroit

Ft. Niagara

L. Erie

PENNA.

N.J.

LOUISIANA (Sp.)

TERRITORY

SCIOTO CO. OPTION
OHIO CO. GRANT

MD.

DEL.

VA.

Ohio R.

0   200 MILES

hard cash, land offices were to be established in all the states.

Surveying and the settlement of Indian claims proceeded slowly. Before the lands were ready for public sale, a group of ambitious and not very scrupulous speculators from New England came to Congress with a proposition. Calling themselves, like an earlier group, the Ohio Company, they offered to buy a million and a half acres, for which they would pay in currency so badly depreciated that the price amounted to less than 10 cents an acre in specie. Presumptuous as the offer was, the United States needed the money desperately, and Congress decided to accept it. The Ohio

Company also agreed to take an option on 5 million additional acres, to be turned over to a subsidiary company known as the Scioto Company. By no coincidence, this company included several congressmen.

To oblige the Ohio Company, Congress passed a new ordinance for governing the Northwest. Jefferson's ordinance of 1784 had never gone into operation, because the area as yet contained no authorized settlers. It did, however, contain many squatters who had helped themselves to public lands and stoutly resisted eviction. Because of the difficulty anticipated in establishing property rights against squatters, and because of the frontier's reputation for violence and disorder, many Easterners believed that congressional rule would be more appropriate than self-government during the initial years of settlement. Accordingly, the Northwest Ordinance of 1787 provided for a period during which a governor, a secretary, and a court of three judges, all appointed by Congress, would hold full powers. Once the population had reached five thousand free adult males, a representative legislature would be established, but none of its actions would be valid without the approval of the governor, who would still be appointed by Congress. The legislature could send a representative to Congress, but he would have no vote. The whole area was to be divided into not fewer than three or more than five territories, each of which would be admitted to the Union on equal terms with the existing states when it attained a population of sixty thousand. Slavery was forbidden throughout the area; no person was to be "molested" for his religious beliefs or mode of worship; and "schools and the means of education" were to be encouraged. Though the ordinance did not say how the encouragement was to be effected, the Land Ordinance of 1785 had already reserved one lot in each township "for the maintenance of public schools."

The Northwest Ordinance, if less liberal than the one drafted by Jefferson, nevertheless established for the United States a Western policy that embodied the most cherished American principles. Though the ordinance applied to only a part of the West, it set a precedent that guided the territorial expansion of the nation until the end of the nineteenth century.

National humiliation. One serious obstacle stood in the way of Congress' noble aspirations for the American West: the United States held only a tenuous grip on the area. England had never completely evacuated the Northwest, nor had Spain recognized American possession of any territory south of the Ohio. As the weakness and poverty of the new nation grew more apparent, European statesmen intrigued to push its western boundary back to the Appalachians.

When England made peace in 1783, she was not fully persuaded — nor was the rest of Europe — that the United States would last. While the king officially proclaimed the treaty and commanded his subjects to comply with it, his ministers sent secret orders to the governor-general of Canada to retain Britain's trading posts and military garrisons in the Northwest. The United States, with its own armies disbanded and the French forces gone, was in no position to compel the British to withdraw. To excuse their continued occupation of the posts, the British charged that the Americans had violated the treaty.

Again the weakness of the national government was to blame. The treaty required that neither side make laws impeding the collection of private debts contracted before the war, and it required that Congress "earnestly recommend" to the states the restoration of confiscated loyalist property. Congress did recommend the restitution, and the fact that the states did not follow the recommendation was not technically a violation of the treaty. But when some states passed laws impeding the collection of British debts, they violated the treaty as surely as England did in keeping troops on American territory. Congress was as helpless to prevent one violation as the other. It sent John Adams to England as American minister; and he protested the British garrisons with characteristic Adams vigor, but in vain, for England knew that no American troops stood behind him.

England showed her contempt for the government of her former colonies by failing to establish a legation in the United States to match the American legation in London. More ominously she dickered with the influential Allen brothers, Ethan and Levi, for help in acquiring Vermont. Claimed by both New Hampshire and New York, Vermont had asserted its independence of both and applied for statehood. Congress was reluctant to antagonize either claimant by admitting Vermont into the Union, and there was danger that the Vermonters might attach themselves to Canada (Vermont was not admitted until 1791).

In the Southwest, Spain was grasping for the area that later became the states of Kentucky and Tennessee. Americans were moving into it at such a rate that by 1790 it contained more than a hundred thousand of them, but their presence was hardly a guarantee of permanent American possession. Barred by the mountains from trade with the East, the settlers relied on the Mississippi River to float their produce to market at New Orleans. New Orleans belonged to Spain, and so did the lower Mississippi. The Spaniards had gained Louisiana in 1763, the Floridas in 1783; and they maintained forts on the west bank of the Mississippi as far north as St. Louis, on the east bank as far as the present site of Memphis. Anyone who wanted to use the river had to do business with Spain.

Although commercial exports from the Southwest were still meager, everyone in the region was expecting future prosperity through the Mississippi trade. Spain was well aware of that expectation. In 1784 she closed the river to navigation by Americans and waited for the settlers to abandon their feeble Congress for the solid commercial advantage of Spanish citizenship. For a time it seemed that the settlers might do just that, for they were far from pleased with the way Eastern Americans were treating them. In 1772, by the Watauga Compact, pioneers in the Tennessee area had formed a government of their own, which lasted until 1776, when North Carolina organized them into Washington County. In 1784, after her land-speculators had established claims to the most valuable land, North Carolina ceded the region to Congress in order to avoid the expense of protecting it from the Indians. The next year she changed her mind and decided to take it back. Meanwhile, the settlers had resumed their own government as the independent state of Franklin and had asked to be admitted to the Union. When Congress failed to act on their request and North Carolina tried to regain possession, many settlers grew disgusted and began to look favorably toward Spain. In Kentucky, the Western region of Virginia, there was a similar secessionist movement, and a similar flirtation with Spain threatened to disrupt the Union.

As the Southwest began to draw away from the United States, Spain in 1785 sent Don Diego de Gardoqui to wring from Congress a formal recognition of her exclusive control over the Mississippi. Congress instructed its Secretary of Foreign Affairs, John Jay, to insist in his negotiations with Gardoqui on the right of Americans to navigate the Mississippi through Spanish territory to its mouth. This was a subject about which the two men had tilted inconclusively once before, during the Revolution,

when Jay had gone to Spain in search of assistance in the war against England. Jay now found Gardoqui as adamant as ever about refusing to recognize an American right of navigation but willing to make other concessions. The Spaniards would agree to recognize American territorial rights as far south as the old border of British West Florida and as far west as the Mississippi and to give American merchants a few trading privileges in Spain. In return, he asked only that the United States agree to give up navigation of the Mississippi for twenty-five years. The offer was attractive to Easterners. Jay was ready to accept, and so were a majority in Congress. But ratification of a treaty required the approval of nine states, and the five Southern states would not agree to it. Now Gardoqui's shrewdness became apparent; for though the treaty failed, Spain still gained an advantage: the willingness of the Northern states to give up the Mississippi further weakened the Southwest's attachment to the Union.

While Gardoqui led Jay into alienating the Westerners, the Spanish governor of Louisiana, Esteban Rodríguez Miró, was wooing them with bribes and privileges. General James Wilkinson, a veteran of the Revolutionary War and a consummate double-dealer, took a trip to New Orleans in 1787. While there, he took a secret oath of allegiance to Spain in return for trading concessions. The following year he accepted a Spanish pension, with the understanding that he would lead his neighbors in the Tennessee region to repudiate the United States. Wilkinson was not the only Southwestern traitor. Daniel Boone, James Robertson, and John Sevier all accepted Spanish gold. Instead of doing what they were paid to do, however, they cheerfully deceived both sides while they waited to see what was going to happen. If, as seemed likely, the United States should break up, they were ready to learn Spanish.

The United States had troubles even in the Mediterranean. For years European countries had been protecting their Mediterranean shipping from pirates by paying an annual tribute to the rulers of Morocco, Algiers, Tripoli, and Tunis. As long as American ships carried the British flag, they were safe; but after 1776, when they began to fly the Stars and Stripes, pirates swarmed out upon them. The captured American captains and crews were put on the auction block and sold as slaves. Congress bought protection from Morocco in 1787 but had neither money nor guns to stop the other African pirates.

Nor were pirates the only difficulty to beset American trade. The whole American economy was in a precarious position. With the coming of peace, American merchants had sensed a huge demand for the British dry goods and hardware to which American consumers had been accustomed before the war. The merchants placed their orders, and warehouses and stores were soon bulging, with the British extending liberal credits. The American merchants in turn extended credit to retailers and consumers, and the country indulged itself in a buying spree. Only when it came time to pay the bills did the Americans discover their situation.

The colonial economy had been a complex one, in which Americans paid for British imports by carrying their own and other people's goods to market in various ports throughout the world, but mostly within the empire. Now they were no longer a part of the empire, and Britain closed her West Indian ports to American vessels. Prices of American produce dropped, merchants found themselves cut off from usual channels of trade, and depression settled over the land — while British merchants called for payment.

Americans blamed themselves and their merchants. Having won their political independence, they had promptly mortgaged it by extravagant purchases from their old masters. It seemed that the British, by craftily extending liberal credits and closing their ports to Americans, had rewon economically the position of dominance that they had lost politically. Congress instructed John Adams to ask England for a commercial treaty, but he was no more successful in this than in pressing for the evacuation of British garrisons in the Northwest.

There were loud demands for retaliation against the British restrictions on American trade, and some states passed laws to discourage imports. But such partial legislation by single states only added to the difficulties by injuring the economies of sister states. As John

Sullivan confessed concerning the New Hampshire law, "It was a blow aimed at Britain but wounds us and our friends." What was needed was an overall national regulation of commerce, not simply to discourage unnecessary imports, but to create a balanced economy in which manufacturing, agriculture, and commerce would all find their place. Only in this way could the United States become economically as well as politically independent and insure herself against domination by Britain or any other nation. But the American Congress, with no power to regulate commerce, could not even begin to direct the economy toward such a goal.

THE CRISIS OF AMERICAN NATIONALITY

Many Americans found the impotence of the national government intolerable. The Revolution had widened their vision beyond the affairs of town or county or colony and had taught them to think, as Alexander Hamilton put it, "continentally." They knew that the only way to solve the difficulties of the United States was to strengthen the national government — they had known it before the ink was dry on the Articles of Confederation. Now, as the weakness of the government became more and more embarrassing, they spoke out ever more loudly.

Thinking continentally. The Americans had had plenty of practice in making and breaking governments. Their usual method had been to call an extralegal convention — like the Stamp Act Congress or the Continental Congress or the provincial congresses that replaced the royal governments. Conventions were also summoned whenever the people of a state or region wanted to achieve a public purpose for which their regular government had proved inadequate. Several interstate conventions had met during the war in an effort to regulate prices. Connecticut held a convention in 1783 to protest the founding of the Society of the Cincinnati and the granting of extra pay to army officers. And, as we have seen, Massachusetts called a convention to draft a state constitution.

It was only natural, then, for men who had begun to think "continentally" to turn to a convention for the purpose of strengthening the continental government. As early as 1784 they had talked of it, but at that time public sentiment was overwhelmingly against it. The opposition did not arise from a deficiency of national patriotism or from too much local patriotism. Nationalism, which has proved the most lively — and deadly — force in the modern world, attached itself in America to the Union rather than to the states. Thomas Paine, in his first publication after the peace, wrote: "I ever feel myself hurt when I hear the Union, the great palladium of our liberty and safety, the least irreverently spoken of. . . . Our citizenship in the United States is our national character. Our citizenship in any particular state is only our local distinction."

This sentiment was echoed by statesmen, poets, painters, and schoolmasters. George Washington, the nation's hero, was a great Virginian but a greater American. "We are known by no other character among nations," he declared in 1783, "than as the United States." Connecticut during the 1780's produced a host of brilliant young men who celebrated in literature and art not their own state but America. John Trumbull depicted the great events of the American Revolution in a series of historical paintings. Joel Barlow attempted an American epic in *The Vision of Columbus*. Noah Webster wrote schoolbooks designed to teach American English. Jedidiah Morse published an *American Geography*. And Ezra Stiles, the president of Yale, preached of *The United States Elevated to Glory and Honor*. Some authors, to be sure, wrote the history of their own states (Jefferson, for example, published his *Notes on the State of Virginia* in 1785), but the local pride they exhibited was different in kind from the national pride that was evident throughout the Union.

Yet however proud of their country's past and confident of its future, Americans needed leadership and a government capable of elevating the United States to the glory and honor they wanted for it. National policy was drifting, and continental-minded men warned that the nation faced collapse or conquest if its government was not strengthened. But their appeals met stout resistance from people who feared that a stronger government might become aristocratic or tyrannical; it might threaten the principles that had brought the Union into being — the principles of equality and of responsible, republican government. In 1785, for example, when the legislature of Massachusetts proposed a general convention to strengthen the national government, her delegates in Congress objected. Would-be aristocrats, they argued, would use such a convention to establish a government based on special privilege, loaded with lucrative positions for themselves, and bolstered by a standing army.

Because of such sentiments on the part of honest and patriotic men, a national constitutional convention, though often talked of, had failed to materialize. By 1786, however, Americans had become so impatient with British trade restrictions, conflicting state commercial laws, and national economic helplessness that they arranged for an interstate meeting at Annapolis, Maryland, to consider the extension of national authority to the regulation of commerce. The first delegates to arrive at Annapolis told one another that the contemplated revision of the national government was insufficient; those from New Jersey had even been instructed to ask for a general overhaul of the Articles of Confederation. When representatives from five states had convened, though more were on the way, they drew up a proposal to Congress and the several states and dissolved the convention. What they proposed was another convention the next year at Philadelphia for the larger purpose of making "the constitution of the Federal Government adequate to the exigencies of the Union."

The message reached the states along with some alarming news from Massachusetts. In the summer of 1786 the citizens in the economically depressed western part of the state, laboring under a heavy burden of debt, had called a number of local conventions to demand changes in the state government: they objected to the state senate (the upper house of the legislature) as a needless expense and an aristocratic influence; they objected to the heavy taxation of land; and they objected to the high fees charged by lawyers and county courts. After the conventions had voiced their protests and adjourned, mobs prevented the county courts from sitting and thus put an end to the collection of debts. Then, during the winter of 1786–87, some two thousand Western farmers rose in armed rebellion under the leadership of Daniel Shays, a veteran of the Revolutionary War.

Though Shays' Rebellion was easily quelled by the loyal militia of Massachusetts, it alarmed Americans in every part of the United States. Other states too had depressed areas and discontented debtors; it was widely feared that the whole country might be teetering on the edge of anarchy. This might be only the beginning of a series of uprisings to intimidate the courts and state legislatures everywhere. One incident in the rebellion dramatically emphasized the weakness of the national government: a United States arsenal at Springfield had been threatened by the rebels, and there was no United States army to protect it or to come to the aid of the militia had they been unable to stop the rebellion.

By threatening law and order, Shays' Rebellion threatened property: the closing of the courts in western Massachusetts had halted mortgage foreclosures and deprived creditors of property owed to them. Property was also endangered from other directions. In several states, the coming of peace had brought no end to the flood of paper money that inflated values and defrauded creditors. Rhode Island made it illegal for a man to refuse the state's worthless paper money as payment for debts owed him.

Even before Shays' Rebellion people were saying that something must be done about this undermining of property rights. It would be a mockery of the national purpose if Americans who had undertaken a revolution to defend property, should themselves destroy property through irresponsible government. After the shock of Shays' Rebellion every state but Rhode Island agreed to send delegates to Philadelphia to revise the Articles of Confederation.

The great convention. The United States in the Revolutionary period produced six men of indisputable greatness: Franklin, Washington, Jefferson, Madison, Hamilton, and John Adams. Four of them — Franklin, Washington, Madison, and Hamilton — were among the fifty-five delegates sent by the state governments to the convention that met in Philadelphia from May 25 to September 17, 1787. Jefferson and Adams would doubtless have been there too if they had not been representing the United States in Europe, for the convention was an extraordinary assemblage of talent. The delegates had a wealth of experience and tradition to draw upon: the heritage of British political and constitutional ideas stretching back to Magna Carta and beyond; the experience of five generations of colonists in representative assemblies, town meetings, and county courts; the searching debates about authority that preceded the Declaration of Independence; the drafting of state constitutions; the running of state governments and of a rudimentary national government. In no period of American history could a group have been gathered with more sophistication in political thought or with more practical experience in the construction and reconstruction of governments.

Almost without exception the delegates were men who thought continentally; and they were eager for a central government that would preserve and embody the national feeling that had grown out of the Revolution, a government that would be respected at home and abroad. The only way to achieve that end, they believed, was to give the central government more authority than Congress had been allowed. It had to be able to levy taxes so that it could support itself and not be starved into impotence, so that it could raise the armies and build the navy that might one day be needed to defend the independence so dearly won. It had to be able to regulate commerce so as to bargain effectively with foreign nations. It had to offer better protection to private property than the existing national or state governments did. And it had to have coercive powers to enforce its decrees.

The delegates, while agreeing on these objectives, realized that two obstacles stood in the way of attaining them. The first was the fear of the American people that a national government, if given enough power to do its job, would quickly seize more than enough, that it would fall into the hands of a select group of wealthy and clever men who would use it to their own advantage and to the disadvantage of ordinary men. The American people would not accept an effective central government unless they could be sure of controlling it.

The second obstacle was rivalry among the states. Each state feared that a strong national government might give unfair advantage to the others. For example, it might levy taxes that would injure one state and benefit another. Fortunately quarrels over the West were momentarily at a minimum because of Virginia's renunciation of claims to the Northwest and because the status of future states in the territory was determined by Congress (in the Northwest Ordinance) while the convention was sitting. The convention itself, after preliminary debates, skirted the knotty question of whether new states should be equal to old and decided simply that "New States may be admitted by the Congress into this Union."

But another form of state rivalry could not be bypassed and threatened to deadlock the convention: in a national government composed of states, how was representation to be apportioned? Under the Articles of Confederation, each state, no matter what its size, had one vote in Congress (this manner of voting was also followed in the convention). Such an arrangement gave undue advantage to the citizens of small states: 68,000 Rhode Islanders had the same influence on decisions as 747,000 Virginians. The large states would not be satisfied with any national government in which their influence was not at least approximately commensurate with their size. But the small states believed that unless they retained an equal vote the large states would be able to advance their own interests at the expense of the small states.

When the convention opened, Edmund Randolph of Virginia presented a plan, drafted by his colleague James Madison, that was designed to overcome both the fears of the people and the fears of the states. Madison, who at thirty-six was the most astute political thinker of his day, perceived that what the small states took for a problem was partly an illusion: the people of a small state did not necessarily have different interests from those of a large state. There was a serious, though not irreconcilable, difference between the economic interests of the Southern states and the Northern, but there was no serious difference between the interests, say of the people in Pennsylvania and those in Delaware. Madison proposed, therefore, to rest the government on the people rather than on the state governments and to make representation in the national government proportionate to population.

To keep the government from seizing more power than it was assigned, Madison proposed to divide it into different branches that would check and balance one another: a two-house legislature, an independent executive, and an independent judiciary. Each would have specific functions and would see to it that the others did not overstep their bounds. Thus the most distant constituent in America would have guardians within the government itself watching to make sure that it did not get out of hand. The Americans had already endorsed the principle of separation of powers in their state governments, but their discussions of national government had usually revolved around the granting of further powers to the existing unicameral Congress. Only a few, like Jefferson and John Jay, had seen the need for separation of powers in the national government itself; but as soon as Madison made the proposal, its advantages were obvious, and many of the fears about the government's escaping control were dispelled. Pierce Butler, a delegate for South Carolina, said that "he had opposed the grant of powers to Congress heretofore, because the whole power was vested in one body. The proposed distribution of the powers into different bodies changed the case, and would induce him to go great lengths."

The delegates spent two weeks revising Madison's plan and working out its details, without altering its basic structure. They decided, among other things, that members of the lower house of the legislature should be popularly elected and those of the upper house appointed by the state legislatures. And they agreed that representation in both houses should be according to population. Then on June 15 William Paterson of New Jersey suddenly came up with a new plan calling for a continuation of the existing unicameral Congress with increased powers, but with each state retaining its equal vote. Paterson and his supporters would allow Congress the power to tax, to regulate trade, and to enforce its own decrees, but they wanted the national government to remain what it had been, an assembly of the states, not of the people, its members chosen by the state governments, not by popular election. Paterson's plan was rejected, but the small-state delegations had rallied to it and finally threatened to bolt the convention unless each state was given an equal vote in at least one house of the national legislature. To pacify them, the other members of the convention agreed on July 16 that all the states would have equal representation in the upper house, but to this concession they attached several provisions: representation in the lower house and direct taxation would be apportioned according to population, with five slaves to be considered the equivalent of three free men; all bills for raising or spending money would originate in the lower house; a census would be taken every ten years. The last two provisions had not been discussed earlier, but the convention had agreed on the others before the Paterson plan was introduced.

Once they had made this Great Compromise (which was actually a concession to the illusions of the small states) there was no longer any serious danger that the delegates would fail in their attempt to strengthen the national government. They had started out in substantial agreement about what needed to be done, and they had overcome, in large measure at least, both the rivalry of the states and the fear of tyranny. They still argued about many things: an executive (one or more? elected by the people, by Congress, or by the state legislatures? elected how often?), slavery, trade duties, the ratio of representation, terms of office, and more. But these were details, and, within three and a half months of assembling, the convention had finished drafting the new constitution.

The Constitution provided for a national government with authority to collect taxes, make treaties with foreign countries, maintain an army and a navy, coin and borrow money, regulate commerce among the states and with foreign nations, and make any laws necessary to carry its powers into execution. The United States Constitution and all the treaties and laws made under it were to be the supreme law of the land, superior to state laws and binding on state courts. Moreover, the federal government would have its own executive and its own courts to enforce its treaties, Constitution, and laws, and to settle disputes between states. As a last resort it could call on the militia for help.

The national legislature, or Congress, was to consist of an upper house, or Senate, and a House of Representatives. Each state was to have two senators, both appointed by the state legislature for six-year terms, and one representative for every thirty thousand persons, to be popularly elected for a two-year term by the same persons who were qualified to vote for members of "the most numerous branch of the State Legislature." The executive, known as the President, was to be elected every four years by an electoral "college" to which each state might appoint (in any way its legislature prescribed) as many members as the total of its representatives and senators in Congress. It was intended, of course, that the members of this body should exercise their own discretion in selecting the best man in the country. The man who received the second largest number of votes became the Vice-President, who was to preside over the Senate.

The Constitution hedged both the federal and the state governments with specific prohibitions. To protect private property, it forbade the state governments to pass laws impairing the obligation of contracts, or to coin money, issue paper money, or make anything but gold and silver legal tender in payment of debts. To prevent the states from encroaching on the sphere of the federal government, it forbade them to make treaties, levy import or export duties, or engage in war unless actually invaded. Conversely the states were protected by clauses prohibiting the federal government from levying direct taxes except in proportion to population, from levying export taxes at all (a protection for the tobacco- and rice-exporters of the South), and from restricting immigration "or Importation of such Persons as any of the States now existing shall think proper to admit" before the year 1808 (a protection for the slave trade until that time). Republicanism and individual rights were protected by clauses forbidding either the states or the federal government to grant titles of nobility, or to pass bills of attainder or ex post facto laws. And the federal government could not make any religious test a qualification for public office or suspend the writ of habeas corpus "unless when in Cases of Rebellion or Invasion the public Safety may require it."

Apart from these prohibitions, the Constitution did not contain any guarantee of individual rights such as freedom of speech or religion or trial by jury. In the last days of the convention Elbridge Gerry of Massachusetts

Something must be done to preserve your liberty and mine. The Confederation, this same despised government, merits, in my opinion, the highest encomium. It carried us through a long and dangerous war; it rendered us victorious in that bloody conflict with a powerful nation; it has secured us a territory greater than any European monarch possesses: and shall a government which has been thus strong and vigorous, be accused of imbecility, and abandoned for want of energy?...

When the American spirit was in its youth, the language of America was different: liberty, sir, was then the primary object.... We drew the spirit of liberty from our British ancestors: by that spirit we have triumphed over every difficulty. But now, sir, the American spirit, assisted by the ropes and chains of consolidation, is about to convert this country into a powerful and mighty empire. If you make the citizens of this country agree to become the subjects of one great consolidated empire of America, your government will not have sufficient energy to keep them together. Such a government is incompatible with the genius of republicanism.

From Patrick Henry, Speech at the Virginia Ratifying Convention, 1788.

and George Mason of Virginia proposed that this omission be corrected, but their colleagues rejected the suggestion as unnecessary on the grounds that the Constitution defined and limited the powers of the national government to specified actions and that the state constitutions already contained bills of rights. But in case experience should prove this or any other of their decisions to be unwise, the convention provided a means of correction: the Constitution could be amended if two-thirds of both houses of Congress and three-fourths of the state legislatures agreed. The convention adjourned on September 17, after sending a copy of its work to Congress for transmission to the states.

Ratification. The constitution drafted at Philadelphia was the greatest creative triumph of the Experimental Period, and it showed how much its authors had learned during those experimental years. After the war the initial reaction against monarchy and aristocracy had led Americans to create state governments with feeble executives and ineffective upper houses; the new Constitution proposed a powerful executive and a Senate equal in power to the House of Representatives. The Articles of Confederation had created a national government controlled by the state governments and having no direct relation to the individual citizen; the new Constitution proposed a national government independent of the state governments, with a House of Representatives elected directly by the people of the United States and with federal courts acting directly on them. The Articles of Confederation had placed the national government in the hands of a single congress of delegates and had provided it with little authority; the new Constitution split up the national government to prevent abuses and gave it real authority.

The members of the Philadelphia Convention had been empowered only to revise the Articles of Confederation. Actually, they had drawn up a completely new government to take the place of the debating society that Congress had become. Knowing that their ambitious plan would meet opposition, and unwilling to have it defeated by the stubbornness of a few states, the delegates boldly proposed that as soon as nine states had accepted the new Constitution it should go into effect among those nine (revisions of the Articles of Confederation required unanimous approval). The convention also proposed the revolutionary technique of bypassing the state legislatures, where power-hungry state politicians and pressure groups might exert an influence as pernicious as the speculators had exerted against ratification of the Articles of Confederation. In each state the people would elect a special convention to judge the new constitution. The state government would issue the call for the ratifying convention but would have no part in accepting or rejecting the Constitution. The new national government, if adopted, would thus be authorized directly by the people; its power would derive from them.

The prestige of its authors, especially Washington and Franklin, as well as its intrinsic merits assured the Constitution a hearing. But its adoption was not at all certain. Several members of the convention, including the influential Edmund Randolph, had refused to sign the completed document. When it reached Congress, Richard Henry Lee took an immediate dislike to it. Why, he asked, should Congress approve its own dissolution? Why should nine states be allowed to withdraw from the Confederation to form a new and dangerously powerful government? Before transmitting the document to the states, Lee proposed at least the insertion of a bill of rights.

Lee's proposal was defeated by what he termed "a coalition of monarchy men, military men, aristocrats and drones whose noise, impudence and zeal exceeds all belief." When the Constitution reached the American people, many reacted as Lee had. But in every state the legislature eventually, if sometimes reluctantly, issued the necessary call for a popular ratifying convention.

The opponents of the Constitution were moved less by a desire to perpetuate the superiority of the state governments than by the old fear that a strong national government would escape from popular control and become oppressive. The system of checks and balances, they felt, was not adequate insurance against tyranny. The House of Representatives was too small to represent so many people. And the failure to include a bill of rights seemed an ominous indication of the direction the national government would take. Madison had argued at the convention, and now wrote in the newspapers, to persuade people that there were no grounds for the long-accepted notion that a large republic would fall into tyranny. In a large republic there would be so many different groups with such varied and opposing interests that they would be unable to submerge their differences and combine into a tyrannical majority. The danger of a tyrannical coalition was far greater in a small republic, Madison pointed out, because of the fewer divergent interests and the greater ease of communication.

The supporters of the Constitution were generally more aggressive than their opponents, and sometimes their tactics were unworthy of their cause. In Pennsylvania they pushed through the call for a convention after the legislature had voted to adjourn; they rounded up a quorum only by forcibly detaining two members. Everywhere they campaigned with a vigor and invective born of urgency. This, they felt, was the crisis of American nationality.

A Case for Ratification

Among the numerous advantages promised by a well-constructed Union, none deserves to be more accurately developed than its tendency to break and control the violence of faction. The friend of popular governments never finds himself so much alarmed for their character and fate as when he contemplates their propensity to this dangerous vice. He will not fail, therefore, to set a due value on any plan which, without violating the principles to which he is attached, provides a proper cure for it....

The influence of factious leaders may kindle a flame within their particular States, but will be unable to spread a general conflagration through the other States. A religious sect may degenerate into a political faction in a part of the Confederacy; but the variety of sects dispersed over the entire face of it must secure the national councils against any danger from that source. A rage for paper money, for an abolition of debts, for an equal division of property, or for any other improper or wicked project, will be less apt to pervade the whole body of the Union than a particular member of it; in the same proportion as such a malady is more likely to taint a particular county or district than an entire State.

In the extent and proper structure of the Union, therefore, we behold a republican remedy for the diseases most incident to republican government.

From James Madison, *The Federalist,* No. 10, 1787.

If the Constitution failed of adoption, the Union might be doomed.

Opposition to the Constitution was generally weakest in the small states, which would have more than their share of power in the new government. But the Federalists, as the supporters of the Constitution called themselves, knew that it was imperative to win over the four largest states: Massachusetts, Pennsylvania, New York, and Virginia. For any one of them to abstain would imperil the success of the new government. Pennsylvania, in spite of determined opposition, fell in line first, on December 12, 1787. Massachusetts ratified on February 6, 1788, by a narrow majority, which included several anti-Federalist delegates. They had been persuaded after John Hancock proposed that a recommendation for a bill of rights accompany ratification.

In Virginia the opposition, led by Patrick Henry, was weakened when Edmund Randolph swung back in favor of adoption. The state accepted the Constitution by a vote of eighty-nine to seventy-nine on June 26. Meanwhile every other state but New York, North Carolina, and Rhode Island had voted for ratification. Several had, like Massachusetts, included recommendations for amendments. In New York Alexander Hamilton, John Jay, and James Madison had campaigned for the Constitution in an impressive series of newspaper articles, known as *The Federalist*. Though these were perhaps the most searching discussion of the Constitution ever written, they did not prevent the election of a hostile ratifying convention. Only after news of Virginia's decision reached New York was Hamilton able to persuade a small majority to follow suit on July 26. North Carolina did not ratify until November 21, 1789; and Rhode Island withheld its approval until May 29, 1790. But the rest of the country did not wait for them. As soon as the four big states had given their assent, Congress arranged for its own demise by ordering national elections to be held in January 1789.

The United States was at last to have a government that would embody on a national scale the American principle of responsible representative government. The world had said that republican government was impossible for a country the size of the United States, that only a federation of republics or a powerful monarchy or aristocracy could extend so wide. But here was a new kind of republic, a federation that would be more than a federation, a government that would remain responsible to the people though its territory and population expanded tenfold, a union in which the people would be joined not as citizens of rival states but as a nation of equals.

SUGGESTIONS FOR READING

Two good introductions to the military history of the Revolution are Howard Peckham, *The War for Independence** (1958), and Willard Wallace, *Appeal to Arms** (1951). J. R. Alden, *The American Revolution** (1954), while treating the whole Revolution, gives generous consideration to military history. The standard account of naval operations is G. W. Allen, *Naval History of the American Revolution*, 2 vols. (1913), but for the exploits of John Paul Jones see S. E. Morison, *John Paul Jones: A Sailor's Biography** (1959). T. G. Frothingham, *Washington, Commander in Chief* (1930), assesses the general's military genius, but a more complete, day-by-day account is D. S. Freeman, *George Washington*, 7 vols. (1948–57). The story of the war as seen by participants is told, with extensive quotations, by G. F. Scheer and H. F. Rankin in *Rebels and Redcoats** (1957).

The classic account of the diplomacy of the Revolution is S. F. Bemis, *The Diplomacy of the American Revolution** (1935, 1957). Richard B. Morris gives a lively and detailed narrative of the peace negotiations in *The Peace Makers* (1965). On the loyalists, C. H. Van Tyne, *The Loyalists in the American Revolution* (1902), should be supplemented by W. H. Nelson, *The American Tory** (1961), Wallace Brown, *The King's Friends* (1965), and L. W. Labaree, *Conservatism in Early American History** (1948). Clarence Ver Steeg, *Robert Morris* (1954), deals largely with the financing of the Revolution. A more extensive study is E. J. Ferguson, *The Power of the Purse: A History of American Public Finance, 1776–1790* (1961).

Since 1909, when Carl Becker offered his opinion that the Revolution, in New York at least, was a contest about who should rule at home, many historians have addressed themselves to the effect of the Revolution on social conflicts within the participating states. J. F. Jameson, *The American Revolution Considered as a Social Movement** (1926), argued that the Revolution acted

* Available in a paperback edition.

as a leveling movement in the direction of greater democracy and accelerated social change. Studies of individual states in the period from 1776 to 1789 do not all bear out this contention. For example, Richard McCormick, *Experiment in Independence: New Jersey in the Critical Period, 1781–1789* (1950), finds little evidence of class conflict, but E. W. Spaulding, *New York in the Critical Period* (1932), finds a good deal, as does Staughton Lynd, "Who Should Rule at Home? Dutchess County, New York, in the American Revolution," *William and Mary Quarterly*, 3rd series, XVIII (1961), 330–59. Robert Brown, *Middle-Class Democracy and the Revolution in Massachusetts* (1955), argues that there was little democratizing of Massachusetts during the Revolution, because Massachusetts already had democratic government, with the vast majority of adult males enjoying the right to vote. Chilton Williamson, *American Suffrage from Property to Democracy, 1760–1860* (1960), finds that the majority of males in most colonies had the right to vote but that the majority became larger during the Revolution as a result of reductions in the property qualifications. E. S. Morgan, *The Birth of the Republic** (1957), emphasizes the growth of common principles rather than conflicts among Americans of the period 1763–89. J. T. Main, *The Social Structure of Revolutionary America* (1965), contains valuable statistical information about the distribution of property.

John Fiske, *The Critical Period of American History, 1783–1789* (1883), painted a black picture of the United States under the Articles of Confederation and told of the nation's rescue by the Constitution of 1787. Merrill Jensen, *The Articles of Confederation** (1940) and *The New Nation** (1950), sought to redeem the reputation of the Articles, which he saw as a true embodiment of the principles of the Declaration of Independence. Edmund Burnett, *The Continental Congress** (1941), covers the activities of Congress before and after adoption of the Articles. Irving Brant, *James Madison the Nationalist, 1780–1787* (1948), gives a view of the period through the eyes of one of America's most perceptive statesmen.

Most modern accounts of the Constitutional Convention take their point of departure from Charles Beard, whose *Economic Interpretation of the Constitution** (1913) exercised a powerful influence. Beard maintained that the authors of the Constitution had invested heavily in public securities and sought to bolster the national government in order to gain protection for the economic interests of their own class. In recent years Beard's thesis has been attacked and all but demolished by Robert Brown, *Charles Beard and the Constitution** (1956), and Forrest McDonald, *We the People: The Economic Origins of the Constitution** (1958). In *E Pluribus Unum* (1965) McDonald gives his own view of the economic and political maneuvering that brought about the Philadelphia convention, while J. T. Main in *The Antifederalists** (1961) examines the forces of opposition. Max Farrand, *The Framing of the Constitution of the United States** (1913), is a good account of the convention itself, but there is no substitute for the records of the convention and of the debates in it, which are published in Max Farrand, ed., *Records of the Federal Convention of 1787*, 4 vols.* (1911–37), and C. C. Tansill, ed., *Documents Illustrative of the Formation of the Union of the United States* (1927). Jacob E. Cooke, ed., *The Federalist** (1961), is the definitive edition of these papers, which are also available in a reliable paperback edition by Clinton Rossiter (1961).

For the reader who wishes to approach this period through the original sources, a wealth of material, besides *The Federalist* and the *Records* of the convention, is readily available in complete modern editions, now in process of publication, of the *Papers* of the period's great men. These editions, besides printing everything that a man wrote, include letters and communications written to him. Among the men whose *Papers* are thus being published are Thomas Jefferson (Julian P. Boyd, ed.), John Adams (Lyman Butterfield, ed.), Benjamin Franklin (L. W. Labaree, ed.), Alexander Hamilton (H. C. Syrett, ed.), and James Madison (W. T. Hutchinson and W. M. E. Rachal, eds.).

* Available in a paperback edition.

6

The Establishment of National Institutions

by Congress. He was extremely reluctant to use his veto power and did so only twice during his Presidency. It was his business, he believed, to administer the laws, not to make them. Consequently, while he established the authority and independence of executive action within the range allowed by the Constitution, he took no active part in the formation of public policy by legislation.

In the absence of presidential initiative three men guided Congress: Madison, Hamilton, and Jefferson. For the first five months Madison had the job to himself, for no other member of Congress combined the requisite political talents with the imagination that the new situation demanded. Hamilton acquired a position of leadership by his appointment to the Treasury on September 11, 1789, because in creating that department Congress had provided for a close connection between the Secretary and the legislature. At Madison's insistence, Congress had authorized the Secretary to prepare plans for collecting revenue and sustaining public credit and to present them to the House of Representatives, which under the Constitution had the sole right to initiate money bills. Washington approved Hamilton's active participation in the affairs of the House for, though he refrained from legislative matters himself, he did not think it necessary or desirable that his department heads should do so.

Jefferson did not accept the Secretaryship of State until January 1790 and did not arrive in New York until two months later. His office was less closely connected with legislative affairs than Hamilton's. Moreover, while Hamilton ran the Treasury pretty much by himself, Washington took an active part in the management of foreign affairs and frequently overruled his Secretary of State. Nevertheless, Jefferson's close friendship and alliance with Madison gave him considerable influence in Congress.

The Bill of Rights. In ratifying the Constitution, six states had suggested amendments to specify the popular rights that the government must never invade. Many of the legislators who had been elected to the first Congress under the new Constitution arrived in New York prepared to carry out the suggestions. Although Madison had opposed a bill of rights

both before and during ratification, when it became clear to him that the people of the United States were determined to have one he decided to draft it himself.

Madison had initially opposed a bill of rights for two reasons. First, he thought that declarations of popular rights, while useful against a monarch, would be ineffective against a republican government, in which the people themselves were ultimately the lawgivers. Second, he feared that any explicit statement of rights would prove too narrow and might be used to limit freedom instead of limiting authority: a wayward government might construe the specified rights as the only rights of the people. The debates over ratification had introduced another ground for fear: many advocates of amendment, including some members of Congress, wanted to reduce the authority of the federal government in relation to that of the state governments. In order to forestall amendments that might weaken the new government or ones that might undermine American freedom, Madison wanted to frame the bill of rights himself.

From the proposals he first presented to Congress in June 1789 there emerged the first ten amendments to the Constitution, which were ratified by the necessary number of states in December 1791. Known as the Bill of Rights, the amendments protected freedom of religion, of speech, and of the press, and the rights to assemble, to petition the government, to bear arms, to be tried by a jury, and to enjoy other procedural safeguards of the law (see p. 858). They forbade general warrants, excessive bail, cruel or unusual punishments, and the quartering of troops in private houses.

To prevent the government from ever claiming that the people had no rights except those specifically listed, the Ninth Amendment provided that "The enumeration in the Constitution of certain rights shall not be construed to deny or disparage others retained by the people." The Tenth Amendment reassured the state governments about their relationship to the federal government by affirming, "The powers not delegated to the United States by the Constitution, nor prohibited by it to the States, are reserved to the States respectively, or to the people."

Madison fought hard for his amendments,

because in preparing them he had convinced himself that a bill of rights might be more effective than he had originally supposed. If a republican legislature proved hard to control, specific prohibitions would at least form a rallying point around which popular resistance could gather. The amendments would also assist the executive and judiciary branches in checking the legislature, for the amendments would be part of the Constitution, which every officer of government must swear to uphold. Even the state governments might be brought into action to resist encroachments, a thought that recurred some years later to Madison and Jefferson alike (see p. 162).

While Madison guided the Bill of Rights through Congress, the Senate passed a judiciary bill establishing the Supreme Court and thirteen inferior district courts. When the bill came to the House of Representatives, some members wanted to eliminate the provision for district courts and leave the everyday enforcement of federal laws to the state courts. But Madison persuaded the majority that the states could not be trusted in the matter. The Judiciary Act of 1789 as finally passed established thirteen district courts and three circuit courts with both concurrent and appellate jurisdiction. It also explicitly provided that the Supreme Court should review decisions of state courts and nullify state laws that violated the United States Constitution or the laws and treaties made under it.

THE SHAPING OF DOMESTIC POLICY

By adopting the Bill of Rights and by establishing federal courts to uphold the Constitution, Americans completed the work of the Constitutional Convention and made secure the inheritance that the preceding generation had won for them. The next pressing problem was to recover the nation's economic credit.

National credit and national debt. At the Constitutional Convention it had been understood that the new government would levy taxes to pay not only its own expenses but the debts of the old government. The debts were the debts of the nation, regardless of which government contracted them. On July 4, 1789, Congress established customs duties on all imports and two weeks later placed a tonnage duty on all shipping, with high rates for foreign vessels, low ones for American. When Alexander Hamilton took office at the Treasury, it became his task to apply the income from these duties to the national debt.

Hamilton found that the United States owed $54,124,464.56, including interest. It was widely assumed that the amount would be scaled down, at least the amount owed to creditors who were themselves citizens of the United States. Much of the domestic debt was in the form of certificates that had been either issued as pay to soldiers during the Revolution or bought by patriotic citizens to further the war effort. But by now most of the certificates were held by speculators or merchants who had secured them at a considerable discount when the credit of the government fell and hard times forced the owners to sell. The restoration of national credit, it seemed to many Americans, did not require payment at face value to men who had themselves discounted that value. Hamilton thought otherwise. In his Report on Public Credit, presented to Congress on January 14, 1790, he proposed to fund the entire national debt, both foreign and domestic, at its face value. Existing certificates of indebtedness would be redeemed by interest-bearing government bonds worth the original value plus the unpaid interest, calculated at 4 per cent.

The very boldness of the proposal won acclaim, and there was no real opposition to the full payment of the nation's obligations. The only question — and a large one — was who should be paid. On this question Madison and Hamilton came to a parting of the ways.

Hamilton insisted that payments be made to whoever held the certificates. Many of his associates, including members of Congress, had known that his report would contain such a recommendation and had begun buying up certificates wherever they could be found. Madison, shocked by the scramble, rose in the House of Representatives to offer an alternative to Hamilton's scheme. There were, he said, four kinds of creditors who held or had held the certificates: (1) original holders who still held them, (2) original holders who had sold them at less than face value, (3) present holders who had bought them from someone other than the government, and (4) intermediate holders, who had bought them and sold them. The first group, Madison agreed, should be paid in full. The fourth group, he agreed, should be paid nothing. But he did not agree that full value should be paid to the third group and that nothing should be paid to the second. Instead, he proposed that the third group, which included the speculators, be paid the highest market value that the certificates had formerly commanded (50 cents on the dollar) and that the difference between this amount and the face value be paid to the second group, the Revolutionary soldiers and patriots who had been obliged to part with the certificates at less than face value because of the government's inability to maintain its credit.

Madison's plan would not have reduced by a penny the amount paid by the government. In fact, Madison proposed to pay the original interest rate of 6 per cent, instead of the 4 per cent advocated by Hamilton. But Madison's plan would have offered partial compensation to the original certificate-holders instead of giving a bonus to speculators. Unhappily for Madison, and not by accident, the speculators included many members of Congress, who did not hesitate to wrap their own shady transactions in the national honor. Men who had agents combing the country for certificates stood on the floors of Congress and denounced Madison's proposal as an attempt to make the government evade its just obligations. Madison, hitherto the master of Congress, now saw his motion defeated in the House of Representatives by a vote of thirteen to thirty-six.

Madison's proposal, while it would have been more equitable than Hamilton's, probably never had a chance of acceptance, because it would have jeopardized the basic purpose of funding the debt: to restore national credit. Congressional speculators, however personally interested they may have been in the outcome, were right at least in insisting that the credit of the government ought to be sustained without regard to the motives or merits of its creditors. When the government had need for more money than it could obtain by current taxation (and every government has such a need in national emergencies), it would have to rely on bankers and speculators, men with

Alexander Hamilton: Architect of the national economy.

money to lend. Their confidence had to be purchased in advance.

Before bringing Hamilton's funding scheme to a vote, Congress took up an even more controversial matter, which Hamilton had also recommended in his report — the assumption by the national government of debts owed by the state governments. Such a move was not necessary to sustain national credit, and many supporters of the funding measure failed to see the point of it. Gouverneur Morris, a stanch conservative, was in London when he heard of the scheme and wrote back in puzzlement: "To assume the payment of what the States owe, merely because they owe it, seems to my capacity not more rational, than to assume the debts of corporations, or of individuals." Senator Robert Morris of Pennsylvania, to whom the letter was written, had other views. "By God," he said, "it must be done."

The crucial difference between Gouverneur Morris and Robert Morris was that one was in England and the other in America. Robert, like other speculators in America, had an opportunity to take advantage of assumption before it became a fact. During the Revolutionary War the states, like the national government, had borrowed money by issuing securities. Many of these state securities had since depreciated even more than national ones. Speculators, including congressmen, now rushed to buy them. And with the prospect of making fortunes they lined up behind the assumption of state debts as they did behind the funding of the national debt.

But there was more opposition to assumption than to funding because Hamilton's proposition contained no allowance for states that had already paid a large proportion of their debt by accepting public securities in payment of taxes. These states included Virginia, Maryland, North Carolina, and Georgia. The largest debts were owed by Massachusetts and South Carolina. As a result, Virginians, for instance, having been taxed by the state government to pay its debt, would be taxed again by the federal government to help pay the debts of Massachusetts and South Carolina.

The inequity of the scheme enabled Madison to muster a small majority against it on a test vote in the House. But he did not dare to push his advantage, because the speculative interests threatened to vote against funding unless they got assumption as well. Much as he disliked Hamilton's funding plan, Madison knew that the rejection of funding altogether would mean the total destruction of national credit and possibly of the national government itself.

Both funding and assumption were still undecided when Jefferson arrived to take up his duties as Secretary of State. Hamilton approached him to arrange a bargain with Madison. Congress had been arguing for some time about whether the national capital should be permanently located at New York, Philadelphia, Baltimore, or at a site on the Potomac River. Hamilton suggested that his speculators would deliver Northern votes for the Potomac site favored by Virginia, with a ten-year interim period at Philadelphia, provided Virginia and Pennsylvania would furnish enough votes to pass assumption. Convinced that funding could not pass without assumption and that without funding the nation faced catastrophe, Madison consented to supply the votes. The bargain was fulfilled in July 1790 when Congress agreed to assumption, funding, and the ultimate location of the capital on the Potomac. The final measure included a partial allowance for states that had already paid a large part of their debts.

The fact that the two sides had been able to reach a compromise was heartening, but the line of division was ominous: Hamilton spoke for the merchants and creditors of the North, who would benefit enormously from funding and assumption, because they had accumulated most of the government's certificates of indebtedness; Madison and Jefferson spoke for the planters and farmers of the South, whose taxes would flow steadily north to pay the debt. The differing interests of North and South, which Madison had already perceived in 1787, were beginning to affect national policy.

The Hamiltonian program. Hamilton's victory, for it amounted to that, was not simply a successful swindle. The speculative frenzy set off by his measures was a calculated part of one of the boldest programs ever envisaged for the development of the nation and the nation's economy. Hamilton believed that the future of the United States depended on a large-scale expansion of industry and commerce. The suspension of imports from England during the war had forced the growth of manufacturing in America; and the production of hardware and textiles had continued in some measure afterward. To effect the kind of growth that Hamilton wanted the primary need was capital, capital in large quantities concentrated in the hands of men willing to risk investing it. By means of funding and assumption Hamilton created just such a group of wealthy investors, or, to use a less attractive word, profiteers. Hamilton was no profiteer himself — he was too interested in power to give much attention to his own finances. But he was well satisfied with the huge speculative profits that others reaped from his measures, for those profits meant capital for business investment. Moreover, funding and assumption, by restoring national credit, would make investment in American enterprises more attractive to foreign capital.

Hamilton's measures were prompted not merely by economic considerations but by his consistent determination to strengthen the national government and to overcome the centrifugal force of the state governments. He anticipated that all the capitalists created by funding and assumption would be eager to maintain the national credit and the national government, if only to protect their investments. By the same token, the assumption of state debts would deprive the state governments of such support. The national government, working hand in glove with powerful investors, would grow strong as industry and commerce grew.

Hamilton's scheme generated its own support. The opportunity to get rich easily and by methods not strictly illegal was more than congressmen could resist. Washington was disturbed by the rumor that "The funding of the debt has furnished effectual means of corrupting such a portion of the Legislature as turns the balance between the honest voters whichever way it is directed." Hamilton, who was doing the directing, assured the President that "there is not a member of the Legislature who can properly be called a stock-jobber or a paper-dealer. . . . As to improper speculations on measures depending before Congress, I believe never was any body of men freer from them." Washington believed him.

Hamilton's next objective was a national bank with capital supplied partly by the government and partly by private investors. But since the investors would be permitted to pay in government bonds for three-fourths of the bank stock they purchased, the bank's notes would rest very largely on the national debt. With the government furnishing most of the capital and assuming most of the risk, the bank could offer an irresistible invitation to wealthy men to invest their money. Furthermore, the national debt, if utilized for a bank, could be a national advantage. In arguing for funding and assumption, Hamilton had emphasized the fact that where a national debt "is properly funded, and an object of established confidence, it answers most of the purposes of money." He intended to make it serve this purpose through the bank: notes issued by the bank would serve as a much needed medium of exchange (specie being scarce) and would greatly facilitate business and the financing of new commercial and industrial enterprise. Besides acting as a central exchange, the bank would handle government finances; and it would expedite borrowing both by the government and by individuals. Through this government-sponsored expansion of credit, the bond between private capital and the national government would be tightened.

When the bill to charter the bank came before the House early in February 1791, Madison attacked it with arguments he would not have used two years earlier. Before the adoption of the Constitution, he had argued strenuously that Congress should assume all the powers it needed to do its job. Under the new government he had hitherto taken a generous view of the extent of congressional authority. By now, however, he was thoroughly worried over the emerging shape of Hamilton's program and intent on stopping it. He argued that because the Constitution did not specifically empower Congress to issue charters of incorporation it had no right to do so. Hamilton answered that the Constitution empowered the government to do anything "necessary and proper" to carry out its assigned functions.

This was the first great debate over strict, as opposed to loose, interpretation of the Constitution. Congress readily accepted Hamilton's loose construction and passed the bill. Washington weighed the question more seriously, listening carefully to Madison and Jefferson as well as to Hamilton. Though he remained doubtful to the end, at the last minute, on February 25, 1791, he signed the bill. Hamilton's program moved ahead another step.

Having provided capital and credit Hamilton was now ready to direct the expansion of manufacturing. In December he presented to Congress his Report on Manufactures, a scheme to make investment in industry attractive by means of protective tariffs and bounties. It was Hamilton's aim to direct the nation toward a balanced economy that would include manufacturing as well as agriculture and commerce. Only through such a balance could the United States make the most of its resources, reduce its foreign debt and its reliance on foreign nations, and attain true independence. But Hamilton was not allowed to add this capstone to his economic edifice. Farmers and merchants, fearing that protective tariffs would prompt retaliatory action by other countries against American agricultural exports, preferred free competition to keep down the price of manufactures. And almost everyone wondered whether the United States could afford a measure that would discourage importation, since the government's principal income came from import duties. To raise them to protective levels might reduce the volume of imports so drastically as to endanger the national credit. Moved by these considera-

Hamilton's View of the Good Society

It is now proper ... to enumerate the principal circumstances from which it may be inferred that manufacturing establishments not only occasion a positive augmentation of the produce and revenue of the society, but that they contribute essentially to rendering them greater than they could possibly be without such establishments. These circumstances are:

1. The division of labor.
2. An extension of the use of machinery.
3. Additional employment to classes of the community not ordinarily engaged in the business.
4. The promoting of emigration from foreign countries.
5. The furnishing greater scope for the diversity of talents and dispositions, which discriminate men from each other.
6. The affording a more ample and various field for enterprise.
7. The creating, in some instances, a new, and securing, in all, a more certain and steady demand for the surplus produce of the soil.

Each of these circumstances has a considerable influence upon the total mass of industrious effort in a community; together, they add to it a degree of energy and effect which are not easily conceived.

From Alexander Hamilton, Report on Manufactures, 1791.

tions, Congress dealt Hamilton his first defeat by shelving his report.

Madison and Jefferson, who engineered the defeat, were both alarmed by the apparent intent of Hamilton's program. No one had done more than Madison to resuscitate and strengthen the central government a few years earlier at the Constitutional Convention, but in the Hamiltonian system he saw the beginnings of a national government so strong that it would endanger the individual liberties he had been trying to protect in the Bill of Rights. Jefferson, even more than Madison, was wary of governmental power.

To this distrust of government, Jefferson joined a dislike of cities and of the merchants and manufacturers who thrived in them. Farmers, he believed, enjoyed a greater virtue and a closer contact with their Maker than

did the inhabitants of cities. From Paris he had written to Madison in 1787, "I think our governments will remain virtuous for many centuries; as long as they are chiefly agricultural. ... When they get piled upon one another in large cities, as in Europe, they shall become corrupt as in Europe." Jefferson and Madison were both convinced that the federal government would have all the strength it needed and would be less likely to exceed its authority if it depended not on an alliance with powerful creditors but on the support of the producing classes, especially the farmers, who formed the bulk of the population. Opponents of the Constitution had feared that a strong central government would be manipulated to bring power and wealth to a few. Hamilton seemed bent on justifying their fears, which he and Madison had earlier joined to combat in *The Federalist*. Moreover, Hamilton's program was driving a wedge between the North, where capital and credit were accumulating, and the South, whose farmers and planters feared that the accumulation was at their expense. Almost all the stock in Hamilton's United States Bank was purchased by Northern and European creditors; and Hamilton made it plain that the bank was intended to assist the expansion of commerce and industry, not agriculture, which in his view needed no encouragement. He dismissed out of hand a proposal that the bank lend money to Southern planters on the security of tobacco warehouse receipts.

Thus within three years of the inauguration of the national government its leaders had reached a fundamental disagreement over its scope and policy. Washington stood above the quarrel, and both sides could still join in persuading him to accept another term of office when the national elections were held in 1792. But the gap between the views of Hamilton on the one hand and of Jefferson and Madison on the other was about as wide as constitutional government could stand. During Washington's second term the dissension spread from domestic to foreign affairs with growing bitterness that threatened to split the Union.

FOREIGN AFFAIRS UNDER WASHINGTON

The Constitution assigned to the President the conduct of relations with Europeans and Indians, and, where Washington gave Hamilton a free hand in developing financial policy and refused to meddle in congressional enactments of that policy, he gave Jefferson no such freedom as Secretary of State. He turned to Jefferson for advice, but he sought advice from other department heads as well. As foreign affairs assumed greater and greater complexity, he began the practice of calling together the Attorney General and the Secretaries of State, War, and the Treasury to discuss policy. During these meetings, from which grew the Cabinet as an institution, Jefferson and Hamilton again revealed their differing conceptions of the national welfare.

Jeffersonian neutrality. The discord in foreign affairs first showed itself in 1790, when a threatened war between Spain and England offered the United States an opportunity to press American claims against both countries. Spain had seized three British vessels trading in Nootka Sound, Vancouver Island, which had been Spanish territory ever since its discovery. England demanded the return of the ships, reparation for damages, and recognition of British trading rights in the area. It seemed likely that Spain would fight rather than submit.

Washington's advisers all agreed that the United States should remain neutral in case of war, but they did not agree on what the United States should do if England decided to march troops through American territory in the Mississippi Valley in order to attack the Spaniards in Florida and Louisiana. Since Hamilton had just tied his funding program to duties on British trade, he was reluctant to do anything that might offend England and was ready to declare American neutrality at once. Jefferson, on the other hand, had just come from five years as the United States Ambassador to France, where he had seized every opportunity to bargain for national advantages. He wanted to bargain now, to keep both Spain and England guessing about America's intentions and to make them bid high for her neutrality.

As it happened, Spain gave in to the British ultimatum, and no war occurred. But another European war was clearly in the making, and mounting tensions in Europe generated a notable increase in the cordiality of European countries toward the United States. In 1791 Eng-

Jefferson's View of the Good Society

Those who labor in the earth are the chosen people of God, if ever He had a chosen people, whose breasts He has made His peculiar deposit for substantial and genuine virtue. It is the focus in which he keeps alive that sacred fire, which otherwise might escape from the face of the earth. Corruption of morals in the mass of cultivators is a phenomenon of which no age nor nation has furnished an example. It is the mark set on those, who, not looking up to heaven, to their own soil and industry, as does the husbandman, for their subsistence, depend for it on casualties and caprice of customers. Dependence begets subservience and venality, suffocates the germ of virtue, and prepares fit tools for the designs of ambition. This, the natural progress and consequence of the arts, has sometimes perhaps been retarded by accidental circumstances; but, generally speaking, the proportion which the aggregate of the other classes of citizens bears in any State to that of its husbandmen, is the proportion of its unsound to its healthy parts.... While we have land to labor then, let us never wish to see our citizens occupied at a workbench, or twirling a distaff.... For the general operations of manufacture, let our workshops remain in Europe.

From Thomas Jefferson, *Notes on the State of Virginia*, 1782.

land sent a minister plenipotentiary, George Hammond, to reside in Philadelphia; the United States in turn sent Thomas Pinckney to London. Full diplomatic relations had thus been established between England and the United States when war finally did break out in 1793 between England and France — and something close to war between Hamilton and Jefferson.

Thomas Jefferson, as American minister to France during the 1780's, had learned to admire French civilization and French people. Just before returning to the United States late in 1789, he had witnessed the beginnings of their revolution. At first he was skeptical that a people who had lived so long under absolute monarchy could successfully undertake republican government. But as the Revolution progressed, he became increasingly enthusiastic. When he took up his post as Washington's Secretary of State, he brought with him a warm sympathy for the French and their cause, a sympathy that was not destroyed by the execution of Louis XVI in 1793 or by the reign of terror that followed.

Hamilton, by contrast, watched with horror as the French Revolution overturned the foundations of society, destroying monarchy and aristocracy, exalting democracy and demagogues. His horror mounted when the French Revolutionists launched the "war of all peoples against all kings," with England and Spain as primary targets. England, even under King George III, seemed to Hamilton a safer friend for Americans than mob-wracked republican France. Hamilton was moved not simply by his repugnance for the French Revolution but by the belief that, if the United States had to choose sides, England was more to be feared than France, because England had the stronger navy. American commerce was more vulnerable to English sailors than to French soldiers.

Hamilton agreed with Washington's other advisers that the United States should stay out of the war, but he wanted to use the crisis as an opportunity to scrap the French alliance. The treaties of 1778, he argued, had been made with the French monarchy and were no longer binding now that the monarchy had been overthrown. The United States should therefore declare its neutrality and refuse to receive the minister, Edmond Genêt, sent by the new French republic early in 1793.

Jefferson argued that the treaties had been made with the French nation and were still binding. He was as certain as Hamilton that the United States should stay out of the war but wanted the country to do so without publicly announcing its intention. A declaration of neutrality would affront the French and would destroy the possibility of bargaining with the British, who still had troops stationed in the American Northwest and still withheld trading privileges in the empire. Washington decided the matter on April 22, 1793, by issuing a proclamation of neutrality addressed to American citizens only and not actually mentioning the word "neutrality." The treaties with France were not repudiated, and Citizen Genêt was accorded formal recognition. But the bargaining power that Jefferson valued was gone. Shortly afterward he announced that he would retire at the end of the year.

Genêt was a fool. From the moment of his arrival he assumed powers that no independent country could permit a foreign envoy: he commissioned American ships to sail as privateers under the French flag; he set up courts to condemn the ships they captured; he arranged an expedition of Western frontiersmen to attack Spanish New Orleans. Jefferson tried hard to like him but gave up in disgust. Finally Washington demanded Genêt's recall.

While Genêt was losing friends for France, the British government was losing them for England. Americans claimed the right as neutrals to carry noncontraband goods (including naval stores) to and from the ports of belligerents. France had lifted some of her mercantilist restrictions regulating trade with her West Indian islands, and American ships were swarming there to take advantage of the new opportunity. But England did not recognize the principle (cited in the Franco-American treaties) that "free ships make free goods." Instead she adhered to a rule of 1756 that trade closed in peacetime could not be opened in wartime. In December 1793, without warning, her naval vessels began seizing American ships trading with the French West Indies.

The seizures combined with an Indian episode in the Northwest to bring the United States, in spite of Hamilton, to the brink of war with England. The record of Washington's government in dealing with hostile Indians had not been good. He had arranged a treaty with Alexander McGillivray, the half-breed chieftain of the Creeks, but the Creeks had broken it as soon as it was made. He had sent General Josiah Harmar to crush the Miamis in Ohio, but they had crushed him. He had sent Arthur St. Clair with a much larger force in 1791, but St. Clair, like Braddock in 1755, had been surprised just short of his objective and completely routed. In February 1794, as General Anthony Wayne gathered a force to try again, the governor-general of Canada, Lord Dorchester, made a speech to the Indians in which he in effect exhorted them to do their worst. Reports of the speech reached Congress along with news of the Caribbean seizures.

The House of Representatives was then debating whether restrictions against British commerce (suggested by Jefferson shortly before his resignation) might lead England to reduce her own restrictions against American commerce. News of the seizures precipitated an overwhelming demand for much stronger anti-British measures, to which Hamilton felt sure England would react by declaring war on the United States — if indeed the United States did not declare war first. The country was swept by war hysteria; volunteer defense companies sprang up. Mobs mistreated English seamen and tarred and feathered pro-British Americans. To prevent a plunge into actual warfare, Hamilton urged Washington to send a special mission to England. Hamilton seems to have thought of heading it himself, but Washington gave the job to Hamilton's alter ego, John Jay.

A Hamiltonian treaty. Although Jay had had abundant experience as a diplomat, in the eyes of most Americans it had been unsuccessful experience. As envoy to Spain during the Revolution, he had failed to gain either alliance or recognition of American independence. As Secretary for Foreign Affairs under the Articles of Confederation, he had conducted the nearly disastrous negotiations with Gardoqui. In both cases failure arose less from lack of skill on his part than from the fact that the other side held all the cards. This time, with England engaged in a major European war, Jay was in a strong position to play the game that Jefferson had recommended all along: namely, to convince England that unless she made concessions she could not count on continued American neutrality. Edmund Randolph, the new Secretary of State, agreed with the Jeffersonian strategy. He instructed Jay to consult with Russia, Sweden, and Denmark about the possibility of an armed-neutrality agreement in order to bring pressure on England to stop seizures of neutral shipping.

Once again, however, Jay found himself on the losing side through no fault of his own. Denmark and Sweden, which shared the American view of the rights of neutral ships, took the initiative, and just after Jay's departure for Europe the United States received an invitation from them to join in forming an alliance of neutrals. Randolph wanted to accept, for he felt that such backing would strengthen Jay's hand. But Hamilton persuaded Washington to decline, on the grounds that the alliance would jeopardize Jay's mission by antagonizing the British. Not content with rejecting the assistance of other neutrals, and eager to create a friendly climate of opinion in England, Hamilton weakened Jay's position still further by informing George Hammond, the British minister in America, of Washington's decision.

With this information to guide him, Lord Grenville, the British foreign minister, felt safe in conceding little. He promised again to surrender the Northwest posts — provided the United States permitted the continuation of the English fur trade with the Indians in the area; he promised recompense for the American ships that had been seized without warning in December 1793 in the Caribbean — provided the United States compensated British creditors for prerevolutionary debts whose collection had been impeded by state governments. He refused to compensate American slave-owners for slaves kidnapped or liberated by the British during the Revolution, and he refused to give any guarantee against the British navy's practice of stopping American vessels to impress alleged British subjects as seamen. Instead of stopping the seizure of neutral ships he required the United States to give up her own view of neutral shipping rights for the duration of England's war with France and for two years thereafter. He consented to reciprocal trading rights between England and America but restricted American trade with the British West Indies to vessels of no more than seventy tons, and even these he allowed only in return for an American promise to ship no molasses, sugar, coffee, cocoa, or cotton from the islands or from the United States to any other part of the world. The only generosity he showed was at the expense of the Spanish: it was agreed that both British subjects and Americans should have the right to navigate the Mississippi through Spanish territory to the sea.

When the treaty containing these terms reached Washington on March 7, 1795, Hamilton was no longer at the Treasury. He had resigned at the end of January, a little more than a year after Jefferson, but he retained as much influence over the President out of office as in. His replacement, Oliver Wolcott, Jr., had been his assistant and continued to consult him on every important matter. Hamilton

The Treaty of Greenville, 1795

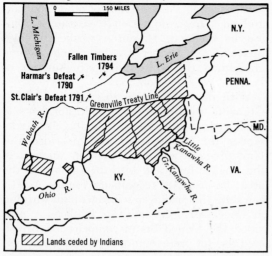

Lands ceded by Indians

thought that the treaty was satisfactory and that failure to ratify it would mean war. Washington reluctantly agreed, but he could see that other Americans might not. To avoid a premature hardening of opposition, he tried to keep the terms secret until he could present the treaty for ratification at a special session of the Senate called for June 8. It was impossible. By the time the Senate met, rumors of the contents had produced wide public hostility, which increased as the details became known. Nevertheless, the senators, after striking out the clause regarding trade with the West Indies, accepted the treaty by the exact two-thirds majority required.

As the treaty came before Washington for his signature, the press was denouncing Jay, the treaty, the Senate, and even the President. Popular meetings in Boston, Philadelphia, New York, and other cities urged Washington to reject it. In the Cabinet everyone but Randolph urged him to sign. Dismayed by the public antagonism, Washington hesitated. In the meantime, the British minister handed to Oliver Wolcott some intercepted dispatches written by the French minister, Jean Fauchet. In them Fauchet, referring to some transactions with Randolph, seemed to imply that Randolph had turned over state secrets to him for money. Although the dispatches had nothing to do with the treaty, they discredited the only Cabinet member who opposed it. Washington signed the treaty, and, after confronting

Randolph with the dispatches, refused his explanations and accepted his resignation.

The winning of the West. Jay's Treaty was the low-water mark of foreign affairs under Washington. General Wayne had defeated the Indians of the Northwest at the Battle of Fallen Timbers (August 20, 1794) and had gone on to devastate their settlements. At the Treaty of Greenville (August 3, 1795) they gave up most of the territory that was to become the state of Ohio. In the next year the British at last honored their agreement to evacuate their posts in the Northwest.

Meanwhile, Spain had become fearful that the United States would throw her small weight on the British side in the precarious European balance. The clause about the Mississippi in Jay's Treaty suggested that England and the United States might be contemplating joint action against Louisiana. Taking advantage of this fear, the American envoy, Thomas Pinckney, who was sent to negotiate a treaty, won for the United States everything she had been seeking from Spain: free navigation of the Mississippi, permission for American traders to deposit goods for shipment at the mouth of the river, acknowledgment of the American southern boundary at the thirty-first parallel and the western boundary at the Mississippi,

Pinckney's Treaty, 1795

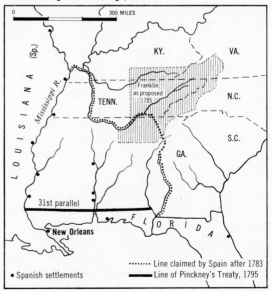

.... Line claimed by Spain after 1783
——— Line of Pinckney's Treaty, 1795

• Spanish settlements

and an agreement by each country to prevent Indians within its territory from making incursions into the territory of the other.

The Senate accepted Pinckney's Treaty unanimously on March 3, 1796. With it the danger of secession in Kentucky and Tennessee (admitted to the Union in 1792 and 1796) disappeared; with the Mississippi open to trade, any attachment to Spain lost its charm for the Americans of the Southwest. Although Washington's foreign policy had produced some vastly unpopular concessions to Britain, it must be credited with the restoration of reciprocal trading rights and with achieving at last recognition by both Spain and Britain of United States sovereignty over the area first won from Britain in 1783.

FEDERALISTS VERSUS REPUBLICANS

Alexander Hamilton, by dictating domestic policy to Congress and foreign policy to the President, gave the national government its initial direction. Although Madison and Jefferson managed to modify some of his measures, in all essentials Hamilton prevailed. But in their efforts to defeat him, Madison and Jefferson set a pattern of political action that in ten years' time gave them control of the government and thereafter became the only way of gaining or keeping control. They started a political party.

The Republican challenge. The framers of the Constitution, Madison included, had not thought well of parties. "Faction" was the word generally used for party in the eighteenth century, and a faction meant, by Madison's own definition, a group of men organized to procure selfish advantages at the expense of the community. Denunciation of factions or parties was a standard ingredient in every discussion of politics in the eighteenth century, as safe and as platitudinous as denunciation of corruption and praise of honesty.

The parties of the time deserved denunciation. In the British House of Commons, and to some degree in the colonial assemblies, politicians had joined forces from time to time in order to make legal raids on the public purse. Because neither Madison nor Jefferson had any such end in view, they did not at first think of

New States 1791–96

VERMONT 1791

KENTUCKY 1792

TENNESSEE 1796

their opposition to Hamilton as constituting a party. Madison, to be sure, had a following in the House of Representatives and was an old hand at collecting votes in support of his measures. But in lining up opposition to indiscriminate funding and wholesale assumption, neither Jefferson nor Madison anticipated a continuing, organized opposition.

It was only as the full dimensions of Hamilton's program revealed themselves that the two men deliberately set out to gather and consolidate their strength against him inside the government and out. Jefferson was aware that Washington consulted Hamilton on every kind of measure, including matters that seemed to belong properly in the Department of State; in response, he tried to extend his own influence within the executive departments. Washington liked Jefferson, as did most of the other members of the presidential entourage. And yet Jefferson made little headway in his campaign. Though he succeeded in having the Mint established under the State Department instead of the Treasury, his attempts to get the Post Office transferred to the State Department failed, and so did his efforts to get his friend Tench Coxe appointed as Comptroller and Thomas Paine as Postmaster General.

Madison was more successful. In the House

of Representatives he was often defeated, but every defeat strengthened the loyalty of his followers. Though he lacked Jefferson's personal charm and was not eloquent in debate, he knew how to work in the corridors; and on the floor his colleague from Virginia, William Giles, was an able spokesman of his views. John Beckley, the perennial Clerk of the House, who seemed to know everybody's secrets, turned over valuable information to him. As the Madison forces hardened, they began to call themselves the "republican interest," and by 1792 they even dared to say the "republican party" — a phrase that gradually acquired capital letters.

Their opponents, not considering themselves a party, appropriated the name of Federalists, which had been used earlier by the advocates of the Constitution of 1787. This maneuver identified the Republicans with the anti-Federalists of that period. Actually there was no connection. The leaders of the Republican party had supported the Constitution in 1787 and still did; the Federalists of the early 1790's were distinguished, not by any special reverence for that document, but by a conception of the national welfare that included a permanent national debt, a national bank, and dependence on England.

Madison and Jefferson believed that the source of Federalist strength, apart from Washington's support of Hamilton, was typical of faction or party in the traditional sense: it lay in the corruption of congressmen through the speculative opportunities that accompanied funding and assumption. Their own strength, they believed, lay with the people at large. Perhaps because they assumed that the people were on their side, they did not at first organize their party except within the government itself; they did, however, take steps to let the people know, through the press, what their side was.

Before 1791 the *Gazette of the United States* was the only newspaper that gave full coverage to national politics, and its editor, John Fenno, was an ardent Hamiltonian. Madison and Jefferson persuaded the poet Philip Freneau, whom they knew to be Republican in sentiment, to establish a newspaper that would report national issues from their point of view. On October 31, 1791, the first issue of the *National Gazette* was published, and the Republicans gained a medium for spreading attacks on the Hamiltonian program (some of them written by Madison) throughout the country.

At the same time spontaneous popular societies began to form that might have furnished the basis for Republican party organization at the local level. Admiration for the French Revolution and discontent with the government's evident bias in favor of England prompted the formation of these "Democratic Clubs," first in Pennsylvania and then all over the country. The clubs, which were imitations of the Jacobin societies in France, felt that they were continuing the tradition of the Sons of Liberty of the 1760's and 1770's. They sympathized with the French Revolution and passed resolutions against the government's pro-British foreign policy; they supported the Republicans in Congress and in elections for Congress. But before Madison and his friends could capitalize on their support, the Federalists found an opportunity to discredit the clubs and capture a wide popular following for themselves.

The Federalist response. The Federalist opportunity arose from a tax on whiskey passed by Congress in 1791 to help pay the expenses of funding and assumption. Excise taxes, especially on alcoholic beverages, were unpopular in the eighteenth century. A cider tax nearly caused rebellion in England in 1763, and so did a rum tax in Massachusetts in 1754. By 1794 the federal excise tax on liquor did cause rebellion, or what looked like it, in Pennsylvania. Farmers in the western part of the state generally turned their surplus grain into whiskey. This could be transported over the mountains more easily than wheat or corn, and it brought a better price in the Eastern markets. But the profit was small, and there was much evasion of the tax. In July 1794 the United States marshal, summoning offenders to court, met with mass resistance.

The governor of the state, Thomas Mifflin, thought that the courts could handle the situation. But Washington, urged on by Hamilton, decided that the challenge to national authority called for military action, and in October he marched fifteen thousand militiamen to western Pennsylvania. No rebel fired a shot against him, and Washington returned to Philadelphia, leaving Hamilton to complete the arrest of the ringleaders.

When Congress assembled shortly after his return, Washington delivered an address that made clear his contempt for all organized opposition to the policies of the national government, whether from whiskey rebels, Democratic Clubs, or Republicans. Although there is no evidence that the clubs had anything to do with the rebellion, Washington had somehow got the notion that they had. In spite of the fact that the Constitution guaranteed the right to assemble, he rebuked the clubs as "self-created societies." Dismayed by his disapproval, many of them dissolved at once, and the rest expired within a year or two.

National Authority and Individual Loyalty

The unity of government which constitutes you one people is also now dear to you. It is justly so; for it is a main pillar in the edifice of your real independence, the support of your tranquility at home; your peace abroad; of your safety; of your prosperity; of that very liberty which you so highly prize. But as it is easy to foresee, that from different causes and from different quarters, much pains will be taken, many artifices employed, to weaken in your minds the conviction of this truth; as this is the point in your political fortress against which the batteries of internal and external enemies will be most constantly and actively (though often covertly and insidiously) directed, it is of infinite moment, that you should properly estimate the immense value of your national Union to your collective and individual happiness....

To the efficacy and permanency of your union, a Government for the whole is indispensable.... This Government, the offspring of your own choice uninfluenced and unawed ... has a just claim to your confidence and your support. Respect for its authority, compliance with its laws, acquiescence in its measures, are duties enjoined by the fundamental maxims of true liberty....

Towards the preservation of your Government ... it is requisite, not only that you steadily discountenance irregular oppositions to its acknowledged authority, but also that you resist with care the spirit of innovation upon its principles however specious the pretexts.

From George Washington, The Farewell Address, 1796.

Washington's personal popularity was thus revealed as the strongest weapon in the Federalist arsenal. The Republicans were not fully aware of how strong it was or of how it could be used against them. Nor was Washington aware. He continued to regard himself as standing above party and seems never to have realized that as he came more and more to rely on Hamilton he was choosing sides in a party conflict. Hamilton did realize it and used Washington's prestige to turn popular opinion against the Republicans.

When the President signed Jay's Treaty, in spite of popular meetings that urged him not to, the Republicans, instead of conceding defeat, carried the battle to the House of Representatives. Although the Constitution gave

President and general: Washington at the time of the Whiskey Rebellion.

only the Senate the authority to approve or reject treaties, the House, under Madison's leadership, asserted its right to examine treaties before appropriating funds to implement them. On this basis, the House demanded copies of the papers that had passed to and from Jay during the negotiations. Washington, defending the integrity of the executive department, indignantly refused; Hamilton, by decrying the demand of the House as an insult to the President and a step toward war, soon had Congress flooded with petitions supporting the President. Republican efforts to secure counterpetitions were less successful, and Madison saw his majority dwindle to a minority. The House in the end supported the treaty.

The election of 1796. When the Republicans attacked the treaty in the House of Representatives, they had an eye on the presidential election that was to take place later in the year. In the elections of 1788 and 1792 there had been no serious contest for the Presidency. In 1796 it was probable, though not certain, that Washington would retire. If he did, the Republicans would have a chance to challenge Hamilton at the polls. But the Republican hope of unseating the Federalists received a strong setback when Madison's attack on the treaty foundered against Washington's popularity.

As the election approached, Washington gave the Federalists another advantage by delaying his decision to withdraw. The Republicans were wary of advancing any candidate of

their own unless the still insuperable national hero was out of the race. It was understood that if Washington chose not to run, Adams would be the Federalist candidate; for Hamilton, though influential among politicians, did not have a wide enough popular following to assure election. For the same reason the Republicans had settled on Jefferson rather than Madison. In September Washington finally announced his retirement and delivered a farewell address written by Hamilton. The address contained a strong warning against partiality for foreign countries on the one hand (i.e., for France) and against political parties on the other (i.e., the Republicans). Washington still refused to think of the Federalists as a party.

Having secured Washington's support for a Federalist successor, Hamilton set about substituting a more pliable candidate for the prickly, independent Adams. Because of Adams' popular following, Hamilton could not renounce him publicly, but he hoped to achieve his purpose by manipulating the electoral vote.

The maneuver was made possible by the peculiar constitutional provisions for electing the President. Each state could select its members for the Electoral College in any manner it saw fit. Six did it by popular vote, nine by vote of the state legislature, and one, Massachusetts, by a combination of the two. Most candidates for the college announced beforehand for whom they would vote; but this practice was not universal, and the college as an institution retained some small measure of choice. Each elector cast two ballots, without specifying which man he preferred for President; the candidate who received the largest vote became President, and the candidate with the second-largest vote became Vice-President. Since this was a system designed for a partyless government, complications arose when political parties appeared. If all the electors who favored the strongest party voted for both its candidates, a tie vote would result. In order to elect the party's preferred presidential candidate some electors had to divert their second vote from the party's vice-presidential candidate to some other candidate. This could be dangerous: if too many votes were diverted from the party's vice-presidential candidate he might be left with fewer than the presidential candidate of the opposing party, who would then become Vice-President instead. There was also the possibility that if both parties wanted the same man for Vice-President, he might receive more votes than either presidential candidate and thus become President.

It was this latter possibility that led Hamilton to arrange for Adams' running mate on the Federalist ticket to be Thomas Pinckney of South Carolina. Pinckney, who had just returned in triumph from his Spanish mission, enjoyed great popularity in the South, where the Republicans were strongest. Southerners would certainly give most of their votes to Jefferson, but they might be persuaded to designate Pinckney as second choice. If a substantial number of electors did so, the combined Federalist-Republican vote might be large enough to put Pinckney into the Presidency.

But Hamilton was not the only one who knew the deficiencies of the electoral system. When the votes of the Electoral College were cast, it appeared that his advocacy of Pinckney had failed. Adams' friends in Connecticut and New Hampshire, refusing to endanger his success, had all scattered their second votes, and the Southern Republicans had actually given Pinckney nothing. Even so, he had fifty-nine votes; but Adams with seventy-one became President and Jefferson with sixty-eight became Vice-President. Jefferson's running mate, Aaron Burr of New York, had only thirty.

Had the Federalist electors of Connecticut and New Hampshire given Pinckney their second votes, Hamilton's strategy could have succeeded. Pinckney would have tied Adams' vote, and tied presidential elections, according to the Constitution, were to be decided in the House of Representatives. There, with Jefferson out of the contest, Southern Republicans might have joined with Hamilton's forces to make Pinckney President. For Adams it was a bitter thing to have come so close to losing and to know that Hamilton was to blame.

THE PRESIDENCY OF JOHN ADAMS

The new President was a man of conflicting emotions, ideas, and loyalties. Round of face and frame, he looked like an English country squire and often behaved like one, lashing out at those who crossed him as though he were lord of the manor. Yet he was sometimes remarkably patient when there was real cause for anger. Like Washington and Jefferson and George III, he loved the land and found high office uncongenial and inconvenient. Yet no man wanted the Presidency more or would have found defeat more humiliating.

Adams had had a distinguished career during the Revolution, both in the Continental Congress and in negotiating the peace treaty. His political experience and his study of history had given him strong ideas about the proper form of government: liberty, he believed, could be preserved only where a strong executive presided over a legislature divided into two houses, the upper representing the wealthy and well born, the lower representing the people at large. This idea, expounded at length in his *Defence of the Constitutions of the United States* (1787), had influenced the Philadelphia convention and had helped produce the strong executive office that Adams inherited from Washington. As President, Adams continued to think that the executive must stand above the other branches of government and mitigate differences between them.

The President and the politicians. Adams, like his contemporaries, spoke of political parties only to condemn them. Though he had been elected in a contest between parties, the circumstances were not such as to endear either side to him. The Republicans had branded him a monarchist because of his openly avowed advocacy of a strong executive, while the Federalists had almost betrayed him for Thomas Pinckney.

In his inaugural address Adams did his best to minimize party differences. Answering for the first time the accusations that had been made against him during the campaign, he assured the Republicans that he did not want a monarchical or aristocratic or indeed any but a republican government. Lest anyone think him an enemy of the French alliance, so dear to Jefferson, he affirmed his personal esteem for the French nation, "formed in a residence of seven years, chiefly among them"; and his "sincere desire to preserve the friendship which has been so much for the honor and interest of both nations."

The Republicans were delighted. Newspaper editors who had been warning of the approach of tyranny suddenly discovered the President's "incorruptible integrity," his intelligence, his patriotism. Jefferson had always liked Adams. The two had become estranged in 1791 when one of Jefferson's friends published a private letter from him criticizing Adams' political writings. Before the inauguration they made it up and took rooms in the same Philadelphia boardinghouse. In assuming office as Vice-President, Jefferson hailed the man "whose talents and integrity have been known and revered by me through a long course of years."

The political backers of both men were suspicious of the new harmony and uneasy about the effect it might have on the party organizations they had been building. Before coming to Philadelphia, Jefferson had drafted an open and generous letter to Adams, declaring his pleasure in the outcome of the election. He had always served as a junior to Adams and would be glad to continue doing so. He sent the letter to Madison to deliver at his discretion. Madison thought it best not to: if made public, it might alienate Jefferson's supporters and embarrass him in a future contest. Jefferson himself avoided getting too close to the Administration: the separation of powers; he decided, should prevent his sitting in the President's Cabinet.

Federalist leaders, equally cautious, were worried about Adams' charity toward the Republicans and pulled him up sharp when he proposed appointing Madison as special envoy to France. Adams, who had already told Jefferson of his intention, with some embarrassment withdrew the nomination when Oliver Wolcott, Jr., the Secretary of the Treasury, threatened to resign in protest. Thereafter relations between the President and the Vice-President cooled off, for Adams' behavior seemed to indicate that in spite of his good beginning he would not stand very far above party.

It might, in the end, have been better for Adams if he had used his famous temper on Wolcott. Since there was as yet no tradition requiring Cabinet officers to submit their resignations when a new President took office, Adams inherited the Cabinet that Washington left behind. And a sorry lot they were. Besides Wolcott at the Treasury, there was James McHenry in the War Department and Timothy Pickering at State. Hamilton, in suggesting McHenry's appointment to Washington, had said that "he would give no strength to the administration, but he would not disgrace the office." Three years later, Hamilton had to admit that "my friend McHenry is wholly insufficient for his place." Timothy Pickering had originally served as Postmaster, a position that strained his talents to their limits. When Randolph resigned, Washington gave Pickering the State Department temporarily but was unable to persuade a more competent man to take the job.

Apart from their palpable mediocrity, the only thing that Wolcott, McHenry, and Pickering had in common was that they all took orders from Hamilton. Adams was too keen a man not to perceive the quality of their minds, but he did not realize that the advice they gave him came by mail from New York. Even had he known, he might have hesitated to drop them. They had been appointed by the great Washington, and it would have been brash for a President who had barely won the office to cashier the advisers whom the national hero had thought adequate. Even if Adams had let them go, he might have had difficulty replacing them. Cabinet officers received a salary of only $3,000 a year, and a man of talent who could earn much more in private business might be reluctant or unable to make the financial sacrifice, especially since there was as yet little prestige in any appointive office. Washington had kept second-rate men simply because he could not get first-rate ones.

Surrounded by incompetent advisers who remained loyal to a politician who had betrayed him, Adams could have preserved the strength of the executive department only by showing a resolute determination to make his own decisions. Instead, he spent much of his time at home in Quincy, Massachusetts, leaving the members of his Cabinet to deliberate by themselves. Consequently his Administration drifted into policies with which he did not fully agree and from which he finally extricated it only at the expense of his political career.

The end of the French alliance. In the opening months of his Administration Adams' cordiality for France as for Jefferson cooled rapidly. During Washington's Presidency the French government had become increasingly angered by the apparent partiality of its American ally for England. Although the commercial treaty of 1778 stated that the United States would give no nation greater trading privileges than it gave to France, Congress had never given France anything more than equality with other nations — and that only on paper. In operation, the laws that Congress passed consistently favored England. Jay's Treaty had outraged France, and the French minister to America, Pierre Adet, had warned that his country would henceforth treat American ships "in the same manner as they suffer the English to treat them." Actually the French had already intercepted several American vessels bound for England and had impounded them in French harbors. Now France announced that she would no longer recognize the treaty principle that free ships made free goods and that she would treat American sailors serving on British ships as pirates. She went even further: she refused to have anything to do with the American minister, Charles Cotesworth Pinckney (brother of Thomas).

President Adams proposed to meet the crisis diplomatically by sending a three-man mission to France, the mission for which he had considered Madison. The members of his Cabinet were at first opposed not only to Madison but to any mission. Only after Hamilton cautioned them not to get too far ahead of public opinion did they fall in with Adams' plan. The com-

John Adams: Always honest, often wise.

missioners appointed were the Virginia Federalist lawyer, John Marshall; the rejected minister to France, C. C. Pinckney; and an astute but unpredictable Massachusetts politician, Elbridge Gerry. To announce the mission the President called a special session of Congress in May and delivered a message that the Cabinet, speaking for Hamilton, had thought the only proper accompaniment to negotiations. It called for strengthening coastal defenses, arming merchant vessels, completing three frigates begun in 1794, and establishing a provisional army.

The message put an end to Republican sympathy for the President. Jefferson, the former advocate of bargaining from strength, now thought that the recommendations would be offensive to France and would make the mission's task impossible. As it turned out, neither American nor French belligerence but French corruption prevented the mission's success. The

French minister of foreign affairs, Talleyrand, after keeping the envoys waiting for several weeks, informed them through three unaccredited go-betweens, known only as X, Y, and Z, that the price of negotiating would be $250,000 for himself. The price of a treaty would be several million dollars for France. "Not a sixpence," said Pinckney, as he and Marshall departed, leaving Gerry to continue the futile conversations until he was ordered home.

When Adams reported the XYZ Affair, incredulous Republicans in Congress demanded to see the commission's papers. Adams did not follow Washington's example in the case of the Jay's Treaty papers, probably because he knew that the record would fully sustain him. He turned the papers over, and Congress supported the President in retaliating against France by actions just short of war. The treaties of 1778 were repudiated. Commercial intercourse was suspended. American ships were authorized to seize French armed vessels, and for the next two years French and American ships fought an undeclared war on the seas.

It would have been foolhardy to go such lengths without preparing for full-scale war. But the President and his advisers could not agree on the kind of preparation to make. The most ardent Federalists saw in the crisis an opportunity to strengthen themselves as well as the government at the expense of the Republicans. They wanted a large standing army, not merely to repel a French invasion but to overawe and if necessary to suppress their political opponents. Hamilton also dreamed of leading an army of conquest into Florida and Louisiana. Adams, while denouncing the French and their American friends, had a more realistic and more comprehensive view of the national interest. He thought it wise to keep a small army in readiness, but he discounted the possibility of a French invasion, and he had no ambition to rule by military force or to conquer territories peopled by Frenchmen and Spaniards. What the country really needed, he believed, was a navy to defend its commercial interests in the shifting tides of European conflict. To concentrate on an army would leave the United States no choice but to side always with the country whose navy dominated the seas, in other words, with England. Though Adams' own sympathies lay with England, he thought it was bad policy to let the safety of American commerce depend on the good will of any foreign country. Accordingly, in May 1798 he persuaded Congress to establish a Department of the Navy, with Benjamin Stoddert, a Maryland merchant, as Secretary. In Stoddert Adams gained his first loyal adviser in the Cabinet.

While Adams and Stoddert proceeded with the construction and commissioning of warships, the High Federalists, as the more extreme branch of the party came to be called, continued their buildup of the army, dragging the reluctant President with them, and levying heavy taxes to pay for it. Washington was persuaded to accept command again, and Hamilton was eager to join him. Adams agreed to make Hamilton a general but refused at first to rank him above Henry Knox, Daniel Morgan, and Benjamin Lincoln, Hamilton's seniors in the Revolutionary army. Hamilton, perhaps with more than military ends in view, declined to play second fiddle to anyone but Washington and made his refusal a test of strength. When Washington, still willing to play Hamilton's game, joined the Cabinet in demanding that Hamilton be his second in command, Adams was forced to back down.

After this victory, the High Federalists pressed hard for a declaration of war against France. The harder they pressed, the more apparent it became that their aims were domestic rather than foreign. England's depredations against American shipping had continued unabated, while France, according to reports from Elbridge Gerry, had become far more conciliatory in response to the violent American reaction to the XYZ Affair. Gerry was denounced by the Federalists upon his return in 1798, but he was courted by the Republicans and heeded by the President. George Logan, an ex-Quaker from Philadelphia who had conducted an unauthorized peace mission of his own, confirmed Gerry's view of the shift in France's attitude. Adams objected to private citizens meddling in the country's foreign relations and got the Logan Act passed to prevent it in the future, but he was impressed by what Logan told him. Similar reports were arriving from the President's son, John Quincy Adams, also in Europe, and from Rufus King, the American minister in London, and from William Vans

Murray at The Hague. In January the President received from Murray a letter sent by Talleyrand to the French chargé at The Hague, specifically stating that an American envoy to France would "undoubtedly be received with the respect due to the representative of a free, independent and powerful nation."

Adams did not assume that Talleyrand's character had improved, but he suspected that American firmness had worked a change in French policy. To declare war now would be to lose all the advantages of neutrality, to sacrifice the national interest to party politics. To make a gesture toward peace, on the other hand, would still leave the United States a free hand and would reduce party tensions at home. Such a reduction would not please the High Federalists, who had visions of a Republican rebellion that the new army commanded by old heroes would crush. That way, Adams believed, lay disaster for the Union, and he decided for once to be President. In February 1799, without consulting his Cabinet further, he sent to the Senate the nomination of William Vans Murray as minister to negotiate a new agreement with France.

Having done so, Adams went off to Quincy, leaving the High Federalists furious and frustrated and the Republicans delighted. With party tensions eased, Adams was not in any hurry to get his mission under way. He was by no means sure that it would succeed, and he wanted to have his new naval vessels ready in case it should fail. By October, three squadrons were fit for duty, and Adams gave orders for Murray's departure. Murray was accompanied now by Oliver Ellsworth (Chief Justice of the United States) and William R. Davie (former governor of North Carolina). When the three-man commission arrived in France, they found Bonaparte in control. He was eager to line up a coalition of neutral nations against England and ready to renew Franco-American relations on terms advantageous to the United States. France was willing to declare the old treaties of 1778 void, thus formally freeing the United States of its only permanent alliance. France was also willing to accept again the principle of free-ships–free-goods and, on September 30, 1800, the negotiators signed a convention that put an end to French spoliation of American commerce. The President's declaration of in-

dependence from his Cabinet had thus saved his country from a needless war and gained it greater freedom on the seas.

The Alien and Sedition laws. In sending the mission to France, John Adams had risen above party, as he believed a President should. But he never fully admitted, even to himself, how much he had been and still remained a member of the Federalist party. After his initial *rapprochement* with Jefferson had faded, his very devotion to the national interest and to the dignity of his office betrayed him, as it had Washington, into regarding himself and his supporters as impartial patriots and the Republican opposition as a criminal conspiracy.

After the disclosure of the XYZ Affair, Adams had been deluged by addresses from groups of patriotic citizens declaring their readiness to fight the French. In his public replies he commended his correspondents and deplored the "few degraded or . . . deluded characters" who viewed the crisis differently. "These lovers of themselves," he announced, "who withdraw their confidence from their own Legislative Government, and place it on a foreign nation, or Domestic Faction, or both in alliance, deserve all our contempt and abhorrence." The references to Republicans were oblique but unmistakable. Even Hamilton thought the President might be pushing anti-Republican sentiment a little too far. But other Federalist leaders (without specific encouragement from either Adams or Hamilton) persuaded Congress to pass legislation designed to harass, if not destroy, the Republican opposition.

The Alien Acts, three in number, were passed in June and July 1798. One, the Alien Enemies Act, was a nonpartisan measure that simply provided for the restraint of enemy aliens in time of war. Since war was never declared against France, the act did not operate during Adams' Presidency. The other two were partisan measures aimed against immigrants, who were widely suspected of being Republican in politics. The Naturalization Act required that an alien seeking citizenship must have resided for fourteen years in the United States, five of them in the state where naturalization was sought. The Alien Friends Act, which was to run for two years only, gave the President power to deport any alien whom he considered dangerous to the welfare of the country.

The Sedition Act, which was passed in July 1798, was one of the most repressive measures ever directed against political activity in the United States. It provided fines and imprisonment for persons unlawfully combining or conspiring "with intent to oppose any measure or measures of the government of the United States," or counseling or advising such opposition, or writing, printing, uttering, or publishing "any false, scandalous, and malicious writing or writings against the government of the United States, or the President of the United States, with intent to defame . . . or to bring them or either of them, into contempt or disrepute." The blatant political purpose of the act was admitted in the date it was to expire: March 3, 1801, when the next President would be inaugurated. The act would last long enough to gag Republican criticism of the Administration until the next election was safely over; it would expire soon enough to permit Federalist criticism in case the election brought in a Republican administration.

The first victim of the Sedition Act was Matthew Lyon, Republican representative from Vermont. On the floor of the House, Lyon and the Connecticut Federalist Roger Griswold had already engaged each other with canes, fire tongs, and spit. In the autumn following the passage of the Sedition Act, Lyon, who was up for reelection, directed his campaign against the Federalist party's conduct of the government. Although his attacks were returned measure for measure by his opponent, Lyon was indicted, convicted, and sentenced (by a Federalist judge) to four months in jail and a $1,000 fine. He was reelected while serving his jail sentence.

The Republicans were alarmed — and rightly so. The Alien and Sedition Acts demonstrated that the Federalists were prepared to abandon the principles of the Enlightenment, of the Revolution, and of the Constitution. When Madison sponsored the first amendments to the Constitution, he had recognized that they might one day have to be defended against an ambitious executive or legislature. He had suggested that the federal courts might protect them, but thus far the courts had shown a disposition to restrain the states more than the national government. They had declared a few state laws unconstitutional, and in the case of *Chisholm v. Georgia* (1793) the Supreme Court had awarded judgment against the state of Georgia in a suit brought by citizens of South Carolina. This affront to state sovereignty caused so many protests that an eleventh amendment to the Constitution was adopted to deny federal jurisdiction in suits brought against a state by foreigners or by citizens of another state.

The Eleventh Amendment, which was ratified in January 1798, was a direct blow at the federal courts, whose prestige was already at a low ebb. Men of high talents refused to serve on them. John Jay had resigned as Chief Justice of the United States in 1795 in order to run for the governorship of New York. The judges who remained and who presided at sedition trials had no more scruples about the constitutionality of the Alien and Sedition Acts than John Adams had had when he signed them.

Since there seemed to be no other way of protecting the Constitution from the Federalists, Madison and Jefferson turned to the state governments. With the election of Adams, Madison had retired temporarily from Congress and returned to Virginia. In the Virginia legislature, he now secured passage (December 24, 1798) of a series of resolutions affirming the authority of the states to judge the constitutionality of federal legislation and declaring the Alien and Sedition Acts unconstitutional.

Madison's resolutions did not go beyond the statement of unconstitutionality. But Vice-President Jefferson had framed another set, for the state of Kentucky (November 16, 1798), which declared the acts to be "void and of no force." When the other states declined to support Virginia and Kentucky, Kentucky reaffirmed in another set of resolutions (November 22, 1799) that "nullification" by the states was the proper remedy for unconstitutional actions by the federal government. But the other states still refused to follow suit and allowed the Alien and Sedition Acts to expire under their own terms. Though the resolutions of Kentucky and Virginia failed in their immediate object, they posed a question that would trouble the nation for many years to come. The Philadelphia convention had not decided which was sovereign, state governments or national government, and the resolutions were a reminder that the question was still open.

The election of 1800. The steadily declining fortunes of the Republicans convinced them that in order to survive they would have to build a national organization. As a result of the XYZ Affair they had lost congressional seats in the elections of 1798; even Virginia, the Republican stronghold, had returned five "certain Federalists" and three moderates who leaned toward Federalism. With Jefferson directing party strategy, the Republicans resolved to do better in the next election. Following regional patterns of local government, they appointed county committees in the South and township committees in the North to instruct the voters about the vices of Federalists and the virtues of Republicans. The local committees were supervised by state committees, which in turn took their direction from a caucus of Republican congressmen at Marache's boardinghouse in Philadelphia. By now there were Republican newspapers scattered throughout the country, the most prominent of which was Philadelphia's *Aurora*. The editors, defying the Sedition Act, charged the government with aristocratic and monarchical pretensions and with levying heavy taxes to support an expensive navy, a standing army, and a corrupt funding system.

The charges struck home, for they were substantially correct. Armies and navies are always expensive, and in 1798 the Adams Administration had levied an extremely unpopular direct tax on houses, lands, and slaves to pay the rising costs. What was worse, in 1799 the army had been ordered into action to enforce collection of the tax, after a mob led by one John Fries released two tax-evaders from prison in Northampton County, Pennsylvania. Although the army, as in the case of the Whiskey Rebellion, could find no one to fight, the use of it lent support to Republican accusations of tyranny.

Federalist newspapers replied by calling Republicans the tools of the godless French. Federalist attorneys and judges made full use of the Sedition Act to silence Republican editors, but the wheels of the law did not turn rapidly enough to make more than a few martyrs. The Federalists also caucused at Philadelphia and tried to organize support at the local level. But

The Election of 1800

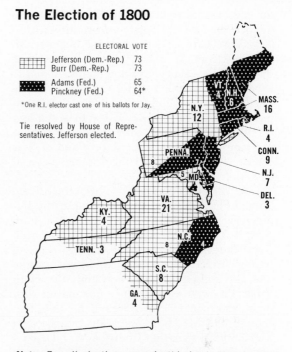

ELECTORAL VOTE

Jefferson (Dem.-Rep.) 73
Burr (Dem.-Rep.) 73

Adams (Fed.) 65
Pinckney (Fed.) 64*

*One R.I. elector cast one of his ballots for Jay.

Tie resolved by House of Representatives. Jefferson elected.

Note: For all election maps in this book, the electoral vote will be given within each state. When a state's electoral vote is split, as were the votes of Pennsylvania, Maryland, and North Carolina in this election, the split will be shown with the number of electoral votes going to each candidate. The graphic presentation in such cases is not intended to indicate the geographic distribution of votes within the state.

their efforts were hampered by their own divisions. The rank and file of the party approved John Adams' peace mission to France and would have been outraged by a proposal to support any other candidate for the Presidency. The High Federalists, however, considered Adams a traitor. Pickering thought that the mission to France would "subvert the present administration and with them the government itself." Hamilton declared he would never again support Adams and even wrote a pamphlet attacking him.

In spite of the defection in his own camp, Adams made a strong bid for reelection. By the spring of 1800 it had become probable that he would take New England and New Jersey, that Jefferson (the natural Republican candidate) would win most of the South, and that a deadlock would neutralize Pennsylvania. New York and South Carolina, both uncertain, held the balance. In New York the legislature chose the presidential electors, and the state was so divided that the thirteen representatives from New York City held the balance of power in the legislature. In 1800 Aaron Burr, perhaps the Republicans' best working politician on the local level, was able to offer the city a slate of thirteen extremely influential and popular candidates for representative. They took the city by five hundred votes, thus assuring Republican control of the state legislature and of New York's electoral votes in the coming national contest.

New York City had hitherto been the private preserve of Alexander Hamilton, and the significance of his defeat was not lost on John Adams. The President knew that he had been right about the peace mission, regardless of party considerations; but he knew now that he was also right politically and that the High Federalists were wrong. After putting up with their insolence for three years, he had had enough. On May 6 he asked for and received McHenry's resignation from the War Department. On May 10 he asked for Pickering's; when Pickering refused, Adams simply discharged him.

While Adams was cutting loose from the High Federalists, the Republicans had decided that Aaron Burr would again make the best running mate for Jefferson. The Federalists' vice-presidential candidate was Charles Cotesworth Pinckney. Hamilton, who had been responsible for the choice, used the same strategy as in 1796: to throw support to a vice-presidential candidate in the hope that he would overtake both presidential candidates.

The outcome of the election was in doubt for some time, for electors were still chosen at different times and in different ways; but when the ballots were finally counted, Adams had sixty-five electoral votes, and Pinckney sixty-four. The Republican machine, working a little too well, had given Jefferson and Burr each seventy-three. It had been understood that Burr was the vice-presidential candidate, but no Republican elector had diverted one of his two ballots to preclude a tie. To prevent this situation from recurring, the Twelfth Amendment to the Constitution, adopted in 1804, required the Electoral College to vote separately for President and for Vice-President. But in February 1801, as directed by the Constitution,

the choice between Jefferson and Burr was thrown to the House of Representatives, with each state allowed only one vote. Voting went on for a week through thirty-five ballots without the necessary nine-state majority being reached. Finally Hamilton, who considered Jefferson a lesser evil than Burr, persuaded some of the latter's supporters to cast blank ballots. Jefferson was declared elected.

Since Republican candidates for Congress were also victorious, the election of 1800 brought to an end Federalist control of the national government. Nevertheless, the Federalists could look forward to a continuing influence: the United States judiciary, manned by Federalist appointees, enjoyed a lifetime tenure. The last acts of the Adams Administration made the most of this fact. A new judiciary act of February 27, 1801, created sixteen circuit courts; and Adams, instead of leaving the appointment of the new circuit judges to his successor, filled the offices with loyal Federalists. Even more significantly Adams in January 1801 appointed as Chief Justice of the United States John Marshall of Virginia, an ardent Federalist. Under Marshall the Court was to rise to new heights of prestige and power, to the considerable annoyance of Marshall's fellow Virginian in the White House.

Jefferson liked to think of his election as the "Revolution of 1800." But the election had been no landslide. John Adams had only eight votes fewer than the winners. If he had taken either New York or South Carolina, he would have won; and he might have taken them had he parted sooner from the High Federalists. Actually John Adams' capture of the Federalist party marked as great a political change as Jefferson's triumph at the polls, a change possibly more crucial to the preservation of national unity. Hamiltonian policies, tied to urban business interests at home and to Great Britain abroad, had repeatedly threatened to divide the nation. By sending the mission to France and by repudiating Hamilton, Adams reduced the gap between Federalist and Republican views of the national interest. His action came too late to win an electoral majority for himself or his party, but it did ensure peace, not only between the United States and France, but between two groups of Americans who had drifted dangerously far apart.

SUGGESTIONS FOR READING

The period covered by this chapter is surveyed by J. C. Miller, *The Federalist Era** (1960), and by Nathan Schachner, *The Founding Fathers** (1954). Leonard White, *The Federalists** (1948) assesses the achievements of the Washington and Adams administrations in establishing the bureaucratic machinery of national government. The political foundations of Federalist power are analyzed in Manning Dauer, *The Adams Federalists* (1953). In *The Economic Origins of Jeffersonian Democracy** (1915), Charles Beard saw the rise of the Republican party as a continuation of the small-farmer hostility to the Constitution, which he had described in his *Economic Interpretation of the Constitution** (1913). Joseph Charles, *The Origins of the American Party System** (1956), denies that there was any such continuity. Noble Cunningham, *The Jeffersonian Republicans* (1957), describes the political organizing activities of the Republicans and is particularly good on the election of 1800. A good general account of the first parties is W. N. Chambers, *Political Parties in a New Nation** (1963).

Two aspects of political discontent during the 1790's are treated in E. P. Link, *Democratic-Republican Societies* (1942), and L. D. Baldwin, *The Whiskey Rebels* (1939). R. A. Rutland, *The Birth of the Bill of Rights** (1955), discusses the origins of the first ten amendments. Irving Brant, *The Bill of Rights* (1965), is more comprehensive and deals with the later interpretations of the amendments. L. W. Levy, *Legacy of Suppression** (1960), shows that the First Amendment offered less firm protection for freedom of speech and the press than has generally been supposed. J. M. Smith, *Freedom's Fetters** (1956), is the most complete account of the Alien and Sedition Acts. Adrienne Koch and Harry Ammon, "The Virginia and Kentucky Resolutions," *William and Mary Quarterly*, 3rd series, V (1948), 145–76, is a good account of that subject.

S. F. Bemis, *Jay's Treaty** (1923) and *Pinckney's Treaty** (1926, 1960), definitively treats two important episodes in foreign relations in the Federalist decade. Felix Gilbert, *To the Farewell Address** (1961), discusses the origins of attitudes classically expressed in Washington's warning against alliances. Alexander DeConde, *Entangling Alliance* (1958) and *The Quasi-War* (1966), L. M. Sears, *George Washington and the French Revolution* (1960), Charles Hazen, *Contemporary American Opinion of the French Revolution* (1897), and L. S. Kaplan, *Jefferson and France* (1967), discuss relations with France. In *Number 7* (1964) Julian Boyd gives evidence of Hamilton's efforts in the Nootka Sound crisis to turn American policy in favor of the British.

So many men of large stature shared in the making of public policy during the 1790's that much of the history of the period has been written in the form of biography. D. S. Freeman, *George Washington*, 7 vols. (1948–57), is the most complete account; Vol. VII was written after Freeman's death by J. A. Carroll and M. W. Ashworth. J. C. Miller, *Alexander Hamilton: Portrait in Paradox* (1959), is the best biography of Hamilton. Hamilton's great reports are conveniently gathered in J. E. Cooke, ed., *The Reports of Alexander Hamilton** (1964). Irving Brant, *James Madison: Father of the Constitution, 1787–1800* (1950), the third volume of a six-volume study of Madison, contains a wealth of new information about the formation of the Republican party. Gilbert Chinard, *Honest John Adams** (1933), is good, but C. P. Smith, *John Adams* (1962), is more definitive. J. R. Howe, *The Changing Political Thought of John Adams* (1966), is a sensitive interpretation. Stephen Kurtz, *The Presidency of John Adams** (1957), is very good on the election of 1796; Zoltan Haraszti, *John Adams and the Prophets of Progress** (1952), is a charming account of Adams' notes in the margins of his books. Dumas Malone, *Jefferson and His Time*, 3 vols. (1948, 1952, 1962), covers Jefferson's career up to his election as President. A stimulating interpretation of Jefferson's thought is D. J. Boorstin, *The Lost World of Thomas Jefferson** (1948). Other good studies are Frank Monaghan, *John Jay* (1935); F. B. Tolles, *George Logan* (1953); George Dangerfield, *Chancellor Robert R. Livingston* (1960).

* Available in a paperback edition.

7
Jeffersonian Republicanism

For more than a decade, with mounting indignation, Thomas Jefferson and his followers had been protesting against the trend of Federalist policies: against fiscal measures that allegedly spawned a moneyed aristocracy and put an unjust burden on the agrarian "producing classes"; against the "monarchical aristocratical" tendencies of the federal bureaucracy; against the subversion of civil liberties; against "national consolidation" and encroachments on the rights of the states. Now, on March 4, 1801, the first Republican President was obliged to spell out a set of policies of his own. This, in broad outline, Jefferson accomplished in a brilliant inaugural address (the first to be delivered in the new capital on the banks of the Potomac) that affirmed his liberal democratic philosophy and his faith in the wisdom of the people.

Jefferson soothed jittery Federalists by assuring them that no Jacobin reign of terror would follow the "Revolution of 1800" and by inviting them to join Republicans "in common efforts for the common good." He cautioned Republicans that though the will of the majority must prevail, "the minority possess their equal rights, which equal law must protect." He reminded members of both parties that in spite of the acrimonious campaign just past

> every difference of opinion is not a difference of principle. We have called by different names brethren of the same principle. We are all Republicans, we are all Federalists. If there be any among us who would wish to dissolve this Union or to change its republican form, let them stand undisturbed as monuments of the safety with which error of opinion may be tolerated where reason is left free to combat it.

Yet, even as he tried to conciliate his political foes, Jefferson was stressing a difference between them and him, for Federalists did not share his confidence that reason ruled the minds of men.

ECONOMY AND SIMPLICITY

The new regime. The rustic simplicity and democratic manners that Jefferson thought proper for the leaders of an agrarian republic

Rustic simplicity and democratic manners.

seemed appropriate in a crude, half-built capital city that lacked the social and cultural opportunities of Philadelphia. Though the President was a cultivated gentleman to the manner born, his plain informality was natural and uncontrived. Unlike his predecessors, he sent his annual messages to Congress to be read by a clerk, lest reading them in person should suggest that he was imitating the British monarch delivering his speech from the throne. Jefferson abandoned the elegant weekly presidential levees that had previously been such a delight to the capital's aristocracy. At his infrequent state dinners and receptions and in his dealings with the diplomatic corps he avoided anything that smacked of the pomp and pretentiousness of European courts. In the White House he lived simply and made himself accessible to countrymen who had business with him.

Although Jefferson believed in the sovereignty of the people and tended to romanticize the independent farmer, he did not assume that untrained men could handle the responsibilities of important administrative posts. He rejected the theory of government by a political élite, and yet the men in his Administration were of as high a caliber as their Federalist predecessors. Actually he discharged few Federalists from nonpolicymaking offices, and most of his new appointees were educated, talented, and experienced upper-class Republicans. James Madison, Jefferson's close friend and political collaborator, a Virginia aristocrat who had led the political fight against the Federalists, joined the new Administration as Secretary of State. Albert Gallatin of Pennsylvania, a gifted and devoted Jeffersonian, accepted the crucial office of Secretary of the Treasury and served with such distinction that he won the respect of even the Federalists.

Jefferson, like Washington and Adams, had doubts about the wisdom of political parties, but far more than his predecessors he played the dual role of President and party-leader. As party-leader he was concerned about the weakness of the Republicans in the Northern states, where Federalists had identified them with the interests of the South. In order to strengthen his party in the chief bastion of Federalism, Jefferson appointed three New Englanders to major offices: Levi Lincoln of

Thomas Jefferson: Confident that reason ruled the minds of men.

Massachusetts as Attorney General, Henry Dearborn of Massachusetts as Secretary of War, and Gideon Granger of Connecticut as Postmaster General. He also made skillful use of the patronage to this end, and in 1804 the Republicans won a majority of Northern votes.

Republican policies. Jefferson repudiated most of Hamilton's mercantilist theories in favor of a general policy of laissez faire. His ideal was "a wise and frugal Government, which shall restrain men from injuring one another . . . [and] leave them otherwise free to regulate their own pursuits of industry and improvement." The principal responsibilities of such a government, Jefferson explained, would be to honor the Bill of Rights, seek equal justice for all men, respect the rights of the states, "the surest bulwarks against antirepublican tendencies," and practice strict economy, "that labor may be lightly burthened."

But the Jefferson Administration soon discovered — as would future administrations when political supremacy passed from one party to another — that it could reverse the actions and repudiate the commitments of its

predecessor only at the risk of serious confusion. Republicans, therefore, thought it best not to tamper with some of Hamilton's economic measures. The Bank of the United States, for example, continued its operations undisturbed until 1811, when its charter expired. By then many Republicans, including Madison and Gallatin, favored granting the Bank a new charter, a proposal that failed in each house of Congress by a single vote. Nor did the Republicans reverse Federalist measures for refunding the national debt, or for federal assumption of the Revolutionary debts of the states, or for encouraging American shipping.

Without changing his opinion about the primacy of agriculture, Jefferson as President developed a greater respect for other economic pursuits. In his first message to Congress he referred to manufacturing, commerce, and navigation, along with agriculture, as "the four pillars of our prosperity"; and he even suggested, though somewhat vaguely, that "within the limits of our constitutional powers" their protection from "casual embarrassments" might be "seasonably interposed."

The "Revolution of 1800" did not, however, lack substance, for the Republicans lost no time in disposing of some of the Federalists' pet measures. They refused, of course, to renew the Alien Act when it expired in 1801. They reduced the residence requirement for naturalization from fourteen years to five; once again America became, in Jefferson's words, an "asylum" for "oppressed humanity." The Sedition Act also expired in 1801, and Jefferson saw to it that those who had been imprisoned for violating it were freed and that all fines were refunded. The Republican Congress repealed the Judiciary Act of 1801 and abolished, as a needless extravagance, the new circuit judgeships that act had created. Thus, defeated ("lame duck") Federalists to whom Adams had given "midnight appointments" in the judicial branch lost their jobs; and the courts, as one Republican explained, ceased to be a "hospital for decayed politicians." The House of Representatives then turned on the Supreme Court and, in 1804, impeached Associate Justice Samuel Chase, an arch-Federalist who had used the bench as a political stump. But the Senate did not interpret Chase's offense as a misdemeanor within the meaning of the Constitution and refused to remove him. Henceforth, the Republicans relied on new appointments in their efforts to reform the courts.

The Jeffersonian revolution also wrought a significant change in fiscal policy. There is a tendency for governments, the new President said, "to multiply offices . . . and to increase expense" — to leave to labor only a small portion of its earnings and to "consume the whole residue of what it was instituted to guard." Unlike Hamilton, Jefferson regarded a public debt and the accompanying interest charges as beneficial only to a small class of investors and felt that it was a "mortal canker" on the rest of the community. With the able support of Secretary of the Treasury Gallatin, he strove to retire the whole public debt, which had grown to $83 million, at the earliest possible date — in sixteen years, according to the original plan. Since the excise tax had been repealed, the only way to retire the debt was through revenues from import duties and the sale of public lands and through the most rigid government economy. To cut costs in the executive department Jefferson reduced the number of officers in the diplomatic corps and revenue service. He urged Congress to abolish other public offices, to replace wasteful general appropriations with grants of "specific sums to every specific purpose," and to hold the Treasury Department responsible for all funds spent.

Jefferson was convinced, too, that military and naval expenditures could be cut without jeopardizing national defense. America, he said, was fortunately "separated by nature and a wide ocean from the exterminating havoc" of the Old World and consequently needed no large standing army. For defense against invasion, the country should rely on "the body of neighboring citizens as formed into a militia." Accordingly, the regular army was reduced from four thousand to twenty-five hundred officers and men. Jefferson realized, however, that the state militia systems needed to be improved, and in 1808 the federal government began to take a hand in reorganizing them and in defraying part of the cost of arms and equipment. Moreover, in 1802 Jefferson was instrumental in establishing the United States Military Academy at West Point.

Turning to the navy, the new Administration proceeded to sell some ocean-going vessels, lay up others, and halt construction on still others; it discharged many Navy Department employees, reduced the number of officers and enlisted men, and abandoned the improvement of navy yards and dry docks. Shore defense was to be maintained by coastal fortifications and by a fleet of small, inexpensive gunboats serving as a kind of naval militia. This policy was designed, Jefferson explained, "merely for defensive operations," not to protect commerce or to establish the United States as a sea power. The quarreling European states would thus be kept "at a distance" and at little cost.

Here, in short, was Jefferson's formula for an agrarian utopia: simplicity, frugality, and "a government founded not on the fears and follies of man, but on his reason" — a government whose authority the ordinary citizen would scarcely feel. For a time all worked according to plan, and in his second annual message Jefferson congratulated Congress for the "pleasing circumstances . . . under which we meet." The United States had become a nation of peaceful, prosperous citizens "managing their own affairs in their own way and for their own use, unembarrassed by too much regulation, unoppressed by fiscal exactions." Unfortunately, this idyllic picture of rustic innocence was but a brief and passing phase.

FERMENT IN THE WEST

The westward movement. In his vision of America as the ideal republic, Jefferson projected upon the nation at large an image of the stable, mellow society of Virginia's rural gentry. This image, however, did not fit much of the rest of the country — not even the trans-Appalachian West in whose future Jefferson placed such confident hopes. In 1800 nearly a million settlers were living in the vast area between the Appalachians and the Mississippi River; a new land act that year encouraged others to come by offering land for sale in individual tracts of 320 acres and by permitting four-year credits with a down payment of 25 per cent. A revision of this law in 1804 reduced the minimum tract to 160 acres; thus, with public land selling at a minimum price of $2 an acre, a buyer could obtain a farm for an initial payment of $80. This generous federal policy brought a steady tide of immigrants into the West, whose rich lands Jefferson thought would afford "room enough for our descendants to the thousandth and thousandth generation." As the forests were cleared and farms and villages dotted the land, new states were created from time to time — Kentucky in 1792, Tennessee in 1796, and Ohio in 1803.

Most of the Westerners liked Jefferson's politics and found much in his philosophy that pleased them, but they had mixed feelings about his economics and scarcely understood his agrarian dream — in fact, they did much to destroy it. Jefferson's ideal of a stable, self-sufficient yeomanry free of the corrupting influences of commercialism was hardly the ideal of the traders and speculators who infested the West — or, for that matter, of many of the farmers. Soon after they arrived, most Westerners began to dream not of self-sufficiency but of cash crops, of outlets to markets, and of the comforts and luxuries of the East.

The problem of transportation. Between the Western settlers and their ambitions stood two major obstacles: the mountains, which cut them off from the East, and the French, who were taking over from Spain possession of New Orleans and the mouth of the Mississippi. Before Jefferson left office, he was to find solutions to both these problems — solutions that in the long run helped to undermine his original goal of a simple agrarian society. In 1806 Congress authorized the building of a road from Cumberland, Maryland, across the mountains to Wheeling, Virginia, as a government-financed "internal improvement." Jefferson approved the measure, even though, without the constitutional amendment he had urged, it required a stretching of federal power to do so. Construction on the National Road, as it was called, began in 1811 and was completed in 1818. In subsequent years the road was extended westward to Vandalia, Illinois.

The second problem — navigation of the Mississippi River — forced Jefferson to take vigorous action that compromised not only his constitutional scruples but his fiscal policy, his foreign policy, and perhaps even his principles of public ethics. Since 1763 the mouth of the Mississippi and the immense territory of Louisiana, stretching westward to the Rockies, had been held by a declining and enfeebled Spain; and Spain, in Pinckney's Treaty of 1795, had opened the Mississippi to American navigation and granted Western flatboatmen the right to deposit their cargoes at New Orleans for shipment abroad. This arrangement satisfied the Westerners, who saw in Spain no serious threat. But they were bound to react violently if Louisiana were to fall into the hands of a stronger power or if their river outlet were cut off. As Madison explained: "The Mississippi is to them every thing. It is the Hudson, the Delaware, the Potomac, and all the navigable rivers of the Atlantic states, formed into one stream."

The Louisiana Purchase. Soon after Jefferson became President two events shocked and angered the Western settlers. The first was the revelation that Napoleon, in the secret Treaty of San Ildefonso (1800), had negotiated the transfer of Louisiana from Spain to France (though formal possession by France was long delayed). The second was a proclamation by the Spanish intendant at New Orleans, on October 16, 1802, that the right of deposit was to be suspended. Taking this as a foretaste of Napoleon's future policy, indignant Westerners looked to Jefferson for support.

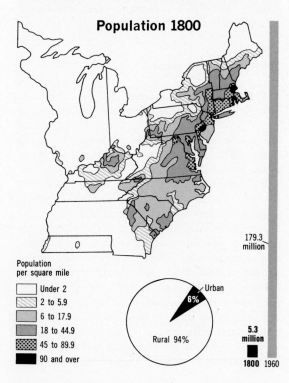

Population 1800

Population per square mile

Under 2
2 to 5.9
6 to 17.9
18 to 44.9
45 to 89.9
90 and over

Urban 6%
Rural 94%

179.3 million

5.3 million

1800 1960

The Louisiana Purchase and Explorations of the Far West

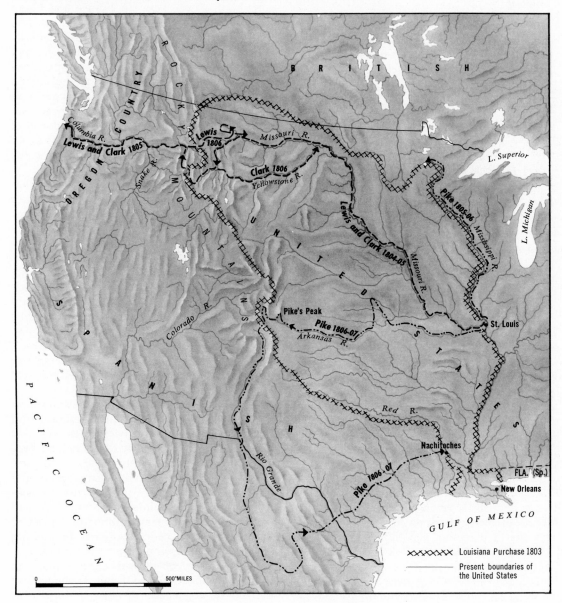

Alarmed, Jefferson feared for a time that Napoleon might force him to reconsider his basic foreign policy, perhaps even to abandon temporarily his opposition to "entangling alliances." The United States, he told Robert R. Livingston, the American minister in Paris, has always looked upon France as her "natural friend"; but there was on the globe one single spot, the possessor of which is our natural and habitual enemy. It is New Orleans, through which the produce of three-eighths of our territory must pass to market. . . . France placing herself in that door, assumes to us the attitude of defiance. The day that France takes possession of New Orleans . . . [we will be forced to] marry ourselves to the British fleet and nation.

To Congress he spoke of "the danger to which our peace would be perpetually exposed whilst so important a key to the commerce of the Western country remained under foreign power."

But before taking any drastic steps, Jefferson tried to negotiate peacefully with France. He instructed Livingston to offer to purchase New Orleans and West Florida; he obtained from Congress an appropriation of $2 million for vaguely defined expenses; and he sent James Monroe, who had the confidence of Westerners, as a special envoy to assist Livingston. Monroe arrived in Paris on April 12, 1803, two days after Talleyrand, negotiating for France, had startled Livingston by asking whether the United States would like to buy the whole of Louisiana! The two American diplomats, whose instructions were essentially to buy a city, hesitated, though only momentarily, before agreeing to buy an empire that would double the size of their country.

There were several reasons for Napoleon's sudden decision to abandon his imperial ambitions in America and to concentrate on Europe. First, he suffered a major disaster when his troops failed to crush a slave insurrection, led by Toussaint L'Ouverture, in the French colony of Santo Domingo. Second, the Peace of Amiens of 1802 had really settled nothing, and a renewal of war between France and Great Britain seemed all but inevitable. Third, Napoleon needed money, and it was obviously wise to sell a province that the British navy could prevent France from occupying in any case. Finally, selling Louisiana to the United States would remove a source of friction and avoid an Anglo-American *rapprochement*. Accordingly, on April 11 Napoleon told one of his ministers: "I renounce Louisiana. It is not only New Orleans that I will cede, it is the whole colony without any reservation."

Livingston and Monroe soon decided that this was a poor time to quibble over the letter of their instructions. On April 30, 1803, after some higgling over price, they made the purchase for $15 million and a promise (written into the purchase treaty) to give citizenship and religious freedom to the Catholics residing in Louisiana. The boundaries of Louisiana were then only vaguely defined, and the treaty merely stated that they were to be the same as they had been when Spain possessed it. "You have made a noble bargain for yourselves," said the realistic Talleyrand, "and I suppose you will make the most of it." In later years the United States did precisely that.

Westerners were delighted with the terms of the treaty, and their devotion to Jefferson and confidence in the federal government grew correspondingly stronger. But New England Federalists, viewing the West as enemy territory, criticized Jefferson severely for accepting a treaty that was tainted with duplicity. In making the sale, they pointed out, Napoleon had violated the French constitution and a promise to Spain not to cede Louisiana to another power. Yet Jefferson approved the transaction knowing this to be the case — knowing, too, that the Constitution did not explicitly authorize the acquisition of new territory. Federalists also complained that the purchase of these worthless lands was a wasteful expenditure and meant a staggering addition to the public debt.

Jefferson was sensitive to such criticism, especially to the charge that he was exceeding the limits of the Constitution strictly construed. His first impulse was to urge an amendment to the Constitution expressly granting the power to acquire territory; but the amending process was painfully slow, and Livingston warned that Napoleon might have a change of heart. Moreover, some Republicans argued that the power to acquire territory might be *implied* from the power to make treaties. Such an argument could hardly have satisfied Jefferson, but he concluded that Congress would be wise to cast aside "metaphysical subtleties and . . . throw themselves on their country for doing for them unauthorized what we know they would have done for themselves, had they been in a situation to do it." Trusting that "the good sense of our country will correct the evil of [constitutional] construction when it shall produce evil effects," Jefferson submitted the treaty to the Senate.

During the debate Federalists and Republicans reversed their former positions on questions of constitutional interpretation — a few extreme Federalists even spoke of dissolving the Union. But the treaty was ratified by a vote of twenty-four to seven, and the House appropriated the money required to fulfill its terms. Thus the United States acquired the whole of the Mississippi River and its tributaries, some 828,000 square miles of territory, millions of acres of rich farmland, and a vast store of natural resources. Moreover, the purchase of Louisiana removed a major source of American concern about the internal politics of Europe; and, in the long run, it produced a basic shift in the national balance of political power. After the treaty was ratified, Jefferson seemed to forget quickly his anxieties about it — except to regret that Spanish West Florida had not been part of the bargain. Though for the present neither threats nor money — he tried both — could pry the Floridas loose from Spain, Jefferson was confident that it was America's destiny to obtain them, too, "and all in good time."

Western exploration. On December 20, 1803, just a few weeks after France had taken formal possession of Louisiana from Spain, the French prefect at New Orleans turned the lower part of the territory over to the United States. The transfer of the upper part was delayed until the spring of 1804, when, at St. Louis, Meriwether Lewis, Jefferson's private secretary, accepted it in behalf of the United States. But Lewis was not there for that specific purpose; in fact, his presence was the result of presiden-

---

Thomas Jefferson on the Louisiana Purchase

Congress witnessed, at their last session, the extraordinary agitation produced in the public mind by the suspension of our right of deposit at the port of New Orleans.... Previous, however, to this period, we had not been unaware of the danger to which our peace would be perpetually exposed while so important a key to the commerce of the western country remained under foreign power. Difficulties, too, were presenting themselves as to the navigation of other streams, which arising within territories, pass through those adjacent. Propositions had, therefore, been authorized for obtaining, on fair conditions, the sovereignty of New Orleans, and of other possessions in that quarter interesting to our quiet....

The property and sovereignty of all Louisiana ... have on certain conditions been transferred to the United States.... While the property and sovereignty of the Mississippi and its waters secure an independent outlet for the produce of the Western States, and an uncontrolled navigation through their whole course, free from collision with other powers and the dangers to our peace from that source, the fertility of the country, its climate and extent, promise in due season important aids to our treasury, an ample provision for our posterity, and a wide-spread field for the blessings of freedom and equal laws. With the wisdom of Congress it will rest to take those ulterior measures which may be necessary for the immediate occupation and temporary government of the country; for its incorporation into our Union; for rendering the change of government a blessing to our newly-adopted brethren; for securing to them the rights of conscience and property; for confirming to the Indian inhabitants their occupancy and self-government, establishing friendly and commercial relations with them, and for ascertaining the geography of the country acquired.

From Thomas Jefferson, *Third Annual Message to Congress,* 1803.

---

tial plans that antedated the Louisiana Purchase.

In January 1803 Congress had secretly appropriated money for an expedition to explore the upper reaches of the Missouri River and from there westward to the Pacific — though none of this territory at the time belonged to the United States. The expedition, which Jefferson had been trying to promote for many years, had several purposes. The President assured the Spanish minister that it would "have no other view than the advancement of geography"; and, to be sure, his scientific curiosity about the great unexplored interior was genuine. Lewis and his fellow explorer, William Clark (a brother of George Rogers Clark), were instructed to make astronomical observations, to study the flora and fauna, and to compile the fullest possible records. But they were to be alert to more practical matters, too, especially trading opportunities and mineral deposits. Moreover, Jefferson was fully aware that explorations had diplomatic value when nations laid claims to unsettled lands.

The Lewis and Clark expedition, which took more than two years to complete, was a remarkable success. The party of forty-five men ascended the Missouri River to the Great Falls, crossed the Rockies, and descended the Snake and Columbia Rivers to the Pacific. The explorers brought back with them an enormously expanded factual knowledge of Western North America (first made available to the public when their journals were published in 1814), a large botanical collection, information of value to American fur-traders, and a strengthened foundation for an American claim to the Oregon country. This was only one of several Western explorations that Jefferson promoted. Two others were led by Zebulon Pike: one in 1805 up the Mississippi River in search of its source, and a second in 1806 up the Arkansas River to the Rockies in what is now Colorado. All of them combined the scientific and practical interests that Jefferson himself personified.

POLITICAL COMPLICATIONS

Even though Jefferson accommodated his political and economic principles to some of the realities of American life, he never managed to appease the more ardent Northern Federalists. Timothy Pickering described Jefferson as a "cowardly wretch," a "Parisian revolutionary monster, prating about humanity" while plotting "the utter destruction of his opponents." Hamilton publicly described the Administration as composed of "indolent and temporizing rulers, who love to loll in the lap of epicurean ease, and seem to imagine that to

govern well, is to amuse the wondering multitude with sagacious aphorisms and oracular sayings."

On the other hand, some Republicans, notably the uncompromising state-righters of Virginia, felt that Jefferson had moved too far toward Federalism. His good friend John Taylor observed with dismay that "Federalism . . . has gained a new footing, by being taken into partnership with republicanism." Jefferson's most persistent Virginia critic was the brilliant but erratic John Randolph of Roanoke, who would tolerate not the slightest deviation from the principles of the Kentucky Resolutions of 1798 (see p. 162). "Asking one of the States to surrender part of her sovereignty," he said, "is like asking a lady to surrender part of her chastity." After grumbling about several measures backed by the Administration, Randolph broke with Jefferson over a proposal to use federal funds to settle the claims of certain land-speculators organized into the so-called Yazoo Land Companies. These speculators had corruptly obtained a large grant from the Georgia legislature before the state, in 1802, ceded its Western lands to the federal government. Jefferson's desire to facilitate the transfer by compensating the Yazoo claimants, even though many of them were Northern speculators and their claims were tainted with fraud, drove Randolph and a small faction of Republicans into open rebellion. The "Tertium Quids," as these Republican rebels were called, blocked the settlement of the Yazoo claims for many years and tormented Jefferson with accusations of apostasy.

Meanwhile, Vice-President Aaron Burr, who had lost all influence in Republican councils after the disputed election of 1800 (see p. 164), seemed ready for almost any reckless maneuver that might improve his political fortunes. By 1804 he was willing to accept the support of the Federalists in his campaign for the governorship of New York. Some of the more irresponsible Federalists, especially the "Essex Junto" in Massachusetts and the "River Gods" in Connecticut, had been toying with a scheme to unite New York and New England in an independent Northern confederacy; and now they hoped to enlist the services of Burr. But Hamilton exposed and denounced the plot and played a major role in Burr's defeat in New

York. The enraged Burr then challenged his old New York rival to a duel, in which Hamilton, on July 11, 1804, was mortally wounded. In the presidential election of that year, Jefferson and his new running mate, George Clinton of New York, crushed the discredited Federalists. Charles Cotesworth Pinckney, the Federalist candidate, carried only Connecticut and Delaware.

The talented Burr had wrecked a promising political career by overreaching himself; he now courted final disaster by involving himself in a quixotic intrigue whose exact nature was obscured in a maze of conflicting reports. The British minister had heard that for a half-million dollars Burr would separate the Western part of the United States from the East; the Spanish minister had heard that he planned to establish a buffer state between Louisiana and Mexico; others had heard that he planned to conquer Mexico and establish an empire. Whatever his scheme was, Burr won the support of two confederates: General James Wilkinson, who commanded the American troops in Louisiana and had a greater taste for conspiracy than Burr; and Harman Blennerhassett, a wealthy Irish exile who lived on an island in the upper Ohio River. In the summer of 1806 Burr and some sixty men on thirteen flatboats departed from Blennerhassett's Island and floated down the Ohio and Mississippi for some unknown purpose to some nameless glory.

The enterprise collapsed when General Wilkinson shifted sides and sent Jefferson a report that Burr was plotting treason. On Jefferson's orders the fleeing Burr was caught and taken to Richmond, where, in 1807, he was indicted for treason and conspiracy. In the curious trial that followed, Jefferson seemed determined to get a conviction whether or not the evidence warranted it; and the presiding judge, John Marshall, a Federalist, seemed as interested in discrediting Jefferson as in giving Burr justice. In the end Burr was acquitted, for the case against him did not fulfill the terms of the Constitution's definition of treason. According to the Constitution, treason consists in "levying war" against the United States or in "adhering to their enemies, giving them aid and comfort." A conviction for treason requires "the testimony of two witnesses to the same overt act." In his charge to the jury, Marshall insisted that the witnesses must have directly implicated Burr in a specific "overt act" of treason, not merely in planning treason or just loosely in organizing "a military assemblage." Since the witnesses had failed to do this, Marshall's charge prepared the way for Burr's acquittal. It also set an important precedent that made convictions for treason extremely difficult and indictments rare.

TROUBLE ON THE HIGH SEAS

War and American trade. When Jefferson became President in 1801, he was determined that the United States pursue its destiny free from "entangling alliances" and from the wars and diplomatic duplicity of the Old World. Yet he found himself entangled in world affairs throughout most of his second Administration, and he left office with the country fast approaching total involvement. The abrogation of the French alliance in 1800, it appeared, did not mean that America had closed the door on Europe. Since she exported foodstuffs and raw materials, imported foreign manufactured goods, and sent merchant ships to distant ports, America was bound to be affected by the course of international politics and the state of the world economy.

Even during Jefferson's first Administration the Barbary pirates, operating from bases on the coast of North Africa, had provoked the pacifistic President into surprisingly vigorous action. For many years these corsairs had been harrying American vessels and forcing the federal government, like the governments of Europe, to buy immunity by paying tribute to the rulers of Morocco, Algiers, Tunis, and Tripoli. To Jefferson this costly and humiliating practice was intolerable, and in 1801 he dispatched a naval squadron to the Mediterranean. For several years the United States was engaged in virtual war with Tripoli, until the Pasha, in 1805, was obliged to make a satisfactory peace. Tribute payments to other Barbary states, however, did not cease altogether until 1816.

The Tripolitan War, though a minor affair, had forced Jefferson to modify his naval policy. But the resumption of hostilities between Great Britain and France in 1803 — a conflict that raged without interruption for the next eleven years — provided a far more strenuous test of the President's pacifism. In a larger sense, it was a test of how much the American people were ready to endure and sacrifice to remain at peace, for peace has its price as well as war. As Jefferson warned Congress, with "the flames of war lighted up again in Europe . . . the nations pursuing peace will not be exempt from all evil." To him the price was not too great, and he thanked "that kind Providence which . . . guarded us from hastily entering into the sanguinary contest and left us only to look on and to pity its ravages." America's sole interest and desire, he said, would be "to cultivate the friendship of the belligerent nations by every act of justice and of innocent kindness." Of them he would ask only respect for the rights to which American vessels and citizens were entitled as neutrals under international law. Since American friendship and trade were useful to them, Jefferson was certain that "it can not be the interest of any to assail us, nor ours to disturb them."

While Jefferson professed confidence in his country's capacity to bring "collisions of interest to the umpirage of reason rather than force," the European belligerents were locked in a conflict whose stakes seemed to justify any means that promised ultimate victory. In 1805 Napoleon's smashing victory over the armies of Austria and Russia at Austerlitz made him for the time master of much of the European continent, while Lord Nelson's decisive defeat of the French and Spanish fleets at the Battle of Trafalgar gave Britain control of the high seas. Thereafter, in a savage war of attrition, neither antagonist showed much concern for the rights of neutrals or the punctilios of international law. Both rained blows on American shipping interests and insults on sensitive patriots.

Trouble began in 1805, when a British court ruled that goods from the French West Indies bound for Europe on American vessels, even though shipped by way of the United States, were subject to seizure. When the commercial provisions of Jay's Treaty of 1794 expired in 1807 and American diplomats were unable to negotiate a new agreement satisfactory to Jefferson, British interference with American shipping increased. Meanwhile Napoleon had developed a program of economic warfare; his so-called Continental System, elaborated in his Berlin Decree of 1806 and Milan Decree of 1807, closed the European ports under his control to British goods and stated that neutral ships complying with British trade regulations would be confiscated. The British government retaliated with a series of Orders in Council, the most important of which proclaimed a blockade of the ports of France and of the nations under her control. Thereafter American ships bound for western Europe risked seizure by one or the other of the belligerents, depending on whose rules they flouted. In the three years prior to 1807 the British seized at least a thousand American merchantmen and the French half that many.

To Americans the most grievous British wrong was the revival and vigorous application of the centuries-old system of impressment, by which the Royal Navy procured its manpower. In times of crisis British law permitted the commander of a warship, when he needed men, to draft able-bodied subjects of the king wherever they could be found. In enforcing the system British warships stopped American merchantmen on the high seas to search for deserters; they took off British-born sailors who had become Americans by naturalization; and in the process they heedlessly impressed an unknown number of native-born Americans as well. The issue reached a crisis in June 1807, when the British frigate *Leopard* overhauled the United States frigate *Chesapeake* within sight of the Virginia coast and demanded the right to search her for deserters. When the commander of the unprepared *Chesapeake* refused, the *Leopard* fired three broadsides that killed three Americans and wounded eighteen others. The crippled *Chesapeake* submitted to the seizure of four deserters and then returned to Norfolk. This humiliation of an American frigate infuriated both Federalists and Republicans. "Never, since the battle of Lexington," wrote Jefferson, "have I seen this country in such a state of exasperation as at present." Judging from the tone of the press and the speeches of politicians, the country seemed ready to unite behind a war policy. But Jefferson asked for less: he ordered British warships out of American waters and demanded reparations and an apology.

The embargo. Jefferson asked something of Americans, too. He called for a supreme effort, not to win a war, but to achieve what he considered the nobler goal of keeping the country at peace. He believed that denying the belligerents the benefits of American trade would cause them so much distress that they would abandon their encroachments on American neutral rights. For this purpose, and to avoid further provocative incidents, Jefferson proposed a policy that he had long cherished as an alternative to war, a policy he described as "peaceable coercion." On December 22, 1807, in response to his urgent plea, Congress passed the Embargo Act, which stopped the export of American goods and prohibited all ships from clearing American ports for foreign ports. This act, in effect, required shipowners to abandon their risky but extremely profitable wartime trade and obliged planters and farmers to give up their rich European export market.

Jefferson asked for a greater sacrifice than most Americans seemed ready to make. Angry New England merchants, preferring risks and insults to commercial stagnation, denounced the embargo as an unconstitutional expansion of federal power. Many of them defiantly engaged in an illicit trade that severe enforcement measures could not altogether suppress. Some again hinted at secession. Among them was Federalist Senator Timothy Pickering of Massachusetts, who described Jefferson as capable of almost any "nefarious act" and called on the states to resist "the usurpations of the general government." The agricultural interest was equally distressed when farm commodities began to accumulate at the ports and prices declined. John Randolph's assaults on the Administration matched those of the Federalists.

Eventually Congress yielded to overwhelming pressure and passed an act repealing the embargo. On March 1, 1809, a disappointed Jefferson signed it. The failure of "peaceable coercion" to win the needed public support should not obscure the fact that it had kept the country at peace; moreover, there is reason to believe that, given time, the embargo might even have wrung concessions from the British.

"Nature intended me for the more tranquil pursuits of science by rendering them my supreme delight," wrote the weary Jefferson at the close of his second Administration. Retirement was a welcome relief not only from the vicissitudes of domestic politics, in which he counted more successes than failures, but from the trials of international affairs, in which he suffered his greatest defeat.

THE DECISION FOR WAR

By declining to run for reelection in 1808, Jefferson helped to establish the two-term tradition; but he also set the precedent by which a retiring President intervened in the selection of his successor. Jefferson won the Republican nomination for his Secretary of State, James Madison. Though the Federalists, who again nominated Charles Cotesworth Pinckney, regained control of New England and increased their strength in the new Congress, Madison won the Presidency by a decisive majority of 122 to 47 in the Electoral College. His inaugural address reflected the changing conditions of the preceding eight years, especially in its concern for the promotion of commerce and industry; but in spirit it was still a thoroughly Jeffersonian document, which endorsed the domestic and foreign policies of his predecessor. Few Presidents have brought to the White House such rich experience in public life as did Madison; none, save John Adams, was so profound a student of political philosophy. Yet, though Madison had contributed much to the formulation of Republican doctrine and had never been Jefferson's mere pliant tool, the scholarly Virginian lacked Jefferson's political acumen and administrative skill.

The failure of diplomacy. The overshadowing problem confronting the new President and Congress was the continuing European holocaust, which still created difficult situations for neutrals. Although the embargo had been repealed, the policy of "peaceable coercion" persisted in less drastic forms. The Madison Administration blundered badly in applying it, however. The first substitute for the embargo was a Nonintercourse Act, passed in 1809, which reestablished trade with all nations except Great Britain and France so long as the latter continued to enforce their obnoxious orders and decrees. This act encouraged the British government to try negotiation. David Erskine, the friendly and sympathetic British minister, concluded an agreement that was

James Madison: A greater man than President.

highly satisfactory to the United States, though he violated his instructions in doing so. On June 10, 1809, the delighted President renewed trade with Great Britain without waiting for the agreement to be approved in London, and hundreds of American ships cleared their home ports for the first time in many months. Unfortunately the British government repudiated the Erskine "treaty" as soon as it arrived and recalled its too-generous minister. Madison, embarrassed and humiliated, then proclaimed the restoration of nonintercourse, and Anglo-American relations worsened.

On May 1, 1810, nonintercourse gave way to a new policy incorporated in a curious measure called Macon's Bill Number 2. This bill restored trade with both Great Britain and France but threatened to resume nonintercourse with either of them whenever the other agreed to respect America's neutral rights. Now it was Napoleon's turn to try some shifty diplomacy. Proclaiming his love for Americans and his concern for their prosperity, he announced that on November 1, 1810, the French

commercial restrictions would be repealed — but he attached conditions that made his promise almost meaningless. Madison fell into Napoleon's trap and on February 2, 1811, reestablished nonintercourse with Britain, though, in fact, the French continued to seize American ships. Unable to get Britain to repeal her Orders in Council, Madison recalled the American minister, William Pinkney, and thus virtually severed diplomatic relations.

Ironically, a few months later the policy of "peaceable coercion" won a striking victory. On June 16, 1812, beset by an economic crisis at home, the British foreign minister announced the immediate suspension of the Orders in Council (though not impressment). But the announcement came too late. On June 1 Madison had asked for a declaration of war against Great Britain, and Congress soon complied: the House on June 4 by a vote of 79 to 49, the Senate on June 18 by a vote of 19 to 13.

The motives of the War Hawks. The geographical distribution of the vote for and against war raises some difficult questions about its causes. In the House, Pennsylvania and the southern and frontier states, including Vermont, voted 65 to 15 for war; New York, New Jersey, and the New England maritime states voted 14 to 34 against. The Federalist commercial interests, though directly affected by British impressment and interference with American shipping on the high seas, nevertheless considered war with Great Britain the ultimate folly. War would be more devastating to their trade than the Orders in Council had been — and the blow would be dealt by their own government. Moreover, to them Britain was not only a profitable market but the defender of conservatism, stability, and order against the obscenities of Napoleonic France. Sharing these views with the Federalists was a handful of Republicans representing Southern coastal districts. John Randolph, a severe critic of the war policy, urged Republicans to live up to their principles of economy and retrenchment and not to become "infatuated with standing armies, loans, taxes, navies, and war."

An able and highly articulate group opposed the declaration of war, but the majority seemed to support it. Although the center of this majority was in the agricultural South and West, rather than in New England, neutral rights and impressment were issues of major importance in the decision to go to war. The grievances Madison stressed in his war message were "the injuries and indignities which have been heaped upon our country" — the British actions "hostile to the United States as an independent and neutral nation." Patriotic Southerners and Westerners felt these insults keenly and resented the implicit unwillingness of the British to concede the reality of American independence. According to one Kentuckian, "we must now oppose the farther encroachments of Great Britain by war, or formally annul the Declaration of our Independence, and acknowledge ourselves her devoted colonies." Neutral rights involved economic interests, too; as Madison explained, British policy struck not only at commerce but at agriculture as well. By closing European markets to American staples, the British threatened the prosperity of farmers and planters who lived hundreds of miles from the sea and might never have seen an ocean-going vessel. "The interests of agriculture and commerce are inseparable," said Representative Langdon Cheves of South Carolina.

In the Congress that voted for war there was a remarkable little band of youthful Republicans from the Southern and Western states. Some of them had taken their seats for the first time in November 1811 and had at once begun to badger the President and harangue their colleagues with appeals for war. They managed to elect Henry Clay of Kentucky Speaker of the House; and Clay in turn gave important committee assignments to the young War Hawks — among them, Richard M. Johnson of Kentucky, Felix Grundy of Tennessee, and John C. Calhoun of South Carolina. These second-generation Republicans were critical of the pacifistic measures of Jefferson and Madison; indifferent to the state-rights political tradition embodied in the Resolutions of 1798; nationalistic to a degree exceeding the Federalists in their prime; and eager for geographic expansion and economic growth, with none of the anxieties that Jefferson sometimes seemed to feel. To them war was a way of asserting American power, a means of redressing intolerable wrongs too long endured: impressment, violations of America's neutral rights,

interference with her foreign trade. But it was also an opportunity to capitalize on Europe's strife and advance the American frontier.

The insatiable Southern and Western demand for land was one of the impelling forces behind the War Hawks. The American frontier was not advancing in a slow, orderly manner, with contiguous tracts of the public domain successively opened for sale and then compactly settled. Rather, farmers and speculators rushed into new areas, often before Indian claims were cleared and surveys completed, and sought out the most fertile parcels. With such an abundance of good land, few buyers were interested in land of second- or third-rate quality. Hence, the government was under constant pressure to open additional tracts even before those already open had been properly settled.

An unfortunate consequence of this planless expansion was that the Western Indians were being cajoled into making treaties whose terms they rarely comprehended, treaties by which they surrendered more and more of their hunting grounds. Jefferson's hope of incorporating the Indians in the body politic — of introducing among them "the implements and the practice of husbandry and of the household arts" — never had a chance to materialize. The white invasion was too swift; moreover, the Westerners preferred simply to drive the Indians farther and farther west. In the Ohio Valley alone, during the first decade of the nineteenth century, the Indians had been obliged to cede more than a hundred million acres of land. In 1809, Governor William Henry Harrison, of the Indiana Territory, negotiated the last of a series of cessions under particularly dubious circumstances, bargaining with the demoralized remnants of several tribes for nearly 3 million acres in the lower Wabash Valley. The Indians realized that if they were ever to make a stand east of the Mississippi, it would have to be now.

At this crucial time two Shawnees of uncommon ability, Tecumseh and his brother "the Prophet," managed to unite the tribes east of the Mississippi for resistance against further white encroachments. Tecumseh supplied political leadership, while the Prophet provided spiritual inspiration and a call for moral regeneration. Together they organized an efficient Indian confederation supported by braves determined to preserve their lands and uncorrupted by the white man's proffered gifts of liquor. Terror spread along the frontier. In the summer of 1811, when Tecumseh went south to bid for the support of the Creeks, Governor Harrison decided to take advantage of his absence. He advanced with a force of a thousand men to the outskirts of Prophetstown, the chief Indian settlement, on the Wabash River near the mouth of Tippecanoe Creek. There, on November 7, after repelling an Indian attack, his men destroyed the town. The Battle of Tippecanoe marked the beginning of a long and savage Indian war and was directly related to the American declaration of war on Great Britain.

In his war message Madison expressed an opinion held by the majority of Westerners: that the Indians had been receiving arms and encouragement from the British in Canada. The War Hawks were certain of it. "I can have no doubt of the influence of British agents in keeping up Indian hostility" and of encouraging them "to murder our citizens," cried Richard M. Johnson of Kentucky. Felix Grundy of Tennessee agreed, adding, moreover, that there would be no peace on the frontier until the British were driven out of Canada. "We shall drive the British from our continent," Grundy affirmed; "they will no longer have an opportunity of intriguing with our Indian neighbors. . . . That nation will lose her Canadian trade, and, by having no resting place in this country, her means of annoying us will be diminished." To Westerners, the rich lands of Upper Canada were not the least of the prizes to be won in a successful war with the British. "Agrarian cupidity, not maritime rights, urges the war," was the acid but exaggerated comment of John Randolph. In Congress he had "heard but one word — like the whip-poorwill, but one eternal monotonous tone — Canada! Canada! Canada!"

There was in fact a second tone — Florida — which for Southerners provided the harmony. East and West Florida were still in the possession of Spain, Great Britain's ally, and their conquest might well be another reward of a war policy. They contained fertile cotton lands, and through them flowed the navigable rivers of the Mississippi Territory. As early as 1810, Madison, in collusion with American settlers, had seized a portion of West Florida; but nothing short of the whole of the Floridas would now satisfy the expansionists of the Southwest.

In a letter summarizing the causes of the war, Andrew Jackson mentioned neutral rights, impressment, national vindication, Indian pacification, and the desire for territorial conquest. He then condensed all these motives into two phrases: "to seek some indemnity for past injuries, some security against future aggression." Jackson seems to have reflected the sentiment of the majority in the Southern and Western states, and in the presidential election of 1812 they, along with Pennsylvania and Vermont, endorsed the war policy by giving their electoral votes to Madison. De Witt Clinton of New York, the candidate of the Federalists and Peace Republicans, carried the rest of the New England and Middle states.

The Aims of the War Hawks

Before we relinquish the conflict, I wish to see Great Britain renounce the piratical system of paper blockade; to liberate our captured seamen on board her ships of war; relinquish the practice of impressment on board our merchant vessels; to repeal her Orders in Council; and cease, in every other respect, to violate our neutral rights; to treat us as an independent people. The gentleman from Virginia (Mr. Randolph) has objected to the destination of this auxiliary force — the occupation of the Canadas, and the other British possessions upon our borders where our laws are violated, the Indians stimulated to murder our citizens, and where there is a British monopoly of the peltry and fur trade. I should not wish to extend the boundary of the United States by war if Great Britain would leave us to the quiet enjoyment of independence; but, considering her deadly and implacable enmity, and her continued hostility, I shall never die contented until I see her expulsion from North America, and her territories incorporated with the United States.... This deep rooted enmity to Great Britain arises from her insidious policy, the offspring of her perfidious conduct toward the United States. Her disposition is unfriendly; her enmity is implacable; she sickens at our prosperity and happiness.

From Richard M. Johnson of Kentucky, Speech in the House of Representatives, December 11, 1811.

The War of 1812: Northern Campaigns, 1812–14

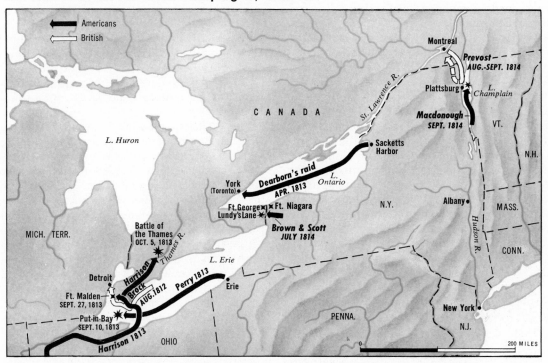

Madison's rather narrow margin in the Electoral College (128 to 89 — the shift of one state, Pennsylvania, could have changed the result), together with the bitter resentment of the commercial centers, meant that the country went to war dangerously divided. No patriot, wrote a Boston editor, "conceives it his duty to shed his blood for Bonaparte, for Madison or Jefferson, and that Host of Ruffians in Congress." New England Federalists wanted no part of "Mr. Madison's war."

THE WAR OF 1812

National unpreparedness. The War Hawks were convinced that the war could be won with little effort and a minimum of sacrifice. Henry Clay announced that "the militia of Kentucky alone are competent to place Montreal and Upper Canada at your feet." His friends in Congress must have believed him, for they led into war a country that was not only internally divided but hopelessly unprepared. As war approached, the Madison Administration loy-

ally adhered to Jefferson's policy of relying on small gunboats and continued to neglect the regular navy; even in his message to Congress of November 1811 Madison made no recommendation for naval expansion. The following January two-thirds of the representatives who were to vote for war five months later helped to defeat a modest proposal to add ten frigates to the navy. During the debate on this measure, Richard M. Johnson of Kentucky, one of the War Hawks, vowed that he would not vote a penny for a naval force "destined to entail upon this happy Government perpetual taxes and a perpetually increasing public debt."

Congress made no effort to increase American naval power until months after the outbreak of war, and the new forty-four-gun frigates and seventy-four-gun ships of the line then provided for were not ready for action until the war had ended. Indeed the United States had an ocean-going navy of only sixteen vessels fit for service with which to challenge the world's foremost sea power, whose warships numbered in the hundreds. The American navy had the advantage of a talented, well-trained group of officers but suffered from a serious shortage of experienced seamen. It had no real fleet organization, each ship operating more or less as an independent unit. Moreover, since most of the ships were expected to function as commerce-raiders, the question of naval strategy seemed superfluous.

But the War Hawks, after all, were thinking primarily of a land war, not of challenging Britain's naval supremacy. With Florida weakly defended, with less than 5,000 British troops in Canada, and with war raging in Europe, the odds seemed to favor the Americans. Had the United States trained, equipped, and put in the field an army of only 50,000 men — no serious strain on the country's resources — it might have conquered Canada and Florida with relative ease. Congressional action seemed adequate enough: it authorized an expansion of the small regular army by the recruitment of 25,000 five-year volunteers; provided for the raising of an additional 50,000 one-year volunteers; and made repeated calls on the state militias, which numbered, on paper, some 700,000 men.

Even in the regions most enthusiastic for war, however, Americans were reluctant to abandon their civilian pursuits; neither coercion nor persuasion, such as offers of cash bounties and land grants, had much effect. Never during the war did the army number more than 35,000 men, and even this small force was poorly trained and unimaginatively commanded by over-age veterans of the Revolution and incompetent militia officers. Militiamen, moreover, generally felt that their duty was limited to state defense, and some refused to leave their states for operations across the frontier.

Congress, including the War Hawks, hesitated to adopt the fiscal measures demanded by a war policy. Eventually Congress doubled tariff rates and levied a new excise tax, a stamp tax, and a direct tax on the states, but these unpopular measures brought the government little revenue until near the end of the war. It authorized loans, but the Treasury Department managed to market the bulk of about $80 million in securities only at a discount and at high interest rates. Since most New England capitalists opposed the war, and since the Bank of the United States had been abolished in 1811, Secretary of the Treasury Gallatin had

to rely on state banks, which were poorly equipped to handle business of this sort. In short, the whole configuration of Republican policy over the past decade had been designed for a simple agricultural nation at peace with the world; the War Hawks, in effect, attempted to apply Jeffersonian means to a non-Jeffersonian end. In so doing, they barely escaped national disaster.

The military campaigns. Plans for the conquest of Canada (which Southern Republicans, incidentally, had never viewed with much enthusiasm) ended in a complete fiasco. Effective strategy called for a concentration of forces in an attack on Montreal, whose fall would have cut British communications along the St. Lawrence and the Great Lakes and made the British position in Upper Canada untenable. But, in response to the Western demand for protection from Tecumseh's Indian confederation, the nation's forces were diffused. As a result, the military campaign of 1812 was a feeble, poorly planned, uncoordinated attempt to invade Canada at three separate points. General William Hull marched an army from Detroit toward the British garrison at Malden. But, doubting the wisdom of an invasion before winning control of Lake Erie, and hearing that Tecumseh and his warriors had joined the British, Hull soon lost his nerve and returned to Detroit. There, on August 6, a brilliant British commander, General Isaac Brock, surrounded Hull's army and forced him to surrender without firing a shot. A second invasion across the Niagara River culminated in defeat and surrender when New York militiamen refused to enter Canada to reinforce their countrymen. Finally, General Henry Dearborn led an advance along Lake Champlain toward Montreal. When he reached the Canadian border he found that his militiamen would not cross it and was obliged to march back to Plattsburg. So ended the land campaigns of 1812. If they had made no conquests and won no glory, at least they had cost few lives.

Things went little better the next year. Canadians astonished their would-be "liberators" by vigorously supporting British efforts to drive the invaders out. Two events, however, enabled the Americans to recover lost ground on the Northwest frontier and all but eliminate the danger of another British offen-

"We have met the enemy": Battle on Lake Erie, 1813.

sive there. The first was Captain Oliver Hazard Perry's notable victory at Put-in-Bay on Lake Erie, September 10, 1813. When Perry reported, "We have met the enemy and they are ours," he gave the Americans control of the Great Lakes and made the British position at Detroit hopeless. The second event was General Harrison's victory over the retreating British at the Battle of the Thames, October 5, 1813. Here the great Indian leader Tecumseh was killed; with his death the Indian confederacy collapsed, and the Northwest frontier was secure. But the conquest of Canada was as remote as ever.

By 1814 the Americans were striving desperately to prevent the British from invading their land and, perhaps, taking a slice of it. With the defeat of Napoleon and his exile to Elba, the British were able for the first time to turn their undivided attention to the American war and to send some of their best troops across the Atlantic. Their plan was to harass the cities on the Atlantic coast with amphibious operations while launching invasions at

three points: Niagara, Lake Champlain, and New Orleans.

The most ambitious coastal attack was a thrust up Chesapeake Bay culminating in the capture of Washington on August 24. As the President and other Administration officials fled, the British burned the Capitol, the White House, and other public buildings. Having avenged an earlier American raid on York (Toronto) with this crowning humiliation, the British withdrew. The military significance of the raid was negligible, but it underscored the utter failure of the War Hawks' schemes.

The British invasion plans, however, seriously miscarried, for by 1814 the Americans had found some vigorous young officers and no longer had to rely on untrained, undisciplined militia units. The projected British offensive at Niagara was thwarted by the aggressive operations of General Jacob Brown and his able young subordinate, Winfield Scott. The Battle of Lundy's Lane, near Niagara Falls, on July 25, was itself indecisive, but it ended the British invasion threat from that position.

In August a powerful force of British veterans commanded by Sir George Prevost advanced toward Lake Champlain with the apparent purpose of cutting off the New England states from the rest of the Union. Early in September Prevost paused before the strong American fortifications at Plattsburg to await the outcome of a bitter duel between British and American flotillas on Lake Champlain. On September 11 Captain Thomas Macdonough's American fleet won a decisive victory, forcing Prevost to abandon his campaign and retire to Canada. Clearly, the war on the Canadian frontier had reached a stalemate.

The final campaign took place in the Southwest. Here Andrew Jackson of Tennessee, an authentic self-trained military genius, somehow managed to make soldiers out of militiamen and to furnish them with supplies. Jackson had already smashed the military power of the Southwestern Indians by defeating the Creeks at the Battle of Horseshoe Bend, on March 27, 1814, and had also forced them to cede some of their richest lands in Mississippi Territory. Next he captured and destroyed Pensacola in Spanish Florida to prevent the British from using it as a base and then marched his army to New Orleans to meet the invaders. Placing his men behind earthworks and bales of cotton, he awaited the attack of

The War of 1812:
Southwestern Campaigns, 1813–15

eight thousand seasoned British troops commanded by Sir Edward Pakenham. Contemptuous of Jackson's motley army of militiamen, sailors, and pirates, Pakenham, on January 8, 1815, led his men in tight formation in a rash frontal assault. American rifles and artillery raked the British columns with a deadly fire. Before the British withdrew, the Americans had killed the British commander and inflicted more than two thousand casualties, while suffering little more than a dozen of their own. The Battle of New Orleans was the last engagement of the war — in fact, it was fought two weeks after a treaty of peace had been signed. But it helped sweeten the bitter taste of the defeats and disappointments of the previous two and a half years, and it launched Andrew Jackson, the Hero of New Orelans, on his dazzling career.

On the high seas in the early months of the war the tiny American navy won a series of stunning victories in single-ship engagements, bolstering public morale during the disasters on the Canadian frontier. The most spectacular of these victories were those of the American frigate *Constitution* (Old Ironsides) over the British frigates *Guerrière* and *Java*, and of the *United States* over the *Macedonian*. These successes shocked the British public, which had heard the American navy described as a "few fir-built frigates, manned by a handful of bastards and outlaws"; but they constituted no real challenge to British naval supremacy, nor did they have any great strategic significance.

By 1813 most of the American men-of-war were bottled up in their home ports by an effective British blockade, and by the end of the war only the *Constitution* and a few smaller vessels were still at sea. American cruisers and privateers continued to prey on British commerce and altogether captured more than a thousand merchantmen. These commerce-raiders were a costly annoyance to the British but fell far short of seriously crippling her overseas trade or disrupting her economy. The decisive fact of the naval war was the British blockade of the American coast, which dealt an almost mortal blow to the American carrying trade. In 1814 exports and imports fell to less than 10 per cent of what they had been in the peak year of 1807. Flour exports

Victory at New Orleans: Occasion for capital rejoicing.

declined from 1,443,000 barrels in 1812 to 193,000 barrels in 1814. The blockade was equally disastrous to American interstate commerce, most of which still moved along coastal waterways. Francis Wayland described the devastating impact of the blockade on the whole economy: "Our harbors were blockaded; communications coastwise between our ports were cut off; our ships were rotting in every creek and cove where they could find a place of security; our immense annual products were mouldering in our warehouses; the sources of profitable labor were dried up." If the land war was a stalemate, the war on the high seas culminated in a British victory that was well-nigh complete. Floating in the wreckage was Jefferson's gunboat policy.

Disaffection in New England. These disasters were what antiwar Federalists in the Northeast had anticipated — what Josiah Quincy of Massachusetts had in mind when he said, "This war, the measures which preceded it, and the mode of carrying it on, are all undeniably southern and western policy, not the policy of the commercial states." Feeling betrayed by their own government, convinced that the Madison Administration had deliberately set about to destroy their political and economic power, New England Federalists throughout the war regarded the Republican politicians in Washington, not the British, as their mortal enemies. And, having regained political control of all the New England states, they were in a position to translate their angry polemics into defiant deeds.

Federalist governors contested federal calls on the state militias, insisting that their proper function was to repel invasion, not to invade foreign territory. Federalists discouraged voluntary enlistments; and when Congress de-

Daniel Webster on Conscription and Federal Tyranny

I would ask, sir, whether the supporters of these measures have well weighed the difficulties of their undertaking. Have they considered whether it will be found easy to execute laws which bear such marks of despotism on their front, and which will be so productive of every sort and degree of misery in their execution? For one, sir, I hesitate not to say that they cannot be executed.... The operation of measures thus unconstitutional and illegal ought to be prevented by a resort to other measures which are both constitutional and legal. It will be the solemn duty of the State Governments to protect their own authority over their own militia, and to interpose between their citizens and arbitrary power. These are among the objects for which the State Governments exist; and their highest obligations bind them to the preservation of their own rights and the liberties of their people....

In my opinion, sir, the sentiments of the free population of this country are greatly mistaken here. The nation is not yet in a temper to submit to conscription. The people have too fresh and strong a feeling of the blessings of civil liberty to be willing thus to surrender it. You may talk to them as much as you please, of the victory and glory to be obtained in the enemy's provinces; they will hold those objects in light estimation if the means be a forced military service.

From Daniel Webster, Speech in the House of Representatives, December 9, 1814.

bated a militia draft they defended state sovereignty against national tyranny. "Where is it written in the Constitution," asked Daniel Webster, a young Federalist congressman from New Hampshire, "that you may take children from their parents, and parents from their children, and compel them to fight the battles of any war in which the folly or the wickedness of government may engage it?" Federalists resisted tax measures and boycotted government loans. According to a Boston editor, "any man who lends money to the government at the present time will forfeit all claim to common honesty." Meanwhile, New Englanders defiantly continued to trade with Canada and even furnished supplies to the British fleet. The more extreme dissenters favored either a separate peace and the withdrawal of New England from the war or else secession from the Union.

In 1814 British depredations along the New England coast and the belief that the federal government would do nothing to check them precipitated a serious political crisis. In October the Massachusetts legislature called for a convention of the New England states, asserting that the federal Constitution "has failed to secure to this commonwealth, and as they believe, to the Eastern sections of this Union, those equal rights and benefits which are the greatest objects of its formation." Twenty-six delegates, most of them from Massachusetts, Connecticut, and Rhode Island, assembled in Hartford on December 15 and deliberated secretly for nearly three weeks. A few reckless men, such as Timothy Pickering, were ready to take desperate measures; but the moderates, led by Harrison Gray Otis, gained control and adopted a final report that was relatively mild.

The report began with a gloomy account of the evils the country had endured under the "withering influence" of the Republicans. The Jeffersonians, it claimed, had debauched the civil service; destroyed "the balance of power which existed among the original states" by creating new Western states; and entertained a "visionary and superficial theory in regard to commerce, accompanied by a real hatred but a feigned regard to its interests." As a remedy for these grievances the Hartford report demanded a series of constitutional amendments abolishing the three-fifths compromise, requiring a two-thirds vote of both houses of Congress to declare war and to admit new states, prohibiting embargoes lasting for more than sixty days, excluding the foreign born from federal offices, limiting the President to one term, and prohibiting the election of two successive Presidents from the same state. If these demands were ignored and the war continued, the report recommended that another convention be called and given "such powers and instructions as the exigency of a crisis so momentous may require."

When representatives from the Hartford Convention arrived in Washington with their ultimatum, they found the capital rejoicing over Jackson's victory at New Orleans and over the signing of a treaty of peace. Under the circumstances their complaints seemed pointless, and their demands were ignored. But the Hartford Convention was remembered; to nationalists it symbolized the disloyalty, the narrow, selfish provincialism, of the Federalists. Consequently, the Federalist party itself was one of the casualties of the War of 1812.

Oddly enough, New England, in spite of her political disaffection, was the only region that profited materially from the war. Since the British blockade was not enforced along her coast until 1814, she received the bulk of foreign imports. Gold from the rest of the country flowed to her banks, which were thus able to maintain specie payments while other banks were forced to suspend payments. Above all, the war gave a strong impetus to New England manufacturing; between 1810 and 1814 the number of cotton spindles in the area increased sixfold. A war that was launched in part to acquire more land for the farmers and planters of the Northwest and South ended without an acre of new territory but with many thousands of spindles whirling in New England factories.

PEACE NEGOTIATIONS

The Treaty of Ghent. Almost from the start of this curious conflict there had been talk of peace. As early as September 1812 the czar of Russia, anxious that the British give their full attention to Napoleon, offered to act as mediator. President Madison responded favorably and, early in 1813, sent Albert Gallatin and James A. Bayard to work with John Quincy Adams, the American ambassador in St. Petersburg. The British declined the Russian offer — Russia could not be trusted to support the British position on neutral rights — but soon indicated a willingness to negotiate directly with the Americans. This, too, was acceptable to Madison, though he did not hear of the suggestion until January 1814. He then appointed Henry Clay and Jonathan Russell to join the three commissioners already in Europe, and in August negotiations began in the city of Ghent.

The British diplomats, an unimpressive group, were under the strict control of the Foreign Office in London. The Americans, superior in talent, had received from their government broader powers and greater freedom to negotiate. But they found it difficult to agree among themselves on matters of policy, and during the tedious months of negotiation their personal relations sometimes became tense. Adams' colleagues found him an irritating companion, and Adams, in turn, took a dim view of them, especially of Clay with his taste for cards and late hours. "They sit after dinner and drink bad wine and smoke cigars, which neither suits my habits nor my health, and absorbs time which I cannot spare," wrote the austere New Englander. Gallatin turned out to be the chief peacemaker in dealings not only with the British but with his own colleagues.

Had the two delegations adhered to their initial instructions, the negotiations would have been brief and the result complete failure. The Americans were to insist that the British abandon impressment, agree to respect international law in setting up blockades, and pay indemnity for their illegal seizure of American ships. The British, anticipating decisive military victories in the campaigns of 1814, presented a list of terms that would have jeopardized the sovereignty and future growth of the United States. They demanded territorial cessions in northern New York and Maine, the surrender of American control of the Great Lakes, the creation of an autonomous Indian buffer state south of the Great Lakes, the right to navigate the Mississippi River, and the relinquishment of American fishing rights off the coasts of Newfoundland and Labrador. The Americans made it clear that if the British insisted on these terms the war would continue. "Our negotiations may be considered at an end," wrote Gallatin to his government.

But the British did not insist. News of Macdonough's victory on Lake Champlain and Prevost's retreat from Plattsburg drastically changed the military picture, and the Duke of Wellington, when consulted by the British ministry, argued that failure to gain control of the Great Lakes made the British demands unreasonable. "I confess," he said, "that I think you have no right, from the state of the war, to demand any concession of territory from America." British merchants and manufacturers, eager to resume trade with the United States, favored an end to hostilities. The tax-burdened British public, too, had had enough of war.

As negotiations proceeded, the diplomats

dropped one demand after another and eventually agreed to a peace treaty that settled nothing but simply restored the status quo ante bellum. The Treaty of Ghent, signed on December 24, 1814, was silent on impressment and neutral rights, boundaries and fisheries, trade and indemnities — although it referred some of these questions to joint commissions for future settlement. In submitting the treaty to the Senate for ratification, Madison claimed no victory. "The late war," he said with more than a little ambiguity, "has been waged with a success which is the natural result of the wisdom of the legislative councils, of the patriotism of the people, of the public spirit of the militia, and of the valor of the military and naval forces of the country." As Adams described the document, "Nothing was adjusted, nothing was settled — nothing in substance but an indefinite suspension of hostilities was agreed to." Clay, though he signed it, described it as a "damned bad treaty."

Nevertheless, Americans looked back on the war with pride and satisfaction. They ignored the fact that the British had yielded nothing on neutral rights or impressment, because these issues lost their significance when the war ended in Europe. In the selective memories of patriots the military defeats, the bungling of the Canadian campaigns, and British supremacy on the high seas faded into insignificance; the early exploits of American frigates and privateers, Perry's victory on Lake Erie, and, best of all, Jackson's victory at New Orleans were remembered vividly as the crucial events of the war. The very fact that no territory had been lost — that the British had abandoned their extreme demands — contributed to this myth of military success. Moreover, the death of Tecumseh, the collapse of the Indian confederation, and the destruction of Indian military power east of the Mississippi meant that at least one purpose of the war had been fully achieved. Finally, the rise of manufacturing made the country more self-sufficient, and the preservation of their threatened independence gave the Americans a greater feeling of national identity than ever before. As Gallatin observed: "The war has renewed and reinstated the national feelings and character which the Revolution had given. . . . The people now have more general objects of attachment. . . . They are more Americans; they feel and act more as a nation."

Postwar settlements. Though memories of the war were to keep alive an undercurrent of Anglo-American hostility for many years, several specific issues that might have caused trouble were resolved soon after the stalemate at Ghent. In 1815 a commercial treaty removed most of the restrictions on Anglo-American trade (except with the British West Indies). An agreement of 1817, signed by Richard Rush, the Acting Secretary of State, and Charles Bagot, the British minister, provided for naval disarmament on the Great Lakes. Though either side could terminate it on six months' notice, the Rush-Bagot Agreement became a permanent policy and eventually was applied to the land frontier as well. Another agreement the following year reopened the coasts of Newfoundland and Labrador to American fishermen, established the forty-ninth parallel as the northern boundary of the Louisiana Purchase from the Lake of the Woods to the Rocky Mountains, and provided for a joint occupation of Oregon for the next ten years. Neither the British nor the Americans could have guessed it then, but these postwar negotiations, rather than the War of 1812, were to set the pattern for subsequent Anglo-American relations.

Another long-standing source of diplomatic friction was removed when Spain finally agreed to give up the Floridas. Internally weak and rapidly losing her once great empire in South and Central America, Spain maintained only a tenuous hold on the Floridas. Her feeble garrison was unable to control the Seminole Indians or to prevent white outlaws and runaway slaves from using the region as a sanctuary. In 1818 Andrew Jackson, giving the broadest possible interpretation to vague instructions from his government, led a military force into the Floridas to punish the Seminoles for depredations along the American frontier. In the process he seized St. Marks and Pensacola, deposed the Spanish governor, and raised the American flag; he also arrested two British subjects for inciting the Indians, tried them by court-martial, and executed them. At home Jackson's highhanded conduct added to his popularity, but it immensely complicated matters for Secretary of State John Quincy Adams,

Boundary Treaties, 1818–19

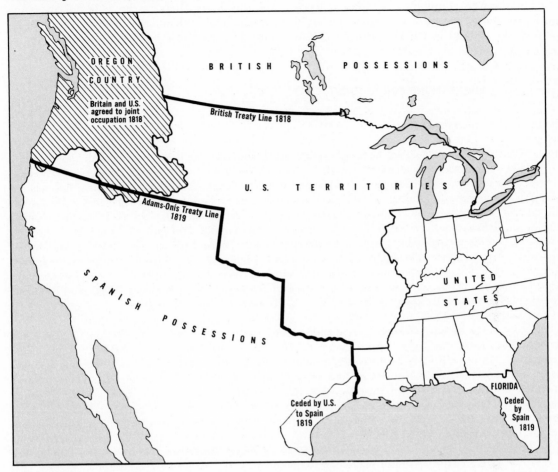

OREGON COUNTRY

Britain and U.S. agreed to joint occupation 1818

BRITISH POSSESSIONS

British Treaty Line 1818

U. S.   T E R R I T O R I E S

Adams-Onís Treaty Line 1819

S P A N I S H   P O S S E S S I O N S

UNITED STATES

Ceded by U.S. to Spain 1819

FLORIDA Ceded by Spain 1819

who had been negotiating with the Spanish minister, Luis de Onís.

Making the best of a bad situation, Adams brazened his way through. He not only refused to apologize for Jackson's behavior but threw responsibility on the Spanish for failing to preserve order in the Floridas. Spain, he insisted, must either govern the provinces efficiently or cede them to the United States, for they had become "a derelict, open to the occupancy of every enemy, civilized or savage, of the United States, and serving no other earthly purpose than as a post of annoyance to them." This was a challenge that the Spanish were in no position to accept, and in 1819 the Adams-Onís Treaty arranged for the transfer of the Floridas to the United States. In exchange, the Ameri-

can government agreed to assume payment of $5 million worth of claims that American citizens held against the Spanish government. The treaty also drew a boundary between the Louisiana Territory and Spanish possessions in the Southwest. The line followed the Sabine, Red, and Arkansas rivers to the Rocky Mountains, then the forty-second parallel west to the Pacific. Thus the United States gave up her claim to Texas (as part of the Louisiana Purchase) and Spain her claim to territory in the Pacific Northwest. Ratification of the treaty was delayed for two years, but in 1821 Jackson triumphantly reentered the Florida Territory as the first American governor.

Those who had moral sensibilities about the rough tactics of Jackson and Adams soothed their consciences with the argument that since the Floridas were contiguous to American territory Providence intended that America should have them. A later generation would call this argument "Manifest Destiny." Even so, the age of the Jeffersonians, who believed in man's reason and disliked the cynicism of the Old World, was closing on a slightly sour note.

SUGGESTIONS FOR READING

Jefferson in Power

Jefferson's political philosophy has had an enduring influence on American thought; it is analyzed sympathetically in C. M. Wiltse, *The Jeffersonian Tradition in American Democracy** (1935), and Adrienne Koch, *The Philosophy of Thomas Jefferson** (1943). How it has been interpreted and used by subsequent generations is explained in Merrill Peterson, *The Jefferson Image in the American Mind** (1960). The best completed biography of Jefferson is Nathan Schachner, *Thomas Jefferson: A Biography*, 2 vols. (1951). Two earlier biographies, A. J. Nock, *Thomas Jefferson** (1926), and Gilbert Chinard, *Thomas Jefferson, The Apostle of Americanism** (1929), are still valuable. The contributions of Jefferson's two ablest lieutenants can be studied in three works of genuine distinction: Adrienne Koch, *Jefferson and Madison: The Great Collaboration** (1950), Irving Brant, *James Madison: Secretary of State, 1800–1809* (1953), and Raymond Walters, Jr., *Albert Gallatin: Jeffersonian, Financier and Diplomat* (1957).

The Republican era is covered in three brief, well-written surveys: Marcus Cunliffe, *The Nation Takes Shape, 1789–1837** (1959), C. M. Wiltse, *The New Nation, 1800–1845** (1961), and Morton Borden, *Parties and Politics in the Early Republic, 1789–1815** (1967). A brilliant analysis of the Republican era, in spite of its hostility to Jefferson and Madison, is Henry Adams, *History of the United States During the Administrations of Jefferson and Madison*, 9 vols. (1889–91). The balance is more than redressed in C. G. Bowers' vivid but partisan account, *Jefferson in Power* (1936). Two excellent accounts of the party battles and Republican party organization are W. N. Chambers, *Political Parties in a New Nation, 1776–1809** (1963), and Noble Cunningham, *The Jeffersonian Republicans in Power: Party Operations, 1801–1809* (1963). The role of the Federalist opposition is traced in D. H. Fischer, *The Revolution of American Conservatism: The Federalist Party in the Era of Jeffersonian Democracy* (1965). L. D. White, *The Jeffersonians: A Study in Administrative History, 1801–1829** (1951), is an expert analysis of Republican administrative organization. J. S. Young, *The Washington Community, 1800–1829* (1966), stresses the failure of the Jeffersonians, because of certain negative attitudes, to develop an effective federal government. Alexander Balinky, *Albert Gallatin: Fiscal Theories and Policy* (1958), is a sharply critical evaluation of Jeffersonian finance.

An unfriendly biography of John Randolph, Jefferson's chief Republican critic, is Henry Adams, *John Randolph** (1882); a sympathetic analysis of his ideas is Russell Kirk, *Randolph of Roanoke: A Study in Conservative Thought* (1951). The case for Aaron Burr is presented in Nathan Schachner, *Aaron Burr: A Biography** (1937); the case against him, in T. P. Abernethy, *The Burr Conspiracy* (1954).

Foreign Policy and the War of 1812

The two most useful works on the Louisiana Purchase are E. W. Lyon, *Louisiana in French Diplomacy, 1759–1804* (1934), and, by the same author, *The Man Who Sold Louisiana: The Life*

* Available in a paperback edition.

of François Barbé-Marbois (1942). Two earlier books should also be consulted: J. K. Hosmer, *History of the Louisiana Purchase* (1902), and F. A. Ogg, *The Opening of the Mississippi* (1904). The best accounts of the conflict with the Barbary pirates are G. W. Allen, *Our Navy and the Barbary Corsairs* (1905), and R. W. Irwin, *Diplomatic Relations of the United States with the Barbary Powers* (1931).

Several excellent works are available on the problems of American neutrality. A good place to begin is with Irving Brant's study of Madison as Secretary of State, mentioned above, and with the same author's *James Madison: The President, 1809–1812* (1956). Outstanding monographs include W. W. Jennings, *The American Embargo* (1921); J. F. Zimmerman, *Impressment of American Seamen* (1925); L. M. Sears, *Jefferson and the Embargo* (1927); Harry Bernstein, *Origins of Inter-American Interest, 1700–1812* (1945); and Bradford Perkins, *First Rapprochement: England and the United States, 1795–1805* (1955).

The view that the War of 1812 was caused by Western and Southern expansionism and fear of the Indians is developed in J. W. Pratt, *Expansionists of 1812* (1925). The case for impressment and neutral rights as the fundamental causes of the war is presented, with varying emphases, in A. L. Burt, *The United States, Great Britain, and British North America from the Revolution to the Peace after the War of 1812* (1940); Bradford Perkins, *Prologue to War: England and the United States, 1805–1812* (1961); and Reginald Horsman, *The Causes of the War of 1812** (1962). R. H. Brown, *The Republic in Peril: 1812* (1964), stresses the desire of Jeffersonians to defend Republican institutions as a force leading to war. The careers of two of the leading War Hawks can be studied in Bernard Mayo, *Henry Clay: Spokesman of the New West* (1937), and C. M. Wiltse, *John C. Calhoun: Nationalist, 1782–1828* (1944).

Irving Brant, *James Madison: Commander-in-Chief, 1812–1836* (1961), strongly defends the President's wartime leadership. The best general account of the war is F. F. Beirne, *The War of 1812* (1949). A good brief survey is H. L. Coles, *The War of 1812** (1965). A. T. Mahan, *Sea Power in Its Relation to the War of 1812,* 2 vols. (1919), is the classic study of the naval war. Marquis James, *Andrew Jackson: The Border Captain** (1933), provides an absorbing account of the campaigns in the Southwest. Federalist disaffection is treated perceptively in George Dangerfield, *The Era of Good Feelings** (1952), and S. E. Morison, *The Life and Letters of Harrison Gray Otis,* 2 vols. (1913). An excellent analysis of the peace negotiations is in S. F. Bemis, *John Quincy Adams and the Foundations of American Foreign Policy* (1949).

* Available in a paperback edition.

8
Nationalism and Economic Expansion

One might have expected the War Hawks to be discredited by their failure to capture Canada and their general mishandling of military affairs. But at the end of the War of 1812 the Republican party, with the young nationalists at the helm, was still firmly in power. Though the record of Madison's wartime Administration was somewhat less than brilliant, the country was still intact, and the people were prospering. Southern planters were regaining their European markets, and a growing number of Western farmers were taking advantage of cheaper transportation to send their agricultural surpluses to markets in the South, the Northeast, and overseas. Farm-commodity prices were good, and land values were rising. Settlers were swarming into the West, and within a few years after the Treaty of Ghent five new states — Indiana (1816), Mississippi (1817), Illinois (1818), Alabama (1819), and Missouri (1821) — entered the Union. A new economic interest, manufacturing, was growing in importance and striving to expand at the rate it had achieved during the wartime dearth of British goods. Shipping, though it would never again dominate the economy of the Northeastern maritime states as it once had, was gradually recovering from the blows the embargo and the war had dealt.

This vast land, with its burgeoning economy and its optimistic, nationalistic people (9½ million of them by 1820), was no longer the plain, uncomplicated republic that Jefferson had once so much admired. Jefferson's party was changing with the country and now counted manufacturers, factory workers, and other urban groups, as well as farmers and planters, among those it had to serve. Henry Clay, John C. Calhoun, and John Quincy Adams were impatient with the old-fashioned Virginia Republicans' emphasis on constitutionalism, state rights, and agrarianism. They had a vision of national growth, economic expansion, and social progress that required a more dynamic federal government pursuing more positive and imaginative policies than had been contemplated in traditional Republican philosophy. In fighting their political battles, postwar Republicans still used Jeffersonian rhetoric, but the old creed had lost

Lockport on the Erie Canal, 1836.

much of its substance. In 1801 Jefferson's remark that "We are all Republicans, we are all Federalists" was only a loose figure of speech; in 1816 it was almost a fact.

THE TRIUMPH OF NEO-FEDERALISM

The American System. Circumstances had forced Madison, time after time, to compromise traditional Republicanism. In his seventh annual message to Congress, December 5, 1815, his surrender to the nationalists was well-nigh complete; Hamilton himself could hardly have composed a message that embraced orthodox Federalist doctrine more fully. In the name of national defense, Madison urged an expansion of the navy, a reorganization of the militia, and an enlargement of the Military Academy at West Point. Without a blush he recommended federal assumption of certain state debts incurred for militia expenses during the recent war. To establish a uniform national currency, he suggested that "a national bank will merit consideration." A federal tariff should provide industry with the protection that "is due to the enterprising citizens whose interests are now at stake." Finally, Madison urged Congress to finance such internal improvements as required "a national jurisdiction and national means," thus "binding more closely together the various parts of our extended confederacy."

Congressional leaders had few qualms about this program of neo-Federalism, and Henry Clay soon labeled it the "American System." The trouble with the prewar economy, thought Clay and his supporters, had been its dependence on the exchange of American raw materials for European manufactured goods, a dependence that exposed it to the whims of other powers and made it the victim of every international crisis. "Dame Commerce," said Clay, "is a flirting, flippant, noisy Jade and if we are governed by her fantasies, we shall never put off the muslins of India and the cloths of Europe." Hence the foundation of Clay's American System was a protective tariff to stimulate domestic manufacturing and to create an enlarged domestic market for the agricultural products of the South and West. Internal improvements, financed with tariff

New States 1812–21

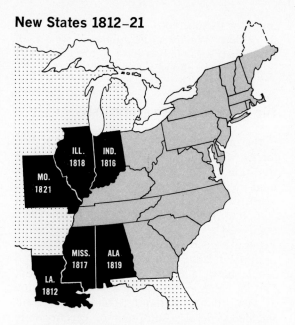

ILL. 1818
IND. 1816
MO. 1821
MISS. 1817
ALA 1819
LA. 1812

revenues, would encourage interstate commerce, and a national bank would provide the currency and accumulate the capital required for economic growth. This nationalistic program, Clay believed, would bring to all sections of the country both prosperity and independence from the outside world.

The Tariff of 1816. The first postwar Congress, one of the most fruitful of the nineteenth century, took long strides toward Clay's goal of an American System. By 1816 the Republican party numbered in its ranks a large cluster of interest groups, both urban and rural, clamoring for protective duties on foreign manufactured goods entering the American market. Leading the protectionists were those who had invested in New England textile mills and Pennsylvania iron-smelters when the embargo and war had choked off European supplies. Seconding them were the hemp-growers of Kentucky, the wool-growers of Ohio and Vermont, and an assortment of Southerners and Westerners who hoped either to promote industry or to expand their domestic market behind a tariff wall.

The cries of the protectionists increased when British exporters, seeking to dispose of surpluses accumulated during the war and to drive competing American manufacturers out of business, flooded the American market with low-priced goods. A member of Parliament

suggested that British goods might even be sold at a loss for a time, in order "to stifle in the cradle, those rising manufactures in the United States, which war has forced into existence, contrary to the natural course of things." In the critical years immediately following the war, British competition forced many small, less efficient American manufacturers to close their doors. Protectionists claimed that the British were plotting to wreck the American economy and asserted that a higher tariff was essential for national economic survival. America's "infant industries" were fragile things, they said, requiring the tender care of the federal government while they matured.

Congress responded with the Tariff of 1816, the first fiscal measure specifically designed to provide protection as well as revenue. In the House the Western and Middle states gave the bill overwhelming support; New England divided seventeen to ten for it, the South twenty-three to thirty-four against. Webster and other Federalists, speaking for the shipping interests, opposed higher duties as an obstacle to foreign trade; John Randolph, like most Southerners, vowed that he would not "agree to lay a duty on the cultivator of the soil to encourage exotic manufactures." On the other hand, Calhoun, the South Carolina nationalist, hoped that the manufacturing interest would "at all times, and under every policy . . . be protected with due care." In 1816 a considerable minority in the South shared Calhoun's point of view; within a few years, as conditions and expectations changed, Southern support for the tariff — and for the American System in general — almost vanished.

The second Bank of the United States. Republican leaders, chastened by their fiscal experiences during the war, made their most dramatic surrender to Federalism when they revived both Hamilton's plan and his arguments for a national bank. When the first Bank of the United States perished in 1811, its business had fallen to the state-chartered banks; within five years the number of these banks had increased from 88 to 246, their issues of bank notes from $28 million to $68 million. Since most state-chartered banks did not maintain adequate specie reserves (gold and silver), their notes usually circulated at a discount. The bewildering variety of notes, their fluctuating value, and an epidemic of counterfeiting brought the country to the edge of fiscal chaos. The final blow came when the state banks, except those in New England, suspended specie payments altogether during the war — and showed no disposition to resume specie payments with the restoration of peace.

Meanwhile, the federal government lacked a safe depository for its funds, a reliable agency to transfer them from place to place, and adequate machinery to market securities when it needed to borrow. The absence of a uniform paper currency was a severe handicap to businessmen engaged in interstate commerce. Even some of the old Republican agrarians, though they opposed all banks that issued paper currency, favored chartering a new national bank as the lesser of two evils. Madison discarded his constitutional doubts and decided that the question had been settled "by repeated recognitions . . . of the validity of such an institution, in acts of the legislative, executive, and judicial branches of the government, accompanied by . . . a concurrence of the general will of the nation." Calhoun, taking a thoroughly nationalistic position, attacked the state banks for usurping the federal government's exclusive power to issue and regulate the country's currency. Clay, who had opposed rechartering the first Bank, confessed that he had not anticipated the evils its demise had caused.

In 1816 a bill to grant a twenty-year charter to a second Bank of the United States passed both houses of Congress over the opposition of state banking interests, Federalist partisans, and Virginia agrarians. The functions and structure of the second Bank were essentially the same as those of the first, except that its capital was increased from $10 million to $35 million. The federal government again held one-fifth of the stock, and the President appointed five of the twenty-five directors. The Bank's headquarters were to be in Philadelphia, but it could establish branches elsewhere. Its liabilities were not to exceed its capital, one-fifth of which must be in specie; and it was to report annually to the Treasury Department and open its books for periodic inspection.

This powerful banking corporation could serve a number of useful purposes: it could assist the government in its fiscal business by helping to market federal securities and by providing a depository for federal funds; it could regulate the state banks; and it could encourage business enterprise by providing a sound paper currency in national-bank notes and by making available long- and short-term credits. But as the largest capitalistic institution in the country, exercising immense power over the national economy, depending as it did upon the government for special favors, it was essential that the Bank be responsibly directed and that its operations be subjected to adequate federal control. Lacking these, it was bound to find itself in political trouble, for it would then loom as a threat to democracy and an instrument of economic tyranny. Indeed, even under the best of circumstances, the Bank, because of its size and strength, was always a tempting political target.

Internal improvements. The War of 1812, by disrupting coastal shipping, had demonstrated the inadequacy of the country's internal transportation system for both interstate commerce and national defense. The West, where high transportation costs still deprived many farmers of outside markets and tied them to an economy of pioneer self-sufficiency, was the most persistent solicitor of federal funds for internal improvements. New England, suffering a loss of population and a decline of political strength, was the center of opposition. President Madison, stretching his constitutional scruples to support projects that were national in scope, approved appropriations for the continued building of the National Road to Wheeling, which had been started in 1811. But he doubted that Congress had power to subsidize local roads and canals without an appropriate amendment to the Constitution. In 1817 Congress ignored his doubts and passed a bill to distribute among the states for local internal improvements a $1,500,000 bonus that the Bank of the United States had paid the government for its charter. For Madison this was going too far, and in one of his last presidential acts he vetoed the so-called Bonus Bill. Calhoun, disgusted with this narrow view of things, grumbled that the Constitution "was not intended as a thesis for the logician to exercise his ingenuity on . . . it ought to be construed with plain good sense." But Madison's veto stalled this crucial phase of the Ameri-

James Monroe: A last nostalgic look.

its narrow particularism, and the Republican pirating of its program all contributed to its death.

James Monroe, a representative of the small-planter class of the Virginia piedmont, reached the Presidency at the age of sixty-one after many years of devoted, though not brilliant, public service. Once the favorite of John Randolph and the Quids (see p. 174), Monroe continued to interpret the Constitution more narrowly than the nationalists in his party, especially when it came to internal improvements. He accepted the tariff and the banking legislation passed during Madison's last year in office, but while he was President the American System made only limited progress. Though he was less talented than his distinguished predecessors, Monroe's contemporaries found something solid and reassuring in this member of the Revolutionary generation. In Monroe, with his wig, his cocked hat, and his knee-length pantaloons, the postwar generation had a last nostalgic look at the eighteenth century.

The year of Monroe's inauguration, 1817, found the country in a complaisant mood. On a good-will tour that ultimately carried him into once-hostile New England, the new President saw everywhere abundant signs of national unity. His warm reception in Boston caused the *Columbian Centinel*, a Federalist paper, to speak of an "Era of Good Feelings," thus giving a popular label to Monroe's Administrations. Political factionalism was at a low ebb, and there was relative harmony among the sections. Above all, as Monroe observed in his first message to Congress, the country was in a "prosperous and happy condition. . . . The abundant fruits of the earth have filled it with plenty." The "Era of Good Feelings" lasted, however, only about two years — until the middle of Monroe's first Administration — when party strife and sectional bitterness suddenly revived, and the national prosperity came to an abrupt and shocking end.

JOHN MARSHALL AND THE SUPREME COURT

Marshall's role. In these postwar years still another Virginian played a key role in the formulation of public policy and in the molding

can System. Local internal improvements remained, for the time being, the responsibility of the individual states and private enterprise.

The Era of Good Feelings. Nearing the end of his second term, Madison supported another Virginian, his Secretary of State, James Monroe, to succeed him to the Presidency. The Randolph Republicans preferred William H. Crawford of Georgia, and some Northern Republicans fretted about the long domination of their party by the "Virginia Dynasty." But Madison had his way, and Monroe won an easy victory over his Federalist opponent, Rufus King of New York. Four years later with the Federalists too feeble even to run a candidate, Monroe was reelected without opposition.* After a few more years of activity in scattered localities, the Federalist party was extinct. The party's war record, the failure of its older leaders to adjust to new conditions,

* One elector from New Hampshire voted for John Quincy Adams.

of the American political structure. This was John Marshall, Chief Justice of the United States Supreme Court from 1801 to 1835, who gave the judicial branch of the government the prestige it had previously lacked and who, unlike most of his fellow Virginians, supported nationalistic measures with unqualified enthusiasm. Born in 1755, Marshall saw military service during the Revolution and then went home to become one of the most successful lawyers before the Richmond bar. In 1792 Jefferson, already suspicious of Marshall's politics, suggested to Madison that Marshall ought to be appointed a judge to keep him out of mischief. As it turned out, Jefferson understood his man — Marshall became a Federalist — but he could scarcely have been more mistaken about how to render him harmless. After a term in Congress and brief service as John Adams' Secretary of State, Marshall received his appointment as Chief Justice shortly before the last Federalist President left office. The Supreme Court, at least, would remain in Federalist hands!

In personal appearance and social intercourse Marshall impressed one as a plain, homespun democrat, for he was the most unpretentious of men, an amiable lover of sports and other simple pleasures. But underneath he was a resolute Federalist, suspicious of popular government and contemptuous of what he considered Jefferson's sentimental trust in the people. Marshall was in no sense a scholar or philosopher of the law; he lacked the patience for intensive study and the imagination for metaphysical speculation. But he had a keen intelligence and a tough mind that readily discovered the logic of a case and swiftly drove to its core. According to Joseph Story, whom Madison made an Associate Justice in 1811, Marshall "examines the intricacies of a subject with calm and persevering circumspection and unravels its mysteries with irresistible acuteness." His personal magnetism and intellectual powers gave him enormous influence over his colleagues on the bench, including those appointed by Republicans. Marshall's domination of the Court is evident from the fact that during his thirty-four years as Chief Justice he wrote almost half the decisions and dissented from the majority opinion only eight times. Caring little for precedents, avoiding legal

John Marshall: A tough mind.

jargon, using crisp prose and careful reasoning, Marshall delivered a series of the most momentous decisions in American judicial history.

Judicial review. Soon after assuming his new office, Marshall found an opportunity to pronounce a vigorous and, in the long run, decisive opinion on a matter of prime importance for a federal government based on a written constitution. While the Federalists were in power there had been a persistent but inconclusive debate over who was to decide when Congress had exceeded its delegated powers or encroached upon the rights of the states. Since the Constitution is not explicit on this point, the answer had to be found by inference rather than from the plain language of the document. Probably the majority of delegates to the Constitutional Convention had expected the Supreme Court to pass on the constitutionality of the acts of Congress, and Hamilton, in one of the articles in *The Federalist*, had upheld the principle of judicial review. Jeffersonian Republicans, however, had argued that the federal government was the agent of the sovereign states and that those who had created it must define its powers. The individual states, said Jefferson in the Kentucky Resolutions of 1798, would decide when the Constitution had been violated, as well as "the mode and measure of redress."

John Marshall on Judicial Review

If Congress remains at liberty to give this court appellate jurisdiction, where the constitution has declared their jurisdiction shall be original; and original jurisdiction where the constitution has declared it shall be appellate; the distribution of jurisdiction, made in the constitution, is form without substance....

The question whether an act repugnant to the constitution can become the law of the land, is a question deeply interesting to the United States; but, happily not of an intricacy proportioned to its interest....

The constitution is either a superior paramount law, unchangeable by ordinary means, or it is on a level with ordinary legislative acts, and, like other acts, is alterable when the legislature shall please to alter it.

If the former part of the alternative be true, then a legislative act contrary to the constitution is not law; if the latter part be true, then written constitutions are absurd attempts, on the part of the people, to limit a power in its own nature illimitable.

Certainly all those who have framed written constitutions contemplate them as forging the fundamental and paramount law of the nation, and consequently the theory of every such government must be that an act of the legislature repugnant to the Constitution is void.

From Marbury v. Madison, 1 Cr. 137, 1803.

This is where things stood when, in 1803, Marshall gave the Court's decision in the case of *Marbury v. Madison.* Intrinsically of minor importance, this case related to a section of the Judiciary Act of 1789 that, according to Marshall, expanded the Court's original jurisdiction beyond what the Constitution intended it to be. "The question whether an act repugnant to the constitution can become the law of the land, is a question deeply interesting to the United States," Marshall wrote. His answer to the question was clear: The wording of the Constitution establishes the principle "that a law repugnant to the constitution is void; and that courts, as well as other departments, are bound by that instrument." Moreover, "It is emphatically the province and duty of the judicial department to say what the law

is. Those who apply the rule to particular cases must of necessity expound and interpret that rule."

Marbury v. Madison thus established a precedent for the Supreme Court to determine the constitutionality of congressional legislation and to act as the final authority on the meaning of the Constitution. This doctrine of judicial review has been challenged many times, but it has weathered all the storms and survives to this day. Having established the precedent, Marshall never again disallowed an act of Congress — more than a half-century passed before the Supreme Court exercised this power again. But Marshall frequently applied the positive side of judicial review — that is, he reviewed and *approved* congressional legislation as constitutional.

National supremacy. As a nationalist Marshall was, in fact, eager to interpret the powers of Congress as broadly as possible and to assert the federal government's supremacy over the states. For example, in two important cases, *Martin v. Hunter's Lessee* (1816) and *Cohens v. Virginia* (1821), the Marshall Court affirmed its right to review and reverse decisions of state courts when they concerned issues arising under the federal Constitution. On thirteen occasions it voided state laws as violations of "the supreme law of the land." One of the most significant of these cases, *Gibbons v. Ogden* (1824), involved a New York law giving a steamboat company a monopoly of the business of carrying passengers on the Hudson River to New York City. In rejecting the law Marshall gave the term "commerce" an extremely broad definition and came close to saying that the power of Congress over interstate commerce is absolute. This power, he ruled, "is complete in itself, may be exercised to its utmost extent, and acknowledges no limitations other than are prescribed in the constitution."

But the Chief Justice expounded the nationalist doctrine most fully in the case of *McCulloch v. Maryland* (1819), which tested the constitutionality of the second Bank of the United States. Conceding that the Constitution does not explicitly grant Congress authority to charter a bank, Marshall insisted that Congress must have some discretion in exercising the powers it does possess. Surely the authority could be implied from the "necessary and proper" clause. Then Marshall made a classic statement of the doctrine of "loose construction": "Let the end be legitimate, let it be within the scope of the Constitution, and all means which are appropriate, which are plainly adapted to that end, which are not prohibited, but consist with the letter and spirit of the constitution, are constitutional." The nationalist advocates of the American System could scarcely have asked for a warmer endorsement.

Sanctity of contracts. As a conservative defender of property rights, Marshall also sought to make the federal courts a sanctuary of the propertied classes whenever they were harassed by unfriendly state legislatures. He sympathized with creditors and entrepreneurs who considered contracts sacred and inviolable, and he admired the clause in the Constitution that prohibited states from "impairing the obligation of contracts." In the case of *Fletcher v. Peck* (1810), Marshall gave evidence of the extremes to which he would go to defend this principle. As we have seen (p. 174), the Georgia legislature, in 1795, had granted a large tract of Western land to the Yazoo Land Companies. The following year a new legislature, discovering bribery and fraud, repudiated the grant and thus provoked litigation that ultimately reached the Supreme Court. To Marshall the case was perfectly clear: the grant of land was a binding contract, and the circumstances under which it was negotiated did not concern the Court. The withdrawal of the grant, therefore, was an unconstitutional violation of the obligation of contract.

Another case, *Dartmouth College v. Woodward* (1819), enabled Marshall to make an equally extreme application of the contract clause. The case originated in an attempt of the New Hampshire legislature to revise Dartmouth's charter, which dated back to colonial days, and to transform the college into a state institution. The trustees went to court and employed Daniel Webster, a Dartmouth alumnus, to represent them. Webster's sentimental plea in behalf of his alma mater brought tears to the eyes of the unsentimental Chief Justice, who ruled that a charter was a contract and could not be violated. This decision won praise from the promoters of business corporations, for it

---

John Marshall on National Supremacy

If any one proposition could command the universal assent of mankind, we might expect it would be this: that the government of the Union, though limited in its powers, is supreme within its sphere of action. This would seem to result necessarily from its nature. It is the government of all; its powers are delegated by all; it represents all, and acts for all.... The nation, on those subjects on which it can act, must necessarily bind its component parts. But this question is not left to mere reason: the people have, in express terms, decided it, by saying, "this constitution, and the laws of the United States, which shall be made in pursuance thereof," "shall be the supreme law of the land," and by requiring that the members of the State legislatures, and the officers of the executive and judicial departments of the States, shall take the oath of fidelity to it.

The government of the United States, then, though limited in its powers, is supreme; and its laws, when made in pursuance of the constitution, form the supreme law of the land, "anything in the constitution or laws of any State, to the contrary, notwithstanding."

From McCulloch v. Maryland, 4 Wheat. 316, 1819.

---

now appeared that their charters, once granted, could not be tampered with.

Some old-line Republicans believed that Marshall's decisions had dealt "a deadly blow to the sovereignty of the states." Judge Spencer Roane of Virginia sent angry dissenting opinions to the newspapers, and John Taylor waged a pamphlet war against the Supreme Court. To Jefferson the federal justices were a "corps of sappers and miners" steadily undercutting the powers of the states. "The Constitution," he wrote, "is a mere thing of wax in the hands of the judiciary, which they may twist and shape into any form they please." Yet, except for Marshall's interpretation of the contract clause (which later courts have modified), there was little in these decisions that the dominant element in the postwar Republican party really cared to criticize. Giving his blessing to the nationalistic trend of Republican legislation, Marshall used the Constitution as a flexible instrument adaptable to conditions that the Founding Fathers could never have anticipated. If judicial review was a usurpation, no majority in Congress ever agreed on any alternative to it. As for Marshall's defense of property rights, the Republicans could hardly have been called enemies of property.

THE MONROE DOCTRINE

Revolutions in Latin America. One of the most striking expressions of postwar American nationalism was in the field of foreign policy. While Spain was preoccupied with France during the Napoleonic wars, her South and Central American colonies had had a pleasant taste of freedom from her strict political and commercial control. Their appetite whetted, the colonies revolted and soon expelled the Portuguese from Brazil and the Spanish from all their American possessions save Cuba and Puerto Rico. When, in 1820, a revolution broke out in Spain and Portugal, all hope of recovering the lost colonies perished — unless other European powers could be induced to intervene.

To the people of the United States this was 1776 all over again. Henry Clay, a warm admirer of the Latin-American patriots, rejoiced at "the glorious spectacle of eighteen millions of people, struggling to burst their chains and to be free." When a modest commerce developed with South America, Clay, optimistic about its further expansion, incorporated Pan-American trade into his American System. Both justice and self-interest, thought Clay, required quick recognition of the revolutionary governments.

After 1815 the State Department had pursued a policy of neutrality that recognized the revolutionists as belligerents and permitted them to purchase supplies in the United States; but a Neutrality Act of 1818 prohibited American citizens from serving in the rebel armies. Impatient with Secretary of State Adams' coolness toward the rebel cause, Clay introduced a resolution in the House giving the *de facto* governments of Latin America immediate recognition. The resolution alarmed Monroe and Adams, who feared that it would end the negotiations then in progress for the purchase of Florida or even lead to war. After the President and Secretary of State exerted their influ-

ence against the resolution, the House finally voted it down. Recognition came in 1822, after the Florida negotiations had been completed and after the new governments in South America had shown themselves capable of maintaining their independence. To Clay this recognition was disgracefully late, but the United States was nevertheless the first nation to grant it.

The fear of foreign intervention. Granting recognition at that time was in fact a bold step. Thus far the British had refrained from establishing diplomatic relations with Latin America and had even indicated a willingness to see Spain reestablish her authority there. Moreover, the reactionary governments of Russia, Prussia, Austria, and France had formed an alliance pledged not only to preserve the status quo and to suppress liberalism but to intervene in the internal affairs of any country that threatened the peace and security of Europe. Under this mandate Austria had invaded Italy and France had invaded Spain to liquidate revolutionary movements for which many Americans felt a deep sympathy. Perhaps the alliance would now apply its policy to the New World and assist Spain in the reconquest of her colonies. France, it was rumored, had an eye on Cuba as a reward for intervening in Spain; and Russia seemed intent on spreading her influence southward from Alaska along the Pacific coast. Actually there was not much danger that any European power would intervene in Latin America without British support, and, when Adams warned Russia that the Western Hemisphere was closed to further colonization, the two countries soon negotiated a satisfactory agreement. Nevertheless, the time seemed appropriate for formulating some kind of policy that would cover all contingencies.

By 1823 Great Britain, too, was ready to take a stronger stand. Her liberals resented the reactionary schemes of the continental alliance, and her merchants and manufacturers were determined to maintain the profitable markets they had established in Latin America. Accordingly, the British foreign minister, George Canning, approached the American minister in London, Richard Rush, with a proposal that their governments make a joint statement of policy. Canning told Rush that his govern-

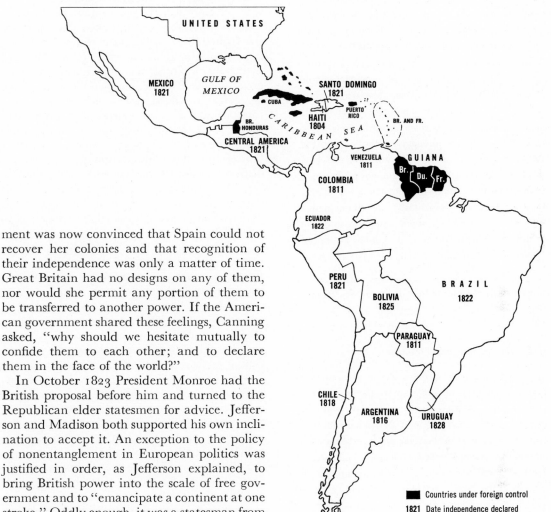

Countries under foreign control
1821 Date independence declared

ment was now convinced that Spain could not recover her colonies and that recognition of their independence was only a matter of time. Great Britain had no designs on any of them, nor would she permit any portion of them to be transferred to another power. If the American government shared these feelings, Canning asked, "why should we hesitate mutually to confide them to each other; and to declare them in the face of the world?"

In October 1823 President Monroe had the British proposal before him and turned to the Republican elder statesmen for advice. Jefferson and Madison both supported his own inclination to accept it. An exception to the policy of nonentanglement in European politics was justified in order, as Jefferson explained, to bring British power into the scale of free government and to "emancipate a continent at one stroke." Oddly enough, it was a statesman from New England, the traditional center of pro-British sentiment, who objected most strenuously to accepting British leadership in the Western Hemisphere. Secretary of State Adams opposed any agreement by which the United States would, in effect, commit itself not to annex additional territory. With an eye on Texas and Cuba, Adams argued that "we should at least keep ourselves free to act as emergencies may arise." Moreover, he disliked a joint statement that would make the United States appear "to come in as a cockboat in the wake of the British man-of-war." After long discussion in the Cabinet, Adams noted with satisfaction that his position "was acquiesced

in on all sides." The President, it was agreed, would make a statement of *American* policy emphasizing the separateness of the Old World and the New.

The American response. Monroe incorporated his famous doctrine rather unsystematically in his annual message to Congress on December 2, 1823, a message that dealt with many other topics as well. With some rearranging, the relevant passages run substantially as follows: First, wherever American sympathies may lie,

Thomas Jefferson: Advice to Monroe

Our first and fundamental maxim should be, never to entangle ourselves in the broils of Europe. Our second, never to suffer Europe to intermeddle with cis-Atlantic affairs. America, North and South, has a set of interests distinct from those of Europe, and peculiarly her own. She should therefore have a system of her own, separate and apart from that of Europe. While the last is laboring to become the domicile of despotism, our endeavor should surely be to make our hemisphere that of freedom. One nation, most of all, could disturb us in this pursuit; she now offers to lead, aid, and accompany us in it. By acceding to her proposition, we detach her from the band of despots, bring her mighty weight into the scale of free government, and emancipate a continent at one stroke, which might otherwise linger in doubt and difficulty. Great Britain is the nation which can do us the most harm of any one, or all on earth; and with her on our side we need not fear the whole world.

From Thomas Jefferson, Letter to President Monroe, October 24, 1823.

John Quincy Adams: Advice to Monroe

We have no intention of seizing either Texas or Cuba. But the inhabitants of either or both of them may exercise their primitive rights, and solicit a union with us. They will certainly do no such thing to Great Britain. By joining with her, therefore, in her proposed declaration, we give her a substantial and perhaps inconvenient pledge against ourselves, and really obtain nothing in return. Without entering now into the enquiry of the expediency of our annexing Texas or Cuba to our Union, we should at least keep ourselves free to act as emergencies may arise, and not tie ourselves down to any principle which might immediately afterwards be brought to bear against ourselves....

It would be more candid, as well as more dignified, to avow our principles explicitly to Russia and France, than to come in as a cock-boat in the wake of the British man-of-war....

The answer to be given to Baron Tuyll, the instructions to Mr. Rush relative to the proposals of Mr. Canning, those to Mr. Middleton at St. Petersburg, and those to the Minister who must be sent to France, must all be parts of a combined system of policy and adapted to each other.

From Memoirs of John Quincy Adams, November 7, 1823.

it does not comport with American policy to intervene in the "internal concerns" or the wars of European powers when they involve matters only "relating to themselves." Second, the United States will not interfere with "existing colonies or dependencies" in the Western Hemisphere. Third, with the Latin-American governments "whose independence we have . . . acknowledged, we could not view any interposition for the purpose of oppressing them, or controlling in any other manner their destiny, by any European power in any other light than as the manifestation of an unfriendly disposition toward the United States." Fourth, "the American continents, by the free and independent condition which they have assumed and maintain, are henceforth not to be considered as subjects for future colonization by any European powers." Finally, Monroe warned the autocrats of Europe that "we should consider any attempt on their part to extend their [political] system to any portion of this hemisphere as dangerous to our peace and safety." In brief, the essence of this nationalistic pronouncement was the concept of two worlds, each of which was to refrain from intervening in the internal affairs of the other.

Monroe and Adams, of course, were responsible for the precise phrasing of these principles, but they owed much to earlier Presidents and Secretaries of State. They had brought together the elements of an American foreign policy that had been gradually evolving since the Revolution. To European diplomats, the promulgation of a policy that the young republic lacked the power to enforce was a piece of presumptuous impertinence. Canning, who knew that British diplomacy and the British navy had been decisive in preventing continental powers from meddling in America, was particularly annoyed. He was aware that Monroe's unilateral statement could be invoked against Great Britain as well as against other nations. Yet, though the response of the American people was overwhelmingly favorable, within a few years the President's dramatic message had been nearly forgotten. A generation later it would be rediscovered and identified as the Monroe Doctrine; and for many years thereafter it would be accepted as the authoritative and almost definitive statement of American foreign policy.

THE WESTWARD MOVEMENT

These displays of nationalism in domestic politics and foreign policy reflected the underlying optimism of the American people — their confidence in the destiny a kind Providence planned for them. To be sure, their nationalistic creed also embraced an awareness of their past: they had their nostalgic and sentimental side; they gloried in their traditions each Fourth of July; and they were deeply stirred when a Webster waxed eloquent upon the Constitution and the Founding Fathers. But most Americans would have agreed with Jefferson when he affirmed that he liked "the dreams of the future better than the history of the past." America was still primarily a promise: as Ralph Waldo Emerson rejoiced, it was "a country of beginnings, of projects, of designs, of expectations."

The general confidence and optimism of the American people were rooted both in a popular belief that man's potentialities were unlimited when he was free to develop them and in the practical social and economic realities of nineteenth-century America. One of the most important of these realities was the virgin land — the seemingly unlimited space and inexhaustible resources that promised a life of greater dignity and abundance than Europe's common people had ever dreamed of. The West — the untapped wealth of the great interior stretching from the Appalachians to the Rockies — helped to give the future its rosy hue; and the West became one of the central interests of the American people in the decades after the Treaty of Ghent.

Advance of the agricultural frontier. The story of the westward movement of population is, in the main, the story of the expansion of American agriculture — of the development of new areas for the cultivation of wheat, corn, tobacco, cotton, and wool. After 1815 improved transportation drew more and more Western farmers out of a self-sufficient way of life and into a national market economy. Farmers involved in this kind of commercial agriculture specialized in a "money crop" — one produced for sale in distant markets — and used the proceeds to buy consumer goods manufactured in the Northeast or in Europe. During periods when commodity prices were high, the rate of

westward migration, the sale of public lands, and eventually the supply of Western staples increased spectacularly.

"Old America seems to be breaking up and moving westward," observed an English visitor in 1817, during the first great wave of postwar migration. After falling off for a few years during the depression following the Panic of 1819 (see p. 218), the number of emigrants increased again and reached a peak in the 1830's. Whereas in 1810 only a seventh of the American people lived west of the Appalachians, by 1840 more than a third lived there. Below is a table showing population growth in the new Western states between 1810 and 1840:

	1810	1840
Ohio (1803)	230,760	1,519,467
Louisiana (1812)	76,556	352,411
Indiana (1816)	24,520	685,866
Mississippi (1817)	40,352	375,651
Illinois (1818)	12,282	476,183
Alabama (1819)		590,756
Missouri (1821)	20,845	383,702
Arkansas (1836)	1,062	97,574
Michigan (1837)	4,762	212,267

Some of the people who settled the great Mississippi Valley were recent immigrants from Europe, but most of them came from the older states. Kentuckians and Tennesseeans moved to the new cotton lands of the Southwest or crossed the Ohio River into the Northwest; migrants from New England and the Middle states generally settled in the Great Lakes region; and people from the South Atlantic states (the largest group of all) invaded southern Ohio, Indiana, and Illinois, as well as the Southwest. By and large those who moved west came from the lower middle classes and traveled with their few worldly possessions loaded on wagons or flatboats — or even on pack horses or pushcarts.

Factors encouraging migration. Why were these hundreds of thousands of settlers — most of them farmers, some of them artisans — drawn away from the cleared fields and established cities and villages of the East? Apart from the fact that the West happened to be an inviting land of opportunity, certain characteristics of American society help to explain this remarkable migration. The European ancestors of the American people had lived century after century rooted to the same village or the same piece of land until some religious or political or economic crisis uprooted them and drove them across the Atlantic. Those who experienced this sharp and devastating break tended thereafter to lack the ties that had bound them and their ancestors to a single place. Moreover, in the relatively stratified European society men inherited the occupations and social status of their fathers, but in American society there was a less rigid class structure. Men changed occupations easily and believed that it was not only possible but almost a moral duty to improve their social and economic position. As a result, Americans were, as many European visitors observed, an inveterately restless, rootless, and ambitious people.

The Frenchman Alexis de Tocqueville, who published a remarkably penetrating study of American society after a tour in the early 1830's, was impressed with these traits.

> In the United States, a man builds a house in which to spend his old age, and he sells it before the roof is on . . . he brings a field into tillage and leaves other men to gather the crops . . . he set-

tles in a place, which he soon afterwards leaves to carry his changeable longings elsewhere.

The reasons for this "strange unrest," Tocqueville believed, were, first, the American "taste for physical gratifications"; second, a social condition "in which neither laws nor customs retain any person in his place"; and, third, a pervasive belief that "all professions are open to all, and a man's own energies may place him at the top of any one of them." These social traits helped to produce the nomadic and daring frontiersmen who kept pushing westward beyond the fringes of settlement, as well as the less adventurous immigrants who followed them across the mountains in search of new homes, material success, and a better life.

The West had plenty of attractions for a people conditioned to appreciate them. The alluvial river bottoms, the fecund soils of the rolling forest lands, and the black loams of the prairies were tempting to New England farmers working their rocky, sterile acres and to Southeastern farmers plagued with soil exhaustion. The Indian menace east of the Mississippi was now substantially reduced; after

A center of Western power: Cincinnati, 1848.

Transportation to the West, about 1840

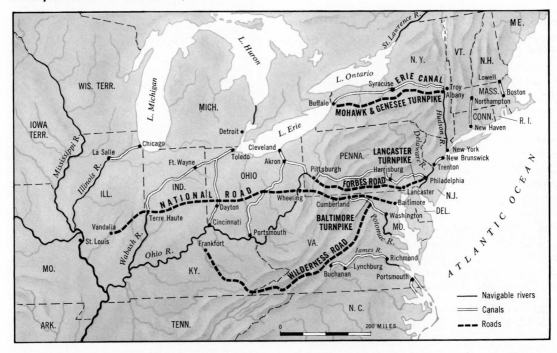

1815 the helpless tribes made a succession of treaties ceding lands, which the government surveyed and put up for sale. In 1820 a new land law ended the credit system but reduced the minimum tract for individual sales to eighty acres and the minimum price to $1.25.* Now it was possible for a man to buy a farm for $100, and the continued proliferation of state banks made it relatively easy for those without cash to negotiate loans in paper money. Western farmers borrowed with the confident expectation that the expanding economy would keep farm prices high, thus making it easy to repay the loans when they fell due.

Transportation was becoming less of a problem for those who wished to move west and for those who had farm surpluses to send to market. Prior to 1815 Western farmers who did not live on waterways were connected with the outside world only by dirt roads and mountain trails. High-value products, such as whiskey and furs, might be carried profitably on pack

*New lands, however, were first put up at auction, and the best sold for a good deal more than the minimum price.

horses or by wagon across the mountains, but the cost of transporting bulky grains in this fashion was several times greater than their value in Eastern markets. Goods could even be shipped across the Atlantic for less than the cost of transportation from western New York or western Pennsylvania to cities along the seaboard.

The first step toward an improvement of Western transportation was the construction of graded and paved turnpikes. Built by private corporations that charged tolls, most of the turnpikes were designed to connect Eastern cities, but a few served the tramontane West. By the 1820's migrants could follow the Baltimore Turnpike to Cumberland, Maryland, and then the National Road to Wheeling (a decade later, to Vandalia, Illinois); the Lancaster Turnpike and Forbes Road to Pittsburgh; or the Mohawk and Genesee Turnpike to Lake Erie. These roads made possible a substantial reduction in transportation costs and thus stimulated the commercialization of agriculture along their routes.

Two developments brought an end to the era of turnpikes and started a transportation revo-

Fulton's "Paragon": Steamboat on the Hudson.

lution that resulted in increased regional specialization and the growth of a national market economy. First came the steamboat. In 1811, four years after Robert Fulton's *Clermont* made its celebrated voyage up the Hudson River, Nicholas J. Roosevelt launched the steam-powered *New Orleans* at Pittsburgh and sent it on a successful voyage down the Ohio and Mississippi. A witness found it an awesome spectacle: "a boat moving without appearance of sail, oar, pole, or any manual labor — moving within the secrets of her own mechanism and propelled by power undiscoverable." Within twenty years some two hundred shallow-draft sternwheelers were plying the Western waters and had superseded all other craft in the carrying of passengers and freight. Steamboats were not only faster but transported upriver freight for about one-tenth of what it previously had cost on hand-propelled keelboats.

Next came the Erie Canal, which spanned the three hundred fifty miles between Buffalo on Lake Erie and Albany on the Hudson River. With the support of Governor De Witt Clinton and funds from the New York legislature, construction began in 1817 and was completed in 1825. After the Erie Canal went into operation the cost per mile of transporting a ton of freight between Buffalo and New York City declined from nearly 20 cents to less than 1 cent. Until the 1840's the canal was used primarily by the farmers of western New York, but eventually the Western states diverted much of their produce from the rivers to this shorter route to Eastern markets.

The Erie Canal's immediate success (tolls enabled the state to recover the cost within seven years) launched the country into the Canal Age. New York's rivals, such as Philadelphia and Baltimore, strove to tap the West with their own canal systems, but with less success; Ohio and Indiana built canals to connect the Ohio River with the Great Lakes. Between 1815 and 1840 (after which construction declined), various states invested about $125 million in three thousand miles of canals. By the 1830's the country had a complete water route from New York City to New Orleans. By then, however, a new marvel, the railroad, promised an even more dazzling answer to the West's transportation needs (see p. 309).

In all phases of this transportation revolution government provided a large proportion of the needed funds. State and local governments helped finance the turnpike companies by subscribing to their stocks; the states built all the important canals; federal and state governments paid for all river and harbor improvements; and federal, state, and local governments gave so much support to the Western railroads that they became semipublic enterprises. Thus even in the years of alleged laissez faire the states had begun to play an active role in the nation's economic life, supplementing the dynamic federal role urged by Henry Clay in his American System.

Life on the frontier. Only hope could make bearable the hardships of a farmer getting his start on the Western frontier. The propaganda literature of the land-speculators abounds in descriptions of the salubrious climate, the health-giving waters, the ease with which one could make the land bloom, and the increasing comforts of civilization. The realities, for some years at least, were quite different. To clear a piece of land for cultivation — girdling the trees to kill them, cutting the branches and rolling the logs into great piles to burn, grubbing out the stumps, and breaking the root-infested ground with primitive plows — meant backbreaking labor for pioneer families. Disease and death hung over the Western settlements; trained doctors were scarce, and the only resort was to home remedies or the patent-medicine panaceas of itinerant quacks. Malaria, dysentery, pneumonia, smallpox, yellow fever, cholera, and dietary deficiencies took a heavy toll; travelers often commented on the pale and sickly appearance of Westerners. Living in primitive lean-tos or floorless cabins, surviving on a diet mainly of corn and salt pork, making their own clothing from home-spun and deerskin, enduring the almost unmitigated bleakness of frontier life, these pioneers would have been hard put to discover the Arcadian quality that some romanticists see in their isolated, self-sufficient agrarian society. A prospective migrant to Illinois warned his family: "What awaits you in this region, which, as of now, is not much better than a wilderness, is a life full of hardships, want and toil. By this choice we shall close ourselves off from the rest of the world for many years."

But the settlers looked beyond the ordeal of these early years, and eventually better times did come. Life softened for them as schools and churches were built, as neighbors became less remote, as transportation improved and Eastern manufactured goods became cheaper and more plentiful, and as the growing villages and county seats acquired printing presses and newspapers, developed small local industries, and offered social diversions to the surrounding countryfolk. These cultural amenities, the modest comforts earned from operating a family-size farm, and the feeling of independence derived from landownership, were the ultimate rewards of many who made their homes in the Western wilderness.

For many others, however, this was not enough. The more ambitious Westerners, if they came to farm, thought of agriculture as a business enterprise and of themselves as small capitalists producing for the market. Moreover, to those who invaded the West in search of wealth, farming was only one way — and perhaps the slowest — to gain their end. Along with the yeomen came the frontier boomers, the speculators in real estate to whom land was simply a commodity to be bought and sold for a profit. The greatest rewards in the West were not always earned by industrious and thrifty farmers; they were often won by shrewd operators who knew how to exploit the vagaries of federal land policy or to buy favors at the local land offices. A long chapter in the history of the West belongs to the land companies — one of the earliest forms of large-scale American business enterprise — whose agents spied out the best tracts, bought them at public auction, and then sold them at higher prices to authentic settlers.

Other Westerners engaged in the fascinating business of promoting towns at strategic trading sites. Many of these wilderness metropolises never materialized, and often the giddy purchasers of unseen town plots wound up with a "business block" knee-deep in swamp water. But important urban centers, such as Cincinnati, Cleveland, Detroit, Indianapolis, St. Louis, and Chicago, did grow with amazing speed. To them came not only promoters and speculators but men with capital to invest in banking, commerce, and manufacturing. Surprisingly early these cities became the centers of Western political and economic power, and of Western culture when it pushed out its first tender shoots.

The significance of the frontier. What impact did the New West make on American society? Not much in the way of political innovation, for state and local government in the West was for the most part modeled after the East. Apparently the forces generating the trend toward increased political democracy in these years were as much Eastern as they were Western. Socially and culturally the West was dependent on the East and again showed a greater tendency to copy than to innovate. This was natural enough, for those who moved west were less often critical of the fundamental structure of Eastern society than dissatisfied with their position in it.

But the impact of the New West was not insignificant. Because of its lack of local traditions, its interior position, and its need for protection and improved transportation, the West was the most nationalistic section of the country. Certainly the problems that settlers faced on a raw frontier encouraged them to develop to a high degree such qualities as individualism and resourcefulness. By stripping Eastern and European civilization down to its fundamentals, Westerners exposed some of its shams and discarded some of its superficialities. Though the West did not produce a society of social and economic equals, it did give added emphasis to the notion that all artificial barriers to advancement must be removed — that all must have an equal chance to make their way in the world. Moreover, the West showed uncommon respect for the man who, starting with little, achieved success in the competitive struggle.

Above all, the New West was America's treasure house of unused land and untapped re-sources. It was a major, though not exclusive, factor in producing the social mobility, economic expansion, and steadily rising standard of living from which all white Americans profited more or less. When the historian Frederick Jackson Turner, near the end of the nineteenth century, called his colleagues' attention to the significance of the frontier in American history, he perhaps claimed too much. But there is some truth in his assertion that "this expansion westward with its new opportunities" accounted for the "fluidity of American life." These Western wilds, Turner wrote, "constituted the richest free gift that was ever spread out before civilized man."

SLAVERY AND THE COTTON KINGDOM

Southern expansion. The migration into Alabama, Mississippi, and Louisiana was, as we have seen, a part of the westward movement; and the great majority of the early settlers were pioneer farmers, mostly from Virginia and the Carolinas, who endured the same hardships and cherished the same ambitions as those who settled north of the Ohio River. They engaged in subsistence farming to begin with, and many of them never managed to produce more than occasional small surpluses for the market. But enterprising farmers in the Southwest knew that cotton-planters in the South Carolina and Georgia piedmonts had been making fortunes ever since Eli Whitney, in 1793, invented a gin that efficiently separated seeds from the lint of "upland," or short-staple, cotton. Before Whitney solved this technological problem, most of the cotton used in European textile mills had come from Egypt and Asia. Southerners had grown small amounts of high-quality "sea-island" cotton on the coast of South Carolina and Georgia, but this variety could not be grown inland. In 1793 the South produced only about 10,000 bales of cotton; but by the 1820's, with the Cotton Kingdom spreading westward, the South's annual production rose to a half-million bales.

Since cotton prices before 1837 seldom fell below 15 cents a pound and often rose much higher, those who obtained suitable land soon devoted at least part of their time to cotton cultivation, usually with the labor of Negro

Agricultural Regions of the South

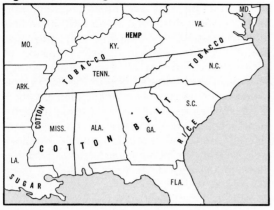

slaves. Eventually a fortunate few — some beginning as small farmers, others bringing slaves with them from the Southeast — established large plantations on the rich, silt-loamed prairies of the Alabama-Mississippi Black Belt, or on the alluvial bottom lands of the Mississippi and Yazoo delta. These great cotton-planters, together with the rice-planters of coastal South Carolina and Georgia and the sugar-planters of Louisiana, developed agriculture to the highest levels of efficiency, complexity, and commercialization to be found anywhere in nineteenth-century America.

After 1815 the economy of the South was tied to the cultivation of cotton, for investments in new cotton lands brought higher returns than any of the possible alternatives. Fluctuations in the price of cotton were responsible for the periodic surges and declines in westward migration and land sales. Indeed, during the next few decades cotton was a crucial factor in the whole developing national market economy and in the economic growth of all regions. It accounted for more than half the country's exports and thus paid for most of its imports. The cotton plantations provided a substantial market for foodstuffs from the West and manufactured goods from the Northeast, and the marketing of Southern cotton gave the Northeastern commercial interests their most profitable trade.

Within two decades after the War of 1812 the booming Gulf states were ceasing to be part of the New West and were becoming increasingly identified with the Old South, even though they differed socially from Virginia and the Carolinas in many significant ways. Their identification with the South Atlantic states came at a time when Southerners were becoming more, rather than less, conscious of their special sectional problems and interests.

The survival of slavery. What was it that made the Old South unique? Not physical isolation, for it lacked natural frontiers separating it from the rest of the country; nor geographic and climatic uniformity, for it had great diversity of soils, topography, mean temperatures, growing seasons, and average rainfalls. Not a difference in population origins, for the South, like the North, was originally settled by middle- and lower-class people; nor contrasts in religion or political philosophy, for here, too, the similarities outweighed the differences. Not even the economies of North and South were altogether unlike, for, although there were important differences, the majority of the white people of both sections were independent yeomen farmers who worked their own lands. In contrast to the Western farmers, however, few Southern farmers benefited from improved transportation and became part of the national market economy. Wealth was less evenly distributed in the South than in the West; less money was invested in education; and the rate of illiteracy was higher. Fewer towns and less local industry developed, with the result that much of the income of the cotton-planters flowed out of the region to pay for goods and services provided by the West and Northeast. In short, the Old South remained more rural and economically less diversified than the North, and a larger proportion of its small farmers lived a life of pioneer self-sufficiency.

But all these differences between North and South were of secondary importance. By far the most significant difference was the presence and survival in the South of Negro slavery, which Southerners themselves called their "peculiar institution." More than anything else, it was slavery, with all its ramifications, that eventually gave the Old South its identity and Southerners their feeling of separateness from the rest of the Union.

In the eighteenth century, of course, Southern slavery had not been a peculiar institution, for it existed in the Northern colonies and throughout the Western Hemisphere. During or soon after the Revolution, however, the Northern states abolished it; and in the first half of the nineteenth century slaves gained their freedom in most of Central and South America. Many Southerners of Washington's and Jefferson's generation also were critical of slavery; as late as the 1820's there were numerous emancipation societies in the Upper South that carried on a discreet but steady agitation. In Virginia, in the late eighteenth and early nineteenth centuries, a prolonged agricultural depression resulting from low tobacco prices and soil exhaustion led some to believe, or hope, that slavery would soon die. In August 1831, Southampton County, Virginia, was the scene of the South's bloodiest slave insurrection, led by a bondsman named Nat Turner, in which sixty whites and scores of Negroes (including Turner) were killed. This event precipitated an earnest debate in the Virginia legislature the following January during which various legislators denounced slavery as a social canker, an economic blight, and a moral evil, and demanded a program of gradual emancipation. But the Virginia emancipationists, like those in other Southern states, were defeated; and soon after 1832 Southern critics were either silenced or driven into exile.

Southern slavery, then, did not die of natural causes; it did not even decline. Instead, with the rise of the Cotton Kingdom and the eventual improvement of agriculture in the seaboard states, it flourished and seemed to have the vitality to survive indefinitely. Since the federal Constitution recognized slavery as a local institution within the jurisdiction of individual states, Southerners saw nothing to prevent them from introducing it into the Southwest. Some moved there with their Negroes, while others stayed behind and operated new plantations as absentee owners. Still others took advantage of high slave prices resulting from the labor shortage in the Southwest and sold a portion of their Negroes to professional traders who took them to the busy markets in New Orleans and Natchez. There at the slave auctions the self-made men of the Cotton Kingdom, some of whom had started with no slaves at all, purchased "prime field hands" to work their growing estates.

Negro slaves thus became an important element in the migration to the Southwest and played a major role in clearing the land for cultivation. By 1840 almost half the population of Alabama and Louisiana and more than half the population of Mississippi (by then the leading cotton-producing state) consisted of Negro slaves. Yet at all times nearly three-fourths of the white families in the South as a whole held no slaves and depended on their own labor alone. Moreover, the great majority of slaveholders owned just a few slaves; as late as 1860 only ten thousand Southern families belonged to the planter aristocracy operating large estates with slave gangs numbering more than fifty.

Why did Southern slavery survive far into the nineteenth century? Not because Negroes were natural slaves; nor because white labor could not adjust to the Southern climate and successfully cultivate the Southern crops; nor because the Negroes' health was not adversely affected by living in the malarial swamps, where the sugar and rice plantations and many of the cotton plantations were located. The reasons the South clung so tenaciously to slavery are to be found in the fears, ambitions, and aspirations of Southern white men.

By the nineteenth century the South's peculiar institution was two hundred years old, and to abolish it would have brought painful changes in long-established habits and attitudes. Those who would destroy slavery, warned a Georgian, "would have to wade knee-deep in blood"; indeed, slavery is "so intimately . . . mingled with our social conditions that it would be impossible to eradicate it." To some, who thought that Negroes were naturally shiftless and immoral, slavery was a system of controlling an inferior race. To non-slaveholders slavery symbolized their link with the privileged caste of white men and the Negroes' social and legal subordination. "Now suppose they was free," explained a poor Southern farmer to a Northern visitor, "you see they'd all think themselves as good as we." To the master class the possession of slaves brought great prestige, for in the South the ownership of a plantation worked by slave labor was the sign of success and high social position.

But, above all, slavery survived because it was a viable and profitable labor system and because it represented an enormous investment of Southern capital. Slavery, of course, did not make every master a rich man, nor did every master strive to wring the last ounce of profit from his toiling bondsmen. Nevertheless, most slaveholders earned good returns on their investments — and this accounts for the generally heavy demand for slaves and for their high price in the market. The system, moreover, was highly adaptable. Slaves were employed, not only in agriculture and as domestics, but as skilled artisans, as laborers in construction gangs, and as workers in iron foundries, textile mills, and tobacco factories. In short, the master class had no compelling economic reason for wanting to abolish slavery.

The nature of slavery. In governing their bondsmen most masters were neither inordinately cruel nor remarkably indulgent; they simply dealt with their human property in the manner they deemed necessary to make the system work. They bought and sold slaves, used them as security for loans, and divided them among heirs. In these transactions husbands were often separated from their wives and children from their mothers, for state laws gave slave marriages no recognition. Except for the deliberate killing or maiming of a slave, the master's power to administer physical punishment was virtually unlimited, and planters could delegate this power to white overseers employed to manage their estates. Most slaveholders used the whip for "moderate correction" only when they believed it essential to maintain discipline; but an element of cruelty was inseparable from slavery, as even many of its defenders recognized. Some slaves fell into the hands of brutal masters, or of men who were corrupted by the power the institution conferred upon them. Since a Negro was unable to give testimony against a white man, the justice he received in court was, at the best, very eccentric.

The average slave's standard of living was near the subsistence level. He lived on a diet mainly of corn and pork, adequate in bulk but unbalanced and monotonous; he wore coarse, skimpy clothing made from some variety of cheap "Negro cloth"; and he lived in a cabin that was too often drafty, cramped, and scantily furnished. His labor routine kept him at work from dawn to dusk. By nineteenth-century standards, he was not often worked excessively, but a long day of hard toil was usually exacted from him. The slave was most in danger of being overworked to the detriment of his health on the large cotton and sugar plantations managed by overseers.

One cannot pretend to know all that being a slave meant to the Negroes; one certainly must be cautious about assuming that they accepted slavery as their natural lot. No doubt they made certain psychological adaptations to their condition; no doubt they enjoyed the occasional holidays and simple pleasures that most masters permitted them; no doubt their untrained intellects seldom dwelt on freedom as a philosophical abstraction. But to conclude from this that they had no idea of the meaning of freedom, no comprehension of its practical advantages, no desire to obtain it, would be quite unwarranted. The evidence of their submission and obeisance suggests not so much contentment as the superior power of the white caste and the effectiveness of its elaborate techniques of control. The swift and ruthless suppression of Nat Turner's followers drove home to the slaves the futility of organized rebellion. But it did not deter some of the bolder ones from less spectacular forms of protest. Of these, running away was among the most common — and certainly the most irksome to the master class.

White men paid a high price for slavery: artisans and yeoman farmers suffered from the competition of cheap slave labor; most white Southerners were more or less distressed by the obvious paradox of slavery in a republic whose moral commitment was to individual freedom and natural rights; and all were bedeviled by a nagging fear of slave rebellions, a fear that is endemic wherever bondage exists. But the Negro paid an even higher price. Apart from his exposure to cruelty and his meager rewards, slavery afforded him little opportunity for cultural advancement. It gave him some vocational training, indoctrinated him with a crude form of Christianity that provided more emotional release than spiritual nourishment, and exposed him to some of the external forms of white civilization. But slavery also made the Negro family unstable, encouraged sexual promiscuity, and exposed Negro women to the lust of white men. It robbed the Negro of his manhood, encouraged infantile and irresponsi-

The Missouri Compromise, 1820

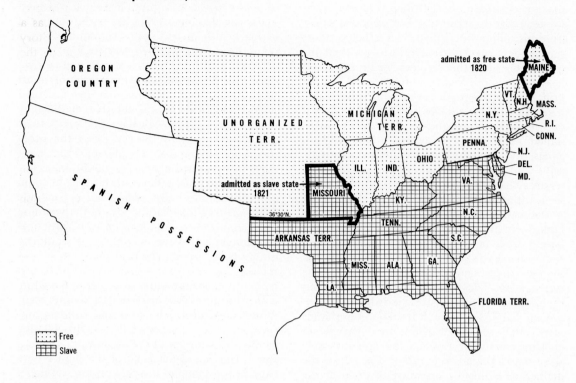

- Free
- Slave

ble behavior, and put a premium on docility. In short, slavery deprived a whole race of the opportunity to develop its potentialities and of the freedom that white men treasured so highly.

Missouri and the issue of slavery expansion. Eventually the South's peculiar institution was to have a tragic impact upon the whole nation, and a few intimations of the ultimate tragedy were evident even in the early years. Slavery was a topic of debate at the Constitutional Convention of 1787, and just what would happen to it under the new Constitution was a subject of inquiry at Southern ratifying conventions. The compromise by which Southerners obtained congressional representation for three-fifths of their slaves (see p. 135) provoked repeated complaints, especially from New England. Antislavery Northerners frequently resisted enforcement of the Fugitive Slave Act of 1793, which enabled Southern masters to recover runaways in the free states. In the Deep South some doubted the wisdom of a federal law that closed the African slave trade

on January 1, 1808, and the law was often flagrantly violated thereafter.

But these were minor irritants compared to the succession of crises generated by the steady march of slavery into the Southwest. Before 1820 five additional slave states (Kentucky, Tennessee, Louisiana, Mississippi, and Alabama) had been admitted to the Union; these increased the total number to eleven, which, as it happened, was balanced by eleven free states. The resulting political equilibrium in the Senate was threatened, however, when the territory of Missouri, settled mostly by pro-slavery Kentuckians and Tennesseeans, petitioned for admission as a slave state. In February 1819 a House committee reported an enabling act; but Representative James Tallmadge, Jr., a Republican from New York, proposed an amendment to prohibit the introduction of additional slaves into Missouri and to provide gradual emancipation for those already there. The Tallmadge Amendment passed the House on a sectional vote but was defeated in the Senate. When neither chamber would yield, slavery's critics and defenders plunged into an ill-tempered debate that showed the existence of a deep sectional cleavage.

Much of the Missouri debate revolved around constitutional issues. Southerners, especially Virginians, insisting that new states had the same sovereign rights as the old, denied that Congress could make the abolition of slavery a condition of admission. Northerners claimed that the Founding Fathers had thought of slavery as a temporary institution and had not intended that it should spread into the Western territories. In the heat of the debate angry Southerners accused Federalists of deliberately fomenting a crisis in order to win popular support in the North and revive their dying party. Jefferson, who strongly opposed the Tallmadge Amendment, was convinced that the Federalist leader Rufus King was "ready to risk the Union for any chance of restoring his party to power and wriggling himself to the head of it." Northern opposition to slavery expansion, wrote Charles Pinckney of South Carolina, "sprang from the love of power, and the never ceasing wish to regain the honors and offices of the government."

No doubt political advantage and sectional power — the North already had a substantial majority in the House — were basic ingredients of the Missouri controversy. But the crisis might have looked less portentous had this been all there was to it. Tallmadge himself appeared to have no crass political motive; rather, he seems to have acted from a conviction that slavery was a moral evil that should not be permitted to spread. So did many others whose humanitarian impulses were aroused by the apparent vitality of Southern slavery. According to a resolution of the Pennsylvania legislature, to admit Missouri as a slave state would be to open "a new and steady market for the lawless venders of human flesh"; it would be a "covenant with crime, contrary to duty, to God, and to the fathers of the Republic." Never before had the peculiar institution been so severely attacked — and so vigorously defended — on moral grounds as it was during the Missouri debate.

The basic issue was not resolved on this occasion; it was simply postponed by a compromise in whose passage Henry Clay played a leading role. In 1820 Congress finally agreed to admit Missouri as a slave state, but it preserved the balance by admitting Maine as a free state. It divided the remaining territory acquired in the Louisiana Purchase along the line 36°30′ north latitude. North of that line, except for Missouri, slavery was "forever prohibited."

The Missouri crisis made some Americans apprehensive about the future of the federal Union. John Quincy Adams foresaw the possibility of a realignment of political parties along sectional lines, hastening the "emancipation of all . . . [Southern] slaves, threatening in its immediate effect that Southern domination which has swayed the Union for the last twenty years." Tallmadge, said a Georgia congressman, had "kindled a fire which all the waters of the ocean can not put out, which seas of blood can only extinguish." And Jefferson, showing hardly a glimmer of his earlier antislavery sentiments, poured his indignation on Northerners for opening this sensitive issue. "All, I fear, do not see the speck on our horizon which is to burst on us as a tornado, sooner or later. The line of division lately marked out between different portions of our confederacy is such as will never, I fear, be obliterated." Writing thus in 1821, Jefferson had, in effect, formulated the doctrine of an "irrepressible conflict" between North and South.

Even in an era of nationalism and expansion, then, slavery hung like a menacing shadow over the young republic. And in the South the conflict between slavery, which Southerners would not abolish, and the American liberal tradition, which they claimed as their birthright, created tensions that were ultimately to become unbearable.

ANOTHER FRONTIER: INDUSTRY AND TECHNOLOGY

Beginnings of the factory system. The western edge of settlement was not the only frontier that attracted Americans and promised a future of increased abundance. Since the War of 1812 growing numbers had been drawn to the thriving towns and cities of the New England and Middle Atlantic states. Here lived the pioneers of the American Industrial Revolution — the men who devoted their lives to the develop-

Weaving by power loom.

ment of large and intricate forms of business enterprise and to the application of science and technology to the twin goals of lightening the burdens of labor and multiplying the comforts of human life. Their efforts gradually rendered obsolete the system of domestic manufacturing that had been almost universal in colonial days. Under this system farmers outside the market economy had made their own clothes and household necessities, while village artisans had produced items such as cloth, shoes, hats, and tools for sale to consumers in local markets. The independent artisan survived longer in some crafts than in others, and household manufacturing was always a part of life on the isolated agricultural frontier; but after 1815 both were clearly doomed by the factory and the spreading market economy.

In a sense the Industrial Revolution, in America as in Europe, was merely an acceleration of technological changes that had no clear beginning and as yet have no foreseeable end. It involved the development and increasing use of power-driven machines in industrial production; the location of these machines in factories that tended to grow in size and complexity;

and, with the decline of transportation costs, the distribution of their products in ever widening mass markets. As the domestic market expanded, manufacturing enterprises became increasingly specialized. The early textile mills, for example, marketed their own products and constructed their own machinery; but eventually they concentrated on spinning and weaving, selling their products to wholesalers and buying their machinery from independent machine shops. The essential features of the Industrial Revolution, then, were mechanization, specialization, and national distribution.

American industrial technology was in part copied from England and in part an indigenous outgrowth of the genius of American scientists, inventors, skilled mechanics, and entrepreneurs. Manufacturers found an impelling incentive for mechanization in the high cost of domestic labor, whose wages in the early nineteenth century were from 30 to 50 per cent higher than wages in Great Britain. The dearness of labor was the direct result of the high productivity of American agriculture, which forced industry to pay wages comparable to what could be earned on the land. Another incentive was the presence of cheap water-power to which machinery could easily be harnessed. Moreover, the optimistic American entrepreneurs, anticipating continued technological advances, usually built machines that wore out quickly, thus making it relatively inexpensive to retool. Nowhere in Europe did environmental conditions provide so many inducements for mechanical innovation; nowhere was there a society so free from the sort of hampering traditions that impede technological change. "Everything new is quickly introduced here," wrote a European visitor in the 1820's. "There is no clinging to old ways; the moment an American hears the word 'invention' he pricks up his ears."

The Northeastern states, for a variety of reasons, were the first to industrialize to a significant degree. In the years before the embargo and War of 1812, their profitable foreign trade had enabled them to accumulate the necessary capital and to build the banks and other commercial facilities that were now useful to industry. Their substantial urban centers provided large local markets, and the turnpikes gave them early access to the hinterland. In addition, the Northeast had superior entrepreneurial talent, a relatively abundant and well-educated labor supply, easy access to Southern cotton, and rich resources in the waterpower of New England and the iron and coal of Pennsylvania. In the years after 1815 manufacturing rapidly superseded commerce as this region's primary economic concern.

What the pioneers in technology accomplished lacked the romance and drama of the Western frontiersman's elemental struggle for survival. Yet their work was equally vital to national growth and expansion, and its long-run social and economic consequences were, if anything, greater. In the field of transportation, for example, the builders of turnpikes experimented with various kinds of road-surfacing and with truss-type and suspension bridges; engineers on the Erie Canal designed new excavating equipment and developed a special cement for use in its eighty-eight locks; and Henry M. Shreve, among others, built flat-hulled steamboats of shallow draft especially adapted to service on the Western rivers. Meanwhile, a patent act adopted by Congress in 1790 (revised in 1793) encouraged numerous

men to pursue fame and fortune through the improvement or invention of devices useful to mankind. As Hamilton claimed in his Report on Manufactures, there did seem to exist "in the genius of the people of this country, a peculiar aptitude for mechanical improvements."

The factory system in the United States had its beginnings during the Presidency of Washington. In 1790 Samuel Slater, an English immigrant who knew the secrets of English textile machinery, built a cotton-spinning mill at Pawtucket, Rhode Island, for the merchant Moses Brown. This first successful American factory contained seventy-two spindles tended by nine children, and its machinery was soon harnessed to waterpower. After years of slow and faltering growth, Jefferson's embargo and the War of 1812 gave the American cotton-textile industry a chance to become a significant part of the national economy. By the end of the war cotton factories were counted in the hundreds, most of them in New England, and the number of spindles in operation approximated 130,000. Immediately after the war many of these mills failed because of renewed British competition; but others survived, and by 1840 the number of spindles in operation exceeded 2 million.

In the years of expansion constant improvements were made in the machinery for carding the raw cotton and for spinning it into yarn and thread. But the weaving long continued to be done in the homes of small craftsmen, who sold the cloth in their own shops or who worked for wages for merchant capitalists. After 1814, however, the introduction of the power loom soon brought weaving as well as spinning into the factory. Many American mills specialized in the manufacture of a coarse white cloth called "sheeting," which was in wide demand and could be mass produced. American manufacturers of sheeting could compete successfully with the British in the domestic market, and by the 1830's they were even selling in foreign markets.

From cotton textiles the factory spread to other industries. In 1793, at Byfield, Massachusetts, John and Arthur Schofield, who came to the United States from Yorkshire, England, built the first factory to manufacture woolens. War in Europe, a series of improvements in carding, napping, and shearing machines, and the introduction of waterpower soon placed the American woolens industry on a secure foundation. Meanwhile, merchant capitalists were taking the manufacture of shoes out of the cobblers' shops and into the homes of semi-skilled workers who specialized in making a single part of the finished product. Eventually, when the shoe industry began to be mechanized, the workers were brought into factories where their role changed from that of craftsmen to that of tenders of machines. Similarly, in the iron industry Pennsylvania's furnaces and rolling mills were fast supplanting the small local forges and blacksmith shops.

In 1804 Oliver Evans of Philadelphia, one of the most remarkable pioneers of American technology, developed a high-pressure steam engine that was adaptable to a great variety of industrial purposes. Within a few years it was being used not only in steam navigation but to run sawmills, flour mills, and printing presses — and, in 1828, steam power replaced waterpower at the Slater cotton mills. Evans also experimented with the techniques of mass production and built the first completely mechanized flour mill. In 1798 Eli Whitney applied these techniques to the manufacture of guns and conceived the idea of interchangeable parts. He taught his workers to make identical parts from metal molds, or "gigs"; now guns could be assembled in a fraction of the time required by a skilled gunsmith. Whitney then introduced his system in the clock industry, and Connecticut manufacturers were soon mass-producing inexpensive clocks for a national market.

To build a factory equipped with expensive machinery run by steam or waterpower required more capital than the average individual entrepreneur could obtain. As a result, business partnerships increased in number, but the ultimate answer to this financial problem was the corporation. Chartered under state laws, corporations could accumulate capital from numerous small investors; and the stockholders enjoyed "limited liability" — that is, they were financially responsible for the corporation's debts only to the extent of their investment. Used first by bankers and the builders of turnpikes, bridges, and other internal improvements, the corporate form slowly spread to manufacturing, especially textiles, after the War of 1812. In 1813 a group of wealthy merchants known as the Boston Associates, including Francis Cabot Lowell, Nathan Appleton, and Patrick Tracy Jackson, formed the Boston Manufacturing Company in Waltham, Massachusetts. With capital exceeding a half-million dollars and an efficient managerial staff, these men built the first integrated textile factory that performed every operation from the carding of the raw cotton to the weaving of the cloth with power looms. A decade later the Boston Associates shifted the center of their activities to Lowell, "the Manchester of America," where they chartered the Merrimack Manufacturing Company. During the 1820's and 1830's they chartered additional companies in Massachusetts and New Hampshire, until they and their imitators had made the manufacturing corporation an entrenched economic institution.

In other areas, too, the American economy began to show the effects of advancing technology. Eastern merchants used improved transportation and marketing techniques to compete for the trade of the hinterland, with New York merchants rapidly outstripping their rivals. The New York group siphoned much of the Western trade through the Great Lakes and the Erie Canal and captured most of the cotton trade between the South and Europe. The skill of Yankee shipbuilders and the initiative of New York merchants combined to improve transatlantic service for passengers and cargo. The New York packet lines, beginning with the Black Ball Line in 1818, were the first to post sailing dates and observe them regardless of weather. The sleek vessels in this service were built for speed and maximum cargo; they were, said an English reporter, "probably the finest and fastest sailing vessels in the world . . . beautifully modeled and of the best workmanship." The whaling industry, concentrated at New Bedford and Nantucket Island, Massachusetts, was also more highly organized after the War of 1812 than before, because the depletion of the Atlantic supply necessitated long, expensive voyages to the Pacific. Still another sign of the new era was John Jacob Astor's American Fur Company, a million-dollar corporation chartered in New York in 1808. Until the 1830's, when the fur supply of the

Northwest began to near exhaustion, Astor used efficient organization and ruthless methods to destroy his weaker competitors and lay the foundation for the first great American fortune.

As mechanical devices played an increasingly important part in the lives of the American people, applied science began to invade the precincts of American education. A network of mechanics' institutes, beginning with one in Boston in 1795, spread through American cities to train men in the mechanical arts. When President Madison, like his predecessors, urged the founding of a national university, he stressed its potential value as a "temple of science" to diffuse "useful knowledge." Nothing came of this, but several private colleges soon added applied science to their curricula. At Harvard, in 1814, Dr. Jacob Bigelow began to lecture on "The Elements of Technology" and tried to awaken his students to the possibilities of this exciting frontier. At Yale, Benjamin Silliman brought a similar message not only to his students but to a wider audience through his *American Journal of Science*, founded in 1818, and through his enormously popular public lectures. In 1825 Rensselaer Polytechnic Institute, the first of its genre, opened its doors at Troy, New York, "for the purpose of instructing persons who may choose to apply themselves in the application of science to the common purposes of life."

If newspapers and periodicals accurately reflected public opinion, the American people were proud of their technological achievements and fascinated by the many useful products of applied science. The promise of a rising standard of living encouraged them to rationalize agriculture, to build great internal improvements, to mechanize industry, and to widen commercial horizons. Looking back at the half-century of economic growth following independence, Tocqueville concluded that "no people in the world had made such rapid progress in trade and manufactures as the Americans; they constitute at the present day the second maritime nation in the world"; their manufacturing makes "great and daily advances"; "the greatest undertakings and speculations are executed without difficulty. . . . The Americans arrived but as yesterday on the territory which they inhabit, and they have already changed the whole order of nature for their own advantage."

Capital and labor. Yet, while they found the promises of the Industrial Revolution irresistible, many Americans were at the same time a little uneasy about what had been happening to their society since industry got a foothold. Carrying with them into the new age the assumptions of a simple agrarian society, they watched apprehensively the paper-money speculations, the growth of cities, and the movement of young people from the land to the factory. They wondered whether the American tradition was somehow being betrayed, whether the craving for material success was undermining their morals and compromising their virtue. To be sure, these fears were still rather vague and sporadic, for in the 1820's and 1830's the cities and the factories were not very large, and the urban industrial population was a small fraction of the whole. But the trend was clear.

A particularly conspicuous consequence of the factories and machines was the emergence of two new social classes. The first were the industrial capitalists, whom the agrarian gentry regarded as vulgarly ambitious and dangerously powerful. With their wealth they burrowed their way into government, made politicians their vassals, and, as James Fenimore Cooper complained, substituted their "fluctuating expedients for the high principles of natural justice." Industrialists operated in mysterious ways through corporations, those cold, impersonal institutions "having neither a body to be kicked nor a soul to be damned." The second new social class were the factory workers, the hirelings who tended machines for a weekly wage and had no personal contact with either owners or ultimate consumers. They were recruited from the farms and, increasingly by the 1830's, from among newly arrived immigrants. Less and less the nonagricultural "laboring population" meant the village artisans and mechanics; more and more it meant the miners, construction gangs, and urban factory employees.

Thanks to a chronic labor shortage, workingmen's living conditions were far better in America than in Europe. Visitors to Lowell often commented on the attention that the Boston Associates gave to the welfare of the young women who worked in their mills. The "Lowell girls" lived in comfortable boarding-houses built by the company; their morals were strictly supervised; and they were provided with recreational facilities, educational opportunities, and religious instruction. They published their own monthly magazine, the *Lowell Offering*, "as a repository of original articles, written by females employed in the mills." After a visit to Lowell, Charles Dickens reported that he had seen "no face that bore an unhealthy or an unhappy look." According to Anthony Trollope, Lowell was "the realization of a commercial utopia," where the women were "taken in, as it were, to a philanthropical manufacturing college."

But industrial paternalism soon declined in the Lowell mills as professional managers fought competitors by cutting costs and making increased use of immigrant labor. Even in the 1830's the working day at Lowell was thirteen hours in summer and from sunrise to sunset in winter. Another visitor had a less happy report about conditions among the women employees: "The great mass wear out their health, spirits, and morals without becoming one whit better off than when they commenced labor." Children under sixteen, who constituted two-fifths of the labor force in New England textile mills, worked twelve or more hours a day. Real wages declined; in 1830 it was estimated that some twenty thousand of the lowest-paid women in Eastern cities worked sixteen hours a day for $1.25 a week. The callousness of the factory system in a laissez faire economy began to be reflected, too, in the crowded dwellings of drab factory towns.

Such conditions produced disturbing social fissures and a greater awareness of class interests and class identity than had been the case before the rise of the factory. When workingmen tried to improve their status through united action, unprecedented tensions developed in the relations between labor and capital. In the 1790's the carpenters, printers, and cordwainers had begun to organize in several cities; in the early nineteenth century other skilled trades followed their example. The next step was the formation of city federations of craft unions, six of which united, in 1834, to form the short-lived National Trades' Union. Strikes for higher wages usually failed, first, because labor organizations were still weak and inexperienced and, second, because state courts usually treated them as criminal conspiracies under common law.* Turning briefly to political action in the 1820's, workingmen's parties, especially in New York and Philadelphia, agitated for free public education, shorter working hours, and other social reforms to aid the laboring class. Distressed by such novel phenomena as trade unions and workingmen's parties, some conservatives might well have recalled Jefferson's pessimistic predictions about the evil consequences of industrialization.

Economic crisis. The Panic of 1819 introduced the United States to still another hazard of a commercial-industrial economy: the modern business cycle. When Americans first began to experience the rhythmic rotation of booms, panics, and depressions, they were so mystified that many of them turned to the supernatural for an explanation. An angry deity, they said, periodically brought hard times to punish man for his moral delinquencies — extravagance, speculation, and greed. This first modern panic followed several years of postwar prosperity. In the boom years, when cotton sold for more than 30 cents a pound and wheat for $2 a bushel, land speculation financed by the state banks became a national disease. Soon the Bank of the United States caught the spirit of the times; rather than acting as a stabilizing force, it extended credit generously to speculators and business-promoters in both the East and the West. Public land sales rose sharply; and between 1814 and 1819, under the impetus of high prices, cotton production doubled.

At length an accumulation of adverse economic forces brought these flush times to a sudden end. First came a decline in the European demand for American agricultural products, especially cotton, then a shrinking of the market for textiles. Early in 1819 the Bank of the United States, now under new and more

---

* The common law, introduced to America from England in colonial days, consists of a body of judicial decisions based on custom and precedent. It became the basis of the legal system in all the states except Louisiana. In the early nineteenth century, state courts repeatedly used common-law precedents to find guilty of criminal conspiracies the combinations of workmen attempting to force employers to bargain with them over wages and working conditions.

conservative management, began to call in its loans and to exert pressure on the state banks to redeem their notes with specie. The Bank's attempt to save itself from its own recent follies was the immediate cause of a financial panic that forced many state banks to close their doors. In the subsequent depression prices fell disastrously — in 1823 cotton sold for less than 10 cents a pound — and public land sales nearly ceased. Thousands of farmers and planters saw their lands sold at public auction to satisfy the claims of creditors; numerous speculators and business-promoters forfeited property to the Bank of the United States for failing to repay their loans. In the Eastern cities a half-million workers lost their jobs when factories closed down or curtailed their operations.

Those suffering from economic distress turned to government for relief. Manufacturers demanded higher tariff protection, and after a long battle Congress came to their aid with the Tariff of 1824. To help Western farmers who had bought public land on credit, Congress permitted them to delay payments or to keep as much of the land as they had paid for. Several Southern and Western states passed "stay laws" postponing the time when creditors could foreclose on the property of debtors. The demand for "stay laws" and other measures of debtor relief became bitter issues in the politics of various states, especially Kentucky and Tennessee.

By the mid-twenties prosperity had returned, but not before the panic and depression had created angry feelings that were reflected in national politics. Many accused the Bank of the United States of coldly sacrificing thousands of innocent victims to protect the selfish interests of its wealthy stockholders. Thereafter much of the anxiety about the new economic order was focused on the monopolistic Bank, the most powerful of the "soulless" corporations. Senator Thomas Hart Benton of Missouri pictured the Bank as a ruthless "money power" to which the Western cities were enslaved: "They may be devoured by it at any moment. They are in the jaws of the monster! A lump of butter in the mouth of a dog! One gulp, one swallow, and all is gone!"

The ground had been prepared for the growth of the Jacksonian movement, which, in a strange way, benefited from both the acquisitive impulses that the new order had aroused in the American people and the lingering doubts they felt about its results.

SUGGESTIONS FOR READING

Postwar Nationalism

George Dangerfield has written two superb books on the period from the War of 1812 to the election of Andrew Jackson as President: *The Era of Good Feelings** (1952), and *The Awakening of American Nationalism, 1815–1828** (1965). Two older works are still useful: K. C. Babcock, *Rise of American Nationality* (1906), and F. J. Turner, *Rise of the New West** (1906). P. C. Nagel, *One Nation Indivisible: The Union in American Thought, 1776–1861* (1964), is a study of the intellectual roots of American nationalism. An excellent study of the postwar decline of the Federalists is Shaw Livermore, Jr., *The Twilight of Federalism* (1962). The period may also be studied through several good biographies of Republican leaders: W. P. Cresson, *James Monroe* (1946); C. M. Wiltse, *John C. Calhoun: Nationalist, 1782–1828* (1944); G. G. Van Deusen, *The Life of Henry Clay** (1937); and Clement Eaton, *Henry Clay and the Art of American Politics** (1957). Sympathetic and authoritative accounts of the chartering of the second Bank of the United States and its role in the American economy are R. C. H. Catterall, *The Second Bank of the United States* (1903), and Bray Hammond, *Banks and Politics in America from the Revolution to the Civil War* (1957).

* Available in a paperback edition.

The role of the Supreme Court in the Marshall era is treated fully in A. J. Beveridge's distinguished biography of the great Chief Justice, *The Life of John Marshall*, 4 vols. (1916–19). Some of the best of the briefer studies are E. S. Corwin, *John Marshall and the Constitution* (1919); Charles Warren, Vol. I of *The Supreme Court in United States History*, 2 vols. (1937); and C. G. Haines, *The Role of the Supreme Court in American Government and Politics, 1789–1835* (1944). E. T. Mudge, *The Social Philosophy of John Taylor of Caroline: A Study in Jeffersonian Democracy* (1939), presents the view of one of Marshall's ablest contemporary critics.

The most authoritative book on the Monroe Doctrine is A. P. Whitaker, *The United States and the Independence of Latin America, 1800–1830** (1941). Three other excellent monographs are Dexter Perkins, *The Monroe Doctrine, 1823–1826* (1927); E. H. Tatum, *The United States and Europe, 1815–1823* (1936); and C. C. Griffin, *The United States and the Disruption of the Spanish Empire* (1937). Two fine biographies should also be consulted: J. H. Powell, *Richard Rush: Republican Diplomat, 1780–1859* (1942), and S. F. Bemis, *John Quincy Adams and the Foundations of American Foreign Policy* (1949). Frank Thistlethwaite, *The Anglo-American Connection in the Early Nineteenth Century* (1959), describes the economic and intellectual ties of the United States and Great Britain.

The Westward Movement

General histories of the westward movement with useful chapters on the period following the War of 1812 are R. E. Riegel and R. G. Athearn, *America Moves West* (1964); R. A. Billington, *Westward Expansion* (rev. ed., 1967); and T. D. Clark, *Frontier America* (1959). A good synthesis covering this period is F. S. Philbrick, *The Rise of the West, 1754–1830** (1965). The classic statement of the importance of the West to the whole of American society is F. J. Turner, *The Frontier in American History** (1920). R. A. Billington, *America's Frontier Heritage* (1966), is a sympathetic appraisal of the Turner thesis in the light of modern scholarship. The best study of public land policy in the West is R. M. Robbins, *Our Landed Heritage: The Public Domain** (1942). Agricultural development in the Northwest is traced in P. W. Bidwell and J. I. Falconer, *History of Agriculture in the Northern United States, 1620–1860* (1925); in the Southwest, in L. C. Gray, *History of Agriculture in the Southern United States to 1860*, 2 vols. (1933). A comprehensive study is P. W. Gates, *The Farmer's Age* (1960). The importance of urban development in the West, long neglected, is stressed in R. C. Wade, *The Urban Frontier** (1959). R. C. Buley, *The Old Northwest: Pioneer Period, 1815–1840*, 2 vols. (1950), provides an exhaustive study of social conditions in the West.

Three general studies of transportation have much detail on efforts to deal with this problem in the West: Seymour Dunbar, *A History of American Travel*, 4 vols. (1915); B. H. Meyer, C. E. MacGill, and others, *History of Transportation in the United States before 1860* (1917); and G. R. Taylor, *The Transportation Revolution, 1815–1860* (1951). L. C. Hunter, *Steamboats on the Western Rivers* (1949), is a classic. Other valuable studies are P. D. Jordan, *The National Road* (1948); L. D. Baldwin, *The Keelboat Age on Western Waters* (1941); Carter Goodrich and others, *Canals and American Economic Development* (1961); and R. E. Shaw, *Erie Water West: A History of the Erie Canal, 1792–1854* (1966).

The Old South and Slavery

The best surveys of the Old South are Clement Eaton, *A History of the Old South* (2nd ed., 1966), and F. B. Simkins, *A History of the South* (1953). There is a brilliant essay on the Old South in the first section of W. J. Cash, *The Mind of the South** (1941). Clement Eaton has written two

* Available in a paperback edition.

perceptive studies of the social and cultural life of the Old South: *The Growth of Southern Civilization** (1961), and *The Mind of the Old South** (1964). W. R. Taylor, *Cavalier and Yankee: The Old South and American National Character** (1961), is a study of the evolution of the Southern legend. U. B. Phillips, *Life and Labor in the Old South** (1929), is a somewhat sentimental description of life on the plantations. F. L. Owsley, *Plain Folk of the Old South** (1949), deals with the life of the nonslaveholders, whom Phillips almost ignored. An indispensable book, based on extensive travels in the South in the 1850's, is F. L. Olmsted, *The Cotton Kingdom* (1861). A new edition of Olmsted, edited by A. M. Schlesinger, was published in 1953.

Slavery may be studied from several perspectives in U. B. Phillips, *American Negro Slavery** (1919); K. M. Stampp, *The Peculiar Institution** (1956); Stanley Elkins, *Slavery: A Problem in American Institutional and Intellectual Life** (1959); and E. D. Genovese, *The Political Economy of Slavery* (1965). Three of the best books on special aspects of slavery are Frederic Bancroft, *Slave-Trading in the Old South* (1931); R. C. Wade, *Slavery in the Cities* (1964); and W. K. Scarborough, *The Overseer: Plantation Management in the Old South* (1966). The best study of the Missouri Compromise is Glover Moore, *The Missouri Controversy** (1953).

Industry and Technology

Several surveys of American economic history have good sections on the beginnings of industrialization: F. A. Shannon, *America's Economic Growth* (rev. ed., 1951); E. C. Kirkland, *A History of American Economic Life* (rev. ed., 1951); and H. U. Faulkner, *American Economic History* (rev. ed., 1954). Useful specialized surveys are V. S. Clark, *History of Manufactures in the United States*, 3 vols. (1928), and J. W. Oliver, *History of American Technology* (1956). Books especially valuable for their interpretations are Roger Burlingame, *The March of the Iron Men** (1938); L. M. Hacker, *The Triumph of American Capitalism** (1940); T. C. Cochran and William Miller, *The Age of Enterprise** (1942); D. C. North, *The Economic Growth of the United States, 1790–1860** (1961); and Stuart Bruchey, *The Roots of American Economic Growth** (1965). H. J. Habakkuk, *American and British Technology in the Nineteenth Century* (1962), is a penetrating analysis of the relationship between high labor costs and mechanization.

Two outstanding studies of the early textile industry are A. H. Cole, *The American Wool Manufacture*, 2 vols. (1926), and C. F. Ware, *The Early New England Cotton Manufacture* (1931). The beginnings of the corporation can be studied in E. M. Dodd, *American Business Corporations until 1860* (1954). The best treatment of the early labor movement is in J. R. Commons and others, Vol. I of *History of Labor in the United States*, 4 vols. (1918–35). The best work available on the Panic of 1819 is M. N. Rothbard, *The Panic of 1819: Reactions and Policies* (1962).

* Available in a paperback edition.

9
Politics for the Common Man

The rapid economic growth and social change that followed the War of 1812 soon began to influence the nation's political life. In the 1820's, after the death of the Federalists (see p. 196), the Republican party split to form two new parties: the Democrats and the National Republicans (renamed the Whigs in the 1830's). During the subsequent growth of vigorous two-party politics, control of public affairs became less exclusively the business of select groups of prudent gentlemen than it had been before. The Democratic party, under the leadership of Andrew Jackson, made skillful appeals to the fears and aspirations of the common man; but the Whig party, under the leadership of Clay and Webster, also made an effective bid for mass support and became equally adept in the use of new political tactics. The politics of the Jacksonian era was enlivened by bitterly fought presidential contests, by disputes over who were the friends and who the enemies of the people, by ill-tempered conflicts between nationalists and state righters, and by a heightened sectionalism. Political wars were waged with intense fervor, and each faction predicted that the victory of its rival would bring disaster to the nation. Although the heated rhetoric of political partisans cannot be taken at face value, these party battles did in fact involve basic issues of public policy.

THE NEW DEMOCRACY

The rise of the common man. The Jacksonian era, it has been claimed, marked the "rise of the common man." But precisely how did he rise? One way, of course, was for an ambitious and energetic young man to take advantage of the tempting opportunities to achieve material success in his fluid and thriving society. With economic affluence he would, more than likely, soon gain social prestige and political influence as well. This was the road followed by numerous men who began with modest means — in effect, they emerged from the ranks of common men and pushed their way into the ranks of the élite, as Jackson himself did.

But if this is what is meant by the rise of the

"Stump-speaking."

common man, there would be nothing remarkable about the Jacksonian era. For in this sense common men had been rising ever since the colonial period. We have seen that the people who came to America carried little in the way of worldly possessions and social prestige. Here they found cheap land and rich resources, neither a feudal tradition nor an aristocracy of birth; in short, unprecedented opportunities to accumulate wealth were open to those who wished to make a career of accumulating it. The fact that America had a class of wealthy merchants and landowners by the end of the eighteenth century indicates that success had already rewarded the enterprise of many. In the years of prosperity and expansion after the War of 1812, common men continued to flourish and rise by engaging in manufacturing in New England, or by speculating in land in the West, or by growing cotton with slave labor in Alabama and Mississippi. And some common men would continue to rise by piling up riches long after the Jacksonian era had closed.

But the great majority of common men, in this era as in those that preceded and followed it, neither grew rich nor rose to high social position. Instead they managed only to make a more or less comfortable living and continued to be common men. So the social mobility in Jackson's America was not unique; nor was it the means by which the *average* common man enhanced his prestige. To be sure, a major goal of the Jacksonians was to remove obstacles to success and to provide equal opportunities for all to prosper materially. But the special significance of the Jacksonian era was that the power and influence of the common man increased while he *remained* a common man. The base of American democracy was broadened to give him a greater voice in politics without his first having to achieve uncommon economic success. Then, for the first time, politicians were obliged to square their goals with the desires and tailor their rhetoric to the tastes of a mass of ordinary voters. More than ever before, they celebrated the sovereign people's moral virtue and common-sense wisdom. "Never for a moment believe," said Jackson, "that the great body of the citizens . . . can deliberately intend to do wrong."

Democratic reforms. This was not the beginning of American democracy, only its expansion; nor was the expansion initiated by President Jackson, for the trend had been evident long before. The impulse came in part from the newly settled West, where conditions of life encouraged a spirit of equalitarianism; but it also came from the cities of the East, where middle-class reformers, small businessmen, and spokesmen for urban artisans demanded that government be not only *for* the people but *of* and *by* the people as well. Armed with the Declaration of Independence and the doctrine of natural rights, they argued that they were seeking no radical innovations but merely harmonizing political practices with the principles on which the nation was founded. Restrictions on the popular will, insisted one reformer, "arose from British precedents." Moreover, America was safe for political democracy, because there were no mass poverty, no sharp class lines, and no need for ambitious men to remake society before they could advance in it. Indeed, conservative property-holders could yield, if sometimes grudgingly, to the democratic upsurge without fearing that they were paving the way to their own destruction.

When, for example, political reformers urged the removal of property restrictions on the suffrage, they invariably stressed the argument that no one would be hurt. A delegate to the New York constitutional convention of 1821 agreed that if manhood suffrage would in fact impair the rights of property "this would be a fatal objection." But this was not the case: "Will not our laws continue the same? Will not the administration of justice continue the same? And if so, how is private property to suffer?" Unlike Europeans, said another delegate, "We have no different estates, having different interests, necessary to be guarded from encroachments. . . . We are all of the same estate — all commoners."

The best-remembered protest against manhood suffrage was that of Chancellor James Kent, a New York Federalist. Though Kent warned of the "tendency in the poor to covet and to share the plunder of the rich," he did not advocate the rule of a small aristocracy of large property-holders. Rather, he accepted the election of the governor and the lower house of the state legislature by manhood suffrage and asked only that the upper house be chosen by owners of freehold estates worth at least $250. In defending his position he sounded more like a Jeffersonian than a champion of a capitalist plutocracy, for he spoke of the "freeholders of moderate possessions" as the "safest guardians of property and the laws." Like Jefferson, Kent feared "the crowds of dependents connected with great manufacturing and commercial establishments, and the motley and undefinable population of crowded ports." In large cities like New York, "one master capitalist with his one hundred apprentices, and journeymen, and agents, and dependents will bear down at the polls an equal number of farmers of small estates who cannot safely unite for their common defense." Another New York conservative professed "great veneration for the opinions of Mr. Jefferson," quoted his view that cities are "ulcers on the body politic" and expressed fear that manhood suffrage "would occasion political demoralization, and ultimately overthrow our government." But these conservatives frightened few and went down to overwhelming defeat.

Indeed, it is remarkable how easily the reformers carried the day — how feeble the resistance of the conservatives proved to be. The constitutions of the new Western states provided for white manhood suffrage — or at least enfranchised all taxpayers, which was almost the same thing. The Eastern states had originally restricted the suffrage to property-holders, but one by one they gave way, until, in the 1850's, the last of them, Virginia and North Carolina, adopted manhood suffrage. Only in Rhode Island did the movement for reform result in violence — in the so-called Dorr Rebellion — but even there, by 1843, the conservatives had surrendered.

Manhood suffrage alone, however, had only a minor impact on American politics until the mass of qualified voters began to take a personal interest in it. Since the Revolution, a large proportion of the voters had been apathetic; save for an occasional state election, they turned out in limited numbers and seemed willing to accept the leadership of a small political élite. To the mass of village artisans and self-sufficient farmers, both federal and state governments seemed remote, and in an age of laissez faire neither visibly affected their daily lives. Politics was the business of wealthy men who had things at stake and had the experience necessary for the management of public affairs. State governments, therefore, were often controlled by a few great families, who ruled through factional alliances and only occasionally faced the challenge of an aroused electorate.

But when ordinary voters became involved in the money economy as small entrepreneurs, industrial wage-earners, or farmers producing for the market, they developed a greater personal interest in questions of public policy such as the tariff, internal improvements, and banking. The shock of the Panic of 1819 and the depression that followed intensified their political concerns and shook their confidence in the old political leadership. The Virginia Dynasty came to an end in 1825, and soon after party politics took on a new vitality. Inexpensive party newspapers appeared in every town to arouse and educate the people; and a different breed of politician, skilled in the art of popular appeal, emerged to lead an awakening mass electorate. In this new political era attendance at the polls began to rise. When Jackson was elected President in 1828, 56 per cent of the adult white males voted, which was more than double the percentage of 1824; and in 1840, 78 per cent of them voted. Since no state yet had the secret ballot, ordinary voters were still subject to the influence of powerful neighbors. Nevertheless, an increasing number paid less deference to the gentry and became more independent in exercising their political rights.

Another democratic reform gave the common man a more direct role in the selection of the President. From the time of Jefferson, Federalists and Republicans had named their candidates in secret congressional caucuses. This system was used for the last time in 1824; by 1832 King Caucus had given way to the national nominating convention, which in theory gave the party rank and file a voice in choosing candidates. Meanwhile, one state after another transferred the election of presidential electors from the legislature to the voters, and by 1832 only South Carolina adhered to the old system. The states also made an increasing number of state offices elective rather than appointive. Finally, the idea of a trained — and therefore, presumably, aristocratic — civil service was repudiated so that common men could aspire to state and federal offices as a reward for faithful party service. "To the victors belong the spoils" was the slogan of the New York Jacksonians; and in its day the "spoils system" appeared to be another step toward the democratization of American politics. The anti-Jacksonians were critical of this debasing of the civil service, but when they came to power they found the system irresistible and used it with equal enthusiasm.

"The day of the multitude is now dawned," observed a Jacksonian politician who saw the rise of the common man as one of the most notable achievements of his generation. As voters and as officeholders ordinary citizens now had a part in the shaping of public policy.

JOHN QUINCY ADAMS
AND NATIONAL REPUBLICANISM

The election of 1824. As the end of his second term approached, President Monroe tried to name his own successor, as both Jefferson and Madison had done. He chose William H. Crawford, his Secretary of the Treasury, a Virginian by birth though a resident of Georgia, and a state-rights representative of the planter class. A sparsely attended congressional caucus nominated Crawford as the official Republican candidate. But this time there were other ambitious politicians in the field — all professed Republicans — whose supporters repudiated the caucus system as undemocratic and won endorsements for their candidates from state legislatures and mass meetings. Crawford's competitors included John Quincy Adams, the talented Secretary of State, a nationalist, and the favorite of New England; Henry Clay, Speaker of the House, champion of the American System, and a man of captivating charm; and Andrew Jackson, a military hero with wide popular appeal, though at the time with rather vague political views. With four competing candidates, each attracting somewhat different sections and interests, the Republican party quickly disintegrated as a national political organization.

In the election Jackson won a plurality of the popular vote and ninety-nine electoral votes; he had substantial support everywhere except

The Election of 1824

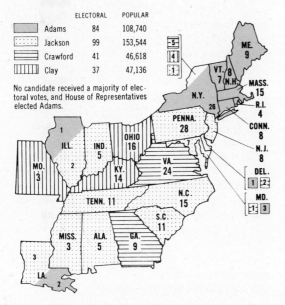

	ELECTORAL	POPULAR
Adams	84	108,740
Jackson	99	153,544
Crawford	41	46,618
Clay	37	47,136

No candidate received a majority of electoral votes, and House of Representatives elected Adams.

in New England. Adams' eighty-four electoral votes came chiefly from New York and New England, Crawford's forty-one from the Southeast, and Clay's thirty-seven from the Northwest.* Since none of the four polled a majority in the Electoral College, the choice had to be made by the House of Representatives from among the three leading candidates, with the congressional delegation from each state casting one vote. Clay, who had come in fourth, was thus eliminated from the competition, and a serious illness had put Crawford out of the running. The choice was between Adams and Jackson.

Clay, because of his power in the House and his control over the three states he had carried, could swing the election either way. Jackson's friends approached Clay and argued that their man had the stronger claim, because he had polled the largest popular vote; and the Kentucky legislature instructed Clay to support the Hero of New Orleans. But Clay not only feared Jackson as a formidable competitor in Western politics but doubted that he was qualified to be President — doubted, too, that he would support the American System. Adams, meanwhile, was tortured by a conflict between his ambition

* Calhoun easily won election as Vice-President.

to be President and his distaste for the political higgling that was required to win the prize. Eventually his ambition triumphed: he made the necessary promises and had an interview with Clay that seemed to satisfy the President-maker and win his support. Adams and Clay were as different as two men could be, and their personal relations had been far from cordial; but Adams was still the logical man for Clay to favor, because he shared Clay's views on public policy. Accordingly, when the House voted on February 9, 1825, Adams, with Clay's backing won a clear majority on the first ballot (Adams thirteen, Jackson seven, Crawford four).

When President Adams appointed Clay Secretary of State, the disappointed Jacksonians immediately detected a shocking case of political jobbery. Adams, they claimed, had purchased Clay's support by giving him the post from which he could best hope to succeed to the Presidency. It was, said John Randolph, an alliance "of the puritan and the black-leg." The nation's political virtue, wrote an angry Jacksonian editor, had died "of poison administered by the assassin hands of John Quincy Adams, the usurper, and Henry Clay." For the next three years the enemies of the Adams Administration charged that "bargain and corruption" had betrayed the plain will of the people. Though Adams doubtless had reached a political understanding with Clay, he had in fact made no corrupt bargain. But neither man ever successfully refuted the accusation. Jackson resigned his seat in the Senate, the Tennessee legislature again nominated him for the Presidency, and the political campaign of 1828 was under way almost as soon as Adams was settled in the White House.

The Adams Administration. Adams' term as President was a tragic episode in an otherwise brilliant public career, which included service as a diplomat, as Secretary of State, and in later years as a congressman from Massachusetts. Unfortunately the superb talents of this son of John Adams did not include a sensitivity to trends in public opinion or the adroitness, tact, and personal warmth essential to presidential leadership. As a result he met with a series of political disasters. This was all the more unfortunate because Adams represented a point of view on the federal government's role in the national economy, and on its responsibilities to the states and the people, that deserved to be considered on its own merits.

The new President was an enthusiastic champion of national economic growth, especially of commercial and manufacturing expansion, and he looked benevolently upon the new capitalistic enterprises that were spawned by the Industrial Revolution. He was, moreover, as he made clear in his first annual message, a nationalist who believed that the Constitution gave the federal government ample power to direct and encourage this growth and to undertake numerous projects "for the common good." Adams spoke in support of the American System with as much fervor as Clay, especially when he urged the use of federal funds for internal improvements. Citing the National Road as a precedent, he asked: "To how many thousands of our countrymen has it proved a benefit? To what single individual has it ever proved an injury?" After the retirement of the public debt he would use the proceeds from the sale of public lands for roads and canals to facilitate communication "between distant regions and multitudes of men." More, he would build a great national university at Washington for "moral, political, and intellectual improvement," finance explorations of the interior and of the Northwest coast, and establish an astronomical observatory. Adams believed that Congress might even pass laws designed to promote "the elegant arts, the advancement of literature, and the progress of the sciences." Congress would, in fact, betray a sacred trust by not doing so; nor should it use as an excuse for inaction "that we are palsied by the will of our constituents." The time was ripe for action, said Adams confidently, for "the spirit of improvement is abroad upon this earth."

But these very sentiments prompted his critics to assail him as a tyrant and an aristocrat. Crawford found them "replete with doctrines which I hold to be unconstitutional." Jefferson accused Adams of seeking to establish "a single and splendid government of an aristocracy . . . riding and ruling over the plundered ploughman and beggared yeomanry." Congress responded to the President's proposals with little enthusiasm — even his friends thought he had gone too far — and after the congressional election of 1826 his enemies had full control of the

John Quincy Adams: Scrupulous nationalist.

Senate and the House. Appropriations for internal improvements far surpassed those provided during previous administrations but fell short by a great deal of Adams' grand design. A new tariff, enacted in 1828, sponsored by both Administration and anti-Administration congressmen from the Middle and Western states, was not the judicious measure he had called for. The bill was poorly drawn, and because of its concessions to the extreme protectionists the Southern cotton interest called it the "tariff of abominations." Yet Adams signed it.

Somehow his good intentions always seemed to lead him to personal disaster. He conscientiously repudiated a fraudulent Indian treaty, by which the Creeks were to be shorn of all their lands in Georgia, and ordered the negotiation of a new one. But his scrupulous concern for the rights of Indians irritated both Southerners and Westerners. Worse, when the governor of Georgia defied the federal government and threatened to take jurisdiction over the disputed lands, Adams flouted the principle of state rights: he warned that it was the President's duty to vindicate federal authority "by

The Election of 1828

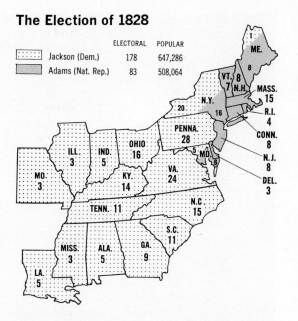

	ELECTORAL	POPULAR
Jackson (Dem.)	178	647,286
Adams (Nat. Rep.)	83	508,064

all the force committed for that purpose to his charge." Even in foreign affairs, in spite of Adams' rich experience, the Administration failed to achieve its goals. In 1826, chiefly for partisan reasons, Congress obstructed Clay's attempt to send delegates to a conference at Panama in order to strengthen ties with Latin America. Adams also failed to persuade the British to open their West Indian islands to American trade. And at home, while his foes continued their unmerciful attack, Adams further weakened his position by refusing to use the patronage weapon in his own defense. Many hostile politicians continued to hold office in his Administration — including Postmaster General John McLean, whose appointment policy seemed to be to reward the President's enemies and punish his friends.

The triumph of the Jacksonians. Adams realized that his chances for reelection in 1828 were slim; "the base and profligate combination" of his critics, he wrote bitterly, would probably succeed in defeating him. During the preceding three years the anti-Administration forces had rallied around Andrew Jackson. Included in this heterogeneous group were those who disliked the nationalistic American System or had been alienated by the President's inept handling of public affairs and public relations. Though political divisions did not follow clear occupational lines, the Jacksonians included a

large proportion of the planters and farmers in the South and West, small entrepreneurs in all parts of the country, and artisans and factory workers in the towns and cities. What strength remained to Adams was concentrated in the Northeast, mostly in New England. Thinking it proper to remain aloof from electioneering, the President gave little help to those who ran his campaign. But his lieutenants were no match in any case for the able and hard-hitting Jacksonian leaders, among whom were three senators: Martin Van Buren of New York, Thomas Hart Benton of Missouri, and John H. Eaton of Tennessee; and three newspapermen: Amos Kendall and Francis Preston Blair of Kentucky and Isaac Hill of New Hampshire. These men and their associates skillfully exploited the fears and prejudices as well as the ideals of the mass electorate.

In the background of the campaign were a number of specific public-policy issues: the tariff, internal improvements, banking, land policy, and at the local level the question of bankruptcy laws and debtor-relief laws. But the politicians and party editors were usually vague on these issues, first, because they feared to divide their friends and hoped to win over the doubtful and, second, because they found other appeals that seemed better calculated to win votes. In a campaign that revolved largely around personalities, few political leaders showed much respect for the intelligence of the American electorate.

Jacksonians described the election as a contest between democracy and aristocracy. Old Hickory was a man of the people who had their interests at heart. Adams was a monarchist, an enemy of the people, a parasite who had lived off the taxpayers all his life, the head of a band of rascally officeholders, an extravagant waster of public funds for his own pleasure, and the darling of the old Federalists. Voters were also reminded of the "corrupt bargain" of 1825 and of the need to vindicate the will of the people. Friends of Adams retaliated by describing Jackson as an inexperienced, hot-tempered incompetent — a demagogue having no program and totally unfitted for the responsibilities of the Presidency. At a still lower level campaign-leaders resorted to mud-slinging and character assassination.

Somehow, in spite of these unedifying exchanges, most of those who voted came to the conclusion that Jackson would better protect the interests of the people against special privilege. Though scarcely more than half the adult males went to the polls, they gave Jackson a substantial popular majority: 647,286 to 508,064. The electoral vote was 178 to 83, with Adams carrying only New England, New Jersey, Maryland, and Delaware. Observing the boisterous celebration in Washington on the day of Jackson's inauguration, men with different perspectives came to different conclusions. Some saw the start of the reign of King Mob, others the triumph of the common man. Webster observed dryly, "People have come five hundred miles to see General Jackson, and they really seem to think that the country has been rescued from some dreadful danger."

JACKSONIAN DEMOCRACY

The new President. Andrew Jackson was a controversial figure in his own day and has been one ever since. This may be explained in part by the complexity of the man, in part by the divergent goals of those who supported him, and in part by the fact that he soon became not only a man but an abstraction — a symbol and a myth. Jackson's original appeal was not as an experienced statesman with a clear-cut program but as a nationally popular figure who embodied numerous American virtues and towered above the ranks of "mere" politicians. To some his election represented a victory for the nationalistic West, to others a victory for the state-rights South, and to still others a victory for those everywhere who would dislodge entrenched privilege from positions of power.

Above all, Jackson's victory was interpreted as a vindication of the common man. Born in poverty to Scotch-Irish immigrant parents in the Carolina back country, lacking formal schooling, he had moved to Tennessee and made his own way as a lawyer, land-speculator, and planter. He was the first President who did not come from a well-established American family in comfortable circumstances. Jackson was, in fact, the first President to embody the American success story in its most romantic form: from a log cabin to the White House.

This does not mean, however, that he was at the time of his election still a crude and simple frontiersman, as his political enemies described him. For he had already held several public offices; he had accumulated lands and slaves and lived in a mansion, "The Hermitage," near Nashville; and he had been allied with affluent speculators and creditors in Tennessee politics. In fact, Jackson had entered the ranks of the gentry of the Southwest and with advancing years had become increasingly mellow and perhaps a little pompous. A visitor who met him after his inauguration reported that he had seen dukes and princes and kings, "but none of such elegance and courtliness of manners, and of so commanding presence, as were possessed by General Jackson."

Nevertheless, Jackson was closer to the people than any of his predecessors had been, and his view of himself as their special defender was not a mere demagogic pose. As the one officer of the federal government chosen in a truly national election, he felt that he was in a position of peculiar responsibility. He was not intimidated by congressmen, whose acts, he felt, were too often controlled by small, selfish groups of powerful constituents, and he used his veto power more freely than had any previous President. Nor would Jackson agree that the Supreme Court had the final word on matters of constitutional interpretation, for he believed that the President's oath bound him to support the Constitution "as he understands it, and not as it is understood by others." The decisions of the Court were entitled "to have only such influence as the force of their reasoning may deserve." Beyond being governed by the dictates of his own judgment, Jackson professed to know of no tribunal to which a public man "can appeal with greater advantage or more propriety than the judgment of the people."

As the guardian of the people's interests, Jackson promised to use his appointive power to "reform" the civil service and to make it more responsive to the public will. He would discharge all "unfaithful or incompetent" officeholders who had acquired a "habit of looking with indifference upon the public interest" or who had come to regard their offices "as a species of property" and "a means of promoting individual interests." Long tenure in the civil service, he said, was corrupting; a rotation

Andrew Jackson: Commanding Democrat.

of civil servants every four years would force them to "go back to making a living as other people do." Jackson saw little to be gained from long incumbency, for in general the duties were "so plain and simple that men of intelligence may readily qualify themselves for their performance; and I can not but believe that more is lost by the long continuance of men in office than is generally to be gained by their experience."

Jackson thus elevated the spoils system to a democratic principle, though its practical purpose was to reward loyal party workers with public offices. His rejection of an experienced civil service was not a major disaster in an age when the functions of government were relatively few and uncomplicated; but it did nothing to encourage efficiency or to increase the devotion of officeholders to the public interest. One Democrat observed with dismay that "office-seeking and office-getting was becoming a regular business, where impudence triumphed over worth." Clay indignantly described the "lank, lean, famished" Jacksonians who descended on Washington in 1829 with

the cry: "Give us bread! Give us treasury pap! Give us our reward!" But Clay and other critics exaggerated the thoroughness with which Jackson applied his principle. In practice he left 80 per cent of the officeholders undisturbed during his eight years at President, and at least a few of the removals were not for political reasons but for dereliction of duty. Though Jackson used the spoils system more freely than his predecessors, subsequent administrations used it with far less restraint than he.

In selecting heads of departments Jackson drew on the various regions and factions that had elected him. But save for Van Buren, who became Secretary of State, the men he appointed were an undistinguished lot, and he never consulted them as an organized group of Cabinet advisers. Instead he counseled informally with a shifting group of men in whom he had confidence, among them the shrewd, talented, ambitious Van Buren; the Second Auditor of the Treasury, Major William B. Lewis of Tennessee, who lived with Jackson in the White House; Francis Preston Blair of Kentucky, who came to Washington to edit the Washington *Globe* as an Administration organ; Isaac Hill, editor of the New Hampshire *Patriot;* and the Fourth Auditor of the Treasury, Amos Kendall, a man of great influence, who helped Jackson prepare many of his state papers. This so-called Kitchen Cabinet, which was not a Cabinet in any formal sense, played an important role in the development of Administration policies and ideas.

The Jacksonian philosophy. Much of what may be called the ideology of Jacksonian Democracy can be found in the President's inaugural addresses, annual messages to Congress, and veto messages. The Jacksonians lived in a vastly more complex society than had Jefferson, and they favored the advances in political democracy that individual states had recently achieved. Yet they were strikingly traditional and conservative on most questions of public policy. In a sense, John Quincy Adams had endorsed a more radical program for national economic growth and social progress with the aid of a vigorous federal government. Adams' call for government action was in sharp contrast to Jackson's warning: "To suppose that because our government has been instituted for the benefit of the people it must therefore have the power to do whatever may seem to conduce to the public good is an error into which even honest minds are too apt to fall." Jackson repeatedly emphasized that the federal government was one of limited powers and cautioned against "overstrained constructions" of the Constitution. He would guard against "all encroachments upon the legitimate sphere of State sovereignty."

Federal intervention in the affairs of the people, Jackson believed, usually came in the form of special favors to influential minorities or of encouragement to monopolistic corporations. There would always be distinctions in society, he conceded, as a result of "superior industry, economy, and virtue . . . but when the laws undertake to add to these natural and just advantages artificial distinctions, to grant titles, gratuities, and exclusive privileges, to make the rich richer and the potent more powerful, the humble members of society — the farmers, mechanics, the laborers — who have neither the time nor the means of securing like favors to themselves, have a right to complain of the injustice of their Government."

As an exponent of laissez faire, Jackson promised to reduce the government "to that simple machine which the Constitution created." Experience had vindicated the Founding Fathers in their decision to withhold "the power to regulate the great mass of the business and concerns of the people" and to leave them to "free enterprise . . . aided by the State sovereignties." The people would find happiness not in a "splendid government . . . but in a plain system, void of pomp, protecting all and granting favors to none, dispensing its blessings, like the dews of Heaven, unseen and unfelt save in the freshness and beauty they contribute to produce."

Some Jacksonians favored this formula of state sovereignty, strict construction, and laissez faire because they hoped for a return to old-fashioned, agrarian-oriented Jeffersonianism. On numerous occasions Jackson, unlike Adams with his enthusiasm for economic and social progress, looked back wistfully to the simpler, and presumably purer, young republic of Jefferson's day. He praised "the examples of public virtue left by my illustrious predecessors"; he suggested that it was "time to pause in our career to review our principles"; and,

disillusioned by his own earlier speculations and resulting bankruptcy, he expressed a desire "to revive and perpetuate those habits of economy and simplicity which are so congenial to the character of republicans." Like Jefferson, Jackson idealized an agrarian society. He described the agricultural interest as "superior in importance" to all others and the cultivators of the soil as the "best part" of the population. "Independent farmers are everywhere the basis of society and true friends of liberty."

But the agrarian ideal was already hopelessly out of date. Reducing the government's role in the economy made it harder for favored groups to win special privileges, but it also gave free rein to irresponsible entrepreneurs in a period of frantic economic activity. At best, Jackson's followers had mixed feelings about his conception of the ideal society. Many of them doubtless shared his nostalgia, but few could resist the temptations of their age. Indeed, more often than not they liked Jackson because, in one way or another, they expected him to help them get ahead in the world — and it was not Jefferson's world that interested them.

INDIANS, INTERNAL IMPROVEMENTS, AND PUBLIC LANDS

After his inauguration in 1829, Jackson faced a problem that nearly every President in American history has faced: that of holding together the disparate groups that elected him. The Democratic party of Jackson's day was, as the two major parties have always been, an unstable coalition of men from many regions with differing needs and interests. Insofar as voters had favored Jackson over Adams for rational reasons, they preferred what they believed would be his stand on most, but seldom all, of the issues that concerned them. Moreover, the Democrats were loosely organized at the national level, and party discipline was correspondingly lax. Not even the Democratic majority in Congress shared Jackson's view on every issue, and it seldom voted as a unit. Those who differed with the President on questions of secondary importance might rebel momentarily but still remain in the party and continue their general support of the Administration. But those who differed with him on a crucial issue might break away entirely and join the opposition party. This is what actually happened to many of the men who had supported Jackson in 1828, while some of his original opponents turned to him because of his stand on one or another major issue.

Indian removals. Indian policy caused the President relatively little political trouble, because his critics were a minority of humanitarians concentrated in the Northeast, most of them already affiliated with the anti-Jackson party. Jackson, to the delight of land-hungry Southerners and Westerners, vigorously enforced a plan, favored by both Monroe and Adams and approved by Congress, to remove all the Indian tribes to lands west of the Mississippi. Removal would be better for the Indians themselves, said Jackson, because they were not only unhappy living among the whites but threatened with extinction. "Doubtless it will be painful to leave the graves of their fathers," he conceded, but we need only "open the eyes of those children of the forest to their true condition" to make them appreciate the "humanity and justice" of removal. "Rightly considered," Jackson concluded, "the policy of the General Government toward the red man is not only liberal, but generous."

These unctuous words covered a policy that was callous in its conception and often brutal in its execution. Most of the tribes were more or less coerced into signing removal treaties; usually the lands they received in the West were inferior to those they gave up; the migrations themselves were poorly planned and caused much suffering; and in some cases the Indians were literally driven from their old homes by military force. Only a few tribes put up organized resistance. In 1832 about a thousand Sac and Fox Indians, led by Chief Black Hawk, defiantly returned to Illinois, but militiamen and army regulars easily drove them back across the Mississippi. This so-called Black Hawk War was hardly more than a skirmish, but the resistance of the Seminoles in Florida was a good deal more formidable. In 1835 many of them, led by Chief Osceola and supported by scores of runaway slaves, rose in rebellion· and thus began a costly war that dragged on into the 1840's. The highly civilized Cherokees of Georgia, on the other hand, tried resistance through legal action. When the gov-

ernment of Georgia refused to recognize their autonomy and threatened to seize their lands, the Cherokees took their case to the Supreme Court and won a favorable decision. Marshall's opinion for the Court majority was that Georgia had no jurisdiction over the Cherokees and no claim to their lands. But Georgia officials simply ignored the decision, and the President refused to enforce it. At length the Cherokees had to leave, too, and when Jackson retired from office he counted the near completion of Indian removals as one of his major achievements.

The Maysville veto. On another issue, internal improvements, Jackson was bound to antagonize either his friends in the West who favored federal support or his friends in the South and in New York and Pennsylvania who opposed it. He gave a full statement of his position in 1830 when he vetoed a bill to subsidize the construction of a sixty-mile road from Maysville on the Ohio River to Lexington, Kentucky. In this veto message as well as in other state papers, apparently in part because of the influence of Van Buren, he opposed in principle federal spending for internal improvements of any kind. But, like Madison and Monroe, Jackson insisted that if such appropriations were to be made without a constitutional amendment, they must be for projects that were national and not local in character. The Maysville Road, he protested, had "no connection with any established system of improvements; is exclusively within the limits of a State . . . and even as far as the State is interested . . . [it gives] partial instead of general advantage."

Federal appropriations for such purposes, Jackson feared, would bring corruption and wasteful spending; they would lead to a consolidated government with powers so vast as to endanger the liberties of the people. It would be far better for the government, after the public debt was retired, to distribute its surplus revenues among the states and permit them to manage their own internal improvements. Yet, in spite of these views, Jackson did not veto all the internal-improvement bills that Congress passed, not even all that were for local projects. At most it can be said that his Maysville veto checked the acceleration of such appropriations. But this was enough to give the National Republicans an issue, which they exploited effectively in the West, where the need for improved transportation determined the political affiliations of many voters.

Land policy. On the question of public land policy Jackson redeemed himself somewhat in the West. In general, Westerners wanted the government to encourage the rapid settlement of unoccupied lands by offering generous terms rather than to seek maximum revenue for the federal treasury. With this in mind, Senator Thomas Hart Benton of Missouri advocated a gradual reduction of the minimum price of public lands of inferior quality from $1.25 to 50 cents an acre, after which any lands still unsold might be given free to actual settlers. Another favorite scheme of Westerners was to permit "squatters" — that is, men who had settled on the public domain before the land was surveyed and offered for sale — to purchase at the minimum price the land they had improved. Neither the first of these schemes (called "graduation") nor the second (called "preemption") was enacted into law during Jackson's Administration, but the President clearly shared the Western point of view. In his message to Congress in 1832 he urged that "the public lands shall cease as soon as practicable to be a source of revenue." To give everyone a chance to obtain a freehold, land should be sold to settlers in small tracts at a price barely sufficient to cover the cost of surveys and clearing Indian titles. More, Jackson recommended that each new state be given that portion of the public domain that lay within its boundaries.

Easterners, especially the manufacturers, hoped to slow down the westward movement and the resulting depletion of the labor supply. They strongly opposed both graduation and preemption and even looked with favor on a proposal to stop temporarily the survey and sale of new Western lands. Henry Clay, seeking a plan that would satisfy all sections, suggested that rather than giving public lands to individual Western states the proceeds from the sale of the lands should be distributed among all the states, to be used as each saw fit. In 1833 Congress passed such a bill, but the President vetoed it. Land policy was thus an unsettled issue when Jackson left office, but the position he had taken weakened him politically among the industrial interests of the East.

THE TARIFF AND NULLIFICATION

Disaffection in South Carolina. Jackson favored a fiscal policy that, in its broad outlines, was consistent with old-fashioned Republican principles: he promised rigid economy and a swift reduction of the public debt in order to "counteract that tendency to public and private profligacy" encouraged by large federal expenditures. But on one critical issue, the tariff, he wavered. Some of his early statements gave aid and comfort to the protectionists — for example, in his first inaugural address he endorsed protective duties on all products "that may be found essential to our national independence." As Southern opposition increased, however, Jackson's position began to change. By 1832 he advocated a tariff designed primarily to provide the government with revenue, one that would give only "temporary and, generally, incidental protection"; and he warned manufacturers not to expect the people to "continue permanently to pay high taxes for their benefit." This shift in favor of tariff reduction antagonized the Northern protectionists. Subsequently, however, when South Carolina resorted to direct action to force a reduction of duties, Jackson firmly denounced her and thereby alienated many Southerners who believed in free trade and extreme state rights.

Though the tariff was never a clear-cut sectional issue, protectionist sentiment was concentrated in the North and free-trade sentiment in the South. By the 1820's most Southerners, especially the cotton-growers, were convinced that the protective tariff was a discriminatory tax — designed, according to a public meeting in Charleston, to elevate the manufacturing interest "to an undue influence and importance" and thus to benefit "one class of citizens at the expense of every other class." Clay's American System, Southerners believed, gave no advantage to the South, because the South had built few factories and because it exported two-thirds of its cotton crop to European markets. Southern exports paid for most of the country's imports, and the federal government supported itself chiefly by taxing this exchange. Hence Southerners complained that they were paying more than their share of federal taxes; and, to make matters worse, much of the income from the tariff was spent on internal improvements, mostly in the North. In short, the tariff was a peculiar tax on Southern farmers and planters, a tax that raised the price of everything they consumed and the cost of everything they produced. Such an arrangement, many Southerners soon concluded, was unconstitutional. They agreed that the Constitution had empowered Congress to levy moderate duties on imports, but the purpose was to provide the government with revenue, not to protect industry.

These were the opinions of cotton-growers everywhere, but nowhere were they so strongly held as in South Carolina. Here a combination of economic disaster and social anxiety caused a reaction not only against the tariff but against nationalism generally. Looming large in the background was the fear — widespread in this state, whose Negro population outnumbered the white by a considerable margin — that federal power might somehow be used to weaken or destroy slavery. The Missouri debate had increased the concern of white South Carolinians; and in 1822 rumors (which had some basis in fact) of a formidable slave conspiracy, led by Denmark Vesey, a Charleston free Negro, created a veritable frenzy. Throughout the 1820's white South Carolinians were inordinately sensitive to the slightest criticism of the peculiar institution from any source. The tariff, many said, was only the first dangerous manifestation of federal usurpation; the same arguments that justified protection might subsequently justify congressional emancipation.

More immediately, however, South Carolina was in the midst of a severe economic crisis. Prior to 1819 the state had flourished, and its proud and aristocratic planters had made fortunes from the cultivation of rice and cotton. But the Panic of 1819 and the subsequent depression were cruel blows, for they brought a sharp decline in cotton prices — a decline that hit South Carolina planters with exceptional force. Facing the competition of the new cotton states in the Southwest, South Carolinians found production costs on their long-used lands relatively high and their crop yield per acre and profit margin correspondingly low. Charleston's commercial interest was languishing, and the state's population had almost stopped growing as farmers moved west in search of better land. Economic adversity, along with worries about slavery, caused political unrest and a swing to extreme state rights.

The majority of white South Carolinians had a simple explanation for their plight. Not soil exhaustion, not the competition of the Southwest, but the high tariff and other federal encroachments on the rights of the states, they said, were to blame. They looked suspiciously at their leading politician, John C. Calhoun, who had supported the Tariff of 1816 (see p. 194) and still in the early 1820's gave evidence of being a nationalist and protectionist. To have a political future in his state Calhoun had no choice but to revise his views; to advance his ambitions in national politics he had to find some remedy that would satisfy the South without alienating all his friends in the North and West. He faced this challenge while he was still Vice-President under Adams, and he faced it even more after the passage of the high Tariff of 1828 while he was seeking reelection with Jackson.

Calhoun and state interposition. By then Calhoun had changed his mind and adopted the Southern position that the protective tariff was not only discriminatory but unconstitutional. Now, in 1828, he proposed a remedy in an essay entitled *The South Carolina Exposition and Protest*, which the state legislature published without revealing the name of its author. This document indicated that Calhoun had abandoned much of his earlier nationalism and that he had become a conservative spokesman for the Southern planter class. From his new state-rights position he found the way by which a numerical minority, such as the South, could protect itself from obnoxious legislation adopted by the majority. His solution was the doctrine of nullification, or state "interposition," which he offered as a procedure less drastic than a dissolution of the Union. It was his hope that this remedy would find approval in other sections and thus enable him to protect the interests of the South and to continue his pursuit of the Presidency.

Calhoun was an able student of political theory and a skillful logician. The premises on which he based his doctrine of nullification, however, were not altogether original, for he borrowed much from Madison's and Jefferson's Virginia and Kentucky Resolutions of 1798 (see p. 162). As they had, Calhoun argued that before 1787 the states had been completely sovereign and that in framing and ratifying the new Constitution they had not given up their sovereignty. Rather, they had merely formed a "compact" and created the federal government as their "agent" to execute it. This agent had only limited powers, and the sovereign states, not the Supreme Court, were the judges of what powers had been delegated to it.

From these premises Calhoun concluded that if Congress exceeded its delegated powers by enacting, say, a protective tariff, any one of the states might interpose state authority to block enforcement of the law. To accomplish this the people of a state would elect delegates to a state convention; if the convention decided that the act in question was unconstitutional, it would declare the act null and void within the state's boundaries. Congress might then choose between acquiescing in nullification or proposing a constitutional amendment specifically granting to the government the desired power. Thus whenever a single state challenged the constitutionality of an act of Congress, the cumbersome amending process, requiring ratification by three-fourths of the states, would be the government's only recourse. This system, thought Calhoun, would provide a sufficient safeguard for the interests of the minority South. True democracy, he said, was not the rule of an absolute, or numerical, majority, for such a majority could ride roughshod over the rights of minorities. Instead, he proposed rule by the "concurrent" majority, with the people of each state having a veto over federal legislation. Minority rights would thereby be protected, and only legislation beneficial to all sections would be enacted.

Calhoun's ingenious system had a full review in the United States Senate early in 1830 during a debate that began over public land policy but soon centered on the nature of the federal Union. Robert Y. Hayne of South Carolina and Daniel Webster of Massachusetts, both brilliant orators, were the chief contestants, while Vice-President Calhoun listened carefully as presiding officer of the Senate. Hayne explained and defended the doctrine of nullification, enumerated his section's grievances, appealed to the West to join the South

in resisting the avarice of the Northeast, and reminded New Englanders that they themselves had toyed with both nullification and secession during the War of 1812. Webster, now an intense nationalist, denied that the Constitution was a mere compact to be interpreted as individual states might please. The people, not the states, had created it, and the Supreme Court was the proper authority to settle disputes over its meaning. Nor was the federal government simply an agent of the states; in exercising its powers it was sovereign and acted directly on the people. "It is," he said, "the people's Constitution, the people's government, made for the people, made by the people, and answerable to the people." The Union was not a voluntary federation of sovereign states; it was intended to be perpetual, and any attempt to dismember it would be treasonable and would lead to civil war. There may have been flaws in Webster's logic and in his history, but he understood better than Hayne the direction of events and the views of the majority. The South sympathized with Hayne's expression of its grievances, but outside South Carolina few Southerners showed much sympathy for his remedy.

The cold response of Congress to the doctrine of nullification disappointed Calhoun, but the response of President Jackson produced a major crisis in Calhoun's political career. Jackson had a deep respect for the rights of the states, and he was now convinced that Southerners had reason to complain about the existing tariff; but to talk of nullification or secession, as South Carolinians did, was another matter. Soon after the Webster-Hayne debate, at a public banquet, Jackson rose, looked squarely at Calhoun, and proposed his famous toast: "Our *Federal* Union — *It must be preserved.*" This incident was only one of numerous signs of a growing rift between the President and the Vice-President, a rift that Secretary of State Van Buren encouraged in his effort to supersede Calhoun as Jackson's successor to the Presidency. Even a petty social tiff among Administration wives contributed to Calhoun's downfall. Mrs. Calhoun, a South Carolina aristocrat, snubbed the wife of the Secretary of War, Peggy Eaton, the attractive daughter of a Washington tavernkeeper. Jackson had no patience with this kind of snobbery, and Van Buren, a widower, made it clear that he shared the irritated President's admiration for Mrs. Eaton. Meanwhile, Calhoun's enemies let Jackson know that back in 1818, Calhoun, as Secretary of War, had denounced Jackson for his high-handed invasion of Florida. Explanations were offered and rejected. In 1831 there was a Cabinet reorganization, and Calhoun's friends were forced out of the Administration. Van Buren was now Jackson's candidate to succeed him, and Calhoun found himself pushed more and more out of his role of national leadership into the position of chief defender of the South.

The nullification crisis. The doctrine of nullification was put to the test in 1832, when Congress passed a new tariff bill that conceded little to the Southern demand for lower duties. After Jackson signed the bill, South Carolina's congressmen sent an address to their constituents stating that "all hope for relief from Congress is irrecoverably gone," and Calhoun

now openly announced his support of nullification. The nullifiers won control of the South Carolina legislature, and when it met in October it ordered the election of delegates to a state convention. On November 24, 1832, the convention, by an overwhelming majority, adopted an ordinance that pronounced the tariffs of 1828 and 1832 "unauthorized by the Constitution" and therefore "null, void, and no law, nor binding upon this State, its officers or citizens." The ordinance prohibited state or federal officers from enforcing the tariff laws after February 1, 1833, forbade appeals to federal courts, and warned that any federal attempt to coerce the state would force South Carolina to secede from the Union. At this juncture Hayne resigned from the Senate to become governor of South Carolina, and Calhoun resigned as Vice-President to take Hayne's place and lead the fight on the Senate floor. The tariff issue had precipitated a serious national crisis.

But South Carolina's position was an uncomfortable one, for no other Southern state was prepared at that time to approve of her radical action. And the angry President reacted vigorously: he threatened to hang Calhoun, he sent a warship and revenue cutters to Charleston harbor, and he announced his readiness to take the field personally in case of a clash of arms. In a proclamation to the people of South Carolina, Jackson endorsed Webster's position on the nature of the Union and warned them of the serious consequences of their action. Nullification, he said, was "incompatible with the existence of the Union, contradicted expressly by the letter of the Constitution, unauthorized by its spirit, inconsistent with every principle on which it was founded, and destructive of the great objective for which it was formed." As President he had no choice but to see that the laws of the United States were executed.

Tension increased when the legislature of South Carolina defiantly replied that Jackson's views were "erroneous and dangerous" and that the state would "repel force by force ... and maintain its liberty at all hazards." It increased further when Congress considered a "force bill" authorizing the President, if necessary, to use the army and navy to enforce the laws. Yet Jackson hoped to avoid violence except as a last resort, and South Carolina politicians, feeling their isolation, were eager to find a way to escape from their predicament without losing face. At length Henry Clay came forward with a compromise tariff, the details of which he worked out in consultation with Calhoun. It provided that tariff schedules would be gradually reduced over a period of nine years, until by 1842 no duty would exceed 20 per cent. On March 1, 1833, Congress passed both the compromise tariff and the force bill, and Jackson signed them. On March 15, the South Carolina convention accepted the compromise and withdrew its nullification of the tariff; but, yielding nothing in principle, it solemnly declared the force bill null and void. Since the crisis had passed, Jackson had the good sense to overlook this final petulant gesture.

Though Jackson irritated both the uncompromising protectionists and the state-rights followers of Calhoun, nationalists in subsequent sectional crises remembered him fondly for his bold action against the nullifiers. At the same time, even though most Southerners rejected nullification, the fight over the tariff made them more conscious than ever before of their minority position. Looking back at the tariff crisis, Chancellor Harper of South Carolina was pessimistic about the future:

> It is useless and impracticable to disguise the fact that the South is a permanent minority, and that there is a *sectional* majority against it — a majority of different views and interests and little common sympathy. . . . We are divided into slave-holding and non-slave-holding states; and . . . this is the broad and marked distinction that must separate us at last.

THE BANK WAR

Criticism of the Bank. Before the controversy over the tariff and nullification had been resolved, Congress and the Administration were engaged in an equally bitter dispute over whether the charter of the Bank of the United States should be renewed when it expired in 1836. Jackson had been hostile to the Bank long before he became President, criticized it repeatedly during his first term in office, made it a basic issue in his campaign for a second

Daniel Webster: The Nature of the Union

If the government of the United States be the agent of the state governments, then they may control it, provided they can agree in the manner of controlling it; if it be the agent of the people, then the people alone can control it, restrain it, modify, or reform it.... The people of the United States have declared that this Constitution shall be the supreme law. We must either admit the proposition or dispute their authority. The states are, unquestionably, sovereign so far as their sovereignty is not affected by this supreme law. But the state legislatures, as political bodies, however sovereign, are yet not sovereign over the people.... So far as the people have restrained state sovereignty, by the expression of their will, in the Constitution of the United States, so far, it must be admitted, state sovereignty is effectually controlled.... The fact is that the people of the United States have chosen to impose control on state sovereignties. There are those, doubtless, who wish they had been left without restraint; but the Constitution has ordered the matter differently.

From Daniel Webster, Second Reply to Hayne, January 26, 1830.

term, and gave it so much attention after his reelection that he seemed almost obsessed with a desire to destroy it. To many agrarian-oriented Jacksonians the Bank was by far the most crucial problem, for it went to the very heart of their philosophy; and Jackson himself doubtless counted his ultimate victory over "the Monster" his greatest single accomplishment. To his critics, however, the destruction of the Bank was a major blunder in public policy, a singularly irresponsible exercise of presidential power that did incalculable harm to the country. The merits of the two positions still remain a subject of lively historical debate.

After a shaky start this powerful financial institution had settled down to become, in the decade after the Panic of 1819, a conservative, prosperous, and reasonably responsible business enterprise. Since 1823, the president of the Bank had been Nicholas Biddle, an aristocratic, cultivated, and talented Philadelphian, whose acumen as a banker was unfortunately matched by his ineptitude in dealing with politicians. Many of his admiring contemporaries

Defense of the Bank

The national bank, though not properly a *political* institution, is one of the most important and valuable instruments that are used in the practical administration of the government. ... As the fiscal agent of the executive, it has exhibited a remarkable intelligence, efficiency, energy, and above all, INDEPENDENCE. This ... has been its real crime. As the regulator of the currency, it has furnished the country with a safe, convenient and copious circulating medium, and prevented the mischiefs that would otherwise result from the insecurity of the local banks. As a mere institution for loaning money, it has been ... the Providence of the less wealthy sections of the Union.... Through its dealings in exchange at home and abroad, the bank has materially facilitated the operations of our foreign and domestic trade. The important advantages which have thus been derived from this institution have been unattended by any countervailing evil. As its term advanced, and its officers acquired additional experience, it has been constantly gaining on the public favor.

From the Boston *Daily Advertiser*, September 1832.

credited him with developing the Bank and its twenty-nine branches into an effective regulator of the expanding American economy. The Bank marketed government bonds and served as a reliable depository for government funds; it was an important source of credit for the business community; its bank notes provided the country with a sound paper currency; and it exerted a restraining influence on the state banks by forcing them to back their notes with adequate specie reserves. The source of its power was its control of one-fifth of the bank notes and one-third of the bank deposits and specie of the country.

But it was in part the Bank's possession of this vast economic power that made it so vulnerable politically. Many Jacksonians had not forgotten its seemingly selfish behavior during the Panic of 1819 (see p. 219), and they believed that democracy was in peril when so much power was concentrated in a single corporation. During the 1820's Biddle ran the Bank with considerable restraint, but he tactlessly admitted to a congressional committee

that most state banks might have been "destroyed by an exertion of the powers of the [United States] Bank." Moreover, its influence over the national economy was not subjected to sufficient government control. Senator Benton complained that it was to this privileged monopoly that "the Federal Government, the State Governments, and great cities, must, of necessity, apply, for every loan which their exigencies may demand." Biddle's enemies also accused him of corrupting the nation's political life, because many influential politicians and editors were indebted to the Bank for loans. Webster was not only a heavy borrower but was on the Bank's payroll as a legal counsel. "I believe my retainer has not been renewed or *refreshed* as usual," he once wrote to Biddle. "If it be wished that my relation to the Bank should be continued, it may be well to send me the usual retainer."

Thus, by the time Jackson became President the Bank had incurred the hatred of numerous groups for either practical or ideological reasons. Curiously, it antagonized both those who favored "soft money" (more state-bank notes) and those who favored "hard money" (only gold and silver coins). The former included some state banking interests, land-speculators, and small entrepreneurs who felt that their needs were best served by an abundant paper currency. The latter included Eastern workingmen who resented receiving their wages in paper of uncertain value, and agrarian-oriented Southerners and Westerners, such as Senator Benton, who considered any currency other than gold and silver dishonest. The hard-money men were hostile to banks of any kind, state or national, that issued bank notes; they tended to look upon banking as a parasitic enterprise. Among them was Jackson, who once told Biddle, "I do not dislike your Bank any more than all banks." By using gold and silver in ordinary business transactions, he told Congress, the country would avoid "those fluctuations in the standard of value which render uncertain the reward of labor."

Veto of the Bank bill. Jackson's first two messages to Congress left little doubt that he would veto any bill to recharter the Bank. In his first message, in December 1829, he affirmed that "both the constitutionality and the expediency of the law creating this bank are well questioned by a large portion of our fellow-citizens." A year later he again pointed to the dangers posed by the Bank as it was then organized. If a national bank was needed, he suggested that it be established as a branch of the Treasury Department, to act simply as a bank of deposit without power to issue notes, make loans, or acquire property. Such a bank, "having no stockholders, debtors, or property," would raise no constitutional objections. To be sure, the Supreme Court had already affirmed the constitutionality of the present Bank, but to Jackson this was irrelevant. "I have read the opinion of John Marshall," he said, "and could not agree with him."

Biddle, in his campaign to save the Bank, could not avoid getting deeply involved in national politics. He had started as a Jeffersonian Republican and had tried to appease Jackson by appointing some of his supporters to directorships of the branch banks. But Jackson's hostility drove Biddle into the camp of the opposition, and Biddle's loans to congressmen and newspaper editors became increasingly motivated by politics. At length, in 1832, he took the advice of Clay and Webster and applied for a new charter, though the old one would not expire for four more years. Clay assured Biddle that Congress would pass the bill, and he was ready to make a presidential veto an issue in the coming campaign. The bill to recharter the Bank, amended to meet some of Jackson's objections, easily passed both houses of Congress with the support of a substantial minority of the Democrats. Jackson accepted the challenge. "The Bank," he told Van Buren, "is trying to kill me, but I will kill it."

Jackson's veto message, a powerful political document, maintained that the Bank was unconstitutional in spite of the changes in its charter and described the dangers of "such a concentration of power in the hands of a few men irresponsible to the people." Much of the stock was held by foreigners, "and the residue is held by a few hundred of our own citizens, chiefly of the richest class." Their demands for "grants of monopolies and special privileges" had "arrayed section against section, interest against interest, and man against man, in a fearful commotion which threatens to shake the foundations of the Union." Webster bitterly denounced the President for executive

Death of the Bank

The Bank of the United States ... enjoys ... a monopoly of ... favor and support, and, as a necessary consequence, almost a monopoly of the foreign and domestic exchange. The powers, privileges, and favors bestowed upon it in the original charter, by increasing the value of the stock far above its par value, operated as a gratuity of many millions to the stockholders....

The modifications of the existing charter proposed by this act are not such, in my view, as make it consistent with the rights of the States or the liberties of the people.... All the objectionable principles of the existing corporation, and most of its odious features, are retained without alleviation. ... Already is almost a third of the stock in foreign hands and not represented in elections. It is constantly passing out of the country, and this act will accelerate its departure. The entire control of the institution would necessarily fall into the hands of a few citizen stockholders....

If we can not at once ... make our Government what it ought to be, we can at least take a stand against all new grants of monopolies and exclusive privileges, against any prostitution of our Government to the advancement of the few at the expense of the many, and in favor of compromise and gradual reform in our code of laws and system of political economy.

From Andrew Jackson, Veto of the Bank Bill, July 1832.

usurpation and for seeking "to inflame the poor against the rich," but the veto stood and became a central issue in the presidential election of 1832. Indeed, Clay, Biddle, and the National Republicans helped to make it so by giving the veto message wide circulation, mistakenly thinking that it would serve to discredit Jackson. Whatever the weaknesses of its reasoning, however it may have exposed Jackson's limitations as a student of money and banking, the election showed that Jackson knew how to reach the ordinary voter better than they.

Jackson vindicated. The campaign of 1832 was notable not only for its vindication of Jackson but for two political innovations: the appearance of the first American third party, the Anti-Masonic party, and the holding of the first national nominating conventions. The new party, like so many third parties, focused on a single issue: opposition to secret societies, especially the Society of Freemasons. The party's strength was concentrated in the rural districts of New England and the Middle states, where its supporters objected to the secrecy, exclusiveness, and allegedly undemocratic character of these societies. In 1826 William Morgan of Batavia, New York, a former Mason who was about to publish an exposure of the secrets of Freemasonry, suddenly vanished, and rumors spread that members of the society had murdered him. The resulting popular indignation eventually took the form of a political movement designed to drive the "grand kings" of Freemasonry out of public office. In September 1831 the Anti-Masonic party held a national convention at Baltimore and nominated William Wirt of Maryland for President, the first candidate to be selected in this fashion. The new party, in spite of its democratic assaults on a presumably privileged group, was essentially anti-Jacksonian — Jackson was himself a Mason — and in a short time most of its leaders joined the National Republicans.

Wirt hoped to win the nomination of the National Republicans, too, but in December 1831 this party held its own convention in Baltimore and nominated Henry Clay for President and John Sargeant of Pennsylvania for Vice-President. Its national platform attacked Jackson for abusing the patronage and the veto power, endorsed Clay's American System, and boldly demanded the rechartering of the Bank. The Democrats also met in Baltimore, in May 1832, but Jackson had already been renominated by numerous local conventions, and a party platform seemed superfluous. All that remained was to nominate a candidate for Vice-President, and Jackson saw to it that his choice, Van Buren, was selected. Jackson was then at the peak of his popularity, and with Wirt taking votes away from Clay the outcome of the campaign was never in doubt. Jackson won by a comfortable majority in the popular vote, and in the Electoral College he polled 219 votes to Clay's 49. Wirt carried only Vermont, while the disaffected leaders of South Carolina gave their state to John Floyd of Virginia. To Jackson the significance of the election was clear: he had been given a mandate to press his war against the Bank of the United States until this "Hydra of corruption" had been destroyed.

The Bank destroyed. Nicholas Biddle was not yet ready to surrender. "This worthy President," he said, "thinks that because he has scalped Indians and imprisoned judges, he is to have his way with the Bank. He is mistaken." So the battle went on, and in its final phase the friends and enemies of the Bank fought so recklessly that they impaired the stability of the entire American economy.

Jackson refused to wait for the Bank's charter to expire, for he feared that Biddle might still use its political and economic power to buy a new charter from Congress. Soon after the election Jackson decided to deprive the Bank of federal support for its financial operations by ceasing to use it as a depository for government funds. He justified his decision on the grounds of the Bank's "misconduct" — its attempt to influence the outcome of the election by playing on "the distress of some and the fear of others." Jackson had to get rid of two uncooperative Secretaries of the Treasury before he found a man in complete sympathy with his scheme: Roger B. Taney, the former Attorney General. The gradual removal of federal funds from the Bank was accomplished simply by paying government expenses from the existing deposits and by refusing to place current revenues in its vaults. These revenues were now distributed among numerous state banks — eventually, eighty-nine of them — which critics called "pet banks." The use of state banks of varying degrees of soundness was, as Jackson himself admitted, an unsatisfactory expedient subject to strong political pressures.

Jackson's enemies struck back hard. In the Senate Clay mustered a majority in 1834 to pass a resolution censuring the President for removing the deposits and thus assuming power "not conferred by the constitution and the laws." Not until 1837 were indignant Jacksonians able to get this partisan resolution expunged from the Senate record. Meanwhile, as federal deposits diminished, Biddle began calling in the Bank's loans and contracting credit, in part to protect himself and in part as a deliberate means of creating economic distress in order to force the government to return the deposits and renew the charter. The resulting credit shortage caused unemployment and business failures and brought delegations of businessmen to Washington to petition for relief. But the angry President told them to "go to Biddle." "I never will restore the deposits," he vowed, "I never will recharter the United States Bank, or sign a charter for any other bank, so long as my name is Andrew Jackson." At length the businessmen turned against Biddle and forced him to relax his credit policy, but not before he had managed to increase his unpopularity and thus to destroy even the faint hope that a drastically revised federal charter could be obtained. In 1836 Biddle received a charter from the state of Pennsylvania, which enabled the Bank to continue in business until 1841, when, because of the economic depression and unwise speculations, it was finally forced to close its doors.

The Bank war was over, and Jackson's victory was complete. The anti-Jacksonians fumed at his highhanded tactics; they spoke indignantly of the "reign of King Andrew I"; they renamed themselves the "Whigs" in imitation of the British party that, in the eighteenth century, had sought to reduce the power of the monarch; and they formed a loose coalition of those who opposed the Administration. In 1836, in their extremity, they held no national convention and drew up no platform; party strategists decided to run not one but three presidential candidates: Webster to appeal to New England, Hugh Lawson White of Tennessee to appeal to the South, and General William Henry Harrison of Ohio to appeal to the West. The Whigs hoped thus to throw the election into the House of Representatives, where they might unite behind a single candidate. The Democrats held a convention at Baltimore, dutifully nominated Van Buren, and presented him on Jackson's record without a formal platform. After a dull campaign, Van Buren won by a slim majority in the popular vote and by 170 electoral votes to 124 for his several opponents.

PANIC AND DEPRESSION

Economic crisis. Jackson remained in Washington to witness Van Buren's inauguration, and Benton observed dryly that "the rising was eclipsed by the setting sun." It was not easy to follow the dynamic Jackson into the Presidency, not even for Van Buren, whose political adroitness had earned him the title of "the Little Magician." Like Jackson, this New Yorker of Dutch descent was a self-made man from a rural family of modest means. After a successful law career that gave him financial independence, Van Buren turned to state politics and soon became the leader of an efficient Republican machine called the Albany Regency; following the presidential campaign of 1824, he linked his political fortunes with Jackson's and rose with him as a faithful advocate of his principles. But Van Buren was a pale copy of his chief: he lacked Jackson's forcefulness and popular appeal and had to rely on his tact and his skill in the management of men. Unfortunately neither these talents nor the Jacksonian philosophy enabled him to cope with the serious economic problems that beset the nation while he was President. Jackson was fortunate to have left office when he did, for within two months the country plunged into a panic and depression whose intensity was attributable at least in part to the policies of his Administration. Van Buren thus had the misfortune of being remembered as a "depression President."

During Jackson's two Administrations, except for the brief "Biddle panic" of 1833–34, the country enjoyed a period of glorious prosperity and unprecedented economic expansion. Southerners found a seemingly limitless market for their cotton at good prices, and planters and slaves poured into the states of the Southwest to open up vast new cotton lands. Between 1831 and 1836, because of rising prices and expanded production, the value of cotton exports trebled. In the West farmers, finding good markets for their foodstuffs on the Southwestern plantations, continued to be drawn into the spreading money economy. Western cities experienced a phenomenal growth as they developed commercial facilities and manufacturing enterprises to serve local needs. In the Northeast merchants prospered from the flourishing cotton trade, and manufacturers expanded to supply their growing Southern and Western markets. Land prices shot up as speculation once again became a national mania; between 1834 and 1836 the speculators were responsible for a fivefold increase in government land sales. Meanwhile, the states and

Martin Van Buren: "The Little Magician."

private entrepreneurs undertook ambitious canal and railroad projects.

Funds for all this economic activity came from British capitalists, who invested in both private and state securities, and from the multiplying state banks, which expanded note issues and liberalized loan policies once they had been freed from the control of Biddle's Bank. Between 1829 and 1837 the number of state banks more than doubled, their note issues trebled, and their loans quadrupled. In an economically "underdeveloped" country with a rapidly growing population, much of this business activity was healthy. But some of it was reckless and speculative — and the economy now lacked even the modest control that the Bank of the United States had exercised.

Before Van Buren took office, the Jackson Administration, besides trying to divorce the government from business, had adopted fiscal policies that intensified the crisis when it came. First, as Jackson himself observed, the deposit of federal funds in numerous "pet banks"

tended to multiply state-chartered banks and "had a great agency in producing a spirit of wild speculation." Many state banks, especially in the West, where they were almost unregulated, indulged in "wildcat financiering" by failing to maintain adequate specie reserves for their note issues and by making loans without demanding adequate collateral. Speculators borrowed paper of dubious value from Western banks and gave it to the government land offices for new lands; the government in turn deposited the paper in the "pet banks," which made the money available again for further speculation. This was a happy situation for those who favored soft money, but it distressed the hard-money men who, as Benton said, had not joined "in putting down the paper currency of a national bank in order to put up a paper currency of a thousand local banks." Jackson shared this point of view and, in July 1836, suddenly intervened with his so-called Specie Circular. In the future, he ordered, the federal land offices would accept only gold and silver in payment for public lands. This was a severe blow to the speculators, and for a time land sales almost ceased and inflated land prices dropped precipitately.

Next, the Congress, with Jackson's approval, gave an enormous stimulus to costly internal-improvement projects launched by the states. In 1836, with the federal government out of debt and with a surplus of almost $40 million, an act provided that beginning on January 1, 1837, the surplus above $5 million was to be distributed among the states in proportion to population in four quarterly installments. Many states, assuming that they would receive a similar subsidy each year and ignoring the fact that the federal funds were intended to be only a loan, immediately designed ambitious projects that exceeded the limits of their own resources. At the same time, the act deprived the "pet banks" of the bulk of their federal deposits and, in consequence, obliged them to call in their loans from private borrowers.

But there were causes other than federal fiscal policy for the economic crisis. In the years of prosperity and free spending, imports of consumer goods increased, the balance of trade was upset, and specie flowed out of the country. Hard times in Great Britain caused British investors to withdraw their support and led to a decline in the demand for American cotton just as the opening of new Western lands caused a sharp increase in the supply. Business conditions in the United States had been deteriorating for some months, but the real panic began in May 1837, when New York banks, soon followed by banks in the rest of the country, suspended specie payments. The Panic of 1837 was followed by a brief period of economic recovery, but in 1839 the collapse of cotton and other agricultural prices and the decline of foreign investments brought on one of the most severe depressions in American history. Banks and business houses failed by the hundreds, factories closed and unemployment mounted, cotton sold for as low as 6 cents a pound, internal-improvement projects were abandoned, and some states either stopped payments on their debts or repudiated them outright. The most feverish economic activity was among lawyers and auctioneers who arranged the foreclosure sales of farms, plantations, and urban business properties. Recovery did not come until the middle of the 1840's.

The independent Treasury. Understanding of the causes of business cycles had advanced very little since the depression following the Panic of 1819 — President Van Buren attributed the present crisis to "overbanking" and "overtrading." The idea that government might give assistance to distressed farmers, workers, and businessmen was not yet seriously considered. In so far as the government did react to the crisis, it adopted fiscal policies that served to deepen the depression and heighten economic distress. Distribution of funds to the states for internal improvements was stopped, federal spending was curtailed, and the President concentrated on getting the government out of debt. Van Buren also rejected pleas for the withdrawal of the Specie Circular and continued the hard-money policy of his predecessor; he scorned the argument that the crisis justified the chartering of a new national bank. He thus identified himself with the radical, or Locofoco,* wing of his party — the extreme

* "Locofoco" was a popular name for the newly invented friction matches. The radical Democrats once carried "locofocos" to a party meeting, because they feared that the conservatives would try to break it up by turning off the gas lights. This incident explains how the Locofocos got their name.

hard-money, antibank, antimonopoly faction that was especially strong among workingmen and reformers in his own state of New York.

The chief aim of the Locofocos was to divorce the federal government from banking altogether by denying all private banks the use of federal deposits. Van Buren urged such a step repeatedly, and finally, in 1840, Congress passed the Independent Treasury Act. This act authorized the establishment of subtreasuries in various cities where government funds could be placed in vaults for safekeeping. Although this system insured the government from loss, it made economic recovery more difficult, because it deprived the banks of funds that otherwise could have been used for private loans.

Banking was now entirely in the hands of the states. A few, notably New York and the New England states, managed to establish reasonably satisfactory and responsible state banking systems; a couple of Western states adopted the Locofoco philosophy and for a time abolished banking altogether. In many states the Jacksonians established "free banking" systems, which enabled promoters to secure a bank charter without a special act of the legislature. Free banking and so-called general incorporation laws were important aspects of Jacksonian Democracy at the state level. By eliminating the need for small entrepreneurs to have political influence in order to obtain state charters, these laws were expected to provide equal opportunities for all.

The election of 1840. As the presidential campaign of 1840 approached, the country was still deep in economic depression; the Democrats were bound to lose the support of many voters who would express their discontent by turning against the party in power. The Democratic national convention at Baltimore was a gloomy affair. The delegates renominated Van Buren unanimously, but with restrained enthusiasm, and adopted a platform reaffirming the party position on state rights, banking, internal improvements, and the Independent Treasury. The Democrats were on the defensive throughout the campaign.

The Whigs, however, were in an optimistic mood when their convention assembled at Harrisburg, Pennsylvania. Having been branded the enemies of the common man, a party of

The Election of 1840

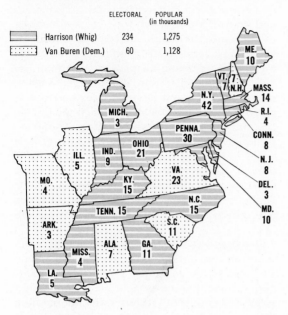

	ELECTORAL	POPULAR (in thousands)
Harrison (Whig)	234	1,275
Van Buren (Dem.)	60	1,128

Ohio country gentleman in a sixteen-room mansion, the Whigs transformed "Old Tippecanoe" into a simple frontier farmer and man of the people. When a blundering Democratic editor sneered that Harrison would be satisfied to retire to a log cabin with a barrel of hard cider, the Whigs happily accepted the statement as true. They praised his simple tastes, made log cabins and cider barrels their party symbols, and boasted of their own log-cabin backgrounds. (Webster apologized for not having been born in one.) The Whigs described Van Buren as a squanderer of public funds on lavish entertainment, a man of expensive aristocratic tastes who fancied fine wines, ate from gold plates, and effeminately scented his whiskers with cologne. They dazzled the voters with boisterous mass meetings, barbecues, and torchlight processions; they nicknamed Van Buren "Martin Van Ruin" and "Sweet Sandy Whiskers"; they promised to cleanse the civil service of corruption and to restore prosperity; and they chanted their campaign slogans: "Tippecanoe and Tyler too" and "Van, Van is a used-up man." If this was the way to win democratic elections, the Whigs proved that they had mastered the technique as well as their opponents.

The voters responded by turning out in larger numbers than in any previous presidential election — even Jackson had not attracted so large a proportion to the polls. Harrison's popular majority was small, but he won overwhelmingly in the Electoral College: 234 votes to 60 for Van Buren. After twelve years of Democratic supremacy, the Whigs were to have their turn.

The Supreme Court under Taney. But the Democrats, like the Federalists in 1801, retained a firm hold on the third branch of the federal government: the judiciary. While he was President, Jackson had appointed six new Associate Justices to the Supreme Court, all of them staunch Democrats; and when Chief Justice Marshall died in 1835, Jackson had selected Roger B. Taney, a state-rights agrarian, to replace him. Jacksonians thus controlled seven of the nine positions on the Court, and conservatives such as Webster feared an irresponsible and radical new departure from the constitutional doctrines laid down by Marshall. Actually, though the Taney Court modified

aristocrats and monopolists, having endured a succession of humiliating defeats, they now looked forward to giving the Democrats some of their own medicine. They had already attributed the depression to Democratic fiscal measures, charged that the Independent Treasury scheme was a callous attempt of the government to protect itself without regard for the welfare of the country, and accused Van Buren of indifference to the suffering of the people. Now, having learned much from the tactics of their enemies and from their own mistakes, they prepared to out-Jackson the Jacksonians in a bid for popular support. The Whigs passed over Clay in favor of a military hero: William Henry Harrison of Ohio, who had defeated the Indians at the Battle of Tippecanoe and the British at the Battle of the Thames. With an eye on the South, they nominated John Tyler of Virginia, a conservative, state-rights Whig, for the Vice-Presidency. They adopted no platform, for the campaign they planned was to have little relevance to concrete issues.

The Democrats were guilty of much low-level electioneering, but their campaign seemed almost dignified compared to the antics of the Whigs. Though Harrison was descended from an aristocratic Virginia family and lived as an

Marshall's opinions on the rights of corporations and the sanctity of contracts, the main corpus of his decisions remained almost intact. Even the doctrine of judicial review went unchallenged; in several important cases the Court threw out state and (on one occasion) federal legislation that it found to be unconstitutional.

The chief departure from the extreme nationalism of Marshall was the new Court's tendency to give the states greater power to regulate corporations. This change is best illustrated in the case of *Charles River Bridge v. Warren Bridge* (1837). The issue was whether the state of Massachusetts, having given a charter to the Charles River Bridge Company to build and operate a toll bridge, could now grant a charter to a second company to build and operate another and competing bridge. The first company contended that this would constitute a breach of contract, but the Court disagreed and held that the rights of corporations are subordinate to the interests of the community — "that the community also have rights, and that the happiness and well-being of every citizen depends on their faithful preservation." The Court thus provided an admirable statement of several of the basic goals of Jacksonian Democracy: encouragement to new entrepreneurs, an attack on special privilege and entrenched "monopoly," and the promotion of the happiness and welfare of all the people.

TYLER AND PARALYSIS

The Whig disaster. As the Whigs organized their first administration, they looked forward to a period of progress along the lines of Whig principles. Harrison, who appeared to favor the goals of the American System, seemed ready to accept guidance from Webster and Clay, for he made Webster Secretary of State and gave most of the other Cabinet posts to followers of Clay. Then disaster struck. Only a month after his inauguration the sixty-eight-year-old President died of pneumonia, and for the first time the Vice-President rose to the Presidency. Unfortunately for the Whigs, their new President, John Tyler, a Virginia aristocrat, sympathized with the Southern planters who opposed nearly everything the Whig majority hoped to accomplish. As a result, within less than a year, the Whig party was so torn by factionalism that it accomplished little, and the country had to suffer through a period of almost complete political stalemate.

Tyler had once been a Democrat but had broken with Jackson over nullification and the removal of federal deposits from Biddle's Bank. He drifted over to the Whigs because they were dominated by affluent men of high social status and because he opposed the radical, Locofoco tendencies of the Democrats under Jackson and Van Buren. Tyler was thought to be a political friend of Clay's, but he made it clear that the imperious Kentuckian was not going

Political barbecue of 1840.

to run his Administration; none of his messages showed any sympathy for Clay's views on banking, tariffs, or internal improvements.

Clay, however, confidently planned a legislative program that would at last put his American System into full operation. In 1841 he introduced a bill to distribute the proceeds from the sale of public lands among the states to finance internal improvements. In a bid for Western support, this bill also contained a provision for preemption by which squatters on the public domain could purchase 160 acres of the land they had improved at the minimum price of $1.25 an acre when the land was put up for sale. To get his bill adopted, Clay had to agree that the distribution of proceeds from land sales would cease if tariff schedules were increased. A year later, in 1842, the Whigs tried to raise the tariff without repealing distribution. But a presidential veto forced them to give up distribution in order to get the increase in duties for which manufacturers were clamoring. Tyler then reluctantly approved the Tariff of 1842 to solve the government's need for more revenue, though it restored the level of duties provided in the Tariff of 1832. The new tariff was virtually the only Whig achievement — Tyler not only forced the abandonment of distribution but vetoed internal-improvement bills with essentially the same arguments Jackson had used.

The final disappointment came when Clay and the majority of Whigs attempted to establish a third Bank of the United States. Tyler approved the repeal of the Independent Treasury Act, but it was well known that he would not accept a new system of national banking in its place. Hence the Whigs tried to disguise their purpose by using other names. First they provided for the creation of a "Fiscal Bank," but Tyler was not deceived and vetoed the bill; then they proposed the chartering of a "Fiscal Corporation," only to be thwarted by another presidential veto. With that, national banking ceased to be a serious issue in national politics for two decades. The angry Whigs in Congress formally read Tyler out of the party, the Cabinet resigned (except Webster, who was involved in diplomatic negotiations with the British), and Clay gave up his seat in the Senate to try again for the Presidency. After making a fiasco of the Whig victory, Tyler and his Southern allies began to drift back to the Democratic party, where in subsequent years they would challenge the Jacksonians for control.

Foreign affairs under Tyler. The political paralysis at home did not prevent the Tyler Administration from solving several problems in the country's foreign relations. Jackson, in spite of his blunt tactics, had already disposed of two issues that had survived the negotiations following the War of 1812: he managed to persuade the British to permit American merchants to trade with their West Indian islands; and he made a satisfactory settlement of claims against France for damages inflicted on American shipping during the Napoleonic wars. But new sources of friction in Anglo-American relations had begun to appear during the 1830's and had reached serious proportions by the time Tyler became President. The traditional undercurrent of hostility, heightened by British travelers who made disparaging comments on American culture and by local politicians bidding for the Irish vote, made it dangerous to permit disagreements to go unsettled.

Trouble began in 1837, when an insurrection broke out in the eastern provinces of Canada. Though many Americans hoped the uprising might ultimately lead to annexation, the British suppressed it with relative ease. But while it was in progress Americans along the frontier aided the rebels and afterward gave the defeated rebel leaders refuge. When raids across the border continued from American bases on the Niagara River, Canadian officials one night impetuously crossed the river, killed one American, and burned an American steamer, the *Caroline*, which had been carrying supplies to the rebels. In spite of growing tension, the British government ignored the American demand for reparations and an apology. Then, in 1840, a Canadian named Alexander McLeod was arrested in New York on suspicion of being a member of the party that had attacked the *Caroline;* he was brought to trial for murder and arson. The British government responded with a vigorous protest: it assumed responsibility for the attack on the *Caroline* and warned that McLeod's conviction would have serious consequences. Fortunately McLeod established an alibi and was acquitted, much to the relief of the State Department.

Meanwhile, a long-standing controversy

over the Maine boundary flared up when, in 1838, American and Canadian lumberjacks battled for possession of part of a disputed area along the Aroostook River. Another dispute grew out of a British request that its naval patrols along the west coast of Africa be permitted to stop and search ships flying the American flag to determine whether they were engaging in the slave trade. This request revived memories of British practices during the Napoleonic wars, and the American government would not agree to it. Finally, in 1841, a group of slaves being transported from Virginia to New Orleans on the American brig *Creole* mutinied and sailed to Nassau, where British officials freed them. Prodded by angry Southerners, Secretary of State Webster demanded that the slaves be returned, but the British refused.

At this point a new British government decided that the time had come for negotiations and sent Lord Ashburton to Washington as a special envoy. Ashburton was a happy choice, for he was friendly to the United States and a man of infinite tact; moreover, he had met Webster in England, and the two men liked each other. Neither was an experienced professional diplomat, but both were in a conciliatory mood, and their patient and highly informal negotiations culminated in the important Webster-Ashburton Treaty of 1842.

Except for Oregon, which remained under joint occupation, the treaty settled all border controversies by awarding seven-twelfths of the disputed territory along the Maine boundary to the United States and by making minor adjustments around Lake Champlain and between Lake Superior and the Lake of the Woods. The treaty also included an agreement for the mutual extradition of fugitives accused of any of seven major crimes. As for the slave trade, the United States did not agree to British search of her vessels but did agree to maintain a squadron off the African coast to apprehend slavers flying the American flag. Neither the *Caroline* nor the *Creole* affair was dealt with in the treaty, but Ashburton disposed of them through an exchange of notes that Webster chose to accept as satisfactory. With regard to the *Caroline* affair, Ashburton simply expressed regret "that some explanation and apology for this occurrence was not immediately made."

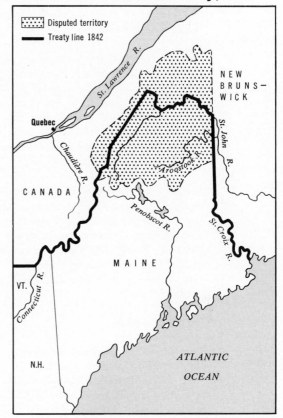

The Webster-Ashburton Treaty, 1842

▒ Disputed territory
━━ Treaty line 1842

In the case of the *Creole*, the slaves were not to be returned, but he promised that in the future there would be no "officious interference" with American vessels forced to enter British ports by "violence or accident."

Webster, after concluding these negotiations and seeing the treaty ratified by both governments, followed the example of the other Whigs and resigned from Tyler's Cabinet. Thereafter the Tyler Administration, disrupted and lacking congressional support, looked rather futile in the face of an increasingly powerful drive for the moral reform of American society. This drive would have a shattering effect on both national parties and, eventually, on the federal Union itself. In the critical years ahead, disheartened patriots would remember the strength and firmness of Andrew Jackson with growing admiration. As the country moved from crisis to crisis, the cry that would be heard with increasing frequency was "Oh, for an hour of Old Hickory."

SUGGESTIONS FOR READING

The Advance of Democracy

The most perceptive contemporary analysis of the workings of American democracy in the Jacksonian era is Alexis de Tocqueville, *Democracy in America,** 2 vols. (1945). Moisei Ostrogorski, *Democracy and the Organization of Political Parties,** 2 vols. (1902), is the best general work on the democratization of American politics. The advance of democracy in two important states can be studied in D. R. Fox, *The Decline of Aristocracy in the Politics of New York** (1919), and A. B. Darling, *Political Changes in Massachusetts, 1824–1848* (1925). Chilton Williamson, *American Suffrage from Property to Democracy, 1760–1860* (1960), supersedes all other works on the extension of the suffrage.

The disputed election of 1824, as well as the goals and misfortunes of the Adams Administration, are described with rich detail in George Dangerfield's two books: *The Era of Good Feelings** (1952), and *The Awakening of American Nationalism, 1815–1828** (1965). Two biographies are essential for an understanding of these years: G. G. Van Deusen, *The Life of Henry Clay** (1937), and S. F. Bemis, *John Quincy Adams and the Union* (1956). A fascinating personal record of Adams' Presidency can be found in C. F. Adams, ed., *The Memoirs of John Quincy Adams*, 12 vols. (1874–77). R. V. Remini, *The Election of Andrew Jackson** (1963), is the best study of the election of 1828.

The Age of Jackson

Two recent surveys, based on modern scholarship, deal with Jacksonian Democracy: G. G. Van Deusen, *The Jacksonian Era** (1959), and C. M. Wiltse, *The New Nation, 1800–1845** (1961). C. G. Bowers, *Party Battles of the Jackson Period* (1922), is a highly partisan, pro-Jackson account. Marquis James, *Andrew Jackson: Portrait of a President** (1937), is a sympathetic and lucid biography of the presidential years. Two of Jackson's strongest supporters in Congress are the subjects of distinguished biographies: C. G. Sellers, Jr., *James K. Polk: Jacksonian, 1795–1843* (1957); W. N. Chambers, *Old Bullion Benton: Senator from the West* (1956); and E. B. Smith, *Magnificent Missourian: The Life of Thomas Hart Benton* (1958). There are also excellent biographies of two of the key figures in the Jackson Administration: C. B. Swisher, *Roger B. Taney* (1936), and W. B. Hatcher, *Edward Livingston: Jeffersonian Republican and Jacksonian Democrat* (1940). An authoritative study of administrative organization is L. D. White, *The Jacksonians: A Study in Administrative History, 1829–1861** (1954). The growth of the spoils system is traced in C. R. Fish, *The Civil Service and the Patronage* (1905). R. P. McCormick, *The Second American Party System: Party Formation in the Jacksonian Era* (1966), is an important revisionist study of Jacksonian politics.

The meaning of Jacksonian Democracy is still the subject of an animated controversy. The following books, all of them of major importance, provide a sample of the various ways in which Jacksonian Democracy can be viewed: A. M. Schlesinger, Jr., *The Age of Jackson** (1945); T. P. Abernethy, *From Frontier to Plantation in Tennessee* (1932); Richard Hofstadter, *The American Political Tradition** (1948); J. W. Ward, *Andrew Jackson: Symbol for an Age** (1955); Joseph Dorfman, *The Economic Mind in American Civilization*, 3 vols. (1946–49); Marvin Meyers, *The Jacksonian Persuasion** (1957); H. C. Syrett, *Andrew Jackson: His Contribution to the American Tradition* (1953); and Lee Benson, *The Concept of Jacksonian Democracy: New York as a Test Case** (1961).

* Available in a paperback edition.

All the above books are concerned with Jackson's views on banking and are important to a study of the controversy over the second Bank of the United States. But the key work on this topic is Bray Hammond, *Banks and Politics in America from the Revolution to the Civil War* (1957). Two other works merit consultation: R. C. H. Catterall, *The Second Bank of the United States* (1903), and W. B. Smith, *Economic Aspects of the Second Bank of the United States* (1953). The best possible case for Nicholas Biddle is presented in T. P. Govan, *Nicholas Biddle: Nationalist and Public Banker* (1959).

The tragedy of Indian removals is the subject of Angie Debo, *The Road to Disappearance: A History of the Creek Indians* (1941), and Grant Foreman, *Indian Removal: The Emigration of the Five Civilized Tribes* (1932). F. P. Prucha, *American Indian Policy in the Formative Years* (1962), is a history of federal legislation. Land policy in the Jacksonian era is treated fully in R. G. Wellington, *The Political and Sectional Influence of the Public Lands, 1828–1842* (1942), and R. M. Robbins, *Our Landed Heritage: The Public Domain** (1942).

The Nullification Controversy

C. S. Sydnor, *The Development of Southern Sectionalism, 1819–1848* (1948), analyzes the nullification crisis in the broad setting of Southern history. The best study of nullification is W. W. Freehling, *Prelude to Civil War* (1966). Three older studies are D. F. Houston, *A Critical Study of Nullification in South Carolina* (1896); C. S. Boucher, *The Nullification Controversy in South Carolina* (1916); and Frederic Bancroft, *Calhoun and the South Carolina Nullification Movement* (1928).

Calhoun's ideas can be studied in a collection of his writings edited by R. K. Crallé: *Works of J. C. Calhoun*, 6 vols. (1851–55). Sympathetic analyses are provided in A. O. Spain, *The Political Theory of John C. Calhoun* (1951); C. M. Wiltse, *John C. Calhoun, Nullifier, 1829–1839* (1949); and M. L. Coit, *John C. Calhoun: American Portrait** (1950). More critical appraisals appear in Richard Hofstadter, *The American Political Tradition** (1948); G. M. Capers, *John C. Calhoun, Opportunist* (1960); and R. N. Current, *John C. Calhoun** (1966).

Depression and the Whig Interlude

The best available biographical studies of Van Buren are Holmes Alexander, *The American Talleyrand* (1935), and R. V. Remini, *Martin Van Buren and the Making of the Democratic Party* (1959). These should be supplemented by Van Buren's relatively candid account of his own life: *The Autobiography of Martin Van Buren*, ed. by J. C. Fitzpatrick (1920). The best studies of the panic and depression are R. C. McGrane, *The Panic of 1837** (1924), and W. B. Smith and A. H. Cole, *Fluctuations in American Business, 1790–1860* (1935).

The origin and growth of the Whig party are traced in detail in three monographs: A. C. Cole, *The Whig Party in the South* (1913); E. M. Carroll, *Origins of the Whig Party* (1925); and G. R. Poage, *Henry Clay and the Whig Party* (1936). Three biographies of Whig leaders also need to be consulted: the biography of Clay by Van Deusen, cited above; C. M. Fuess, *Daniel Webster*, 2 vols. (1930); and R. N. Current, *Daniel Webster and the Rise of National Conservatism** (1955). R. G. Gunderson, *The Log-Cabin Campaign* (1957), is a brisk account of the election of 1840. The Tyler Administration is treated competently in O. D. Lambert, *Presidential Politics in the United States, 1841–1844* (1936), and O. P. Chitwood, *John Tyler: Champion of the Old South* (1939). A. B. Corey, *The Crisis of 1830–1842 in Canadian-American Relations* (1941), and J. B. Brebner, *North Atlantic Triangle* (1945), are good monographs on foreign policy under Tyler.

* Available in a paperback edition.

10

An Era of Reform

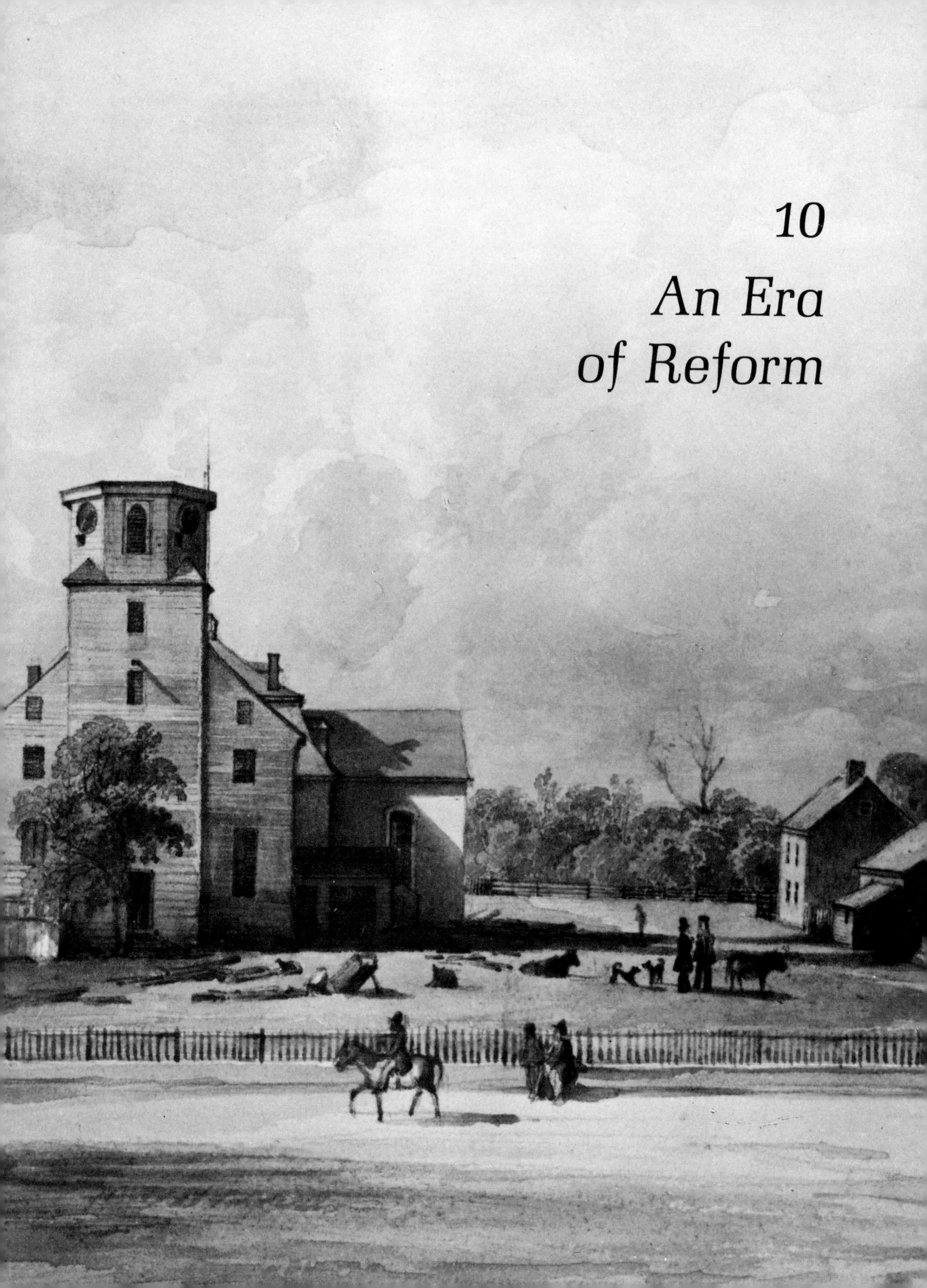

Many nineteenth-century Americans believed that the destiny of their country concerned not only themselves but all mankind. In America's congenial environment man would reveal his capacity to govern himself, to live in harmony with the laws of God's universe, and to eradicate social injustice; he would build an ideal society led by righteous men motivated by disinterested benevolence. In achieving these noble goals America would serve as a model for the rest of the world. To fail would be to betray a sacred trust.

This belief in a divine mission, together with a nagging awareness of their shortcomings, made Americans inordinately sensitive to criticism from European visitors. Tocqueville noted that their "irritable patriotism" caused them to take offense at any comment that was even mildly unfavorable. Outsiders could not speak freely, without risking resentment, "of anything at all except, perhaps, the climate and the soil; and even then Americans will be found ready to defend both as if they had cooperated in producing them."

But if Americans regarded criticism by outsiders as impertinent, they periodically displayed an ample capacity for self-criticism. For they knew that their society had not yet achieved that state of near-perfection toward which so many of them hopefully aimed. Though they cherished an optimistic belief that a benign providence made progress inevitable, improvements did not always come fast enough to satisfy them, and they sometimes tried to give providence a helping hand. "We could not retard the great forward movement of Humanity if we would," wrote Horace Greeley, editor of the New York *Tribune*, "but each of us may decide for himself whether to share in the glory of promoting it or incur the shame of having looked coldly and indifferently on."

In the 1820's movements for moral uplift and social reform began to attract people who were unwilling to compromise with evil and were impatient with the slow pace of progress. The causes they championed were by no means peculiarly American — British reformers influenced reformers across the Atlantic — but there was a millennial quality about the American crusades that was unique. Theodore

New Harmony, 1832.

Parker, a distinguished Boston clergyman, described the aims of the reformers who kept the country in a turmoil for a whole generation: They looked to a society

> full of industry and abundance, full of wisdom, virtue, and the poetry of life; a state with unity among all, with freedom for each; a church without tyranny, a society without ignorance, want, or crime, a state without oppression; yes, a world with no war among the nations to consume the work of their hands, and no restrictive policy to hinder the welfare of mankind.

The goals of this perfectionist program, the reformers believed, not only were attainable but could be achieved without violent upheaval. There existed in America, one of them explained, "abundant elements for progress, and a field of action comparatively free from those obstacles which so impede reform elsewhere." Other countries might have to resort to violence in order to overthrow tyranny, but here "the better course of effecting reform by moral and intellectual means is more trustingly expected." The proper agencies of reform were the churches and benevolent societies, rather than revolutionary movements or even political parties. To be sure, some clergymen frowned on the crusaders, but many of them thought it their proper function to help realize the promise of American life by advancing the cause of reform.

THE RELIGIOUS BACKGROUND

The decline of orthodox Calvinism. Tocqueville believed that there was "no country in the world where the Christian religion retains a greater influence over the souls of men than in America." Certainly the Americans of the first half of the nineteenth century were still deeply religious, and the church was still a powerful force in their lives. But the various Protestant sects, especially those that had been based on Calvinist theology, had gone through some critical times during the century since the Great Awakening and Jonathan Edwards' stout defense of orthodoxy. By the start of the nineteenth century many of the Puritan dogmas — predestination, infant damnation, and the total depravity of man — had already been rejected, or at least qualified, by a more liberal theology that replaced Calvin's God of wrath with a benevolent God of love. The conservatives fought back: they admonished the faithful to "guard against the insidious encroachments of innovation — that evil and beguiling spirit which is now stalking to and fro in the earth, seeking whom it may devour." But this was no more than a rear-guard action.

Even in the eighteenth century certain heresies had begun to trouble the minds of a few New England clergymen: Arminianism, which raised doubts about some of the tenets of Calvinism and eventually became the theology of the Methodists; Arianism, which questioned the divinity of Christ; and Socinianism, which rejected both the Trinity and predestination. These early challenges were fortified by the rationalism of the Enlightenment and the more optimistic view of human nature expressed by the philosophers of the American and French revolutions. Respect for the dignity of the individual, confidence in man's capacity to improve himself, and belief in the idea of progress led to a decline in otherworldliness and a growing interest in temporal affairs. Life on earth, according to this new view, was not a mere preparation for the hereafter, at best a kind of winnowing of the saved from the damned; rather, it had its own beauty and value.

These intellectual trends caused orthodox Calvinism to give way to a theology that was at once more rational and more humanistic. Many leaders of the Revolutionary generation, such as Jefferson and Franklin, withdrew from the established churches and became deists. Deism, which originated in Europe in the early eighteenth century, rejected the Trinity, the divinity of Christ, the idea of original sin, and the Bible as divine revelation. It held that God had created the universe but had then withdrawn to let it run by natural laws. The humanistic implications of deism were evident in Thomas Paine's *The Age of Reason:* "I believe in the equality of man, and I believe that religious duties consist in doing justice, loving mercy, and endeavoring to make our fellow creatures happy." Paine accepted the creed of no church; indeed, he described the established churches as "human inventions set up to terrify and enslave mankind and monopolize power and profit." But few intellectuals were prepared to carry rationalism this far, and most

church leaders saw no difference between deism and atheism.

Unitarianism. In the long run those who worked for a liberalized theology within the churches had a broader influence than the freethinkers who deserted organized Christianity entirely. These liberalizers rebelled especially against the deterministic Calvinist doctrine of salvation only for the elect in favor of the more hopeful doctrine of free will and salvation open to all. The revolt against traditional Calvinism produced several new sects, including the Universalists and Campbellites (Disciples of Christ), and a division of the Presbyterians into Old and New schools. But the largest and most influential of the organized religious groups produced by eighteenth-century rationalism and humanism was the Unitarian Church. An offshoot of Congregationalism, it appealed chiefly to the better-educated and more affluent descendants of the New England Puritans. It showed its greatest vitality and grew most vigorously in the early decades of the nineteenth century. Unitarians, as their name indicates, did not believe in the Trinity — Jesus was mortal, the founder of a great religion but not the son of God. They denied that man was conceived in sin or that he was totally depraved; rather, he was by nature good. God was a merciful and loving Father, not a vindictive and arbitrary deity who predestined the mass of mankind to damnation. Unitarians were skeptical of fine-spun theological systems and urged each individual to search the Scriptures for truth. And once he had found it, he must not pervert it into dogma to be imposed on others. Instead, Unitarians preached tolerance of differences among sincerely devout men.

William Ellery Channing (1780–1842), pastor of the Federal Street Church in Boston, was the most eminent Unitarian clergyman of the early nineteenth century. Channing stressed the primary responsibility of man to his own conscience and helped to link the liberal Unitarian creed with humanitarianism. To him the essence of religion was "the adoration of goodness." Since he believed in the excellence of man and denied original sin, Channing found the doctrine of atonement preposterous — it was as if "the Creator, in order to pardon his own children, had erected a gallows in the centre of the universe, and had publicly executed upon it . . . an Infinite Being, the partaker of his own Supreme Divinity." Channing supported humanitarian reform, "because I have learned the essential equality of men before the common Father . . . because I see in him a great nature, the divine image, and vast capacities." In Channing, Unitarianism found its ideal leader, for he balanced its rationalism and tolerance with a humanistic warmth and with an active concern for the welfare of mankind.

The transcendentalists. In the course of time, however, Unitarianism began to crystallize into a new orthodoxy. The Church's well-fed members, though more reasonable and tolerant than their Puritan ancestors, became at least as smug; though given to philanthropy, they were free to pursue individual gain with far less restraint. Unitarianism struck a growing number of New England intellectuals as distressingly cold, formal, and passionless and its communicants as more concerned with material than with spiritual well-being. Moreover, eighteenth-century rationalism, the foundation of Unitarianism, was succumbing to a romantic movement that was associated with the German philosophers Immanuel Kant and Georg Wilhelm Friedrich Hegel and with the British men of letters Samuel Coleridge, Thomas Carlyle, and William Wordsworth. The romanticists rejected experience and pure reason as the keys to truth and substituted for them intuition, or spiritual insight, which they believed gave man knowledge that he could not derive through his senses. They idealized the natural, spontaneous man rather than the educated, sophisticated man. In a sense, Jacksonian Democracy, with its faith in the good judgment of the common man, was the political manifestation of romanticism in America.

During the 1830's, a small group of intellectuals living in and around Concord, Massachusetts, met at the home of the former Unitarian minister, Ralph Waldo Emerson, to exchange ideas about philosophy and theology. In addition to Emerson, this distinguished group included, at one time or another, clergymen such as Theodore Parker, George Ripley, and James Freeman Clark; literary figures such as Henry Thoreau, Amos Bronson Alcott, Nathaniel Hawthorne, and Orestes Brownson; and talented women such as Margaret Fuller and Elizabeth Peabody. The Concord neighbors of this little band of idealists, in good-natured amusement, began to refer to them as the Transcendental Club. The members of the club were appalled by the crass materialism of a country preoccupied with economic development and were concerned that spiritual progress was not keeping pace. They were too individualistic and too hostile to institutional restraints to start a church of their own, but the philosophy of transcendentalism was shot through with theological implications. It was clearly an outgrowth of Puritanism and Unitarianism (with a touch of Quakerism and oriental mysticism) as well as of romanticism.

The transcendentalists, like the Unitarians, rejected Calvinist dogma and hopefully believed in man's essential goodness and in a God of love. But their idealism was warm and affirmative, not the bland concoction of "pale negations" that Emerson found so unsatisfying in Unitarianism. As Theodore Parker explained, transcendentalists held that man has "faculties which give him ideas and intuitions which transcend sensational experience; ideas whose origin is not from sensation, nor their proof from sensation." The mind of man "is not a smooth tablet on which sensation writes its experience, but is a living principle which of itself originates ideas." Moreover, God dwells in every man, and human nature, therefore, is not simply excellent but divine. Since the transcendentalists discovered no evil in the mind of man and had faith in his intuitive knowledge of right and justice, they urged everyone to follow his conscience even if he was thus driven to defy church or state. "To know what is right," said Parker, "I need not ask what is the current practice, what say the Revised Statutes, what said holy men of old, but what says conscience? what, God?" Thoreau, in his famous *Essay on Civil Disobedience*, asked: "Must the citizen ever for a moment, or in the least degree, resign his conscience to the legislator? Why has every man a conscience, then?" Carrying an old Jeffersonian slogan to what he thought was its logical conclusion, he argued: "That government is best which governs not at all."

The transcendental belief that God, or the Oversoul, permeated both matter and spirit,

Ralph Waldo Emerson: The Infinite Capacity of Man

Genius is that which belongs of right to every one. A man should know himself for a necessary actor.... Is it for him to account himself cheap and superfluous, or to linger by the wayside for opportunities? Did he not come into being because something must be done which he and no other is and does? If only he *sees,* the world will be visible enough. He need not study where to stand, nor to put things in favorable lights; in him is the light, from him all things are illuminated to their centre. What patron shall he ask for employment and reward? Hereto was he born, to deliver the thought of his heart from the universe to the universe; to do an office which nature could not forego, nor he be discharged from rendering, and then immerge again into the holy silence and eternity out of which as a man he arose.... Here art thou with whom so long the universe travailed in labor, darest thou think meanly of thyself whom the stalwart Fate brought forth to unite his ragged sides, to shoot the gulf, to reconcile the irreconcilable?

From Ralph Waldo Emerson, "The Method of Nature," 1841.

that man had in him a spark of divinity, and that his potentialities were limitless had several consequences. It led to a celebration of individualism and self-reliance and to an admiration of men who had the strength and confidence to strike out on their own. In this spirit Thoreau, in 1845, built a cabin on Walden Pond near Concord, where he lived for two years to illustrate that man can rely on himself and live a full life apart from society. Transcendentalism also produced a rather naive faith that in the long run everything would turn out well. As Emerson wrote: "An eternal beneficent necessity is always bringing things right. . . . The league between virtue and nature engages all things to assume a hostile front to vice."

But although the transcendentalists were optimists, they did not ignore the shortcomings of American society or wait complacently for an inevitable progress to produce the remedies. Instead, they were severe critics of govern-

ments, laws, social institutions, and debasing commercialism — whatever prevented man from realizing his full potential. "Their quarrel with every man they meet," said Emerson, "is not with his kind, but with his degree." Hence the transcendentalists, though they were not given to organizing or joining reform societies, nonetheless contributed to the country's intellectual climate of reform. Emerson asked,

> What is man born for but to be a Reformer, a Remaker of what man has made; a renouncer of lies; a restorer of truth and good, imitating that great Nature which embosoms us all, and which sleeps no moment on an old past, but every hour repairs herself, yielding to us every morning a new day, and with every pulsation a new life?

The Protestant sects and revivalism. If Unitarianism was too cold, transcendentalism was too intellectual (and perhaps too cheerful) to attract a large following. Most Americans remained in the Congregational, Presbyterian, Baptist, and Methodist churches or joined one of the numerous evangelical sects that proliferated in the nineteenth century. Even at the popular level, however, the hard tenets of orthodox Calvinism began to soften. Devout Protestants continued to believe in man's sinful

Emerson, Hawthorne, and Thoreau:
A hostile front to vice.

condition, but they accepted the doctrine of a benevolent God who offered all men the chance of salvation through the experience of spiritual conversion and through faith. Moreover, the material opportunities that lay before Americans in a growing and flourishing society discouraged otherworldliness and tempted them to expect virtue to be rewarded on earth as well as in heaven.

Even so, much of orthodoxy still survived in the religion of the common man. In his cosmology, the Copernican revolution in astronomy notwithstanding, the earth was still the center of the universe; and God continued to be actively and intimately involved in the affairs of man. The ordinary churchgoer still believed in the Trinity, in the Bible as divine revelation, and in a literal heaven and hell. He might doubt man's total depravity, but he could never accept the transcendentalist's extreme optimism about human nature. For the reality of evil in the world was too manifest, human frailty in the face of temptation too obvious. The continued prevalence of endemic and epidemic diseases, and the resulting short life expectancy and high infant mortality, made the average man acutely conscious, sometimes almost obsessed, with the imminence of death. This awareness helps explain the persistence of

Ralph Waldo Emerson: The Goodness in Man

The intuition of the moral sentiment is an insight of the perfection of the laws of the soul. These laws execute themselves. They are out of time, out of space, and not subject to circumstance. Thus in the soul of man there is a justice whose retributions are instant and entire. He who does a noble deed is instantly ennobled. He who does a mean deed is by the action itself contracted. He who puts off impurity, thereby puts on purity. If a man is at heart just, then in so far is he God; the safety of God, the immortality of God, the majesty of God do enter into that man with justice.... Good is positive. Evil is merely privative, not absolute: it is like cold, which is the privation of heat. All evil is so much death or nonentity. Benevolence is absolute and real. So much benevolence as a man hath, so much life hath he. For all things proceed out of this same spirit, which is differently named love, justice, temperance, in its different applications.... Whilst a man seeks good ends, he is strong by the whole strength of nature. In so far as he roves from these ends, he bereaves himself of power, or auxiliaries; his being shrinks out of all remote channels, he becomes less and less, a mote, a point, until absolute badness is absolute death.

From Ralph Waldo Emerson, "Divinity School Address," 1838.

a measure of gloom and pessimism in his outlook on life; it intensified his religious fervor and turned him to the church for strength and solace.

With few exceptions, notably the Quakers, the various Protestant sects actively proselytized those who were seeking comfort and salvation. Some sects had greater success than others. After the Revolution the Protestant Episcopal Church, formerly the Anglican Church, was discredited by the fact that much of its clergy had been Loyalist; it grew only slowly, appealing mostly to well-to-do Eastern conservatives. The Congregationalists of New England lost members to the Unitarians. In the newly settled regions of the West they joined with the Presbyterians in 1801 to adopt a Plan of Union, by which they agreed to establish united churches that might select either Congregational or Presbyterian ministers. In the long run the Plan of Union benefited the Presbyterians, because most of the united churches entered their fold. Although the Presbyterians thus experienced a considerable growth, they were far surpassed by two other Protestant denominations. One of these, the Baptists, had phenomenal success with their system of autonomous congregations and with an untrained, uneducated clergy that spoke the language of the common man. Their ministers brought a primitive but passionate message of hellfire for sinners and redemption for those who experienced conversion and admitted God into their souls. The second, and most successful of all, were the Methodists, each of whose itinerant ministers rode a circuit of several congregations in the scattered settlements of the West and preached an equally simple Christianity.

After the Great Awakening of the mid-eighteenth century, revivalism became a periodic phenomenon. During these interludes of religious enthusiasm Presbyterians, Baptists, and Methodists won new converts by the thousands. In the course of the Second Awakening, which began around 1800, the religious frenzy spread with increasing intensity from east to west. An innovation of this revival was the camp meeting, which brought crowds together for several days of uninterrupted preaching and prayers. Under the emotional influence of exhorters who called for repentance, many experienced conversion. Since the battle with Satan was often violent, a familiar spectacle at the camp meetings was the jumping, shouting, and moaning of tortured souls. When the battle had been won and Satan put to rout, as one witness observed, "hundreds were prostrate upon the earth before the Lord."

The 1820's witnessed still another period of revivalism, but this time many of its leaders combined a desire to save souls with an active interest in social reform. The greatest preacher of this revival was the Reverend Charles G. Finney, who gathered his first harvest of converts from the fertile soil of upstate New York, a land of transplanted New Englanders. Finney preached not only salvation through faith but the importance of good works and the obligation of the churches to take "right ground . . . on all the subjects of practical morality which come up for decision from time to time." To him original sin was a "deep-seated but voluntary . . . self-interest. . . . All sin consists in selfishness; and all holiness or virtue, in disinterested benevolence." Salvation was not the end but the beginning of life — a life of useful work and benevolent activity. Since Finney's doctrine, as one contemporary observed, encouraged mankind "to *work* as well as to *believe*," Finney became a powerful influence for social reform. In addition to winning the support of many established preachers, he sent out a remarkable group of young converts to advance his work, notably Theodore Dwight Weld, who went into the West to preach and to advance the cause of moral reform.

In 1830 Finney brought his revival to New York City, which he regarded as carrying the Gospel into the precincts of hell itself. Here he met two remarkable brothers, Arthur and Lewis Tappan, wealthy merchants and pious men who were already devoting most of their energy and fortunes to philanthropy. The Tappans welcomed Finney and organized an Association of Gentlemen to give financial support to both his religious and his reform work. Lewis Tappan, once a Unitarian, had become dissatisfied with that faith and had moved not toward transcendentalism but back to evangelical Protestantism. He had concluded, he explained, that the Unitarians "did not, in an equal degree, consider themselves as stewards, and their property as consecrated to the cause of Christianity; and that they were deficient in a devotional frame of mind."

Religion thus encouraged reform in two different but parallel trends. First, the transcendentalists celebrated the divinity of man and called on him to trust his conscience in his quest for right and justice. Thoreau wrote: "It is not desirable to cultivate a respect for the law, so much as for the right. The only obligation which I have a right to assume is to do at any time what I think right." Second, the evangelical Protestantism of the revivalists made good works a manifestation of holiness and of the experience of conversion, and reform a vital function of the churches. "And what is to reform mankind but the truth?" asked Finney. "And who shall present the truth if not the church and the ministry? Away with the idea that Christians can remain neutral and keep still, and yet enjoy the approbation and blessing of God."

THE MOVEMENT FOR REFORM

The nature of the movement. William Ellery Channing observed that one of the remarkable circumstances of his age was "the energy with which the principle of combination, or of action by joint forces, by associated numbers, is manifesting itself. It may be said, without much exaggeration, that everything is done now by Societies. . . . You can scarcely name an object for which some institution has not been formed." Though the benevolent societies were numerous, there was a considerable overlapping of both leaders and members. Active reformers tended to be attracted to several causes, and the same names appeared repeatedly among the directors of the various reform organizations.

The reformers, for a variety of reasons, were severely criticized by their conservative contemporaries and have been treated unsympathetically by some historians as well. In the first place, as a leading reformer himself noted, there is a "tendency of every reform to surround itself with a fringe of the unreasonable and half-cracked"; and the reformers had within their ranks a full quota of cranks whose bizarre crusades exposed the whole movement to ridicule. Some devoted their energies to

stopping the wearing of corsets; others to food fads, such as the eating of whole-wheat bread; and still others to the "science" of phrenology. Reformers were accused, too, of being more concerned with denouncing evil than with advancing constructive remedies. Their movement, it has been said, was a vehicle for righteous men to assert their righteousness — for teetotalers to deplore the use of alcohol, and for the virtuous to denounce immorality. Moreover, as Emerson complained, many of them were "narrow, self-pleasing, conceited men" given to petty bickering and "personal and party heats." They often exhibited an uncompromising inflexibility that made them unattractive as human beings and ineffective in striving toward their own goals.

From the perspective of the twentieth century, these reformers have also been criticized for their naive optimism about human nature and for their confidence that social problems could be solved simply by exposing them and by appealing to the innate goodness in man. In addition, most of them were blind to the problems of the growing class of urban factory workers. Reform leaders usually came from the old middle-class families of rural and small-town New England; their social backgrounds and economic assumptions made them singularly insensitive to conditions in the industrial centers — or prone to blame the plight of the workingman on his use of liquor and tobacco. Indeed, it has been suggested that in a sense they were themselves victims of the Industrial Revolution. Belonging to families that in the past had been accustomed to social recognition and leadership in public affairs, they were now losing status and being displaced by the rising merchants and manufacturers. Presumably the discontent provoked by their loss of prestige found an outlet in movements for reform. This psychological interpretation can be neither proved nor disproved, but the dislocations of a period of economic growth and social change undoubtedly contributed to the reform impulse.

Though the shortcomings of the reformers were real enough, the crusade they launched cannot be written off as an enterprise of impractical, shortsighted cranks and neurotics. There were in the ranks of reform many dedicated men and women who demonstrated a keen understanding of, and sensitivity to, some of the social problems of their day. They reacted to objective conditions, not merely to their own internal need for self-expression. Their goals were noble, their accomplishments far from negligible. If the reformers were a trial to their friends, it was in part because their work, by its very nature, forced them to "disregard the peace and proprieties of the social world." Each reformer seemed to bear a burden of personal guilt for the evils in his society and felt driven to do something to eliminate them. This sense of individual responsibility, which can easily be lost in a mass society, was in itself a thing of inestimable value.

Treatment of criminals and the insane. Humane and sensitive men and women who investigated the care of paupers, criminals, and the insane in their own communities found an ample field for reform. These social derelicts, the victims of public ignorance or indifference, were treated almost as they had been in the Middle Ages. In atrocious jails and dungeons young offenders were thrown together with hardened criminals and the violently insane; in neglected almshouses idiots and the destitute were left to the mercy of low-paid, untrained attendants. Humanitarians managed at least to start the painfully slow process of providing prisons with better physical accommodations. With their more enlightened approach to penology, they urged, with some success, that the community concentrate on reforming, rather than punishing, criminals. Meanwhile, the states, one by one, responded to the new spirit by abolishing several vestiges of primitive justice: the imprisonment of debtors, public floggings, and public executions.

Since little was known about the causes of insanity, or about therapy, society provided almost no mental hospitals; the insane were either cared for by relatives or committed to jails and almshouses. Among those who took an interest in the treatment of the insane, Dorothea Dix, a Boston schoolmistress, was the most active advocate of state-supported mental hospitals and of experiments in therapy. In 1841 she launched her crusade by investigating the condition of the insane in her own state. Two years later, she presented the legislature with an eloquent but factual memorial that described "the present state of insane persons confined in this Commonwealth, in cages, closets, cellars, stalls, pens! Chained, naked, beaten with rods, and lashed into obedience." Until her death in 1887 she worked with tireless patience to arouse public officials throughout the country, and her sincerity and command of the facts won her considerable success.

Temperance. Concern for criminals, paupers, and the insane was intimately related to another goal of the reform movement: temperance. It was commonly believed that excessive drinking was a basic cause of the condition of these unfortunates, as well as of the poverty that plagued city workers. Temperance, therefore, would not merely redeem the individual sinner but would advance the whole program of social reform. There can be no doubt that drunkenness was a genuine problem, for this was an age of heavy drinking in which the per capita consumption of whiskey, hard cider, and rum was staggering. The temperance movement began with the formation of numerous local societies, which, in 1826, combined to form a national organization, the American Society for the Promotion of Temperance. Some leaders merely preached moderation in the use of liquor, but others sought converts who would pledge total abstinence. Some relied on the voluntary decisions of individuals; others urged the use of the coercive power of state governments. In 1846 Maine passed the first prohibition law; within the next decade a dozen other Northern and Western states followed Maine's example, but most of these laws remained in force for only a few years. At its height the temperance movement resembled a religious revival; its flavor is suggested by a stanza from one of its popular songs, "One Glass More":

> Stay, mortal, stay! nor heedless thus
> Thy sure destruction seal;
> Within that cup there lurks a curse,
> Which all who drink shall feel.
> Disease and death forever nigh,
> Stand ready at the door,
> And eager wait to hear the cry —
> "O give me one glass more!"

Women's rights. Women took a special interest in temperance, but when they tried to participate actively in this or other reform movements they confronted a wall of prejudice and

The reform crusade: Women's Rights Convention, New York.

the rebuff that woman's place was in the home. The American man characteristically treated women with deference but would not accept them as equals. Woman's inferiority was sanctioned by laws recognizing the husband as the dominant figure in the family and even giving him control over the property his wife brought to the marriage. Except for female seminaries where the daughters of the well-to-do could learn the social graces, schools were closed to girls. Women were excluded from the professions. They could neither vote nor hold public office. Indeed, it was considered unfeminine for them even to speak in public places or to offer prayers in church. In 1840 a group of American women, including Elizabeth Cady Stanton and Lucretia Mott, went as delegates to a World Antislavery Convention in London, but they were denied the right to participate. This and similar experiences provoked a women's rights movement that became at once an integral part of the general reform crusade and a divisive issue among male reformers, some

of whom favored and some of whom opposed permitting women to join their organizations.

In 1848 the first Women's Rights Convention was held at Seneca Falls, New York. Here the delegates adopted a statement that paraphrased the Declaration of Independence and proclaimed that "all men and women are created equal." The history of mankind, it said, "is a history of repeated injuries and usurpations on the part of man toward woman, having in direct object the establishment of an absolute tyranny over her." After listing women's specific grievances, the statement closed with a demand that women "have immediate admission to all the rights and privileges which belong to them as citizens of the United States."

In the years before the Civil War, the women of the United States did make some limited gains. A few states gave married women control over their own property, and everywhere one profession, elementary education, was opened to them. They secured admission to a few high schools and normal schools, and in 1837 Oberlin College became the first coeducational college. Also in 1837 the first women's college, Mount Holyoke, opened its doors. But most important was the example set by a courageous group of women who defied prejudice and played an active and constructive role in public affairs. Dorothea Dix, as we have seen, contributed to improved treatment of the insane; Dr. Elizabeth Blackwell won distinction as a physician; Margaret Fuller for a time edited the transcendentalist journal, *The Dial*, and then served as literary editor of the New York *Tribune;* Emma Willard campaigned for educational reform; Lucy Stone was a popular lecturer as well as a crusader for equal suffrage; and a small host of women, notably Frances Wright, Elizabeth Cady Stanton, and Lucretia Mott, worked to abolish slavery. Most men (and more than a few women) sneered at these "unsexed" women, citing Mrs. Amelia Bloomer's wearing of pantalettes as evidence of where it would all end. But the feminists had effectively challenged the myth that women were physically and intellectually unfitted for any useful activity outside the home.

Education. The reform movement revealed its debt to Jacksonian Democracy, and the reformers their concern for the welfare of the common man, in the crusade for free, tax-supported public education. In the early nineteenth century, except in Massachusetts, the children of the poor obtained their elementary education at home or in church or charity schools, and the children of the rich in private schools or from tutors. The lack of public support, together with the fact that most teaching was done by low-paid, untrained young men who regarded it as a temporary occupation, left a mass of people, both urban and rural, in a state of semiliteracy. In the two decades after 1830 the crucial battle to establish public responsibility for elementary education was fought and won, though in many states it took much longer for the idea to be translated into reality.

Opposition came from those who considered education a private concern, from taxpayers who objected to paying for the education of other people's children, and from religious groups that maintained their own schools. Support came from practical men in an increasingly commercial society, where more and more occupations required the ability to read, write, and cipher. It came, too, from those who believed that mass education was essential to a political system based on manhood suffrage. Further support came from those who viewed public education as a means of providing the common man with better opportunities to advance. They hoped thus to achieve a more general diffusion of property ownership and a softening of class lines. In 1848, Horace Mann, in one of his celebrated reports as secretary of the Massachusetts Board of Education, noted the alarming contrasts of wealth and poverty in his state; he maintained that "nothing but Universal Education can counterwork this tendency to the domination of capital and the servility of labor." Educate the workingman, and he will improve his position and acquire property, for "such a thing never did happen, and never can happen, as that an intelligent and practical body of men should be permanently poor." Education, Mann concluded, "is the great equalizer of the conditions of men — the balance wheel of the social machinery. . . . It does better than to disarm the poor of their hostility toward the rich; it prevents being poor." The city workers themselves made state-supported education one of their prime demands. A resolution adopted by the mechanics of Philadelphia in 1830 declared "that there can be no real liberty without a wide diffusion of real intelligence . . . [and] that until means of equal instruction shall be equally secured to all, liberty is but an unmeaning word, and equality an empty shadow."

By the 1850's the states were committed to making tax-supported public education available to all without the stigma of charity. Some of the states had already passed laws requiring local communities to establish elementary schools, and most of the others had at least required that when schools were established they must admit all children, not just those able to pay tuition. One of the decisive battles was fought in Pennsylvania, where in 1834 a state school law was passed. But opposition to the law was so formidable that the legislature seemed ready to repeal it in favor of one providing free education only for the poor. After a bitter struggle, the law was saved largely through the efforts of a young Whig legislator, Thaddeus Stevens, whose brilliant defense of free education carried the day. Similar battles were fought and won in other states. As a result, outside the South, where the movement was impeded by rural conditions and the indifference of the planter class, a steadily growing number of children found free public schools available to them.

But this was only the beginning, for compulsory-attendance laws had not yet been passed, school terms were short, the curriculum was thin, and teaching methods were still based on rote memorization and corporal punishment. Massachusetts led the way in remedying these conditions in 1837 by establishing a state Board of Education, with Horace Mann as secretary. Mann had devoted many years to teaching and the study of education, and during his eleven years as secretary his annual reports made him the most influential man in the public-school movement. In Massachusetts he did much to improve the curriculum and teaching methods, lengthen the school year, raise teachers' salaries, establish the first state-supported normal school for teacher-training, and organize a state association of teachers. Other states appointed their own boards or superintendents of education, who tried, with varying degrees of success, to achieve similar reforms.

For most American children formal education ceased after a few years in an elementary school. Secondary education was limited to those who could afford to pay the tuition to a private academy, where, in preparation for college, they took courses in mathematics, rhetoric, and the classics. In 1827 Massachusetts passed a law requiring every town of five hundred or more families to set up a public high school, and the other New England states soon followed suit. But as late as 1860 there were only slightly more than three hundred public high schools in the United States, with almost a third of them in Massachusetts and only a scattering in the South and West.

In higher education, which was less influenced by reform, the most notable development was the proliferation of private denominational colleges throughout the country. In the two decades between 1830 and 1850 about eighty of these colleges were founded. Most of them had meager endowments, small student bodies, and incompetent faculties; but every village seemed determined to have a college, and every religious sect wanted a network of colleges to train its clergy and indoctrinate its youth. The idea of state-supported institutions of higher learning was an old one, and four states (Vermont, North Carolina, Georgia, and Tennessee) chartered them in the late eighteenth century. The first one actually to win academic distinction, however, was the University of Virginia, founded in 1819. By the 1850's numerous state universities, most of them in the South and West, had been founded, but few were in reality more than small colleges limping along on slender budgets.

Both state and private colleges offered a traditional liberal-arts curriculum, which stressed Latin, Greek, science, mathematics, moral philosophy, and political economy. True universities in the modern sense, with professional schools, graduate teaching, and emphasis on scholarly research, did not emerge until after the Civil War. Too many colleges were founded during these years, and few of them had the libraries and scholars they needed to become centers of creative intellectual life. The idea of academic freedom, moreover, had few defenders, and countless instructors fell victim to the political and sectarian controversies of the age.

Since the colleges served only a tiny fraction of the population, the mass of adults with a thirst for learning searched for other and more accessible avenues to cultural advancement. The "penny press," which began in 1833 when the New York *Sun* went on sale at a penny a copy, put newspapers within the reach of everyone and served up a mixed fare of sensationalism, news, and essays on practical and scientific subjects. Hundreds of magazines catered to all tastes, but the best of them offered essays, poetry, and fiction by the most distinguished European and American writers. This was an era of organized efforts for self-improvement, and most communities had their debating societies, literary societies, and library associations. The lyceum movement, a nationally organized program of adult education initiated in 1826 by a New Englander, Josiah Holbrook, was the most ambitious of these enterprises. The original plan was to encourage local lyceums to assemble libraries, study scientific subjects, and form discussion groups, but most of them soon concentrated on lecture courses. Though many a fraud and charlatan managed to get on the lyceum lecture circuit, men of letters such as Emerson and Charles Dickens, scientists such as Harvard's Louis Agassiz, and a host of reformers made the program a useful instrument of mass education.

The peace movement. Reformers not content with the piecemeal alleviation of domestic social ills turned to more ambitious projects, such as the cause of world peace. Remembering the dreadful suffering and waste of the Napoleonic wars, some reformers were attracted to the pacifist principles of the Quakers or at least hoped to find nonviolent ways of settling international disputes. Local peace societies, which had begun to appear soon after the War of 1812, united in 1828 to form the American Peace Society. William Ladd, the Maine merchant who founded the national organization, proposed the formation of a Congress of Nations to interpret international law and a Court of Nations to apply it. Most peace men, however, distinguished between the use of

William Lloyd Garrison: Harsh as truth.

force for aggressive and for defensive purposes and condemned only the former. In 1838 the peace movement split when the "ultraists," headed by Henry Clark Wright and William Lloyd Garrison, formed a Non-Resistance Society committed to oppose violence even in self-defense. Their constitution denounced military service, forceful resistance to tyranny, capital punishment, and actions at law for civil damages. This millennial program was designed to put Christian precepts into immediate action — to prepare the way "for the full manifestation of the reign of Christ on earth." It would secure "the reconciliation and salvation of a warring and lost world."

Communitarianism. Other perfectionists worked for the complete regeneration of society by building model communities that they hoped would form the nuclei of a better social order. Early communitarian projects had been undertaken by several small religious sects, such as the Shakers, with the goal of achieving holiness through a form of Christian communism. In 1825 Robert Owen, a Scottish textile-manufacturer and philanthropist, established the first significant nonreligious communitarian enterprise at New Harmony, Indiana. Owen hoped to abolish poverty and crime through cooperative labor and the collective ownership of property, but within two years New Harmony proved an economic failure. Communitarianism reached its peak during the 1840's, when the ideas of the French reformer Charles Fourier were embraced by many transcendentalists and popularized by his chief American champion, Albert Brisbane. The transcendentalists were attracted by Fourier's optimistic view of human nature, his goal of social harmony, and his plan of voluntary associations, or "phalanxes," free of governmental intervention. Association, explained the idealistic Brisbane, offered "the means of effecting peaceably and in the interest of all classes, a complete transformation in the social condition of the world." The successful establishment of only one association, he believed, would inspire men to form others. At last the movement would become universal, and there would emerge "a true Social and Political Order in the place of the old and false one." Of the many phalanxes that briefly put Fourier's ideas into practice, the best remembered was Brook Farm near Boston, founded in 1841 by George Ripley. Until its abandonment in 1847 a number of transcendentalists repaired to it, as Ripley explained, "to prepare a society of liberal, intelligent, and cultivated persons" who could lead "a more simple and wholesome life, than can be led amidst the pressures of our competitive institutions."

Young Nathaniel Hawthorne was one of the transcendentalists who went to Brook Farm, but he left with doubts about the divinity of man and a conviction that the reformers did not understand the true source of evil in the world. "The heart, the heart," he wrote, "there was the little yet boundless sphere wherein existed the original wrong of which the crime and misery of this outward world were merely types." His caution to the perfectionists is perhaps more understandable to our generation than it was to his: "The progress of the world, at every step, leaves some evil or wrong on the path behind it, which the unrest of mankind, or their own set purpose, could never have found the way to rectify."

THE CRUSADE AGAINST SLAVERY

The beginnings of abolitionism. In Boston on January 1, 1831, William Lloyd Garrison began publishing a weekly newspaper, *The Liberator*, dedicated to the immediate abolition of Southern Negro slavery without compensation to the masters. This event, though an important turning point, did not mark the beginning of the crusade against slavery, for organized activity, especially among the Quakers, dated back to the eighteenth century. Pressure from antislavery groups had already achieved the abolition of slavery in the Northern states, and in the 1820's a manumission movement in the Upper South had called for gradual, compensated emancipation with colonization of the free Negroes in Africa. Benjamin Lundy, a New Jersey Quaker, organized local societies in Kentucky, Tennessee, North Carolina, and Virginia and at the same time edited an antislavery newspaper, *The Genius of Universal Emancipation*, in Baltimore. Garrison got his start writing for Lundy's paper, but he was a man of different temperament who brought a new stridency and militancy to the attack. He

set the tone for his crusade in the prospectus printed in the first issue of *The Liberator:*

> I *will* be as harsh as truth, and as uncompromising as justice. On this subject, I do not wish to think, or speak, or write with moderation. . . . I am in earnest — I will not equivocate — I will not excuse — I will not retreat a single inch — AND I WILL BE HEARD.

In 1832 Garrison organized the New England Antislavery Society and a year later helped to establish a national organization, the American Antislavery Society. During the next few years abolitionist agents were busy establishing local societies, until by 1840 a network of some two thousand of them with nearly two hundred thousand members stretched across the North. To many, Garrison was the embodiment of abolitionism, and the angry response of the South to his harsh words kept him in the public eye. But he was more an editor and publicist than a leader and tactician, and the movement soon grew too large for him to control. Other abolitionists were at least as important as Garrison: Wendell Phillips in New England, Gerrit Smith and the Tappans in New York, and Theodore Dwight Weld in the West. Weld, a product of the Finney revival in upstate New York, was perhaps the most successful of the abolitionist organizers. In 1833, at the Lane Theological Seminary in Cincinnati, Weld persuaded the students to engage in a prolonged debate on the subject of slavery. In the course of the debate many students became converts to abolitionism, and in subsequent years they joined Weld as agents and organizers for the American Antislavery Society. Using the techniques of the revivalists, these men had notable success in New York, Pennsylvania, and the Old Northwest; they won thousands of converts and sometimes managed to abolitionize entire communities.

At length, in 1840, resentment against Garrison, disagreement over his effort to admit women to full participation, and differences over program caused a split in abolitionist ranks and led to the withdrawal of the anti-Garrisonians from the American Antislavery Society to form a society of their own. Thereafter abolitionism was only loosely organized at the national level, and the real force of the crusade came from the state and local groups.

By the end of the 1830's, for several reasons,

abolitionism had become the most popular cause of the whole reform movement. Most of the reformers had come to agree that slavery was the greatest social evil in the way of the nation's moral regeneration. In this romantic age they found particularly obnoxious a system that denied the individual control over his own destiny. To prove its wickedness, the abolitionists dwelt on the cruelties of slavery, for they were always less interested in presenting a balanced picture than in winning converts. Slavery provided them with plenty of illustrations of cruelty. In 1839 Weld published a powerful abolitionist tract, *Slavery As It Is*, which was simply a documented compilation of incidents reported in Southern newspapers and court records. The Southern states made themselves especially vulnerable to criticism by refusing to eliminate the system's worst abuses: its physical cruelty, its failure to give legal recognition to slave marriages, the separation of children from their parents, the callous practices of the interstate slave-traders, and the denial to Negroes of opportunities for self-improvement.

Abolitionism also attracted Northern reformers because the Southern manumission societies had failed to accomplish their purpose; slavery, it appeared, would never be destroyed without intervention by the North. It no longer seemed to be a weak and declining institution that could be left to die a natural death; instead it was flourishing and spreading westward into new territories and states. The reformers were shocked by the Southerners' growing tendency to regard slavery as a desirable and permanent institution and by their increasingly harsh treatment of even native Southern critics. One reformer expressed his dismay at "the sentiments openly expressed by the southern newspapers, that slavery is not an evil . . . [and] that it is criminal toward the South . . . to indulge even a hope that the chains of the captive may some day or other, no matter how remote the time, be broken." Moreover, the reformers were acutely conscious of the hypocrisy of America's posing as a model of liberal institutions while remaining one of the last countries in the Western world to tolerate human bondage. Finally, the success of British abolitionists in securing emancipation in the British West Indies (1833) stimu-

lated the reformers to undertake a similar crusade in America.

One small group of Americans, the free Negroes, needed no prodding from white reformers to support abolitionism, and in the North they made a significant contribution to the movement. In Boston, in 1829, David Walker, a free Negro born in North Carolina, published an angry *Appeal to the Colored Citizens of the World*, justifying violence to destroy slavery and warning white masters of the consequences of holding Negroes in bondage. Northern free Negroes always constituted the majority of subscribers to Garrison's *Liberator*, and after the organization of the American Antislavery Society three Negroes always served on its executive committee. Among the most prominent Negro abolitionist agents and orators were Samuel Ringgold Ward, who escaped from slavery in Maryland; Lunsford Lane, who was born a slave in North Carolina and bought his own freedom; Sojourner Truth, who was born a slave in New York and was freed by the state emancipation act; Charles Lenox Remond, a well-educated Massachusetts Negro who lectured in Great Britain as well as in the United States; and Frederick Douglass, who escaped from slavery in Maryland to become editor of an antislavery newspaper, one of the greatest of all antislavery orators, and the preeminent American Negro leader of the nineteenth century. Countless free Negroes guided fugitives to freedom over the so-called underground railroad. Among them was Harriet Tubman, who escaped from slavery in Maryland but returned nineteen times to help several hundred slaves flee from their bondage.

Abolitionist tactics. The tactics of the abolitionists were determined by their assumptions about human nature, by their belief in the power of truth, and by the political structure within which they had to operate. They were confronted with the problem that the federal Congress, unlike the British Parliament, had no constitutional power to interfere with slavery. At the same time, the pacifism of most abolitionists discouraged the use of force. In its statement of principles, the New England Antislavery Society affirmed that "we will not operate on the existing relations of society by other than peaceful and lawful means; and that we will give no countenance to violence or insurrection." Abolitionists, therefore, relied on "moral suasion." Their first goal was to persuade slaveholders that slavery was both a sin and a denial of the "unalienable rights" with which, according to the Declaration of Independence, all men are endowed. When the abolitionists failed to impress the slaveholders, when they found it nearly impossible to carry their message into the South, they turned to building up antislavery opinion in the North. Their propaganda hammered relentlessly at their central argument: every person of full age and sane mind has a right to freedom unless convicted of a crime; "mere difference of complexion is no reason why any man should be deprived of any of his natural rights"; "man cannot, consistently with reason, religion, and the eternal and immutable principles of justice, be the property of man"; "whoever retains his fellow-man in bondage is guilty of a grievous wrong." Abolitionists sometimes spoke of the alleged economic waste of slavery, but their indictment was chiefly moral and religious.

Whether moral suasion might be supplemented by some form of political action was a question on which abolitionists differed. Garrison's nonresistance principles turned him against government as an instrument of force and therefore against involvement in politics. Moreover, he viewed the political parties as tools of the slaveholders, the Union as their protector, and the Constitution as a proslavery document (in his words, "a covenant with death and an agreement with hell"). Most abolitionists, however, though recognizing that Congress could not touch slavery in the states, believed that some things might be accomplished through political action — for example, the abolition of slavery in the District of Columbia, the outlawing of the interstate slave trade, and the exclusion of slavery from federal territories. Hence they took an active part in politics and put pressure on congressional candidates to take antislavery positions. In 1840 a group of political abolitionists organized the Liberty party and nominated James G. Birney for the Presidency, but the small vote the party attracted in this and subsequent elections indicated that most abolitionists preferred to operate through existing parties. With the growth of political abolitionism there was a notable decline in pacifist sentiment, and the sectional conflict of the 1850's prepared many abolitionists to turn from moral suasion to force as the ultimate remedy.

Another issue that divided abolitionists was the proper interpretation of the term "immediate emancipation." Abolitionists were, by definition, "immediatists" — slaveholding was a sin, and moral men could not advocate abandoning it gradually. To the Garrisonians immediate emancipation meant exactly what the term implied: slavery should be totally eradicated at once. But the majority of abolitionists took what they considered to be a more realistic position. They believed that the actual implementation of emancipation might take a little time, because there would probably have to be a period of transition while the Negroes were being prepared for their new status as freemen. Their definition of "immediatism," therefore, was a program of emancipation "promptly commenced" but "gradually accomplished." Even Garrison once admitted privately that though he demanded immediate abolition, "it will, alas, be gradual abolition in the end. We have never said that slavery would be overthrown by a single blow: that it ought to be, we shall always contend." But the theoretical immediatism to which abolitionists were committed strengthened the conviction of indignant Southerners that they were reckless incendiaries seeking to bring ruin upon the South.

During the 1830's most Northerners, too, regarded the abolitionists as irresponsible fanatics, and antislavery meetings were frequently broken up by violence. In 1834 a mob invaded Lewis Tappan's house and destroyed the furnishings; in 1835 a Boston mob treated Garrison so roughly that authorities took him to jail for his own protection; and in 1837 a mob in Alton, Illinois, murdered Elijah Lovejoy, an abolitionist editor. Northern businessmen, viewing antislavery agitation as a threat to their profitable trade with the South, more than once joined or encouraged the mobs. Race prejudice was nearly as intense in the North as in the South, and Northern free Negroes were subjected to many forms of discrimination. They were excluded from most trades and professions and forced into menial occupations; they were barred from the public schools or sent to segregated schools; they were assigned

Slavery: An Apologist's View

The negro slaves of the South are the happiest, and, in some sense, the freest people in the world. The children and the aged and infirm work not at all, and yet have all the comforts and necessaries of life provided for them. They enjoy liberty, because they are oppressed neither by care nor labor. The women do little hard work, and are protected from the despotism of their husbands by their masters. The negro men and stout boys work, on the average, in good weather, not more than nine hours a day.... Besides, they have their Sabbaths and holidays. White men, with so much of license and liberty, would die of ennui; but negroes luxuriate in corporeal and mental repose. With their faces upturned to the sun, they can sleep at any hour; and quiet sleep is the greatest of human enjoyments.... The free laborer must work or starve. He is more of a slave than the negro, because he works longer and harder for less allowance than the slave, and has no holiday, because the cares of life with him begin when its labors end. He has no liberty, and not a single right.

From George Fitzhugh, *Cannibals All!* 1857.

segregated seats in white churches and on public transportation; they were denied the ballot except in five New England states and in New York (where they had to meet a property qualification not required of whites); and they were prohibited from settling in several Western states. Even some of the abolitionists were unable to free themselves entirely from the prevailing prejudice and shrank from personal contacts with Negroes; but as a group their racial attitudes were so liberal that their contemporaries often denounced them as "nigger-lovers."

A broadening appeal. Though abolitionists had only limited success in reducing Northern prejudice against Negroes, the growing sectional tension of the 1840's and 1850's caused Northerners to listen more sympathetically to what they had to say about the evils of slavery. Eventually abolitionist agitation helped to persuade the great majority of Northerners that slavery was morally wrong and therefore could not be accepted as a permanent institution. This agitation also produced an image of slaveholders as undemocratic, arrogant, immoral, cruel. The slaveholders and their political henchmen, said the abolitionists, formed a sinister "Slave Power" that ruled the South and conspired to rule the entire Union in order to destroy freedom. Theodore Parker described the Slave Power as

the blight of this nation, the curse of the North and the curse of the South. . . . It confounds your politics. It has silenced your ablest men. It has muzzled the pulpit, and stifled the press. It has robbed three million men of what is dearer than life; it has kept back the welfare of seventeen million more.

Meanwhile, as the abolitionists braved mobs to defend freedom of assembly and of the press, they began to win admiration as champions of civil liberties not only for Negroes but for white men. They aroused sympathy when Southern mobs broke into post offices to seize and destroy packages of antislavery pamphlets, for now the right of minority groups to disseminate their ideas through the mails seemed to be at stake. In 1836, when the abolitionists deluged Congress with petitions urging the abolition of slavery in the District of Columbia, Southerners forced through the House a so-called gag rule, which provided that petitions relating to slavery were to be laid on the table without being printed, referred to committee, or debated. Until the repeal of the gag rule in 1844, abolitionists stood as defenders of another sacred liberty: the right of petition.

Most Northerners also sympathized with the more or less systematic efforts of abolitionists to assist fugitive slaves to freedom along the routes of the underground railroad. Few could help but feel compassion for the pathetic fugitive seeking his own liberty, and even a Negro-phobe might resent the activities of the professional slave-catchers who roamed the free states. In 1842 an important case (*Prigg v. Pennsylvania*) involving the constitutionality of the Fugitive Slave Act of 1793 came before the Supreme Court. Though the Court ruled that the act was constitutional, it conceded that a state might prohibit its own officers from helping to enforce it. Thereafter a number of states, under pressure from the abolitionists, adopted "personal-liberty laws" that withheld assistance in the capture of fugitives.

On one issue — whether slavery should be introduced into new territories and states —

the abolitionists eventually gained overwhelming Northern support. Northerners continued to agree that the Constitution prevented federal interference with slavery in the Southern states, but by the 1850's they were strongly of the opinion that slavery ought to be confined to its present limits. Often this sentiment sprang less from sympathy for the Negro than from a determination of free white farmers to keep slaveholders out of the territories they coveted. But the abolitionist indictment of slavery proved a handy weapon for them to use against Southern expansionists.

In one fundamental respect the abolitionist crusade was a failure. Since it did not convert the slaveholders, it never achieved its original goal: peaceful abolition through the triumph of truth over evil. But in another respect the crusade was a success. Though it was launched by pacifists, by 1861 abolitionism had armed the Northern population morally for the terrible struggle that lay ahead.

THE PROSLAVERY ARGUMENT

Slavery a positive good. In January 1837 Senator John C. Calhoun boldly took a position toward which many Southerners had been drifting:

> I hold that in the present state of civilization, where two races of different origin, and distinguished by color and other physical differences, as well as intellectual, are brought together, the relation now existing in the slaveholding states between the two is, instead of an evil, a good — a positive good.

There would be no more apologies — no concessions that slavery was at best a necessary evil — as Southern dialecticians spun out the arguments affirming the benign qualities of their peculiar institution. Never before had the justification of human bondage been presented with so much moral fervor and in such elaborate detail as in the ante-bellum South. Indeed the proslavery argument was one of the most impressive products of its intellectual life. Southern poets, theologians, moral philosophers, social theorists, jurists, and scientists combined their talents to uphold slavery and denounce heresy and radicalism.

Slavery: An Abolitionist's View

The slaves in the United States are treated with barbarous inhumanity ... they are overworked, underfed, wretchedly clad and lodged, and have insufficient sleep ... they are often made to wear round their necks iron collars armed with prongs, to drag heavy chains and weights at their feet while working in the field ... they are often kept confined in the stocks day and night for weeks together, made to wear gags in their mouths for hours or days, have some of their front teeth torn out or broken off, that they may be easily detected when they run away ... they are frequently flogged with terrible severity, have red pepper rubbed into their lacerated flesh, and hot brine, spirits of turpentine, &c., poured over the gashes to increase the torture ... they are often stripped naked, their backs and limbs cut with knives, bruised and mangled by scores and hundreds of blows with the paddle, and terribly torn by the claws of cats, drawn over them by their tormentors.

From Theodore Dwight Weld, *Slavery As It Is,* 1839.

This body of proslavery literature is significant not only because it was one of the principal contributions of Southern men of letters but because it was a rare expression in nineteenth-century America of deep pessimism about human nature, of doubt about the liberal tradition, and of skepticism about progress. One Southerner wrote with sarcasm:

> No word in the English language is so much used as the dissyllable *progress.* In America we use it so much, that we have made a verb of it. This is an age of progress — a country of progress — a people of progress. Progress is synonymous with enlightenment, and he who falls into the rear rank, is considered recreant to the cause of civilization.

And yet, insisted another Southerner, "it cannot be denied that we must still look to antiquity for the noblest deeds and grandest thoughts that illustrate the race of men." Romanticism, which found expression in the North in the reform movement and in a remarkable burst of literary productivity, found expression in the South in a cult of chivalry and in the identification of the planter class with traditional aristocratic values.

The nature of the defense. Since the average slaveholder was highly religious, a theological defense of slavery was fully developed and almost invariably incorporated in the numerous treatises on the subject. Out of the mass of Scriptural arguments, three were of crucial importance. The first identified the Negroes as the descendants of Canaan, the son of Ham, of whom Noah said, "Cursed be Canaan; a servant of servants shall he be unto his brethren." The second pointed to Mosaic law, which authorized the Jews to make bondsmen "of the heathen that are round about you." The third noted that neither the prophets of the Old Testament nor Christ and his apostles ever condemned slavery. Rather, they repeatedly admonished servants to obey their masters and to submit to their earthly lot. The proper role of the church, therefore, was to bring spiritual salvation to the slaves and to urge benevolence on their masters.

Turning to history, the defenders argued that slavery had always existed in some form and that it had been the foundation of all the great civilizations of antiquity. Aristotle, whose thought permeates the proslavery argument, taught that in every organized society the men of superior talents would become masters over those of inferior talents. Slavery thus enabled a class to emerge that could devote its genius to

Calhoun on slavery.

JOSHUA, COMMANDING THE SUN TO STAND STILL.

art, literature, and other intellectual pursuits. "It is a common remark," wrote George Fitzhugh of Virginia, "that the grand and lasting architectural structures of antiquity were the results of slavery."

Since Southern slaves were descended from Africans, proof that Africans were innately inferior to whites would presumably provide conclusive justification for the peculiar institution. By a curious combination of comparative anatomy and the pseudo-science of phrenology Southern ethnologists attributed to Negroes certain distinct physical and psychic traits that suggested their inferiority to the whites. In the Negro, claimed a Georgia doctor, "the animal parts of the brain preponderate over the moral and intellectual," which explains why he is "deficient in reason, judgment and forecast . . . thoughtless of the future, and contented and happy in the enjoyment of the mere animal pleasures of the present moment." The inevitable conclusion was that "nothing but arbitrary power can restrain the excesses of his animal nature: for he has not the power within himself." These and other alleged racial diversities established the master-slave relationship between whites and Negroes as a natural condition, its abolition a profound disaster to both.

Belief in the Negro's inferiority led to the conclusion that the affirmations of the Declaration of Independence, the provisions of state bills of rights, and the benefits of citizenship did not and were not intended to apply to him. More, in its extreme form, the proslavery argument brought under attack the whole eighteenth-century philosophy of natural rights. Borrowing heavily from Edmund Burke and Thomas Carlyle, proslavery writers idealized a stable society in which men fell naturally into social gradations and enjoyed liberty only to the extent to which they could use it wisely. "It is a great and dangerous error to suppose that all people are equally entitled to liberty," said John C. Calhoun. Liberty had to be earned; it was "a reward reserved for the intelligent, the patriotic, the virtuous and deserving." Society must have a class "to perform the drudgery of life," affirmed James H. Hammond of South Carolina, a class "requiring but a low order of intellect," a class that "constitutes the very mud-sill of society." Boldly accepting a principle that Jefferson had passionately denied,

George Fitzhugh proclaimed that "some were born with saddles on their backs, and others booted and spurred to ride them — and the riding does them good."

The South had found in slavery, argued its defenders, a way to avoid the dangers to order and property posed by the laboring classes in free society. Slavery served as a conservative bulwark against all the radical "isms" that threatened the North with revolution. "There are two kinds of labor, hireling labor and slave labor," explained a writer in the Charleston *Courier*. "The task of each is the same — continued hard work. The promised reward of each is the same also — subsistence." In the North and in Europe the hirelings were discontented; they clamored for change, for "communism, socialism, the organization of labor." In the South the slaves were "orderly and efficient," and society had within it no element of disharmony. "It is the only condition of society in which labor and capital are associated on a large scale in which their interests are combined and not in conflict. Every plantation is an organized community . . . where *all work*, where *each member gets subsistence and a home*." Slavery, in short, was a practical form of socialism.

In every respect, said Southern apologists, the slaves were better off than so-called free laborers. They were happy and contented, because they were well treated, well fed, well housed, and well clothed; they were cared for in childhood, in old age, and in times of sickness. The free-labor system, which left the worker to shift for himself, was far more cruel and heartless. "I may say with truth," said Calhoun, "that in few countries so much is left to the share of the laborer, and so little exacted from him." Indeed, wrote a Virginian, "a merrier being does not exist on the face of the globe, than the Negro slave of the United States."

The endorsement of such ideas in the South at a time when a great reform movement was agitating the North produced an ideological conflict between the sections that threatened the survival of the Union. Slavery was no longer open to discussion in the South, and slaveholders intensely resented its denunciation on moral grounds in the North. Not even the two largest Protestant churches were able to bear the strain, and the slavery issue led to a split along sectional lines — the Methodists in 1844, the Baptists in 1845. Eventually the national political parties would also disintegrate, and thus another major institutional tie would be broken. Abolitionists and proslavery polemicists had raised a moral issue — the right and wrong of slavery — that stubbornly resisted the best efforts of a generation of able politicians and statesmen to resolve.

SUGGESTIONS FOR READING

Religion

The surveys of American cultural and intellectual history devote much space to religion in the first half of the nineteenth century. One of the earliest and most spirited of them, V. L. Parrington, *Main Currents in American Thought,** 3 vols. (1927–30), though dated, is still decidedly worth reading. Among the good recent surveys are M. E. Curti, *The Growth of American Thought* (rev. ed., 1951); R. H. Gabriel, *The Course of American Democratic Thought* (rev. ed., 1956); and Harvey Wish, *Society and Thought in Early America* (1950). I. H. Bartlett, *The American Mind in the Mid-Nineteenth Century** (1967), is brief and readable. Several useful general studies of American religion are available, among them W. W. Sweet, *The Story of Religion in America* (1920); H. K. Rowe, *The History of Religion in the United States* (1924); W. L. Sperry, *Religion in America** (1946); E. S. Gaustad, *A Religious History of America* (1966); and J. W. Smith and A. L. Jamison, eds., *Religion in American Life,* 4 vols. (1961). Alexis de Tocqueville, *Democracy in America,** 2 vols. (1945), makes some interesting comments about religion and the American people.

The revolt against orthodox Calvinism can be traced in H. M. Morais, *Deism in Eighteenth Century America* (1934); Albert Post, *Popular Free Thought in America* (1943); Conrad Wright, *The Beginnings of Unitarianism in America** (1955); G. W. Cooke, *Unitarianism in America* (1902); R. L. Patterson, *The Philosophy of William Ellery Channing* (1952); D. P. Edgell, *William Ellery Channing* (1955); and M. H. Rice, *Federal Street Pastor: The Life of William Ellery Channing* (1961). Transcendentalism is examined in the surveys of American intellectual history cited above and in two distinguished works on American literature covering this period: V. W. Brooks, *The Flowering of New England, 1815–1865** (1936), and F. O. Matthiessen, *American Renaissance* (1941). Three other books worth consulting are: O. B. Frothingham, *Transcendentalism in New England** (1876); H. C. Goddard, *New England Transcendentalism* (1908); and H. W. Schneider, *History of American Philosophy** (1946). There are good biographies of several transcendentalist leaders: H. S. Commager, *Theodore Parker: Yankee Crusader** (1936); A. M. Schlesinger, Jr., *Orestes A. Brownson: A Pilgrim's Progress** (1939); J. W. Krutch, *Henry David Thoreau** (1948); and R. L. Lusk, *The Life of Ralph Waldo Emerson* (1949). Perry Miller, *The Transcendentalists** (1950), is an excellent collection of transcendentalist writings.

A good survey of Protestant revivalism is W. W. Sweet, *Revivalism in America** (1944). Much valuable detail is added in W. R. Cross, *The Burned-Over District** (1950); C. A. Johnson, *The Frontier Camp Meeting* (1955); and B. A. Weisberger, *They Gathered at the River** (1958). Two important books tie revivalism to the reform movement: C. C. Cole, Jr., *The Social Ideals of the Northern Evangelists, 1826–1860* (1954), and T. L. Smith, *Revivalism and Social Reform in Mid-Nineteenth Century America* (1957).

* Available in a paperback edition.

Reform

A. A. Ekrich, *The Idea of Progress in America, 1815–1860* (1944), is a critical analysis of one of the reformers' basic assumptions. A. M. Schlesinger, *The American as Reformer* (1950), is a perceptive introduction to the reform movement. The best general treatment is A. F. Tyler, *Freedom's Ferment: Phases of American Social History to 1860** (1944). Other useful books are: C. R. Fish, *The Rise of the Common Man, 1830–1850* (1927); Meade Minnigerode, *The Fabulous Forties, 1840–1850* (1924); E. D. Branch, *The Sentimental Years, 1836–1860** (1934); R. E. Riegel, *Young America, 1830–1840* (1949); and C. S. Griffin, *Their Brothers' Keepers: Moral Stewardship in the United States, 1800–1865* (1960).

In the vast literature on specific reforms, the following are among the best: Blake McKelvey, *American Prisons: A Study in American Social History Prior to 1915* (1936); H. E. Marshall, *Dorothea Dix: Forgotten Samaritan* (1937); J. A. Krout, *The Origins of Prohibition* (1925); F. L. Byrne, *Prophet of Prohibition: Neal Dow and His Crusade* (1961); Paul Monroe, *The Founding of the American Public School System* (1940); L. H. Tharp, *Until Victory: Horace Mann and Mary Peabody* (1953); Carl Bode, *The American Lyceum* (1956); M. E. Curti, *The American Peace Crusade* (1929); and A. E. Bestor, Jr., *Backwoods Utopias: The Sectarian and Owenite Phases of Communitarian Socialism in America, 1663–1829* (1950).

Abolition and Proslavery

An exhaustive and highly sympathetic study of every aspect of abolitionism is D. L. Dumond, *Antislavery** (1961). Excellent brief surveys are available in Allan Nevins, *Ordeal of the Union,* 2 vols. (1947), and Louis Filler, *The Crusade Against Slavery** (1960). G. H. Barnes, *The Antislavery Impulse, 1833–1844** (1933), is a pioneer work that stresses the role of Theodore Dwight Weld at the expense of Garrison. Lawrence Lader, *The Bold Brahmins* (1961), is a vivid, anecdotal account of the antislavery crusade in New England. D. G. Mathews, *Slavery and Methodism* (1965), traces the conflict in one of the largest Protestant denominations. An important facet of abolitionism is examined in R. B. Nye, *Fettered Freedom: Civil Liberties and the Slavery Controversy, 1830–1860** (1949). Two stimulating essays on the nature of the movement are in David Donald, *Lincoln Reconsidered** (1956), and Stanley Elkins, *Slavery: A Problem in American Institutional and Intellectual Life** (1959). D. B. Davis, *The Problem of Slavery in Western Culture* (1966), is a brilliant study of the intellectual origins of the American antislavery movement. Martin Duberman, ed., *The Antislavery Vanguard* (1965), is a valuable collection of essays by scholars sympathetic to abolitionism. L. F. Litwack, *North of Slavery: The Negro in the Free States, 1790–1860** (1961), is an excellent empirical study of race prejudice in the North.

Among the best biographies of abolitionist leaders are R. V. Harlow, *Gerrit Smith: Philanthropist and Reformer* (1939); B. P. Thomas, *Theodore Weld: Crusader for Freedom* (1950); Betty Fladeland, *James Gillespie Birney: Slaveholder to Abolitionist* (1955); W. M. Merrill, *Against Wind and Tide: A Biography of William Lloyd Garrison* (1963); J. L. Thomas, *The Liberator: William Lloyd Garrison* (1963); Oscar Sherwin, *Prophet of Liberty: The Life and Times of Wendell Phillips* (1958); and I. H. Bartlett, *Wendell Phillips: Brahmin Radical* (1961).

W. S. Jenkins, *Pro-Slavery Thought in the Old South* (1935), is a comprehensive analysis of the proslavery argument. Harvey Wish, *George Fitzhugh: Propagandist of the Old South* (1943), is an excellent biography of a leading defender of slavery. A special aspect of proslavery thought is analyzed by Richard Hofstadter in his essay on Calhoun in *The American Political Tradition** (1948).

* Available in a paperback edition.

11
Expansion and Sectional Crisis

The acquisition of Louisiana and Florida in the early nineteenth century temporarily quieted the American urge for geographic expansion. Feeling secure from foreign intervention, and satisfied that there was ample space for a growing population, most Americans who moved west in the 1820's and 1830's were content to take up the vacant lands in their already immense country. They occupied the unsettled regions of Mississippi, Missouri, and Illinois and poured into new territories that soon would become states: Arkansas (1836), Michigan (1837), Florida (1845), Iowa (1846), and Wisconsin (1848). The vast area beyond Missouri and Arkansas, stretching out to the Rocky Mountains, was then of no interest to the westward-moving settlers. Because explorers reported that the land was too arid for farming, cartographers labeled it the "Great American Desert," and white Americans presented it as a "permanent" gift to the Indians. The donors felt there was room enough and plenty for white men to the east of this "Indian Country."

Or so it seemed until the 1840's, when the impulse to expand suddenly stirred anew. Actually, few Americans had ever assumed that the boundaries of the United States would stand forever unchanged, though it is surprising that the desire for more territory revived so soon. Some Americans pressed expansion more aggressively than others, but few challenged the idea that providence had destined their country to continued growth. Expansion in itself was not an issue that seriously divided the electorate. But it had a vexatious consequence: it raised the touchy question of whether slavery should be permitted to spread into the territories that were acquired. Much of the controversy recently generated by proslavery and antislavery propagandists began to center on this problem, and by the end of the 1840's it had precipitated a national crisis. In 1850, after months of bitter debate, a compromise was painfully constructed — a makeshift arrangement that settled nothing but that somehow served to hold the Union together for another decade.

Spanish church at the Santa Fe mission.

WESTWARD TO THE PACIFIC

Manifest Destiny. The reasons for the revived interest in territorial expansion were several. The first and most obvious was that the American people, with their sense of mission, were sorely tempted by the boundless tracts of unsettled or sparsely settled land lying just beyond the borders of their country. All through the 1820's and 1830's American fur-trappers, in their search for beaver streams, had been blazing trails, searching out passes through the mountains, and ranging over the fertile valleys of the Far West. The publicity they gave to the region beyond the Great American Desert at once strengthened the myth of the West as a land of romance and adventure and aroused interest in its agricultural possibilities. A second reason was a growing desire to develop trade with the Far East and the belief, as one expansionist politician expressed it, that along the valley of the Columbia River "lies the North American road to India." Many Eastern businessmen began to look covetously at the three best natural harbors on the Pacific coast, at San Diego, San Francisco, and Puget Sound. A third reason — and the one that probably explains the rebirth of expansionism at this precise time — was renewed fear of foreign intervention in lands bordering the United States, especially of British activity in Texas, California, and Oregon. Once again freedom and republican institutions in North America seemed threatened by the aggressive meddling of Europeans.

The expansionist drive was further strengthened by a mystical and romantic concept that, though hardly new, now received an attractive label. In 1845 a New York editor wrote exuberantly that it was America's "manifest destiny to overspread and to possess the whole of the continent which Providence has given us for the development of the great experiment of liberty and federated self-government entrusted to us." This doctrine of Manifest Destiny, quickly taken up by the press and politicians, was in part the kind of rationalization that nationalists everywhere have used to justify imperialist expansion. Nationalists invariably celebrate the superiority of their own culture and insist that their conquests are merely the fulfillment of a divine mission impelled by

Manifest Destiny

Texas has been absorbed into the Union in the inevitable fulfilment of the general law which is rolling our population westward.... It was disintegrated from Mexico in the natural course of events, by a process perfectly legitimate on its own part, blameless on ours.... [Its] incorporation into the Union was not only inevitable, but the most natural, right and proper thing in the world....

California will, probably, next fall away from ... Mexico.... Imbecile and distracted, Mexico never can exert any real governmental authority over such a country.... The Anglo-Saxon foot is already on its borders. Already the advance guard of the irresistible army of Anglo-Saxon emigration has begun to pour down upon it, armed with the plough and the rifle, and marking its trail with schools and colleges, courts and representative halls, mills and meeting houses. A population will soon be in actual occupation of California, over which it will be idle for Mexico to dream of dominion.... All this without agency of our government, without responsibility of our people — in the natural flow of events, the spontaneous working of principles, and the adaptation of the tendencies and wants of the human race to the elemental circumstances in the midst of which they find themselves placed.

From the *Democratic Review*, July 1845.

forces beyond human control. So did Americans when they spoke of their Manifest Destiny, and editors and stump-speakers often advocated expansion in terms so extravagant as to make the United States sound like a nation of swashbucklers. "Make way, I say, for the young American Buffalo," shouted a New Jersey politician, "he has not yet got land enough."

But running through the boasts and the threats was a thread of idealism that tied expansion to America's supposed mission to serve as a model of political democracy. Expansion in these terms was simply a means of "extending the area of freedom," to quote a popular phrase of the day. America's destiny was not merely to teach by precept but to bring more land and more people under the nation's jurisdiction — in short, to spread its democratic institutions over the entire North American continent. Thus, as one politician explained,

America would become "a vast theatre on which to work out the grand experiment of Republican government, under the auspices of the Anglo-Saxon race."

Texas. The first area outside the United States to which settlers moved in substantial numbers was Texas. Many Westerners had been disappointed when the national government, in the Florida-purchase treaty of 1819, accepted the Sabine River as a southwestern boundary, thereby surrendering whatever vague claim the government might have had to Texas, as part of the Louisiana Purchase. Mexico, after winning her independence from Spain in 1822, twice rejected American offers to buy this sparsely settled province; but during the 1820's she welcomed Americans who would submit to her jurisdiction and abide by her laws. Among the promoters of settlement, the first and most successful was Stephen F. Austin, who obtained a huge land grant from Mexico and planted a flourishing colony on the banks of the Brazos River. Most of the immigrants were Southern yeoman farmers and small slaveholders who were attracted by the rich lands suitable for cotton culture and available for a few cents an acre. By 1830 eastern Texas had been occupied by nearly twenty thousand whites and a thousand Negro slaves from the United States.

The Mexican government soon had cause to regret its hospitality, for the American settlers had no intention of giving their allegiance to a nation whose culture was so different from their own. Among numerous sources of friction, one of the most irritating was the fact that Texas did not have its own state government but remained a part of the state of Coahuila, whose legislature the Mexicans controlled. Moreover, the Americans were suspicious of Mexican land titles, which were unlike those they had been used to in the United States. In 1830 the mounting tension had prompted the Mexican government to make a drastic switch in policy: it prohibited further immigration from the United States, stopped the importation of slaves, placed heavy duties on American goods, and dispatched troops to the frontier to see that these laws were enforced. The final blow came when General Santa Anna, who had seized political power in Mexico, not only repudiated his promise to give Texas separate statehood but nearly abolished the nation's federal system.

To the Texans the parallel between British oppression under George III and Mexican oppression under Santa Anna was clear, and revolution was the obvious and justifiable remedy. For a short time they pretended to be fighting in defense of the old Mexican constitution, but on March 2, 1836, they declared their independence. The struggle was brief. Santa Anna moved into Texas with a large army and won a few minor skirmishes, the most notable being the extermination of a small garrison of Texans at the Alamo mission in San Antonio. But on April 21, 1836, at the Battle of San Jacinto, an army commanded by General Sam Houston decisively defeated the Mexicans and took Santa Anna prisoner. Santa Anna was forced to sign a treaty recognizing Texan independence; and though Mexico later denounced the treaty as having been signed under duress, she made no further attempt to reestablish her authority. The new Republic of Texas then framed a constitution, but in September 1836, when the voters ratified it, they also indicated overwhelming support for annexation to the United States. President Houston forthwith began negotiations with the government at Washington, first for recognition and then for annexation.

American volunteers and supplies had contributed to the Texans' victory over Santa Anna, and proannexation sentiment was strong, especially in the South and West. But opposition to the admission of another slave state began to grow among Whigs and abolitionists in the Northeast. Some practical Whig politicians feared that annexation would lead to war with Mexico and objected that it would increase the South's power to block legislation favorable to Northern economic interests. Abolitionists charged that the settlement of Texas, the revolution, and the movement for annexation were all parts of a slaveholders' plot to enlarge their empire and open new markets for the vendors of human flesh. Texas thus became an issue between the critics and the defenders of slavery.

President Jackson was an ardent annexationist, but he acted cautiously lest he impair Van Buren's chances of winning the presidential election of 1836. Jackson even delayed recog-

nition of Texan independence until the eve of his retirement from office, and Van Buren refused to recommend annexation during his term as President. Rebuffed by the United States, Texas in 1838 turned to Europe for recognition and aid; her leaders began to talk boldly of creating a nation that would expand to the Pacific and rival the United States in size and strength. This was a pleasing prospect to the British, who saw in Texas a buffer to American expansion, a threat to the American cotton monopoly, and a promising new market. Moreover, British abolitionists hoped to persuade the Texans to abolish slavery and prove that cotton could be produced with free labor. As Texan leaders doubtless expected, British interest in their affairs alarmed the United States government, and the talk of abolition angered the slaveholders of the South.

These developments spurred President Tyler to reopen negotiations with Texas, and he worked vigorously to get a treaty of annexation before his term expired. By April 1844 Tyler's new Secretary of State, John C. Calhoun, had secured the desired treaty, and it was submitted to the Senate for ratification. Unfortunately Calhoun also sent a note to the British government concerning its interest in Texas, in which he defended slavery as a positive good and thus strengthened the abolitionist claim that annexation would be the culmination of a proslavery plot. This, along with the continued anxiety about war with Mexico, doomed the treaty; only sixteen senators voted for it, while thirty-five voted against. Annexation was again delayed, and Texas became an issue in the approaching presidential election.

The Santa Fe trade. Meanwhile, a resourceful group of small entrepreneurs had aroused American interest in another of Mexico's remote provinces: New Mexico. The Spanish outpost at Santa Fe on the upper Rio Grande, planted in the seventeenth century, was hundreds of miles from the nearest Mexican settlements, and Spain's rigid trade restrictions had long deprived it of supplies from the United States. In the 1820's, however, the independent Mexican government had opened the Santa Fe trade to Americans. Every spring for the next two decades petty merchants assembled their wagons at Independence, Missouri, for the long journey along the Santa Fe Trail.

Only a few merchants engaged in the trade — usually not many more than a hundred — but they always found a highly profitable market for their goods. In 1844, to the dismay of the traders, bad feeling generated by the Texas question caused Santa Anna again to exclude Americans from Santa Fe. By then, however, the trade had enlarged the American vision of Manifest Destiny to encompass New Mexico. Though few of the traders had actually settled in Santa Fe, they had opened a route into the Far West, demonstrated that heavily laden wagons could cross the plains, and developed a system of organized caravans for protection against the Indians. Another sparsely settled territory seemed ripe for American plucking.

Oregon. Far to the northwest, in the Oregon country, during the 1830's and early 1840's, merchants, fur-trappers, and missionaries were awakening Americans to the potentialities of still another area, one to which the United States had a solid, though not exclusive, claim. That claim was based on the voyages of Boston merchants to the Oregon coast to buy furs from the Indians in the late eighteenth century; on Captain Robert Gray's discovery of the mouth of the Columbia River in 1792; on the explorations of the Lewis and Clark expedition between 1804 and 1806; and on the founding of Astoria on the Columbia River in 1811 by John Jacob Astor's Pacific Fur Company. In addition, the United States had acquired the French claim to Oregon in the Louisiana Purchase treaty of 1803 and the Spanish claim in the Florida-purchase treaty of 1819. But the British claim was at least as good as the American. Sir Francis Drake, the British insisted, had discovered the Oregon coast in 1579; Captain James Cook and Captain George Vancouver had visited it again in the eighteenth century; and Alexander Mackenzie had made the first overland trip to Oregon in 1793 as an agent of British fur-trading interests. Moreover, by a treaty of 1825, the British had acquired the Russian claim to Oregon. Thus the Americans and British were the sole claimants to a huge territory bounded on the south by the forty-second parallel, on the north by the line of 54° 40′, on the east by the Rocky Mountains, and on the west by the Pacific Ocean.

In the early nineteenth century, though neither the British nor the Americans claimed the whole of Oregon, they were unable to agree on a line of division. On several occasions the United States proposed an extension of the forty-ninth parallel to the Pacific, while the British suggested that the line follow the Columbia River from the forty-ninth parallel to its mouth. In 1818 the two countries postponed the settlement of this question and agreed to leave Oregon "free and open" to the citizens of both for a period of ten years. In 1827 they extended the agreement indefinitely, with the proviso that either country could terminate it on a year's notice. There the matter rested until the 1840's.

For many years Americans showed little interest in Oregon, and British fur-traders had the area largely to themselves. After 1821 the Hudson's Bay Company monopolized the fur trade, establishing its headquarters at Fort Vancouver on the north bank of the Columbia and sending Dr. John McLoughlin there to serve as its chief factor. For more than twenty years McLoughlin gave Oregon the only government it had; he was scrupulously fair in dealing with the Indians, and under his efficient direction the company flourished. In the 1830's, however, agents of the Hudson's Bay Company operating in the Rockies began to encounter fierce and ruthless competitors: the intrepid Mountain Men, who hunted beaver skins for the Rocky Mountain Fur Company, directed by Thomas Fitzpatrick, James Bridger, and Milton Sublette. The Mountain Men, along with the agents of Astor's American Fur Company, were the advance guard of American overland penetration of Oregon.

Efforts by several Eastern promoters to stimulate American migration to Oregon in the 1820's and 1830's ended in failure. But the impulse for settlement soon came from another source. In 1833 an Eastern religious periodical published a report that the Indians of the Oregon country were eager for instruction in the Christian faith. In response to this report (which had little substance to it) the Methodists sent the Reverend Jason Lee, who established a mission in the fertile Willamette Valley; the Presbyterians sent the Reverend Marcus Whitman, who was active farther east, near Fort Walla Walla; and the Catholics sent Father Pierre Jean de Smet, a Jesuit priest from St. Louis, who worked among the Indians

Trails to the Far West

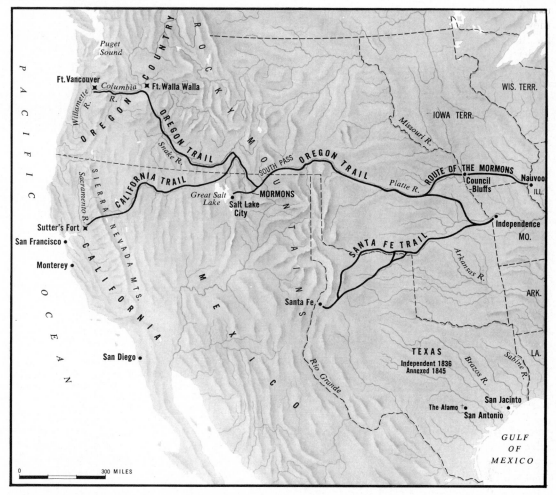

in the Rockies. Dr. McLoughlin gave the missionaries a cordial welcome and much assistance, but the Indians showed little interest in the Gospel. Indeed, the religious work of the missions proved to be less important than the publicity they gave to Oregon. Scores of missionary letters and reports filled with reference to Oregon's fecund soil and salubrious climate found their way into the Eastern press.

As word spread that the Willamette Valley was a new Garden of Eden, the people of the Mississippi Valley began to catch the "Oregon fever." In the late 1830's a trickle of emigrants began to follow the Oregon Trail in quest of free virgin land; in 1841 the first substantial caravan of covered wagons made the two-thousand-mile journey; and by 1843 the movement to Oregon was taking on the dimensions of a mass migration. The Oregon Trail began at Independence, Missouri, ran northwest to the Platte River, followed the Platte and its north fork into southern Wyoming, made an easy crossing of the Rockies at South Pass, followed the Snake River to a cutoff that led to the Columbia River, and then followed the Columbia to the Willamette Valley. By 1845 at least five thousand Americans had reached Oregon along this route; they had already formed a provisional government and were now demanding that the United States establish exclusive jurisdiction over them. Joint occupation with the British was no longer a

A Wagon Train

First, near the bank of the shining river, is a company of horsemen.... Then the wagons form a line three quarters of a mile in length.... Next comes a band of horses; two or three men or boys follow them, the docile and sagacious animals scarce needing this attention.... Not so with the large herd of horned beasts that bring up the rear; lazy, selfish and unsocial....

Nothing of the moving panorama, smooth and orderly as it appears, has more attractions for the eye than the vast square column in which all colors are mingled.... But the picture, in its grandeur, its wonderful mingling of colors and distinctness of detail, is forgotten in contemplation of the singular people who give it life and animation.... They have undertaken to perform, with slow moving oxen, a journey of two thousand miles. The way lies over trackless wastes, wide and deep rivers, rugged and lofty mountains, and is beset with hostile savages. Yet, whether it were a deep river with no tree upon its banks, a rugged defile where even a loose horse could not pass, a hill too steep for him to climb, or a threatened attack of an enemy, they are always found ready and equal to the occasion, and always conquerors.

From Jesse A. Applegate, *A Day with the Cow Column,* 1843.

satisfactory formula, and a final settlement could not be delayed much longer.

California. South of Oregon lay California, another of Mexico's remote provinces and the fourth area in the Far West where Manifest Destiny seemed to beckon Americans. In the eighteenth century the Spanish, in order to strengthen their control over California and to convert the Indians to Christianity, had encouraged Franciscan friars to build a chain of missions along the coast from San Diego to San Francisco. The missions were highly successful both in their religious work and as large-scale agricultural enterprises; but in 1834 the Mexican government deprived them of their lands, and the mission system fell apart. Under a succession of weak, inefficient, and often corrupt secular administrators, California sank into political chaos. But the sparse Mexican population of approximately seven thousand settlers, most of them ranchers, still managed to live in easygoing comfort.

The first American contacts with California were made by merchant ships putting in along the coast for modest trading, and by whaleboats stopping for supplies. Now and then an American sailor deserted his ship and settled down; an occasional party of Mountain Men found their way to California on a trapping expedition; and by the 1830's a few merchants had come to trade with the Indians and Mexicans. Among the merchants was Thomas O. Larkin, who arrived at Monterey in 1832, built a flourishing trade, and worked tirelessly to promote American immigration to California. In the 1840's a few emigrants began to leave the Oregon Trail near the Snake River to follow the California Trail across the Nevada desert and the Sierra Nevada to the Sacramento River Valley. Invariably their goal was Sutter's Fort, the center of a private empire ruled by John A. Sutter, a German-born immigrant who had acquired Mexican citizenship and was a law unto himself. Sutter welcomed the Americans, furnished them with supplies, and helped them find land. By 1845 California was the home of about seven hundred Americans, almost none of whom expected to give up their American citizenship or to remain beyond the jurisdiction of their government very long.

The "California fever" had become almost as virulent as the "Oregon fever." Emigrants were attracted by the abundance of fertile, unoccupied land and by extravagant descriptions of California as "the richest, the most beautiful, and the healthiest country in the world." Eastern businessmen became increasingly interested in the commercial opportunities, and the American government coveted the harbors at San Diego and San Francisco — the latter was described as "capacious enough to receive the navies of all the world." Reports of British designs on California, though inaccurate, gave the matter a special urgency. In 1842 Commodore Thomas ap Catesby Jones, commander of the United States Pacific squadron, somehow got the impression that his country had gone to war with Mexico and that British warships were moving toward California. Accordingly, he sailed into Monterey Bay, seized the city, ran up the American flag, and proclaimed the annexation of California to the United States. The embarrassed State Depart-

Land of the lizard: Salt Lake City, 1853.

ment disavowed Jones' act and made apologies to the Mexican government, but the incident was a clear sign of what the expansionists had in mind.

The Mormon migration. One group of emigrants to the Far West had no interest in Manifest Destiny — indeed, they sought to escape the jurisdiction of the United States. These were the Mormons, who in 1847 crossed into Mexican territory and established a settlement in the isolated Great Salt Lake basin. The Mormon migration followed nearly two decades of persecution, which had begun in the 1820's in western New York, where Joseph Smith had founded the sect. The Church of Jesus Christ of Latter-Day Saints, as it was officially called, was based on miraculous revelations that Smith claimed to have received from God and that he incorporated in the Book of Mormon. From the beginning the Mormon Saints annoyed the "gentiles" about them with their close-knit communitarian social pattern, their thriving economic life, and their contempt for other religious sects. In their search for a Zion where they could escape this hostility and live in peace, they first moved from New York to Kirtland, Ohio, then to Missouri, then (in 1839) to Nauvoo, Illinois, where their numbers soon grew to fifteen thousand. In 1844, after five prosperous years, a new crisis developed when Smith received another revelation, this one justifying polygamy. The result was a schism in the Church, a rash of violence, and Smith's arrest and imprisonment. On June 27, 1844, an anti-Mormon mob took him

from jail and murdered him. Once more the Mormons were obliged to abandon their homes and renew their wanderings.

Leadership now passed to Brigham Young, a brilliant, strong-willed man, who organized the most remarkable migration and settlement in the annals of the American West. In 1846 Young led almost the whole Mormon community across Iowa to the Council Bluffs on the Missouri River; the next year he sent the first band to the Salt Lake basin, which he had selected for the new Zion. No place could have appeared less promising; the first to arrive saw only "a broad and barren plain . . . a seemingly interminable waste of sagebrush . . . the paradise of the lizard, the cricket and the rattlesnake." But within a decade the Mormons, under the stern leadership of Young and the theocratic control of the Church, had transformed the landscape. Substituting cooperative labor for the individual effort of the typical pioneer, they built a thriving city and an efficient irrigation system with which they made the desert bloom. In the critical early years their economy benefited from the sale of supplies to emigrants passing through on their way to California. When their lands were annexed to the United States soon after they arrived, the Mormons tried first to organize their own state of "Deseret." Failing, they acquiesced when Congress created the Territory of Utah. Even then, however, the Mormon Church continued to be the dominant political as well as religious force in the land of the Saints.

POLK AND THE TRIUMPH OF MANIFEST DESTINY

The election of Polk. The presidential election of 1844 exposed a variety of tensions that had been growing in American society in recent years. First, the long depression following the Panic of 1837 had kept alive issues of national policy concerning money, banking, and public lands, issues that sometimes divided labor and capital, sometimes farm and city. Second, the entrance of the abolitionist crusade into politics had given sectional differences a moral dimension that made compromise increasingly difficult to achieve. Third, the doctrine of Manifest Destiny was reaching the height of its influence, and the drive for expansion to the Pacific was becoming an irresistible force. The complexity of these issues, all of which were more or less interrelated, sorely tried the national party system and led ultimately to a fragmentation of both the Whig and the Democratic organizations.

In 1844 Henry Clay and Martin Van Buren expected to receive the presidential nominations of their respective parties. They found the unsettled Texas question a source of embarrassment, because it had become involved in the slavery controversy. Hence they tried to eliminate it as a campaign issue by making separate but very similar statements (apparently after private consultation) opposing the annexation of Texas at that time without the consent of Mexico. The Whig convention unanimously nominated Clay and adopted a platform that avoided taking a stand either on Texas or on most other national issues. But the Democratic convention, where expansionist sentiment was stronger, denied Van Buren the nomination he coveted. Instead, the delegates chose James K. Polk of Tennessee, whose commitment to territorial expansion was clear and unqualified. To avoid the accusation of sectional favoritism, the Democratic platform cleverly united a demand for the admission of Texas with a demand for the acquisition "of the whole of the Territory of Oregon." The platform also made the dubious assertion that the United States had a clear title to both. It followed, therefore, "that the re-occupation of Oregon and the re-annexation of Texas at the earliest practicable period are great American measures, which this convention recommends to the cordial support of the Democracy of the Union."

By combining the expansionist desires of South and West, the Democrats had found a winning formula. Throughout the campaign Manifest Destiny transcended all other issues, so much so that Clay began to shift his position on Texas. He would favor annexation after all if it could be accomplished without war and upon "just and fair terms." But this commitment still sounded halfhearted when compared with the spread-eagle oratory and aggressive slogans of the Democrats. Clay converted few of the expansionists but lost some antislavery votes to the Liberty party (see p. 265), especially in New York. In the election Polk won by a small plurality of thirty-eight thousand in the popular vote and by a margin of 170 to 105 in the Electoral College.

Though Polk is remembered as the first "dark-horse" presidential candidate, the term is valid only in the sense that he had not been considered for the nomination before the Democratic convention. He was far from a political unknown in 1844. Born in North Carolina, he had moved to Tennessee as a young man and soon became a successful lawyer and planter. He entered politics as a Jacksonian Democrat and served seven terms in the House of Representatives (two as Speaker) and one term as governor of Tennessee. As President, Polk displayed neither extraordinary talent nor a striking personality, but by hard work and stubborn determination he had remarkable success in redeeming the pledges his party had made during the campaign. His inaugural address was unimaginative — a mere reiteration of the principles with which Jefferson and Jackson had been identified. Polk promised a passive domestic role for government "by abstaining from the exercise of doubtful or unauthorized implied powers."

Polk's Administration reflected both the continuing influence of Jacksonian principles on the Democratic party and the growing power of the South within the party. As a planter and slaveholder Polk shared the Southern hostility toward abolitionists; if they achieved their goal, he warned, "the dissolution of the Union . . . must speedily follow." He favored a low revenue tariff, and in 1846 his Secretary of the Treasury, Robert J. Walker of Mississippi, helped to frame such a measure, which Congress passed. The Walker Tariff delighted the South, but it angered Northern protectionists and increased their hostility to further strengthening the antiprotectionists by the admission of any more slave states. Polk shared Jackson's views on national banking and persuaded Congress to reestablish the Independent Treasury system, which it had abolished during the Tyler Administration. On two occasions, to the intense annoyance of Westerners in the Great Lakes region, he vetoed internal-improvements bills. In short, Polk blocked every effort to revive the American System of Henry Clay and John Quincy Adams, and in his last message to Congress he devoted much space to attacking that system and celebrating its demise.

The acquisition of Texas and Oregon. Important as these domestic policies were, the Polk

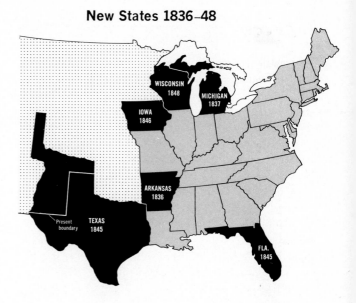

New States 1836–48

Administration's primary concern was with geographic expansion. The Texas question was the first to be disposed of, for Congress had virtually settled the matter shortly before Polk's inauguration. After the presidential election Tyler assured Congress that the verdict of the voters had been in favor of annexation, and he proposed now that the two houses accomplish it by a joint resolution. Annexation would thus require only a simple majority, rather than the two-thirds majority needed in the Senate to ratify a treaty. The introduction of a resolution for this purpose provoked a heated debate between proslavery and antislavery congressmen, but it finally passed the House by a vote of 120 to 98 and the Senate by a vote of 27 to 25. President Tyler signed the joint resolution on March 1, 1845. Polk approved of this action, and within a few months Texas had accepted the terms of annexation. In December 1845 Texas was admitted to statehood.

The problem of Oregon was not so easily resolved, for the Americans and British still had not agreed on a line of division. Indeed, the restless settlers in Oregon and the expansionists in the East were growing increasingly belligerent in their demand that the government make no division at all but, as the Democratic platform of 1844 had insisted, take the whole territory to its northern limits. Apparently ready for another war with the British, they repeated

The Oregon Controversy, 1818–46

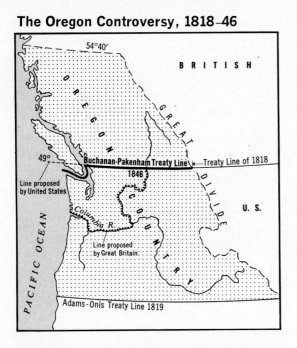

the slogans "All of Oregon or none" and "Fifty-four forty or fight." "We want thirty thousand rifles in the valley of the Oregon," cried Senator Benton of Missouri. "They will make all quiet there . . . and protect the American interests." In January 1845 the British government, realizing that continued joint occupation was impossible, proposed arbitration, but the State Department rejected the offer.

In referring to the Oregon question in his inaugural address, Polk seemed to stand firmly on his party's platform; it would be his duty, he said, "to assert and maintain by all constitutional means the right of the United States to that portion of our territory which lies beyond the Rocky Mountains. Our title to the country of the Oregon is 'clear and unquestionable,' and . . . those rights we are fully prepared to maintain." Meanwhile, there was a good deal of irresponsible saber-rattling on both sides of the Atlantic, and the situation threatened to get out of hand.

But Polk did not want war with England at a time when there was danger of war with Mexico; accordingly, he soon decided to abandon the Democratic platform and try for a compromise. In July 1845 he notified the British minister in Washington, Richard Pakenham,

that the United States was willing to renew its offer to divide Oregon along the forty-ninth parallel. Pakenham, without even consulting his government, rejected the offer and held firm to the earlier British demand for a division at the Columbia River. The indignant President then withdrew his offer, concluded that "the only way to treat John Bull was to look him straight in the eye," and decided to pursue "a bold and firm course." In his message to Congress that December, Polk recommended that the British government be given the year's notice required to end joint occupation. He also invoked the almost forgotten Monroe Doctrine to fortify his case: "it should be distinctly announced to the world as our settled policy that no future European colony or dominion shall with our consent be planted or established on any part of the North American continent." Once Congress had approved the termination of joint occupation of Oregon, the only remaining hope for a peaceful settlement seemed to be an offer of concessions on the part of the British.

Fortunately the British Foreign Office disapproved of Pakenham's blunt rejection of Polk's offer to compromise, for it did not believe that the disputed segment of Oregon between the Columbia River and the forty-ninth parallel was worth a war. Indeed, the flood of American settlers and the depletion of the fur resources had already prompted the Hudson's Bay Company to transfer its headquarters from Fort Vancouver on the Columbia northward to Fort Victoria on Vancouver Island. In June 1846 Secretary of State James Buchanan received from Pakenham the draft of a proposal to divide Oregon at the forty-ninth parallel but to retain for the British all of Vancouver Island and the right to navigate the Columbia River. Polk was at first inclined to reject the proposal, but he decided to submit it to the Senate and let that body assume responsibility for the decision.

After an angry debate the Senate advised acceptance; the treaty was signed on June 15, and the Senate ratified it by a vote of 41 to 14. Most of the opposition came from Western Democrats who bitterly criticized Polk for backing down on the demand for the whole of Oregon. But most of the country was satisfied with the settlement, for the British, rather than the Americans, had given up their original claim. Eastern business interests had no taste for a war to secure the area north of the forty-ninth parallel; nor did the Southerners, whose interest in Oregon waned once Texas had been safely annexed. Besides, the United States was already at war with Mexico and had a richer prize in view.

WAR WITH MEXICO

The background. Among the causes of the war with Mexico were the inability of United States citizens to obtain compensation for claims against the Mexican government, the anger of Mexican patriots over American annexation of Texas, a dispute over the southern and western boundaries of Texas, and the instability of the Mexican government, which made negotiation with it difficult and irritating. But even more important was the determination of Polk (and of the expansionists generally) to obtain the provinces of New Mexico and California — with money if possible, by force if necessary. Though Mexico was far from blameless for the war that came — indeed, welcomed it — the central cause was nevertheless the readiness of Americans to resort to arms to fulfill their Manifest Destiny.

As soon as the United States annexed Texas, Mexico broke off diplomatic relations, thus closing the normal channels of negotiation. Yet there was need for negotiation, because Texas was not satisfied with its traditional southern boundary, which in Spanish days had been the Nueces River, but claimed instead the Rio Grande. Polk, convinced that the Texas claim was justified, ordered General Zachary Taylor to take fifteen hundred troops into the disputed area. By the summer of 1845, Taylor's small army was encamped at Corpus Christi on the Nueces River; in March of the following year it obeyed Polk's command and advanced to the Rio Grande. To Mexican patriots this act, following soon after what they considered the illegal seizure of Texas, was a further aggressive invasion of their territory, and the war spirit grew among them.

There was now little hope that Polk could persuade Mexico to give up California and New Mexico peacefully, but he decided to try nonetheless. In the fall of 1845 he explored the possibility of resuming diplomatic relations. When he learned that Mexico would receive an American commissioner to settle the Texas dispute, he appointed John Slidell of Louisiana as envoy extraordinary and minister plenipotentiary with authority to discuss not only Texas but California and New Mexico as well. Slidell was instructed to offer (1) the assumption by the United States of all claims of its citizens against Mexico if Mexico would accept the Rio Grande boundary; (2) $5 million for the rest of New Mexico west of the Rio Grande; and (3) as much as $25 million for California. Since the Mexican government needed money and since its hold on these distant territories was weak, to Polk it seemed the course of wisdom for Mexico to sell.

When Slidell reached Mexico City on December 6, 1845, news about his purpose had already leaked out, and Mexican nationalists were furious at this brazen attempt to dismember their country. The existing government was collapsing, in part because of its alleged lack of firmness in dealing with the United States, and a new revolutionary government came to power pledged to uphold the national dignity. Neither the old nor the new government would receive Slidell. Mexico, he was reminded, had agreed only to receive a commissioner to negotiate on Texas, and until that question was settled there could be no regular diplomatic relations. The Slidell mission had failed. "Be assured," the angry diplomat wrote Polk, "that nothing is to be done with these people until they shall have been chastised."

Polk apparently agreed. On May 9, 1846, he told his Cabinet that the unpaid claims and the snubbing of Slidell would justify a declaration of war, and he began at once to prepare a war message to Congress. That evening news arrived that on April 25 Mexican troops had crossed the Rio Grande and engaged in a skirmish in which sixteen American soldiers were killed or wounded. Polk hastily revised his war message and sent it to Congress on May 11. After reviewing recent relations between Mexico and the United States, his message concluded: "The cup of forbearance had been exhausted even before the recent information from the frontier. . . . But now, after reiterated menaces, Mexico has passed the

The Mexican War, 1846–48

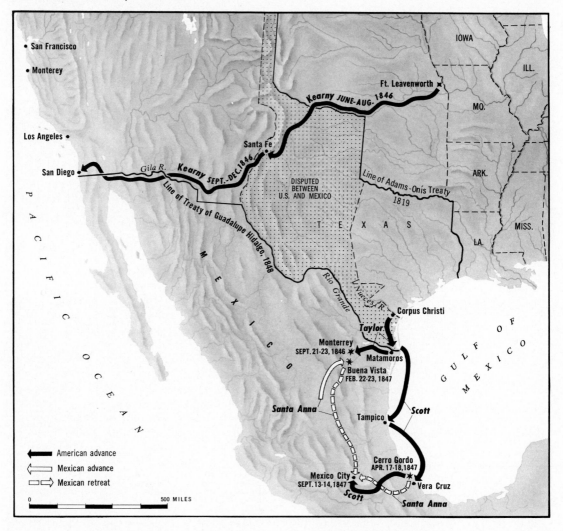

boundary of the United States, has invaded our territory and shed American blood on the American soil." Therefore, "war exists, and, notwithstanding all our efforts to avoid it, exists by the act of Mexico herself." Two days later Congress passed a declaration of war, the Senate by a vote of 40 to 2, the House by a vote of 174 to 14. It then appropriated $10 million for war purposes and authorized the recruitment of an army of fifty thousand volunteers.

The country went to war somewhat less united than these votes in Congress indicated. Though most Whig politicians felt they had no choice but to support the military measures,

they showed less enthusiasm for the conflict than the Democrats. War sentiment was strong in the Southwest, but it diminished to the east and north. Abolitionists and antislavery Whigs (who called themselves Conscience Whigs) denied that Polk had tried to avoid war and insisted that American blood had been shed not on American soil but on disputed soil that American troops should never have occupied. Senator Tom Corwin of Ohio accused Polk of involving the country in a war of aggression, and added bitterly: "If I were a Mexican, I would tell you, 'Have you not room in your own country to bury your dead men? If you come into mine, we will greet you with bloody hands and welcome you to hospitable graves.' " Abolitionists viewed the war as another attempt of the Slave Power to enhance its strength. In 1847 the Massachusetts legislature resolved that the war was "unconstitutionally commenced by the order of the President" and that it was being waged for the "dismemberment of Mexico" with "the triple object of extending slavery, of strengthening the slave power, and of obtaining the control of the free states." A new sectional crisis thus began to take shape almost as soon as the war commenced.

The military campaigns. In all probability the Mexicans entered the war with greater unity and enthusiasm than the Americans. They had concluded that war was the only way to check Yankee aggression, and they were confident that their regular army, vastly superior in numbers to the American, could easily defeat the invaders. But the Mexicans were sadly deluded, for they did not take into account their outdated weapons, their limited supplies and inferior resources, and their oversupply of incompetent generals. The United States War Department was inefficient enough, but the Mexican was even more so. Though the United States had a regular army of less than eight thousand officers and men, it was able quickly to raise a force of sixty thousand volunteers. With this manpower, with superior equipment, and with at least one gifted military commander, General Winfield Scott, the Americans won the war with relative ease.

Polk, who planned the military operations himself, hoped that a few quick victories would persuade Mexico to make the desired territorial cessions. According to Senator Benton, Polk "wanted a small war, just large enough to require a treaty of peace." In the first of three major campaigns, General Taylor crossed the Rio Grande, captured Matamoros, and pushed on to Monterrey. There, in a severe battle (September 21–23, 1846), Taylor defeated the Mexican garrison but permitted it to withdraw rather than surrender. Because of these early victories, Old Rough and Ready, as Taylor's men affectionately called him, became a national hero, but he had betrayed limitations as a tactician and a tendency to be overcautious — serious flaws in a commanding officer.

As a result, Polk lost confidence in him, took away half his army for a new offensive at Vera Cruz, and would have been content to let him remain idle for the rest of the war. But Santa Anna, who had regained power in Mexico, moved north to attack Taylor's weakened forces. At the Battle of Buena Vista (February 22–23, 1847) Taylor added to his national popularity by defeating Santa Anna and forcing him to return to Mexico City. This action ended the war in northern Mexico, but the decisive victories were still to be won elsewhere.

The second offensive was designed to bring the coveted Mexican provinces under American occupation before a peace treaty was negotiated. In the summer of 1846 a force of seventeen hundred men, commanded by Colonel Stephen W. Kearny, marched from Fort Leavenworth to Santa Fe and, on August 18, captured it without firing a shot. After proclaiming the annexation of New Mexico to the United States, Kearny sent part of his troops to join Taylor, left a small garrison at Santa Fe, and took the rest to California. There the American settlers, in the "Bear Flag Revolution," had already declared the independence of California; and Captain John C. Frémont, who had arrived earlier at the head of an exploring expedition, was in command of the rebels. Meanwhile, naval forces had landed at Monterey and raised the American flag. Hence, when Kearny arrived late in 1846 the only remaining task was to subdue scattered resistance to American authority in southern California. By January 1847 the United States had virtually undisputed possession of both New Mexico and California.

It took a third American campaign to force Mexico to accept these realities. In March 1847 an army commanded by General Scott landed near Vera Cruz, forced that city to surrender after an eighteen-day siege, and then began a slow and difficult advance toward Mexico City. Scott won a decisive victory over Santa Anna at Cerro Gordo (April 17–18, 1847), and by August he was on the high plateau before the Mexican capital. On September 14 American troops forced their way into the city, and soon after Mexico surrendered.

The Treaty of Guadalupe Hidalgo. A new Mexican government was now ready to sign a treaty of peace. In anticipation of this outcome, Polk had sent Nicholas P. Trist, chief clerk in the State Department, along with Scott's army "to take advantage of circumstances, as they might arise to negotiate a peace." Trist was instructed to offer essentially the same terms that Slidell had offered. In November 1847, after a long and irritating delay, negotiations were about to begin when Trist received orders from the impatient President to return to Washington. But Trist, convinced that he was on the verge of getting all he had been sent for, decided to ignore his orders and enter into negotiations. On February 2, 1848, he signed the Treaty of Guadalupe Hidalgo, by which the United States obtained California, New Mexico, and the Rio Grande boundary for $15 million and the assumption of the claims of United States citizens against Mexico. Trist then hurried back to Washington, but he got no thanks from the President. Instead, Polk denounced him as an "impudent and unqualified scoundrel" for disobeying orders and dismissed him from his job.

But Polk could find no fault with the treaty and, notwithstanding "the exceptional conduct of Mr. Trist," decided to submit it to the Senate. By then some of the more rabid expansionists were asking why the United States should settle for only California and New Mexico. Why not take the whole of Mexico? As one partisan of Manifest Destiny asked, why "resign this beautiful country to the custody of the ignorant cowards and profligate ruffians who have ruled it for the last twenty-five years?" But after a volley of bombastic oratory, the Senate, on March 10, 1848, ratified the treaty by a vote of 38 to 14. Thus, as one disgruntled Whig observed, the Mexican War ended with a peace "negotiated by an unauthorized agent, with an unacknowledged government, submitted by an accidental President to a dissatisfied Senate." Through it the United States gained possession of more than a half-million square miles of territory.

CRISIS AND COMPROMISE

The issue of slavery expansion. On August 8, 1846, shortly after the outbreak of the Mexican War, the House of Representatives had under consideration a bill appropriating $2 million to facilitate the acquisition of territory from Mexico when a peace treaty was negotiated. The bill appeared to be harmless enough until David Wilmot, a Jacksonian Democrat from Pennsylvania, rose to move an amendment making it "an express and fundamental condition" that "neither slavery nor involuntary servitude shall ever exist in any part of said territory." The Wilmot Proviso, as the amendment was called, twice passed the House but each time failed in the Senate, and on numerous other occasions it was reintroduced and bitterly debated. During the next fifteen years the issue of the expansion of slavery, which had been a latent source of trouble ever since the Missouri controversy, was to drive a wedge ever deeper between North and South.

What personal motives Wilmot may have had for introducing his proviso is of no great historical importance, because other Northern congressmen were prepared to offer similar proposals had not Wilmot acted first. The important question is whether the long and angry controversy over slavery expansion involved a genuine problem or was simply a flight from reality. Polk was the first of many contemporaries to denounce the Wilmot Proviso as "mischievous and foolish" and to accuse "Southern agitators and Northern fanatics" of raising a false issue merely for political advancement. He and other conservatives held that, since none of the territory acquired from Mexico was geographically suitable for plantation agriculture with slave labor, any legislation to exclude slavery from it would be unnecessarily provocative, because it would needlessly reenact a "law of nature." From this, presumably, it followed that irresponsible demagogues were creating a great national crisis and endangering the Union over a mere abstraction.

By the end of the 1840's the Southern plantation system may well have reached its natural geographic limits within the existing boundaries of the United States, but it does not necessarily follow that the debate over slavery expansion was therefore meaningless. Though the politicians who had to deal with the problem may not have handled it well, many of them were convinced that the problem had substance to it. In the first place, not all Northerners and Southerners were sure that geography alone would keep slavery out of California and New Mexico. Some believed that even if the familiar plantation system could not be developed in these areas, slavery might still be introduced there in other forms of agriculture, as well as in industry and mining. In the second place, few Americans thought that their country's growth had stopped with the territory acquired in the Treaty of Guadalupe Hidalgo. There was a widespread conviction that at least Cuba would one day become part of the United States, and perhaps other Caribbean islands and Central America as well. In these tropical lands slavery would certainly not be a merely academic question. Indeed, much of the controversy over slavery expansion was waged with an eye on future annexations and with the understanding that laws excluding slavery from existing territories would provide significant precedents.

Finally, and perhaps most important, the issue had meaning in terms of the moral positions of the two sections. The debate over slavery expansion was in reality an extension of the debate over slavery where it already existed. When Northerners with antislavery sentiments argued that it would be morally wrong to legalize slavery in New Mexico, they were by implication arguing that it was also morally wrong to tolerate it in Virginia. Southerners understood this perfectly well, which explains in part why they so vigorously opposed any move by Congress to prohibit slavery in territories where they knew it would never be established. For example, Southern congressmen delayed for two years (until 1848) the passage of a bill creating Oregon Territory, because the bill contained a clause excluding slavery.

Much of the debate over the Wilmot Proviso centered on the question of how much power the Constitution had given Congress to govern the territories. Antislavery Northerners cited the clause authorizing Congress to "make all needful rules and regulations respecting the Territory or other Property belonging to the United States." Until the 1840's, as Henry Clay observed, this clause had been accepted as giving Congress power over slavery in the territories "by the uniform interpretation and action of every department of our government, legislative, executive, and judicial." Moreover, the power had repeatedly been used. The First Congress had reenacted the Ordinance of 1787, which prohibited slavery in the Northwest Territory; a later Congress had applied the same restriction to the Illinois and Michigan territories when they were created; and overwhelming majorities in the House and Senate had voted in 1820 to prohibit slavery in that portion of the Louisiana Purchase north of the line 36° 30'. After the Mexican War, when President Polk and many other Southern moderates suggested extending the Missouri Compromise line to the Pacific, they were in effect agreeing that Congress did have authority to regulate slavery in the territories.

Calhoun, however, led proslavery Southerners toward an extreme state-rights position similar to the stand that some Virginians had taken during the Missouri debates. In 1847 he introduced a series of resolutions in the Senate asserting that the territories were the common property of all the states; that Congress had no power to deprive the citizens of any state of their right to migrate to the territories with their property, including slaves; and that only when a territory was ready for statehood could it constitutionally prohibit slavery. Calhoun's position, therefore, was that *all* the territories must be open to slavery — which made even the Missouri Compromise unconstitutional. Some of his supporters went a step further and insisted that it was the duty of Congress to *protect* slavery in the territories if necessary. This being the case, the Wilmot Proviso was, in the words of one Southern congressman, "treason to the Constitution," and its adoption would justify the secession of the South.

Between these uncompromising antislavery and proslavery doctrines, a third doctrine, called "popular sovereignty," began to win the support of moderates in all sections but especially in the Old Northwest. With two Democratic senators, Lewis Cass of Michigan and Stephen A. Douglas of Illinois, its chief advocates, popular sovereignty was designed in part to remove the explosive territorial question from the halls of Congress. Why not respect the American tradition of local self-government, these moderates asked, and permit the people who actually settled in a territory to decide the question of slavery for themselves? Congress could then organize new territories without reference to slavery. Southerners would escape the humiliation of congressional prohibition, while Northwestern farmers might hope that their numerical superiority over Southern slaveholders would enable them to win the territories for freedom.

The election of 1848. Meanwhile, as the debate over the territorial question dragged on, California and New Mexico were left without government, and the issue was injected into the Presidential campaign of 1848. President Polk had failed to unite the Democrats behind his Administration, and as the election approached the party was torn by factionalism. Calhoun led a group of Southern-rights men unwilling to accept anything less than his extreme position on slavery expansion. Martin Van Buren commanded a faction of disaffected New York Democrats, called the "Barnburners" (presumably because they would burn the barn to get rid of the rats), who had thirsted for revenge ever since Polk defeated Van Buren for the presidential nomination in 1844. Throughout the North, especially in the Northeast, groups of free-soil Democrats endorsed the Wilmot Proviso. When the Democratic convention met in Baltimore, the party leaders, having decided that a Northern candidate was essential, threw the nomination to Lewis Cass of Michigan, a colorless old party wheel horse whose opposition to the Wilmot Proviso and support of popular sovereignty would appease the Southern moderates. The platform praised Polk for his territorial acquisitions and domestic policies but was silent on the slavery question. As a result, the Barnburners and pro-Wilmot delegates left the convention prepared for revolt.

The Whigs, meeting in Philadelphia, again staked their chances on a military hero, General Zachary Taylor. Born in Virginia and now a Louisiana slaveholder, Taylor was expected to reassure Southern Whigs who had grown uneasy about the antislavery sentiments of Northern Whigs. Old Rough and Ready had spent his whole career in the regular army; he had neither political principles nor political experience — and, indeed, had discovered only recently that he was a Whig ("but not an ultra Whig"). After nominating Taylor on the fourth ballot, the convention tried to avoid controversy by writing no platform at all. But this surrender to expediency was more than the Northern Conscience Whigs could bear. Many of them decided that rather than support a slaveholder whose views were unknown and who was uncommitted to a platform they would bolt their party.

Antislavery leaders saw in the disgruntled Van Buren Barnburners, free-soil Democrats, Conscience Whigs, and political abolitionists the elements of a powerful third party, one that would take a firm stand on the territorial question and make a broader appeal than the Liberty party had made in the two preceding elections. In August 1848 delegates representing all these groups met in Buffalo, organized the Free-Soil party, and nominated Van Buren for President and Charles Francis Adams (a Conscience Whig, the son of John Quincy Adams) for Vice-President. The platform bluntly demanded that slavery be excluded from the territories and opposed any additional concessions to the Slave Power. It supported federal appropriations for internal improvements and the passage of a homestead act giving actual settlers free farms from the public domain. In a concluding statement the platform summarized the principles of the new party as "Free Soil, Free Speech, Free Labor, and Free Men." Among the Free-Soilers were numerous self-seeking politicians, but the organization also reflected much of the idealism of the antislavery crusade.

In spite of the intensity of feeling about the territorial question, the campaign itself was unexciting, the voters apathetic. Taylor defeated Cass by a small plurality in the popular vote (1,360,967 to 1,222,342) and by a majority of 36 in the Electoral College (163 to 127). The Free-Soil party failed to carry a single state, but its popular vote of 291,263 was impressive for a party organized less than three months before the election. A dozen Free-Soilers were elected to Congress, among them Ohio's new senator, Salmon P. Chase.

Taylor and the crisis. President Taylor was a man of honesty, integrity, and determination; he was capable of quick action, and he had a store of plain common sense. But these virtues were not sufficient to offset his limitations as chief executive in a time of crisis: his lack of training in politics and civil administration, his ignorance of public affairs — above all, his tendency to oversimplify complex problems. In

California gold rush, 1849.

a brief and vacuous inaugural address, he promised to devote his Administration "to the welfare of the whole country, and not to the support of any particular section or merely local interest." This pledge he tried conscientiously to fulfill; though he was a Southerner, he was a nationalist with no strong sectional loyalties.

When Taylor came into office, California and New Mexico, still lacking civil government, were being ruled by army officers directly responsible to the President. The settlers found this situation annoying under the best of circumstances, but it became intolerable soon after the discovery of gold in California. James Marshall had made the discovery in January 1848, along the American River about forty miles from Sutter's Fort; within six months San Francisco and other coastal towns were all but deserted as men rushed headlong to the "diggings" in the Sierra. By the end of 1848 the news had spread to the East, and during the next year some eighty thousand "fortyniners" came to California from the Mississippi Valley, from the Atlantic coast, and from Europe, Asia, and Australia. Most of them followed the overland trails across the continent, others took the easier but more expensive route by ship around Cape Horn, and still others risked death by taking a short-cut through the jungles of Panama. The miners dreamed of fortunes in gold as they worked the beds of streams with picks, shovels, and wash-pans; a few struck it rich, but most of them gained only modest returns from their backbreaking labor and their months of discomfort in primitive mining camps. Much of the gold ultimately found its way into the pockets of merchants in San Francisco and Sacramento, who in effect mined the miners by selling them supplies at exorbitant prices.

By the end of 1849 California's population had grown to one hundred thousand, and in the absence of civil government crime and violence were endemic in the cities and mining camps. With military authorities unable to restore law and order, with Congress seemingly paralyzed by the slavery issue, President Taylor decided to take matters into his own hands. As he saw it, there was a simple solution to the problem that had bedeviled Congress ever since the introduction of the Wilmot Proviso. He proposed to avoid the territorial issue by encouraging California and New Mexico to frame constitutions and apply for immediate admission to the Union as states. Californians wasted

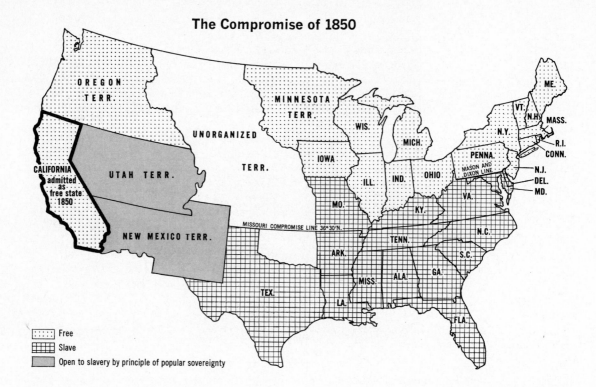

The Compromise of 1850

OREGON TERR.

MINNESOTA TERR.

UNORGANIZED TERR.

CALIFORNIA admitted as free state 1850

UTAH TERR.

NEW MEXICO TERR.

MISSOURI COMPROMISE LINE 36° 30'N.

ME.

VT. N.H. MASS.

N.Y. R.I. CONN.

WIS.

MICH.

IOWA

PENNA.

MASON AND DIXON LINE

ILL. IND. OHIO

N.J. DEL. MD.

VA.

MO. KY.

N.C.

TENN.

S.C.

ARK.

MISS. ALA. GA.

TEX.

LA.

FLA.

Free
Slave
Open to slavery by principle of popular sovereignty

no time in taking Taylor's advice; by October 1849 they had drafted and ratified a constitution prohibiting slavery, and soon after they elected state officers to whom the military gladly yielded its political authority. The people of New Mexico took more time, but by May 1850 they too had adopted a free-state constitution. Thus, when Congress met in December 1849, Taylor congratulated the country on the fact that the problem had been solved. All that remained was for Congress to admit California as a free state at once, and New Mexico as soon as it was ready.

The Compromise of 1850. Taylor had miscalculated. Rather than settling the matter, he helped precipitate one of the most bitter sectional debates in American history, one that carried the country dangerously close to disunion and civil war. Southerners denounced Taylor as an apostate and a tool of the abolitionists, while the followers of Calhoun vowed that they would break up the Union rather than see slavery excluded from California and New Mexico. Several other issues intensified the crisis: Texans and New Mexicans were on the verge of a private war over their common

boundary; abolitionists were gaining Northern support for their demand that slavery be abolished in the District of Columbia; and Southerners were clamoring for a more effective fugitive-slave law. Legislatures and mass meetings in both the North and the South adopted fiery resolutions, and violence threatened to break out in the halls of Congress. A Massachusetts convention of Democrats and Free-Soilers resolved that "we are opposed to slavery in every form and color, and in favor of freedom and free soil wherever man lives." Mississippi contributed to the atmosphere of crisis by issuing a call for a convention of the Southern states to meet at Nashville in June 1850. Many feared that the friends of Calhoun would use the convention to expedite Southern secession.

Moderates in both sections were convinced that nothing short of a comprehensive settlement of all outstanding issues could save the Union. And it was to Henry Clay, then in his seventy-third year and near the end of his long career, that lovers of the Union looked almost instinctively for a just and durable compromise. On January 29, 1850, Clay offered the Senate a series of resolutions proposing (1) that California be admitted as a free state; (2) that territorial governments be provided for the rest of the Mexican cession without any restriction on slavery; (3) that Texas abandon its claim to the eastern portion of New Mexico; (4) that the federal government compensate Texas by assuming the public debt Texas had contracted before annexation; (5) that the use of the District of Columbia as a depot in the interstate slave trade be prohibited; (6) that slavery in the District of Columbia be abolished only with the consent of its residents and of the state of Maryland and with compensation to the slaveholders; (7) that a new and more rigorous fugitive-slave act be adopted; and (8) that Congress declare that it had no power to interfere with the interstate slave trade. Among the many moderates who labored long and hard to secure the adoption of these compromise proposals, Stephen A. Douglas of Illinois was second only to Clay.

Congress debated the proposals for more than seven months, with the moderates under constant attack from both proslavery and anti-

slavery opponents of compromise. Clay opened the memorable debate in February. For two days he spoke in defense of his measures and urged mutual concessions for the sake of the Union. He asked Northerners why they insisted on the Wilmot Proviso when they had a stronger force working for them: "You have got nature itself on your side." He warned Southerners that they would gain nothing and lose a great deal by secession — that secession was certain to lead to civil war, "furious, bloody, implacable, exterminating." On March 4 John C. Calhoun, ill and close to death, listened to a colleague read his last address to the Senate. The present crisis, Calhoun insisted, was due to a breakdown of the old sectional equilibrium, to Northern aggression against the South, and to the destruction of the rights of the states and the creation of a consolidated government. Nothing could save the Union but an end of antislavery agitation, a faithful enforcement of the Fugitive Slave Law, equal rights for the South in the territories, and a constitutional amendment restoring the bal-

Webster and Clay: They loved the Union.

1850: John C. Calhoun

The Union cannot ... be saved by eulogies on the Union, however splendid or numerous. The cry of "Union, Union, the glorious Union!" can no more prevent disunion than the cry of "Health, health, glorious health!" on the part of the physician, can save a patient lying dangerously ill....

How can the Union be saved? There is but one way by which it can with any certainty; and that is, by a full and final settlement, on the principle of justice, of all the questions at issue between the two sections....

But can this be done? Yes, easily; not by the weaker party, for it can of itself do nothing — not even protect itself — but by the stronger. The North has only to will it to accomplish it — to do justice by conceding to the South an equal right in the acquired territory, and to do her duty by causing the stipulations relative to fugitive slaves to be faithfully fulfilled — to cease the agitation of the slave question, and to provide for the insertion of a provision in the Constitution, by an amendment, which will restore to the South, in substance, the power she possessed of protecting herself before the equilibrium between the sections was destroyed by the action of this Government....

If you, who represent the stronger portion, cannot agree to settle them on the broad principle of justice and duty, say so; and let the States we both represent agree to separate and part in peace. If you are unwilling we should part in peace, tell us so; and we shall know what to do, when you reduce the question to submission or resistance.

From John C. Calhoun, Speech in the Senate, March 4, 1850.

ance between the two sections. If these points were not conceded, if the South were forced to choose between "submission or resistance," it would know how to act.

On March 7, three days after Calhoun had sounded his grim protest against Clay's compromise, Daniel Webster delivered the last great oration of his career. To the dismay of his antislavery constituents, he repudiated his free-soil sentiments and announced that he would speak "not as a Massachusetts man, nor as a northern man, but as an American." Though Webster refuted Calhoun's charges against the North, his speech was clearly an attempt to make the compromise palatable to his own section. He denounced antislavery agitation, urged Northerners not to insist on the Wilmot Proviso when slavery would not expand into the new territories in any case, called for an end to resistance to the Fugitive Slave Act, and concluded with a tearful plea for the Union. Webster's speech immensely strengthened the forces of compromise, but for the remaining two years of his life antislavery men vilified him for his apostasy. Most of the Northern Conscience Whigs stood firm. Senator William H. Seward of New York spoke for them when he denounced compromise as "radically wrong and essentially vicious." There was only one way to end antislavery agitation, he said, and that was by "yielding to the progress of emancipation." In reply to Calhoun's constitutional defense of the right to carry slaves into the territories, Seward appealed to "a higher law than the Constitution," a divine law that intended these rich lands to be enjoyed by free men.

As the debate wore on and the House and Senate considered numerous variations of Clay's proposals, it became increasingly evident that opinion in favor of a compromise of some kind was steadily building up in both North and South. Northern businessmen, frightened by the talk of secession, favored a compromise in order to protect their Southern trade and investments. The country had recovered from the depression of the 1840's, and practical men longed for a political peace so that they could make the most of a new era of prosperity and economic growth. The compromisers were further strengthened when the moderates won control of the Southern convention at Nashville and indicated that they were ready to accept a fair settlement. Now the most formidable obstacle to compromise was President Taylor, who bitterly resented Clay's rejection of the Administration's recommendations on New Mexico and California in favor of proposals of his own. The possibility of a presidential veto loomed until Taylor's sudden death on July 9 after an attack of cholera morbus. His successor, Vice-President Millard Fillmore, though a New York Whig of free-soil proclivities, immediately allied himself with Webster and Clay and used his influence in favor of compromise.

Even then the adoption of a compromise was not easy. When Clay's major proposals had been combined in an "omnibus bill," they were threatened with defeat by a combination of Free-Soilers, antislavery Whigs, and Southern-rights men. But the moderates discovered that each of the measures might be enacted separately, for the moderates could then combine with those who opposed the compromise as a whole but favored individual parts of it. In the final weeks of the battle, Senator Douglas replaced the exhausted Clay as leader of the compromisers, and by September 1850 all the measures had been passed and signed by President Fillmore. The Compromise of 1850 as it was finally adopted was essentially like the one Clay had proposed the January before: California was admitted as a free state; the territories of New Mexico and Utah were created from the rest of the Mexican cession, with no restriction on slavery; the Texas boundary was fixed as it exists today; Texas was paid $10 million from the federal treasury as compensation for yielding to New Mexico in their boundary dispute; slave-trading was prohibited in the District of Columbia; and a more severe fugitive-slave act replaced the old one of 1793.

1850: Daniel Webster

I wish to speak to-day, not as a Massachusetts man, nor as a northern man, but as an American, and a member of the Senate of the United States.... I speak to-day for the preservation of the Union. "Hear me for my cause"....

In the excited times in which we live, there is found to exist a state of crimination and recrimination between the North and South. There are lists of grievances produced by each....

I should much prefer to have heard, from every member of this floor, declarations of opinion that this Union could never be dissolved, than the declaration of opinion that in any case, under the pressure of circumstances, such a dissolution was possible. I hear with pain, and anguish, and distress, the word secession....

Instead of speaking of the possibility or utility of secession, instead of dwelling in these caverns of darkness ... let us come out into the light of day.... Let us cherish those hopes which belong to us.... Let us make our generation one of the strongest, and brightest links in that golden chain which is destined, I fully believe, to grapple the people of all the States to this Constitution, for ages to come.

From Daniel Webster, Seventh of March Speech, 1850.

THE AFTERMATH

Public reaction to the compromise. Few Northerners or Southerners were altogether satisfied with the Compromise of 1850, and some in each section spurned it as an unclean thing. Abolitionists and Free-Soilers refused to be bound by its terms and denounced as unprincipled tools of the Slave Power the Northern congressmen who had voted for it. Emerson publicly declared that no man could obey the new Fugitive Slave Law "without loss of self-respect and forfeiture of the name of a gentleman." In 1851 the Massachusetts legislature delivered a stern rebuke to Webster (who had joined Fillmore's Cabinet as Secretary of State) by electing Charles Sumner, a radical Free-Soiler and enemy of the compromise, to the United States Senate.

In the South, "fire-eaters" like Robert Barnwell Rhett of South Carolina and William L. Yancey of Alabama termed the compromise a fatal defeat for their section and called for drastic action. The position of the South in the Union was now hopeless, they said, and the proper remedy was immediate secession. In South Carolina the secessionists were defeated with the greatest difficulty, and then only because the "moderates" insisted that action be delayed until other Southern states were ready for independence. A state convention in Georgia adopted a series of resolutions, known as the Georgia Platform, that were probably an accurate expression of public opinion in the Deep South. These resolutions accepted the Compromise of 1850 but warned that Georgia would resist, "even (as a last resort) to a disruption of every tie which binds her to the Union," any act abolishing slavery in the District of Columbia, refusing to admit a slave state, excluding slavery from the territories, or repealing the Fugitive Slave Law.

But most Americans in both sections, though doubting the wisdom of some provisions of the compromise, accepted it with great relief and hoped for a respite from sectional agitation.

Mass meetings throughout the country celebrated its passage, and the merchants of New York City formed a Union Safety Committee to mobilize public opinion in its defense. Stephen A. Douglas announced that he had resolved "never to make another speech on the slavery question. . . . Let us cease agitating, stop the debate, and drop the subject." In his annual message of December 1850 President Fillmore told Congress that he regarded the compromise measures as "a final settlement of the dangerous and exciting subjects which they embraced." And forty-four congressmen of both parties signed a pledge to respect the terms of the compromise and never to support a candidate for public office who threatened to disturb it.

Franklin Pierce. The presidential election of 1852 gave further evidence of the widespread hope that the Compromise of 1850 would in fact be a "final settlement." The Democrats adopted a platform that endorsed the compromise without qualification and promised to resist "agitation of the slavery question, under whatever shape or color the attempt may be made." After many futile ballots the convention dropped the leading candidates — Douglas, Cass, and James Buchanan of Pennsylvania — and nominated another "dark horse," Franklin Pierce of New Hampshire. The Whig party, with its Northern and Southern wings now almost hopelessly divided, wrangled over a platform that unenthusiastically "acquiesced in" the compromise and therefore pleased almost no one. The convention rejected Fillmore and turned to another military hero, General Winfield Scott of Virginia, whose friendship with Seward and whose failure to endorse the compromise made him suspect in the South. The election dealt a crushing blow to the Whig party — a blow from which it never recovered. Though Pierce's popular majority was not overwhelming, he carried twenty-seven states with 254 electoral votes, while Scott carried only four states with 42 electoral votes. The Barnburners had returned to the Democratic fold, and the Free-Soil party, with John P. Hale of New Hampshire as its candidate, polled only about half as many votes as it had four years earlier.

Pierce was a Jacksonian Democrat of amiable disposition, modest talent, and almost no capacity for executive leadership. His close ties with Southern Democrats, especially with his Secretary of War, Jefferson Davis, and his sympathy for their views on questions of public policy caused antislavery leaders to damn him as a "doughface" — "a northern man with southern principles." But his promise in his inaugural address that the provisions of the Compromise of 1850 would be "unhesitatingly carried into effect" suited the popular mood. In his first message to Congress, in December 1853, Pierce rejoiced that the recent compromise had "given renewed vigor to our institutions and restored a sense of repose and security to the public mind." With the country prospering, with the sectional issues hopefully disposed of, some optimists went so far as to predict a new era of good feelings.

Surviving sources of friction. But very soon there were abundant signs that the truce would be short. The disintegration of the Whig party after its defeat in 1852 snapped another of the ties holding the Union together. The admission of California had upset the sectional balance in the Senate — prior to 1850 there had been fifteen slave and fifteen free states — and the admission of several more free states could not be long delayed. The immigrants who poured into the United States during the 1840's and 1850's (see p. 305) shunned the South and thus further increased the North's numerical majority, and railroad-building and industrial expansion gave the North an accelerating economic supremacy. Now secessionists could argue that the rights and interests of the minority South were at the mercy of a hostile and overbearing North.

To Southern-rights men the controversy that began at once over the enforcement of the new Fugitive Slave Act proved their point. This provision of the Compromise of 1850 was the one Southerners regarded as their principal gain and the one Northerners found most difficult to accept. It was a harsh measure that subjected alleged fugitives to summary hearings before federal commissioners without trial by jury or the right to testify in their own behalf. Since a commissioner received a fee of $10 if he ruled that a Negro prisoner was a slave but only $5 if he ruled that the Negro was free, abolitionists charged that the commissioners were being bribed to collaborate with kid-

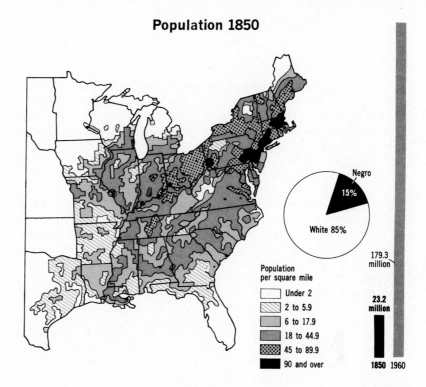

Population
per square mile

☐ Under 2
▨ 2 to 5.9
▦ 6 to 17.9
▦ 18 to 44.9
▦ 45 to 89.9
■ 90 and over

napers who sought to sell free Negroes back into slavery. In the Northern strongholds of antislavery sentiment the new law simply could not be enforced; during the 1850's abolitionists executed a series of dramatic rescues of fugitives and sent them on to Canada and freedom. Moreover, various Northern states passed personal-liberty laws that nullified the Fugitive Slave Act or at least interfered with its enforcement. This was an assertion of state rights and a form of nullification that Southerners scarcely appreciated.

Above all, the Compromise of 1850 could not stop the pens or quiet the voices of the abolitionists. Indeed, less than two years after the compromise was passed the most eloquent and influential appeal in behalf of the slave ever to be written appeared in Harriet Beecher Stowe's justly celebrated novel, *Uncle Tom's Cabin*. Mrs. Stowe was the daughter of a New England clergyman, sister of seven others, and wife of still another. Her anger over the Fugitive Slave Act prompted her to declare: "I will write something. I will if I live." First published serially in an antislavery weekly, her novel appeared in book form in March 1852.

By the end of the year, three hundred thousand copies had been sold. Thereafter the novel, together with its various adaptations for the stage, won thousands of converts to the antislavery cause. *Uncle Tom's Cabin* has more than a few flaws as a piece of literature: its situations are contrived; its dialogue is unreal; its slaves are romanticized. Mrs. Stowe knew almost nothing of slavery firsthand, but she understood clearly its tragic aspects; moreover, she had the wisdom to direct her moral indictment against the institution itself rather than against the Southern men and women who were caught in its toils. Indeed, the chief villain of her plot, the cruel overseer Simon Legree, was Northern born. But these subtleties made the book no more attractive to Southern slaveholders than the cruder forms of abolitionist propaganda.

Slavery, then, still threatened the nation's peace and unity. On the eve of the Civil War Abraham Lincoln wrote to Alexander H. Stephens of Georgia: "You think slavery is right and ought to be extended, while we think it is *wrong* and ought to be restricted. That I suppose is the rub."

SUGGESTIONS FOR READING

Westward to the Pacific

Among the surveys of the westward movement, R. A. Billington, *Westward Expansion* (rev. ed., 1967), is especially good on American penetration of the Far West. General coverage of the diplomacy of expansion is provided in S. F. Bemis, *A Diplomatic History of the United States* (rev. ed., 1955); T. A. Bailey, *A Diplomatic History of the American People* (6th ed., 1958); J. W. Pratt, *A History of United States Foreign Policy* (1955); and Alexander DeConde, *A History of American Foreign Policy* (1963). The best books dealing comprehensively with expansion in this period are R. A. Billington, *The Far Western Frontier, 1830–1860** (1956), and J. A. Hawgood, *America's Western Frontiers* (1967). N. A. Graebner, *Empire on the Pacific* (1955), stresses the desire for Pacific ports as a motive for expansion. A. K. Weinberg, *Manifest Destiny** (1935), is an excellent analysis of the ideology of expansionism. Frederick Merk has written two important books on the motivation and rationalization of expansionism: *Manifest Destiny and Mission in American History: A Reinterpretation** (1963), and *The Monroe Doctrine and American Expansionism; 1843–1849* (1966). H. N. Smith, *Virgin Land** (1950), brilliantly analyzes the place of the West in American literature and thought.

The two basic works on the American occupation of Texas are E. C. Barker, *Mexico and Texas, 1821–1835* (1928), and W. C. Binkley, *The Texas Revolution* (1952). A good popular account of the Santa Fe trade is R. L. Duffus, *The Santa Fe Trail* (1930). The best introductions to the fur trade of the Far West are H. M. Chittenden, *The American Fur Trade of the Far West*, 3 vols. (rev. ed., 1935); R. G. Cleland, *This Reckless Breed of Men: The Trappers and Fur Traders of the Southwest* (1950); D. L. Morgan, *Jedediah Smith and the Opening of the West** (1953); P. C. Phillips, *The Fur Trade*, 2 vols. (1961); and G. G. Cline, *Exploring the Great Basin* (1963). Missionary activity in Oregon can be studied in two competent biographies: C. J. Brosnan, *Jason Lee: Prophet of the New Oregon* (1932), and C. M. Drury, *Marcus Whitman: M.D., Pioneer and Martyr* (1937). Two books on the overland trails, reliable and well written, are W. J. Ghent, *The Road to Oregon* (1929), and Jay Monaghan, *The Overland Trail* (1937). A superb contemporary account, Francis Parkman, *The California and Oregon Trail* (1849), is available in several modern editions under the title *The Oregon Trail*.* The American occupation of Oregon is treated adequately in R. C. Clark, *History of the Willamette Valley, Oregon*, 3 vols. (1927), and O. O. Winther, *The Great Northwest* (1947). Early American interest in California is covered in three general histories: J. W. Caughey, *California* (1940); R. G. Cleland, *From Wilderness to Empire: A History of California, 1542–1900* (1944); and A. F. Rolle, *California: A History* (1963). Wallace Stegner, *The Gathering of Zion: The Story of the Mormon Trail.* (1964), is an excellent account of the Mormon migration. The best history of the Mormon settlement in the Salt Lake basin is Nels Anderson, *Desert Saints: The Mormon Frontier in Utah** (1942). F. M. Brodie, *No Man Knows My History: The Life of Joseph Smith* (1945), is an outstanding biography. Preston Nibley, *Brigham Young: The Man and His Work* (1936), is warmly sympathetic.

Polk and the Triumph of Manifest Destiny

The authoritative study of the election of 1844 and the first two years of the Polk Administration is Charles Sellers, *James K. Polk: Continentalist, 1843–1846* (1966). Polk's presidential years can also be studied in E. I. McCormac, *James K. Polk* (1922), and in Allan Nevins, ed., *Polk: The Diary of a President, 1845–1849* (1952). A lively and readable introduction to the expansionism of the Polk era is Bernard De Voto, *The Year of Decision, 1846** (1943). Two books deal with negotiations for the annexation of Texas: J. H. Smith, *The Annexation of Texas* (1911), and

---

* Available in a paperback edition.

J. W. Schmitz, *Texan Statecraft, 1836–1845* (1945). M. C. Jacobs, *Winning Oregon* (1938), is a good summary of the Oregon dispute and its settlement. The standard works on the background of the Mexican War are J. S. Reeves, *American Diplomacy under Tyler and Polk* (1907), and G. L. Rives, *The United States and Mexico, 1821–1848*, 2 vols. (1913).

The fullest and most authoritative work on the Mexican War is J. H. Smith, *The War with Mexico*, 2 vols. (1919). Three later books contribute few fresh interpretations but are brief and readable: A. H. Bill, *Rehearsal for Conflict: The War with Mexico, 1846–1848* (1947); R. S. Henry, *The Story of the Mexican War* (1950); and O. A. Singletary, *The Mexican War** (1960). The military campaigns are traced in two excellent biographies: C. W. Elliott, *Winfield Scott* (1937), and Holman Hamilton, *Zachary Taylor: Soldier of the Republic* (1941). Allan Nevins, *Frémont: Pathmarker of the West* (1955), is valuable for military operations in California.

Crisis and Compromise

Allan Nevins, *Ordeal of the Union*, 2 vols. (1947), contains a full, incisive, and well-written account of the issue of slavery expansion and of the Compromise of 1850. Other useful works include T. C. Smith, *The Liberty and Free-Soil Parties in the Northwest* (1897); J. M. White, *The Secession Movement in the United States, 1847–1852* (1916); R. H. Shryock, *Georgia and the Union in 1850* (1926); J. T. Carpenter, *The South as a Conscious Minority* (1930); and A. O. Craven, *The Growth of Southern Nationalism, 1848–1861* (1953). The election of 1848 and the Taylor Administration are treated thoroughly in two good biographies: Brainerd Dyer, *Zachary Taylor* (1946), and Holman Hamilton, *Zachary Taylor: Soldier in the White House* (1951).

Of the many books on the California gold rush, the following are among the best: R. W. Paul, *California Gold: The Beginning of Mining in the Far West** (1947); J. W. Caughey, *Gold Is the Cornerstone* (1948); O. C. Coy, *The Great Trek* (1931); A. B. Hulbert, *Forty-Niners* (1931); and J. H. Jackson, *Anybody's Gold: The Story of California's Mining Towns* (1941).

The best study of the Compromise of 1850 is Holman Hamilton, *Prologue to Conflict: The Crisis and Compromise of 1850** (1964). The crisis and Compromise can also be studied through the numerous biographies of national political leaders. Among the most useful are: C. B. Going, *David Wilmot, Free-Soiler* (1924); W. Y. Thompson, *Robert Toombs of Georgia* (1966); Frederic Bancroft, *The Life of William H. Seward*, 2 vols. (1900); F. B. Woodford, *Lewis Cass: The Last Jeffersonian* (1950); G. F. Milton, *The Eve of Conflict: Stephen A. Douglas and the Needless War* (1934); G. M. Capers, *Stephen A. Douglas: Defender of the Union* (1959); C. M. Fuess, *Daniel Webster*, 2 vols. (1930); R. N. Current, *Daniel Webster and the Rise of National Conservatism** (1955); G. G. Van Deusen, *The Life of Henry Clay** (1937) and *Thurlow Weed: Wizard of the Lobby* (1947); J. H. Parks, *John Bell of Tennessee* (1950); Rudolph Von Abele, *Alexander H. Stephens: A Biography* (1946); and C. M. Wiltse, *John C. Calhoun: Sectionalist, 1840–1850* (1951).

* Available in a paperback edition.

12
America at Mid-Century

From the Mexican War to the Civil War the major political themes in the history of the United States were sectional conflict and national disintegration. But this period was also notable for the burgeoning of the American economy and for the quality of American literature. The first writers to win more than local recognition — Washington Irving and James Fenimore Cooper — had exploited American themes, but they had spent much of their lives abroad and had observed the conventions of Europe's men of letters. Indeed, Cooper had little confidence in the future of literature in America: "There is scarcely an ore which contributes to the wealth of the author, that is found, here, in veins as rich as in Europe."

In the 1840's and 1850's, however, American writers began to heed Emerson's advice to stop imitating the "courtly muses of Europe" and to produce a distinctive literature of their own. "Our day of dependence . . . draws to a close," exulted Emerson. "The millions that around us are rushing into life, cannot always be fed on the sere remains of foreign harvests. Events, actions arise, that must be sung, that will sing themselves." Theodore Parker maintained that an American literature would be an inevitable product of American democracy, "for we are not always to be pensioners of other lands, doing nothing but import and quote."

Accordingly, the essays of Emerson and Thoreau marked a turning away from Europe, a trend still more apparent in the novels of Nathaniel Hawthorne and Herman Melville and in the poetry of Walt Whitman. These writers gave this age of distinguished American literature its finest expression. Their masterpieces — Hawthorne's *The Scarlet Letter* (1850), Melville's *Moby Dick* (1851), Thoreau's *Walden* (1854), and the first edition of Whitman's *Leaves of Grass* (1855) — conveyed the best spirit of America at mid-century to a limited but appreciative audience of educated men and women. That audience, of course, has constantly grown, for the great works of the "American Renaissance" combine a nobility of expression and aspiration that invigorates each successive generation of American readers.

The mass of Americans, however, were during the 1850's too busy with practical affairs to

"Getting things done."

give much time to literature; they seldom thought about the philosophical questions that worried Hawthorne and Melville — the nature of man and the source of evil — for there was work to do. They were occupied with ships and railroads and machines and farm implements, with the settlement and development of the West, and with geographic expansion and Manifest Destiny. Stephen A. Douglas, energetic and tough-minded, idol of a bumptious element in the Democratic party that called itself Young America, cared little for literature, less for the moral issue of slavery. In the early 1850's Douglas struck a popular note when he urged his countrymen to forget the sectional quarrel and turn to the main business of building a prosperous and powerful nation. Young America was, to be sure, concerned about its soul, but it was concerned even more about getting things done.

INTIMATIONS OF IMPERIALISM

In his inaugural address President Pierce served notice that the acquisition of Oregon, California, and New Mexico was not the complete fulfillment of his country's Manifest Destiny. There were other areas that circumstances might force the United States to acquire, and Pierce announced that his Administration would not shrink from further expansion because of "any timid forebodings of evil." In part he was expressing the continuing belief that eventually all or part of Canada and the rest of Mexico would be annexed to share the blessings of American democracy. But by mid-century some expansionists were looking beyond these adjacent territories to Cuba, Central America, and Hawaii, where commercial and strategic considerations fortified the hunger for land. This was a sign that Manifest Destiny might easily be converted into a doctrine of imperialism.

Cuba. The Spanish colony of Cuba, a land of slaves and plantations, interested Southerners who hoped to acquire it in order to increase their political and economic power. Cuba also attracted certain Northern commercial interests, especially a small but active group of business-speculators in New York. Moreover, its proximity to Florida and its commanding position at the mouth of the Caribbean Sea and the Gulf of Mexico gave it great strategic importance. The United States had always been apprehensive about the possibility that Cuba might pass from Spain to a stronger power. As early as 1810 President Madison had warned that his country "could not be a satisfied spectator" if Cuba were to fall to some European government "which might make a fulcrum of that position against the security and commerce of the United States."

Until the 1840's the chief aim of American diplomacy had been merely to keep Cuba out of the hands of Britain and France. After the Mexican War, however, proannexation sentiment became so strong that the government changed its policy. In 1848 James Buchanan, Polk's Secretary of State, instructed the American minister at Madrid to offer as much as $100 million for Cuba. The Spanish government responded with a cold refusal; indeed, the foreign minister vowed that he would sooner see the island sunk in the ocean than sold.

Failing to gain Cuba by diplomacy, some expansionists (mostly Southerners) were ready to try force. In 1848 General Narciso López, a Venezuelan adventurer, appeared in New Orleans to find arms and recruits for a filibustering expedition against Cuba. The next year, in spite of federal attempts to stop him, López invaded the island with two hundred fifty volunteers, mostly Mexican War veterans, but Spanish troops quickly repulsed them. In 1851 López tried again with a force of four hundred men, but once more he was defeated; this time Spanish authorities executed him and fifty other captives as pirates. Disappointed sympathizers in New Orleans retaliated by destroying the Spanish consulate, and the American and Spanish governments exchanged angry notes. Eventually the United States paid an indemnity for the damage committed by the New Orleans mob, and Spain pardoned the rest of the captured filibusters. But the government did not disavow its interest in Cuba; indeed, it rejected a British and French proposal for a tripartite agreement designed to assure the island's continued possession by Spain.

The Pierce Administration made the acquisition of Cuba one of its chief goals. It sent Pierre Soulé of Louisiana, a flamboyant French exile and ardent expansionist, as minister to Spain, and it gave him cause to believe that his mission was to acquire the island regardless of methods. Secretary of State William L. Marcy authorized Soulé to renew the attempt to purchase Cuba, this time for $130 million; failing in this, he might try to "detach" it from Spain by intrigue. Lacking the most elementary qualifications of a diplomat, the impetuous minister soon engaged in a bitter dispute with the Spanish government. In February 1854 an American merchant vessel, the *Black Warrior*, was seized at Havana for a technical violation of Spanish customs laws. Soulé promptly demanded a disavowal of the act and an indemnity; when he received no immediate reply, he renewed his demands in the form of a virtual ultimatum. The Spanish foreign minister simply ignored Soulé and negotiated a settlement directly with Washington and with the owners of the *Black Warrior*.

At this point Soulé might well have been replaced by a more skillful minister. Instead,

Marcy showed no outward sign of disapproval and gave him an even more delicate assignment. Soulé was to confer with John Y. Mason, minister to France, and James Buchanan, minister to Great Britain, about methods of acquiring Cuba and of dealing with possible British and French opposition. In October 1854 the three ministers met for a few days at Ostend and then for a week at Aix-la-Chapelle. They sent their recommendations to the Secretary of State in a confidential memorandum, but its contents were soon known to the public — and the document itself was quite inaccurately named the Ostend Manifesto. Largely the work of Soulé, the memorandum declared that the United States would benefit from the possession of Cuba, while Spain would be better off without it. Accordingly, it proposed that another effort be made to purchase the island. If Spain again refused to sell, the United States would have to consider whether Cuba was a threat to her internal peace. If it were found to be such a threat, "then by every law human and divine, we shall be justified in wresting it from Spain, if we possess the power."

The Ostend Manifesto delighted Southern expansionists and the Young America element in the Democratic party, and it played no small part in Buchanan's presidential nomination two years later. But the criticism from abroad and the indignation of antislavery Northerners forced the Pierce Administration to repudiate it. Marcy sent a strong rebuke to Soulé, and the shocked and humiliated minister resigned. But Cuba was not forgotten; the Democratic platform of 1856 favored annexation, and in three of his annual messages to Congress President Buchanan urged another attempt to purchase it. Cuba, however, had become a sectional issue, and any further action was impossible.

Central America. For centuries men had dreamed of joining the Atlantic and Pacific by cutting a canal through Panama or Nicaragua, but the United States did not become seriously interested in the idea until after the Mexican War and the acquisition of California. In 1846 the need for faster communication between the East and the Far West led to the signing of a treaty with New Granada (Colombia), which gave the United States transit rights through Panama in exchange for a guarantee of New

---

Individualism: Thoreau

The authority of government ... must have the sanction and consent of the governed. It can have no pure right over my person and property but what I concede to it. The progress from an absolute to a limited monarchy, from a limited monarchy to a democracy, is a progress toward a true respect for the individual. Is a democracy, such as we know it, the last improvement possible in government? Is it not possible to take a step further towards recognizing and organizing the rights of man? There will never be a really free and enlightened State, until the State comes to recognize the individual as a higher and independent power, from which all its own power and authority are derived, and treats him accordingly. I please myself with imagining a State at last which can afford to be just to all men, and to treat the individual with respect as a neighbor; which even would not think it inconsistent with its own repose, if a few were to live aloof from it, not meddling with it, nor embraced by it, who fulfilled all the duties of neighbors and fellow-men. A State which bore this kind of fruit, and suffered it to drop off as fast as it ripened, would prepare the way for a still more perfect and glorious State, which also I have imagined, but not anywhere seen.

From Henry David Thoreau, *Essay on Civil Disobedience*, 1849.

Granada's sovereignty over this isthmian province. By 1855 a group of American promoters had built a railroad across Panama; until the completion of the first transcontinental railroad in 1869, this was the easiest route to the Pacific coast.

Meanwhile, American diplomats, speculators, and adventurers had become deeply involved in the affairs of the small and politically unstable Republic of Nicaragua, which seemed as promising a site for a canal as Panama. Here, however, the Americans met a formidable competitor in Great Britain, whose worldwide trade, large navy, and extensive colonial possessions gave her a keen interest in an isthmian canal. Indeed, because of the enormous cost of such a project, many assumed that when a canal was built, British capitalists would finance and control it. The British government, watching American movements suspiciously, established a foothold at the mouth of the San

Juan River (the probable eastern terminus of a Nicaraguan canal) and claimed a protectorate over the Mosquito Indians on the eastern coast of Nicaragua. This action alarmed the American government, and in the resulting diplomatic exchanges each country warned that it would not permit the other to have exclusive control over an isthmian canal. In 1850 the dispute was settled when Sir Henry Lytton Bulwer, the British minister to the United States, and John M. Clayton, President Taylor's Secretary of State, agreed to the terms of a treaty. It provided, first, that any canal built through Panama or Nicaragua was to be unfortified, neutral in time of war, and open to the ships of all countries on equal terms; second, that neither country was to colonize or establish dominion over any part of Central America.

The Clayton-Bulwer Treaty was ratified by the Senate and remained in force for the next half-century, but it was unpopular from the start. Expansionists disliked the commitment not to acquire territory in Central America which meant, they said, that the United States had voluntarily applied the Monroe Doctrine against itself. This concession, together with the implicit recognition that Britain had equal interests in Central America, provoked critics to accuse Clayton of having been outwitted by Bulwer — Buchanan suggested that Clayton ought to be rewarded with elevation to the British peerage. Resentment increased when the British government maintained that the treaty applied only to the future and was not an obligation to abandon its existing protectorate over the eastern coast of Nicaragua. Impulsive Southern expansionists applauded when, in 1855, William Walker, a Tennesseean by birth, led a filibustering expedition into Nicaragua and seized control of her government. Walker was soon driven out, and when he tried to return in 1860 he was captured and executed.

In spite of the criticism, the Clayton-Bulwer Treaty was not a bad bargain for the United States, given the circumstances of the time. The British government removed one cause of complaint when in 1859 it voluntarily gave up its protectorate over the Mosquito Indians. Then and later the treaty avoided a race between the two countries for possessions in Central America. Above all, it assured the United States equal access to an isthmian canal at a time when she was in no position to ask for more.

Hawaii. Even before the acquisition of Oregon and California made the United States a Pacific power, some Americans had developed an interest in Hawaii. Merchantmen engaged in trade with the Far East, and whaling ships, had stopped there for supplies; by the 1830's missionaries had begun to arrive; other Americans had come in search of land or commercial opportunities. In these early years there was little talk of annexation, but the government was uneasy about the intentions of the British and the French. In 1849, when France seemed ready to seize the islands, Secretary of State Clayton, though denying that the United States desired to establish her sovereignty over them, warned that she "could never with indifference allow them to pass under the dominion or exclusive control of any other power." The Pierce Administration, however, pursued a more aggressive policy; in 1854 Secretary of State Marcy negotiated a treaty of annexation with the Hawaiian government. But British protests and Senate opposition caused Pierce to drop the matter. Thereafter, until the 1880's, the United States seemed content merely to keep Hawaii free from foreign control.

The Gadsden Purchase. The only tangible result of the various expansionist schemes of the 1850's was the purchase from Mexico of another slice of land in the Southwest. In 1853 the War Department made a survey of possible routes for a transcontinental railroad. The survey revealed that if a line were to be built westward from a Southern city it would probably have to enter Mexican territory south of the Gila River. Realizing that this would be an effective argument for a Northern route, Secretary of War Jefferson Davis persuaded President Pierce to send James Gadsden, a Southern railroad-promoter, to negotiate with Mexico. When Gadsden arrived in Mexico City, he found Santa Anna back in power and in need of money. In 1853 they signed a treaty giving the United States a forty-five-thousand-square-mile strip of desert land below the Gila for $10 million. Except for Alaska, the Gadsden Purchase rounded out the continental frontiers of the United States.

INTERNATIONAL TRADE

Europe. American merchants and shipowners recovered only slowly from the disasters they had suffered during the War of 1812, and they were severely hurt again by the long depression following the Panic of 1837. By the mid-1840's however, economic recovery and several other favorable developments combined to encourage a revival of foreign trade. The repeal of the British Corn Laws in 1846 opened a large market for American wheat; the passage of the low Walker Tariff the same year (followed by a still lower tariff in 1857) encouraged the flow of European manufactured goods to the United States; and a spectacular rise in immigration kept American ships filled to capacity on the homeward voyage. As a result, the combined value of American exports and imports increased from $222 million in 1840 to $318 million in 1850; during the next decade they more than doubled, to reach $687 million in 1860.

More than two-thirds of this commerce was with Europe, and the most valuable part of it was the exchange of American cotton, wheat, and flour for the products of British factories. In 1860 finished manufactured goods constituted only 10 per cent of United States exports but nearly half of her imports. As is typical of an agricultural country, the value of imports usually exceeded the value of exports — by $29 million in 1850. This unfavorable trade balance forced the United States to send a large part of the gold mined in California to Europe. Nevertheless, foreign trade was vital to the whole national economy. Though Americans still concentrated on their own internal development, they were bound to the outside world by important commercial ties.

China. As late as 1860 scarcely more than 5 per cent of American trade was with Asia. Ever since the late eighteenth century, however, many New York and New England merchants had been dazzled by the profits they anticipated from the penetration of Far Eastern markets. As we have seen, their hope of developing this trade was related to the desire for ports on the Pacific coast. By the early nineteenth century, American merchant ships were stopping in the Philippines, Java, and India, and in 1833 the United States signed a trade treaty with Siam. But the center of activity was at Canton, the one Chinese port open to foreigners, where furs were traded for tea, spices, and nankeens.

Though the United States government never took the initiative in wringing commercial concessions from China, it always capitalized on opportunities afforded by the encroachments of others. When Britain, after the Opium War of 1839–42, forced open several additional Chinese ports and gained various other advantages, American merchants demanded that their government intervene in their behalf. President Tyler responded by sending Caleb Cushing of Massachusetts, a man of rare diplomatic talent, to negotiate with China. In the Treaty of Wanghia (1844) Cushing won access to the ports that had been opened to the British; he established the right of extraterritoriality, which enabled resident Americans accused of crimes to be tried in American rather than Chinese courts; and he obtained a promise of "most favored nation" treatment for the United States, whereby privileges granted to other powers would also be granted to her. In subsequent years, as the British and French forced China to make further concessions, American merchants were thus able to claim similar rights. Since the United States merely asked to be given what others had seized by force, however, relations with China remained friendly.

Japan. From the sixteenth century to the middle of the nineteenth century Japan's only contact with the outside world had been a limited trade with the Dutch East India Company through the port of Nagasaki. The military Shoguns, who dominated the weak emperors, had excluded foreign merchants, missionaries, and diplomats in order to preserve a feudal society. But during the 1840's some Americans began to take an interest in Japan. The Pacific whaling industry needed a treaty to assure proper treatment of shipwrecked sailors cast upon Japanese shores; merchants engaged in the China trade hoped to make Japan a port of call; and textile-manufacturers were eager to exploit the Japanese market.

In 1852 pressure from these groups caused President Fillmore to send Commodore Matthew C. Perry to Japan with an imposing fleet of steam warships. Perry bore a letter and gifts to the emperor and an array of gadgets illustrating the wonders of Western civilization. In July 1853 he arrived at Yedo Bay, insisted that his letter be delivered to the emperor, and promised to return in the spring. Perry made his second visit early in 1854 and found Japanese officials conciliatory and ready to negotiate. By combining vague threats of war with skillful diplomacy, he secured a treaty of friendship that opened two small ports to American trade, permitted the establishment of a consulate at one of them, guaranteed the safety of shipwrecked sailors, and gave the United States "most favored nation" treatment. Other Western powers soon negotiated their own treaties and forced Japan to open other ports and make additional concessions.

The State Department sent Townsend Harris, a brilliant diplomat, to Japan as the first American consul. Pointing to the fate of China under foreign domination, Harris assured Japan that the United States had no territorial ambitions and urged her to protect herself by

modernizing and Westernizing under American guidance. "If you accept my proposals," he predicted, "Japan will become the England of the Orient." His case was persuasive, and in 1858 he signed another treaty greatly enlarging the concessions that Perry had won. Ministers were now to be exchanged; American consuls could reside at the six ports then open to foreigners; American citizens could buy property and enjoy freedom of religion at the so-called treaty ports; and Japan could buy warships and merchantmen from the United States. In 1860 the first Japanese diplomatic delegation visited Washington, and soon thereafter Japan began to make rapid strides toward catching up with the modern world.

The clipper ships. The recovery of American foreign trade was immensely aided by a series of dramatic changes in the design of the old three-masted packet ships (see p. 216), changes that produced a fleet of the swiftest and most beautiful sailing vessels ever to engage in ocean commerce. In 1845 the *Rainbow*, a seven-

The clipper ship: Triumph of American practical art.

hundred-fifty-ton ship designed by John Griffith, a naval architect, was completed; it had a long, sleek hull with a concave bow, convex sides, and a rounded stern, and tall masts with an enormous spread of canvas. The launching of the *Rainbow*, a ship that incorporated the advances of several decades, marked the beginning of the era of the famed clipper ships.

Among the builders of clippers, Donald McKay, of Newburyport, Massachusetts, was the most successful; his yards produced scores of vessels, including the 1,783-ton *Flying Cloud*, the 2,421-ton *Sovereign of the Seas*, and the 4,000-ton *Great Republic*. Commanded by daring, hard-driving captains, these ships broke all records for speed. In 1851, on her maiden voyage, the *Flying Cloud* covered 374 miles in a day; then, on a voyage from New York to San Francisco, she made a run of 433 miles in a day to break her own record. The *Sovereign of the Seas* soon surpassed that with 495 miles in a day's run. Another clipper, the *Lightning*, set a record of thirteen and a half days for a voyage from New York to Liverpool; still another, the *Oriental*, set a record of eighty-one days for a voyage from New York to Hong Kong.

From the mid-1840's to the mid-1850's the clippers gave the United States a larger share of the world's carrying trade than ever before, a share that briefly promised to surpass the British. The new ships and their masters took a commanding position in the commerce of both Europe and the Far East. But the most spectacular role of the clippers came in the early 1850's in the growing trade between the Atlantic coast and California. The older sailing vessels had taken more than five months to make the voyage around the Horn, whereas the clippers made it in three.

The era of the clipper ships, however, soon ended, for by the mid-1850's advances in technology were making them obsolete. The opening of the Panama Railroad in 1855 deprived them of the California trade, because cargoes could reach San Francisco along the shorter route in five weeks. Meanwhile the clippers were losing out in the competition with British ironclad steam vessels, which were less beautiful in design but superior in speed and cargo space. American steamship companies had only indifferent success in their rivalry with the British, who now recaptured much of the ocean commerce that they had lost to the clippers. Not until the First World War would the United States again hold the position in the carrying trade that she enjoyed for a decade in the mid-nineteenth century.

IMMIGRATION

The role of the immigrant. Between 1830 and 1860 the population of the United States increased from 12,866,000 to 31,443,000. But in spite of this remarkable growth the country was still sparsely settled and short of manpower. The factories needed more and more hands to tend the machines, and the limited supply and relatively high cost of labor retarded the rate of industrial expansion. Revived programs of internal improvements following the depression of the early 1840's created another heavy demand for workers. Above all, the supply of arable land still seemed to be inexhaustible, and the Western states and territories eagerly welcomed new settlers. Depression created temporary unemployment in the Eastern industrial centers, but most of the time before the Civil War there were not enough men and women to meet the labor requirements of cities and farms.

The manpower problem would have been even more acute had it not been for a sharp increase in European immigration to the United States beginning in the mid-1840's. Until then immigrants had been arriving at a slowly accelerating annual rate — 8,385 in 1820, 23,322 in 1830, and 84,066 in 1840 — but in the decade before 1840 fewer than 600,000 had crossed the Atlantic. In the following decade, however, immigration increased to 1,713,000, and during the 1850's to 2,598,000. Each year between 1850 and 1854 the number of immigrants exceeded 300,000, reaching a peak of 428,000 in 1854 — a figure that would not be surpassed until the 1870's.

The overwhelming majority of immigrants still came from northern and western Europe. During the 1850's slightly more than 300,000 migrated from Great Britain, about 25,000 from the Scandinavian countries. But Germany and southern Ireland had now become the two principal sources. In addition to the usual incentives — technological unemployment, the lure of cheap land, and the vision of the United States as a country of opportunity, freedom, and social equality — several special conditions helped to bring in a tide of Irish and Germans. In Ireland the failure of the potato crop of 1845 began a succession of famine years that caused widespread misery and actual starvation. As a result, in the fifteen years after 1845 approximately a million and a half Irishmen, most of them in extreme poverty, crossed the Atlantic. In Germany the suppression of the liberal Revolution of 1848 brought many political refugees along with those who came in search of improved economic conditions. Between 1850 and 1860 nearly a million Germans arrived.

In the main these immigrants were not systematically recruited, and they were seldom subsidized by organized groups. The Mormon Church helped its converts, and an Irish Pioneer Emigration Fund, supported by British, Irish, and American leaders, paid the passage of a few. In addition, some immigrants helped friends or relatives to join them. But most came on their own. A minority of them were fairly well-to-do middle-class people whose motive for coming, according to one report, was "not want or oppression, but . . . a rage for speculation, or a desire to acquire wealth more rapidly." Usually, however, the immigrants were poor people who could afford to pay their way only because competing merchant ships, needing return cargoes, reduced fares to as low as $30. Immigrants were crowded into steerage quarters, where they suffered from poor food, inadequate sanitary facilities, and the ravages of smallpox, dysentery, and "ship fever."

Much of this immigrant stream poured into the country through New York, some of it through Boston, Philadelphia, Baltimore, and New Orleans. Since there was no public program to help these strangers find homes and jobs or to ease the difficult adjustment to a new environment, many of them at first had unhappy experiences. Until the state of New York, in 1855, gave immigrants some protection by establishing Castle Garden as a controlled landing place, they often fell victim to swindlers who cheated them with exorbitant

"Mexicans shall rule America": Bigotry in Baltimore.

charges for lodgings or transportation or with false promises of employment. Because the Irish seldom had the means to become farmers, they congregated in the slums of New York and Boston and in the factory towns of New England. A much larger proportion of the Germans arrived with enough money to move to the Middle West, where they acquired farms or established business enterprises in cities such as Cincinnati, St. Louis, Chicago, and Milwaukee. Immigrants rarely settled in the South. Most of them debarked at Northern ports, but even those who arrived at New Orleans often took steamboats up the Mississippi to the free states. They were drawn north by their preference for the cooler climate, by their unwillingness to compete with slave labor, and, in the case of many Germans, by their opposition to slavery itself.

Though few immigrants found it easy to settle in a new land, though far too many lived in abject poverty in the cities of the East, in the long run most of them did manage to improve their economic lot, and their contributions to American society were incalculable. From the ranks of the immigrants in subsequent years came many of the country's distinguished leaders in politics, the professions, journalism, the fine arts, banking, industry, and transportation. The English and Germans augmented the short supply of skilled craftsmen; the Welsh and Cornish worked the coal mines of Pennsylvania and the lead mines of Missouri and Wisconsin; the Irish tended the machines in New England factories, built railroads, and dug canals; men and women from all the immigrant groups brought millions of acres of Western land under cultivation. Not the least of the immigrants' contributions was the richness and variety they gave to American society through the customs and amenities they brought with them from their old homes.

Nativism. Notwithstanding the value of the immigrants to a thinly settled country, their growing numbers began to alarm some Americans. By the 1850's aliens constituted half the population of New York City and outnumbered the native-born Americans in Chicago, Milwaukee, and St. Louis. Such conditions helped to produce the first nativist, or anti-foreign, movement in American history, a movement that briefly exerted considerable

influence in both state and national politics.

The causes of nativism were several. A few racists feared that the Celts from southern Ireland would pollute the old American stock, and that the United States would cease to be predominantly an Anglo-Saxon nation. Some criticized the Irish and Germans for their clannishness and for their tendency to preserve Old World customs and habits of dress. Others were distressed by the prevalence of crime and pauperism in the immigrant slums, resented the burden that alien indigents put on public funds and private charity, and accused European governments of deliberately exporting their "undesirables" to the United States. Native workingmen disliked the immigrants as economic competitors whose low standard of living threatened to depress wages. Southerners were unhappy to find them adding to the North's majority in population and congressional representation. Conservatives were concerned about the immigrants' political power, for many states permitted them to vote before they became naturalized citizens. Most immigrants supported the Democratic party as the party of the common man, and in the Eastern cities Democratic bosses used them to build political machines.

Though all these anxieties contributed to the nativist movement, the strongest force behind it was anti-Catholicism. In the early nineteenth century Roman Catholics were a small fraction of the population, but in the 1840's and 1850's nearly all of the Irish and many of the German immigrants were adherents of this faith. With the growth of the Catholic population, there was a corresponding increase in the number of Catholic priests and bishops, convents and monasteries, schools and colleges. Anti-Catholic sentiment among American Protestants was old and deep rooted, having grown from a combination of bigotry and genuine disagreement over Christian doctrine. Frightened nativists viewed every Catholic immigrant as an agent of the pope sent to seize the government and destroy Protestantism. They believed the Church to be the ally of tyranny and reaction in Europe, the enemy of freedom and democracy in America. And their prejudices were confirmed by lurid accounts of immorality in the convents and among the priesthood.

Nativist agitation started in the 1830's. In

New York the Reverend George Bourne edited an anti-Catholic weekly, *The Protestant*, while other clergymen organized a Protestant Association "to promote the principles of the Reformation" and to "unfold the true character of Popery." In 1834 Samuel F. B. Morse, portrait-painter and promoter of the telegraph, published an influential anti-Catholic book, *A Foreign Conspiracy Against the Liberties of the United States*, that went through numerous editions. Urging Protestants to unite against the Catholic menace, Morse advocated stricter immigration laws to "stop this leak in the ship through which the muddy waters from without threaten to sink us." Nativists incited anti-Catholic riots, stoned Catholic institutions, and, in 1834, burned the Ursuline Convent School in Charlestown, Massachusetts.

During the 1840's, when Catholic immigrants began to arrive in large numbers, a bewildering array of secret nativist societies sprang up: the Sons of '76, the Sons of America, the Druids, the Order of United Americans, and many others. Early in the 1850's most of these groups united to form a powerful national organization, the Order of the Star Spangled Banner. Because members were sworn to secrecy and refused to answer questions about their aims and activities, they were usually called the Know-Nothings. It soon became evident, however, that their purposes were to defend Protestantism against Catholicism, to make immigration laws more restrictive, to increase the number of years required for naturalization, and to deprive aliens of the ballot.

Meanwhile, nativism had entered politics and had begun to score successes in local elections. After the presidential election of 1852, many former Whigs joined the movement as their own party disintegrated. Political nativism reached its peak in 1854 and 1855, when the Know-Nothings captured several state legislatures, elected numerous governors, and claimed the allegiance of at least seventy-five congressmen. Their most spectacular victory came in Massachusetts, where they controlled every state office and had an overwhelming majority in the legislature. In 1856 the nativists formed the American party, nominated Millard Fillmore for President, and polled about 25 per cent of the popular vote.

Thereafter, nativism rapidly declined. In Massachusetts most of the Know-Nothing legislators proved to be incompetent, and they were able to write almost none of their demands into law. Nationally the nativists soon lost their appeal as the country became increasingly absorbed in the conflict over slavery expansion — indeed, the American party itself split over this issue. Moreover, the religious bigotry and xenophobia of the Know-Nothings failed to destroy certain traditional American attitudes that soon began to reassert themselves: the belief in religious toleration, the idea of America as a refuge for the oppressed of the Old World, and a confidence that the United States could in time assimilate as many immigrants as came to her shores. Besides, nativism betrayed the Christian ideal of the brotherhood of man — as one critic observed, it "judges men by the accidents of their condition, instead of striving to find a common lot for all, with a common access to the blessings of life." Finally, nativist racism was refuted by a popular argument which held that the mixing of various nationalities was producing a new man, the American, superior to the old by the very fact of the mixing. As Herman Melville observed, "We are the heirs of all time, and with all nations we divide our inheritance."

ECONOMIC DEVELOPMENT

Domestic commerce. The flourishing American foreign trade of the mid-nineteenth century required the movement of huge quantities of bulky raw materials and foodstuffs to the seaports on the Atlantic and Gulf coasts as well as the distribution of finished European goods to the markets of the interior. At the same time, internal trade expanded as the population grew and as the economies of the various regions became increasingly specialized and interdependent. Much of this commerce continued to move along the country's excellent waterways. Coastal vessels carried cotton from Southern ports to New York and New England, while the glamorous Mississippi River steamboats carried more freight and passengers in the 1850's than ever before.

The paths of inland water transportation were rapidly changing, however, for the canals

West from Boston: A locomotive of the fifties on the Fitchburg line.

were diverting a growing amount of business from the rivers to the Great Lakes. The Miami and Erie Canal through Ohio, and the Wabash and Erie Canal through Indiana, both connected the Ohio River with Lake Erie at Toledo, while the Illinois and Michigan Canal united the Mississippi and Illinois rivers with Lake Michigan at Chicago. As trade shifted to the Great Lakes and the Erie Canal, New York replaced New Orleans as the chief outlet for Western commodities destined for European markets, and young cities on the lakes outgrew the older cities on the rivers. In the 1830's Chicago had been a small village; by 1860 it had a population of 109,000.

Meanwhile, all forms of water transportation were beginning to face serious competition from the railroads. The principle of running cars on wooden or iron rails had long been in use in the British mining districts for hauling coal, but until the early nineteenth century men or animals had always provided the power. Experiments with steam engines began soon after 1800, and in 1820 John Stevens of New Jersey demonstrated a steam locomotive that success-

fully pulled a train of cars over a short piece of track. Five years later a small British line, the Stockton and Darlington, became the first commercial railroad to utilize steam power.

This development was enough to stimulate feverish activity in the cities of the Eastern United States, where merchants had been seeking a way to compete with New York for the trade of the interior. In 1828 construction began on the Baltimore and Ohio, and by 1830 a thirteen-mile segment was open for business. A year later the Mohawk and Hudson established service over sixteen miles of track between Albany and Schenectady. In 1833 South Carolina's 136-mile Charleston and Hamburg line was completed and became for a time the longest railroad in the world. Philadelphia soon had a rail connection with the coal fields of central Pennsylvania, Boston with Worcester and other interior New England cities. By 1840 these and other lines had a combined trackage of 2,818 miles; by 1850 the trackage had grown to 9,021 miles, and by 1860 to 30,627 miles.

Emerson once observed that "the Americans take to this little contrivance, the railroad, as if it were the cradle in which they were born." They took to it (after first showing considerable hostility) in spite of such early inconveniences as irregular schedules, frequent breakdowns, and the likelihood of being showered with sparks from the wood-burning locomotives. A major annoyance was the lack of a standard-gauge track — as late as 1860 there were still a dozen gauges in use — which made it impossible for the rolling stock of one railroad to use the tracks of another. Worse than the inconveniences were the disastrous wrecks resulting from soft roadbeds, broken rails, and collapsed bridges.

Construction engineers gradually increased the safety and efficiency of the railroads. They built solid roadbeds using crushed rock for ballast, substituted cast-iron "T" rails for the old wooden rails covered with iron straps, learned how to make curves and negotiate grades, erected sturdier bridges, and improved the design of locomotives and cars. By the 1850's, though accidents still occurred with painful frequency, technological advances had reduced the risks of travel by railroad to a point where they were not much greater than by steamboat. The speed of the railroads (twenty to thirty miles an hour by 1860), their ability to get through the roughest terrain and to tap the remotest markets, their serviceability in winter when the canals froze, made them the ideal solution to the country's transportation needs.

During the 1850's, in addition to an enormous expansion of railroad mileage, considerable progress was made toward the consolidation of small, independent lines to form trunk lines. In the South, although both Norfolk and Charleston had established rail connections with the Mississippi River at Memphis, most lines continued to be short and to serve merely as feeders for river transportation. The railroad network that had emerged by 1860 was largely a system that united the Northwest with the Northeast. The Baltimore and Ohio had now reached the Ohio River at Wheeling, the Pennsylvania Railroad had connected Philadelphia and Pittsburgh, and several lines had given Boston access to the Erie Canal and the Great Lakes. Meanwhile, the Hudson River Railroad from New York to Albany, together with the New York Central, formed by the consolidation of seven lines between Albany and Buffalo,

had given New York a through route to the West. A second railroad, the Erie, had been built across southern New York State from Jersey City to Buffalo. Powerful corporations, controlled by railroad capitalists like Erastus Corning of Albany and John Murray Forbes of Boston, directed the construction and consolidation that produced the trunk lines. Most of the funds came from American and British investors, a little from state and local government subsidies.

In the West, where most of the railroad construction of the 1850's took place, various lines in Ohio, Indiana, and Illinois linked the Ohio and Mississippi rivers with the Great Lakes. The most important of these north-south lines was the Illinois Central, which by 1858 had given Chicago a connection with the rivers at Cairo. Other railroads ran eastward from Chicago, now the transportation hub of the West, to meet the Eastern trunk lines. By 1860 both the Erie and the New York Central either controlled or had agreements with a series of lines that gave them access to Chicago. Railroad bridges now spanned the Mississippi River, and new lines had penetrated as far west as Burlington, Iowa, and St. Joseph, Missouri.

Railroad-builders in the West depended on public support more than those in the East. State and local governments aided them with loans, subsidies, and stock subscriptions, and in 1850 Congress passed a momentous bill providing the first of many railroad land grants. This act, whose chief sponsor was Senator Stephen A. Douglas, was for the benefit of the Illinois Central; it gave the state of Illinois three square miles of land in alternate sections on both sides of the proposed line (six square miles for each mile of track), with the understanding that the land would be turned over to the company as the railroad was built. Southern support was obtained by making a similar grant for a line from the Ohio River to Mobile. By 1860 approximately 28 million acres from the public domain had been granted to various states for railroad construction.

After 1850 there was much talk of a transcontinental railroad to be built with a federal subsidy, but sectional disagreement over the location of the route delayed action until after the start of the Civil War. Meanwhile, in 1855 the firm of Russell, Majors & Waddell, aided

The Growth of the Railroad Network, 1850–60

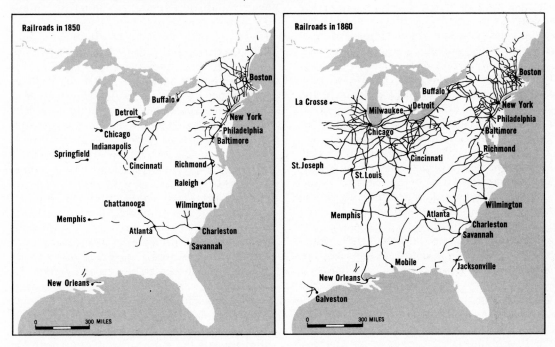

by a government subsidy, established regular overland freight service by wagon train between Kansas and California. Three years later the Butterfield Overland Mail Company began to run subsidized semiweekly stagecoaches between St. Louis and San Francisco. In the spring of 1860 Russell, Majors & Waddell introduced the pony express, which carried mail from St. Joseph, Missouri, to Sacramento in ten days. But in less than a year and a half the pony express was put out of business by a device that was revolutionizing communication: the electric telegraph. In 1844 Samuel F. B. Morse had demonstrated its practicality, and by 1860 the country had been tied together with fifty thousand miles of telegraph wire. In October 1861, when the Pacific Telegraph Company completed its line to San Francisco, communication between the Atlantic and Pacific coasts became a matter of minutes.

Agriculture. The revolution in transportation, the rapid growth of industry, and advances in agricultural technology profoundly affected the life of the American farmer. In New England the rural population declined as many families moved west in search of better land, or

to the cities to find employment in factories. Even so, in the 1850's a large proportion of the country's raw wool came from New England, while much wheat and corn were grown in New York and Pennsylvania. But farmers in the Northeast were rapidly turning from these crops to the production of fruits, vegetables, and milk for the growing cities nearby. Railroads enabled the owners of orchards, truck gardens, and dairy herds to make daily shipments to city markets from considerable distances. In this highly specialized and commercialized form, Eastern agriculture found new life and became a rewarding enterprise.

In the South the 1850's were prosperous years for the producers of the great staples (tobacco, rice, sugar, and cotton) with slave labor. By then the heart of the Cotton Kingdom had shifted from the Southeast to the Alabama-Mississippi Black Belt, the Mississippi Delta, the valleys of the Arkansas and Red rivers, and the prairies of eastern Texas. With cotton selling for 10 to 12 cents a pound, production rose from 2,469,000 bales in 1849 to 5,387,000 bales in 1859, and the South came near to monopolizing world markets. Able-bodied young slaves sold for $1,500 in the New Orleans market. In eastern Virginia, where a generation earlier soil exhaustion had produced agricultural stagnation, conditions had greatly improved. The slave-plantation system gained new vitality from the introduction of fertilizers, improved methods of cultivation, and systems of crop rotation, but the sale of surplus slaves in the markets of the Southwest continued to be vital to the economy of the older plantation districts. Throughout the South the plantations, though highly commercialized agricultural enterprises, were less affected by technological changes than the farms of the Northeast and Northwest. Planters continued to cultivate the staples with gangs of unskilled slaves using simple hoes and plows. As for the mass of non-slaveholding yeoman farmers, they often planted a few acres in cotton or tobacco, but in the main they raised corn and hogs for their own subsistence and remained outside the market economy.

By 1860 the Old Northwest had become the center of wheat, corn, beef, and pork production. Responding to the needs of old markets in the plantation South and to the growing de-

mands of the East and of Europe, native-born farmers and German and Scandinavian immigrants had opened up the virgin lands of northern Illinois and Indiana, southern Michigan and Wisconsin, and eastern Iowa and Minnesota. With their help the corn crop had increased from 592 million bushels in 1849 to 839 million bushels in 1859, the wheat crop from 100 million bushels to 173 million bushels. Illinois and Indiana now led in hog production, Illinois in corn production, and Illinois, Indiana, and Wisconsin in wheat production.

Widening markets, the high cost of labor, and the abandonment of self-sufficient agriculture for specialized crops stimulated the improvement of farm implements and mechanization. To cut through the tough prairie sod, Western farmers needed plows that were more efficient than the old ones made of wood or cast iron and drawn by slow-moving oxen. In 1847 John Deere began to supply this need when he opened a factory at Moline, Illinois, to manufacture light steel plows that cut deeper furrows and could be drawn by horses. The fifties also saw the substitution of grain drills for hand planting and the introduction of mowers

Testing McCormick's reaper, 1831.

A New England mill, 1850.

to harvest the hay crop. Most important for the wheat farmers was the invention of mechanical reapers to replace hand sickles and cradles. In 1831 Cyrus Hall McCormick, a Virginian, built a successful reaper, and in 1847 he moved to Chicago to begin manufacturing them on a large scale. Mechanization advanced another step when threshing machines began to outmode the old method of flailing wheat by hand.

Having entered the market economy, a growing number of Western farmers thought of agriculture as a business enterprise rather than, in Jefferson's terms, as a way of life. Technological advances enabled them to cultivate more acres but also forced them to make heavier investments in implements and machinery. The railroads opened new markets to them but increased their dependence on the middlemen who financed, transported, stored, and marketed their crops. Specialization made them more efficient but increased their dependence on Eastern manufacturers for things they had once made for themselves. In short, the farmers were being caught up in the capitalist world of merchants, manufacturers, bankers, and railroad-operators, and by 1860 some of them were showing signs of dissatisfaction

with their place in this world. Out of their discontent would grow the farmers' movements of the post-Civil War years.

Industry. In 1851, at London's Crystal Palace Exhibition, the products of American industry and technology were shown to the world. More than a hundred of them won prize medals, including the McCormick reaper, which attracted by far the greatest admiration. The success of the American exhibits was an indication of the rapid progress the country had made in manufacturing since the founding of the first textile mills in the early nineteenth century.

The industrial growth of the 1850's far surpassed that of any previous decade. The capital investment of a half-billion dollars in 1849 had nearly doubled by 1859, the number of manufacturing establishments had increased from 123,000 to 140,000, and the annual value of their products had grown from $1,019 million to $1,886 million. Manufacturing was concentrated in the New England and Middle Atlantic states. The market was almost entirely a domestic one, with the Northeast exchanging its industrial surpluses for the foodstuffs and raw materials of the agricultural South and West.

Work began at five o'clock on summer mornings, and at daylight in the winter. Breakfast was eaten by lamplight, during the cold weather; in summer, an interval of half an hour was allowed for it, between seven and eight o'clock. The time given for the noon meal was from a half to three quarters of an hour. The only hours of leisure were from half past seven or eight to ten in the evening, the mills closing a little earlier on Saturdays. It was an imperative regulation that lights should be out at ten. During those two evening hours, when it was too cold for the girls to sit in their own rooms, the dining room was used as a sitting-room, where they gathered around the tables, and sewed, and read, and wrote, and studied. It seems a wonder, to look back upon it, how they accomplished so much as they did, in their limited allowance of time. They made and mended their own clothing, often doing a good deal of unnecessary fancy-work besides. They subscribed for periodicals; took books from the libraries; went to singing-schools, conference meetings, concerts, and lectures; watched at night by a sick girl's bedside, and did double work for her in the mill, if necessary; and on Sundays they were at church, not differing in appearance from other well-dressed and decorous young women.

From Lucy Larcom, *Among Lowell Mill-Girls: A Reminiscence,* November 1881.

Yet industry in the 1850's had certain characteristics indicating that the United States was still in the early stages of the Industrial Revolution. First, most of the manufacturing involved the processing of the products of American farms and forests. In 1860 the leading industry was the milling of flour and meal, whose value was about one-eighth of the total value of manufactures. Other important industries included lumber-milling, distilling, brewing, leather-tanning, and meat-packing. A second indication of industrial immaturity was the smallness of the typical manufacturing enterprises; on the average they employed fewer than ten workers and had a capital value of less than $7,500. Finally, as we have seen, the United States was still a large consumer of foreign manufactured goods and primarily an exporter of agricultural products.

Nevertheless, by 1860 the direction of Ameri-

can economic development was clear. Textile-manufacturing had already become the core of New England's economy: the investment in mills and machinery was more than $100 million, and the number of cotton spindles in operation had grown to 5,236,000 — a 100 per cent increase since 1840. In 1844 Charles Goodyear had patented a method of "vulcanizing" raw rubber to make it resist heat and cold, and a new rubber-goods industry was soon manufacturing hundreds of products. In 1846 Elias Howe had patented a sewing machine, and five years later Isaac Singer had begun to manufacture and market an improved model. During the 1850's these machines were used in hundreds of factories making shoes and ready-made clothing. The iron industry had expanded to meet the demands of the railroads and the producers of farm machinery. Between 1840 and 1860 pig-iron production rose from 321,000 tons to 920,000 tons a year. Originally the rails and locomotives for American railroads had to be imported, but by the 1840's Pennsylvania iron-manufacturers were able to meet the domestic demand.

During the years of rapid industrial growth in the 1840's and 1850's, the chronic shortage of skilled workers and the relatively high cost of labor kept alive the American manufacturer's keen interest in increased efficiency and technological advances. As a result, by the 1850's the United States had outstripped all other industrial countries in turning out products whose manufacture involved the use of precision instruments. A few industries began to apply the methods of modern mass production. The manufacturers of guns, clocks, sewing machines, and farm implements introduced assembly lines on which unskilled workers, performing standardized tasks, made the finished product from interchangeable parts. During the 1850's, two British commissions visited the United States to study manufacturing techniques, especially the remarkable progress of American technology. The British visitors were struck by the inventiveness of American artisans and by the fact that they seemed to be as fascinated by mechanical improvements as their employers.

Meanwhile, in America's growing industries the corporate form of business organization spread rapidly — during the 1850's the number of manufacturing corporations nearly doubled. Industry and the building and organizing of railroads were rivaling commerce as the road to wealth and economic power. Thus Amos and Abbot Lawrence of Boston, Phelps, Dodge & Company of New York, and many others, got their start in mercantile enterprises but transferred their capital to manufacturing, railroads, and mining. The industrial entrepreneur had already become an important figure in the country's economic life.

By 1860 American factories were employing 1,311,000 workers, the mines and transportation a half-million more. Although skilled labor was still in great demand, each craft felt severely threatened by the steady encroachments of the machines and of mass production. Already the factories had made nearly obsolete several old and honorable crafts, notably those of the cordwainers, coopers, and ironsmiths. As the factories grew in size and the ranks of the unskilled were filled with recent immigrants, the relations of labor and capital became increasingly impersonal. Employers began to think of their workers less as human beings than as commodities to be bought at the lowest price. They paid their employees $6 a week or less for a working day of twelve to fifteen hours. They often ignored feeble state laws fixing maximum hours or regulating the labor of children. And they viewed with indifference the poor sanitary conditions and the high rate of industrial accidents in their factories. Conditions such as these touched the lives of only a small fraction of the population, but by the 1850's there had emerged in the factory slums of Eastern cities an unskilled, propertyless proletariat. The Industrial Revolution thus introduced the United States for the first time to the problem of poverty in an affluent society.

Middle-class reformers who took an interest in the plight of the laboring population usually urged low-paid workers to form their own co-operative workshops or to go west and become farmers. They seldom approved of direct economic action through trade unions. This, however, was the means by which factory workers eventually improved their condition. The promising labor movement of the 1830's (see p. 218) had been destroyed by the depression following the Panic of 1837, and it took many

The Lowell Operatives: Contemporary Testimony

The first petitioner who testified was Eliza R. Hemmingway. She had worked 2 years and 9 months in the Lowell Factories; 2 years in the Middlesex, and 9 months in the Hamilton Corporations. Her employment is weaving — works by the piece.... She is now at work in the Middlesex Mills, and attends one loom. Her wages average from $16 to $23 a month exclusive of board. She complained of the hours for labor being too many, and the time for meals too limited. In the summer season, the work is commenced at 5 o'clock, a.m., and continued until 7 o'clock, p.m., with half an hour for breakfast and three quarters of an hour for dinner. During eight months of the year, but half an hour is allowed for dinner. The air in the room she considered not to be wholesome. There were 293 small lamps and 61 large lamps lighted in the room in which she worked, when evening work is required. These lamps are also lighted sometimes in the morning. About 130 females, 11 men, and 12 children (between the ages of 11 and 14) work in the room with her.... She thought there was a general desire among the females to work but ten hours, regardless of pay.

From Massachusetts House Document No. 50, 1845.

years for another movement to get started. A legal barrier was partially removed when the Massachusetts Supreme Court, in the case of *Commonwealth v. Hunt* (1842), ruled that trade unions were not in themselves conspiracies in restraint of trade, a rule that courts in other states soon accepted. But when workers resorted to strikes or boycotts they still ran into trouble with the courts, which continued to interpret such activities as violations of the old common-law doctrine of conspiracy. Trade unions were also handicapped by a hostile press, by generally unfavorable public opinion, and by the ability of employers to recruit strikebreakers.

In the 1850's, though conditions showed little improvement, only a few American workingmen belonged to trade unions. In 1852 the International Typographical Union was formed, and by the end of the decade the stonecutters, hat-finishers, iron-molders, and machinists had also established national organizations. The other skilled crafts were organized only locally, while the mass of unskilled workers had no unions at all. Strikes for higher wages or shorter hours occurred in the shoe and textile industries and on the railroads, but they usually failed. Though trade unionism had made a new beginning, a formidable labor movement would not emerge until after the Civil War.

ECONOMIC DISCONTENT IN THE SOUTH

The colonial South. On the surface the economic conditions of the 1850's would seem to have given no cause for sectional conflict. The South was prospering, and its economy appeared to be neatly complementary to that of the North — each section needed the products of the other. And yet, throughout the decade, there was in the South an undercurrent of economic discontent.

After the Panic of 1837 Southern cotton no longer played so dynamic a role in the economic development of the country as it had before. Industry now played the role that cotton once played, and both the West and the Northeast were less dependent on the Southern market. In short, the South, though still flourishing, was not keeping pace with the other sections.

Far more than that of the Northeast, even more than that of the Northwest, the economy of the South was based on agriculture. In 1860 the eleven states that were to form the Southern Confederacy produced less than one-tenth of the country's manufactured goods; they contained about half as many manufacturing establishments as the Western states. Moreover, there was little direct trade between Southern and European ports, most of the trade being carried on indirectly through Northern ports and in Northern ships. An Alabama editor complained,

> With us every branch and pursuit of life, every trade, profession, and occupation, is dependent upon the North. . . . In Northern vessels [the Southerner's] products are carried to market, his cotton is ginned with Northern gins, his sugar is crushed and preserved by Northern machinery; his rivers are navigated by Northern steamboats . . . his land is cleared with a Northern axe, and a Yankee clock sits upon his mantel-piece; his

floor is swept by a Northern broom, and is covered with a Northern carpet; and his wife dresses herself in a Northern looking-glass.

Southerners resented this dependency and searched for ways to strengthen their economy. As early as 1837 a group of Georgians had sponsored a convention at Augusta "to attempt a new organization of our commercial relations with Europe." During the 1840's and 1850's a series of commercial conventions urged the establishment of direct trade between Southern and European ports. While some Southerners planned steamship lines, others favored the building of railroads to divert Western trade to Southern cities. Neither goal was achieved.

For a time there seemed to be a better prospect of improving the South's industrial position. During the depression years of the 1840's, when the price of raw cotton was low, interest in manufacturing increased in the older states of the Southeast, and a number of factories were built. William Gregg of South Carolina, a vigorous propagandist for industrialization, demonstrated its profitability at his highly successful cotton factory in Graniteville. In the 1850's, however, the revival of agricultural prosperity made it difficult for industry to compete for capital. Moreover, the Northern manufacturer was usually able to undersell his Southern competitor and to provide a superior product. As a result, the South's economy remained agricultural.

Rumors of a Northern conspiracy. The failure of these various efforts toward economic diversification produced a state of mind in the South that contributed to sectionalism and ultimately to disunion. Agriculture, Jefferson had taught and Southerners believed, was the most productive pursuit of man, and the man who worked the soil was the chief repository of human virtue. Yet the North had surpassed the South in wealth and population and had reduced her to a colonial status. This evil and unnatural condition, many Southerners believed, was the result of a sinister conspiracy planned by a close-knit body of Northern bankers, merchants, and manufacturers. The chief haunts of the conspirators were New York and Washington; their distinguishing characteristics were their essential unproductiveness and their skill in amassing wealth from the labor of others. Their special field of operation was the

South, from which they extracted a major portion of their profits.

The Northern businessman, according to this conspiracy theory, took advantage of the plain, homespun Southerner, who was no match for the artful Yankee in the techniques of chicanery. By exacting exorbitant middlemen's charges, by rigging prices, by manipulating the money market, the Northern capitalists kept much of the wealth produced in the South flowing steadily into their coffers. The price of Southern property, wrote an indignant Virginian, "is dependent upon the speculative pleasure of the Merchants, Bankers, and Brokers of New York. And why? Because Wall Street can depress the money market when it pleases." The South, said a Mississippian, had permitted itself to fall into a condition of "serfdom" and to become "the sport and laughing stock of Wall Street." A Southern editor described New York as "a mighty queen of commerce . . . waving an undisputed commercial scepter over the South." With an "avidity rarely equalled," she "grasps our gains and transfers them to herself."

But Northern capitalists did not make their profits solely from their adroit maneuvers in a free economy. Rather, in advancing their conspiracy they had enlisted the support of the federal government. In November 1860 Senator Robert Toombs, in a speech before the Georgia legislature, described the political side of the Northern conspiracy to prostrate the South. No sooner had the government been organized, he claimed, than "the Northern States evinced a general desire and purpose to use it for their own benefit, and to pervert its powers for sectional advantage, and they have steadily pursued that policy to this day." They demanded, and received, a monopoly of the shipbuilding business; they demanded, and received, a monopoly of the trade between American ports. The New England fishing industry obtained an annual bounty from the public treasury; manufacturers obtained a protective tariff. Through its policy of subsidizing "every interest and every pursuit in the North," the federal treasury had become "a perpetual fertilizing stream to them and their industry, and a suction-pump to drain away our substance and parch up our lands."

By the 1850's the notion that Northern profits were largely a form of expropriation of Southern wealth, that the South was "the very best colony to the North any people ever possessed," was having a powerful effect on Southern opinion. Southerners had convinced themselves, remarked a Northerner, "that in some way or other, either through the fiscal regulations of the Government, or through the legerdemain of trade, the North has been built up at the expense of the South." Not even agricultural prosperity could banish this thought from the Southern mind. When the sectional conflict was reopened in 1854, slavery transcended all other issues. However, as the historian Charles A. Beard has observed, it was not always easy to tell "where slavery as an ethical question left off and economics — the struggle over the distribution of wealth — began."

SUGGESTIONS FOR READING

Expansionism and Foreign Trade

American interests in Cuba, Central America, and the Far East are treated adequately in three general surveys of American foreign policy: S. F. Bemis, *A Diplomatic History of the United States* (rev. ed., 1955); T. A. Bailey, *A Diplomatic History of the American People* (6th ed., 1958); and J. W. Pratt, *A History of United States Foreign Policy* (1955). Allan Nevins, *Ordeal of the Union*, 2 vols. (1947,) is informative on Cuba and Central America. Several excellent monographs may also be consulted: M. W. Williams, *Anglo-American Isthmian Diplomacy, 1815–1915* (1916); Dexter Perkins, *The Monroe Doctrine, 1826–1867* (1933); A. A. Ettinger, *The Mission to Spain of*

* Available in a paperback edition.

Pierre Soulé (1932); and Basil Rauch, *American Interests in Cuba, 1848–1855* (1948). E. S. Wallace, *Destiny and Glory* (1957), is a vivid account of filibustering.

The most useful special studies of American-Far Eastern relations that deal with this period are: Tyler Dennett, *Americans in Eastern Asia* (1941); A. W. Griswold, *The Far Eastern Policy of the United States** (1938); P. J. Treat, *Diplomatic Relations Between the United States and Japan, 1853–1905*, 3 vols. (1932–38); F. R. Dulles, *China and America: The Story of Their Relations Since 1784* (1946); and L. H. Battistini, *The Rise of American Influence in Asia and the Pacific* (1960). Arthur Walworth, *Black Ships off Japan* (1946), is a readable account of the Perry mission to Japan. H. W. Bradley, *American Frontier in Hawaii* (1942), is the best study of early American interest in Hawaii.

The standard works on the growth of American foreign trade are E. R. Johnson and others, *History of Domestic and Foreign Commerce of the United States*, 2 vols. (1915), and J. H. Frederick, *The Development of American Commerce* (1932). The commerce of New England and New York City are the subjects of two distinguished books: S. E. Morison, *Maritime History of Massachusetts** (1921), and R. G. Albion, *The Rise of New York Port, 1815–1860* (1939). The best books on the clipper ships are A. H. Clark, *The Clipper Ship Era* (1910); C. C. Cutler, *Greyhounds of the Sea* (1930); and Robert Carse, *The Moonrakers* (1961).

Immigration and Nativism

Several excellent surveys of immigration to the United States are valuable for this period: G. M. Stephenson, *History of American Immigration* (1926); Carl Wittke, *We Who Built America** (1939); M. L. Hansen, *The Atlantic Migration, 1607–1860** (1940); and M. A. Jones, *American Immigration** (1960). Oscar Handlin, *The Uprooted** (1951), is a sensitive study of the immigrant's problems. Four specific immigrant groups are the subjects of individual volumes: T. C. Blegen, *Norwegian Migration to America*, 2 vols. (1931–40); R. T. Berthoff, *British Immigrants in Industrial America, 1825–1950* (1953); Carl Wittke, *Refugees of Revolution: The German Forty-Eighters in America* (1952); and by the same author, *The Irish in America* (1956). The immigrant populations of two large Eastern cities are studied in Oscar Handlin, *Boston's Immigrants* (1941), and Robert Ernst, *Immigrant Life in New York City, 1825–1863* (1949).

A perceptive account of mid-nineteenth-century nativism is in Nevins, *Ordeal of the Union*, cited above. R. A. Billington, *The Protestant Crusade, 1800–1860** (1938), emphasizes the anti-Catholic aspect of the movement. John Higham, *Strangers in the Land** (1955), deals only briefly with Know-Nothingism in the 1850's, but it should be consulted for its distinctive interpretation. Two special studies are also useful: Sister M. E. Thomas, *Nativism in the Old Northwest, 1850–1860* (1936), and W. D. Overdyke, *The Know-Nothing Party in the South* (1950).

Economic Development

All of the books on agriculture, industry, transportation, and technology listed in the suggested readings for Chapter 8 are useful for this period. There are also several good chapters on the American economy at mid-century in Nevins, *Ordeal of the Union*, cited above, and in A. C. Cole, *The Irrepressible Conflict, 1850–1865* (1934).

A good introduction to the history of the railroads is Slason Thompson, *A Short History of American Railways* (1925). Problems of railroad promotion and finance can be studied in F. A. Cleveland and F. W. Powell, *Railroad Promotion and Capitalization in the United States* (1909);

* Available in a paperback edition.

L. H. Haney, *A Congressional History of Railways in the United States to 1850* (1908); and by the same author, *A Congressional History of Railways in the United States, 1850–1877* (1910); and A. D. Chandler, Jr., *Henry Varnum Poor: Business Editor, Analyst and Reformer* (1956). An outstanding history of the New England railroads is E. C. Kirkland, *Men, Cities and Transportation, 1820–1900*, 2 vols. (1948). Railroad promotion in the Southeast is described in U. B. Phillips, *A History of Transportation in the Eastern Cotton Belt to 1860* (1908). T. C. Cochran, *Railroad Leaders 1845–1890* (1953), contains important material on early railroad-promoters and their social attitudes. The following histories of individual railroads are useful: F. W. Stevens, *The Beginnings of the New York Central Railroad* (1926); P. W. Gates, *The Illinois Central Railroad and Its Colonization Work* (1934); Edward Hungerford, *The Story of the Baltimore and Ohio Railroad, 1827–1927*, 2 vols. (1928); and by the same author, *Men of Erie* (1946); and R. C. Overton, *Burlington West* (1941). Two books deal with the impact of the railroads on the American economy: R. W. Fogel, *Railroads and American Economic Growth* (1964), and Albert Fishlow, *American Railroads and the Transformation of the Ante-Bellum Economy* (1965).

In addition to the listings in the suggested readings for Chapter 8, the following books on industry and technology are worth consulting for this period: G. S. Gibb, *The Saco-Lowell Shops: Textile Machinery Building in New England* (1950); Waldemar Kaempffert, ed., *A Popular History of American Invention*, 2 vols. (1924); Allan Nevins, *Abram S. Hewitt: With Some Account of Peter Cooper* (1935); J. A. Kouwenhoven, *Made in America* (1948); D. J. Struik, *Yankee Science in the Making** (1948); and Mitchell Wilson, *American Science and Invention: A Pictorial History* (1954). The best book on labor in this period is N. J. Ware, *The Industrial Worker, 1840–1860** (1924). Hannah Josephson, *The Golden Threads* (1949), is excellent on the women textile-workers of New England. Two good general treatments are J. G. Rayback, *History of American Labor** (1959), and H. M. Pelling, *American Labor** (1960). R. H. Bremner, *From the Depths** (1956), deals with the emergence of the problem of poverty in America.

The causes of economic discontent in the South can be studied in R. R. Russel, *Economic Aspects of Southern Sectionalism, 1840–1861* (1924); J. G. Van Deusen, *The Ante-Bellum Southern Commercial Conventions* (1926); Herbert Wender, *Southern Commercial Conventions, 1837–1859* (1930); and Clement Eaton, *The Growth of Southern Civilization** (1961).

* Available in a paperback edition.

13
The Gathering Storm

The hardening of tempers, north and south, reduced the chances for finding a peaceful solution to the sectional crisis. Politics, as always the art of the possible, had to operate within a more and more constricted range. Slavery lay at the core of the problem. Sectional differences about national public policies would have existed in the absence of the South's peculiar institution, but the debate could not have taken the turn it did had not the expectations of Americans crystallized around the question of slavery. For all the stubbornness of that issue, however, for all the political difficulties attending a time of tension, men had a choice about their destiny — a choice they continually exercised. The choice was not simple, and the men were not often wise. A harassed generation, they were struggling to control themselves and their destiny. They were testing the unity, the spirit, even the survival of the United States.

THE DIVISIVE ISSUE

The Kansas-Nebraska Act. Ironically, a miscalculated effort to dispose of the problem of slavery in the territories resulted instead in the polarizing of sectional attitudes about that issue. Stephen A. Douglas, a talented Illinois Democrat, senator from that state since 1847, was the chairman of the Committee on Territories. No one had a larger experience with territorial politics; no one was more committed to the rapid settlement of the West; no one was more dedicated to the Union and its peaceful preservation. Douglas rejected alike the free-soilers' demand that Congress prohibit slavery in all territories and the Southern demand that Congress protect it there. He stood instead for settling the question by local self-determination, by letting the majority of the people in each territory vote slavery up or down (see p. 287). This doctrine of popular sovereignty, already applied by the Compromise of 1850 to Utah and New Mexico, struck Douglas and like-minded men as twice blessed. They considered it democratic on its merits; they also believed it to be a practicable middle way between the controversial sectional extremes.

Stars and bars above Sumter.

In January 1854 Douglas reported out a bill for the territorial organization of the Platte country, the area west of Missouri and Iowa. In keeping with his interpretation of the Compromise of 1850, his bill provided that the territorial legislature elected by the people should decide about slavery. Since the Platte, or Nebraska, country lay within the Louisiana Purchase, where the Missouri Compromise had governed the slavery question since 1820, Douglas' proposal tacitly abandoned that longtime sectional settlement. Consequently the bill triggered another sectional debate.

Douglas had hoped that his bill would still rather than inflame tempers. His contemporaries thought he also intended it to advance his ambitions for the Presidency. A cocky, undersized, tireless scrapper, Douglas had a practiced ability for seizing a good political chance. He may have been concerned not only with "a final settlement of the controversy" over slavery in the territories but with capturing Southern support for his candidacy. Probably the Little Giant had still other motives. He said at the time that he had proposed the bill in order to remove the "barbarian wall" of Indians blocking settlement on the plains and to encourage thereby a "continuous line of settlement to the Pacific Ocean." To develop the West, he had to skirt the slavery question, for his influential colleague in the Senate, David R. Atchison of Missouri, had sworn to let the Nebraska area "sink in hell" before permitting it to be organized on a free-soil basis. Douglas, furthermore, was in a hurry. A survey of possible routes for a transcontinental railroad had favored a Southern line, but he was eager to win a Northern route that would enhance the growth of Illinois and especially of Chicago. Perhaps his holdings of real estate in that city enlarged his natural preference for his home state. In any case, if the Nebraska area was to surround a vital railway line, it would have to be organized quickly.

Douglas was no fool. Whatever his motives, he had surely estimated the chances for his bill. He apparently counted on its ambiguity about the moral question of slavery, on the tradition of sectional compromise, and on his own political influence to carry his measure past the objections of both free-soilers and Southerners. Personally opposed to slavery, he was one of those who believed that it could not be adapted profitably to the climate and soil of the plains country, so manifestly inhospitable to cotton or tobacco culture. By temperament an adjuster rather than an agitator, he expected the logic of geography to preclude a theoretical debate on the dominant moral and political question of the day. It was in projecting his own feelings that he erred, for the men who stood on either side of him were not willing to let nature make policy.

The storm broke as soon as the bill reached the Senate in January 1854. Countering a free-soil amendment that reasserted the Missouri Compromise, Southern Democrats and their allies insisted on permitting slavery in the Nebraska country during its territorial phase — that is, until it became a state. Douglas yielded and rephrased his bill to read "that all questions pertaining to slavery in the Territories, and in the new states to be formed therefrom, are to be left to the people resident therein through their appropriate representatives." Still not content, some Southerners demanded a further amendment, to which Douglas agreed, that declared the Missouri Compromise "inoperative and void." Another amendment divided the area into the two separate territories of Kansas and Nebraska. As Douglas said, the revised bill, a considerable departure from his own original, equivocal draft, would "raise the hell of a storm." Yet he apparently expected Northern opposition to be less bitter and divisive than Southern resistance to the unamended bill had been. His efforts, and the persistent influence of the Pierce Administration, took the bill safely through an angry debate. The Senate passed it by a vote of 37 to 14; the House by 113 to 100.

The national response. The debate over the Kansas-Nebraska Act marked the end of the uneasy truce of 1850 and set the tone of the rest of the decade. Douglas had sensed the strength of Northern sentiment against repeal of the Missouri Compromise, but he had failed to realize that the new legislation would intensify the slavery issue. He had supposed that once the first storm had blown itself out, the extension of slavery would be left to popular sovereignty and agitation would cease. But the storm would not blow itself out. A more accurate prophet was William H. Seward of New York, who had warned that the bill would "end a cycle in the history of our country."

Antislavery and free-soil men, their resentment increased by the failure of the Homestead Bill (p. 288), began at once to try to reverse the policy of Congress. Their meetings and petitions denounced Douglas for his "criminal betrayal of precious rights." Never before, one Washington newspaper reported, had "a public man been so hounded and hunted." As Douglas said himself, he could have traveled from Boston to Chicago by the light of his burning effigies.

That temper speeded a portentous political realignment that had already begun. The Whig party, moribund at best, was unable to adjust its heterogeneous factions and policies to the deep division over the issue of slavery in the territories. As the party died, many of its Northern adherents — the Conscience Whigs — joined with more radical free-soilers and abolitionists and with some Northern Democrats disenchanted by Douglas' work. These coalitions then formed local "anti-Nebraska" groups, some of which adopted the name "Republican." One, in Ripon, Wisconsin, called for a new party dedicated to "the sole issue of the non-extension of slavery." Before the end of the summer of 1854, the emergent party had its name and its basic principle. It had also begun to attract men for whom slavery was not the major question of the day — some Whigs who were merely seeking a new vehicle for political power, some nativists, and many temperance advocates (see p. 258). In the new party's early years the last group exercised a considerable influence, but from the first, in spite of the diversity of its membership, the Republican party, not least in the eyes of its opponents, carried the stamp of its central principle. It was "anti-Nebraska"; it was against the extension of slavery.

That stance offended conservative Whigs, north and south. Southern Whigs — Alexander Stephens of Georgia, for one — for the most part now went over to the Democrats, who in any case already dominated the politics of the region. In parts of the North and in the border states, where, as in New York, the local Whig organization was particularly strong, the dying party conducted an uninspired and futile canvass in 1854. But in those same areas many

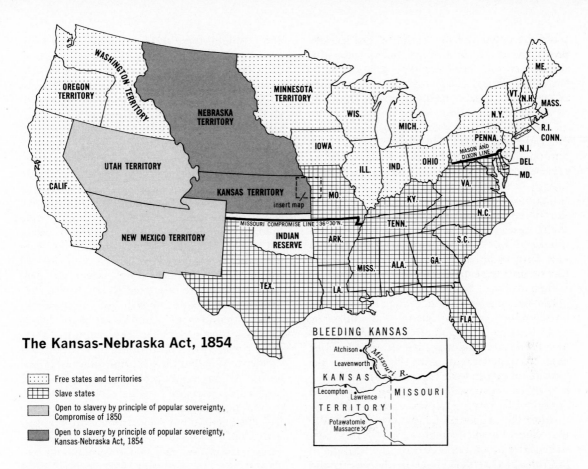

The Kansas-Nebraska Act, 1854

:::::: Free states and territories

▦ Slave states

▨ Open to slavery by principle of popular sovereignty, Compromise of 1850

▨ Open to slavery by principle of popular sovereignty, Kansas-Nebraska Act, 1854

BLEEDING KANSAS

Whigs, partly in order to avoid the slavery issue, partly out of conviction, joined the Know-Nothing Party (see p. 308). That agency of intolerance gained temporary but extraordinary strength, especially in states with urban areas where nativist antipathy to immigrants and to Catholics was highest, as in New England, New York, and the Ohio Valley.

Challenged by the zeal of the Know-Nothings and the Republicans, weakened by the defection of its own "anti-Nebraska" men and by intraparty controversy, the Democrats in 1854 suffered grave reversals. Perhaps most stunning was the plurality the Republicans achieved in the new House of Representatives, where they were to hold 108 seats to 83 for the Democrats and 43 for the Know-Nothings. Indeed that new House, after two months of debate, would elect a Republican Speaker, a former Democrat alienated by the Nebraska Act. Though some Democrats, after election day, took false solace in the disintegration of the Whig party, the Republicans had emerged as serious rivals, while the Democrats themselves, as never before, were separating into Northern and Southern camps. The irony of Douglas' miscalculation had become apparent. In introducing his bill, in bending to Southern amendments to it, he had inadvertently damaged the party — and the nation — he meant to strengthen, weakened the candidacy he wanted to serve, and revived the issue he proposed to bury.

Test in Kansas. The explosive potentialities of the Kansas-Nebraska Act were most immediate within the new territories. The act stipulated that the settlers could decide for themselves whether their territory might or might not contain slavery, but it did not say whether that initial decision would continue to operate once the territory had become a state. The future of slavery in the territories would depend, first, on the sentiment of the majority of original settlers; second, on their ability to mold the policies of the territorial government to their purpose; and, third, on the persisting dominance of their preference at the time of statehood. This situation invited, and the mood of the nation guaranteed, unceasing agitation of the slavery question.

The issue was joined on the plains of Kansas. Nebraska was surrounded by free soil; there geography and climate did decide against slavery. But Kansas adjoined Missouri, and Kansas became a symbol for Southerners determined to stamp out the infection of abolitionism, a symbol for free-soilers resolved to conquer for their cause. Kansas in 1854 was virtually uninhabited, but that summer and fall a rush for new land began to fill the territory. Most of the settlers were from the states adjacent to Kansas; most of them were relatively indifferent to the slavery question, though they brought no slaves to work their farms. They did bring with them, however, other characteristic frontier tensions — conflicts over Indian affairs, land titles, federal and local patronage, the location of county seats, the awarding of army and other contracts. To this powder keg the slavery issue applied a spark.

Since the people of Kansas were eventually to decide whether it should be a free state or a slave state, much depended on the attitude of the interested settlers. Both in the North and in the South determined efforts were made to see that the "right people" moved into the territory. In the East, the Massachusetts Emigrant Aid Company, later the New England Emigrant Aid Company, was set up to encourage and finance the immigration to Kansas of good antislavery men. This organization sponsored some 1,240 settlers, giving them advice and money in the free-soil cause. Similarly, Southern promoters sponsored settlement, including one expedition of several hundred men from Alabama, Georgia, and South Carolina.

The first governor of the territory, Andrew H. Reeder, a Pennsylvania Democrat, found that several thousand settlers had preceded him to Kansas. In the fall of 1854 he called an election to choose a territorial delegate to Congress, and early in 1855 he called another election to name a territorial legislature. But Kansas elections developed unusual features. The Missouri counties that bordered Kansas on the east were strong proslavery areas, and the people in these counties, urged on by leaders like Senator Atchison, did not want a free-soil territory next door. Missourians by the hundreds swarmed across the border to Kansas to vote in the territorial elections. The antislavery settlers, though apparently in the majority, were heavily outvoted. On the face of the returns, the new territory had chosen a proslavery delegate to Congress and had elected a solidly proslavery legislature. The legislature adopted a stringent slave code providing the death sentence for anyone helping a fugitive slave to escape and a prison term for anyone holding that slavery was not legal in Kansas.

Governor Reeder threw out some of the more obviously fraudulent returns, but the principal result of the elections stood. When the proslavery legislature requested Reeder's removal, President Pierce dismissed him and named Wilson Shannon of Ohio in his place. Antislavery settlers now called a convention of their own, drew up a constitution that prohibited slavery and called for the admission of Kansas to the Union as a free state, conducted an extralegal "election," which the proslavery people boycotted, and announced that they had installed a new government in Kansas, with Charles Robinson as governor. The troubled territory now had two governors and two legislatures: one the result of an election dominated by nonresidents, the other without legal basis.

Strong action in Washington might have kept the situation from getting so badly out of hand. Pierce might have asserted federal control, ordered a new election, and established a territorial government designed to win the respect of both parties. Instead, unwilling to use the authority of his office or to risk antagonizing his friends, he let matters drift.

The antagonists in Kansas acted. The roving Missourians who kept crossing the line carried weapons to back up their arguments. New England abolitionists shipped boxes of rifles, "Beecher's Bibles," to the antislavery settlers. (An eminent antislavery clergyman, Henry Ward Beecher, had incautiously remarked that a rifle might be a more powerful moral agent on the Kansas plains than a Bible.) Sporadic shootings and barnburnings culminated, in May 1856, in a raid by Missouri "border ruffians" on the free-soil town of Lawrence. They sacked the place, destroyed the type and press of an antislavery newspaper, and terrorized the inhabitants. A few days later John Brown, a grim abolitionist fanatic, retaliated. He and his sons and companions undertook a foray through the valley of Potawatomie Creek, where they stole horses, murdered five settlers, and mutilated their bodies. Brown claimed that he was an agent of the Lord, assigned to punish those who favored slavery. His atrocities spurred a counterattack by proslavery men, who fell upon Brown's band, killed one of his sons, and burned the settlement at Osawatomie. Though federal troops prevented further private war, the slavery issue had brought blood and terror to Kansas.

His own larger passions aroused, Senator Charles Sumner of Massachusetts, an outspoken abolitionist, delivered, on May 19, 1856, a bitter speech, "The Crime Against Kansas," in which he poured invective on the proslavery men of the South. Sumner denounced South Carolina and, with unstinted personal meanness, one of her absent senators, Andrew Pickens Butler. Two days later Butler's nephew, Congressman Preston Brooks of South Carolina, stalked into the Senate chamber and beat Sumner unconscious with his cane. It was several years before Sumner again took part in Senate debates; meanwhile, Brooks' assault made Sumner a martyr in the eyes of the enemies of slavery, although to most Southerners he seemed a demagogue who had got what he deserved. Coming on the heels of the bloodshed in Kansas, the incident heightened the emotional strain of a nation stumbling to find some way to settle the slavery controversy.

The election of 1856. The Administration of Franklin Pierce, begun in hope, died in futility. The nation, leaderless, was in ferment as the presidential campaign of 1856 approached. Convening at Philadelphia in June, the Republicans were confident. Their new party had already won control of most of the Northern state governments. Turning their back on the South and its votes, they adopted a strong free-soil platform that denounced the repeal of the Missouri Compromise, asserted that it was the duty of Congress to prohibit slavery — a relic of barbarism — in the territories, urged that Kansas be admitted as a free state, and condemned the Ostend Manifesto (see p. 301).

The platform was not, however, an abolitionist pronunciamento. It did not say that the federal government should interfere with slavery in states where it existed. In effect, the Republicans advocated the containment of slavery, asserting only that it must not be allowed to expand any further. In addition, their platform called for internal improvements and federal aid for the construction of a Pacific railroad. As their candidate for President, the Republicans nominated John C. Frémont, an antislavery man who lacked political experience but had won national recognition and some glory as an explorer and soldier in the West.

The Democrats, meeting in Cincinnati, drew their strength from both the North and the South and were eager for a compromise program that would hold the Union together and the party in office. Their platform explicitly denied the power of Congress to interfere with slavery in the states, upheld the Kansas-Nebraska Act — and so, at least by implication, the principle of popular sovereignty — urged the annexation of Cuba, and maintained a discreet silence on the question of whether or not a territorial legislature could outlaw slavery before the formation of a state government. In selecting a candidate, the Democrats passed over Douglas on the ground that he had become too controversial a figure and nominated James Buchanan of Pennsylvania, who had been conveniently out of the country as American minister to England during the Kansas fracas. The choice of Buchanan was another sign of the Democrats' attempt to find a workable compromise; for the last time, the party was trying to win support in both sections by naming a Northern man with Southern principles. Buchanan, elderly and undistinguished, less principled than partisan, fitted the conventional formula.

Buchanan won the election handily with 174 electoral votes against 114 for Frémont; Millard Fillmore, the Whig and Know-Nothing candidate, got only the 8 votes of Maryland. In the popular vote, however, Buchanan had only 45 per cent of the total. Frémont carried all but five of the free states and could have won the election if he had taken Pennsylvania and either Illinois or Indiana. The Republicans had come close to victory without attracting a single Southern state.

THE HOUSE DIVIDED

Dred Scott. When Buchanan took office, the Kansas issue was still alive, bitterness over the slavery question still growing. Popular sovereignty, instead of settling the question of slaveholders' rights in the territories, had made that question more acute. Southerners were arguing that a territorial legislature was powerless to exclude slavery before the territory was ready to enter the Union as a state, for Congress, they contended, lacked that power, and the territories were the creatures of Congress. Some Southerners also maintained that Congress had a positive duty to protect slavery in the territories.

Buchanan, in his inaugural address in March 1857, remarked that the Supreme Court would soon rule on this question, expressed the hope that agitation on the matter might cease, and urged the nation to accept the Court's ruling, when issued, as a final settlement of the matter. This was a disingenuous request, for the President already knew and approved of the Court's decision in the Dred Scott case.

Dred Scott — whose case reached the Supreme Court in 1856 — was a slave whose owner had taken him from Missouri into Illinois and then into Wisconsin Territory, which at the time had been free soil under the Missouri Compromise. Taken back to Missouri, Scott found himself the center of a test case when suit was filed in his behalf asking that he be declared a free man on the ground that his sojourn in free territory had automatically ended his servitude. The Missouri Supreme Court had ruled against this plea, holding that even in Illinois Scott had still been subject to Missouri law. A United States circuit judge, to whom the case next came, held that Scott, because he was a Negro, was not a citizen and therefore not entitled to bring suit under federal jurisdiction. Scott's lawyers then appealed to the United States Supreme Court. In conference in February 1857 the justices decided to dispose of the case by confirming the interpretation of the Missouri Court.

Several justices, however, soon changed their minds. John McLean of Ohio and Benjamin R. Curtis of Massachusetts prepared dissents that, in supporting Scott's plea, reviewed the question of the Missouri Compromise and, in finding that law constitutional, upheld the authority of Congress to regulate slavery in the territories. This antislavery opinion provoked the proslavery justices to spell out their views, which at least one of them — James M. Wayne of Georgia — had apparently resolved to do in any event. The proslavery majority now prepared to dispose of the Dred Scott case on the broadest grounds. Justice John Catron so informed Buchanan, and the President-elect urged Justice Robert C. Grier of Pennsylvania to stand with his five Southern brethren. Buchanan, then, had some responsibility for the Court's seven-to-two decision against Scott just two days after the inauguration.

Though each of the justices issued a separate opinion, five of them concurred with the long, involved, and forceful opinion of Chief Justice Roger B. Taney. In essence, the majority announced that a Negro could not be entitled to the rights of federal citizenship. Negroes, Taney said, had been regarded for more than a century before the Constitution was adopted as "beings of an inferior order" with "no rights which any white man was bound to respect." This doctrine shocked many Northerners, who were equally offended by Taney's second major point. The Missouri Compromise, he held, was unconstitutional, because Congress had no power to prohibit slavery in the territories. Neither did the territorial legislatures. Slaves, Taney went on, were property; the Fifth Amendment guaranteed that no citizen should be deprived of his property without "due process of law"; thus Congress was restrained from forbidding slaveholding, and the law of 1820 was "therefore void." McLean and Curtis dissented. Curtis' powerful rebuttal argued that Negroes had been citizens in several states before the Constitution was adopted and that nothing in the Constitution deprived them of that status. The Constitution, Curtis continued, expressly granted Congress the power to "make all needful Rules and Regulations respecting the Territory . . . belonging to the United States," and the Missouri Compromise was therefore lawful.

Taney's opinion and Curtis' dissent heightened the controversy over slavery. The South rejoiced in the Court's rulings, which fully confirmed that region's attitude about race and about the Constitution. But the majority opinion cut the ground from under the Republican platform on slavery, and Northern Republicans recited Curtis' reasoning to support their own. As advocates of popular sovereignty realized, if Taney was right and Curtis wrong, then Douglas' position was of questionable constitutionality.

Fiasco in Kansas. Whatever its legal merits, popular sovereignty had still to meet the test of application in Kansas. Buchanan, eager to end the bewildering disorder there, named Robert J. Walker of Mississippi as territorial governor. In March 1857 Walker went to Kansas hoping to bring the territory under a legal government acceptable to all and to get a constitution adopted under which the territory could become a state. He summoned a constitutional convention, but he was obliged to turn over to the proslavery legislature all arrangements for the election of delegates. Most of the free-soil settlers, complaining that the election was rigged, boycotted it. Consequently, the convention that met in the fall of 1857 at the temporary capital of Lecompton was controlled by the proslavery group. The delegates first adopted a constitution that made slavery legal in Kansas and then provided that when the constitution was submitted to the electorate no one could vote against it. Voters might accept the constitution as it was or else they might accept a slightly modified version that made slavery legal but forbade importing additional slaves. The ratifying election was also boycotted by the free-soil people, and the Lecompton constitution was adopted by a one-sided vote.

To make matters even more bewildering, another election was held in the summer of 1858 to select members of a territorial legislature. Walker did his best to make this a fair election, and the free-state voters carried it; the new legislature then called a referendum on the Lecompton constitution, which the majority now rejected.

Walker came east to discuss his woes with the Administration. He wanted to cancel everything and start all over again, but Buchanan refused. Though the Lecompton constitution was patently a fraud, Southern leaders in the Democratic party were solidly in favor of it, and Buchanan, unwilling to lose their support, backed them up. Walker resigned, and the President presented the Lecompton constitu-

tion to Congress in a message that cited the Dred Scott decision to prove that Kansas was "as much a slave state as Georgia." The prompt admission of Kansas, he went on, would "restore peace and quiet to the whole country," whereas its rejection would be "keenly felt" by the fifteen slave states. This was too much for Douglas. Breaking with the South and the Administration, he spoke out vigorously against the Lecompton constitution. He was indignant at the highhanded way in which the slavery forces had taken over a territory in which most of the settlers were opposed to slavery, and he felt that his popular-sovereignty doctrine had been distorted beyond recognition. The bill to admit Kansas passed the Senate by a vote of 33 to 25, with Douglas joining the Republican minority, but it had no chance in the House.

Democrats in the lower chamber contrived a compromise, which the Senate accepted. It provided for resubmitting the Lecompton constitution to the people of Kansas, and for a federal land grant if the constitution were adopted. The Republicans denounced the obvious bribe, but it had no discernible effect on the vote. In August 1858 in an honest election, the Kansans rejected the constitution, 11,300 to 1,788. By then, however, Buchanan's habitual concessions to the Southern Democrats had alienated Douglas and his Northern Democratic supporters. The President who was to have cemented the party had helped split it.

The Panic of 1857. Meanwhile, in 1857, the country had experienced a brief but severe economic depression. The new railroad network had been built too far and too fast, with many lines reaching into thinly settled areas where there was no hope for immediate profits. In addition, the land boom that had spread across the Middle West and the Northwest had ended characteristically in a general collapse of land prices, widespread defaulting of mortgages, and a severe strain on the country's flimsy banking structure. On top of all this the end of the Crimean War in Europe deflated the overseas market for farm products, and American farmers found themselves unable to dispose of bumper crops of wheat and meat.

The depression hurt the North more than the South. The network of financial, manufacturing, and transportation interests in the North was much larger and more intricate than

Wall Street: The Panic of 1857.

in the South and hence felt the shock of the depression more keenly. Moreover, since the world market for cotton continued to expand, the Cotton Kingdom weathered the depression very well. All in all, Southerners had reason to conclude that their economy was more stable than that of the North. Their leaders proclaimed that cotton was indeed king, and began to suggest that the South could manage handsomely by itself. They grew more confident that neither New England nor Europe could get along without Southern cotton and that the prospect of losing it would compel the North, Great Britain, and France to accede to demands for "Southern rights."

Many Northern manufacturers, hard hit by the depression, attributed it to the low Tariff of 1857. Some, demanding a protective tariff, moved into the Republican party, giving the South one more reason for hating it. Southerners, already convinced that Republican control of the federal government would bring about a ruinous policy toward slavery, now feared that it would also foster the exploitation of the agricultural South by the commercial and industrial North. As always, moreover, depression

hurt the party in power, and Democrats, especially Southerners, faced the congressional campaign of 1858 anxiously.

The election of 1858. The most memorable of the contests of 1858 occurred in Illinois, where Douglas, the Democratic senatorial nominee, opposed Abraham Lincoln, his Republican rival. Lincoln was by no means unknown. He had served a term in Congress, he had narrowly missed election to the Senate in the early 1850's, and he had received several votes for nomination as Vice-President in the Republican convention of 1856. Not yet a national figure, he had at least emerged from obscurity, and he was the logical candidate of the Illinois Republicans. His rangy body; his homely, rugged features; his crisp, penetrating speech; his frontier background and straightforward ways made him a striking figure on the platform. His long service in the Whig party had given him a broad political acquaintanceship. His thoughtful conservatism tempered his Jeffersonian convictions with practicality. Even for the Little Giant, Lincoln was a formidable opponent, and during the campaign he proved himself a shrewd and effective fighter.

Lincoln challenged Douglas to a series of debates, which focused on the territorial problem, particularly the case of Kansas. By no means an abolitionist, Lincoln was a convinced free-soiler and a telling critic of both popular sovereignty and the Dred Scott decision. The Republicans, he pointed out, considered slavery "a moral, social and political wrong"; the Democrats did not. The Republicans intended to prevent the spread of the blight of slavery; the Democrats did not. At Freeport, Illinois, Lincoln put to Douglas a question much in men's minds: Was there any lawful way in which the inhabitants of a territory could keep slavery from their midst?

Douglas, eagerly rehearsing his own conviction, replied that the answer was simple. The inhabitants could not legally outlaw slavery — that much the Supreme Court had declared — but they could effectively keep it from their midst simply by refusing to adopt the strict slave code that would be needed to protect it. Unless such a code existed, no slave-owner would bring his valuable property into the territory, and the problem of slavery would never arise.

This reply satisfied most Northern Democrats as a logical, practical application of popular sovereignty, but to the proslavery Southern Democrats it seemed outrageous. Douglas had already broken with the Buchanan Administration; he was at war with the Southerners in his party; and he had killed the Lecompton constitution in Congress. Now he was saying that the Dred Scott decision really offered the South nothing. The "Freeport doctrine" was one part of the set of attitudes and purposes that cost Douglas his chance for his party's nomination in 1860. Still, the doctrine sufficed in 1858 in Illinois, where the Democrats won control of the legislature, though they did not poll a majority of the votes, and returned Douglas to his seat.

Through the country, the Democrats held

Stephen A. Douglas: "The Little Giant."

tenuous control of the Senate. The Republicans gained the largest representation in the House, but Know-Nothing congressmen kept them from a majority there. Lincoln, though defeated, earned national Republican acclaim. His interrogation of Douglas had driven deeper wedges between Northern and Southern Democrats. And Lincoln's own program — his insistence on excluding slavery from the territories, his clear denunciation of the immorality of slavery, and yet his promise not to interfere with that institution where it already existed — gave the Republican position the most compelling statement it had known. Lincoln also defined the long-range problem succinctly and in so doing marked the gap between the purpose of his party and that of either of the Democratic factions. " 'A house divided against itself cannot stand,' " he had told the Republican state convention. "I believe that this government cannot endure permanently half *slave* and half *free*."

DENOUEMENT

Harper's Ferry. In the new Congress, the state of mind of the Southern Democrats, who were no longer able to shape public policy, had become alarming. In 1856 they had been content to abide with their interpretation of popular sovereignty and to assert that Congress lacked power to meddle with slavery in the states; now, reacting to the Freeport doctrine, they were close to insisting on a federal slave code for the territories. But the Northern Democrats would accept no such thing. The only national party left in the country was in imminent danger of splitting on a sectional basis. If the 1860 campaign offered only a choice between sectional loyalties, the federal Union would be tested as it had never been before.

In a time of quiet, such a test might have been avoided, or at least postponed. But there was no quiet. During 1859 continued by-elections kept politics at high heat. So did Buchanan's distribution of patronage to Douglas' enemies, and so did Republican proposals for the economic and land programs that Southern Democrats opposed. Most disturbing, in 1859 John Brown struck directly at slavery in the South itself.

The Great Debate: Lincoln

I have stated upon former occasions ... what I understand to be the real issue in this controversy between Judge Douglas and myself. On the point of my wanting to make war between the Free and the Slave States, there has been no issue between us. So, too, when he assumes that I am in favor of introducing a perfect social and political equality between the white and black races. These are false issues.... The real issue in this controversy — the one pressing upon every mind — is the sentiment on the part of one class that looks upon the institution of slavery *as a wrong,* and of another class that *does not* look upon it as a wrong. The sentiment that contemplates the institution of slavery in this country as a wrong is the sentiment of the Republican party.... They look upon it as being a moral, social, and political wrong; and while they contemplate it as such, they nevertheless have due regard for ... the difficulties of getting rid of it in any satisfactory way and to all the constitutional obligations thrown about it. Yet ... they insist that it should, as far as may be, *be treated* as a wrong; and one of the methods of treating it as a wrong is to *make provision that it shall grow no larger.*

From Abraham Lincoln, Speech at Alton, Illinois, October 15, 1858.

Brown in his first fifty-five years had engaged in more than twenty business ventures, most of them failures. Some terminated in bankruptcy, two in crime. He had regularly failed to pay his debts. Since 1855 he had depended for his livelihood on contributions from people whom he persuaded, remarkably, of his integrity and high purpose. Doubtless his fiery passion against slavery blinded his victims to his palpable record of dishonesty. There was evidence of much insanity in Brown's mother's family, and his sister, as well as one of his sons (he had twenty children), was also insane. If he was not himself mad, he was at least a monomaniac about religion and slavery, a psychopathic individual who revealed the symptoms of paranoia and, by his deeds, provoked those symptoms in others.

Brown's plan was to seize some stronghold in the Southern mountains where he could gather slaves together and arm them. This action, he felt, would touch off a general slave

uprising; the slaveholders would be unable to suppress it; the peculiar institution would collapse. Brown had gained financial support from eminent New Englanders who hated slavery; most of them, by no means insane, however vengeful they may have been, were canny enough to keep themselves ignorant of exactly what he was planning, for they did not propose to be accessories before the fact in an insurrection that might fail and come to the gallows. At a hideout in the Maryland hills Brown recruited a handful of followers, collected weapons, and made ready for his stroke.

In October 1859 Brown led his strange company down across the Potomac to seize the government arsenal at Harper's Ferry, Virginia. In theory this bold stroke would give him the armaments he needed, the slaves of Virginia would flock to join him, the nearby mountains would offer a safe retreat, and the great slave uprising would take place. Actually, the old man's planning was so fuzzy that his project never had a chance. He did manage to seize the fire-engine house at the arsenal, and a few bewildered slaves were induced or compelled to join him. In the incidental shooting a few men were killed. Brown himself stayed in the fire-engine house. State militia blocked

John Brown: At the least, a monomaniac.

all his escape routes, while a detachment of United States marines marched up the river from Washington under the command of a regular-army officer, Lieutenant Colonel Robert E. Lee, who chanced to be in the capital at the time. The marines carried the fire-engine house by assault, took Brown and his followers prisoner, and transferred him to Charles Town, Virginia, to stand trial for treason. He was speedily convicted and on December 2, 1859, he was hanged.

The Virginia authorities would probably have been wiser simply to have had Brown adjudged insane and confined in an asylum. By hanging him, they made him a martyr. The one thing John Brown could do well was to die. From the moment of his arrest until the moment of his execution he behaved with dignity, courage, and restraint, and many Northerners who did not themselves believe in fomenting slave uprisings heaped praise upon him.

As a result, the Harper's Ferry raid took on an exaggerated importance. It had been the futile act of a madman, and it had been denounced by most people in the North. But it had touched the South on a particularly sensitive nerve, for the dread of a slave uprising always lay just below the slave-owner's consciousness. John Brown had actually tried to stage one, apparently with the encouragement of antislavery people in the North, and on his death he was hailed there as a martyr, with public ceremonies of mourning. Many thoughtful Southerners were now convinced that the Northerners who wanted to abolish slavery meant also to inflict bloodshed and destruction on the people who held slaves.

The election of 1860. The 1850's drew to a close with a presidential election that, instead of helping to harmonize the differences between the sections, put them almost beyond hope of settlement. At the Democratic convention in Charleston in April 1860 the differences within the party were quickly exposed as past healing.

Senator Douglas was the leading contender for the nomination, but even though a majority of the delegates probably would have accepted him, he could not muster the two-thirds vote the party rules required. The Buchanan Administration fought him as a matter of party politics; neither the President nor such

---

The Great Debate: Douglas

We ought to extend to the negro race ... all the rights, all the privileges, and all the immunities which they can exercise consistently with the safety of society. Humanity requires that we should give them all these privileges; Christianity commands that we should extend those privileges to them. The question then arises, What are those privileges, and what is the nature and extent of them? My answer is, that that is a question which each State must answer for itself.... If the people of all the States will act on that great principle, and each State mind its own business, attend to its own affairs, take care of its own negroes, and not meddle with its neighbors, then there will be peace between the North and the South, the East and the West, throughout the whole Union.

Why can we not thus have peace?... The moment the North obtained the majority in the House and Senate by the admission of California, and could elect a President without the aid of Southern votes, that moment ambitious Northern men formed a scheme to excite the North against the South, and make the people be governed in their votes by geographical lines, thinking that the North, being the stronger section, would outvote the South, and consequently they, the leaders, would ride into office on a sectional hobby.

From Stephen A. Douglas, Speech at Alton, Illinois, October 15, 1858.

---

influential party stalwarts as Howell Cobb of Georgia, John Slidell of Louisiana, or Jefferson Davis of Mississippi would accept a man who had broken with the party leadership on the Lecompton issue, and all the resources of federal patronage were arrayed against him. In addition, the extremists — William L. Yancey of Alabama, Robert B. Rhett of South Carolina, and Edmund Ruffin of Virginia — were determined to accept nothing less than a platform and a candidate explicitly committed to the proslavery position. Specifically, they wanted a federal slave code in the territories, a code that would correct the flaw in the Dred Scott decision that Douglas had spotted at Freeport. The fact that a campaign based on such a program could not hope to win in the North struck them as an advantage rather than a handicap. Above all, they were fighting against any implication that slavery could be

The Election of 1860

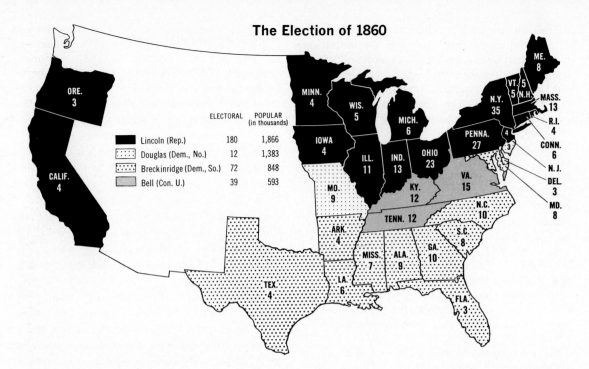

	ELECTORAL	POPULAR (in thousands)
■ Lincoln (Rep.)	180	1,866
▦ Douglas (Dem., No.)	12	1,383
▨ Breckinridge (Dem., So.)	72	848
▦ Bell (Con. U.)	39	593

ORE. 3
CALIF. 4
MINN. 4
WIS. 5
IOWA 4
MICH. 6
ILL. 11
IND. 13
OHIO 23
MO. 9
KY. 12
VA. 15
TENN. 12
ARK. 4
N.C. 10
S.C. 8
MISS. 7
ALA. 9
GA. 10
LA. 6
TEX. 4
FLA. 3
ME. 8
VT. 5
N.H. 5
N.Y. 35
MASS. 13
R.I. 4
CONN. 6
N.J. 4
PENNA. 27
DEL. 3
MD. 8

contained, for they believed that containment would be the first step toward extinction. To avert containment they were ready to split both the party and the Union itself.

Men like Yancey represented only a minority in the South, but it was a determined, tightly organized, ably directed minority that knew exactly what it wanted. It wanted, ultimately, secession of the slaveholding states. Most Southerners in the spring of 1860 were not ready for secession; but if the Democratic convention and the election showed that an all-out "Southern-rights" candidate and platform could not win, then thousands of Southerners who still considered themselves Unionists might be willing to accept secession. This was the goal to which the Yancey group devoted itself at Charleston in April.

The convention fell into a prolonged row over the platform. The Douglas men, a majority of all those gathered, proposed an equivocal plank declaring that the Democratic party would abide by the decisions of the Supreme Court. Yancey and his supporters insisted on an outright declaration that the federal government had to protect slavery in the territories. Anything less, they warned, would provoke them to walk out. When the

Douglas forces nevertheless persisted in their views, Yancey and the Alabama delegation bolted, and most of the cotton-state men followed. The convention, unable under the circumstances to select a nominee, then adjourned after agreeing to meet again in June in Baltimore.

At Baltimore most of the bolters returned but were challenged for their seats by moderate delegates from the same districts. The Douglasites, at first resolved to admit only their allies, soon agreed to a compromise that readmitted substantially all the bolters except those from Alabama and Louisiana. That formula, which the convention adopted, failed to satisfy a substantial minority of delegates, including those from the Deep South, many from the Upper South and border states, and some from the North. The dissatisfied withdrew. The remaining rump nominated Douglas for President. Their antagonists, calling themselves the real Democratic party, held a convention of their own and nominated John C. Breckinridge of Kentucky. Douglas' platform endorsed popular sovereignty; Breckinridge's demanded a federal code to protect slavery in the territories. Now it was all but certain that the Republican candidate would be elected in the fall.

Fully aware of their opportunity and bent on seizing the proffered prize, the Republicans met in Chicago. They had little difficulty agreeing on a platform — calling for a higher tariff, free homesteads, internal improvements, and a Pacific railroad. These planks promised to attract votes in both the industrial East and the agricultural West. Idealists throughout the North could applaud the party's firm stand against any extension of slavery in the territories. For good measure the platform added a denunciation of Southern threats of secession, which were becoming more and more common. Then, looking for a candidate who could pull together the various elements in this still half-formed party, the delegates passed up the most prominent contender, William H. Seward, on the ground that he had been too outspoken, had made too many enemies, and was too closely identified with the militant anti-slavery element. The nomination went instead, in part because of the skillful maneuvering of his floor-managers, to Abraham Lincoln.

Now a fourth party entered the field, a party drawing its support from old-line Whigs, Know-Nothings, and dissident Democrats, calling themselves the Constitutional Union party. They named John Bell of Tennessee as their candidate and prepared to campaign on a program that simply demanded support for the Union and the Constitution.

The campaign was long and bitter. With strenuous determination Douglas stumped the nation — the first presidential candidate ever to do so — from July to November. He sought to reassure the South about his position on slavery, to evoke Unionist support in the North, to make his party, as he represented it, again triumphant as a national party. Secession, he warned, would mean disaster; a Republican victory would provoke secession; the Union had to come first. "Every disunionist in America," he charged, "is a Breckinridge man." Breckinridge, for his part, did not campaign. His organization, confident of his strength in the South, tried also to reach voters in the free states, to whom Breckinridge was presented as the one truly conservative and constitutional candidate. Bell, while pledged to preserve the Union, lacked a strong national party organization, though his middle position and his pleas for brotherhood had

some appeal everywhere and particular attraction in the border states. The Republicans alone made little effort to conduct a national campaign. They focused on the North, where Lincoln's managers and the local party candidates promised citizenship to immigrants, homesteads to farmers in the West, and tariff protection to manufacturers and industrial workers in the East. The Republicans played down the slavery issue in conservative areas

Lincoln the candidate.

The Election of 1860: The Extreme South Speaks

The history of the ... Black Republican party of the North is a history of repeated injuries and usurpations, all having in direct object the establishment of absolute tyranny over the slave-holding States. And all without the smallest ... justification.... Every appeal and expostulation has only brought upon us renewed insults and augmented injuries. They have robbed us of our property ... they have set at naught the decrees of the Supreme Court, they have invaded our States and killed our citizens, they have declared their unalterable determination to exclude us altogether from the Territories, they have nullified the laws of Congress, and finally they have capped the mighty pyramid of unfraternal enormities by electing Abraham Lincoln ... on a platform and by a system which indicates nothing but the subjugation of the South and the complete ruin of her social, political and industrial institutions.

From the New Orleans *Daily Crescent,* November 13, 1860, quoted in D. L. Dumond, ed., *Southern Editorials on Secession,* 1931.

Southern Secession: The Extreme North Speaks

There never was such a set of arrogant and imperious rulers as the slave-driving captains of this Republic.... Such men cannot be created except by Slavery. It is the institution that makes them.... Of all men, they most need the discipline of reverses and the humiliation of defeat. It is their insolence of temper that forbids them to submit to being fairly beaten in a Presidential election. They will not take the position of a defeated party. They will rule or they will ruin.... They will remain in control of the Government, or they will drag it down about our ears, and bury all in a common destruction.

From J. S. Pike in the New York *Tribune,* January 17, 1861, quoted in K. M. Stampp, ed., *The Causes of the Civil War,* 1959.

like Indiana and Illinois but struck strong anti-slavery positions in New England, Wisconsin, northern Ohio, and other regions in which radical tempers prevailed. Lincoln, arguing that he had already made his position clear, maintained a cautious silence. That tactic, doubtless useful in winning Northern moder-

ates, eased none of the worries of Southerners about "black Republicanism."

The election whetted their fears. Lincoln won a decisive majority in the Electoral College — 180 votes to 123 for all the rival candidates together — though his 1,865,593 popular votes came to barely 40 per cent of the total. Lincoln was neither the first nor the last President to win office with a minority of the popular vote — John Quincy Adams, James K. Polk, and James Buchanan had already done so. But Lincoln's victory was obviously sectional: he had received no popular votes in the Deep South and very few in the border states. Douglas, who won a mere handful of electoral votes, ran second with 1,382,713, while Breckinridge and Bell between them polled 1,411,262.

Secession. The election of a Republican President profoundly disturbed the great majority of the people in all fifteen of the slave states. But the South was not, in November of 1860, in complete agreement about what to do next. Extremist leaders like Yancey and Rhett welcomed the Republican victory as justification for the secession they had dreamed of so long and so ardently, but Union sentiment in the South remained strong. Lincoln had denied any intention of trying to free the slaves; a Southern majority still dominated the United States Supreme Court; and the Democrats still controlled the Senate. The South could perhaps be drawn into secession, but not en masse and not without careful leadership. It might not have gone at all if South Carolina had not dramatically exerted that leadership.

Anticipating Lincoln's victory, the South Carolina legislature had remained in session over election day, and immediately thereafter it summoned a state convention. On December 20, without a dissenting vote, the convention passed an ordinance of secession, proclaiming that the union between South Carolina and all the other states was dissolved.

South Carolina obviously could not exist by itself as an independent nation. But if South Carolina could be compelled, by force, to return to the Union, the possibility of peaceful secession would be gone forever. Fundamental to political thinking in the South was the belief that any state could leave the Union if it wanted to, and to many Southerners this right

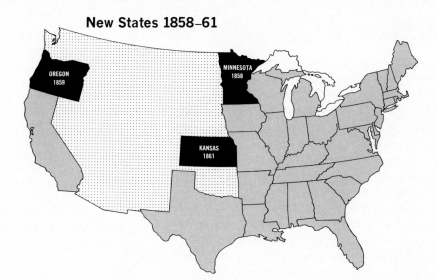

New States 1858-61

OREGON
1859

MINNESOTA
1858

KANSAS
1861

was the ultimate defense against Northern interference with their cherished way of life. The Republican victory pointed to the possibility of such interference, perhaps not at once, but ultimately. Clearly the North had gained the balance of political power. Free population was settling the open territories; California, Minnesota, and Oregon had come into the Union as free states; and urban and industrial development were swelling Northern population and strength. Northern demands for a high tariff, for internal improvements, for a national banking system would soon, given the trend of events, command congressional majorities. All this was portended by Lincoln's election, to which Southern extremists attached still more terrifying omens — the end of state rights, the freedom of the slaves, the violation of Southern white womanhood.

These expectations fed the sectional consciousness of the South and lent persuasion to South Carolina's quick, decisive act. Within six weeks, five other states adopted their own ordinances of secession — Georgia, Florida, Alabama, Mississippi, and Louisiana, though in both Georgia and Alabama a thoughtful minority urged delay. A convention of delegates from the six seceded states met in Montgomery, Alabama, early in February 1861. They formed a new government to be known as the Confederate States of America, adopted a constitution similar to that of the United States, and named Jefferson Davis and Alex-

ander H. Stephens as provisional President and Vice-President. (An election the following November confirmed these choices.)

The Confederacy, to which Texas soon adhered, was made up of the states of the Deep South, where cotton was king both on the small farms that produced most of the crop and on the large plantations of the *nouveau riche*. Here slavery was still a dynamic institution (see p. 210) with an apparently enduring future. Though sentiment in these states was not unanimous for secession, though there was unquestionably more feeling for an undivided Union than was visible on the surface, the secessionist leaders had been well organized and forceful, and the new Confederacy came into existence on a wave of enthusiasm. Its adherents contemplated a rosy future — continuing profits from cotton, a commercial alliance with England, freedom from Northern lenders and sellers, expansion into the Caribbean or Mexico, the fulfillment of Southern reveries. Few men in the Deep South, even among the Unionists, believed that the North would or could resist secession; fewer still thought the North would fight for union; almost none foresaw a terrible war and eventual defeat.

Yet secessionist arguments and expectations were not compelling outside the cotton country. None of the border states at first joined the Confederacy. From Virginia to Missouri, eight slave states refused to secede. Their people

Why the War: Men at Fault?

It is difficult to achieve a full realization of how Lincoln's generation stumbled into a ghastly war.... If one questions the term "blundering generation," let him inquire how many measures of the time he would wish copied or repeated.... Traditional "explanations" of the war fail to make sense when fully analyzed.... Let one take all the factors traditionally presented — the Sumter maneuver, the election of Lincoln, abolitionism, slavery in Kansas, pre-war objections to the Union, cultural and economic differences, etc. — and it will be seen that only by a false display could any of these issues, or all of them together, be said to have caused the war.... If one word or phrase were selected to account for the war, that word would not be slavery, or economic grievance, or state rights, or diverse civilizations. It would have to be such a word as fanaticism (on both sides), misunderstanding, misrepresentation, or perhaps politics.

From J. G. Randall, *Lincoln the Liberal Statesman*, 1947.

---

disliked a Republican administration, but they did not believe that the election, in itself, required them to leave the Union. Many of them considered the secession of the cotton states a political maneuver — a means of inducing the North to make concessions, after which the seceding states would return to the Union with guarantees of Southern rights.

No compromise. While the states of the Deep South were seceding and moving toward the Confederacy, most Americans in the months after the election hoped for a conciliatory solution. Especially in the border states men looked for a compromise that would restore the Union, preclude conflict, and erase the anxieties that had been growing for a decade.

Buchanan denied South Carolina's right to secede, but he also denied his own right to use force to prevent her. The Union, he argued, was perpetual, but it rested upon consent. He hoped negotiations would bring back the seceded states; in contrast, they expected any agreement to legitimize their new status in Northern eyes.

In the Senate, a Committee of Thirteen searched vainly for a compromise. One was submitted to the Senate by John J. Crittenden of Kentucky. It called for a constitutional amendment to prohibit slavery in territories "now held or hereafter acquired" north of the old Missouri Compromise line; it also protected slavery with a federal slave code in territories south of that line; further, it protected the domestic slave trade and endorsed a constitutional amendment prohibiting Congress for all time from interfering with slavery in the states. Lincoln and other leading Republicans opposed this proposal. They had no fear that slavery would ever take root in such territories as New Mexico, but they did fear that Southern expansionists would try to extend slavery and the American flag to Cuba and portions of Mexico and Central America. The Republicans, in short, would accept no program that encouraged the further spread of slavery.

Southerners were wholly dissatisfied with the concessions Lincoln approved. The President-elect was prepared to guarantee enforcement of the Fugitive Slave Law and, if necessary by constitutional amendment, the right of the states to maintain slavery where it existed. When the Southerners rejected these conditions, the impasse moved Crittenden to suggest a national referendum on his program, but the Republicans prevented that.

Efforts at compromise outside Congress also failed. At the request of the Virginia General Assembly, a convention of delegates from twenty-one states met in Washington early in February to seek some settlement. Former President Tyler presided over a company of distinguished men, but their differences quickly proved more marked than their agreements, and their proceedings were handicapped by the absence of delegations from the seceding states and six others. The Peace Convention, after three weeks of deliberation, sent Congress a plan for seven amendments to the Constitution, which, taken together, rehearsed the ill-fated Crittenden proposal and elicited only negligible support.

Now lingering hopes for compromise faded away. Even Buchanan had stiffened and reorganized his Cabinet, replacing state-righters with committed Union men. In his last message to Congress, on January 8, 1861, he appealed for patriotism, rejected the possibility of aggressive war against the seceded states, but also asserted his obligation as President to collect federal revenues and protect federal properties throughout the United States. "The Union," he concluded, "must and shall be preserved by all constitutional means. . . . The present is no time for palliations. Action, prompt action, is required."

In that spirit Buchanan decided to send a ship to reinforce the federal garrison at Fort Sumter, South Carolina. At first he considered dispatching a warship for this purpose, but his advisers persuaded him to send instead an unarmed, and therefore less threatening, merchantman. The *Star of the West*, carrying troops and ammunition, sailed from New York the first week in January. Before she entered Charleston Harbor, the South Carolinians fired upon her, whereupon she came about and steamed away. Major Robert Anderson at Fort Sumter had been about to return the fire and protect the ship. But his guns stayed silent, and his small force was left without reinforcement or adequate supplies. But Fort Sumter remained under federal control, as did Fort Pickens in Florida and a few others. Elsewhere during January 1861 the Confederacy had seized federal forts and arsenals and other establishments. Buchanan failed to protect public property and collect public revenues; Southern independence asserted itself in deed as well as word; and the Confederates, it was clear, were ready to fight for the independence they had declared.

Lincoln takes over. Lincoln's arrival in Washington was inauspicious. At the urging of friends who were afraid he might be assassinated, he reached the city after a secret ride through the night. He seemed preoccupied with patronage, indecisive about the national crisis, an awkward and inept man who would be the agent of powerful advisers like Seward, the designated Secretary of State.

But the new President's inaugural address revealed his true timber. There would be no invasion of the South, he said, no interference with the institution of slavery. Yet "we cannot separate," he maintained; the Union was not dissoluble; and he would use his power "to hold, occupy, and possess the property, and places belonging to the federal government." The "momentous issue of civil war" lay in the hands of the Confederates. Lincoln went on:

Why the War: Slavery the Cause?

Slavery was at the very heart of our disequilibrium. It was the core of the social, the economic, the political, and the constitutional conflicts. But in the fifteen years left to the United States in which to face and solve the problem of slavery, the final decade and a half which ended in civil war, it did not face that problem but faced only a peripheral and even unreal issue that was ancillary to it. The federal powers and the state rights in regard to slavery, the future of slavery, the limitations of and on slavery, the relation of all these to the structure and functioning of our society — were fought out not in regard to themselves, the only way in which there was a possibility that they might be solved peacefully, but in regard to the status of slavery in the territories, where slavery could not exist. There, if you will, is a fact of illimitable importance.

From Bernard De Voto, "The Easy Chair," *Harper's Magazine*, February 1946.

The government will not assail *you*. . . . *You have no oath* . . . to destroy the government, while I . . . have the most solemn one to "preserve, protect, and defend" it. . . . We must not be enemies. . . . The mystic chords of memory . . . will yet swell the chorus of the Union, when again touched, as surely they will be, by the better angels of our nature.

When Lincoln made this statement, he believed that Major Anderson had ample supplies to hold out for several weeks or months. There would be no fighting at Fort Sumter, as he saw it, unless South Carolina (or the Confederacy, which had by now asserted its own control over military matters in Charleston) opened fire and forced the issue. If there was to be a war, the Confederacy would have to start it.

Lincoln immediately learned that his calculations were wrong. Major Anderson's stock of foodstuffs was just about exhausted, and the day after delivering his inaugural address Lincoln was notified that the fort could hold out for only a few more weeks. Unless it could be supplied at once, Anderson would have to surrender. The overt act, as a result, would have to be taken by the federal government, for its efforts to supply Fort Sumter would almost certainly be taken by Jefferson Davis as a warlike step against the new Confederacy.

Up to this point Lincoln had been firm but conciliatory, eager to assert federal authority, reluctant actually to exercise it. To act against Sumter was to risk driving the Upper South to secession. Not to act was to acknowledge disunion. Over Sumter, then, Lincoln and his countrymen faced their great crisis, and over Sumter and what it symbolized, opinion had hardened. The Confederates could not permit reinforcement without jeopardizing their claim to national independence. In the North, patriots believed that the destiny of America, of the whole democratic experiment launched in 1776, depended on preserving the Union. More selfish men had also begun to draw a hard line. Disunity would reduce the value of government securities and weaken the bonds of internal trade and commerce. Consequently the business community felt the need to save the Union even at the cost of war. So also, many abolitionists were ready to risk war, which for them would be a crusade against slavery. And Republican politicians could permit secession only at the cost of destroying their young party.

Yet Lincoln hesitated. Only two of his Cabinet, Secretary of the Treasury Salmon P. Chase and Postmaster General Montgomery Blair, favored sending food to Sumter, and the commanding general of the army, Winfield Scott, advised against such a move. By April 1, most of the Cabinet had come to agree with Blair, but in a note to Lincoln on that day Secretary Seward talked wildly about cementing Union sentiment, north and south, by drawing a European power into war. He had earlier gone as far as to negotiate indirectly on his own with Confederate commissioners in Washington, to whom he sent word that Sumter would be evacuated.

But Lincoln, steady as ever, reached a reasoned decision. Sumter, he concluded, had to be relieved, for anything less testified to Southern independence. But he would not dispatch an armed force. Rather, he would try to get supplies to Sumter peacefully; he would take a chance on war but leave the choice to the South. On April 4 the President completed arrangements for an expedition. He informed Governor Francis W. Pickens of South Carolina that "an attempt will be made to supply Fort Sumter with provisions only . . . if such attempt be not resisted, no effort to throw in men, arms, or ammunition will be made, without further notice, or in case of an attack upon the Fort."

Pickens sent the message, received on April 8, to President Davis in Montgomery. Now the weight of decision lay there. The orders came back at once to demand evacuation, and, if Anderson refused, to "reduce" the place. On April 12 the harbor batteries opened fire, at the command of General Pierre G. T. Beauregard — acting, significantly, as an officer of the Confederacy; it was the Southern nation, not just South Carolina, that had taken the step. Major Anderson's men returned the fire, and the fort was badly battered; on the afternoon of April 13, with his food supplies depleted, Anderson agreed to surrender. The following morning — Sunday, April 14 — he hauled down his flag, and his troops were allowed to embark for New York. Beauregard's forces moved into Fort Sumter. The Civil War had begun.

SUGGESTIONS FOR READING

General

Probably the best introduction to the period covered in this chapter is in the early part of J. G. Randall and David Donald, *The Civil War and Reconstruction* (2nd ed., 1961), a learned, judicious, and comprehensive work that is valuable not least for its treatment of relevant bibliography. There is a longer account of the years 1854–61, distinguished for its clarity and scope and for the movement of its prose, in the latter part of Allan Nevins, *Ordeal of the Union*, 2 vols. (1947), and its sequel, *The Emergence of Lincoln*, 2 vols. (1950). Of equal stature, though

* Available in a paperback edition.

its coverage begins in 1856, and of special significance for its interpretation of politics and the political process, is R. F. Nichols, *The Disruption of American Democracy** (1948). There are other important points of view in A. O. Craven, *The Coming of the Civil War** (1842); H. H. Simms, *A Decade of Sectional Controversy* (1942); and D. L. Dumond, *Antislavery Origins of the Civil War in the United States** (1939). Bruce Catton, *The Coming Fury* (1961), is a spirited narrative.

The Kansas-Nebraska Act and Its Aftermath

A major concern of the general works cited above, the Kansas-Nebraska Act receives central and telling analysis in J. C. Malin, *The Nebraska Question, 1852–1854* (1953), and in a splendid essay, R. F. Nichols, "The Kansas-Nebraska Act: A Century of Historiography," *Mississippi Valley Historical Review*, XLIII, 2 (1956). On the aftermath of the act, again apart from the general works already noted, P. W. Gates, *Fifty Million Acres: Conflicts Over Kansas Land Policy, 1854–1890** (1954), has major significance, as do two studies of John Brown: J. C. Malin, *John Brown and the Legend of Fifty-Six* (1942), and the essay on that disturbed figure in C. V. Woodward, *The Burden of Southern History** (1960). The birth and growth of the Republican party absorb A. W. Crandall, *The Early History of the Republican Party, 1854–1856* (1930), and J. A. Isely, *Horace Greeley and the Republican Party, 1853–1861* (1947), while the same subject, seen from the angle of two New England participants, is illuminated in M. B. Duberman, *Charles Francis Adams* (1961), and David Donald, *Charles Sumner and the Coming of the Civil War* (1960). The latter contains a brilliant analysis of Sumner and his controversial caning.

The Court, the Economy, the Election

The classic studies of the Dred Scott case appear in two books of C. B. Swisher: *Roger B. Taney* (1935) and *American Constitutional Development* (1943), which can be supplemented in Vincent Hopkins, *Dred Scott's Case** (1951), and, with special profit, in the pertinent parts of the books of Nevins and Nichols cited above. Nevins also complements G. W. Van Vleck, *The Panic of 1857: An Analytical Study* (1943). Lincoln in the years 1858–60, as in the other years of his epochal life, has been the subject of a library of books, including the general studies already cited. For the beginning student, an outstanding further reading is the superb biography of B. P. Thomas, *Abraham Lincoln* (1952). A. J. Beveridge, *Abraham Lincoln, 1809–1858*, 2 vols. (1928), remains useful, and R. H. Luthin, *The First Lincoln Campaign* (1944), has instructive depth. For its sentiments and expressions of them, Carl Sandburg, *Abraham Lincoln: The Prairie Years*,* especially the one-volume 1929 edition, continues to win some admirers. For the fascination of the events of 1860–61, see B. Catton, *The Coming Fury* (1961), and G. H. Knoles, ed., *The Crisis of the Union, 1860–61* (1965).

Secession and War

Among the many accounts of secession, three of the best are Nevins, cited above; A. O. Craven, *The Growth of Southern Nationalism, 1848–1861* (1953); and R. A. Wooster, *The Secession Conventions of the South* (1962); while two older works are still admirable for their scope and form: D. L. Dumond, *The Secession Movement, 1860–1861* (1931), and U. B. Phillips, *The Course of the South to Secession** (1939). There is significant additional material in Ollinger Crenshaw, *The Slave States in the Presidential Election of 1860* (1945). On the coming of war, P. S. Foner, *Business and Slavery: The New York Merchants and the Irrepressible Conflict* (1941), sets forth an interesting but, in the end, not entirely persuasive thesis. Much more important are the indispensable and somewhat conflicting analyses of David Potter, *Lincoln and His Party in the Secession Crisis, 1860–1861** (1942), and K. M. Stampp, *And the War Came: The North and the Secession Crisis, 1860–1861** (1950). See, too, R. N. Current, *Lincoln and the First Shot** (1963), for a first-rate study of the Sumter crisis.

* Available in a paperback edition.

14

The Civil War

The Civil War tested the courage and stamina of men and women north and south. It tested the respective strengths of a society still essentially agricultural and of a society increasingly industrialized. It tested the qualities of leadership of dozens of soldiers and civilians who carried the greatest burdens Americans had known since the start of their national history. It tested Northern tolerance for the institution of slavery and Southern commitment to local self-determination. It tested the viability of two constitutions under conditions of crisis. Above all, it tested the meaning and determined the future of the federal Union. It was the great trial of the United States, the crucible from which the mature nation emerged.

THE STAGE FOR WAR

The call to arms. The bombardment of Fort Sumter released the explosive force of the sectional tensions that had accumulated during the preceding decade. Passion galvanized loyalties and dispelled irresolution. On April 15, 1861, President Lincoln called on the governors of the Northern states to furnish seventy-five thousand militia for ninety days to put down what he called the "combinations" of men who had seized control of the seceded South. Early in May he asked for forty-two thousand more volunteers to serve a three-year enlistment. He also enlarged the regular army and navy and declared a blockade of the Confederate coast. As recruitment began, the drums in every community beat the theme of dedication to the Union. Secession, in the view of the Administration, was illegal. The rebellion of Southerners had to be put down. That was the sole issue of the war as the President and later the Congress initially defined it. "The central idea pervading this struggle," Lincoln wrote, "is the necessity of proving that popular government is not an absurdity. We must settle this question now, whether, in a free government, the minority have the right to break up the government whenever they choose." Supporting the President, Horace Greeley of the New York *Tribune*, long preoccupied with the

Army of the Potomac on the march, 1863.

slavery question, for a time made the Union his first cause. And Stephen Douglas, who was soon to die, put the case fervently to a Chicago audience: "There can be no neutrals in this war; only patriots — or traitors."

With comparable fervor, the men of the Confederacy rallied to the flag of secession, to the theory of state rights, including the right to leave the Union, to the emotionally powerful appeal of local self-determination. Responding to Jefferson Davis' call for one hundred thousand troops, Southern volunteers marched forth with the verve and the certitude of their Northern counterparts. The very favor of the ministers of the Lord was thrown into the balance. Of the remaining national churches (some had split during the 1840's and 1850's), only the Roman Catholic and Protestant Episcopal failed to divide along sectional lines as the war began.

Confronted with a choice between two flags, between the attraction of Union and the pull of state rights, Virginia, North Carolina, and Arkansas refused to furnish federal troops and within a few weeks formally joined the Confederacy. Tennessee followed them in June. Kentucky and Missouri likewise refused troops, but remained in a state of indecision, their governors stoutly pro-Confederate, their people split between the two causes. The governor of Maryland was pro-Union, but his state also had divided loyalties, and he announced that Maryland would send men to help defend Washington but not to fight in the South. Of all the slave states, only Delaware remained loyal without qualification.

The border states. The second wave of secession strengthened the Confederacy and made the control of the doubtful border states — Kentucky, Missouri, and Maryland — vital to the Union. Lincoln's vigorous policies held them in line. Until Congress met in July, the President alone made the decisions of government. He decided boldly, improvising where no precedent existed, stretching the authority of his office beyond any previous practice. Besides his calls for troops and his proclamation of blockade, he ordered the disbursement of $2 million for "military and naval measures necessary for the defense and support of the government," and, when he had to, he used force without stint or let.

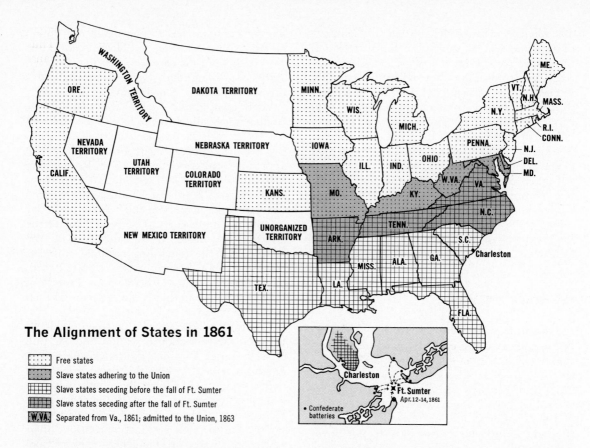

The Alignment of States in 1861

- Free states
- Slave states adhering to the Union
- Slave states seceding before the fall of Ft. Sumter
- Slave states seceding after the fall of Ft. Sumter
- W.VA. Separated from Va., 1861; admitted to the Union, 1863

Charleston

Ft. Sumter
Apr. 12-14, 1861

Confederate batteries

On April 19 the Sixth Massachusetts Infantry, on its way to Washington, passed through Baltimore, a city rife with Confederate sympathies. As the troops marched across town on the way from one railroad station to another, they fell afoul of a mob of disunionists. In the riot that developed, several soldiers and a larger number of civilians were killed. Temporarily, Lincoln ordered additional contingents to bypass Baltimore. But on April 27, 1861, he sent federal troops to occupy the city, authorized suspension of the writ of habeas corpus, and ordered the arrest of suspects. The resort to martial law affected the autumn elections. Union generals then arrested nineteen members of the Maryland legislature, along with the mayor of Baltimore. Further orders called for the arrest also of Southern sympathizers who came to the polls. Union candidates, who were in any case the probable victors, triumphed easily, disunionists fled to the Confederacy, and Maryland became and remained a loyal state.

In Missouri Lincoln followed a similar course. Governor Claiborne Jackson, a leading secessionist, had persuaded the legislature to call a convention to consider secession, but Union sentiment prevailed overwhelmingly. The governor had also called a contingent of state militia into camp on the edge of St. Louis, apparently for the purpose of seizing the federal arsenal there. Lincoln authorized Congressman Francis P. Blair of Missouri to organize a pro-Union "home guard," which was drawn heavily from among German residents of the city. These troops, armed and sworn into federal service and led by Captain Nathaniel Lyon of the regular army, on May 10 forced the surrender of the militiamen without a fight. As Lyon's men marched away, they fell into a riot with St. Louis civilians, and, as in Baltimore, both soldiers and civilians were killed. There followed a period of guerrilla warfare that lasted until federal troops won a commanding victory at Pea Ridge, Arkansas, in March 1862. Meanwhile Jackson and his supporters had proclaimed an independent Missouri government, which seceded, joined the Confederacy, and operated as a government-in-exile in Arkansas and later in Texas. Some 30,000 Missourians ultimately fought for the South, some 109,000 for the North. After Pea Ridge superior Northern power controlled the state, though not without intermittent recourse to martial law.

Kentucky for several months maintained her position of neutrality. As in Missouri, the governor was pro-Confederate, while the legislature was predominantly Unionist. The state contained many Confederate sympathizers, but a majority of the inhabitants probably leaned toward the Union. During the summer, both Lincoln and Davis respected the state's neutrality, at least on the surface, although each executive exerted whatever political pressure he could. Troops for both armies were recruited in Kentucky, but were mustered into service outside the state. Confident that a policy of patience would prevail, Lincoln won his reward in September. Following the occupation of the town of Columbus by a Confederate force, General Grant occupied Paducah for the Union (see p. 352), and in September 1861 the newly elected state legislature authorized a military force to drive out the Confederates. The period of neutrality had ended, and though Southern sympathies remained strong within the state the Union had made a significant gain, for Kentucky was to be a major highway of the war.

Lincoln used still another tactic in western Virginia. Few large plantations and few slaveholders lay beyond the Blue Ridge. For years many of the people who lived there had resented the domination of the state government by the plantation interests of the tidewater region, and now they displayed a strong anti-Confederate sentiment. Capitalizing on this feeling, Lincoln in June ordered an army of twenty thousand volunteers across the Ohio River and into western Virginia. The original aim was to secure the line of the Baltimore & Ohio Railroad, but after the outnumbered Confederates were crushed the Administration encouraged the separatist tendency of the area. In November 1861 the western counties split away and, in an action of questionable legality but unquestionable effectiveness, formed the new state of West Virginia, which Congress formally admitted to the Union in 1863. Thus the Federal authorities secured a major transportation and communication link between the East and the Ohio Valley.

Lincoln's achievement in holding the crucial border states was vital to success in the war. In a revolutionary situation, he had resorted to revolutionary means. Anything less might have surrendered to the Confederacy the margin of ultimate victory.

The Confederacy. Even without the border states, the South was optimistic. It had to wage only a defensive war, as the colonials had against the British. It had only to keep the North from conquest and in that way to establish a separate Southern nation. Confederate leaders expected to protect their territory with relative ease. Though their railroad network was thin except in and near Virginia, they counted on the skill and valor of their troops to repel Northern thrusts anywhere along their front. Their men were conditioned to life outdoors, to shooting and riding; they knew the terrain; they would be fighting to protect their homes. Some Southern leaders also underestimated the bravery and tenacity of the Yankees. Few thought the war would last long, and fewer still realized what a variety of resources it would demand. The dominant belief in speedy triumph rested partly on the expectation of foreign intervention. The South's virtual monopoly of the world's cotton supply was presumed to make England with her textile mills, and France, too, a ready if not a willing potential ally.

The Confederacy also counted heavily on the brilliance of its commanders in the field. General Robert E. Lee and his able lieutenants represented the best in the American military tradition — the best, too, of the alumni of West Point, the cream of the prewar regular army. (In contrast to their officers, the enlisted men for the most part remained loyal to the Union.) Against growing odds — ultimately enormous odds — against opposing commanders of equal dedication and increasing experience and imagination, the Southern generals earned the admiration of their troops and of their enemy. So it was especially with Lee, whose dignity as a man equaled his virtuosity as a soldier.

Yet set off against its assets, the South had telling liabilities. The population of the seceded states was only 9 million, 3½ million of them Negroes, in contrast to the 22 million of the Union. Over the years of war the Confederacy could muster to arms only some 900,000 men, less than half the 2 million soldiers and sailors of the North, and with the attrition and exhaustion of battle this difference told more and more. The Southern share of material resources was even smaller. Confederate troops lacked food, uniforms, supplies, and ammunition. Four-fifths of the nation's manufacturing lay in the North, most of the minerals, most of the total supply of grain and meat. The trans-Mississippi South had no rail route east, whereas the twenty-one thousand miles of track in the North — more than twice the Confederacy's mileage — linked East with West and let both regions carry the Union armies swiftly toward the borders of battle. So also, the North held most of the nation's shipping and most of its banks and financial wealth. And the demands of war, the need for production, the opportunities for economic growth, spurred the industrialization of the Union, while the South, without a pool of skilled labor or capital or business experience, harassed by blockade and attack, remained a country primarily of farms and plantations, of languishing commerce, few cities, and less industry — a fair country, to be sure, but ill equipped for waging war even in its own defense.

The Confederacy suffered not the least from the political theory that had produced it. Its constitution, besides protecting slavery, explicitly recognized state sovereignty and denied to the central government the authority to impose a protective tariff or to finance internal improvements. (Two other innovations set a single, six-year term for the President and gave him the right to veto specific items within a general appropriations act.) The constitution's emphasis on local rights and federal restraints ran counter to the needs of war. The Confederate Conscription Act of 1862, drafting men eighteen to thirty-five years old, as well as later draft acts, met immediate resistance. It exempted various professional men and all owners and overseers of more than twenty slaves, and it permitted a conscripted man to hire a substitute. These provisions, favoring the planters and their friends, alienated the farmers, who had never fully trusted them. The draft also excited the opposition of die-hard state-righters. The governors of Alabama, Georgia, and Mississippi opposed the law and its administration; there was constant evasion of the draft in the nonslaveholding areas; and there were increasing desertions from the army. Though the Union troops deserted more frequently, they were much more easily replaced. The Confederate government, reluctant to impose its authority, waited until 1863 to pass a workable tax law. Earlier and later it resorted largely to borrowing and to printing money to pay its bills. The states also

Robert E. Lee: His achievement was dazzling.

Winslow Homer: Sketch of Union troops.

printed currency, which fed the inflation that crippled the economy, made the various currencies nearly worthless, encouraged hoarding, and eventually hurt morale.

The theory and structure of Confederate government cost the South less than did the shortcomings of its civilian leaders. Alexander H. Stephens of Georgia, the Vice-President, a brilliant neurotic, made a fetish of state rights, opposed the draft and wartime restrictions on civil liberties, and detested President Jefferson Davis. The President's Cabinet, largely undistinguished, squabbled constantly, failed to win the confidence of its chief or the Congress, and suffered from Davis' continuing changes of mind and personnel. Davis was himself ill cast. A native of Kentucky who grew up in Mississippi, he graduated from West Point, served ably in the Mexican War and as Franklin Pierce's Secretary of War, and in the United States Senate spoke ardently and forcefully for Southern aims. He was honest, devoted, and energetic, but also rigid and petty. He had neither the executive experience, the political instincts, nor the flair with people that his trying office demanded. His ego was large, particularly about his military judgment, and that was at best erratic. And Davis was an inveterate meddler.

Indeed his interference and his errors can-

celed out much of the benefit the South might otherwise have garnered from her cotton and from the excellence of her field commanders. In the first year of the war Davis attempted to bring England and France to heel by placing an embargo on shipments of cotton to them. This was an egregious mistake. The Northern navy then still lacked the strength to impose an effective blockade. Davis' decision therefore shut off the best source of Southern revenue and military supplies during the brief period in which they were available. The European textile mills, moreover, had an ample inventory of cotton. Consequently they felt no serious pinch until after the blockade was firm and the course of war had lessened the probability of making a cotton famine into a fulcrum for winning foreign aid. The course of war itself took errant paths, because Davis played favorites, often switched commands out of pique or unreasoning impatience, and, jealous of Lee, paid too little heed to his informed and percipient counsel. The Confederacy, a nation struggling to be born, needed a Washington in charge; Jefferson Davis was not a Washington.

The Union. The ample resources of the Union allowed room for trial and error, of which the war produced an abundance. Obviously far stronger than the South in human and mate-

Confederate volunteers, 1861.

per commented, was "reeling in the whirl of dissipation." Though, as always, most public officials were honorable men, many at every level of government winked at profiteering or shared in fraud. One of them was Lincoln's first Secretary of War, Simon Cameron of Pennsylvania, whom the President had appointed against his better judgment in order to cement his party coalition. In January 1862, to his great relief, Lincoln was able to get rid of Cameron by naming him minister to Russia. His successor, Edwin M. Stanton, while often a difficult man, brought to the War Department the same efficiency that characterized the work of Gideon Welles, the able Secretary of the Navy.

The Union, like the Confederacy, had trouble raising troops. In 1861 the government offered $100 to each volunteer, a bonus later increased to $302 for recruits and $402 for veterans, and states, counties, and cities added bounties of their own. By 1864 a volunteer in New York City could get $375 in addition to the federal bonus, and the total bounty in parts of Illinois came to $1,056. Yet the system did not work well. Enlistments lagged, and "bounty-jumpers" drew their reward, deserted, and then volunteered again under assumed names. Bounties, moreover, did not attract the well-to-do, who preferred civilian life and business profits to the hardships of service. Almost none of the industrial titans of the postwar period ever wore a uniform. Men of their means and temperament were favored by the provisions of the Union Conscription Act of 1863. It applied only to districts that had not supplied their quota of volunteers, a condition that helped to perpetuate the bounty system, and it permitted a drafted man to escape service by hiring a substitute or paying $300. This discrimination, together with persisting antagonism to the principle of conscription, gave rise to opposition to the draft, to widespread draft evasion, and in places to violent protests. A draft riot in New York City, where local machine politics and immigrant hostility to the war inflamed the resentment of workingmen, lasted four days, during which mobs spent their ire partly in attacks on Negroes, whom they blamed for their predicament. Yet in spite of these difficulties, the Union, unlike the Confederacy, had a suffi-

rial resources, the North spent much of its advantage in folly, greed, dissension, and delay. The folly and the delay were frequently attributable to the military. Inadequate organization complicated the problems of the senior generals, who when the war began were by and large second-rate men. Before the war ended, the Union had found commanders in whom it could take pride — Grant, Sherman, Thomas, and Sheridan, among others — but their predecessors too often stumbled through sorry campaigns.

Sorrier still was the greed of Northern warprofiteers — contractors and suppliers who grew rich by overcharging the government and delivering shoddy goods. Never before in American history had the ethics of commerce been worse than during the Civil War; never had public graft more cynically encouraged private immorality. Washington, one newspa-

cient pool of able-bodied men from which to enlist the soldiers it needed.

So it was also with money to finance the war; the North had its troubles, but it got the necessary funds. The Republican commitment to positive government marked the Union's economic policies. By 1864 Congress had boosted tariff rates to 47 per cent, the highest figure in national history to that date. The duties yielded over $300 million during the war and also erected a protective barrier between American industrialists and their European competitors. The absence of Southern representatives in Congress vastly eased the fulfillment of the Republican campaign promise on the tariff. Resulting industrial profits in turn permitted business to pay unprecedented excise taxes, which Congress levied in 1862 and increased two years later. Breaking another precedent, the lawmakers in 1861 imposed a 3 per cent tax on annual personal incomes and later raised that rate to a peak of 5 per cent on incomes from $600 to $5,000 and 10 per cent on additional earnings. Overall, these internal taxes produced some $250 million of wartime revenue. Seeking still more funds, Congress authorized the printing of paper currency, in all $431 million, which depreciated rapidly, though never so dramatically as did Confederate paper. At bottom, in mid-1864, Union greenbacks were worth only 39 cents on the gold dollar, but by the end of the war, as the credit of the government improved with the prospect of victory, their value had risen to about 67 cents. Finally, the Treasury relied on the sale of bonds and notes, which bore the heaviest load of wartime finance — some $2,600 million, almost three times the sum of all other sources of revenue combined.

The need to sell bonds hastened the passage of the National Banking Act of 1863 and major amendments to it in the following year. This legislation also removed most of the confusion and irregularity in the chaotic system of state banks that had developed since Jackson's time. All national banks chartered under the new system had to invest one-third of their capital in federal bonds and deposit these securities with the Treasury Department. They were allowed then to issue bank notes, legal tender, up to 90 per cent of the market value of their bonds. They were also subjected to regular federal inspection, an important protection for depositors. In 1865 Congress extended federal control over banking. A law of that year brought most of the banks under state charters within the national system by imposing a prohibitive 10 per cent tax on their bank notes.

During the war the Republicans also capitalized on their strength in Congress to pass the Homestead Act of 1862, which granted free farms of one hundred sixty acres from the public domain in the West to all citizens and applicants for citizenship who occupied and improved the land for five years. In the same year Congress established the Department of Agriculture and passed the Morrill Act, which offered states a land grant to endow colleges of agriculture and the mechanical arts. These laws, significant in themselves, attracted farmers to the party and to the Union cause. So, too, just as the tariff pleased industry, the railroad legislation of 1862 delighted other business interests. To the companies building the first transcontinental railway — the Union Pacific and the Central Pacific railroads — Congress made large land grants and generous loans on second-mortgage bonds: $16,000 for each mile of level ground covered; $48,000 in the mountains, $32,000 in the high plains, and $22,000 elsewhere. Again public policy followed Republican prescriptions.

In the North partisanship never flagged. A minority of "Peace Democrats" opposed the war and called for a negotiated peace with concessions to the South that would lead to the restoration of the Union. Strongest in the Old Northwest, these Peace Democrats — "Copperheads," in Unionist vocabulary — found a militant leader in Ohio congressman C. L. Vallandigham. Some of them joined secret peace societies. All attacked Lincoln mercilessly. In the Indiana legislature the Copperheads were able temporarily to block important war legislation; for a time they controlled the lower house in Illinois; in 1863 they tried, but failed, to elect Vallandigham — then exiled in Canada — governor of Ohio. The great majority of Democrats, loyal to the Union, supported the war, but they objected to Republican economic policies and kept alive the party organization through which

Lincoln the President: A master of the office.

An Impression of Lincoln

Soon afterwards there entered, with a shambling, loose, irregular, almost unsteady gait, a tall, lank, lean man, considerably over six feet in height, with stooping shoulders, long pendulous arms, terminating in hands of extraordinary dimensions, which, however, were far exceeded in proportion by his feet. He was dressed in an ill-fitting, wrinkled suit of black, which put one in mind of an undertaker's uniform at a funeral; round his neck a rope of black silk was knotted in a large bulb, with flying ends projecting beyond the collar of his coat, and above that, nestling in a great black mass of hair, bristling and compact like a ruff of mourning pins, rose the strange quaint face and head, covered with its thatch of wild republican hair, of President Lincoln. The impression produced by the size of his extremities, and by his flapping and wide-projecting ears may be removed by the appearance of kindliness, sagacity, and the awkward bonhomie of his face; the mouth is absolutely prodigious ... the nose ... a prominent organ ... the eyes, dark, full, and deeply set, are penetrating, but full of an expression which almost amounts to tenderness.

From William Howard Russell, *My Diary, North and South,* 1863.

they expected ultimately to regain power. Horatio Seymour, their outstanding spokesman, won election as governor of New York in 1862 in a campaign addressed to the Democratic slogan "The Constitution as it is and the Union as it was."

Lincoln, in the view of the Democrats, had assumed autocratic authority. They bitterly criticized his denial of habeas corpus in Maryland in 1861 and his further, broader denial, by a proclamation of 1862, wherever any person discouraged enlistment in the army or engaged in any other "disloyal practice." That proclamation also provided for military rather than civil trial. In the case of one Milligan, an Indiana Democrat accused of conspiracy to set free certain Confederate prisoners of war, a military tribunal decreed the death sentence. After the war, in 1866, the Supreme Court annulled that judgment and held that a civilian could not, under the Constitution, be tried by court-martial when regular civil courts were operating "in the proper and unobstructed exercise of their jurisdiction." But that ruling came too late to affect wartime practice, and Lincoln, resolved to restore the Union at any price, regretfully saw no alternative to making civil rights subordinate to victory while the battle raged.

The President's emphasis on union as his overarching objective won the allegiance of most moderate Republicans, the wing of the party that followed his lead in subordinating all other considerations. Though they differed with him about particulars, they were as ready as he was to improvise, to court the support of Union Democrats, to temper partisanship and seek national unity. But the Radical Republicans were of a different mind. By no means unanimous in their attitude toward the legislation of the war years, they were substantially unanimous in deploring the racism of the Democrats, in wanting to make the abolition of slavery one aim of the war, and in demanding the admission of Negroes to the armed forces. These men gave the Union cause much of its idealism. Many of them, like many of the moderates, were also jealous of the prerogatives of the Congress where their forceful and outspoken leaders served, among them Senator Benjamin F. Wade of Ohio, Senator Zachariah Chandler of Michigan, and Thaddeus Stevens of Pennsylvania, a dominant voice in the House. They and their fellows and their friends of the press (Horace Greeley was one) on occasion criticized the President unsparingly. Their special instrument was the Joint Committee on the Conduct of the War, which Congress created in 1861. Its hearings and its demands kept pressure on Lincoln, who needed the Radicals' votes, and agitated the still divisive question of slavery among the people of the North, whose sentiments Lincoln wanted to direct uniformly to the issue of union.

A lesser President might have crumbled; Lincoln, a master of the office, did not. He was a superb conciliator, adept at bending to this force and diverting or isolating that. He was an accomplished tactician, adroit in the use of patronage, persuasive in conference, patient with the foibles of productive men. Neither praise nor abuse turned him, for he lived within himself, supported by his infinite faith in the righteousness of the Lord and of the Union cause. Like any man, he made mistakes and bowed to circumstances, but, while he suffered continual doubts about the thou-

Major Campaigns of the Civil War

Union states
Confederate states
Union blockade of Confederate shipping
Scott's plan to split the Confederacy

Circled numbers ① are keyed to detail maps in the pages which follow. The following symbols are used to designate Union and Confederate forces:

Union advance
Union retreat
Confederate advance
Confederate retreat

MARYLAND

Potomac R.

Johnston

Washington

Arlington

Centreville

Bull Run

McDowell

Alexandria

Beauregard
Manassas Junction

VIRGINIA

0   15 MILES

along the land frontier. An amphibious expedition was to open the Mississippi Valley, restoring the Middle West's traditional outlet to the sea and cutting off such Confederate states as Arkansas, Texas, and Louisiana. Then, separate armies were to strike inland, progressively fragmenting the Southern nation and bringing it at last to full submission.

This strategy obviously would take a great deal of time, and many Northern people wanted decisive action quickly. Scott's plan, implying a slow and remorseless constriction, was dubbed the Anaconda Plan and was subjected to a good deal of derision. Horace Greeley's New York *Tribune* was already urging, "Forward to Richmond" — the new capital of the Confederacy.

Swayed by this sentiment, the Administration early in June decided to attempt an overland advance across Virginia toward Richmond. It had some thirty-five thousand troops available for the operation, under the command of a competent regular-army officer, Brigadier General Irvin McDowell. They were only partly trained, but if they were to fight at all it had to be soon, because most of them were ninety-day militia whose terms would soon expire. Further, the Confederate troops who would oppose them were equally green and undisciplined. The offensive, under way on July 16, moved slowly. On July 21, the raw column met Confederate Brigadier General P. G. T. Beauregard and his army of twenty-five thousand men just beyond the sluggish stream of Bull Run, approximately thirty miles from Washington, and engaged in the first large-scale battle of the war.

McDowell's battle plan was good, but everything went wrong with it. A Union force failed to hold Confederate General Joseph E. Johnston and his twelve thousand men in the Shenandoah Valley. Slipping away, Johnston and most of his men reached Bull Run, where they provided the reinforcements that Beauregard needed. McDowell's flank attack on the Confederates lagged, and, although the untrained soldiers on both sides fought stoutly for several hours, the Union men were exhausted from their march. By mid-afternoon their attack had failed, and when McDowell tried to retreat his army fell apart and streamed back to Washington in a wild rout. Johnston and

sands of decisions that fell to him, he never doubted his mission or wavered in its pursuit. This conviction gave him the boldness that dressed the Constitution in battle armor, gave him the stamina to absorb not only the trials of his task but, much worse for him, the ache of compassion for every sufferer on both sides of the hideous war. The Union, a nation struggling to survive, needed a great leader; it was blessed by the presence of Lincoln.

THE COURSE OF ARMS

The first offensive: Bull Run. Lincoln, as the war began, had to make a difficult choice. To prevent a stalemate that would ensure the survival of the Confederacy, the North had to attack, to destroy the government of the Southern people and bring them back by force into the Union. The President had at hand a long-range plan developed by General Winfield Scott, the commanding general of the army, a veteran of the War of 1812 and the Mexican War, now seventy-four years old, no longer well but not unwise. Scott's plan set a framework within which the Northern war effort could reasonably evolve. Unfortunately, it did not satisfy public opinion.

The plan called for a close blockade of the Confederate coastline, a blockade that the navy began at once feverishly to implement, and for "containment" of the Confederacy all

Beauregard found their own army so disorganized by victory that they could make no effective pursuit. They did not have to. The Union had suffered a humiliating defeat. For months to come, no more would be heard of "Forward to Richmond."

The shock of Bull Run convinced the people of the North that the war could not be won with ninety-day militia. The short-term regiments were sent home, and General George B. McClellan was called from western Virginia to take McDowell's place in command of a huge new force of three-year volunteers. An excellent organizer and administrator, the thirty-four-year-old McClellan devoted himself to the task of creating an army. In the fall Scott retired, and McClellan was made general in chief of all the Union armies. He was determined to undertake no new offensive until his soldiers were fully ready for combat. Lincoln supported him in this resolve, and throughout the summer and fall the war seemed to have an oddly static quality.

Lines for battle. The appearance was deceptive, for away from the Washington-Richmond sector the lines for future battle were forming. While McClellan saw to his training program, the Union in the fall of 1861 launched am-

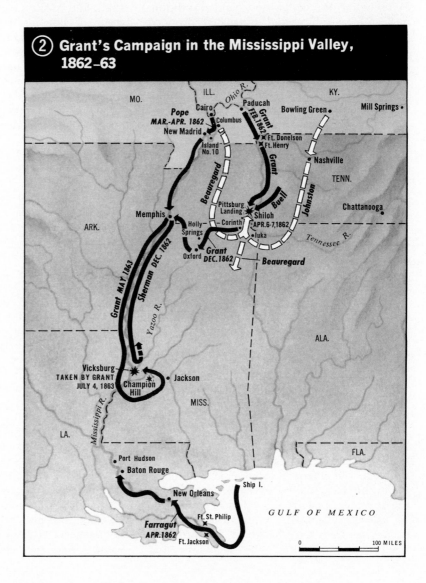

② **Grant's Campaign in the Mississippi Valley, 1862–63**

phibious expeditions to seal off as much as possible of the Confederacy's Atlantic coast-line. On August 29 an army-navy force bombarded, captured, and occupied two Confederate forts at Hatteras Inlet, North Carolina, at one of the approaches to the intricate system of landlocked North Carolina sounds and rivers. During the winter months a second expedition followed, closing the entrances in the long, grass-grown sand dunes that lie between the sounds and the sea, capturing Confederate fortifications on historic Roanoke Island, and effectually shutting off North Carolina except for its most southerly port, Wilmington. Preceding the second expedition, a fleet of warships and transports dropped farther down the coast to seize Port Royal, South Carolina, establishing a secure base for the blockading squadrons and cutting off from ocean traffic all of South Carolina except Charleston itself. Still another expedition, during the winter, took Fort Pulaski at the mouth of the Savannah River in Georgia. By providing numerous federal footholds along the Confederate coast, these sallies compelled Richmond to disperse its troops to guard against sea-borne invasion.

Along the seacoast, the federal government tried to seal in the Confederacy; in the West it wanted to open a path through the Confederacy as General Scott had advised. General John C. Frémont, in command in the West, was limited both as a soldier and as an organizer. But by early autumn 1861 he had begun to build up a powerful Union base at Cairo, Illinois, where the Ohio River joins the Mississippi. He placed an obscure brigadier general from Illinois, Ulysses S. Grant, in charge. Then, unable to get along with the administration, Frémont departed, giving way to sedate, paper-shuffling General Henry Wager Halleck.

The Confederates realized that federal troops at Cairo would soon march south. On September 4 the Confederate commander in the Mississippi area, Major General Leonidas Polk, decided to intervene by occupying Columbus, Kentucky, located on a high bluff overlooking the river, where batteries could deny passage to federal steamboats. Grant countered by occupying Paducah, Kentucky, in order to control the mouths of the Tennessee and Cumberland rivers. Union troops moved into the northern part of the state and Confederates into the southern, and during November and December the lines faced each other, just out of contact, along an east-west line running from Columbus through Bowling Green and off to the Cumberland plateau.

Here was the Confederacy's soft spot. Davis sent the man he considered his best soldier, General Albert Sidney Johnston, to take overall command, but Davis was unable to give him as many soldiers as he needed. Johnston had perhaps fifty thousand men; facing him were Grant, at Cairo, with twenty-five thousand, and Major General Don Carlos Buell, in front of Bowling Green, with some eighty thousand. At St. Louis Halleck had a substantial force, with which he was methodically clearing Missouri of Confederate armies and preparing to reinforce Grant whenever an offensive should take place.

Attack in the West. Just after the end of the year the federal drive began. The left wing of Buell's army, led by Virginia-born Major General George H. Thomas, crushed a small Confederate army under Major General George B. Crittenden in a sharp fight at Mill Springs, Kentucky, on January 19, 1862, destroying the eastern anchor of Johnston's line. Early in February, Grant took fifteen thousand men up the Tennessee River with a flotilla of federal gunboats and captured Confederate Fort Henry, just south of the Kentucky-Tennessee line. This move cut railroad communications between Johnston's center at Bowling Green and his left at Columbus — where General Beauregard of Bull Run fame was now in command — and Johnston was compelled to retire. He placed a substantial fraction of his command at Fort Donelson, Tennessee, on the Cumberland River, and led the rest back to Nashville; but Grant, strongly reinforced by Halleck, on February 16 captured Fort Donelson along with twelve to fifteen thousand Confederate soldiers.

The Union seizure of Forts Henry and Donelson, one of the decisive victories of the war, destroyed Johnston's entire defensive line, compelling him to abandon the strong point at Columbus and to regroup his entire army in northern Mississippi. With virtually all of western Tennessee lost by the Confederacy, the way was open for a federal advance into the deep South. Simultaneously, a portion of Halleck's command drove the Confederates out of southwestern Missouri. Halleck sent another force down the Mississippi under Major General John Pope, who captured New Madrid, Missouri, and early in April took a strong Confederate fort at Island No. 10, in the Mississippi.

Aware that the Confederacy had been knocked off balance, Lincoln tried to get a Union army into eastern Tennessee, where the population showed strong Unionist sentiments. He urged Buell to occupy Knoxville and cut the vital railroad line that connected Virginia with the whole Tennessee area. McClellan supported this strategy, believing that it would help his own projected advance toward Richmond, but Buell refused to undertake it, arguing that the bad roads and the primitive character of the terrain would make it impossible for his army to be supplied. In addition, Halleck was hesitant in following up the Henry-Donelson triumph. Consequently

Johnston and Beauregard gained time to regroup their forces at Corinth, Mississippi, and by the time Halleck at last sent Grant forward up the line of the Tennessee River, the Confederates were ready for him.

Grant established himself with forty thousand men at Pittsburg Landing, Tennessee, a short distance north of the Mississippi line, where he waited for Buell to join him with twenty-five thousand more. Johnston did not wait. With forty-five thousand men he advanced, and on April 6 and 7 his army and Grant's fought the most extensive battle yet seen on the North American continent, in a tangle of woodlands and pastures near a country meetinghouse known as Shiloh Church, not far from Pittsburg Landing. On the first day Grant's army, taken by surprise, was nearly driven into the river, but Johnston was killed in action, Buell's troops began to arrive in the evening, and on the following day the battered Confederates, now under Beauregard, had to retreat to Corinth. The battle had been costly — some thirteen thousand Union casu-

U.S.S. "Cairo" at Memphis.

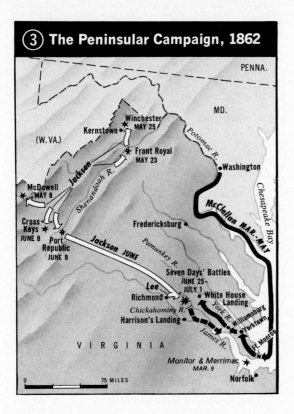

③ The Peninsular Campaign, 1862

PENNA.

MD.

Winchester
MAY 25

Kernstown •

(W. VA.)

Front Royal
MAY 23

McDowell
MAY 8

Jackson

Shenandoah R.

Potomac R.

• Washington

McClellan MAR.-MAY

Chesapeake Bay

Cross
Keys
JUNE 8

Port
Republic
JUNE 9

Jackson JUNE

Fredericksburg •

Pamunkey R.

Seven Days' Battles
JUNE 25-
JULY 1

Lee

Richmond •

Chickahominy R.

Harrison's Landing •

White House
Landing

York R.

Williamsburg

Yorktown

James R.

Ft. Monroe

VIRGINIA

Monitor & Merrimac
MAR. 9

Norfolk •

0   75 MILES

alties, more than ten thousand Confederate — but the victory was momentous. It left the Southern army in the Tennessee region cautiously on the defensive.

More Union victories followed. A powerful Union fleet under Flag Officer David Glasgow Farragut entered the Mississippi River from the gulf and ran past Forts Jackson and St. Phillip, near the mouth. On April 25 Farragut occupied New Orleans, the largest city in the Confederacy and its principal seaport. An army under General Butler followed, taking possession of New Orleans and moving on up the river to seize Baton Rouge; early in June a federal fleet of river gunboats and rams annihilated a Confederate fleet at Memphis, throwing that city into Union possession and opening all of the upper Mississippi River. Halleck came down to Pittsburg Landing, where he assembled a powerful army of approximately 125,000 men, made up of the combined forces of Grant, Buell, and Pope. In a slow, methodical advance he drove Beauregard out of Corinth.

Thus by mid-spring of 1862 the Confederacy was on the verge of disaster. Of the Mississippi River it now controlled only the portion between Vicksburg, Mississippi, and Port Hudson, Louisiana. The area west of the river was fragmented. Halleck was in northern Mississippi with more than twice as many men as the Confederates could bring against him, apparently able to go anywhere he chose. Most of the South's Atlantic coast had been closed, the navy's blockade at the ports that remained open was becoming increasingly effective, and in Virginia General McClellan was finally beginning his advance on Richmond, commanding an army of more than one hundred thousand men. Gloom prevailed in Richmond. In Washington, by contrast, Secretary of War Stanton was so confident that in June he temporarily suspended further recruiting.

Delay along the peninsula. But there was to be no end to the war that summer. The North suffered from the lack of a centralized military command. McClellan had served for approximately five months as general in chief, but in March the Administration, impatient with his reluctance to attack, removed him from the top position and reduced him to the command of the Army of the Potomac. Genuine coordination of the different military theaters did not exist, and as the big drive on Richmond commenced the pressure in the West slacked off. Halleck, who had been given overall command in the West, broke his huge army up into detachments and tried to occupy territory rather than seek out and destroy the opposing Confederate armies. The Union offensive in the West became inactive just when it offered the greatest possibilities.

McClellan set out in mid-March, sending his army down the Potomac River and Chesapeake Bay by steamboat and taking up a position at the tip of the Virginia peninsula, between the York and James rivers, with his base at Fort Monroe. A scientific soldier with a deep streak of caution, he advanced slowly. General Joseph E. Johnston held a strong defensive position at Yorktown, and instead of trying to storm it — he had better than a two-to-one advantage in numbers — McClellan settled down for a methodical siege, moving up heavy mortars and artillery and preparing for a shattering bombardment. Johnston waited until

McClellan had completed his preparations; then, on May 3, he evacuated the Yorktown line and drew off up the peninsula, pausing on May 5 to fight a savage but inconclusive rear-guard action at Williamsburg.

One of McClellan's problems arose from the Confederates' introduction of an ironclad warship into naval warfare. In the spring of 1861 the Federals had abandoned the navy yard at Norfolk, Virginia. At that time they had burned and scuttled the powerful steam frigate *Merrimac*, which was in the yard for engine-room repairs. The Confederates raised and rebuilt this vessel, cutting it down to the berth deck and erecting an iron-plated citadel amidships, mounting powerful guns behind this protection, and equipping the ship with an iron ram at the bow. Rechristened *Virginia* (though it is usually referred to by its old name, *Merrimac*) this ship was slow, clumsy, and unseaworthy; but its four inches of armor made it almost invulnerable to ordinary gunfire, and when it came out into Hampton Roads early in March there was not a wooden warship in the navies of the world that could have stood up to it.

The *Merrimac* on its first appearance caused a near panic. It sank the Union frigate *Cumberland*, forced the frigate *Congress* to surrender, drove the big steamer *Minnesota* aground, and threatened to destroy the whole federal naval force around Fort Monroe. On March 9 this apparently irresistible warship suffered a check when the federal navy brought on an ironclad of its own, the *Monitor*, a singular vessel with low freeboard and a revolving turret mounting two 11-inch guns. The *Monitor's* keel had been laid in October 1861, and she was completed just in time to come down to Hampton Roads and meet the *Merrimac*. The two ships fought a wearing battle, which demonstrated that warships without armor were now obsolete, and which ended the danger that the *Merrimac* might give the Confederacy control of all the lower Chesapeake Bay. But the *Monitor* gained no real advantage, and the *Merrimac* remained on the lower James River, barring that stream to federal shipping and presenting a threat to McClellan's flank as he moved up the peninsula. The ship's existence did much to keep the cautious Union commander from making a bolder advance.

Eventually, however, the obstacle was removed. Johnston's withdrawal, coupled with Union possession of the North Carolina sounds — which opened the back door to Norfolk — compelled the Confederates to evacuate Norfolk on May 9. Since the *Merrimac* drew too much water to go up the James River to Richmond and was not seaworthy enough to go out into the open ocean, her crew had to destroy her once Norfolk was lost.

McClellan repulsed. McClellan, continuing to advance, by the latter part of May had established his army astride the Chickahominy River, with its forward elements less than ten miles from the Confederate capital. Here Johnston attacked him on May 31, at Seven Pines and Fair Oaks Station. The engagement was bloody and indecisive. Johnston himself was seriously wounded, and Jefferson Davis appointed Lee to command Johnston's army, the Army of Northern Virginia. McClellan held his position, waited for reinforcements, and prepared for another methodical advance to within siege-gun range. But now soldierly skill and daring began to reverse the fortunes of war.

McClellan had nearly one hundred thousand men with him, and in northern Virginia — around Washington, in the lower Shenandoah Valley, and elsewhere — there were seventy thousand more federal troops, most of which, McClellan believed, would shortly move overland to join him. But in the Shenandoah Valley the Confederates had fifteen thousand soldiers led by a military genius, General Thomas J. Jackson, nicknamed Stonewall for his steadfast stand at Bull Run. Encouraged by Johnston and Lee, Jackson began a series of dazzling offensive maneuvers, which convinced the Lincoln Administration that he had a larger army than he actually did and that he intended nothing less than the capture of Washington.

In May, alarmed for the safety of Washington, the Administration hastily assembled troops to drive Jackson away, using a substantial number of the men whom McClellan was planning to include in his attack on Richmond. All in all, the Federals put nearly fifty thousand men in the Shenandoah, but Jackson, maneuvering skillfully and swiftly, now eluded them, now attacked and defeated them, leaving them wholly confused about his strength, his whereabouts, and his intentions.

The effect on McClellan's plans was disastrous. McClellan had posted approximately twenty-five thousand of his troops north of the Chickahominy River, believing that strong reinforcements would soon march down from Fredericksburg to join him there. Lee took advantage of the Union commander's awkward position by bringing Jackson and his men down from the Shenandoah. As the last week in June began, Lee found himself with a total force of about eighty thousand men. He was still outnumbered, but he boldly left a quarter of his army to confront McClellan's main body, took all the rest north of the Chickahominy, and on June 26 made a savage assault on McClellan's isolated right wing at Mechanicsville. The next day he made an even heavier attack at Gaines's Mill, driving the Union right wing south of the Chickahominy and compelling McClellan to retreat. Lee followed him, trying to destroy the entire Union army and fighting bitter engagements at Savage Station, Glendale, and Malvern Hill. At the end of a week's spirited combat McClellan had withdrawn to a defensive position at Harrison's Landing, on the James.

In the Seven Days' Battles — as this series of engagements came to be known — McClellan had lost upward of fifteen thousand men, Lee close to twenty thousand. But McClellan's attempt to take Richmond had been repulsed. Outnumbered at all times, Lee had maneuvered in such a way that at the point of contact he had a decisive numerical superiority. With Jackson's aid he had induced the federal government to retain thousands of troops in northern Virginia, a hundred miles and more from the scene of combat. He had grabbed the initiative.

Confederate successes. Lincoln now brought Halleck to Washington as general in chief, a logical step in itself, but a step that led the federal high command to focus its attention entirely on the situation in Virginia, leaving affairs in the West to take care of themselves. General Pope was also brought east and given command of a new army, made up of the elements that had tried so unsuccessfully to destroy Jackson. Pope led them down the line of the Virginia Central Railway. The Union ob-

jective was to catch Lee at Richmond, in a pincers between Pope and McClellan. But the Union commanders would not work in harmony, and Halleck lacked the force of personality to weld them into a proper team. When McClellan characteristically declined to advance on Richmond without strong reinforcements, Halleck early in August ordered him to bring his army back by boat to the Washington area to join Pope.

Lee gave the Federals no time for regrouping. Leaving a contingent to watch McClellan's withdrawal, he marched north, maneuvered Pope into a retreat, forced him to make a stand along the upper Rappahannock River, and then boldly divided the Southern army and sent twenty-five thousand men under Jackson on a daring flanking movement aimed at Pope's rear. On August 28 and 29 Pope was brought to battle on the old field of Bull Run. Wholly undone by Lee's generalship, he was driven back to the fortifications around Washington. McClellan's troops had moved up from the peninsula so slowly that only a part of them had been able to reinforce Pope. Discredited, Pope was relieved, and McClellan was told to take over and save the capital.

Lee's achievement had been dazzling. When he took command early in June, he had been pinned down in Richmond, doomed apparently to a hopeless defensive battle. He had beaten and driven away the attacking army and by the end of August had transferred the scene of action from the environs of Richmond to the shores of the Potomac.

Lee's success in Virginia enabled the Confederacy to regain the initiative in the West. With Halleck's departure for Washington, and with the strong chance that troops from the West might have to be brought east, the whole Union campaign in the West had fallen into the doldrums. Grant was immobilized in western Tennessee, and Buell was making only glacial progress toward Chattanooga. Confederate General Braxton Bragg commanded an army of thirty thousand near Chattanooga, and General Edmund Kirby-Smith had twelve thousand more at Knoxville. While Pope was coming to grief in Virginia, these two suddenly moved north toward Kentucky. Bragg sidestepped Buell, compelling that unhappy officer to follow in his footsteps. In the meantime,

Lee, though his army had been badly mauled, boldly crossed the Potomac River and marched toward Pennsylvania. In the spring the Confederacy had been tottering; by autumn it was on the offensive in the East and in the West.

THE CRISIS OF THE WAR

European problems. Confederate resurgence brought to the point of crisis the deteriorating relations of the North with Great Britain. British opinion about the war in America had been divided, partly along class lines. Many of the nobility viewed the Southern planters as fellow aristocrats and rejoiced in the apparent collapse of popular government in the United States. Many supported the South's claim for self-determination. "The contest," wrote the London *Times*, "is really for empire on the side of the North and for independence on that of the South." But social reformers in Great Britain, engaged in a struggle to democratize their own society, befriended the North and attacked the Slave Power. This was the position also of most of the laboring force, even those textile-workers whose jobs were potentially imperiled by the possibility of a cotton shortage. Self-interest attracted to the side of the Union British exporters of munitions and shippers who took over the carrying trade abandoned by the idled American merchant marine. But neither public opinion nor business considerations in themselves commanded British policy. It responded in the main to the impressions registered by the course of the war and to the negotiations over questions the war raised.

The Union blockade created a first set of problems. In proclaiming it, Lincoln committed a tactical error, for a nation suppressing an "insurrection" does not "blockade" its own ports; it simply closes the ports held by the insurrectionists. The establishment of a blockade acknowledges the existence of a state of war — and, by implication, the existence of an enemy nation. Lincoln hoped to prevent the South from receiving status as a belligerent, but logically enough, the British government met his proclamation of blockade with an announcement that it was extending full belligerent rights to the Confederacy. Now Jefferson Davis

hoped to bring England to grant the Confederacy full recognition as a nation. Yet Davis' tactical error in embargoing cotton at the start of the war (see p. 345) to a degree canceled out Lincoln's mistake, and the question of full recognition remained undecided.

The blockade itself was bound to create friction between the North and a maritime power as important as England. Yet the British kept in mind their own future needs, as a great sea power, for using the weapon of blockade against a continental enemy. They therefore did not deny the authority of the Union to impose a blockade, nor did they press interpretations of international law that might weaken the claims of a blockading country. But the situation nevertheless quickly gave rise to an incident that brought the Union to the verge of war with England. In the fall of 1861 Davis sent abroad two commissioners, James Mason of Virginia and John Slidell of Louisiana, to plead the Confederate cause in England and France. In November Captain Charles Wilkes, in the Union warship *San Jacinto*, stopped the British steamer *Trent*, removed Mason and Slidell, and carried them off directly to the United States, where they were imprisoned. His action, greeted enthusiastically at home, was denounced in London. British troops sailed for Canada, and Lord John Russell, the British foreign secretary, sent a sharp note demanding that the United States make apologies and release the prisoners forthwith. Lincoln could not afford war with England. The seizure of Mason and Slidell, moreover, violated long-standing American doctrine about freedom of the seas. Wisely, Lincoln ordered the release of the prisoners, who presently completed their journey.

Yet tension between the two nations did not much abate. With scant regard for the duties of a neutral, the British in 1862 permitted two crusiers, built for the Confederacy in Liverpool, to slip out to sea. Lincoln's minister to England, Charles Francis Adams, entered a vigorous protest, but the ships, the *Florida* and the *Alabama*, destroyed some $15 million of Northern commerce before the navy could capture them.

Even more disturbing in its long-rum implications was England's association with Spain and France in a military expedition launched against Mexico by Napoleon III. The French emperor, taking advantage of the Civil War, hoped to reestablish his country's hold in the Western Hemisphere by setting up a puppet government in Mexico under Austrian Archduke Maximilian. This violation of the Monroe Doctrine, possible only because of London's permissiveness and Washington's preoccupation, evoked an immediate denunciation from Secretary of State Seward, but French troops remained in Mexico (departing only after the Civil War in 1867, whereupon the Mexicans soon drove out the foreign government), and France, like England, blinked at the construction of Confederate commerce-raiders in her ports. Worse still, Lee's victories in 1862 strengthened the arguments of pro-Southern Englishmen. Late in the summer Lord Palmerston, the prime minister, concluded that the time had come to grant full recognition to the Confederacy, if possible in conjunction with France and other powers, and to urge the Union to negotiate a peace. He decided, however, to await the outcome of Lee's invasion of the North. If it succeeded, the question of recognition would come before the Cabinet, probably to be resolved to the satisfaction of the South.

Again the slavery question. Lincoln, brooding over the potentially ruinous course the war had taken, saw the need to touch men's minds and spirits. The North had not simply been losing battles; the spark and fire seemed to have gone out of the war effort. It was primarily the antislavery men who displayed a vigorous impulse to destroy the Confederacy, and the President sought to engage and disseminate their ardor.

As Lincoln knew, the abolitionists wanted to strike at the South by attacking outright the institution of chattel slavery. In the spring of 1861 fugitive slaves had come into the lines of Major General Benjamin F. Butler of Massachusetts, who then held command at Fort Monroe. The slaves, Butler said, in a novel interpretation of the rules of war, were the property of men in rebellion, and such property was legitimate contraband. He therefore seized the slaves, fed and housed them, and put them to work on his fortifications. Later, in August 1861, General Frémont, then Union commander in Missouri, had announced that,

as a war measure, he would confiscate the property of all rebels in his district and set their slaves free. Lincoln canceled that proclamation, which he feared might otherwise cost the Union the support of loyal slave-owners in the border states. But Congress, on August 6, 1861, enacted a law providing for the seizure of all property, including slaves, used for "insurrectionary purposes." This first Confiscation Act was followed by a second, much more sweeping measure on July 17, 1862, which provided for the confiscation of the property and the emancipation of the slaves of all persons supporting the rebellion. Lincoln had grave reservations about the legality of that act, and his Attorneys General enforced it only rarely.

When the tide of battle turned against him, the President, in order to enlist the drive and energy of the abolitionists, had to make the war a fight against slavery as well as a fight for the Union — a war for human freedom, grounded on a cause lofty enough to evoke a new wave of support. He maneuvered cautiously to that end. He had earlier supported,

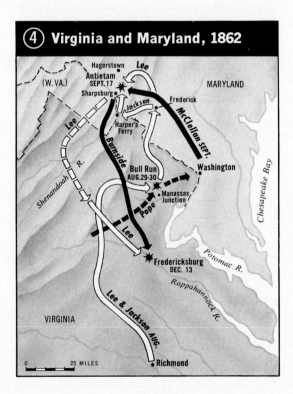

④ **Virginia and Maryland, 1862**

without much success, suggestions for compensated emancipation in the border states. In July 1862 he told the Cabinet that he proposed to use his war powers to issue a general proclamation of emancipation. This would be a purely military measure, offering freedom only to slaves in states that had seceded: it would be, in effect, a means of putting pressure on slaveholders to return to the Union. It might be illegal, but it would commit the federal government to the policy of emancipation; it would portend complete emancipation for all slaves everywhere.

Secretary Seward, though he supported the idea, had urged delay. To issue such a proclamation while the Union armies were staggering from a series of defeats, Seward warned, would sound like a despairing cry for help rather than the bold announcement of a stirring new policy. The army had to win some decisive victory before the proclamation could be made. Lincoln agreed and put the draft of his projected proclamation in his desk, ready for use at an hour of triumph. It was not long in coming.

Antietam. When Lee in September 1862 led his army into western Maryland, pointing toward an invasion of Pennsylvania, his purpose was to demonstrate that the South was going to win the war and that the North should therefore stop fighting. He crossed the Potomac, reached the town of Frederick, Maryland, and then paused. As Lee knew, McClellan and the hastily reorganized Army of the Potomac were coming up from Washington. Yet close at hand there was a garrison of ten thousand Federals at Harper's Ferry. Lying under the shadow of high mountains, Harper's Ferry was indefensible, but Lee could not safely leave its large garrison astride his supply line while he moved north. With characteristic boldness, he once more divided his forces, occupying Hagerstown, Maryland, and the South Mountain passes with half his men, and sending the other half under Stonewall Jackson to take Harper's Ferry.

The scheme might have worked, except that a copy of Lee's orders was lost and got to McClellan, who had nearly reached the South Mountain barrier. Now McClellan found himself between the divided halves of Lee's army; if he moved fast he might destroy them sepa-

Antietam and Emancipation: Lincoln to His Cabinet

I have ... thought a great deal about the relation of this war to Slavery: and ... several weeks ago, I read to you an Order I had prepared on this subject.... I have thought ... that the time for acting on it might very probably come. I think the time has come now. I wish it were a better time.... The action of the army against the rebels has not been quite what I should have best liked. But they have been driven out of Maryland, and Pennsylvania is no longer in danger of invasion. When the rebel army was at Frederick, I determined, as soon as it should be driven out of Maryland, to issue a Proclamation of Emancipation.... I made the promise to myself, and ... to my Maker.... I am going to fulfill that promise.... I do not wish your advice about the main matter.... What I have written is that which my reflections have determined me to say.... I know very well that many others might, in this matter, as in others, do better than I can; and if I were satisfied that the public confidence was more fully possessed by any one of them than by me, and knew of any Constitutional way in which he could be put in my place, he should have it.... But though I believe that I have not so much of the confidence of the people as I had some time since, I do not know that ... any other person has more; and ... I am here. I must do the best I can, and bear the responsibility of taking the course which I feel I ought to take.

From the Diary of Salmon P. Chase, September 22, 1862.

rately and end the war in a week. Though he was not that quick, he did compel Lee to concentrate and give battle on the high ground above Antietam Creek, near Sharpsburg, Maryland, on September 17. (This action did not occur in time to save Harper's Ferry, which Jackson captured with its entire garrison.)

The Battle of Antietam was the bloodiest single day's engagement of the entire war. Of eighty-seven thousand men, McClellan lost thirteen thousand. Lee's army, which had been subject to heavy straggling, numbered probably less than forty thousand and lost at least ten thousand. Tactically the fight was a draw, but strategically it was a Confederate defeat. Lee withdrew into Virginia, his plan to invade the North shattered.

At last Lincoln had the victory he needed. On September 22, 1862, he issued a preliminary emancipation proclamation — an announcement that a final proclamation would be issued on January 1, 1863, unless the Confederacy meanwhile surrendered. The Emancipation Proclamation asserted freedom for slaves in those areas that were not under control of the federal government and left slavery untouched in areas where federal control was effective. It seemed a halting measure of dubious effect and shaky legality, and the Confederates denounced it as a call for a slave revolt. But never again would the federal government consider slavery a question for the states to settle; the Administration now was fighting not only to restore the Union but to make American freedom all-embracing.

Since the time of national independence, the freedom of all Americans had been an essential objective of the nation's best hopes. The fact of slavery had lain below the sectional controversies that rent the Union. The very course of war forced federal troops in slave territory to come to grips with the South's anachronistic institution. Indeed, the waging of war against the Confederacy implied a contest also to abolish slavery, the pillar of the secessionist polity. Now the Emancipation Proclamation declared the American Negro to be "forever free."

After Antietam, the Confederate tide receded in the West as well as in the East. Bragg, invading Kentucky, found that the supposedly prosecessionist populace was not rising in his favor as he had expected it to. At Perryville on October 8 he fought an indecisive battle with Buell and then marched back to Tennessee. Kirby-Smith likewise withdrew, and the menacing counterstroke had come to nothing. Simultaneously, a Confederate army under General Earl Van Dorn, which tried to slip past Grant's army and join Bragg, was checked at Iuka, Mississippi, and soundly defeated in a battle at Corinth. Once more Union control in the West was firmly established.

The Confederacy had passed its high-water mark. Never again would it come so close to outright victory as it had at the beginning of the autumn of 1862. Lacking the sinews to make use of the initiative Lee had gained, it was once more on the defensive.

This reversal cost the South its chance for British recognition. Following Lee's repulse at Antietam, the British government concluded that Southern prospects were dim. Furthermore, so long as the war was fought only for reconstruction of the Union, the British people might have consented to have their government take the Confederate side; but a war fought to end human slavery presented a very different case. The cotton famine — increasing, as the federal blockade grew steadily more effective — brought economic distress to some British workers, who suffered extensive unemployment as the textile mills fell idle. Other workers profited from the boom in the arms trade and the merchant marine. And yet even those who suffered supported their liberal spokesmen, champions of the cause of freedom in America. The British government did not again come close to intervention in favor of the South.

Antietam and the Emancipation Proclamation had still another consequence. The change in Northern policy meant that the war had to be fought to a finish. So long as reunion was the only issue at stake, there had been some possibility of a negotiated peace. But the South would not negotiate the slavery question. After Antietam, the divided nation was committed to an all-out, all-exhausting war.

The attack renewed. As a necessary first step toward the conquest of the South, Lincoln made a series of changes in federal army command. He removed McClellan, appointing to his place Major General Ambrose E. Burnside, who had done well in the earlier operations along the North Carolina coast but who was to prove unfit for command of a large army. McClellan had met strong criticism from antislavery Republicans, including Secretary of War Stanton and Secretary of the Treasury Salmon P. Chase, for his slowness and his apparent reluctance to come to grips with his enemy. Opposed to the Emancipation Proclamation, the general was a hero to Northern Democrats who did not believe in making war to end slavery; and the Administration was now in a mood to equate softness on the slavery question with softness on the field of battle. McClellan went into retirement, his career as a soldier ended. Simultaneously, Lincoln removed one of McClellan's favorite lieutenants,

Major General Firtz-John Porter, who had commanded the Fifth Army Corps and whom Pope had accused of disobeying orders at the second Battle of Bull Run. The President also relieved Major General Buell, a friend of McClellan, who shared McClellan's position on slavery and his slowness to give battle. Buell's place in the West was taken by Major General William S. Rosecrans, who had fought with distinction at Iuka and Corinth.

Lincoln expected the new army commanders to take aggressive action without delay. To their credit, they tried, but with unfortunate results. Burnside, seeking to advance on Richmond by way of Fredericksburg, Virginia, crossed the Rappahannock on December 13, 1862, and made a clumsy assault on Lee's lines. Lee repulsed him with ease, inflicting twelve thousand casualties and suffering less than half that number himself. Burnside sullenly drew back across the river, the morale of his army temporarily shattered. (The soldiers of the Army of the Potomac, immensely fond of McClellan, felt that he would never have driven them into a disaster like that of Fredericksburg.)

In central Tennessee Rosecrans advanced against Bragg, and from December 30 to January 2 the two armies fought fiercely around Stones River near the town of Murfreesboro, Tennessee, thirty miles southeast of Nashville. The Confederates had none the worse of it, but Bragg, unaccountably discouraged, retreated. Though the engagement seemed a Union victory, Rosecrans' army was so badly mangled that it could not resume the offensive for several months.

Grant, meanwhile, set out to capture Vicksburg. He marched south from the Corinth area, following the line of the Mississippi Central Railroad forty miles to the town of Oxford, Mississippi. Grant planned to attack Vicksburg from the east while a subsidiary army led by Major General William T. Sherman went down the Mississippi with a convoy of gunboats and hit the Confederate defenses south of the Yazoo River, just north of Vicksburg. This strategy would catch Confederate General John C. Pemberton between two fires.

The plan came to grief, however, when Confederate Van Dorn slipped behind Grant and on December 20, 1862, captured his base of supplies at Holly Springs. Simultaneously, Confederate cavalry under Major General Nathan Bedford Forrest — an untaught soldier who was rapidly becoming one of the most skilled cavalry-leaders on either side — ranged across western Tennessee, disrupting Grant's line of communications. Grant was temporarily immobilized. Sherman, unaware of this development, reached the mouth of the Yazoo and made his attack, but Pemberton easily drove him off. The campaign against Vicksburg had bogged down.

The failure of the three Union offensives and the heavy casualties suffered in each produced a mood of gloom and discontent. War-weariness fed the doubts of the Peace Democrats and hurt the Republicans in the fall elections of 1862. The growing discontent in the North could, if it persisted, destroy the will to fight. In that case disunion and slavery would survive. Northern disillusionment would abate only if the war itself took a more favorable turn. Thus as 1863 began, the future of the nation, the future of democracy in the United States, depended on the recovery of the federal soldiers in the field.

THE DECISION OF WAR

Gettysburg. In January of 1863, while Rosecrans refitted his battered army at Murfreesboro, Grant regrouped his entire force on the Mississippi River just above Vicksburg and prepared for a new campaign against that fortress. In the East, the Army of the Potomac made ready for another offensive. Its new commander was Major General Joseph Hooker, a dashing, hard-fighting soldier who restored the lost morale of his troops. Hooker planned to take most of his army off on a flanking maneuver, to cross the Rappahannock and Rapidan rivers some miles above Fredericksburg and to come in on Lee from the rear. He had ample manpower, some one hundred twenty thousand men, whereas Lee had no more than half that number.

Hooker moved at the end of April. Holding the river bank opposite Fredericksburg with part of his army, he led the rest upstream to a position on Lee's left and rear at Chancellorsville and sent his cavalry on a long sweep to cut

Lee's supply lines. This plan of battle, he believed, would compel Lee to retreat, and the retreating army could be assailed with overwhelming numbers. But Lee never did the expected. Instead of retreating, he attacked, sending Stonewall Jackson on a wide flanking march that struck and routed Hooker's right on May 1, 1863. After three days of desperate fighting in the wilderness area around Chancellorsville and on the high ground near Fredericksburg, Hooker was thoroughly defeated. The Confederate victory, one of the most spectacular of the war, came at the cost of Stonewall Jackson's life. Wounded in battle, he died shortly after Hooker had retired north of the Rappahannock.

In the Mississippi Valley, however, the Union cause was beginning to prosper. Unable to attack the citadel at Vicksburg from the river, Grant boldly moved his army down the western bank and crossed over to Mississippi some thirty miles below Vicksburg. Cutting loose from his base, he marched to the Mississippi state capital at Jackson to drive off a Confederate force trying to rescue Pemberton. After a sharp fight at Champion Hill, he drove Pemberton and his thirty thousand men into the fortified lines at Vicksburg. With his right wing resting on the Mississippi River above Vicksburg, Grant was again in secure contact with his northern base. Now reinforced, he held entrenched lines that cut

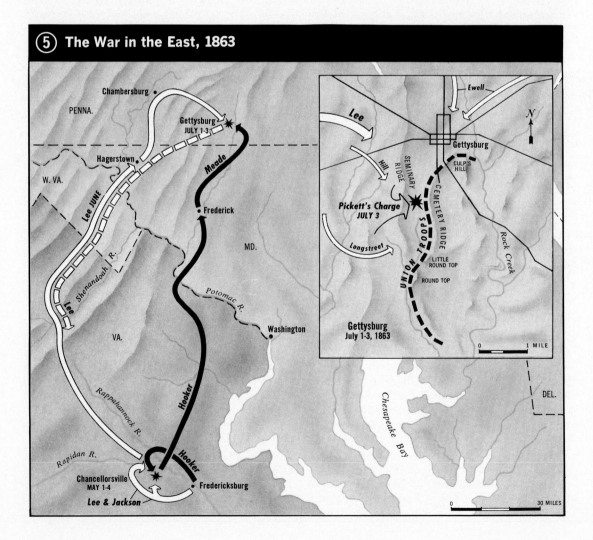

⑤ The War in the East, 1863

Gettysburg
July 1-3, 1863

Union dead after Gettysburg.

Pemberton off from the rest of the Confederacy. He had, moreover, enough men to keep General Joe Johnston (who had been given overall command in the West) from breaking the constricting ring. By the end of May Grant's grip on Vicksburg was so firm that he was bound to capture both the fortress and its defending army unless the Confederacy could muster the strength to intervene.

Davis and Lee decided instead to make one more attempt to invade the North. A Confederate victory in Pennsylvania would imperil Washington and Philadelphia, would probably compel Lincoln to send some of Grant's army east, and might even bring Southern independence. Accordingly, early in June Lee crossed the Blue Ridge, heading for the Potomac. Hooker followed, maneuvering to keep between Lee and the federal capital. On June 28, when Lee had his entire force in Pennsylvania and the Army of the Potomac was grouped in the vicinity of Frederick, Maryland, Lincoln abruptly removed Hooker from

command and gave his army to Major General George Gordon Meade, a sharp-tempered, competent professional soldier. The showdown followed almost at once. On July 1, 1863, Lee's army collided with Meade's at Gettysburg, Pennsylvania, and the biggest battle of the war began.

For three days the Confederates desperately assaulted the Federals, who held a strong position on a chain of rocky hills just south of Gettysburg. Losses on both sides were prodigious. Several times the Union seemed on the very edge of defeat, but Lee lacked the strength to deliver the final blow. The climax came on the afternoon of July 3, when Lee assailed the Federals' center with a column of fifteen thousand men led by Major General George Pickett. The Federals repelled the attack, shattering Lee's offensive power, and on the following day the Confederates began a slow, miserable retreat to Virginia. By mid-July the shattered Army of Northern Virginia was back in the lower Shenandoah Valley, decisively defeated.

Losses on each side had run between twenty and twenty-five thousand men — more than a fourth of the men engaged. The Confederate gamble on invading the North had failed.

Vicksburg and Chattanooga. More important even than the Union victory at Gettysburg was Grant's capture of Vicksburg on July 4, 1863. Pemberton had to surrender his thirty thousand men — a severe loss for the Confederacy, pinched as it was for manpower — and the Mississippi River fell under federal control all the way to the gulf. (The Confederate strong point at Port Hudson surrendered as soon as the fall of Vicksburg became known.) The South west of the great river was irretrievably cut off. Taken together, the defeats at Gettysburg and Vicksburg reduced the Confederacy permanently to defensive warfare.

When Vicksburg fell, General Rosecrans moved his Army of the Cumberland against Braxton Bragg's Army of Tennessee. Maneuvering smartly, he compelled Bragg to retreat all the way to northern Georgia. Following incautiously, Rosecrans gave Bragg an opening for a counterstroke, which Bragg delivered at Chickamauga on September 19 and 20. Rosecrans' army was routed, saved from utter disaster only by the stand of the troops commanded by Major General George H. Thomas. Rosecrans retreated to Chattanooga, where he was replaced by Thomas, and Bragg followed and entrenched on high ground overlooking the city.

If Bragg had attacked vigorously, he might have caused serious trouble, but he was content to wait in his entrenchments, believing that want of supplies would compel Thomas to surrender. Instead Grant, whom Lincoln now named to supreme command in the West, hastened to Chattanooga with substantial reinforcements. On November 24 and 25, in the twin battles of Lookout Mountain and Missionary Ridge, he drove Bragg's army back into Georgia and cemented federal control over Tennessee.

With overwhelming strength the confident Federals awaited the opening of the 1864 campaign. The Union armies were now achieving the constriction and fragmentation of the Confederacy implied in the Anaconda Plan. At Vicksburg and at Chattanooga Grant had demonstrated that Northern resources, remorselessly applied, would bring victory. At Gettysburg, Meade had shown that the South lacked the resources to strike a decisive counterblow. The South was a doomed citadel, waiting to be taken. So persuaded, Lincoln in the spring of 1864 called Grant east and made him general in chief of all Union armies. Now the President had a commander who was prepared to pay whatever price victory might require.

Faltering offensives. Grant set as his objective the defeat of the two major Confederate forces, the Army of Northern Virginia under Lee and the Army of Tennessee, in northern Georgia, led now by General Joseph E. Johnston. Making his headquarters with Meade's Army of the Potomac, Grant on May 4 led it across the Rapidan River to strike at Lee. Simultaneously, Major General William T. Sherman, now commanding the Federals in the West, led a powerful force against Johnston in the vicinity of Dalton, Georgia. These campaigns, proceeding slowly, brought ghastly casualties. The armies of Lee and Grant were in continuous contact for more than a month, fighting some of the most deadly battles in American history — the Wilderness, Spotsylvania Court House, Cold Harbor. In this month the Federals lost fully sixty thousand men, as compared with Confederate losses less than half as great. Grant, unable either to destroy Lee's army or to capture Richmond, settled down late in June to the slow, wearing siege of Petersburg, Virginia — a railroad center whose capture would lead to the fall of Richmond itself. Many people in the North felt that Grant had failed in his purpose and that the casualties his army had suffered were needlessly, intolerably, high. Sherman had had smaller losses, but he had been unable to destroy Johnston's army or to take the city of Atlanta, one of his important objectives. By midsummer a new wave of war-weariness swept the North, endangering Lincoln's reelection.

The election of 1864. Politics in 1864 reflected tensions that had developed during the preceding two years both on the battlefields and on the home front. The Northern economy, stimulated by government purchases of war materials, had boomed. Profits were high, labor by 1864 was in short supply, crops were excellent and in a time of full employment commanded handsome prices. Indeed, by 1864 inflation characterized the economy. The general price index had risen 79 per cent since 1860, the wholesale farm price index 92 per cent, and nonagricultural wages 43 per cent. But the boom carried with it inequities in rewards and inherent frustrations. Farmers complained about the shortage of agricultural labor but rejoiced in high profits. Industrial workers, whose food costs rose more rapidly than their wages, had experienced an actual

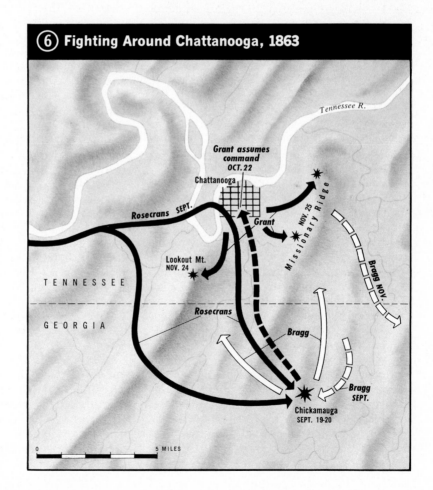

⑥ **Fighting Around Chattanooga, 1863**

Ulysses S. Grant: Victory at any cost.

3 per cent decrease in real income. Both groups, along with the decent majority of businessmen, resented the speculation and war-profiteering that was producing hundreds of newly rich but gross and greedy wartime millionaires, some of whom trafficked brazenly with the enemy. The "hot suns of modern progress," as Harriett Beecher Stowe would later say, were bleaching beyond recognition many of the ideals of a rural past, and in the overheated economy and materialistic society of the war years, the crass and fetid often thrived where high and selfless purpose had been sown. In retrospect, even by materialistic standards, the war was fostering dubious gains. To be sure, manpower shortages spurred mechanization, especially in agriculture, and military needs for guns, ammunition, supporting material, and transport provoked significant new investment in industries that supplied those and related goods and services. But the economy had been industrializing before the war, and the war-born acceleration

distorted the normal flow of investment, over-built some facilities at the expense of others, encouraged the expansion of many marginal plants and techniques, and thereby retarded some desirable innovations, most patently in the steel industry. The industrialization of the North would have proceeded without the war, which at the best hurried it and at the worst led it along fruitless and wasteful paths. At the time, however, such development mattered less to the men and women of the Union states than did their personal responses to the conditions around them — the euphoria of the profiteer over his gains, the pain his critics felt, the unprecedented comfort experienced by many farmers, the squeeze of expenses upon income among industrial workers, particularly those least skilled, the heightened moods of joy and sadness, of identification and alienation, that accompany war and revolution alike.

Those moods related most sharply to political and military rather than to economic questions. Lincoln, as he well knew, could not please all of the people all of the time. His discharge of Frémont had offended many radicals; his Emancipation Proclamation and earlier his suspensions of habeas corpus had distressed many moderates; conscription had influential opponents, Horace Greeley not the least; and in 1864, perhaps above all, the mounting lists of casualties cut at the hearts of bereaved relatives, many of whom blamed their losses on Grant's tactics or on the bungling of other Union generals — and indirectly on Lincoln, the commander in chief. Thousands of men of both parties, grieved and tired of fighting and killing and stalemate, looked for remedy in the peace movements then growing in strength. Hundreds of anti-slavery Republicans, their resolve hardened by the duration of the contest, spurned not only peace but a President they considered too soft.

But Lincoln controlled his party, which in 1864 used the name of "Union" rather than "Republican." To be sure, Wendell Phillips and a small group of German-American Radicals largely from the Middle West convened in May 1864 to nominate Frémont on a platform that denounced the Administration and to run him with an organization bereft of effective politicians. That challenge was weak. Most of the Radicals within the Republican party accepted, often with no great enthusiasm, Lincoln's unanimous renomination at the regular convention. They were generally pleased with the platform, a patriotic document calling for unity in the prosecution of the war, declaring slavery to be the cause of the war and demanding its complete elimination, promising the protection of Negro soldiers, encouraging immigration, and advocating a Pacific railway. However, the Radicals had wanted also to impose on the party their views about the reconstruction of the South, which they incorporated shortly after the renomination in the Wade-Davis Bill (see p. 375), a measure Lincoln subjected to a pocket veto. The Radicals' displeasure with Lincoln grew further when he at last permitted the Radical Secretary of the Treasury, Salmon P. Chase, to resign from the Cabinet.

Yet dissent from the left threatened Lincoln far less than did the rising sentiment for peace. The Democrats postponed their convention during the summer of 1864 while C. L. Vallandigham and others led peace demonstrations in the Middle West, and Horace Greeley importuned Lincoln to treat with representatives of the Confederacy said to be in Canada. The President made the embarrassed Greeley his intermediary, to no end, for Greeley discovered that the supposed representatives had no credentials. Lincoln, who had expected as much, then announced his willingness to consider "any proposition which embraces the restoration of peace, the integrity of the whole Union, and the abandonment of slavery." Those, after all, had long been his terms, and those terms remained anathema to the South. Peace with total union and without slavery could be won only in battle.

Still, the strength of the peace movement and the disunity within the Republican party persuaded Greeley and others that Lincoln could not win reelection and should therefore withdraw in favor of another candidate, Frémont most likely. Those conditions heartened the Democrats, who pleased their war faction by nominating McClellan in their August convention and pleased their peace faction with a platform that described the war as a failure and called for an armistice and for peace negotiations based on a restored Union. It differed from Lincoln's position in two respects — its assumption that peace would be easily negotiable and its exclusion of emancipation as a condition for peace. McClellan in his campaign further narrowed the difference by his dedication to the prosecution of the war until reunion was achieved. The peace movement had no real champion in the field, the Radicals no effective candidate, and Lincoln no intention of withdrawing from the race. But the President was no more optimistic than Greeley. "This morning as for some days past," Lincoln reflected on August 23, "it seems probable that this Administration will not be re-elected."

The war was grinding toward a different conclusion. In August 1864 a federal fleet under Rear Admiral Farragut broke its way into Mobile Bay, closing one of the last ports the Confederacy still possessed. In September and October a Union army, under energetic Major General Philip H. Sheridan, routed the troops of General Jubal A. Early and wrested the rich granary of the Shenandoah Valley from the Confederacy. In Georgia President Davis, tired of General Johnston and his strategically sound delaying tactics, had put the fiery John B. Hood in his place. Hood gave battle to Sherman, lost, and had to abandon Atlanta on September 1. With that victory Northern spirits soared. Frémont retired from

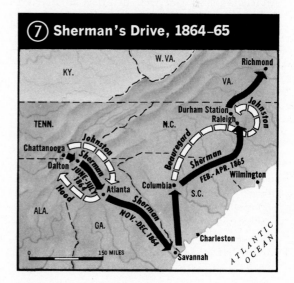

(7) Sherman's Drive, 1864-65

the presidential contest, the Radicals closed ranks behind the President, and in November Lincoln won, polling 55 per cent of the popular vote and carrying the electoral vote 212 to 21. McClellan had run well in areas carried by Breckinridge in 1860 and had drawn most of the immigrant vote. Lincoln had held his support of 1860, gained most of the votes that had then gone to Bell, and attracted native-born farmers, skilled laborers, and professional men. The margin of his victory constituted, for the duration of the war at least, a mandate for his policies.

The bitter end. After the election Lincoln's generals moved swiftly. Sherman, copying the tactics Grant had used below Vicksburg, cut loose from his base at Atlanta and marched across Georgia to Savannah, devastating the country as he went. Hood took his army to northern Mississippi and moved north into Tennessee, hoping by this counterstroke to force Sherman's recall. He suffered a costly check at the Battle of Franklin on November

30, and on December 15 and 16 Thomas struck him at Nashville, driving him away in complete disorder and almost destroying his army. Sherman, meanwhile, moved on, occupying Savannah just before Christmas. When 1865 began, the Confederacy consisted of little more than the Carolinas and the southern half of Virginia. Isolated Confederate armies still existed beyond the Mississippi and in southern Alabama, but they were unable to affect the outcome of the war.

The end, at last in sight, was not long delayed. During the winter of 1865 Sherman marched northward from Savannah, across the Carolinas. Confederate military resources had sunk so low that General Johnston, recalled to oppose him, confessed despairingly: "I can do no more than annoy him." From Tennessee a powerful federal cavalry corps swung down through Alabama, capturing Montgomery and destroying munitions works at Selma. Charleston fell, and a federal army-navy expedition sealed off Wilmington, North Carolina, the South's last seaport. In desperation, Lee attacked Grant's lines before Petersburg, trying to disable his opponent so that he could then break away and join forces with Johnston, but his assault was unsuccessful. On April 2 Grant's troops shattered Lee's right flank in a battle at Five Forks, compelling Lee to evacuate Peters-

⑧ **Grant's Campaign Around Richmond, 1864–65**

burg. Federal troops occupied Richmond, and the Confederate government fled south.

On April 9, at Appomattox Court House in southern Virginia, Lee had to surrender his army to Grant, and the war virtually came to an end. Johnston surrendered to Sherman a few days later. The surrender of the remaining Confederate contingents in the deep South and west of the Mississippi River followed, and by early June the last vestige of Confederate resistance had disappeared. After four years of struggle, after the loss of six hundred thousand lives, after the agony of fratricide, after the awful waste of hatreds, the ravages of destruction and grief, the Union had been restored.

The hour of triumph was marred by tragedy. On April 14, at Ford's Theatre in Washington, a fanatical actor, John Wilkes Booth, murdered Abraham Lincoln. His death dimmed the prospects for his cherished peace of reconciliation. Lincoln had instructed Grant and Sherman to arrange surrender on "the most liberal and honorable terms." Lincoln in his second inaugural address had called on the North to act "with malice toward none, with charity for all." Had he lived, he might not have been able to fashion national policy in the pattern of his magnanimity. But he would doubtless have tried, and, in the manner of his wartime efforts, tried skillfully. His assassination deprived the South of a great friend and the nation of a great leader, possibly the only American who had felt all of the grief and none of the hatred of the four terrible years.

SUGGESTIONS FOR READING

General

Here as in the preceding chapter the best introductory treatment, from the point of view alike of its text and its extensive, critical bibliography, is J. G. Randall and David Donald, *The Civil War and Reconstruction* (2nd ed., 1961). More extensive, but complete only to 1863, is Allan Nevins, *The War for the Union*, 2 vols. (1959–60). Valuable, too, are R. F. Nichols, *The Stakes of Power** (1961), and, especially on military matters, Bruce Catton, *This Hallowed Ground** (1956).

The Confederacy

The outstanding study of the Confederacy is the judicious, trenchant Clement Eaton, *A History of the Southern Confederacy** (1954). E. M. Coulter, *The Confederate States of America, 1861–1865* (1950), is important but less critical. There is a useful short account in C. P. Roland, *The Confederacy** (1960), and a good anthology in A. D. Kirwan, ed., *The Confederacy** (1959). R. S. Henry, *The Story of the Confederacy** (1931), contains a clear narrative focused on military matters. The causes of the South's defeat are the subject of a series of incisive essays in David Donald, ed., *Why the North Won the Civil War** (1960). Among many special studies, one of the most engaging is B. J. Hendrick, *Statesmen of the Lost Cause* (1939), which examines Davis and his civilian associates. A more recent and more sophisticated treatment of the same subject is in R. W. Patrick, *Jefferson Davis and His Cabinet* (1944). Two works of F. L. Owsley are of the first importance: *King Cotton Diplomacy* (1931) and *State Rights in the Confederacy* (1925). Among the many biographies of significance are Hudson Strode, *Jefferson Davis*, 2 vols. (1955), and R. M. McElroy, *Jefferson Davis: The Unreal and the Real*, 2 vols. (1937), as well as R. R. Von Abele, *Alexander H. Stephens: A Biography* (1946).

* Available in a paperback edition.

Lincoln and the Union

The general studies cited above and the Lincoln studies listed here afford among them the appropriate points of departure for understanding the Union during the Civil War. Among additional important works, three bear upon significant diplomatic issues: E. D. Adams, *Great Britain and the American Civil War*, 2 vols. (1925); M. B. Duberman, *Charles Francis Adams* (1961); and the good biography of Seward in S. F. Bemis, ed., *The American Secretaries of State and Their Diplomacy*, 10 vols. (1927–29). F. L. Klement, *The Copperheads in the Middle West* (1960), explains the motivation of the group largely in economic terms, whereas disloyalty and danger are stressed by G. F. Milton, *Abraham Lincoln and the Fifth Column** (1942), and W. Gray, *The Hidden Civil War: The Story of the Copperheads** (1942). There are notable treatments of economic matters in Frederick Merk, *Economic History of Wisconsin During the Civil War Decade* (1916); Sidney Ratner, *American Taxation* (1942); W. C. Mitchell, *Gold, Prices and Wages under the Greenback Standard* (1908); and R. P. Sharkey, *Money, Class, and Party* (1959). Indispensable on its subject is J. G. Randall, *Constitutional Problems under Lincoln** (1926).

There is no end to Lincoln literature. The best short biography is Benjamin Thomas, *Abraham Lincoln* (1952). Among longer biographies, Carl Sandburg, *Abraham Lincoln: The War Years* [abridged version*], 4 vols. (1939), is distinguished for its passion, and J. G. Randall, *Lincoln the President*, 4 vols.* (1945–55), completed by R. N. Current, for its depth and judgment. Among many anthologies, P. M. Angle, ed., *The Lincoln Reader** (1947), stands out for its readability. Two especially incisive collections of essays are David Donald, *Lincoln Reconsidered** (1956), and R. N. Current, *The Lincoln Nobody Knows** (1958). Truly interested students will want to consult R. P. Basler and others, *The Collected Works of Abraham Lincoln*, 9 vols. (1953–55), and the thorough Jay Monaghan, ed., *Lincoln Bibliography, 1839–1939*, 2 vols. (1945). There is a more selective and critical bibliography in P. M. Angle, *A Shelf of Lincoln Books* (1946), and a good selection of Lincoln writings in P. M. Angle and E. S. Miers, eds., *The Living Lincoln* (1955), and R. P. Basler, ed., *Abraham Lincoln: His Speeches and Writings* (1946). Especially significant on Lincoln as a politician are H. J. Carman and R. H. Luthin, *Lincoln and the Patronage* (1943); H. B. Hesseltine, *Lincoln and the War Governors* (1948); and T. H. Williams, *Lincoln and the Radicals** (1941). On Lincoln and military affairs, besides the books listed below, T. H. Williams, *Lincoln and His Generals* (1952), and R. V. Bruce, *Lincoln and the Tools of War* (1956), are particularly rewarding.

Military Events

Just about every significant general, Union or Confederate, and just about every significant engagement at arms, has been the subject of at least one, and ordinarily of several, books or essays. There are further shelves of volumes dealing more generally with the war, many of them memoirs, some of them stirring. The would-be specialist has no convenient terminus in his reading; the neophyte can begin profitably in any one of many places. For an exciting and informed start, an interested student might turn to the writings of Bruce Catton: *Mr. Lincoln's Army** (1951); *Glory Road** (1952); *A Stillness at Appomattox** (1954); *America Goes to War** (1958); *Banners at Shenandoah** (1965); *Centennial History of the Civil War*, 3 vols. (1961–63); *Grant Moves South* (1960); *This Hallowed Ground** (1956); *U. S. Grant and the American Military Tradition** (1954). See also E. S. Miers, *Web of Victory: Grant at Vicksburg* (1955), and F. D. Downey, *Storming the Gateway, Chattanooga, 1863* (1960). Jay Monaghan, *Civil War on the Western Border, 1854–1865* (1955), provides one of the good accounts available of the trans-Mississippi war, and the Northern navy absorbs several authors, among them R. S. West, Jr., *Mr. Lincoln's Navy* (1957), and C. E. Macartney, *Mr. Lincoln's Admirals* (1956) — both general accounts.

* Available in a paperback edition.

There is also an intriguing but more technical study in J. P. Baxter III, *The Introduction of the Ironclad Warship* (1933). Of other accounts of a general nature, an excellent short one is Fletcher Pratt, *Ordeal by Fire: An Informal History of the Civil War* [*A Short History of the Civil War**] (1955), and an excellent long one, K. P. Williams, *Lincoln Finds a General: A Military History of the Civil War*, 4 vols. (1949–56). David Donald has edited an informative picture history, *Divided We Fought: A Pictorial History of the War* (1952), as has R. M. Ketchum, *The American Heritage Picture History of the Civil War* (1960); and the common soldier has had admirable attention from B. I. Wiley, *The Life of Johnny Reb** (1943) and *The Life of Billy Yank** (1952). Also good on that subject is the anthology, H. S. Commager, ed., *The Blue and the Gray: The Story of the Civil War as Told by Participants*, 2 vols. (1950). *The Personal Memoirs of U. S. Grant*, 2 vols. (1885, 1886) are still an impressive testimony to the author's ability and humility, possibly the best of all Civil War memoirs, but W. T. Sherman, *Memoirs*, 2 vols. (1875), is also first rate; and both men have had talented biographers, in particular Lloyd Lewis in his memorable *Sherman, Fighting Prophet* (1932) and *Captain Sam Grant* (1950) — the latter of which Bruce Catton is completing. On the Southern side, the literature, like the valor, balances that of the North, and D. S. Freeman stands out as one of the great historians of the conflict in his two classics, *R. E. Lee, A Biography*, 4 vols. (1934–35) and *Lee's Lieutenants*, 3 vols. (1942–44). Finally, not even a list as brief and selective as this should omit mention of the atlases of the Civil War: the most authoritative, H. S. Commager, 1958 ed. of *Atlas to Accompany the Official Records of the Union and Confederate Armies* (1891–95); the more modern, in its design and use of symbols, V. J. Esposito, ed., *The West Point Atlas of American Wars*, 2 vols. (1959); and the motorists' handy J. B. Mitchell, *Decisive Battles of the Civil War** (1955).

* Available in a paperback edition.

15
The Aftermath
of War

In the decade after Appomattox, the vast social and industrial changes that had begun before the Civil War swept on. The American people continued their uninterrupted movement to the West and, at a quickened pace, to the cities. Immigration, light during the war years, resumed, bringing to the United States unprecedented numbers of Asians and non-English-speaking Europeans. On the farms and in the cities, native born and immigrant alike felt the pressures of personal adjustment to new homes, new neighbors, new machines, new conditions of daily life.

In this time of transition, government, too, faced difficult problems. The war itself had settled three major questions. The triumph of Northern arms had established the Union as indivisible and indissoluble. So also, that victory had wiped out the institution of slavery. And it had assured, at least temporarily, Northern dominance in national politics. But no one was certain how the North would discharge its responsibilities, how the Union would in fact be restored, how the freed slaves would fare. These were thorny questions, especially for a generation that had just fought a fierce war, a struggle imbued with anxiety, death, and hatred. Emotions clouded the judgment of men confronted with the staggering political tasks of the postwar decade. The tensions of the time at once complicated political issues and diverted energies from them. Those who had expected victory to create a brave new world were disappointed.

THE PROBLEM OF RECONSTRUCTION

Diversions. Union soldiers, eager to return to civilian pursuits, welcomed the rapid demobilization that released some eight hundred thousand men in six months. The government also dissolved the rest of its military apparatus. Conscription ceased, the standing army fell off within two years to traditional peacetime levels, the commanding staff scattered or retired, the navy relapsed to the desuetude of the prewar decade. With demobilization, the federal budget dropped about a billion dollars

Richmond: A devastated city.

in one year, government contracts stopped, and over a million employees in wartime industries had to find other work. These adjustments produced a serious but brief economic slump. Recovery came in 1868 as a spurt in railway construction brought demands for iron, steel, lumber, and, consequently, for workers. With reemployment, the need quickened for the produce of farms and for the products of industries that finished foods and textiles. Until 1873, when depression returned, the opportunities of industrial growth and prosperity absorbed millions of Americans.

Prosperity fed a mood of confident materialism. Businessmen in particular exploited the opportunities for riches — new inventions, lucrative tactics for industrial and commercial competition and consolidation, exciting speculations (see Chapter 18). The accumulation of wealth caught the imagination and excited the expectations of many men in all ranks of society. There were each year more symbols to confirm their hopes — more factories, more residential palaces, more railroads and furnaces and bridges to signify the achievements of business and businessmen and the industrial conquest of the continent. Of these symbols perhaps the most stirring was the completion of the transcontinental railroad. The wartime loans and land grants (see p. 347) had sped the construction of the Central Pacific east from California and the Union Pacific west from Nebraska. Gangs of Chinese laborers pushed the tracks of the Central Pacific across the hazardous Sierra Nevada, while Irish immigrants carried the line of the Union Pacific across the plains, often under danger of Indian attack. As the two roads raced for their share of federal subsidies, both subordinated quality to speed. Yet their accomplishment was nonetheless spectacular. The Union Pacific built 1,086 miles of track; the Central Pacific, 689. They met at Promontory Point, just northwest of Ogden, Utah. At ceremonies there on May 10, 1869, the telegraph recorded the blows of a silver sledge that drove in the golden spikes connecting the rails and, with them, the two oceans, now separated by only a week's journey.

The lure of the golden spikes preoccupied most of the talented and ambitious in postwar America. Subsidies to railroads had had their wartime counterparts in the tariff that protected burgeoning industry from European competition and in the Homestead Act, which invited both settlement and speculation in the open West (see p. 426). The itch to gamble, the urge to create, the desire to accumulate wealth and prestige, and the drive for power — all these alone or together moved the majority of men who fashioned an age of enterprise out of the aftermath of war.

This seemed, to many men of noble hope and active conscience, a deplorable diversion from the mission of America. The pursuit of private profit or personal power, whatever its results, strayed wide of the mark of the idealists who had interpreted the war as a struggle for human freedom or a fight to preserve intact the United States and thus the exemplary experiment in democracy. "We hoped," Ralph Waldo Emerson wrote, "that in the peace . . . a great expansion would follow in the mind of the country; grand views in every direction. . . . But the energy of the nation seems to have expended itself." Emerson, of course, meant the nation's moral energy. It was by no means entirely expended, but the diversions of progress cost the nation much of the spirit and concentration needed for the politics of reconstruction and reunion.

The devastated South. The South especially needed the understanding and constructive intelligence of the whole nation. Emancipation had at one stroke wiped out billions of dollars of investment in slaves. It had lifted the Negroes to the status of freedom in a society that had no practice in and no plans for coping with the social and economic conditions of biracial living. Previously the South had counted on slavery to control relationships between white and black; now the South had no controls. But the two races remained, side by side, unaccustomed to their situation.

The South, moreover, was a devastated land. The war had taken the lives of a quarter of a million soldiers. Northern armies had severely damaged and only partially rebuilt the railways; Confederate bankruptcy had forced neglect of most of the roads; horses and mules were in short supply. The shortages of manpower during the war and the havoc of Northern armies on the march had laid waste much of Southern agriculture. Fences, farmhouses,

and outbuildings were burned or in the ruins of disrepair; crops were destroyed; livestock were either killed or left to stray. According to one contemporary report, "the country between Washington and Richmond was . . . like a desert." According to another, the path of General Sherman's march "looked for many miles like a broad, black streak of ruin and desolation." The cities had fared as badly. Industry was crippled or abandoned; financial institutions were bankrupt; resources for business credit were wiped out. Some fifteen thousand people in Atlanta and as many more in Richmond depended on federal relief for subsistence. Charleston, South Carolina, was "a city of ruins, of desolation, of vacant houses, of widowed women, of rotting wharves."

The South was also a conquered territory. Federal troops occupied the major towns, often with an understandable but lamentable disregard for the sensitivities of local citizens. The terms of surrender of course forbade the flying of Confederate flags and the wearing of Confederate uniforms, and the presence of Union blue provided daily reminders of defeat. The federal government imprisoned few Confederate leaders (Jefferson Davis was one), and in all respects the conquerors were, as victors go, not harsh. Indeed Northern relief for the destitute was as spontaneous as it was indispensable. But the evidences of defeat swelled the sorrows of devastation.

The South was on the whole reconciled to the failure of secession. Some die-hards — Confederate Secretary of War and State Judah P. Benjamin and General Jubal A. Early among them — expatriated themselves, others nursed a lifelong sulk, but most of the eminent and the plain alike accepted defeat. While proud of the spirit of the war years, they were ready to return to useful participation in the life of the nation. They immediately displayed remarkable energy in rebuilding the society and economy of their section (see Chapter 16). Over their political rehabilitation, however, they had no authority.

President versus Congress. While the fighting still raged, Lincoln had taken initial steps toward reestablishing loyal governments in the seceded states. He always maintained that insurrectionists had temporarily grabbed power in the Southern states. They had never, in his view, seceded, for secession was impossible. On this theory he proceeded to use military force to set up loyal governments as quickly as he could, even when only a minority of the people of a state were loyal to the Union. He placed military governors over Tennessee, Louisiana, and Arkansas in 1862 and 1863, and in December of 1863 he proclaimed the general procedures by which the Southern people could remake their governments. With the exception of certain high public officials, he offered pardons to any Confederate who would take the oath to support "the Constitution of the United States, and the union of the States thereunder." When in any state one-tenth of the number who had voted in the presidential election of 1860 took this oath, they might establish a government without slavery, which the President would recognize as the "true government." During 1864 Tennessee, Louisiana, and Arkansas, using the "10 per cent plan," set up new state governments.

The Radicals in Congress bitterly opposed Lincoln's plan. They argued that the seceded states had forfeited their rights, and that Congress had to determine the bases for Reconstruction. (Indisputably, Congress alone could pass upon the credentials of its members, a power sufficient to keep the representatives of states rebuilt on Lincoln's plan from taking their seats.) Lincoln, in the view of the Radicals, was much too lenient. In contrast, Benjamin F. Wade, Henry Winter Davis, and their fellows specified severe terms for Reconstruction in a bill that Congress passed in July 1864. By its terms, the provisional governor appointed in each seceded state was to enroll the white male citizens. If a majority of those enrolled took an oath to support the Constitution, they could elect a constitutional convention to form a new state government. No one who had held office in the Confederacy or in any of its states, no one who had voluntarily borne arms against the United States, could vote or serve as a delegate. The new government, moreover, was required to prohibit slavery, repudiate the Confederate debt, and prohibit voting and officeholding by former Confederate officials. Lincoln's pocket veto prevented this measure from becoming law, but the President endorsed its terms "as one very proper plan for the loyal people of any State

Andrew Johnson: Certain of his righteousness.

choosing to adopt it." Southerners naturally preferred the presidential plan, which the Radicals would not accept. The problem called for statesmanship of the highest order, of which Lincoln was capable, but the assassin's bullet at Ford's Theatre put Andrew Johnson in the White House.

Johnson had been born to poverty and ignorance in North Carolina. A courageous, self-taught, energetic man, he had overcome the disadvantages of his background, represented his adopted state, Tennessee, in the House and in the Senate, and served admirably as a loyal Democratic war governor. Though he had not opposed slavery, he detested the planter aristocracy, and he was devoted to the Union. The Radicals, content with his nomination as Lincoln's running mate in 1864, expected to find him a malleable friend. They were wrong. Johnson was to be a pugnacious antagonist, a self-assured, intemperate, aggressive foe, certain of his duty, certain of his righteousness, and uncompromising — as well as frequently inept — in their pursuit.

Congress was in recess when Johnson took

office in April 1865. At first vindictive toward the South, within a month he had adopted Lincoln's conciliatory tone. He retained all of Lincoln's Cabinet, preserved most of Lincoln's plan for Reconstruction (but not the 10 per cent plan), and embraced many of Lincoln's attitudes. Like Lincoln, Johnson considered Reconstruction primarily a presidential function. Like him, he hoped to restore the Southern states to the Union rapidly and on generous terms. Like him, he believed the war had been fought to preserve the Union and free the slaves. Again like Lincoln, he opposed both racial equality and federal policies designed to achieve it, and he had far more confidence in the ability of the South to manage its affairs wisely than did most Republicans, Radicals or moderates.

Within the first weeks of his Presidency, Johnson asserted his constitutional authority to oversee Reconstruction and adopted policies from which he never receded. His policies were expressed, on May 29, 1865, in a Proclamation of Amnesty and in a second proclamation fixing the terms of Reconstruction for North Carolina. The first of these promised a full pardon to all Southerners who would swear an oath of allegiance to the United States. The proclamation listed fourteen classes of persons who were excluded from the amnesty, among them, Confederate office-holders and men with taxable property of over $20,000; but Johnson invited special applications for pardons from persons in these excepted classes and stated that he would give each applicant a fair hearing. In his North Carolina proclamation, Johnson appointed a provisional governor whose duty it was to set rules, as soon as possible, for electing a convention "to be chosen by . . . the people . . . who are loyal to the United States." Loyalty consisted only of a willingness to take the oath described in the amnesty proclamation, a willingness, really, to accept defeat in the war just ended. The convention was to write a new constitution, and either that document or the legislature elected under it was to "prescribe the qualifications of electors and the eligibility of persons to hold office" in the state. In Arkansas, Louisiana, Tennessee, and Virginia the President accepted the governments established according to Lincoln's plan, and for the

remaining Southern states he issued Reconstruction proclamations identical to his North Carolina proclamation. Only later, when his terms provoked criticism in the North, did Johnson request also that the conventions disavow ordinances of secession, repudiate Southern war debts, and ratify the pending Thirteenth Amendment. Approved by Congress the preceding January, that amendment forever ended slavery or involuntary servitude within the United States.

Republican distress was equal and opposite to Southern rejoicing over the President's proclamations of May, for the terms of those documents unconditionally pardoned most Southern men and assured pardons for most of their wartime leaders, left to the Southern states control of their internal policies (not the least, policies relating to the freed Negroes), and offered the South quick and full resumption of its influence in national politics. By December 1865 the Thirteenth Amendment had been adopted, but the Southern states did not comply fully with Johnson's other requests. Some merely repealed their ordinances of secession without declaring them invalid in origin; some tried to avoid repudiating their debts. Further, voters in the South elected to office hundreds of ex-Confederate leaders, many of them celebrated champions of secession. Among them was Alexander H. Stevens of Georgia, the former Confederate Vice-President, whose election to the United States Senate especially rankled Union men. Yet Johnson considered the states reconstructed and also believed, as General Grant put it, that "the mass of thinking men of the South accept the present situation . . . in good faith." Had the decision been his to make, Johnson would unhesitatingly have seated the delegations of Southern congressmen arriving in Washington. Congress was of another mind, as were most Republicans in the North, who feared that developments in the South would cost them the fruits of their victory.

THE SHAPING OF RECONSTRUCTION

Seeds of bitterness. Only the Democrats and a few Republicans were willing to receive the Southerners elected to Congress or to abide with Reconstruction as Johnson had planned it. The other Republicans, moderates and Radicals alike, demanded more than the South had yet yielded. Their attitude reflected the dominant public opinion of the Northern people, who could not believe that the "rebels," enemies in battle for four years, had reformed in nine months. The victors intended to impose stringent terms for Reconstruction, conditions that would set so high a price for disloyalty that it would never occur again. The Radicals proposed to go even further.

In the Congress that reconvened in December 1865, the Radicals were only a minority. But they were determined, personally powerful, politically adroit men, and they had in Thaddeus Stevens one leader distinguished for his parliamentary skill, his pith and sarcasm in debate, and his rancorous commitment to punishing the South. He wanted the South to pay the cost of the war. He wanted to "insure the ascendancy" of the Republican party, on which, he believed, the safety and glory of the nation depended. If he was partisan, he was also a daring champion of Negro rights. He advocated distributing all the public lands in the Southern states, and the private property of the "rebels," too, to the freed Negroes in order to establish each head of a former slave family on his own farm. "Forty acres . . . and a hut," Stevens said, "would be more valuable . . . than the . . . right to vote." But that right also he and the other Radicals eventually demanded for the Negro.

The Radicals were furious over Southern reluctance to accede even to Johnson's lenient recommendations and over Southern suppression of the Negro. The moderates as well as the Radicals objected especially to the return to office of former Confederate leaders and to the "black codes" that the former Confederate states adopted. Those codes represented the initial Southern effort to regulate the economic and social lives of the freed slaves. Many of the Negroes, without experience with freedom, drifted aimlessly about the country, expecting charity and avoiding work, sometimes stealing or carousing. The "black codes" were designed to discourage vagrancy and to minimize race friction. While they permitted the freedmen to make contracts and own property, they treated Negroes as inferior to whites,

Thaddeus Stevens: Rancorous reformer.

segregated schools and some public places, restricted Negro landholding and the movement of Negro servants. They also set special penalties for Negroes who broke labor contracts, and they forbade Negroes to carry arms, serve on juries, or marry whites. To most Northerners these provisions seemed appallingly like the old slave codes. Indeed, in some states and in many respects they were; the South had turned to the past for guidance in managing its problems.

But the past, in the mind of the Republicans, could not give guidance. The war was to have established the conditions of freedom and at least some of the conditions of equality as well. But the "black codes" impaired the freedom of the Southern Negro, and white Southerners manifestly had not even begun to understand the desirability of Negro equality. To be sure, few Northerners were ready to accept Negroes as equals, but Southern disdain for the freed-

It is the opinion of your committee —

I. That the States lately in rebellion were, at the close of the war, disorganized communites, without civil government, and without constitutions or other forms, by virtue of which political relations could legally exist between them and the federal government.

II. That Congress cannot be expected to recognize as valid the election of representatives from disorganized communities, which, from the very nature of the case, were unable to present their claim to representation under those established and recognized rules, the observance of which has been hitherto required.

III. That Congress would not be justified in admitting such communities to a participation in the government of the country without first providing such constitutional or other guarantees as will tend to secure the civil rights of all citizens of the republic; a just equality of representation; protection against claims founded in rebellion and crime; a temporary restoration of the right of suffrage to those who had not actively participated in the efforts to destroy the Union and overthrow the government, and the exclusion from positions of public trust of, at least, a portion of those whose crimes have proved them to be enemies to the Union, and unworthy of public confidence.

From the Report of the Joint Committee on Reconstruction, 1866.

men pushed the moderates in Congress toward the Radical position and away from the President, who unwisely refused to consider any view but his own. Johnson's form of Reconstruction had permitted the Southerners precisely the license Congress would not tolerate. Bitterly, doggedly, Congress struck back.

A bitter year. Although the Republicans in Congress did not break with Johnson at once, they refused to recognize the Southern regimes he had called into being, and they asserted their authority over policy by creating an influential joint committee on Reconstruction. In February 1866 Congress passed a bill to undo the "black codes." This measure enlarged and extended the powers of the Freedmen's Bureau, an agency created by Congress in 1865 to provide humanitarian services for Southern Negroes. The bureau, a kind of guardian for its charges, had been operative in every Southern state, coordinating the work of voluntary benevolent societies, feeding migrants, finding them work and homes, rendering medical aid, establishing schools, sometimes defending freedmen from white terrorists. The new bill permitted the bureau to use military force to protect Negro rights. Though the moderates in Congress considered this step both necessary and equitable, many Southerners distrusted the bureau's agents, of whom a minority were ruthless or corrupt, and President Johnson condemned any resort to the military in time of peace. Vetoing the bill, he argued that the courts would adequately protect the freedmen and that the continuation of the bureau "would inevitably result in fraud, corruption, and oppression."

Though the Senate did not override the veto, Radicals and moderates in April 1866 joined forces to pass a civil-rights bill. It declared all persons born in the United States, with the exception of untaxed Indians, to be citizens of the country and therefore entitled to the legal rights of white persons, regardless of the stipulations of any local statutes. The bill also authorized the use of troops to assure enforcement of its provisions and penalties. Again the President responded with a veto, but this time Congress overrode it. Indeed Congress went on to pass a second Freedmen's Bureau bill, which Johnson also vetoed. This time only three Republicans in the Senate voted to sustain him, and Congress passed the bill over his veto.

Congress next approved, with minor alterations, a constitutional amendment proposed by its joint committee on Reconstruction. The first section of this sweeping amendment — ultimately the Fourteenth Amendment — embodied the substance of the Civil Rights Act, thereby establishing its constitutionality, and went still further. The amendment began by defining American citizenship: "All persons born or naturalized in the United States, and subject to the jurisdiction thereof, are citizens of the United States and of the State wherein they reside." The amendment then prohibited states from passing laws "which shall abridge the privileges or immunities of citizens of the United States"; from depriving "any person of life, liberty, or property, without due process of law"; and from denying "to any person within its jurisdiction the equal protection of the laws." Those provisions, designed to safeguard the rights of the freedmen, were later interpreted by the federal courts as a protection for the privileges of corporations, but the framers of the amendment, judging by the statements they made in 1866, had not intended or envisaged that usage. Rather they were striking out against the "black codes" and against laws that subjected Negroes to special treatment or penalized Negro lawbreakers more than white. Very few congressmen opposed social segregation, though Senator Charles Sumner did, but moderates and Radicals alike opposed inequalities before the law.

The second section of the Fourteenth Amendment tried to force the states to grant Negro suffrage by giving them a choice between enfranchising all male citizens and losing a number of seats in the House of Representatives proportionate to those excluded. Some Radicals would have preferred explicitly to give the Negro the vote, but the moderates, and indeed most Northerners, still opposed that step. The amendment also denied the right to hold office to former Confederates who had been federal or state officials before the war, until Congress should by a two-thirds vote pardon them. This provision postponed indefinitely the return to national politics of the Southern leaders of the 1850's. Finally, the amendment stated that the Confederate war debt was never to be paid, the Union war debt was never to be repudiated, and owners of former slaves were never to be compensated for their loss.

The Fourteenth Amendment was something of a concession to the moderates, who tended to believe that, if ratified, it would put to rest the problems of Reconstruction. But the South would have none of it. Only Tennessee of the former Confederate states ratified the amendment, and Tennessee did so only after the establishment of voting qualifications favoring the Republicans and only after the use of outright force in the legislature. In return Congress readmitted Tennessee to the Union. Elsewhere Southern legislatures rejected the amendment out of hand. These rejections

tended to reinforce Republican belief in Southern intransigence. So did an outbreak of race riots in the South, of which the worst were in Memphis and New Orleans. Although there were provocations on both sides, the spectacle of white mobs killing Negroes for whatever reason hardened the attitude of the North.

Johnson pursued a wholly passive policy during the disturbances in New Orleans. His inaction, based partly on his solicitude for state rights, partly on his misplaced belief that the trouble stemmed primarily from a Radical conspiracy, heightened the antagonism of Northern Republican voters as well as of their congressmen. The President appeared to have enlisted not only with the Democrats, whose support he overtly sought, but with the recent rebels. He seemed to have no interest in Negro rights and no use for the equalitarian principles of the Fourteenth Amendment, which he urged Southerners to reject, or for Northern opinion that embraced those principles. His stance and his obduracy produced during the election campaign of 1866 a truce of political convenience between moderate and Radical Republicans. Johnson's clumsy efforts to use the patronage to assist his few Republican friends and to punish his opponents served only to alienate further the large majority of the party. So, too, did his public classification of Charles Sumner and Thad Stevens as traitors. In a continuing fit of pique the President took the stump against the congressional candidates, particularly the Radicals, who had voted against White House policies. Blustering his way through cities in the East and Middle West, he flashed his temper at hissing audiences and surrendered the dignity of his office to vilification. Again and again he revealed his own prejudice against Negroes. The exhibition played into his enemies' hands. Johnson's outbursts did not move an electorate well informed about the issues of Reconstruction and determined, in the large, to exact from the South a price for Northern victory in the war. The Democrats and the handful of Johnson Republicans were swept to defeat in a major Republican triumph. The verdict was in one sense clear — Johnson had lost; the electorate had repudiated him and his plans. In another sense the verdict was ambiguous, for the magnitude of the victory, which the Radicals interpreted as a mandate for them, was in fact a more general expression of Northern insistence on the admission of the Southern states only on conditions stricter than those the President favored. Moderates in 1866 tended to consider the Fourteenth Amendment a sufficient condition; Radicals demanded more. Now the Republicans in Congress had to reconcile those views.

Congress in control. The outgoing Congress during its final hours in March 1867 put through a stiff Reconstruction bill and quickly repassed it over Johnson's veto. The new Congress in 1867–68 added three supplementary measures to facilitate the administration of the program. These acts rested on the presumption that no lawful governments existed in the ten former Confederate states (the eleventh, Tennessee, had of course been readmitted). The legislation divided the states into five military districts, each of which was placed under a federal commander with authority over police, judicial, and civil functions — au-

thority superior to that of the state governments and including the control of constitution-making. In order to regain representation in Congress, the people of a state had to meet various conditions. In elections for state constitutional conventions, Negroes were entitled to vote, but Confederate officeholders disqualified by the still-pending Fourteenth Amendment were not. The new state constitutions had to establish Negro suffrage and win approval by referendum from the electorate that had chosen the convention delegates and from Congress as well. The state legislatures then elected had to ratify the Fourteenth Amendment. When enough states had done so to make that amendment a part of the Constitution of the United States, and only then, the states that had complied with Congress's demands would be readmitted.

Johnson condemned the Radical program as "without precedent . . . in palpable conflict with the plainest provisions of the Constitution . . . utterly destructive to . . . great principles of liberty." Unquestionably the Republicans were treating the South as a dangerous, conquered province, but as rebels the Southerners were treated with moderation. Still, the firmness of the program occasioned indignation and defiance in the South, thus enlarging the tasks of the military commanders and fanning resentment toward both Yankees and Negroes.

The Radicals, with the necessary support of most moderate Republicans, also expanded congressional power within the federal government. In January 1867, before enacting the Reconstruction legislation, the outgoing Congress authorized a special session of the new Congress to convene in March of that year instead of in December, as was normal. Previously only the President had exercised the right to convene Congress. The outgoing Congress on March 2, 1867, also attached a clause to the Army Appropriation Act that limited Johnson's prerogatives as commander in chief. The President and the Secretary of War, that clause provided, could issue military orders only through the General of the Army, then Ulysses S. Grant. The headquarters of the General of the Army were to remain in Washington, as was he, except by express consent of the Senate to orders taking him elsewhere. Those provisions forestalled the possibility of a military coup, which some Radicals feared Johnson might attempt. Further, Congress on March 2 limited the President's use of patronage by passing the Tenure of Office Act, a measure of dubious constitutionality. It provided that any officeholder appointed with the consent of the Senate was to continue to serve unless and until the Senate approved the nomination of a successor. If the Senate was not in session, the President could suspend an incumbent and name an acting replacement, but when the Senate again convened, the acting officer could serve only with its consent; otherwise the previous incumbent was to resume his duties. The act applied specifically to Cabinet members who, it stipulated, were to hold office, unless the Senate otherwise approved, "during the term of the President by whom they may have been appointed, and for one month thereafter." That clause was intended to keep Johnson from discharging Secretary of War Stanton, the only remaining Cabinet member friendly to the Radicals.

The impeachment of Johnson. Some Radicals wanted to go on to impeach Johnson. The House of Representatives had its Judiciary Committee investigate his conduct, but no actionable charge stood up against examination, and in June 1867 the committee voted 5 to 4 not to recommend impeachment. But the President tried to curtail the powers of the commanders in the five Southern military districts, removed commanders sympathetic to the Radical program, and warned Congress in a message of December 1867 that he "would be compelled to stand on his rights, and maintain them, regardless of consequences." That pugnacity prompted the Judiciary Committee to reverse itself and vote 5 to 4 for impeachment. The House of Representatives rejected the recommendation, largely because Johnson still seemed guiltless of any legally indictable offense. The intemperate President, however, played into the hands of his enemies. In August 1867, while the Senate was adjourned, he had suspended Stanton and made Grant *ad interim* Secretary of War. Johnson wanted to test the Tenure of Office Act, which he expected the courts to void, and he counted on Grant for cooperation. But when the Senate on reconvening declined to approve Stanton's removal, Grant withdrew in confusion. John-

son denounced the general, who comforted himself by accepting the plaudits of the Radicals. Johnson in February 1868 also appointed General Lorenzo Thomas Secretary of War, but Stanton refused to go and instead barricaded himself within the War Department. The outraged Republicans in Congress, aware of the wide support they enjoyed among Northern voters, now took the step from which they had previously drawn back — on February 24 the House of Representatives voted 126 to 47 to impeach Johnson for "high crimes and misdemeanors in office."

That vote preceded the preparation of specific charges or of evidence to sustain them. The charges, drawn up by a special committee, were set out in eleven articles that the House approved in March. Eight of those articles related to the removal of Stanton; a ninth dealt with an alleged, technical violation of the Army Appropriation Act; an eleventh contained a summary charge; the tenth article carried the crux of the case. Johnson, it held, "unmindful of the high duties of his office . . . and of the harmony and courtesies which ought to exist . . . between the executive and the legislative branches . . . did attempt to bring into disgrace, ridicule, hatred, contempt and reproach the Congress of the United States." So, doubtless, from the point of view of Congress, he had, but the charge lacked legal substance; the case against Johnson was political. The crime of which the House had accused him consisted essentially of disagreement with congressional policy. However outrageous his actions, however venomous his enemies, the question was whether two-thirds of the Senate, sitting as a court to judge the matter, would find the President guilty under the Constitution of such a crime. A verdict of guilt might significantly alter the fabric of American constitutional government, the whole concept of a balance of power, by establishing a first precedent for later, political removal of a President.

Indeed the impeachment-managers asserted in one part of their briefs that the action was political rather than judicial, the question one of whether Johnson was "fit to retain the office of President." Yet they also attempted to make a legal case of the removal of Stanton, a case that collapsed when Johnson's counsel pointed out that it was Lincoln who had appointed Stanton, that Stanton had served more than a month beyond Lincoln's term, and that Johnson therefore could dismiss Stanton without violating the Tenure of Office Act, whatever the constitutionality of that measure. Still, the political issue had raised high feelings in Congress and out, and the vote almost went against Johnson. Nineteen senators opposed his conviction, thirty-five supported it — one short of the necessary two-thirds margin. Seven Republicans, at the clear risk of angering their constituents, joined the Democrats to save the President. In the wake of Johnson's escape, Stanton resigned and the Senate adjourned.

No Republican seriously considered renominating Johnson in 1868. The tempers that surrounded the struggle over Reconstruction obscured even his achievements in foreign affairs. Johnson and Secretary of State Seward served the principles of the Monroe Doctrine well. In 1866 the President dispatched fifty thousand veteran troops under General Philip H. Sheridan to the Mexican border, and Secretary of State Seward demanded the withdrawal of French forces from Mexico. France complied, and a year later the Mexicans reestablished their independence. Serving also the spirit of Manifest Destiny, Seward signed a treaty of friendship and commerce with China in 1868 and also negotiated a treaty to buy the Virgin Islands from Denmark for $7,500,000, but the Senate rejected the latter. In 1867 the Senate had almost unanimously approved a treaty for the purchase from Russia of Alaska for $7,200,000. Russia was eager to sell what seemed a barren tract of wasteland, and many Americans joked about Seward's "icebox." But time was to demonstrate the enormous strategic value of Alaska and the richness of her undeveloped resources. Seward had swung a magnificent bargain.

The election of 1868. It was, however, Reconstruction, and not foreign policy, on which the Republican platform focused in 1868. Fashioned by the Radicals, the platform endorsed their policy and damned Johnson and the Democrats. The Radicals' highhanded methods had made them enough enemies to persuade the Republicans to seek a popular hero as their candidate. Unanimously they settled

on Ulysses S. Grant and, as his running mate, Speaker of the House Schuyler Colfax. Grant had no political experience, but he had demonstrated a willingness to accede to the Radicals' advice. From their point of view, he was an ideal choice.

The Democrats had nearly insuperable obstacles to overcome. They had yet to rid their party of the taint of disloyalty. They had yet to find new leaders to replace their ablest prewar spokesmen. For President they nominated Horatio Seymour of New York, a wealthy and conservative man, a war governor with an unjust reputation for disloyalty, but scarcely a compelling candidate. The nomination of Francis P. Blair of Missouri as his running mate added little allure to the ticket. The Democratic platform declared the questions of slavery and secession forever settled but denounced Republican Reconstruction, advocated amnesty for past political offenses, called for the restoration of the Southern states to the Union, and defined the issue of Negro suffrage as belonging properly to the states for settlement, not to the federal government. Those planks exposed the party to Republican charges of softness toward the South, but the Democrats hoped to compensate by focusing attention on the question of money, then under hot debate. During the war the government had issued some $450 million of greenbacks. Then and later that currency fluctuated in value but was always below the value of coins or of gold-backed currency. Between 1866 and 1868, pursuant to an act of Congress of the earlier year, some $100 million of greenbacks had been retired from circulation. Now the Democrats adopted the "Ohio Idea," which demanded the reissuance of those notes to redeem those outstanding war bonds that did not explicitly require redemption in gold. This demand for cheap money appealed to debtors, especially to farmers with long-term mortgages, who stood to benefit from inflation. It appealed also to those who erroneously attributed the economic slump of reconversion from war to the contraction in the supply of money. And it appealed to critics, many of them Democrats, of the "bloated bondholders" — the war profiteers. The Republicans nevertheless pledged themselves to sound money and to redemption of the national debt in gold, a

Reconstruction

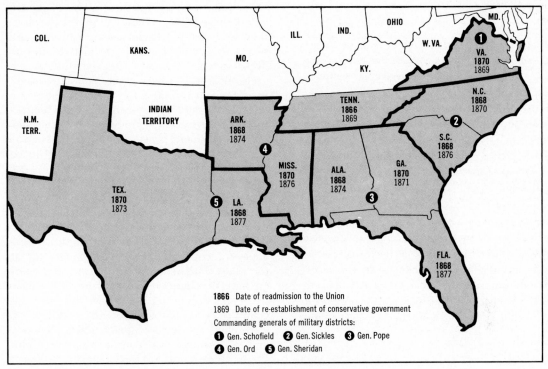

1866 Date of readmission to the Union
1869 Date of re-establishment of conservative government
Commanding generals of military districts:
❶ Gen. Schofield ❷ Gen. Sickles ❸ Gen. Pope
❹ Gen. Ord ❺ Gen. Sheridan

position attractive to conservative financial centers in the East and safe enough in a year when Western farmers, like Northerners in general, vividly remembered the passions of the war.

In a savage campaign, the Republicans concentrated on the alleged treason of the Democratic party and waved the "bloody shirt" of war. The Republicans could count on the support of Southern states dominated by carpetbag governments (see p. 384), on the support, too, of a multitude of federal officeholders and of most Union veterans, to whom they promised generous pensions (a pledge the Democrats made also but less persuasively). Yet in spite of these advantages, and in spite of his appeal as a triumphant soldier, Grant ran just well enough to win. He carried the Electoral College 214 to 80 but received only 52.7 per cent of the popular vote. Without the "bloody shirt" and the support of the six Southern states manipulated by the Radicals, he would have been in trouble. Radical Reconstruction and the "bloody shirt" had brought Republican victory.

THE GRANT ERA

The reconstructed South. The Republican program of military Reconstruction resulted during 1868 in the readmission of most of the Southern states. Each of them met the statutory prescriptions, including approval of the Fourteenth Amendment, which accordingly received the ratifications necessary for adoption. In four states — Georgia, Mississippi, Virginia, and Texas — opposition to the congressional terms delayed Reconstruction and readmission, but military pressure had brought all of them into line by 1870. The Union was then completely restored, and the South was largely under the rule of local administrations subservient to the Radicals and their doctrines.

Now the Radicals could advance their quest for Negro suffrage, a quest that had begun before 1868 and had gained new Republican support because of the importance to the party of the Negro vote in that year. The Fifteenth Amendment, approved by Congress in 1869, secured in 1870 enough ratifications for adoption, including those of subservient Southern states. "The right of citizens of the United States to vote," the amendment provided, "shall not be denied or abridged by the United States or by any State on account of race, color, or previous condition of servitude." Congress, the second section said, had the power "to enforce this article by appropriate legislation." As it developed, Negro voting depended for the while on the permissiveness of the Southern states.

In the South the period of "Black Reconstruction" cut raw wounds. Southerners tended to remember the era as one in which government fell to uneducated Negroes, to selfish Northern transients — "carpetbaggers" — and to a treacherous minority of Southern whites — "scalawags," most of whom had been Unionists during the war. It was a time, according to this memory, of unmitigated public corruption. But the recollection drew on evidence selected to confirm it.

Negroes never dominated the governments of the Southern states. They never held public offices in proportion to their numbers within the population; they had a legislative majority only in the lower house of South Carolina; they won election to no governorship, to only two seats in the United States Senate, to only fifteen in the House of Representatives. Negroes elected to lower offices, to state legislatures, and to positions as justices of the peace, had on the whole qualifications equivalent to the average standard for incumbents in such undistinguished posts. And some Negroes elected to high office were enlightened, talented, forceful men.

In most of the Southern states, a majority of the voters were white, and most of them were not "scalawags." Among the whites who sought and held political power, some were simply renegades, others poor men in quest of social advancement and, possibly, revenge against the planter aristocracy. But many were planters and merchants recruited from the ranks of the prewar Southern elite. Within this last group were many former Southern Whigs who were eager to develop the Southern economy and to promote interracial harmony. They gradually lost out to carpetbaggers who employed less genteel tactics and made less moderate and less practicable promises to the Negroes. Regrettably, the carpetbaggers drove the former Whigs away from the Republican party, which consequently lost its best chance to establish a broad basis in the South and to find a creative leadership there.

Yet the carpetbaggers and their associates in the Reconstruction governments also made positive contributions. Several of the state constitutions they adopted, copied from the best models in the North, endured for several decades. Their policies abetted the Negroes' transition to citizenship; extended social services, including compulsory education, previously unknown in many Southern states; and rebuilt the physical structure essential for economic growth — the cities and roads and railways.

That rebuilding involved letting contracts, granting charters and other privileges, and spending public money. And to each contract let, each charter granted, each dollar of public money spent, large temptations adhered: opportunities for graft and for handsome bribes from rival groups of promoters, especially from competing railroad interests. To those temptations officeholders in parts of the South succumbed. There was graft in public printing, in the sale of public lands, in expenditures for official entertainment, in contracts for hiring prison labor and for marketing public bonds. Fraud and corruption infected all the Reconstruction governments, damaging morale, swelling state debts. But the increases in debt during the period arose mostly from the need to subsidize economic development, particularly the building of railroads, whose properties were often a lien against the obligations the states incurred. The graft and fraud, moreover, were not peculiar to the South and its carpetbag administrations. The Tweed Ring in New York City (see p. 394) and its counterparts in Chicago and Philadelphia were more corrupt than the state-house gangs in Georgia or Florida or Texas. The carpetbaggers simply had no more moral stamina than other Democrats and Republicans the nation over during the era of Grant.

To most Southern whites at the time, however, the pattern of Reconstruction seemed a pattern of oppression, Africanization, and misrule. To relieve their situation they turned to violence. Among the secret terroristic agencies they founded, the most notorious was the Ku Klux Klan. Following its launching in 1866 in Tennessee, the Klan spread throughout the South, reaching its zenith between 1868 and 1870. It adopted weird rituals, a complex scheme of organization, and outlandish titles for its officers — Grand Dragons, Hydras, Titans, Cyclopes. Klansmen in white robes and hoods rode out at night on sheeted horses to intimidate Negroes and punish "scalawags." They often whipped or even killed their victims and sometimes engaged in outright pillage.

Northerners, particularly the Radicals, saw in the activities of the Klan and similar organizations fresh evidence of wickedness in the unrepentant South. Supported by public opinion, Congress passed three disciplinary measures. The Force Act of 1870 imposed severe penalties on anyone using force, bribery, or intimidation to prevent citizens from voting. It also placed congressional elections under federal supervision. A second force bill in 1871 strengthened the terms of the first. In the latter year Congress added a statute defining as high crimes the conspiracies and activities charac-

teristic of organizations like the Klan. This measure authorized the President to suspend habeas corpus in suppressing such "armed combinations," which were deemed comparable to rebellion itself. In executing the act, Grant was for the most part lax, but he did order federal troops to some unruly areas, suspend habeas corpus in nine counties in South Carolina, and appoint commissioners who made hundreds of arrests on the charge of conspiracy. The Supreme Court later severely limited the utility of the disciplinary legislation, but not before the Klan had formally dissolved itself. Many of its previous members, however, continued in their former activities.

The force bills helped the Radicals to preserve hegemony for their friends in the South. Though in several states before 1872 white political leaders found legal ways to unseat the carpetbaggers, elsewhere federal bayonets or the threat of bayonets perpetuated the authority of the Reconstruction administrations.

Southern freedmen:
Their rights were at stake.

This resort to military force in time of peace left a heritage of bitterness at least as deep and rankling as the memory of defeat in battle or fraud in Reconstruction government. The resulting mood contributed to the tension between the races and to the South's antagonism to the Republican party and its works. Reconstruction, by no means empty of achievement, produced as many scars as monuments and failed to attain its finest purposes. Still, the chapters written in the South were not the darkest in the record of the black Grant years.

Government under Grant. No President before 1869 had been so unqualified for office as was Ulysses S. Grant — a man who had no experience in politics, no capacity for absorbing such experience, no sensitivity for statescraft, and little judgment about men. Grant had impeccable personal integrity. He had as a soldier displayed the qualities of leadership and fortitude that won him deserved glory. He had, as his enemies in battle had learned, incomparable courage. But as a public servant Grant was a fool and a failure. He appointed an undistinguished Cabinet, of which several mem-

bers were knaves who duped him shamelessly. He found most matters of public policy utterly bewildering. He did not himself generate the gross and greedy spirit of the time, but a stronger and wiser man would have yielded less readily than Grant to its rapacious temper. Truly pathetic in his inadequacies, he was also singularly obtuse about his choice of friends. He accepted expensive gifts from favor-hunters; he received personal loans from Jay Cooke, whose Northern Pacific Railroad was seeking federal subsidies; he welcomed the company of Jim Fisk, a conscienceless gambler in stocks.

Only one of Grant's official family whom he did not fire performed in the manner of a statesman. Secretary of State Hamilton Fish, an able, honest, dignified gentleman, negotiated the Treaty of Washington of 1871, which resolved issues troubling Anglo-American relations. The treaty put to an end the strident demands of American chauvinists who had talked of acquiring Canada as compensation for the damage done by the *Alabama* and other Confederate commerce-raiders built in England. It referred to arbitration the question of those ships and other matters as well. The German emperor judged one dispute over the international boundary in the channel between Vancouver Island and the state of Washington, deciding in favor of the United States. A special tribunal awarded $2 million to British subjects for damages suffered during the Civil War. The British, in the terms of the treaty itself, expressed "regret" about the *Alabama* and agreed to principles for arbitrating the American claims and for proper neutral behavior in the future. In accord with those principles, a special court awarded the United States $15,500,000. The treaty and the techniques it employed furthered international peace and Anglo-American understanding, achievements of which Secretary Fish could be proud.

The balance of the record of the Grant Administration afforded no occasion for pride. Spokesmen in Washington enjoyed an unparalleled orgy, an orgy that, in the words of the *Nation*, a reform periodical, led to not only "bad appointments but probably some of the worst ever made by a civilized Christian government." The President in 1870 dismissed two of the most culpable of his Cabinet and in 1871 asked Congress for a civil-service law. But he administered that act reluctantly and ineffectively, and in 1873 Congress let expire its appropriation for a commission to supervise federal appointments.

Indeed, Congress during Grant's term enjoyed free rein. The President shared the view of its leaders that it had responsibility for determining federal policy. In this view, it fell to the President to execute the laws but not to take the lead in formulating them. Grant happily rubber-stamped the legislation that came to his desk, legislation in which Congress revealed continuing solicitude for men of wealth. In 1872 it abolished what remained of the wartime income tax, a step that made regressive excise and import taxes the sole source of revenue for repaying the debt and for current account. Responding to the requests of lobbies for various business interests, some of them in conflict with others, Congress in 1869 raised the tariff rate on copper, in 1870 on steel rails, marble, and nickel. In deference to the pending election and to farmer sentiment, Congress lowered most duties by 10 per cent in 1872, but

even then many rates, which in the time of Henry Clay had stood at about 25 per cent, had climbed to 500 per cent, and industrialists were not yet satisfied.

Indeed the greedy were insatiable. Grant's friend Jim Fisk tried to arrange for himself a magnificent bounty built on the ruin of others. With Jay Gould he engineered a fantastic attempt to corner the market in gold. Keeping their role secret, the two men set out to bid up the price of gold and to command the supply of it in New York. They almost succeeded, but on "Black Friday," September 24, 1869, the crash came, the price of gold fell, many speculators and some innocents were ruined, and the conspirators, their plot a failure, escaped only by repudiating their contracts. They managed that repudiation by hiring thugs to intimidate their creditors and bribing officials to refrain from prosecution. Nevertheless, Grant remained friendly with Fisk, who, with Gould, continued his bribing, his manipulating, his frenzied but remunerative finance.

The corruption associated with the Grant Administration in Washington, in New York, and in the South gave rise to a reform movement within the Republican party. In 1870 Carl Schurz, a German immigrant, a Civil War hero, and an emerging statesman, led the group in Missouri who, with Democratic support, carried the state's gubernatorial election. These and other Liberal Republicans (the name they chose) stood for civil-service reform, downward revision of the tariff, and gentler treatment of the South. At the Liberal Republican convention of 1872, however, some of the delegates were protectionists, others merely disappointed office-seekers. A series of squabbles and compromises produced a platform that was silent on the tariff — and it produced as well a grotesque presidential candidate, Horace Greeley, a perfervid protectionist and lifelong castigator of Democrats. Yet the Democrats, still politically bankrupt, buried their reservations about policy and personality and named as their own candidates Greeley and his running mate, Governor B. G. Brown of Missouri.

The election was never in doubt. Grant, the unanimous choice of the Republican convention, had not yet lost his heroic mantle. Seven carpetbag governments in the South were

Horace Greeley: An anomalous candidate.

working for him; the "bloody shirt" remained a persuasive symbol in the North; and business interests provided lavish funds to finance his campaign. The Republican platform, praising tariff protection and Radical Reconstruction, probably counted less than did the appeal of the candidate and the disorganization of the Liberal Republicans and their Democratic allies. Grant polled 55.8 per cent of the popular vote and swept the Electoral College 286 to 63. A few weeks later Horace Greeley died, brokenhearted, aware that never before had poor government won so thunderous an endorsement.

The collapse. In less than a year after Grant's second election, political scandals and economic distress had destroyed the brittle reputation of his Administration. A congressional investigating committee early in 1873 exposed the shocking history of the Crédit Mobilier, a construction company that had been formed allegedly to build the Union Pacific Railroad. Much of the money from contracts it received, however, went straight to its major shareholders. One of its officers, Congressman Oakes

Ames, had sold shares in the company at bargain prices to other congressmen, who had in return prevented inquiries into the company's strange affairs. Among the cooperative beneficiaries were Vice-President Colfax and Congressman — later President — James A. Garfield. The disclosure of the chicanery did not seriously disturb the Republican Congress, which contented itself with a vote of censure against Ames. But the public was troubled, and, though the rascality dated back to 1868, it was associated with the Grant supporters who profited from and condoned it.

More staggering exposures followed apace. Five of them involved Cabinet officers: the Secretary of the Treasury, the Secretary of the Navy, the Attorney General, the Postmaster General, and the Secretary of War. The last of these officials, William W. Belknap, had accepted annual bribes from traders at Indian posts. Though Belknap resigned in 1876, he was impeached by the House and barely saved from conviction by the Senate because several senators argued that their chamber lacked jurisdiction in the case. Grant's new Secretary of the Treasury uncovered the notorious Whiskey Ring, a conspiracy of hundreds of distillers who had bribed Treasury officials in order to evade federal taxes. Grant's private secretary, General Orville E. Babcock, participated in that and other corrupt adventures. "Let no guilty man escape," Grant had ordered, but he provided Babcock with a deposition that helped him to escape punishment. Surely the President had been taken in by his friends, but clearly he could not discriminate between an honest man and a rogue. He richly deserved the criticism he received.

Grant's Administration also earned a share of the blame for the economic collapse that marked his second term. Although the splurge of speculation encouraged by the government contributed to the Panic of 1873, its deeper causes lay in the rapidity of economic expansion in the United States. Entrepreneurs in rails and in industry, foreseeing no end to the soaring profits of the postwar years, had built productive facilities beyond the existing needs of the nation. To assist in those endeavors and to share in their returns, bankers had extended credit beyond the margin of safety. Europe had experienced similar developments. The signal of danger came in September 1873 with the failure of Jay Cooke and Company, a leading financial firm in the United States that had plunged heavily in rails. Panic followed. Within a year eighty-nine railroads had defaulted on their bonds, and business failures had aggregated some $228 million. During the ensuing four years of depression, one of the longest and worst in American history, 3 million laborers lost their jobs, wages fell, agricultural prices sank so low that farmers, unable to pay their mortgages, had to surrender their properties, their homes, their fondest dreams.

Depression and scandal bred protest as well as discontent. The Democrats in 1874 won control in twenty-three states, improved their position in the Senate, and elected a majority of the House of Representatives. Grangerism was flourishing among the harassed farmers of the West (see p. 504). The Republicans met these challenges and the problems of the time by espousing two economic policies that were to hold the dedication of the party for decades to come — high tariffs and hard money. Assisted by the votes of some Eastern Democrats, in 1875 the Republicans restored the duties they had reduced three years earlier. They also reaffirmed their faith in a currency based on, and fully convertible to, gold.

The money issue had received inconsistent treatment. From the time the war ended, most farmers and debtors, but not all of them, favored cheap money, the continued use of the greenbacks issued during the war without gold backing. They believed cheap money would lessen the burden of debt and could sustain or advance the prices of the products they sold. Most, but not all, businessmen favored a return to gold. It would stabilize the value of currency, thus reducing the uncertainty of commerce and exchange, and if it resulted in a deflation of domestic prices of manufactured goods, those lower prices would add some measure of protection against more expensive imports.

The legal status of the greenbacks was uncertain until 1870, when the Supreme Court ruled their issuance unconstitutional. This decision jeopardized the validity of contracts calling for payments in money that had been legal tender since 1862, and it worried those who realized that retiring the greenbacks might overly contract the supply of money. To their satisfaction, the Court in 1871, its membership increased by two Grant appointments, reversed its earlier ruling and declared the greenbacks valid in all respects. That opinion settled the legal question but left open the question of policy.

In 1873, to relieve the deflation that accompanied the panic, the Treasury reissued $26 million of greenbacks retired earlier. The next year Congress, responding to sentiment for further inflation, authorized a further use of paper money up to a limit of $400 million. Now the business interests opposed to that policy persuaded Grant, who had been typically confused and indecisive, to veto the measure. After the congressional elections of 1874, but before the Democrats had assumed control of the House, the Republicans put through a bill drafted by Senator John Sherman and signed by Grant in January 1875. This measure provided for an increase in the number of national banks and in the amount of their bank notes, a change that was intended to meet the demands of the South and the West for a more equitable share of both. The act also provided that after January 1, 1879, the Treasury would, on demand, redeem all legal-tender notes in coin. It permitted the Treasury to prepare for that step by selling bonds (which would, incidentally, furnish a basis for further bank notes). Overlooking the constructive clauses in the act, inflationists condemned it unsparingly and predicted disaster. As it developed, however, the date of resumption coincided roughly with the return of prosperity. That accident strengthened the conviction of Republicans in their "sound-money" policy. It occurred too late, however, to mitigate the unpopularity that the Grant regime had reaped from the depression and from the Administration's steady deference to business and industry.

The twilight of reconstruction. Scandal, depression, and the debates over the tariff and greenbacks during Grant's second term diverted congressional attention from the South. Concurrently, Northern men, preoccupied with their own worries and disenchanted by the corruption and disorder of carpetbag government, lost interest in Radical Reconstruction. The carpetbaggers in some states during these years filched more and more from the public purse, made travesties of elections by bribing Negroes at the polls, padding voting lists, stuffing ballot boxes. Their excesses completed the alienation of white Southerners. Openly now, without hoods or robes, Southern whites of all classes organized to intimidate the Negroes and the remaining scalawags. The carpetbag governments, receiving little support from Washington, gradually toppled. By 1876 Radical rule remained only in Louisiana, South Carolina, and Florida; the rest of the South had achieved "home rule."

Congress did make a last gesture toward the Negro. Senator Charles Sumner had introduced a civil-rights bill in 1872 that was passed in 1875, after his death, in a much denatured form. Sumner had attempted to assure full Negro equality, political rights, and civil liberties. His purpose, however, conflicted with the mood of most white Americans, Northern as well as Southern, and the act of 1875 revealed the stamp of the Republican moderates and of their ambiguous attitude toward the Negro. Without providing a practicable means of enforcement, that act stated a guarantee of equal accommodations in public places, such as inns and theaters, and forbade exclusion of Negroes from jury duty. It promised less than Sumner had advocated, and it carried little sting. Further, in 1883 the Supreme Court declared it invalid for protecting social rather than political rights and ruled also that the Fourteenth Amendment prohibited invasion of civil rights by the states but not by individuals unaided by state authori-

ties. Still, the act of 1875, whatever its weaknesses, established a precedent important for the future, while its very weaknesses disclosed the loss of effective commitment among Republicans to protecting and assisting the Negro.

That loss, like the collapse of the carpetbaggers, would doubtless have occurred even without the collapse of public morals and of the economy. The three debacles, related in time, derived from a common national mood. Avarice, corruption, and vindictiveness in the aftermath of war rotted the splendid fruits of wartime sacrifice and ideals. From victory, the federal government inherited a tripartite positive mission — to cement the Union that had been saved, to develop systematically and equitably the economy that had burgeoned, to provide for the Negro the social and political necessaries of freedom. Sometimes with the best intentions, but often with greed and venom, the men in charge of government failed. In restoring the South, they scarred it. In developing the economy, they delegated opportunity and power to a grasping, gambling, overprivileged few. They set high goals for the freedmen, helped them briefly to reach for those goals, and then left them to the mercy first of demagogues and then of embittered Southern whites. With too many people too intent on private comfort and convenience, with too many public men too susceptible to cupidity or wrath, government of the people and by their elected representatives too rarely and too intermittently directed its energies to the nation's positive good.

SUGGESTIONS FOR READING

General

There is a concise account of Reconstruction and an analysis of the bibliography on that subject in J. G. Randall and David Donald, *The Civil War and Reconstruction* (2nd ed., 1961). That volume also covers the Grant years. Three recent and indispensable studies in the rapidly growing scholarship on Reconstruction are W. R. Brock, *An American Crisis** (1963); D. Donald, *The Politics of Reconstruction* (1965); and K. M. Stampp, *The Era of Reconstruction* (1965). See also J. H. Franklin, *Reconstruction: After the Civil War** (1962), and, for a recent synthesis, R. W. Patrick, *The Reconstruction of the Nation* (1967). Another general treatment of the period

* Available in a paperback edition.

1865–76, stressing social and economic conditions, is in A. Nevins, *The Emergence of Modern America, 1865–1878* (1927). The national politics of the period receive detailed but sometimes jaundiced treatment in M. Josephson, *The Politicos, 1865–1896** (1938). The national mood concerns P. H. Buck, *The Road to Reunion, 1865–1900* (1937).

Johnson, the Radicals, and Reconstruction

H. K. Beale, *The Critical Year: A Study of Andrew Johnson and Reconstruction* (1930), provides a sympathetic analysis of the President and an interpretation of the Radicals emphasizing their economic motives. Johnson is severely criticized in E. L. McKitrick, *Andrew Johnson and Reconstruction* (1960), which takes direct and persuasive issue with Beale's thesis. Of the older studies of Reconstruction, two thorough accounts are marred by their pro-Southern, anti-Negro bias: W. A. Dunning, *Reconstruction: Political and Economic, 1865–1877** (1907), and E. M. Coulter, *The South During Reconstruction, 1865–1877* (1947). W. E. B. DuBois, in *Black Reconstruction** (1935), overstates the achievements of the Negro and views the aftermath of war through a Marxist prism. Also sympathetic to the Negro, but on other issues often curiously oblique, is J. S. Allen, *Reconstruction: The Battle for Democracy, 1865–1876* (1937). Among special studies of particular merit, most of them the product of recent scholarship, are G. R. Bentley, *A History of the Freedmen's Bureau* (1955); L. and J. H. Cox, *Politics, Principle, and Prejudice, 1865–1877* (1963); J. M. McPherson, *The Struggle for Equality: Abolitionists and the Negro in the Civil War and Reconstruction* (1964); W. L. Rose, *Rehearsal for Reconstruction** (1964); V. L. Wharton, *The Negro in Mississippi, 1865–1890** (1947); and J. R. Williamson, *After Slavery* (1965). (General and special literature on the South and its postwar condition and problems through 1900 is listed in connection with Chapter 16, below. On American business, consult the listing following Chapter 18, below.)

The Grant Era

Here there is a dearth of truly satisfactory books. There is a good general study of business in T. C. Cochran and W. Miller, *The Age of Enterprise: A Social History of Industrial America** (1942), which also touches intelligently on public policy. R. Fels, *American Business Cycles, 1865–1897* (1959), is authoritative on the Panic of 1873. For a balanced and significant analysis of the money question, see R. P. Sharkey, *Money, Class, and Party* (1959). Postwar diplomacy has had able attention, especially in D. Perkins, *The Monroe Doctrine, 1876–1907** (1937), and A. Nevins, *Hamilton Fish: The Inner History of the Grant Administration* (1936), which also provides the best account of the topic described by its subtitle. On the scandals of Grant's time and on the responses to them, three worthy studies are D. G. Loth, *Public Plunder: A History of Graft in America* (1938); C. R. Fish, *The Civil Service and the Patronage* (1904); and E. D. Ross, *The Liberal Republican Movement* (1919). There is a first-rate analysis of Grant and the liberals in the beginning chapters of E. Goldman, *Rendezvous with Destiny** (1955). Also useful are C. M. Fuess, *Carl Schurz: Reformer* (1932), and G. G. Van Deusen, *Horace Greeley: Nineteenth Century Crusader** (1953).

* Available in a paperback edition.

Appendix

The Declaration of Independence*

The unanimous Declaration of the thirteen United States of America.

When, in the Course of human events, it becomes necessary for one people to dissolve the political bands which have connected them with another, and to assume, among the Powers of the earth, the separate and equal station to which the Laws of Nature and of Nature's God entitle them, a decent respect to the opinions of mankind requires that they should declare the causes which impel them to the separation.

We hold these truths to be self-evident, that all men are created equal, that they are endowed by their Creator with certain unalienable Rights, that among these, are Life, Liberty, and the pursuit of Happiness. That, to secure these rights, Governments are instituted among Men, deriving their just Powers from the consent of the governed. That, whenever any form of Government becomes destructive of these ends, it is the Right of the People to alter or to abolish it, and to institute new Government, laying its foundation on such Principles, and organizing its Powers in such form, as to them shall seem most likely to effect their Safety and Happiness. Prudence, indeed, will dictate that Governments long established should not be changed for light and transient causes; and, accordingly, all experience hath shewn, that mankind are more disposed to suffer, while evils are sufferable, than to right themselves by abolishing the forms to which they are accustomed. But, when a long train of abuses and usurpations, pursuing invariably the same Object, evinces a design to reduce them under absolute Despotism, it is their right, it is their duty, to throw off such Government, and to provide new

Guards for their future Security. Such has been the patient sufferance of these Colonies; and such is now the necessity which constrains them to alter their former Systems of Government. The history of the present King of Great Britain is a history of repeated injuries and usurpations, all having in direct object the establishment of an absolute Tyranny over these States. To prove this, let Facts be submitted to a candid world.

He has refused his Assent to Laws the most wholesome and necessary for the public good.

He has forbidden his Governors to pass Laws of immediate and pressing importance, unless suspended in their operation till his Assent should be obtained; and when so suspended, he has utterly neglected to attend to them.

He has refused to pass other Laws for the accommodation of large districts of People, unless those People would relinquish the right of Representation in the legislature; a right inestimable to them and formidable to tyrants only.

He has called together legislative bodies at places unusual, uncomfortable, and distant from the depository of their Public Records, for the sole Purpose of fatiguing them into compliance with his measures.

He has dissolved Representative Houses repeatedly, for opposing, with manly firmness, his invasions on the rights of the People.

He has refused for a long time, after such dissolutions, to cause others to be elected; whereby the Legislative Powers, incapable of Annihilation, have returned to the People at large for their exercise; the State remaining in the mean time exposed to all the dangers of invasion from without, and convulsions within.

He has endeavoured to prevent the Population of these States; for that purpose obstructing the Laws for Naturalization of Foreigners; refusing to pass

* Reprinted from Worthington C. Ford, ed., *Journals of the Continental Congress, 1774–1789* (Washington, D.C., 1904–37), Vol. 5, pp. 510–15. The original spelling, capitalization, and punctuation have been retained.

others to encourage their migrations hither, and raising the conditions of new Appropriations of Lands.

He has obstructed the Administration of Justice, by refusing his Assent to Laws for establishing Judiciary Powers.

He has made Judges dependent on his Will alone, for the tenure of their offices, and the amount and payment of their salaries.

He has erected a multitude of New Offices, and sent hither swarms of Officers to harrass our People, and eat out their substance.

He has kept among us, in times of Peace, Standing Armies, without the Consent of our legislatures.

He has affected to render the Military independent of and superior to the Civil Power.

He has combined with others to subject us to a jurisdiction foreign to our constitution, and unacknowledged by our laws; giving his Assent to their Acts of pretended Legislation:

For quartering large bodies of armed troops among us:

For protecting them, by a mock Trial, from Punishment for any Murders which they should commit on the Inhabitants of these States:

For cutting off our Trade with all parts of the world:

For imposing Taxes on us without our Consent:

For depriving us, in many cases, of the benefits of Trial by Jury:

For transporting us beyond Seas to be tried for pretended offences:

For abolishing the free System of English Laws in a neighbouring province, establishing therein an Arbitrary government, and enlarging its Boundaries, so as to render it at once an example and fit instrument for introducing the same absolute rule into these Colonies:

For taking away our Charters, abolishing our most valuable Laws, and altering fundamentally the Forms of our Governments:

For suspending our own Legislatures, and declaring themselves invested with Power to legislate for us in all cases whatsoever.

He has abdicated Government here, by declaring us out of his protection, and waging War against us.

He has plundered our seas, ravaged our Coasts, burnt our towns, and destroyed the Lives of our People.

He is at this time transporting large Armies of foreign Mercenaries to compleat the works of death, desolation and tyranny, already begun with circum-stances of Cruelty and perfidy scarcely paralleled in the most barbarous ages, and totally unworthy the Head of a civilized nation.

He has constrained our fellow Citizens, taken Captive on the high Seas, to bear Arms against their Country, to become the executioners of their friends and Brethren, or to fall themselves by their Hands.

He has excited domestic insurrections amongst us, and has endeavoured to bring on the inhabitants of our frontiers, the merciless Indian Savages, whose known rule of warfare, is an undistinguished destruction of all ages, sexes and conditions.

In every stage of these Oppressions, We have Petitioned for Redress, in the most humble terms: Our repeated Petitions, have been answered only by repeated injury. A Prince, whose character is thus marked by every act which may define a Tyrant, is unfit to be the ruler of a free People.

Nor have We been wanting in attentions to our British brethren. We have warned them from time to time of attempts by their legislature to extend an unwarrantable jurisdiction over us. We have reminded them of the circumstances of our emigration and settlement here. We have appealed to their native justice and magnanimity, and we have conjured them by the ties of our common kindred, to disavow these usurpations, which, would inevitably interrupt our connexions and correspondence. They too have been deaf to the voice of justice and consanguinity. We must, therefore, acquiesce in the necessity, which denounces our Separation, and hold them, as we hold the rest of mankind, Enemies in war, in Peace Friends.

We, therefore, the Representatives of the United States of America, in General Congress assembled, appealing to the Supreme Judge of the World for the rectitude of our intentions, do, in the Name, and by Authority of the good People of these Colonies, solemnly publish and declare, That these United Colonies are, and of Right, ought to be Free and Independent States; that they are Absolved from all Allegiance to the British Crown, and that all political connexion between them and the State of Great Britain, is and ought to be totally dissolved; and that, as Free and Independent States, they have full Power to levy War, conclude Peace, contract Alliances, establish Commerce, and to do all other Acts and Things which Independent States may of right do. And for the support of this Declaration, with a firm reliance on the protection of divine Providence, we mutually pledge to each other our Lives, our Fortunes, and our sacred Honour.

The Constitution of the United States of America*

We the people of the United States, in Order to form a more perfect Union, establish Justice, insure domestic Tranquility, provide for the common defence, promote the general Welfare, and secure the Blessings of Liberty to ourselves and our Posterity, do ordain and establish this CONSTITUTION for the United States of America.

ARTICLE I

SECTION 1. All legislative Powers herein granted shall be vested in a Congress of the United States, which shall consist of a Senate and House of Representatives.

SECTION 2. The House of Representatives shall be composed of Members chosen every second Year by the People of the several States, and the Electors in each State shall have the Qualifications requisite for Electors of the most numerous Branch of the State Legislature.

No Person shall be a Representative who shall not have attained to the Age of twenty-five Years, and been seven Years a Citizen of the United States, and who shall not, when elected, be an Inhabitant of that state in which he shall be chosen.

Representatives and direct Taxes† shall be apportioned among the several States which may be included within this Union, according to their respective Numbers, which shall be determined by adding to the whole Number of free Persons, including those bound to Service for a Term of Years, and excluding Indians not taxed, three fifths of all other Persons.‡ The actual Enumeration shall be made within three Years after the first Meeting of the Congress of the United States, and within every subsequent Term of ten Years, in such Manner as they shall by Law direct. The Number of Representatives shall not exceed one for every thirty Thousand, but each State shall have at Least one Representative; and until such enumeration shall be made, the State of New Hampshire shall be entitled to chuse three, Massachusetts eight, Rhode-Island and Providence Plantations one, Connecticut five, New-York six, New Jersey four, Pennsylvania eight, Delaware one, Maryland six, Virginia ten, North Carolina five, South Carolina five, and Georgia three.

When vacancies happen in the Representation from any State, the Executive Authority thereof shall issue Writs of Election to fill such Vacancies.

The House of Representatives shall chuse their Speaker and other Officers; and shall have the sole Power of Impeachment.

SECTION 3. The Senate of the United States shall be composed of two Senators from each State, chosen by the Legislature thereof, for six Years; and each Senator shall have one Vote.*

Immediately after they shall be assembled in Consequence of the first Election, they shall be divided as equally as may be into three Classes. The Seats of the Senators of the first Class shall be vacated at the Expiration of the second Year, of the second Class at the Expiration of the fourth Year, and of the third Class at the Expiration of the sixth Year, so that one-third may be chosen every second Year; and if Vacancies happen by Resignation, or otherwise, during the Recess of the Legislature of any State, the Executive thereof may make temporary Appointments until the next Meeting of the Legislature, which shall then fill such Vacancies.†

* Original spelling, capitalization, and punctuation have been retained.
† Modified by the Sixteenth Amendment.
‡ Replaced by the Fourteenth Amendment.

* Superseded by the Seventeenth Amendment.
† Modified by the Seventeenth Amendment.

No Person shall be a Senator who shall not have attained to the Age of thirty Years, and been nine Years a Citizen of the United States, and who shall not, when elected, be an Inhabitant of that State in which he shall be chosen.

The Vice President of the United States shall be President of the Senate, but shall have no vote, unless they be equally divided.

The Senate shall chuse their other Officers, and also a President pro tempore, in the absence of the Vice President, or when he shall exercise the Office of the President of the United States.

The Senate shall have the sole Power to try all Impeachments. When sitting for that purpose, they shall be on Oath or Affirmation. When the President of the United States is tried, the Chief Justice shall preside: And· no person shall be convicted without the Concurrence of two thirds of the Members present.

Judgment in Cases of Impeachment shall not extend further than to removal from Office, and disqualification to hold and enjoy any Office of honor, Trust, or Profit under the United States: but the Party convicted shall nevertheless be liable and subject to Indictment, Trial, Judgment, and Punishment, according to Law.

SECTION 4. The Times, Places and Manner of holding Elections for Senators and Representatives, shall be prescribed in each state by the Legislature thereof; but the Congress may at any time by Law make or alter such Regulations, except as to the Places of Chusing Senators.

The Congress shall assemble at least once in every Year, and such Meeting shall be on the first Monday in December, unless they shall by Law appoint a different Day.*

SECTION 5. Each House shall be the Judge of the Elections, Returns and Qualifications of its own Members, and a Majority of each shall constitute a Quorum to do Business; but a smaller number may adjourn from day to day, and may be authorized to compel the Attendance of absent Members, in such Manner, and under such Penalties, as each House may provide.

Each House may determine the Rules of its Proceedings, punish its Members for disorderly Behavior, and, with the Concurrence of two thirds, expel a Member.

Each House shall keep a Journal of its Proceedings, and from time to time publish the same,

* Superseded by the Twentieth Amendment.

excepting such Parts as may in their Judgment require Secrecy; and the Yeas and Nays of the Members of either House on any question shall, at the Desire of one fifth of those Present, be entered on the Journal.

Neither House, during the Session of Congress, shall, without the Consent of the other, adjourn for more than three days, nor to any other Place than that in which the two Houses shall be sitting.

SECTION 6. The Senators and Representatives shall receive a Compensation for their Services, to be ascertained by Law, and paid out of the Treasury of the United States. They shall in all Cases, except Treason, Felony, and Breach of the Peace, be privileged from Arrest during their Attendance at the Session of their respective Houses, and in going to and returning from the same; and for any Speech or Debate in either House, they shall not be questioned in any other Place.

No Senator or Representative shall, during the Time for which he was elected, be appointed to any civil Office under the Authority of the United States, which shall have been created, or the Emoluments whereof shall have been increased, during such time; and no Person holding any Office under the United States shall be a Member of either House during his continuance in Office.

SECTION 7. All Bills for raising Revenue shall originate in the House of Representatives; but the Senate may propose or concur with Amendments as on other bills.

Every Bill which shall have passed the House of Representatives and the Senate, shall, before it become a Law, be presented to the President of the United States; If he approve he shall sign it, but if not he shall return it, with his Objections, to that House in which it shall have originated, who shall enter the Objections at large on their Journal, and proceed to reconsider it. If after such Reconsideration two thirds of that House shall agree to pass the bill, it shall be sent, together with the objections, to the other House, by which it shall likewise be reconsidered, and if approved by two thirds of that House, it shall become a Law. But in all such Cases the Votes of both Houses shall be determined by Yeas and Nays, and the Names of the Persons voting for and against the Bill shall be entered on the Journal of each House respectively. If any Bill shall not be returned by the President within ten Days (Sundays excepted) after it shall have been presented to him, the Same shall be a Law, in like Manner as if he had signed it, unless the Congress by their Adjournment prevent its Return, in which Case it shall not be a Law.

Every Order, Resolution, or Vote to which the Concurrence of the Senate and House of Representatives may be necessary (except on a question of Adjournment) shall be presented to the President of the United States; and before the Same shall take Effect, shall be approved by him, or being disapproved by him, shall be repassed by two thirds of the Senate and House of Representatives, according to the Rules and Limitations prescribed in the Case of a Bill.

SECTION 8. The Congress shall have Power To lay and collect Taxes, Duties, Imposts and Excises, to pay the Debts and provide for the common Defence and general Welfare of the United States; but all Duties, Imposts and Excises shall be uniform throughout the United States;

To borrow money on the credit of the United States;

To regulate Commerce with foreign Nations, and among the several States, and with the Indian Tribes;

To establish an uniform Rule of Naturalization, and uniform Laws on the subject of Bankruptcies throughout the United States;

To coin Money, regulate the Value thereof, and of foreign Coin, and fix the Standard of Weights and Measures;

To provide for the Punishment of counterfeiting the Securities and current Coin of the United States;

To establish Post Offices and post Roads;

To promote the Progress of Science and useful Arts, by securing for limited Times to Authors and Inventors the exclusive Right to their respective Writings and Discoveries;

To constitute Tribunals inferior to the Supreme Court;

To define and punish Piracies and Felonies committed on the high Seas, and Offenses against the Law of Nations;

To declare War, grant Letters of Marque and Reprisal, and make Rules concerning Captures on Land and Water;

To raise and support Armies, but no Appropriation of Money to that Use shall be for a longer Term than two Years;

To provide and maintain a Navy;

To make Rules for the Government and Regulation of the land and naval forces;

To provide for calling forth the Militia to execute the Laws of the Union, suppress Insurrections and repel Invasions;

To provide for organizing, arming, and disciplining the Militia, and for governing such Part of them as may be employed in the Service of the United States, reserving to the States respectively, the Appointment of the Officers, and the Authority of training the Militia according to the discipline prescribed by Congress;

To exercise exclusive Legislation in all Cases whatsoever, over such District (not exceeding ten Miles square) as may, by Cession of particular States, and the acceptance of Congress, become the Seat of the Government of the United States, and to exercise like Authority over all Places purchased by the Consent of the Legislature of the State in which the Same shall be, for the Erection of Forts, Magazines, Arsenals, dock-Yards, and other needful Buildings;—And

To make all Laws which shall be necessary and proper for carrying into Execution the foregoing Powers, and all other Powers vested by this Constitution in the Government of the United States, or in any Department or Officer thereof.

SECTION 9. The Migration or Importation of such Persons as any of the States now existing shall think proper to admit. shall not be prohibited by the Congress prior to the Year one thousand eight hundred and eight, but a tax or duty may be imposed on such Importation, not exceeding ten dollars for each Person.

The privilege of the Writ of Habeas Corpus shall not be suspended, unless when in Cases of Rebellion or Invasion the public Safety may require it.

No Bill of Attainder or ex post facto Law shall be passed.

No capitation, or other direct, Tax shall be laid unless in Proportion to the Census or Enumeration herein before directed to be taken.

No Tax or Duty shall be laid on Articles exported from any State.

No Preference shall be given by any Regulation of Revenue to the Ports of one State over those of another: nor shall Vessels bound to, or from, one State, be obliged to enter, clear, or pay Duties in another.

No Money shall be drawn from the Treasury, but in Consequence of Appropriations made by Law; and a regular Statement and Account of the Receipts and Expenditures of all public Money shall be published from time to time.

No Title of Nobility shall be granted by the United States: And no Person holding any Office of Profit or Trust under them, shall, without the Consent of the Congress, accept of any present, Emolument, Office, or Title, of any kind whatever, from any King, Prince, or foreign State.

SECTION 10. No State shall enter into any Treaty, Alliance, or Confederation; grant Letters of Marque and Reprisal; coin Money; emit Bills of Credit; make any Thing but gold and silver Coin a Tender in Payment of Debts; pass any Bill of Attainder, ex post facto Law, or Law impairing the Obligation of Contracts, or grant any Title of Nobility.

No State shall, without the Consent of the Congress, lay any Imposts or Duties on Imports or Exports, except what may be absolutely necessary for executing its inspection Laws: and the net Produce of all Duties and Imposts, laid by any State on Imports or Exports, shall be for the Use of the Treasury of the United States; and all such Laws shall be subject to the Revision and Control of the Congress.

No State shall, without the Consent of Congress, lay any duty of Tonnage, keep Troops, or Ships of War in time of Peace, enter into any Agreement or Compact with another State, or with a foreign Power, or engage in War, unless actually invaded, or in such imminent Danger as will not admit of delay.

ARTICLE II

SECTION I. The executive Power shall be vested in a President of the United States of America. He shall hold his Office during the Term of four years, and, together with the Vice-President, chosen for the same Term, be elected, as follows:

Each State shall appoint, in such Manner as the Legislature thereof may direct, a Number of Electors, equal to the whole Number of Senators and Representatives to which the State may be entitled in the Congress: but no Senator or Representative, or Person holding an Office of Trust or Profit under the United States, shall be appointed an Elector.

The Electors shall meet in their respective States, and vote by Ballot for two persons, of whom one at least shall not be an Inhabitant of the same State with themselves. And they shall make a List of all the Persons voted for, and of the Number of Votes for each; which List they shall sign and certify, and transmit sealed to the Seat of the Government of the United States, directed to the President of the Senate. The President of the Senate shall, in the Presence of the Senate and House of Representatives, open all the Certificates, and the Votes shall then be counted. The Person having the greatest Number of Votes shall be the President, if such Number be a Majority of the whole Number of Electors appointed; and if there be more than one who have such Majority, and have an equal Number of Votes, then the House of Representatives shall immediately chuse by Ballot one of them for President; and if no Person have a Majority, then from the five highest on the List the said House shall in like Manner chuse the President. But in chusing the President, the Votes shall be taken by States, the Representation from each State having one Vote; a quorum for this Purpose shall consist of a Member or Members from two-thirds of the States, and a Majority of all the States shall be necessary to a Choice. In every Case, after the Choice of the President, the Person having the greatest Number of Votes of the Electors shall be the Vice President. But if there should remain two or more who have equal votes, the Senate shall chuse from them by Ballot the Vice-President.*

The Congress may determine the Time of chusing the Electors, and the Day on which they shall give their Votes; which Day shall be the same throughout the United States.

No person except a natural-born Citizen, or a Citizen of the United States, at the time of the Adoption of this Constitution, shall be eligible to the Office of President; neither shall any Person be eligible to that Office who shall not have attained to the Age of thirty-five years, and been fourteen Years a Resident within the United States.

In Case of the Removal of the President from Office, or of his Death, Resignation, or Inability to discharge the Powers and Duties of the said Office, the same shall devolve on the Vice President, and the Congress may by Law provide for the Case of Removal, Death, Resignation, or Inability, both of the President and Vice President, declaring what Officer shall then act as President, and such Officer shall act accordingly, until the disability be removed, or a President shall be elected.†

The President shall, at stated Times, receive for his Services a Compensation, which shall neither be increased nor diminished during the Period for which he shall have been elected, and he shall not receive within that Period any other Emolument from the United States, or any of them.

Before he enter on the execution of his Office, he shall take the following Oath or Affirmation:— "I do solemnly swear (or affirm) that I will faith-

---

* Superseded by the Twelfth Amendment.
† Modified by the Twenty-fifth Amendment.

fully execute the Office of President of the United States, and will, to the best of my Ability, preserve, protect, and defend the Constitution of the United States."

SECTION 2. The President shall be Commander in Chief of the Army and Navy of the United States, and of the Militia of the several States, when called into the actual Service of the United States; he may require the Opinion, in writing, of the principal Officer in each of the executive Departments, upon any subject relating to the Duties of their respective Offices, and he shall have Power to Grant Reprieves and Pardons for Offenses against the United States, except in Cases of Impeachment.

He shall have Power, by and with the Advice and Consent of the Senate, to make Treaties, provided two thirds of the Senators present concur; and he shall nominate, and by and with the Advice and Consent of the Senate, shall appoint Ambassadors, other public Ministers and Consuls, Judges of the supreme Court, and all other Officers of the United States, whose Appointments are not herein otherwise provided for, and which shall be established by Law: but the Congress may by Law vest the Appointment of such inferior Officers, as they think proper, in the President alone, in the Courts of Law, or in the Heads of Departments.

The President shall have Power to fill up all Vacancies that may happen during the Recess of the Senate, by granting Commissions which shall expire at the End of their next Session.

SECTION 3. He shall from time to time give to the Congress Information of the State of the Union, and recommend to their Consideration such Measures as he shall judge necessary and expedient; he may, on extraordinary occasions, convene both Houses, or either of them, and in Case of Disagreement between them, with respect to the Time of Adjournment, he may adjourn them to such Time as he shall think proper; he shall receive Ambassadors and other public Ministers; he shall take Care that the Laws be faithfully executed, and shall Commission all the Officers of the United States.

SECTION 4. The President, Vice President and all civil Officers of the United States, shall be removed from Office on Impeachment for, and Conviction of, Treason, Bribery, or other high Crimes and Misdemeanors.

ARTICLE III

SECTION 1. The judicial Power of the United States, shall be vested in one supreme Court, and in such inferior Courts as the Congress may from time to time ordain and establish. The Judges, both of the supreme and inferior Courts, shall hold their Offices during good Behaviour, and shall, at stated Times, receive for their Services, a Compensation, which shall not be diminished during their Continuance in Office.

SECTION 2. The judicial Power shall extend to all Cases, in Law and Equity, arising under this Constitution, the Laws of the United States, and treaties made, or which shall be made, under their Authority;—to all Cases affecting ambassadors, other public ministers and consuls;—to all cases of admiralty and maritime Jurisdiction;—to Controversies to which the United States shall be a Party;—to Controversies between two or more States;—between a State and Citizens of another State; * —between Citizens of different States,—between Citizens of the same State claiming Lands under Grants of different States, and between a State, or the Citizens thereof, and foreign States, Citizens or Subjects.

In all Cases affecting Ambassadors, other public Ministers and Consuls, and those in which a State shall be Party, the supreme Court shall have original Jurisdiction. In all the other Cases before mentioned, the supreme Court shall have appellate Jurisdiction, both as to Law and Fact, with such Exceptions, and under such Regulations as the Congress shall make.

The trial of all Crimes, except in Cases of Impeachment, shall be by Jury; and such Trial shall be held in the State where the said Crimes shall have been committed; but when· not committed within any State, the Trial shall be at such Place or Places as the Congress may by Law have directed.

SECTION 3. Treason against the United States, shall consist only in levying War against them, or in adhering to their Enemies, giving them Aid and Comfort. No Person shall be convicted of Treason unless on the Testimony of two Witnesses to the same overt Act, or on Confession in open Court.

The Congress shall have power to declare the Punishment of Treason, but no Attainder of Treason shall work Corruption of Blood, or Forfeiture except during the Life of the Person attainted.

ARTICLE IV

SECTION 1. Full Faith and Credit shall be given in each State to the public Acts, Records, and

* Modified by the Eleventh Amendment.

judicial Proceedings of every other State. And the Congress may by general Laws prescribe the Manner in which such Acts, Records and Proceedings shall be proved, and the Effect thereof.

SECTION 2. The Citizens of each State shall be entitled to all Privileges and Immunities of Citizens in the several States.

A Person charged in any State with Treason, Felony, or other Crime, who shall flee from Justice, and be found in another State, shall on demand of the executive Authority of the State from which he fled, be delivered up, to be removed to the State having Jurisdiction of the crime.

No Person held to Service or Labour in one State, under the Laws thereof, escaping into another, shall, in Consequence of any Law or Regulation therein, be discharged from such Service or Labour, but shall be delivered up on Claim of the Party to whom such Service or Labour may be due.

SECTION 3. New States may be admitted by the Congress into this Union; but no new State shall be formed or erected within the Jurisdiction of any other State; nor any State be formed by the Junction of two or more States, or parts of States, without the Consent of the Legislatures of the States concerned as well as of the Congress.

The Congress shall have Power to dispose of and make all needful Rules and Regulations respecting the Territory or other Property belonging to the United States; and nothing in this Constitution shall be so construed as to Prejudice any Claims of the United States, or of any particular State.

SECTION 4. The United States shall guarantee to every State in this Union a Republican Form of Government, and shall protect each of them against Invasion; and on Application of the Legislature, or of the Executive (when the Legislature cannot be convened) against domestic Violence.

ARTICLE V

The Congress, whenever two-thirds of both Houses shall deem it necessary, shall propose Amendments to this Constitution, or, on the Application of the Legislatures of two-thirds of the several States, shall call a Convention for proposing Amendments, which, in either Case, shall be valid to all Intents and Purposes, as part of this Constitution, when ratified by the Legislatures of three-fourths of the several States, or by Conventions in three-fourths thereof, as the one or the other Mode of Ratification may be proposed by the Congress; Provided that no Amendment which may be made

prior to the Year One thousand eight hundred and eight shall in any Manner affect the first and fourth Clauses in the Ninth Section of the first Article; and that no State, without its Consent, shall be deprived of its equal Suffrage in the Senate.

ARTICLE VI

All Debts contracted and Engagements entered into, before the Adoption of this Constitution, shall be as valid against the United States under this Constitution, as under the Confederation.

This Constitution, and the Laws of the United States which shall be made in Pursuance thereof; and all Treaties made, or which shall be made, under the Authority of the United States, shall be the supreme Law of the Land; and the Judges in every State shall be bound thereby, any Thing in the Constitution or Laws of any State to the Contrary notwithstanding.

The Senators and Representatives before mentioned, and the Members of the several State Legislatures, and all executive and judicial Officers, both of the United States and of the several States, shall be bound by Oath or Affirmation to support this Constitution; but no religious Test shall ever be required as a qualification to any Office or public Trust under the United States.

ARTICLE VII

The Ratification of the Conventions of nine States shall be sufficient for the Establishment of this Constitution between the States so ratifying the same.

Done in Convention by the Unanimous Consent of the States present the Seventeenth Day of September in the Year of our Lord one thousand seven hundred and Eighty seven, and of the Independence of the United States of America the Twelfth. In Witness whereof We have hereunto subscribed our Names.

Articles in Addition to, and Amendment of, the Constitution of the United States of America, Proposed by Congress, and Ratified by the Legislatures of the Several States, Pursuant to the Fifth Article of the Original Constitution.

AMENDMENT I*

Congress shall make no law respecting an establishment of religion, or prohibiting the free exercise

* The first ten amendments were passed by Congress September 25, 1789. They were ratified by three-fourths of the states December 15, 1791.

thereof; or abridging the freedom of speech, or of the press; or the right of the people peaceably to assemble, and to petition the Government for a redress of grievances.

AMENDMENT II

A well regulated Militia, being necessary to the security of a free State, the right of the people to keep and bear Arms shall not be infringed.

AMENDMENT III

No Soldier shall, in time of peace, be quartered in any house, without the consent of the Owner, nor in time of war, but in a manner to be prescribed by law.

AMENDMENT IV

The right of the people to be secure in their persons, houses, papers, and effects, against unreasonable searches and seizures, shall not be violated, and no Warrants shall issue, but upon probable cause, supported by Oath or affirmation, and particularly describing the place to be searched, and the persons or things to be seized.

AMENDMENT V

No person shall be held to answer for a capital or otherwise infamous crime, unless on a presentment or indictment of a Grand Jury, except in cases arising in the land or naval forces, or in the Militia, when in actual service in time of War or public danger; nor shall any person be subject for the same offence to be twice put in jeopardy of life or limb; nor shall be compelled in any criminal case to be a witness against himself, nor be deprived of life, liberty, or property, without due process of law; nor shall private property be taken for public use, without just compensation.

AMENDMENT VI

In all criminal prosecutions, the accused shall enjoy the right to a speedy and public trial, by an impartial jury of the State and district wherein the crime shall have been committed, which district shall have been previously ascertained by law, and to be informed of the nature and cause of the accusation; to be confronted with the witnesses against him; to have compulsory process for obtaining witnesses in his favor, and to have the Assistance of Counsel for his defence.

AMENDMENT VII

In suits at common law, where the value in controversy shall exceed twenty dollars, the right of trial by jury shall be preserved, and no fact tried by a jury, shall be otherwise reexamined in any Court of the United States, than according to the rules of the common law.

AMENDMENT VIII

Excessive bail shall not be required, nor excessive fines imposed, nor cruel and unusual punishments inflicted.

AMENDMENT IX

The enumeration in the Constitution, of certain rights, shall not be construed to deny or disparage others retained by the people.

AMENDMENT X

The powers not delegated to the United States by the Constitution, nor prohibited by it to the States, are reserved to the States respectively, or to the people.

AMENDMENT XI*

The Judicial power of the United States shall not be construed to extend to any suit in law or equity, commenced or prosecuted against one of the United States by Citizens of another State, or by Citizens or Subjects of any Foreign State.

AMENDMENT XII†

The Electors shall meet in their respective States and vote by ballot for President and Vice-President, one of whom, at least, shall not be an inhabitant of the same State with themselves; they shall name in their ballots the person voted for as President, and in distinct ballots the person voted for as Vice-Presi-

* Passed March 5, 1794. Ratified January 8, 1798.
† Passed December 9, 1803. Ratified September 25, 1804.

dent, and they shall make distinct lists of all persons voted for as President, and of all persons voted for as Vice-President, and of the number of votes for each, which lists they shall sign and certify, and transmit sealed to the seat of the government of the United States, directed to the President of the Senate;—The President of the Senate shall, in the presence of the Senate and House of Representatives, open all the certificates and the votes shall then be counted;—The person having the greatest number of votes for President, shall be the President, if such number be a majority of the whole number of Electors appointed; and if no person have such majority, then from the persons having the highest numbers not exceeding three on the list of those voted for as President, the House of Representatives shall choose immediately, by ballot, the President. But in choosing the President, the votes shall be taken by states, the representation from each state having one vote; a quorum for this purpose shall consist of a member or members from two-thirds of the states, and a majority of all the states shall be necessary to a choice. And if the House of Representatives shall not choose a President whenever the right of choice shall devolve upon them, before the fourth day of March next following, then the Vice-President shall act as President, as in the case of the death or other constitutional disability of the President.—The person having the greatest number of votes as Vice-President, shall be the Vice-President, if such number be a majority of the whole number of Electors appointed, and if no person have a majority, then from the two highest numbers on the list, the Senate shall choose the Vice-President; a quorum for the purpose shall consist of two-thirds of the whole number of Senators, and a majority of the whole number shall be necessary to a choice. But no person constitutionally ineligible to the office of President shall be eligible to that of Vice-President of the United States.

AMENDMENT XIII*

SECTION 1. Neither slavery nor involuntary servitude, except as a punishment for crime whereof the party shall have been duly convicted, shall exist within the United States, or any place subject to their jurisdiction.

SECTION 2. Congress shall have power to enforce this article by appropriate legislation.

* Passed February 1, 1865. Ratified December 18, 1865.

AMENDMENT XIV*

SECTION 1. All persons born or naturalized in the United States, and subject to the jurisdiction thereof, are citizens of the United States and of the State wherein they reside. No State shall make or enforce any law which shall abridge the privileges or immunities of citizens of the United States; nor shall any State deprive any person of life, liberty, or property, without due process of law; nor deny to any person within its jurisdiction the equal protection of the laws.

SECTION 2. Representatives shall be apportioned among the several States according to their respective numbers, counting the whole number of persons in each State, excluding Indians not taxed. But when the right to vote at any election for the choice of electors for President and Vice-President of the United States, Representatives in Congress, the Executive and Judicial officers of a State, or the members of the Legislature thereof, is denied to any of the male inhabitants of such State, being twenty-one years of age, and citizens of the United States, or in any way abridged, except for participation in rebellion, or other crime, the basis of representation therein shall be reduced in the proportion which the number of such male citizens shall bear to the whole number of male citizens twenty-one years of age in such State.

SECTION 3. No person shall be a Senator or Representative in Congress, or elector of President and Vice-President, or hold any office, civil or military, under the United States, or under any State, who, having previously taken an oath, as a member of Congress, or as an officer of the United States, or as a member of any State legislature, or as an executive or judicial officer of any State, to support the Constitution of the United States, shall have engaged in insurrection or rebellion against the same, or given aid or comfort to the enemies thereof. But Congress may by a vote of two-thirds of each House, remove such disability.

SECTION 4. The validity of the public debt of the United States, authorized by law, including debts incurred for payment of pensions and bounties for services in suppressing insurrection or rebellion, shall not be questioned. But neither the United States nor any State shall assume or pay any debt or obligation incurred in aid of insurrection or rebellion against the United States, or any claim for the loss or emancipation of any slave; but all

* Passed June 16, 1866. Ratified July 28, 1868.

such debts, obligations, and claims shall be held illegal and void.

SECTION 5. The Congress shall have the power to enforce, by appropriate legislation, the provisions of this article.

AMENDMENT XV*

SECTION 1. The right of citizens of the United States to vote shall not be denied or abridged by the United States or by any State on account of race, color, or previous condition of servitude—

SECTION 2. The Congress shall have power to enforce this article by appropriate legislation.

AMENDMENT XVI†

The Congress shall have power to lay and collect taxes on incomes, from whatever source derived, without apportionment among the several States, and without regard to any census or enumeration.

AMENDMENT XVII‡

The Senate of the United States shall be composed of two Senators from each State, elected by the people thereof, for six years; and each Senator shall have one vote. The electors in each State shall have the qualifications requisite for electors of the most numerous branch of the State legislatures.

When vacancies happen in the representation of any State in the Senate, the executive authority of such State shall issue writs of election to fill such vacancies: *Provided*, That the legislature of any State may empower the executive thereof to make temporary appointments until the people fill the vacancies by election as the legislature may direct.

This amendment shall not be so construed as to affect the election or term of any Senator chosen before it becomes valid as part of the Constitution.

AMENDMENT XVIII§

SECTION 1. After one year from the ratification of this article the manufacture, sale, or transportation of intoxicating liquors within, the importation

thereof into, or the exportation thereof from the United States and all territory subject to the jurisdiction thereof for beverage purposes is hereby prohibited.

SECTION 2. The Congress and the several States shall have concurrent power to enforce this article by appropriate legislation.

SECTION 3. This article shall be inoperative unless it shall have been ratified as an amendment to the Constitution by the legislatures of the several States, as provided in the Constitution, within seven years from the date of the submission hereof to the States by the Congress.

AMENDMENT XIX*

The right of citizens of the United States to vote shall not be denied or abridged by the United States or by any State on account of sex.

Congress shall have power to enforce this article by appropriate legislation.

AMENDMENT XX†

SECTION 1. The terms of the President and Vice-President shall end at noon on the 20th day of January, and the terms of Senators and Representatives at noon on the 3d day of January, of the years in which such terms would have ended if this article had not been ratified; and the terms of their successors shall then begin.

SECTION 2. The Congress shall assemble at least once in every year, and such meeting shall begin at noon on the 3d day of January, unless they shall by law appoint a different day.

SECTION 3. If, at the time fixed for the beginning of the term of the President, the President elect shall have died, the Vice-President elect shall become President. If a President shall not have been chosen before the time fixed for the beginning of his term, or if the President elect shall have failed to qualify, then the Vice-President elect shall act as President until a President shall have qualified; and the Congress may by law provide for the case wherein neither a President elect nor a Vice-President elect shall have qualified, declaring who shall then act as President, or the manner in which one who is to act shall be selected, and such person shall act accordingly until a President or Vice-President shall have qualified.

---

* Passed February 27, 1869. Ratified March 30, 1870.
† Passed July 12, 1909. Ratified February 25, 1913.
‡ Passed May 16, 1912. Ratified May 31, 1913.
§ Passed December 17, 1917. Ratified January 29, 1919.

* Passed June 5, 1919. Ratified August 26, 1920.
† Passed March 3, 1932. Ratified January 23, 1933.

SECTION 4. The Congress may by law provide for the case of the death of any of the persons from whom the House of Representatives may choose a President whenever the right of choice shall have devolved upon them, and for the case of the death of any of the persons from whom the Senate may choose a Vice-President whenever the right of choice shall have devolved upon them.

SECTION 5. Sections 1 and 2 shall take effect on the 15th day of October following the ratification of this article.

SECTION 6. This article shall be inoperative unless it shall have been ratified as an amendment to the Constitution by the legislatures of three-fourths of the several States within seven years from the date of its submission.

AMENDMENT XXI*

SECTION 1. The eighteenth article of amendment to the Constitution of the United States is hereby repealed.

SECTION 2. The transportation or importation into any State, Territory, or possession of the United States for delivery or use therein of intoxicating liquors, in violation of the laws thereof, is hereby prohibited.

SECTION 3. This article shall be inoperative unless it shall have been ratified as an amendment to the Constitution by conventions in the several States, as provided in the Constitution, within seven years from the date of the submission hereof to the States by the Congress.

AMENDMENT XXII†

No person shall be elected to the office of the President more than twice, and no person who has held the office of President, or acted as President, for more than two years of a term to which some other person was elected President shall be elected to the office of the President more than once.

But this Article shall not apply to any person holding the office of President when this Article was proposed by the Congress, and shall not prevent any person who may be holding the office of President, or acting as President, during the term within which this Article becomes operative from holding

the office of President or acting as President during the remainder of such term.

AMENDMENT XXIII*

SECTION 1. The District constituting the seat of Government of the United States shall appoint in such manner as the Congress may direct:

A number of electors of President and Vice President equal to the whole number of Senators and Representatives in Congress to which the District would be entitled if it were a State, but in no event more than the least populous State; they shall be in addition to those appointed by the States, but they shall be considered, for the purposes of the election of President and Vice President, to be electors appointed by the State; and they shall meet in the District and perform such duties as provided by the twelfth article of amendment.

SECTION 2. The Congress shall have power to enforce this article by appropriate legislation.

AMENDMENT XXIV†

SECTION 1. The right of citizens of the United States to vote in any primary or other election for President or Vice President, for electors for President or Vice President, or for Senator or Representative in Congress, shall not be denied or abridged by the United States or any State by reason of failure to pay any poll tax or other tax.

SECTION 2. The Congress shall have power to enforce this article by appropriate legislation.

AMENDMENT XXV‡

SECTION 1. In case of the removal of the President from office or of his death or resignation, the Vice President shall become President.

SECTION 2. Whenever there is a vacancy in the office of the Vice President, the President shall nominate a Vice President who shall take office upon confirmation by a majority vote of both Houses of Congress.

SECTION 3. Whenever the President transmits to the President pro tempore of the Senate and the

---

* Passed February 20, 1933. Ratified December 5, 1933.
† Passed March 12, 1947. Ratified March 1, 1951.

* Passed June 16, 1960. Ratified April 3, 1961.
† Passed August 27, 1962. Ratified January 23, 1964.
‡ Passed July 6, 1965. Ratified February 10, 1967.

Speaker of the House of Representatives his written declaration that he is unable to discharge the powers and duties of his office, and until he transmits to them a written declaration to the contrary, such powers and duties shall be discharged by the Vice President as Acting President.

SECTION 4. Whenever the Vice President and a majority of either the principal officers of the executive department or of such other body as Congress may by law provide, transmit to the President pro tempore of the Senate and the Speaker of the House of Representatives their written declaration that the President is unable to discharge the powers and duties of his office, the Vice President shall immediately assume the powers and duties of the office as Acting President.

Thereafter, when the President transmits to the President pro tempore of the Senate and the Speaker of the House of Representatives his written declaration that no inability exists, he shall resume the powers and duties of his office unless the Vice President and a majority of either the principal officers of the executive department or of such other body as Congress may by law provide, transmit within four days to the President pro tempore of the Senate and the Speaker of the House of Representatives their written declaration that the President is unable to discharge the powers and duties of his office. Thereupon Congress shall decide the issue, assembling within forty-eight hours for that purpose if not in session. If the Congress, within twenty-one days after receipt of the latter written declaration, or, if Congress is not in session, within twenty-one days after Congress is required to assemble, determines by two-thirds vote of both Houses that the President is unable to discharge the powers and duties of his office, the Vice President shall continue to discharge the same as Acting President; otherwise, the President shall resume the powers and duties of his office.

Presidential Elections (1789–1900)

Year	Number of states	Candidates	Parties	Popular vote	Electoral vote	Percentage of popular vote
1789	11	GEORGE WASHINGTON	No party designations		69	
		John Adams			34	
		Minor Candidates			35	
1792	15	GEORGE WASHINGTON	No party designations		132	
		John Adams			77	
		George Clinton			50	
		Minor Candidates			5	
1796	16	JOHN ADAMS	Federalist		71	
		Thomas Jefferson	Democratic-Republican		68	
		Thomas Pinckney	Federalist		59	
		Aaron Burr	Democratic-Republican		30	
		Minor Candidates			48	
1800	16	THOMAS JEFFERSON	Democratic-Republican		73	
		Aaron Burr	Democratic-Republican		73	
		John Adams	Federalist		65	
		Charles C. Pinckney	Federalist		64	
		John Jay	Federalist		1	
1804	17	THOMAS JEFFERSON	Democratic-Republican		162	
		Charles C. Pinckney	Federalist		14	
1808	17	JAMES MADISON	Democratic-Republican		122	
		Charles C. Pinckney	Federalist		47	
		George Clinton	Democratic-Republican		6	
1812	18	JAMES MADISON	Democratic-Republican		128	
		DeWitt Clinton	Federalist		89	
1816	19	JAMES MONROE	Democratic-Republican		183	
		Rufus King	Federalist		34	
1820	24	JAMES MONROE	Democratic-Republican		231	
		John Quincy Adams	Independent Republican		1	
1824	24	JOHN QUINCY ADAMS	Democratic-Republican	108,740	84	30.5
		Andrew Jackson	Democratic-Republican	153,544	99	43.1
		William H. Crawford	Democratic-Republican	46,618	41	13.1
		Henry Clay	Democratic-Republican	47,136	37	13.2
1828	24	ANDREW JACKSON	Democratic	647,286	178	56.0
		John Quincy Adams	National Republican	508,064	83	44.0
1832	24	ANDREW JACKSON	Democratic	687,502	219	55.0
		Henry Clay	National Republican	530,189	49	42.4
		William Wirt	Anti-Masonic	33,108	7	2.6
		John Floyd	National Republican		11	
1836	26	MARTIN VAN BUREN	Democratic	765,483	170	50.9
		William H. Harrison	Whig		73	
		Hugh L. White	Whig	739,795	26	49.1
		Daniel Webster	Whig		14	
		W. P. Mangum	Whig		11	
1840	26	WILLIAM H. HARRISON	Whig	1,274,624	234	53.1
		Martin Van Buren	Democratic	1,127,781	60	46.9

Candidates receiving less than 1 per cent of the popular vote have been omitted. For that reason the percentage of popular vote given for any election year may not total 100 per cent.

Before the passage of the Twelfth Amendment in 1804, the Electoral College voted for two presidential candidates; the runner-up became Vice-President. Figures are from *Historical Statistics of the United States, Colonial Times to 1957* (1961), pp. 682–83; and the U.S. Department of Justice.

Year	Number of states	Candidates	Parties	Popular vote	Electoral vote	Percentage of popular vote
1844	26	JAMES K. POLK	Democratic	1,338,464	170	49.6
		Henry Clay	Whig	1,300,097	105	48.1
		James G. Birney	Liberty	62,300		2.3
1848	30	ZACHARY TAYLOR	Whig	1,360,967	163	47.4
		Lewis Cass	Democratic	1,222,342	127	42.5
		Martin Van Buren	Free Soil	291,263		10.1
1852	31	FRANKLIN PIERCE	Democratic	1,601,117	254	50.9
		Winfield Scott	Whig	1,385,453	42	44.1
		John P. Hale	Free Soil	155,825		5.0
1856	31	JAMES BUCHANAN	Democratic	1,832,955	174	45.3
		John C. Frémont	Republican	1,339,932	114	33.1
		Millard Fillmore	American	871,731	8	21.6
1860	33	ABRAHAM LINCOLN	Republican	1,865,593	180	39.8
		Stephen A. Douglas	Democratic	1,382,713	12	29.5
		John C. Breckinridge	Democratic	848,356	72	18.1
		John Bell	Constitutional Union	592,906	39	12.6
1864	36	ABRAHAM LINCOLN	Republican	2,206,938	212	55.0
		George B. McClellan	Democratic	1,803,787	21	45.0
1868	37	ULYSSES S. GRANT	Republican	3,013,421	214	52.7
		Horatio Seymour	Democratic	2,706,829	80	47.3
1872	37	ULYSSES S. GRANT	Republican	3,596,745	286	55.6
		Horace Greeley	Democratic	2,843,446	*	43.9
1876	38	RUTHERFORD B. HAYES	Republican	4,036,572	185	48.0
		Samuel J. Tilden	Democratic	4,284,020	184	51.0
1880	38	JAMES A. GARFIELD	Republican	4,453,295	214	48.5
		Winfield S. Hancock	Democratic	4,414,082	155	48.1
		James B. Weaver	Greenback-Labor	308,578		3.4
1884	38	GROVER CLEVELAND	Democratic	4,879,507	219	48.5
		James G. Blaine	Republican	4,850,293	182	48.2
		Benjamin F. Butler	Greenback-Labor	175,370		1.8
		John P. St. John	Prohibition	150,369		1.5
1888	38	BENJAMIN HARRISON	Republican	5,447,129	233	47.9
		Grover Cleveland	Democratic	5,537,857	168	48.6
		Clinton B. Fisk	Prohibition	249,506		2.2
		Anson J. Streeter	Union Labor	146,935		1.3
1892	44	GROVER CLEVELAND	Democratic	5,555,426	277	46.1
		Benjamin Harrison	Republican	5,182,690	145	43.0
		James B. Weaver	People's	1,029,846	22	8.5
		John Bidwell	Prohibition	264,133		2.2
1896	45	WILLIAM MCKINLEY	Republican	7,102,246	271	51.1
		William J. Bryan	Democratic	6,492,559	176	47.7
1900	45	WILLIAM MCKINLEY	Republican	7,218,491	292	51.7
		William J. Bryan	Democratic; Populist	6,356,734	155	45.5
		John C. Wooley	Prohibition	208,914		1.5

* Greeley died shortly after the election; the electors supporting him then divided their votes among minor candidates.

Candidates receiving less than 1 per cent of the popular vote have been omitted. For that reason the percentage of popular vote given for any election year may not total 100 per cent.

Presidential Elections (1904–1964)

Year	Number of states	Candidates	Parties	Popular vote	Electoral vote	Percentage of popular vote
1904	45	THEODORE ROOSEVELT	Republican	7,628,461	336	57.4
		Alton B. Parker	Democratic	5,084,223	140	37.6
		Eugene V. Debs	Socialist	402,283		3.0
		Silas C. Swallow	Prohibition	258,536		1.9
1908	46	WILLIAM H. TAFT	Republican	7,675,320	321	51.6
		William J. Bryan	Democratic	6,412,294	162	43.1
		Eugene V. Debs	Socialist	420,793		2.8
		Eugene W. Chafin	Prohibition	253,840		1.7
1912	48	WOODROW WILSON	Democratic	6,296,547	435	41.9
		Theodore Roosevelt	Progressive	4,118,571	88	27.4
		William H. Taft	Republican	3,486,720	8	23.2
		Eugene V. Debs	Socialist	900,672		6.0
		Eugene W. Chafin	Prohibition	206,275		1.4
1916	48	WOODROW WILSON	Democratic	9,127,695	277	49.4
		Charles E. Hughes	Republican	8,533,507	254	46.2
		A. L. Benson	Socialist	585,113		3.2
		J. Frank Hanly	Prohibition	220,506		1.2
1920	48	WARREN G. HARDING	Republican	16,143,407	404	60.4
		James N. Cox	Democratic	9,130,328	127	34.2
		Eugene V. Debs	Socialist	919,799		3.4
		P. P. Christensen	Farmer-Labor	265,411		1.0
1924	48	CALVIN COOLIDGE	Republican	15,718,211	382	54.0
		John W. Davis	Democratic	8,385,283	136	28.8
		Robert M. La Follette	Progressive	4,831,289	13	16.6
1928	48	HERBERT C. HOOVER	Republican	21,391,993	444	58.2
		Alfred E. Smith	Democratic	15,016,169	87	40.9
1932	48	FRANKLIN D. ROOSEVELT	Democratic	22,809,638	472	57.4
		Herbert C. Hoover	Republican	15,758,901	59	39.7
		Norman Thomas	Socialist	881,951		2.2
1936	48	FRANKLIN D. ROOSEVELT	Democratic	27,752,869	523	60.8
		Alfred M. Landon	Republican	16,674,665	8	36.5
		William Lemke	Union	882,479		1.9
1940	48	FRANKLIN D. ROOSEVELT	Democratic	27,307,819	449	54.8
		Wendell L. Willkie	Republican	22,321,018	82	44.8
1944	48	FRANKLIN D. ROOSEVELT	Democratic	25,606,585	432	53.5
		Thomas E. Dewey	Republican	22,014,745	99	46.0
1948	48	HARRY S. TRUMAN	Democratic	24,105,812	303	49.5
		Thomas E. Dewey	Republican	21,970,065	189	45.1
		J. Strom Thurmond	States' Rights	1,169,063	39	2.4
		Henry A. Wallace	Progressive	1,157,172		2.4
1952	48	DWIGHT D. EISENHOWER	Republican	33,936,234	442	55.1
		Adlai E. Stevenson	Democratic	27,314,992	89	44.4
1956	48	DWIGHT D. EISENHOWER	Republican	35,590,472	457	57.6
		Adlai E. Stevenson	Democratic	26,022,752	73	42.1
1960	50	JOHN F. KENNEDY	Democratic	34,227,096	303	49.9
		Richard M. Nixon	Republican	34,108,546	219	49.6
1964	50	LYNDON B. JOHNSON	Democratic	43,126,506	486	61.1
		Barry M. Goldwater	Republican	27,176,799	52	38.5

Candidates receiving less than 1 per cent of the popular vote have been omitted. For that reason the percentage of popular vote given for any election year may not total 100 per cent.

Admission of States

Order of admission	State	Date of admission	Order of admission	State	Date of admission
1	Delaware	December 7, 1787	26	Michigan	January 26, 1837
2	Pennsylvania	December 12, 1787	27	Florida	March 3, 1845
3	New Jersey	December 18, 1787	28	Texas	December 29, 1845
4	Georgia	January 2, 1788	29	Iowa	December 28, 1846
5	Connecticut	January 9, 1788	30	Wisconsin	May 29, 1848
6	Massachusetts	February 6, 1788	31	California	September 9, 1850
7	Maryland	April 28, 1788	32	Minnesota	May 11, 1858
8	South Carolina	May 23, 1788	33	Oregon	February 14, 1859
9	New Hampshire	June 21, 1788	34	Kansas	January 29, 1861
10	Virginia	June 25, 1788	35	West Virginia	June 30, 1863
11	New York	July 26, 1788	36	Nevada	October 31, 1864
12	North Carolina	November 21, 1789	37	Nebraska	March 1, 1867
13	Rhode Island	May 29, 1790	38	Colorado	August 1, 1876
14	Vermont	March 4, 1791	39	North Dakota	November 2, 1889
15	Kentucky	June 1, 1792	40	South Dakota	November 2, 1889
16	Tennessee	June 1, 1796	41	Montana	November 8, 1889
17	Ohio	March 1, 1803	42	Washington	November 11, 1889
18	Louisiana	April 30, 1812	43	Idaho	July 3, 1890
19	Indiana	December 11, 1816	44	Wyoming	July 10, 1890
20	Mississippi	December 10, 1817	45	Utah	January 4, 1896
21	Illinois	December 3, 1818	46	Oklahoma	November 16, 1907
22	Alabama	December 14, 1819	47	New Mexico	January 6, 1912
23	Maine	March 15, 1820	48	Arizona	February 14, 1912
24	Missouri	August 10, 1821	49	Alaska	January 3, 1959
25	Arkansas	June 15, 1836	50	Hawaii	August 21, 1959

Population of the United States (1790–1966)

Year	Total population (in thousands)	Number per square mile of land area (continental United States)	Year	Total population (in thousands)	Number per square mile of land area (continental United States)
1790	3,929	4.5	1835	15,003	
1791	4,056		1836	15,423	
1792	4,194		1837	15,843	
1793	4,332		1838	16,264	
1794	4,469		1839	16,684	
1795	4,607		1840	17,120	9.8
1796	4,745		1841	17,733	
1797	4,883		1842	18,345	
1798	5,021		1843	18,957	
1799	5,159		1844	19,569	
1800	5,297	6.1	1845	20,182	
1801	5,486		1846	20,794	
1802	5,679		1847	21,406	
1803	5,872		1848	22,018	
1804	5,065		1849	22,631	
1805	6,258		1850	23,261	7.9
1806	6,451		1851	24,086	
1807	6,644		1852	24,911	
1808	6,838		1853	25,736	
1809	7,031		1854	26,561	
1810	7,224	4.3	1855	27,386	
1811	7,460		1856	28,212	
1812	7,700		1857	29,037	
1813	7,939		1858	29,862	
1814	8,179		1859	30,687	
1815	8,419		1860	31,513	10.6
1816	8,659		1861	32,351	
1817	8,899		1862	33,188	
1818	9,139		1863	34,026	
1819	9,379		1864	34,863	
1820	9,618	5.6	1865	35,701	
1821	9,939		1866	36,538	
1822	10,268		1867	37,376	
1823	10,596		1868	38,213	
1824	10,924		1869	39,051	
1825	11,252		1870	39,905	13.4
1826	11,580		1871	40,938	
1827	11,909		1872	41,972	
1828	12,237		1873	43,006	
1829	12,565		1874	44,040	
1830	12,901	7.4	1875	45,073	
1831	13,321		1876	46,107	
1832	13,742		1877	47,141	
1833	14,162		1878	48,174	
1834	14,582		1879	49,208	

Figures are from *Historical Statistics of the United States, Colonial Times to 1957* (1961), pp. 7, 8; *Statistical Abstract of the United States: 1962*, p. 5; and *Current Population Reports*, Series P-25 (September 1966), pp. 12, 15.

Year	Total population (in thousands)	Number per square mile of land area (continental United States)	Year	Total population (in thousands)*	Number per square mile of land area (continental United States)
1880	50,262	16.9	1925	115,832	
1881	51,542		1926	117,399	
1882	52,821		1927	119,038	
1883	54,100		1928	120,501	
1884	55,379		1929	121,770	
1885	56,658		1930	123,188	41.2
1886	57,938		1931	124,149	
1887	59,217		1932	124,949	
1888	60,496		1933	125,690	
1889	61,775		1934	126,485	
1890	63,056	21.2	1935	127,362	
1891	64,361		1936	128,181	
1892	65,666		1937	128,961	
1893	66,970		1938	129,969	
1894	68,275		1939	131,028	
1895	69,580		1940	132,122	44.2
1896	70,885		1941	133,402	
1897	72,189		1942	134,860	
1898	73,494		1943	136,739	
1899	74,799		1944	138,397	
1900	76,094	25.6	1945	139,928	
1901	77,585		1946	141,389	
1902	79,160		1947	144,126	
1903	80,632		1948	146,631	
1904	82,165		1949	149,188	
1905	83,820		1950	151,683	50.7
1906	85,437		1951	154,360	
1907	87,000		1952	157,028	
1908	88,709		1953	159,636	
1909	90,492		1954	162,417	
1910	92,407	31.0	1955	165,270	
1911	93,868		1956	168,174	
1912	95,331		1957	171,229	
1913	97,227		1958	174,882	
1914	99,118		1959	177,830	
1915	100,549		1960	179,992	60.1
1916	101,966		1961	183,057	
1917	103,414		1962	185,890	
1918	104,550		1963	188,658	
1919	105,063		1964	191,372	
1920	106,466	35.6	1965	193,795	
1921	108,541		1966	195,857	
1922	110,055				
1923	111,950				
1924	114,113				

* Figures for 1960–66 include Puerto Rico but do not include Armed Forces abroad.

Presidents, Vice-Presidents, and Cabinet Members (1789–1841)

President	Vice-President	Secretary of State	Secretary of Treasury	Secretary of War
George Washington 1789–97	John Adams 1789–97	Thomas Jefferson 1789–94 Edmund Randolph 1794–95 Timothy Pickering 1795–97	Alexander Hamilton 1789–95 Oliver Wolcott 1795–97	Henry Knox 1789–95 Timothy Pickering 1795–96 James McHenry 1796–97
John Adams 1797–1801	Thomas Jefferson 1797–1801	Timothy Pickering 1797–1800 John Marshall 1800–01	Oliver Wolcott 1797–1801 Samuel Dexter 1801	James McHenry 1797–1800 John Marshall 1800 Samuel Dexter 1800–01 Roger Griswold 1801
Thomas Jefferson 1801–09	Aaron Burr 1801–05 George Clinton 1805–09	James Madison 1801–09	Samuel Dexter 1801 Albert Gallatin 1801–09	Henry Dearborn 1801–09
James Madison 1809–17	George Clinton 1809–13 Elbridge Gerry 1813–17	Robert Smith 1809–11 James Monroe 1811–17	Albert Gallatin 1809–14 George Campbell 1814 Alexander Dallas 1814–16 William Crawford 1816–17	William Eustis 1809–13 John Armstrong 1813–14 James Monroe 1814–15 William Crawford 1815–17
James Monroe 1817–25	Daniel D. Tompkins 1817–25	John Quincy Adams 1817–25	William Crawford 1817–25	Isaac Shelby 1817 George Graham 1817 John C. Calhoun 1817–25
John Quincy Adams 1825–29	John C. Calhoun 1825–29	Henry Clay 1825–29	Richard Rush 1825–29	James Barbour 1825–28 Peter B. Porter 1828–29
Andrew Jackson 1829–37	John C. Calhoun 1829–33 Martin Van Buren 1833–37	Martin Van Buren 1829–31 Edward Livingston 1831–33 Louis McLane 1833–34 John Forsyth 1834–37	Samuel Ingham 1829–31 Louis McLane 1831–33 William Duane 1833 Roger B. Taney 1833–34 Levi Woodbury 1834–37	John H. Eaton 1829–31 Lewis Cass 1831–37 Benjamin Butler 1837
Martin Van Buren 1837–41	Richard M. Johnson 1837–41	John Forsyth 1837–41	Levi Woodbury 1837–41	Joel R. Poinsett 1837–41
William H. Harrison 1841	John Tyler 1841	Daniel Webster 1841	Thomas Ewing 1841	John Bell 1841

Secretary of Navy	Postmaster General	Attorney General
	Samuel Osgood 1789–91 Timothy Pickering 1791–95 Joseph Habersham 1795–97	Edmund Randolph 1789–94 William Bradford 1794–95 Charles Lee 1795–97
Benjamin Stoddert 1798–1801	Joseph Habersham 1797–1801	Charles Lee 1797–1801 Theodore Parsons 1801
Benjamin Stoddert 1801 Robert Smith 1801–09	Joseph Habersham 1801 Gideon Granger 1801–09	Levi Lincoln 1801–05 Robert Smith 1805 John Breckinridge 1805–07 Caesar Rodney 1807–09
Paul Hamilton 1809–13 William Jones 1813–14 Benjamin Crowninshield 1814–17	Gideon Granger 1809–14 Return Meigs 1814–17	Caesar Rodney 1809–11 William Pinckney 1811–14 Richard Rush 1814–17
Benjamin Crowninshield 1817–18 Smith Thompson 1818–23 Samuel Southard 1823–25	Return Meigs 1817–23 John McLean 1823–25	Richard Rush 1817 William Wirt 1817–25
Samuel Southard 1825–29	John McLean 1825–29	William Wirt 1825–29
John Branch 1829–31 Levi Woodbury 1831–34 Mahlon Dickerson 1834–37	William Barry 1829–35 Amos Kendall 1835–37	John M. Berrien 1829–31 Roger B. Taney 1831–33 Benjamin Butler 1833–37
Mahlon Dickerson 1837–38 James K. Paulding 1838–41	Amos Kendall 1837–40 John M. Niles 1840–41	Benjamin Butler 1837–38 Felix Grundy 1838–40 Henry D. Gilpin 1840–41
George E. Badger 1841	Francis Granger 1841	John J. Crittenden 1841

Presidents, Vice-Presidents, and Cabinet Members (1841–81)

President	Vice-President	Secretary of State	Secretary of Treasury	Secretary of War
John Tyler 1841–45		Daniel Webster 1841–43 Hugh S. Legaré 1843 Abel P. Upshur 1843–44 John C. Calhoun 1844–45	Thomas Ewing 1841 Walter Forward 1841–43 John C. Spencer 1843–44 George M. Bibb 1844–45	John Bell 1841 John McLean 1841 John C. Spencer 1841–43 James M. Porter 1843–44 William Wilkins 1844–45
James K. Polk 1845–49	George M. Dallas 1845–49	James Buchanan 1845–49	Robert J. Walker 1845–49	William L. Marcy 1845–49
Zachary Taylor 1849–50	Millard Fillmore 1849–50	John M. Clayton 1849–50	William M. Meredith 1849–50	George W. Crawford 1849–50
Millard Fillmore 1850–53		Daniel Webster 1850–52 Edward Everett 1852–53	Thomas Corwin 1850–53	Charles M. Conrad 1850–53
Franklin Pierce 1853–57	William R. King 1853–57	William L. Marcy 1853–57	James Guthrie 1853–57	Jefferson Davis 1853–57
James Buchanan 1857–61	John C. Breckinridge 1857–61	Lewis Cass 1857–60 Jeremiah S. Black 1860–61	Howell Cobb 1857–60 Philip F. Thomas 1860–61 John A. Dix 1861	John B. Floyd 1857–61 Joseph Holt 1861
Abraham Lincoln 1861–65	Hannibal Hamlin 1861–65 Andrew Johnson 1865	William H. Seward 1861–65	Salmon P. Chase 1861–64 William P. Fessenden 1864–65 Hugh McCulloch 1865	Simon Cameron 1861–62 Edwin M. Stanton 1862–65
Andrew Johnson 1865–69		William H. Seward 1865–69	Hugh McCulloch 1865–69	Edwin M. Stanton 1865–67 Ulysses S. Grant 1867–68 Lorenzo Thomas 1868 John M. Schofield 1868–69
Ulysses S. Grant 1869–77	Schuyler Colfax 1869–73 Henry Wilson 1873–77	Elihu B. Washburne 1869 Hamilton Fish 1869–77	George S. Boutwell 1869–73 William A. Richardson 1873–74 Benjamin H. Bristow 1874–76 Lot M. Morrill 1876–77	John A. Rawlins 1869 William T. Sherman 1869 William W. Belknap 1869–76 Alphonso Taft 1876 James D. Cameron 1876–77
Rutherford B. Hayes 1877–81	William A. Wheeler 1877–81	William M. Evarts 1877–81	John Sherman 1877–81	George W. McCrary 1877–79 Alexander Ramsey 1879–81

Secretary of Navy	Postmaster General	Attorney General	Secretary of Interior
George E. Badger 1841 Abel P. Upshur 1841–43 David Henshaw 1843–44 Thomas Gilmer 1844 John Y. Mason 1844–45	Francis Granger 1841 Charles A. Wickliffe 1841–45	John J. Crittenden 1841 Hugh S. Legaré 1841–43 John Nelson 1843–45	
George Bancroft 1845–46 John Y. Mason 1846–49	Cave Johnson 1845–49	John Y. Mason 1845–46 Nathan Clifford 1846–48 Isaac Toucey 1848–49	
William B. Preston 1849–50	Jacob Collamer 1849–50	Reverdy Johnson 1849–50	Thomas Ewing 1849–50
William A. Graham 1850–52 John P. Kennedy 1852–53	Nathan K. Hall 1850–52 Sam D. Hubbard 1852–53	John J. Crittenden 1850–53	A. H. H. Stuart 1850–53
James C. Dobbin 1853–57	James Campbell 1853–57	Caleb Cushing 1853–57	Robert McClelland 1853–57
Isaac Toucey 1857–61	Aaron V. Brown 1857–59 Joseph Holt 1859–61	Jeremiah S. Black 1857–60 Edwin M. Stanton 1860–61	Jacob Thompson 1857–61
Gideon Welles 1861–65	Horatio King 1861 Montgomery Blair 1861–64 William Dennison 1864–65	Edward Bates 1861–63 Titian J. Coffey 1863–64 James Speed 1864–65	Caleb B. Smith 1861–63 John P. Usher 1863–65
Gideon Welles 1865–69	William Dennison 1865–66 Alexander Randall 1866–69	James Speed 1865–66 Henry Stanbery 1866–68 William M. Evarts 1868–69	John P. Usher 1865 James Harlan 1865–66 O. H. Browning 1866–69
Adolph E. Borie 1869 George M. Robeson 1869–77	John A. J. Creswell 1869–74 James W. Marshall 1874 Marshall Jewell 1874–76 James N. Tyner 1876–77	Ebenezer R. Hoar 1869–70 Amos T. Akerman 1870–71 G. H. Williams 1871–75 Edwards Pierrepont 1875–76 Alphonso Taft 1876–77	Jacob D. Cox 1869–70 Columbus Delano 1870–75 Zachary Chandler 1875–77
R. W. Thompson 1877–81 Nathan Goff, Jr. 1881	David M. Key 1877–80 Horace Maynard 1880–81	Charles Devens 1877–81	Carl Schurz 1877–81

Presents, Vice-Presidents, and Cabinet Members (1881–1933)

President	Vice-President	Secretary of State	Secretary of Treasury	Secretary of War	Secretary of Navy
James A. Garfield 1881	Chester A. Arthur 1881	James G. Blaine 1881	William Windom 1881	Robert T. Lincoln 1881	William H. Hunt 1881
Chester A. Arthur 1881–85		F. T. Frelinghuysen 1881–85	Charles J. Folger 1881–84 Walter Q. Gresham 1884 Hugh McCulloch 1884–85	Rogbert T. Lincoln 1881–85	William E. Chandler 1881–85
Grover Cleveland 1885–89	T. A. Hendricks 1885–89	Thomas F. Bayard 1885–89	Daniel Manning 1885–87 Charles S. Fairchild 1887–89	William C. Endicott 1885–89	William C. Whitney 1885–89
Benjamin Harrison 1889–93	Levi P. Morton 1889–93	James G. Blaine 1889–92 John W. Foster 1892–93	William Windom 1889–91 Charles Foster 1891–93	Redfield Procter 1889–91 Stephen B. Elkins 1891–93	Benjamin F. Tracy 1889–93
Grover Cleveland 1893–97	Adlai E. Stevenson 1893–97	Walter Q. Gresham 1893–95 Richard Olney 1895–97	John G. Carlisle 1893–97	Daniel S. Lamont 1893–97	Hilary A. Herbert 1893–97
William McKinley 1897–1901	Garret A. Hobart 1897–1901 Theodore Roosevelt 1901	John Sherman 1897–98 William R. Day 1898 John Hay 1898–1901	Lyman J. Gage 1897–1901	Russell A. Alger 1897–99 Elihu Root 1899–1901	John D. Long 1897–1901
Theodore Roosevelt 1901–09	Charles Fairbanks 1905–09	John Hay 1901–05 Elihu Root 1905–09 Robert Bacon 1909	Lyman J. Gage 1901–02 Leslie M. Shaw 1902–07 George B. Cortelyou 1907–09	Elihu Root 1901–04 William H. Taft 1904–08 Luke E. Wright 1908–09	John D. Long 1901–02 William H. Moody 1902–04 Paul Morton 1904–05 Charles J. Bonaparte 1905–07 Victor H. Metcalf 1907–08 T. H. Newberry 1908–09
William H. Taft 1909–13	James S. Sherman 1909–13	Philander C. Knox 1909–13	Franklin MacVeagh 1909–13	Jacob M. Dickinson 1909–11 Henry L. Stimson 1911–13	George von L. Meyer 1909–13
Woodrow Wilson 1913–21	Thomas R. Marshall 1913–21	William J. Bryan 1913–15 Robert Lansing 1915–20 Bainbridge Colby 1920–21	William G. McAdoo 1913–19 Carter Glass 1919–20 David F. Houston 1920–21	Lindley M. Garrison 1913–16 Newton D. Baker 1916–21	Josephus Daniels 1913–21
Warren G. Harding 1921–23	Calvin Coolidge 1921–23	Charles E. Hughes 1921–23	Andrew W. Mellon 1921–23	John W. Weeks 1921–23	Edwin Denby 1921–23
Calvin Coolidge 1923–29	Charles G. Dawes 1925–29	Charles E. Hughes 1923–25 Frank B. Kellogg 1925–29	Andrew W. Mellon 1923–29	John W. Weeks 1923–25 Dwight F. Davis 1925–29	Edwin Denby 1923–24 Curtis D. Wilbur 1924–29
Herbert C. Hoover 1929–33	Charles Curtis 1929–33	Henry L. Stimson 1929–33	Andrew W. Mellon 1929–32 Ogden L. Mills 1932–33	James W. Good 1929 Patrick J. Hurley 1929–33	Charles F. Adams 1929–33

Postmaster General	Attorney General	Secretary of Interior	Secretary of Agriculture	Secretary of Commerce and Labor	
Thomas L. James 1881	Wayne MacVeagh 1881	S. J. Kirkwood 1881			
Timothy O. Howe 1881–83 Walter Q. Gresham 1883–84 Frank Hatton 1884–85	B. H. Brewster 1881–85	Henry M. Teller 1881–85			
William F. Vilar 1885–88 Don M. Dickinson 1888–89	A. H. Garland 1885–89	L. Q. C. Lamar 1885–88 William F. Vilas 1888–89	Norman J. Colman 1889		
John Wanamaker 1889–93	W. H. H. Miller 1889–93	John W. Noble 1889–93	Jeremiah M. Rusk 1889–93		
Wilson S. Bissel 1893–95 William L. Wilson 1895–97	Richard Olney 1893–95 Judson Harmon 1895–97	Hoke Smith 1893–96 David R. Francis 1896–97	J. Sterling Morton 1893–97		
James A. Gary 1897–98 Charles E. Smith 1898–1901	Joseph McKenna 1897 John W. Griggs 1897–1901 Philander C. Knox 1901	Cornelius N. Bliss 1897–99 E. A. Hitchcock 1899–1901	James Wilson 1897–1901		
Charles E. Smith 1901–02 Henry C. Payne 1902–04 Robert J. Wynne 1904–05 George B. Cortelyou 1905–07 George von L. Meyer 1907–09	Philander C. Knox 1901–04 William H. Moody 1904–06 Charles J. Bonaparte 1906–09	E. A. Hitchcock 1901–07 James R. Garfield 1907–09	James Wilson 1901–09	George B. Cortelyou 1903–04 Victor H. Metcalf 1904–06 Oscar S. Straus 1906–09	
Frank H. Hitchcock 1909–13	G. W. Wickersham 1909–13	R. A. Ballinger 1909–11 Walter L. Fisher 1911–13	James Wilson 1909–13	Charles Nagel 1909–13	

				Secretary of Commerce	Secretary of Labor
Albert S. Burleson 1913–21	J. C. McReynolds 1913–14 T. W. Gregory 1914–19 A. Mitchell Palmer 1919–21	Franklin K. Lane 1913–20 John B. Payne 1920–21	David F. Houston 1913–20 E. T. Meredith 1920–21	W. C. Redfield 1913–19 J. W. Alexander 1919–21	William B. Wilson 1913–21
Will H. Hays 1921–22 Hubert Work 1922–23 Harry S. New 1923	H. M. Daugherty 1921–23	Albert B. Fall 1921–23 Hubert Work 1923	Henry C. Wallace 1921–23	Herbert C. Hoover 1921–23	James J. Davis 1921–23
Harry S. New 1923–29	H. M. Daugherty 1923–24 Harlan F. Stone 1924–25 John D. Sargent 1925–29	Hubert Work 1923–28 Roy O. West 1928–29	Henry C. Wallace 1923–24 Howard M. Gore 1924–25 W. M. Jardine 1925–29	Herbert C. Hoover 1923–25 William F. Whiting 1925–29	James J. Davis 1923–29
Walter F. Brown 1929–33	W. D. Mitchell 1929–33	Ray L. Wilbur 1929–33	Arthur M. Hyde 1929–33	Robert P. Lamont 1929–32 Roy D. Chapin 1932–33	William N. Doak 1930–33

Presidents, Vice-Presidents, and Cabinet Members (1933–   )

President	Vice-President	Secretary of State	Secretary of Treasury	Secretary of War	Secretary of Navy
Franklin Delano Roosevelt 1933–45	John Nance Garner 1933–41 Henry A. Wallace 1941–45 Harry S. Truman 1945	Cordell Hull 1933–44 E. R. Stettinius, Jr. 1944–45	William H. Woodin 1933–34 Henry Morgenthau, Jr. 1934–45	George H. Dern 1933–36 Harry H. Woodring 1936–40 Henry L. Stimson 1940–45	Claude A. Swanson 1933–40 Charles Edison 1940 Frank Knox 1940–44 James V. Forrestal 1944–45
Harry S. Truman 1945–53	Alben W. Barkley 1949–53	James F. Byrnes 1945–47 George C. Marshall 1947–49 Dean G. Acheson 1949–53	Fred M. Vinson 1945–46 John W. Snyder 1946–53	Robert H. Patterson 1945–47 Kenneth C. Royall 1947	James V. Forrestal 1945–47

		Secretary of Defense
		James V. Forrestal 1947–49 Louis A. Johnson 1949–50 George C. Marshall 1950–51 Robert A. Lovett 1951–53

President	Vice-President	Secretary of State	Secretary of Treasury	Secretary of Defense
Dwight D. Eisenhower 1953–61	Richard M. Nixon 1953–61	John Foster Dulles 1953–59 Christian A. Herter 1959–61	George M. Humphrey 1953–57 Robert M. Anderson 1957–61	Charles E. Wilson 1953–57 Neil H. McElroy 1957–61
John F. Kennedy 1961–63	Lyndon B. Johnson 1961–63	Dean Rusk 1961–63	C. Douglas Dillon 1961–63	Robert S. McNamara 1961–63
Lyndon B. Johnson 1963–	Hubert H. Humphrey 1965–	Dean Rusk 1963–	C. Douglas Dilllon 1963–65 Henry H. Fowler 1965–	Robert S. McNamara 1963–68 Clark M. Clifford 1968–

Postmaster General	Attorney General	Secretary of Interior	Secretary of Agriculture	Secretary of Commerce	Secretary of Labor	Secretary of Health, Education and Welfare
James A. Farley 1933–40 Frank C. Walker 1940–45	H. S. Cummings 1933–39 Frank Murphy 1939–40 Robert Jackson 1940–41 Francis Biddle 1941–45	Harold L. Ickes 1933–45	Henry A. Wallace 1933–40 Claude R. Wickard 1940–45	Daniel C. Roper 1933–39 Harry L. Hopkins 1939–40 Jesse Jones 1940–45 Henry A. Wallace 1945	Frances Perkins 1933–45	
R. E. Hannegan 1945–47 Jesse L. Donaldson 1947–53	Tom C. Clark 1945–49 J. H. McGrath 1949–53	Harold L. Ickes 1945–46 Julius A. Krug 1946–49 Oscar L. Chapman 1949–53	C. P. Anderson 1945–48 C. F. Brannan 1948–53	W. A. Harriman 1946–48 Charles Sawyer 1948–53	L. B. Schwellenbach 1945–48 Maurice J. Tobin 1948–53	
A. E. Summerfield 1953–61	H. Brownell, Jr. 1953–57 William P. Rogers 1957–61	Douglas McKay 1953–56 Fred Seaton 1956–61	Ezra T. Benson 1953–61	Sinclair Weeks 1953–58 Lewis L. Strauss 1958–61	Martin P. Durkin 1953 James P. Mitchell 1953–61	Oveta Culp Hobby 1953–55 Marion B. Folsom 1955–58 Arthur S. Flemming 1958–61
J. Edward Day 1961–63 John A. Gronouski 1963	Robert F. Kennedy 1961–63	Stewart L. Udall 1961–63	Orville L. Freeman 1961–63	Luther H. Hodges 1961–63	Arthur J. Goldberg 1961–62 W. Willard Wirtz 1962–63	A. H. Ribicoff 1961–62 Anthony J. Celebrezze 1962–63
John A. Gronouski 1963–65 Lawrence F. O'Brien 1965–68 William M. Watson 1968–	Robert F. Kennedy 1963–65 N. deB. Katzenbach 1965–67 Ramsey Clark 1967–	Stewart L. Udall 1963–	Orville L. Freeman 1963–	Luther H. Hodges 1963–64 John T. Connor 1964–67 Alexander B. Trowbridge 1967–	W. Willard Wirtz 1963–	Anthony J. Celebrezze 1963–65 John W. Gardner 1965–68 Wilbur J. Cohen 1968–

				Secretary of Housing and Urban Development		Secretary of Transportation
				Robert C. Weaver 1966–		Alan S. Boyd 1966–

Source of Illustrations

Index

Boldface numbers refer to maps, charts, or illustrations. When an entry is mentioned both in the text and in the artwork of a single page, the page number is set lightface.

Black Hawk, Chief, 232
Black Hawk War (*1832*), 232
Black Kettle, Chief, 416
Black power, 832
Blackstone, William, 53
Blackwell, Elizabeth, 260
Blackwell, John, 42
Blaine, James G., 393–94, 487, 490, 494, 495, 496, 497, 500, 522–23
Blair, Francis P., 228, 230, 342, 382
Blair, Montgomery, 338
Blake, Eugene Carson, 841
Blake v. Carr, 833
Bland, Richard P., 493, 513
Bland-Allison Act (*1878*), 493, 501, 512
Blennerhassett, Harman, 175
Bliss, Tasker H., 604
Bliss, W. D. P., 514
Bloomer, Amelia, 260
Blue Eagle (NRA), 684
Boleyn, Anne, 9
Bolshevik Revolution, 594, 602, 604, 612
Bonaparte, Napoleon, 161, 170–71, 172, 173, 176, 178, 183
Bonhoffer, Dietrich, 841–42
Bonvouloir, Achard de, 114
Boone, Daniel, 130
Booth, John Wilkes, 369
Booth, William, 474
Borah, William E., 623, 626, 648, 669
Bosch, Juan, 824
Boston, siege of, 23, 104, 109
"Boston Associates," 216, 217
Boston tea party, 99
Boundaries, U.S., 120, **121**, 124–25, **128**, **189**, 247, 282, **559**
"Bourbons." *See* Conservative party, Southern Democratic
Bourne, George, 308
Boutwell, George S., 532, 533
Bow, Clara, 644
Bowles, Chester A., 733, 769
Boxer Rebellion, 535
Boylston, Zabdiel, 70
Braddock, Edward, 82, 150
Bradford, William, 21
Bradley, Omar, 755, 779, 780
Bradstreet, John, **83**, 84
Bragg, Braxton, 356, 360, 364
Brandeis, Louis D., 568, 574, 576, 577, 578, 636, 681, 690, 694
Brando, Marlon, 842
Brannan, Charles F., 776
Brazil, 581, **809**
Breckinridge, John C., 332, 334, 368
Breed's Hill, 103, 111. *See also* Bunker Hill, Battle of
Bretton Woods Conference (*1944*), 750, 765
Briand, Aristide, 648
Bricker, John W., 746
Bridger, James, 276
Brisbane, Albert, 262
British Guiana, 523–24
British West Indies, 89, 264
Britton, Nan, 630
Brock, Isaac, 182

Brook Farm, 263
Brooks, Preston, 325
Brooks, Van Wyck, 653, 701
Brotherhood of Engineers and Trainmen, 769
Brotherhood of Sleeping Car Porters, 734
Browder, Earl, 753
Brown, B. G., 387
Brown, Jacob, **181**, 183
Brown, John, 325, 329–30
Brown, Moses, 215
Brown v. Board of Education of Topeka, 804
Brown Decade, 481
Browne, Robert, 20
Brownson, Orestes, 253
Brussels Pact (*1948*), 715, 727, 773
Bryan, Charles, 643
Bryan, William Jennings, 512–15, 536, 551, 562, 573, 575, 643, 681; and Philippine debate, 532, 533–34; and Scopes trial, 642; as Secretary of State, 578, 583, 586
Bryce, James, 471, 488
Buber, Martin, 841, 844
Buchanan, James, 282, 294, 300, 301, 325; Administration of, 325–31, 336–37
Buchanan-Pakenham Treaty (*1846*), 282
Budget and Accounting Act (*1921*), 626
Buell, Don Carlos, 352, 353, 354, 356, 360
Buena Vista, Battle of, **284**, 285
Buenos Aires Conference (*1936*), 707
Bulgaria, 751, 764
Bull Moose party. *See* Progressive party
Bull Run, Battle of (*1861*), 350–51; (*1862*), **350**, 356
Bulwer, Sir Henry Lytton, 303
Bunker, Ellsworth, 825
Bunker Hill, Battle of, 102, 103
Burchard, Samuel D., 497
Bureau of the Budget, 777
Bureau of Corporations, 550
Bureau of Internal Revenue, 784
Bureau of Labor, 550, 605
Burgess, John W., 521
Burgoyne, John, 103, 113, 114
Burke, Edmund, 101, 269
Burleson, Albert S., 575, 600, 618
Burlingame Treaty (*1880*), 492
Burma, 743, 797
Burnham, Daniel H., 481
Burns, James M., 791
Burnside, Ambrose E., 360, 361
Burr, Aaron, 157, 163, 164, 174–75
Burroughs, William, 840
Bush, Vannevar, 732, 800
Business, 625–27, 633–35, 637–38, 649–51, 769, 781, 829; consolidation of, 637; criticism of, 637, 651; and Eisenhower, 801–02; and financiers, 444–50; and Kennedy, 820–21; and New Deal, 692–93; regulation of,

442–44, 552–53, 627; and '29 crash, 659–62. *See also* Capitalism; Industry; Laissez faire policy; Trusts
Bute, Earl of, 85–87, 88
Butler, Andrew Pickens, 325
Butler, Benjamin F., 354, 358
Butler, Edward, 471
Butler, Pierce, 134
Byrd, Harry F., 804, 811
Byrnes, James F., 617, 733, 747, 764, 770

CCC (Civilian Conservation Corps), 686
CENTO. *See* Central Treaty Organization
CIA. *See* Central Intelligence Agency
CIO. *See* Congress of Industrial Organizations
CORE (Congress of Racial Equality), 832
CPI (Committee on Public Information), 599–600
Cabot, John, 7, 8, 10, **11**
Cage, John, 840
"Cairo," **353**
Cairo Declaration (*1943*), 750, 778
Calhoun, John C., 195, 226n, 287, 288; and annexation of Texas, 275; career of, 234; and Compromise of *1850*, 291–92; and doctrine of nullification, 234–35; and slavery, 234, 267, **268**; and *South Carolina Exposition and Protest*, 234; on the Union, 236; and War of *1812*, 179; and Wilmont Proviso, 291
California: acquisition of, 285, 288; gold rush in, 288–89, 419; settlement of, 7, 278–79; statehood of, 293, 335
California Trail, **277**, 278
Callahan, E. A., 450
Calles, Plutarco Elias, 646
Calvert, Cecilius, 27
Calvert, George, 27
Calvin, John, 9, 20
Calvinism, 65, 66; decline of, 251–52
Cambodia, 797
Cambridge, settlement of, 22
Cameron, Simon, 346
Campbellites, 252
Canada: and Alaska boundary, 559; and American Revolution, 109, 519, 624, 773; as English colony, 99, 129–30, 180; and French, 8, 84, 86; and fur trade, 418
Canal Ring, 394
Canals, 206, 309
Canning, George, 200, 202
Cannon, Joseph G., 552, 566, 567
Cape Breton Islands, 76
Cape Cod, settlement of, 20, 21
Cape Verde Islands, 5
Capitalism: and industrialism, 217–18, 539; and monopolies,

497–500, 507–12, 520, 523–24, 526, 527
Clinton, De Witt, 180, 206
Clinton, George, 175
Clinton, Henry, 103, 110, 116, 117
Clipper ships, 304–05
Coal mining, 550, 551, 627, 691, 733, 769, 829, 830
Cobb, Howell, 331
Coexistence, 792, 808
Cohen, Benjamin, 690
Cohens v. Virginia, 198
Cohn, Roy, 799, 801
Colbert de Croissy, Charles, 75
Cold Harbor, Battle of, 365
Cold War: beginnings of, 752, 767–68, 770, 778, 798; nuclear-test-ban treaty, 819–20; thaw in, 807
Cole, Nathan, 64
Coleridge, Samuel Taylor, 253
Colfax, Schuyler, 382, 388
Collective bargaining, 627, 691, 695, 696
Colleges and universities, 68, 478
Colleton, Sir John, 37–38
Collier, John, 418
Collins, LeRoy, 805
Colombia, 301, 558, 623, **809**, 817
Colonial life: and education, 67–68; and government, 63; on plantation and farm, 53–56, 59–61; and religion, 63–67; in towns and cities, 57–59, 61–62
Colonies, early American, 10–27; assemblies in, 63, 123; corporate, 49; county government in, 60, 63; and Declaration of Independence, 105–06; earliest European settlements in, 8; East-West split in, 88–97; governors in, 49–50; imperial authority over, 87–88; life in, 53–62; political strife in, 42–50; post-Revolutionary governments of, 123; private property in, 122; proprietary, 26–27, 35, 49; religion as factor in proliferation of, 23–25; during Restoration, 35–42; royal, 36, 49; towns in, 57–59; unity of, 93, 103–06. *See also* individual colonies
Colorado, statehood of, **421**
Colored Farmers' National Alliance and Cooperative Union, 504
Columbian Exposition (*1893*), 451, 481, 510
Columbus, Christopher, 3, 4–5, 6, 7
Comanche Indians, 414, 416
Commission on Intergovernmental Relations, 802
Committee on Public Information (CPI), 599–600
Committee on Social and Political Implications, 756
Committee on Un-American Activities, 698
Committee to Defend America by Aiding the Allies, 725
Committees of Correspondence, 100

Commodity Credit Corporation, 505*n*, 775
Common Market, 818
Commons, John R., 545, 643, 653, 654
Commonwealth v. Hunt, 315
Communism, 618, 619, 672, 698–99, 767, 782, 792, 794, 808; challenge of, 771; and containment vs. coexistence, 770–71, 792, 808; and Red scare, 618–21, 782–83, 799–801; and Russo-Chinese split, 820; and uncommitted nations, 777; and underdeveloped nations, 815, 816; and Yalta Conference, 751–53
Communist Labor party, 618
Communist party of America, 619, 643, 672, 676, 698, 711, 719, 753
Communist party congresses: Nineteenth, 795; Twentieth, 795
Communitarianism, 262–63
Community Action program, 830
Compromise of *1850*, 290–95, 321
Comstock, Henry, 420
Concord, 123; Battle of, 102, 111, 120
Confederacy: formation of, 335, 337–38; political theory of, 344–45; and secession, 293, 332, 334–38; surrender of, 369. *See also* Civil War
Confederate States of America. *See* Confederacy
Confederation of Industrial Organizations, 505
Conference for Progressive Political Action, 643
Confiscation Acts (*1861* and *1862*), 358
Congo, 589; Republic of, 816
Congregationalists, 20, 21, 64, 97, 252, 254, 256, 474
Congress, U.S., 126, 134, 135, 679*n*
Congress of Industrial Organizations (CIO), 695–96, 699, 700, 747
Congress of Racial Equality (CORE), 832
Conkling, Roscoe, 393, 487, 490, 491, 492, 494, 495, 497
Connecticut, colony of, 25, 43, 44, 62, 81, 121, 125; charter of, 43; dispute with Pennsylvania, 97; in Dominion of New England, 46–48; settling of, 25
Connecticut, state of, 132
Connor, Eugene, 821
Conquistadors, 5–6
Conservation, 553, 567–68, 686
Conservatism: in government, 491–502, 526, 633, 773–74; and laissez faire doctrine, 452–55; and New Deal, 701–02
Conservative party, Southern Democratic, 395, 398–402, 407, 488
Constitution, English, 123
Constitution, U.S., 124, 131, 133–36, 141, 162; amending of, 136; and Congress, 134, 135; and

executive, 134, 135; and federal and state powers, 134, 135; and judicial review, 197–98, 694; opposition to, 136–37; ratification of, 136–38. *See also* Amendments, constitutional; Articles of Confederation; Bill of Rights
Constitutional Convention (*1787*), 123, 133–38, 141, 142, 144
Constitutional Union party, 333
Continental Army: enlistment of, 109; establishment of, 104; in Revolutionary War, 111–19; and trend toward aristocracy, 121
Continental Congress, First, 100–02; final resolutions of, 101; moderates at, 100; radical contingency of, 100–01
Continental Congress, Second, 104–06, 111; and Continental Army, 104; and French alliance, 114–15, 119–20; and independence, 105; and peace negotiations, 120; in Revolution, 127
Conventions, national nominating, 225, 239
Cook, James, 276
Cooke, Jay, 386, 387, 389, 440
Coolidge, Calvin, 617, 621; Administration of, 633–51, 654–55, 700; and business, 633–35, 637–38, 649–51, 653; and internationalism, 647–49; and Latin-American affairs, 645–46
Coolidge, Grace, 633
Cooper, Anthony Ashley, 38
Cooper, James Fenimore, 217, 299
Copernicus, Nicolaus, 68
Copperheads, 347
Coral Sea, Battle of the, **742**, 743
Corcoran, Thomas G., 690
Corinth, Battle of, 360
Cornell, Alonzo B., 492
Corning, Erastus, 310
Cornwallis, Lord Charles, 110, 117, 118
Coronado, Vásquez, **6**, 7
Corruption, in government, 385, 388, 394, 416, 418, 439, 470–72, 489–90, 491–92, 542, 544, 629–31, 641, 784, 806
Cortelyou, George B., 552
Cortez, Hernando, 5, **6**
Corwin, Thomas, 284
Costigan, Edward P., 671
Cotton, John, 24
Coughlin, Charles E., 689, 693, 734
Coulter, E. Merton, 384
Council of Economic Advisers, 769
Council of Foreign Ministers, 763, 764, 770
Council of National Defense, 598
Council for New England, 20, 22, 26, 27
Country Life Commission, 553
Court of Commerce, 567
Courts, federal district, 144, 162, 168–69, 804
Cowley, Malcolm, 652, 672
Cox, Harvey, 841
Cox, James M., 612, 622

Cox, S. S. "Sunset," 499
Coxey's Army, 510
Cozzens, James Gould, 837
Crawford, William H., 196, 225, 226, 227
Crédit Mobilier, 388
Creek Indians, 3, **73**, 76, **77**, 180, 184
Creel, George, 599–60, 604
Creole, 247
Crèvecœur, Michel Guillaume Jean de, 122
Crime, 784; and growth of cities, 468–69; juvenile, 843; organized, 641, 784, 833
"Crime of *1873*," 493, 507
Crime Investigation Committee, Senate, 784
Crissinger, D. R., 627
Crittenden, George B., 352
Crittenden, John J., 336
Croker, Richard, 471, 473
Croly, Herbert, 574, 599
Cromwell, Oliver, 32, 39, 44, 90
Crystal Palace Exhibition, 313
Cuba, 86, 201, 519, 533, 534, 536, 707; and campaign of *1898*, 529–30; and nineteenth-century imperialism, 287, 299–301, 302; rebel invasion of, 816–17; revolution of, 810, 816; and Soviet Union, 816–18; and Spanish-American War, 525–30; U.S. protectorate of, 556
Cullom, Shelby M., 443
Cumberland Road. *See* National Road
Cummings, Homer, 694
Currency Act (*1764*), 89
Currier and Ives, **427**
Curtis, Benjamin R., 326, 327
Curtis, Charles, 674
Curtis, Edwin U., 472
Curtis, George William, 472, 491, 496, 497
Curtis, S. R., 353
Cushing, Caleb, 303
Custer, George A., 417
Cutting, Bronson, 665
Czechoslovakia, 604, 607, 716, 717, 718, 772, 773

Dadaism, 653
Dakota Indians, 418
Daladier, Edouard, 716
D-Day, **730**
Dale, Thomas, 16
Daniels, Josephus, 725
Darlan, Jean François, 738, 739, 747
Darrow, Clarence, 642, 685, 836
Dartmouth, Lord William, 99, 102
Dartmouth College v. Woodward, 199
Darwin, Charles, 452, 454, 641
Darwinism, social, 453, 454, 455, 473, 521, 544
Daugherty, Harry M., 629, 630, 633
Davenport, James, 65
Davie, William R., 161

Davis, David, 396
Davis, Elmer, 734, 784
Davis, Henry G., 490
Davis, Henry Winter, 375
Davis, James H., 506
Davis, Jefferson, 294, 302, 331; and Confederacy, 335, 338, 341, 345, 352, 355, 357, 363, 367, 374, 394
Davis, John W., 643, 679
Davis, Norman, 710
Davis, Richard Harding, 528, 529
Dawes, Charles G., 626, 647, 670
Dawes Act (*1887*), 418
Dawes Plan, 647
Dean, James, 842
Deane, Silas, 114
Dearborn, Gene Henry, 168, **181**, 182
Debs, Eugene V., 459, 514, 536, 575
Declaration of Independence, 106, 109, 114, 120, 122, 259, 533, 774
Declaration of Lima, 717
Declaration of Moscow, 749
Declaratory Act (*1766*), 92
Deere, John, 312
De Gaulle, Charles, 720, 738, 749, 815, 818
Degler, Carl H., 385
Deism, 252
De La Warr, Lord, 16
Delaware: colony of, 41, 120, 125; statehood of, 134
Democracy: and egalitarianism, 121–23; and contemporary politics, 823; and representative government, 63, 90–91, 101. *See also* Jacksonian democracy; Jeffersonian democracy; New Deal; Populism; Progressivism; Reform movement
Democratic party, 284, 299, 301, 325, 331–32, 333, 367, 377, 382, 394–95, 396, 487, 532, 774–75; and agrarian movement, 505; and Civil War, 347–48; and contemporary politics, 811, 823; early expansionist aims of, 301, 325; in First World War, 600, 601, 603; and immigrant support, 307; Locofoco faction of, 243; and Negro support, 700; and New Deal, 689, 697–98; origin of, 223; and Peace Democrats, 347, 361; and Progressive movement, 568, 573; in Second World War, 734, 746–47; and Southern-rights wing, 322; split of, over slavery, 323, 329; and Treaty of Versailles, 609–12; and '29 depression, 664; and Vietnam War, 827. *See also* Conservative party, Southern Democratic; Elections; Whig party
Dempsey, Jack, 644
Denmark, 429, 773; and Second World War, 719
Dependent Pension Act (*1890*), 501
Dependent Pension Bill (*1887*), 498
Depression: post-Revolutionary, 122; of *1873*, 388–89; of *1879*,

492; of *1893*, 459, 507–11; of *1907*, 554, 576; of *1929*, 662–77, 698–99, 815, 827. *See also* Hoover, Herbert C.; New Deal; Roosevelt, Franklin D.
Desegregation. *See* Civil rights; Segregation
Desert Land Act (*1877*), 426, 427
De Soto, Hernando, **6**, 7
De Voto, Bernard, 337, 701
Dewey, George, 528, 531, 557
Dewey, John, 544, 653, 654
Dewey, Thomas E., 721, 746, 747, 775, 776
Diaz, Bartholomeo, 4
Dickens, Charles, 218, 262
Dickinson, Emily, 481
Diem, Ngo Dinh, 816
Dies, Martin, 698, 783
Dillingham, William Paul, 561, 639
Dingley, Nelson, 515
Dingley Tariff (*1897*), 536, 560
Dinwiddie, Robert, 82
Diplomacy. *See* Foreign policy
Disarmament, 666; J. F. Kennedy's efforts for, 815, 818; F. D. Roosevelt's proposals for, 709–10; naval, 623–24; and outlawing war, 648. *See also* Nuclear weapons
Dix, Dorothea, 258, 260
Dixiecrats. *See* States Rights Democratic party
Dixon, Jeremiah, 42
Dixon-Yates syndicate, 802
Dodd, W. E., 603
Dodge, Grenville M., 396
Dodge, Richard I., 413, 415
Doheny, Edward L., 621, 630, 642
Dolliver, Jonathan, 566, 568
Dominican Republic, 646, 707, 809, 810, 817, 824–25. *See also* Santo Domingo
Dominion of New England, 46–48
Dongan, Thomas, 35
Donnelly, Ignatius, 506, 508, 512
Dorchester, Lord, 150
Dochester Adventurers, 22
Dorr Rebellion, 224
Dos Passos, John, 621, 636, 701, 837
Douglas, Lewis W., 681, 685
Douglas, Stephen A., 287, 291, 292, 294, 310, 341; debates between Lincoln and, 328–29, 330; and election of *1858*, 328–29; and election of *1860*, 332–33; and Kansas-Nebraska Act, 321–22; and popular sovreignty, 287, 320, 325
Douglas, William O., 747
Douglass, Frederick, 264, 398
Drake, Sir Francis, **11**, 12, 14, 276
Dred Scott case, 326–27, 328, 331
Dreiser, Theodore, 543, 837
Druids, 308
DuBois, W. E. B., 542, 617
Duke, James Buchanan, 408
Dukes Laws (*1665*), 36
Dulles, John Foster, 789, 807; and foreign policy, 791–92, 795–96, 797, 799, 800

Dumbarton Oaks Conference (*1944*), 750, 752, 764
Dumond, D. L., 334
Dunne, Finley Peter, 447
Dunkirk, 719, **721**
DuPont de Nemours, E. I., & Co., 549
Dupuy de Lôme, S. C. H. L., 527
Durkin, Martin, 791
Duse, Eleanora, 452
Dutch East India Company, 303
Dutch East Indies, 728
Dutch map of *1635*, **2**
Dutch West India Company, 35
Dylan, Bob, 843

EAC (European Advisory Commission), 749
ECA (Economic Cooperation Administration), 772
EDC (European Defense Community), 795
Eakins, Thomas, 481
Early, Jubal A., 367, 374
East India Company, 98
East Indies, 34
Eaton, Dorman B., 495
Eaton, John H., 228, 235
Eccles, Marriner S., 661, 692, 697
Economic Cooperation Administration (ECA), 772
Economy, U.S.: and capitalism, 437, 445–51; current growth and problems of, 801–03, 820–21, 829–30, 834; and desegregation, 803–05; during First World War, 598–99; Hamilton's funding policy, 144–48; and laissez faire policy, 442, 451; and national expansion, 193–219, 308–11, 316–17; and New Deal, 681; post-Korean War, 781; post-Second World War, 776, 769; during Second World War, 731–35, 769. *See also* Business; Depression; Panic
Ecuador, 810
Eddy, Mary Baker, 474
Eden, Anthony, 749, 791, 795, 798, 799
Edison, Thomas Alva, 450–51, 465
Edmunds, George, 496
Education: in colonial period, 67–68; contemporary, 475–79, 821, 824, 830; and land grants, 129, 347; post-Revolutionary, 120–21, 129; and reform movements, 248–49. *See also* Schools
Edwards, Jonathan, 65, 66, 67, 251
Egalitarianism, 121–23
Egypt, 558, 798–99; and Suez crisis of *1956*, 798–99
Einstein, Albert, 619, 756
Eisenhower, Dwight David, 673, 738, 739, 741, 751, 754, 755, 777, 784, 785, 819, 836; Administration of, **788,** 789–812; and Camp David talks, 807; career of, 789; and desegregation, 803–05; economic policy of, 801–03; foreign

policy of, 791–92, 795, 797; and Korean War, 792–94, 795; and McCarthyism, 799; on the presidency, 789, 791; and Second World War, 738, 739, 741, 753–54, 789; and U-2 incident, 808
El Salvador, 707
Election: of *1792*, 148, 156; of *1796*, 156–57; of *1800*, 164; of *1804*, 175; of *1808*, 177; of *1812*, 180; of *1816*, 196; of *1820*, 196; of *1824*, 225–26; of *1828*, 226, 228; of *1832*, 240; of *1836*, 241; of *1840*, 243–44; of *1844*, 280; of *1848*, 288; of *1852*, 294, 308; of *1856*, 308, 325; of *1858* (congressional), 328; of *1860*, 331; of *1862* (congressional), 361; of *1864*, 365–68; of *1866* (congressional), 380; of *1868*, 382; of *1872*, 387; of *1876*, 394–95, 396; of *1880*, 493; of *1884*, 496–97; of *1888*, 449, 500, 520; of *1890* (congressional), 502; of *1892*, 507; of *1894* (congressional), 511; of *1896*, 514, 515; of *1900*, 536; of *1904*, 551; of *1908*, 562; of *1910* (congressional), 568; of *1912*, 573; of *1916*, 588; of *1918* (congressional), 603; of *1920*, 621; of *1922* (congressional), 629, 643; of *1924*, 638, 642; of *1928*, 654; of *1932*, 674, 676; of *1934* (congressional), 689; of *1936*, 693; of *1940*, 721; of *1944*, 747; of *1946* (congressional) 769, 773, 774; of *1948*, 774; of *1950* (congressional), 784; of *1952*, 784; of *1956*, 806; of *1958* (congressional), 806; of *1960*, 810; of *1962* (congressional), 820; of *1964*, 823–24
Electoral College, 135, 156–57
Eliot, Charles W., 477, 533
Eliot, T. S., 652, 653
Elizabeth I (queen of England), 8, 9, 10, 12, 14, 21
Ellsworth, Oliver, 127, 161
Ely, Richard T., 545
Emancipation Proclamation, 359, 360, 366
Embargo, 712, 713, 714
Embargo Act (*1807*), 177
Emergency Committee for Employment (*1930*), 664
Emergency Price Control Act (*1941*), 733
Emergency Tariff Act (*1921*), 626
Emerson, Ralph Waldo, 203, 253, 257, 262, 293, 299, 309, 374; on Lincoln, 368; on man, 254
Employers' Liability Act (*1906*), 552
Employment Act (*1946*), 769
English, William H., 494
Episcopal Church, 256, 341, 475. *See also* Anglican Church; Church of England
Equal Employment Opportunity Commission, 823

Ericsson, Leif, 3, 4
Erie Canal, **192,** 205, 206, 215, 309, 310
Erie Railroad, 310, 440, 441, 444, 445
Erosion, **687**
Erskine, David, 177–78
Espionage Act (*1917*), 600
"Essex Junto," 174
Estaing, comte d', 116, 117
Estonia, 719
Ethiopia, 522, 712–13
European Advisory Commission (EAC), 749
European Common Market, 818
European Defense Community (EDC), 795
European-recovery program, 772
Evans, Madgar, 822
Evans, Oliver, 216
Ewing, Oscar, 776
Executive, 127, 134, 135, 141–42, 575. *See also* President, U.S.
Exploration: of the New World, 4–8, 10–11; of U.S., **171,** 173. *See also* individual countries
Export-Import Bank, 707, 765

FBI. *See* Federal Bureau of Investigation
FCC (Federal Communications Commission), 835
FEPC. *See* Fair Employment Practices Commission
FPC. *See* Federal Power Commission
FTC. *See* Federal Trade Commission
Factory. *See* Industry
Fair Deal, 768–69, 776–77
Fair Employment Practices Commission (FEPC), 734, 768, 774, 776
Fair Labor Standards Act (*1938*), 697
Fairbanks, Charles W., 551
Fall, Albert B., 629, 630
Fallen Timbers, Battle of, 152
Far East, 532, **561,** 623, 624, 742, 764, 750, 751, 755, **793,** 794–95; and Second World War, 727–28, 735, 742–46, 751
Farley, James, 722
Farm Bureau Federation, 679, 683
Farm Security Administration, 697, 746
Farmer-Labor party, 643
Farmers' Alliance, 504–05
Farmers' Holiday Association, 672, 683
Farmers' Union, 504
Farragut, David Glasgow, 354, 367
Farrell, James T., 837
Fascism, 648, 666, 698, 713
Faubus, Orval, 805
Fauchet, Jean, 152
Faulkner, William, 652, 837
Federal Bureau of Investigation (FBI), 619, 782, 801

Hague Conference (*1907*), 711, 791
Haiti, 519, 522, 579, 646, 666, 707, **809**
Hakluyt, Richard, 12, 13, 31, 34
Hale, Eugene, 532
Hale, John P., 294
Half-Breeds, 393, 487, 491, 494
Halleck, Henry Wager, 352, 353, 354, 356
Halpin, Marie, 497
Hals, Frans, 34
Hamilton, Alexander, 141, 142, 143, 151, 156, 160, 163, 215; and assumption of states' debts, 145–46; and Burr, 174–75; at Constitutional Convention, 133, 138; economic policy of, 146–48, 168, 169; and French Revolution, 150; funding plan of, 144–46; and national bank, 147–48; on society, 148
Hamilton, M. A., 665
Hammarskjöld, Dag, 816
Hammer v. Dagenhart, 628
Hammett, Dashiell, 800
Hammond, George, 149, 151
Hammond, James H., 269
Hampton, Wade, 398, 399
Hancock, John, 137
Hancock, Winfield Scott, 416, 494
Hand, Learned, 800
Hanna, Marcus Alonzo, 490, 512, 514, 515, 536, 547, 549, 550
Hanover, House of, 84, 90, 105
Hanson, Ole, 618
Harding, Warren G., 612, 621, 622, 633; Administration of, 622–31, 700; and agriculture, 626, 628; and business, 625–27; and imperialism, 623; and labor, 627; scandals of, 628–31; and tariff, 626; and taxation, 625, 626; and Washington Conference, 623–25; and World Court, 648
Hardwick, Thomas W., 618
Hariot, Thomas, 12, 14
Harlan, John Marshall, 399
Harmar, Josiah, 150, **152**
Harper's Ferry: Battle of, 359; John Brown's raid at, 329–30
Harriman, E. H., 549
Harriman, W. Averell, 820
Harrington, James, 38, 90
Harrington, Michael, 821
Harris, Joel Chandler, 404–05
Harris, Townsend, 304
Harrison, Benjamin, 487, 507; Administration of, 500–02, 520, 523, 524
Harrison, William Henry, 241, 244, 245, 500; and Indian war, 179, 180, 181, 184
Hartford Convention, 186
Harvard, John, 68
Harvey, George, 621
Harvey, William H., 512
Haugen, Gilbert N., 654
Havana Conference (*1928*), 707
Hawaii, 519, 556, 560; and annexation, 299, 302, 424–25, 531;

bombing of, 728, 731; and Second World War, 743; statehood of, 811
Hawley-Smoot tariff (*1930*), 660, 662
Hawthorne, Nathaniel, 253, **255,** 263, 299, 840
Hay, John, 528, 531, 532, 534–35
Hay-Pauncefote Treaty (*1901*), 558
Hayes, Rutherford B., 394; Administration of, 395–400, 491–94, 520; Cabinet of, 396, 491; career of, 394; monetary policies of, 492; and segregation, 398; and Southern rehabilitation, 395–97
Haymarket riot, 457, 482, 513
Hayne, Robert Y., 235, 236, 237
Hays, Arthur Garfield, 642
Hays, Will, 601, 621
Head Start program, 830
Hearst, W. R., 477, 526
Hegel, Georg W. F., 253
Hemingway, Ernest, 652, 837
Henderson, Leon, 733
Hendrick, Burton J., 544
Hendricks, Thomas A., 394, 496
Henri, Robert, 543
Henry VII (king of England), 7, 8
Henry VIII (king of England), 8–9
Henry, Patrick, 91, 94, 98, 136, 138, 141
Henry Street Settlement, 472
Hepburn Act, 552
Herbart, Johann Friedrich, 475
Herter, Christian A., 807, 808
Higginson, Thomas W., 472
Highway Beautification Act (*1965*), 824
Hill, David B., 500
Hill, Isaac, 228, 230
Hill, James J., 429, 440–41, 445, 549
Hillman, Sidney, 747
Hillsborough, Lord, 96, 97, 99
Himmler, Heinrich, 749
"Hippies," 843–44
Hipsters, 842
Hiss, Alger, 782, 785
Hitchcock, Gilbert, 610, 611
Hitler, Adolf, 669, 705, **706,** 716, 717, 718, 719, 726, 735, 739, 741, 749, 755, 827
Ho Chi Minh, 794, 816
Hoar, George F., 532, 533
Hobart, Garret A., 512
Hobbema, Meindert, 34
Hofstadter, Richard, 463
Holbrook, Josiah, 261
Holding Company Act, 694
Holland, 120; control of seas, 34; exploration of New World, 8; financial assistance from, 127; mercantilism of, 34; and settlement of New York, 35; war between England and, 34. *See also* Netherlands
Holman, William S., 499
Holmes, Oliver Wendell, Jr., 544, 549, 618

Holy See, 474
Home Owners' Loan Act, 686
Homer, Winslow, 345, 481
Homestead Act (*1862*), 288, 322, 347, 374, 407, 425–26, 429
Homestead strike, 446, 459
Honduras, 569
Hooch, Pieter de, 34
Hood, John B., 367, 368
Hooker, Joseph, 361, 362, 363
Hooker, Thomas, 25
Hoover, Herbert C., 621, 625, 629–30, 637–38, 648*n*, 651, 655, 693, 719; Administration of, 658–77, 700; and bank crisis, 661, 663, 665, 667, 670–71; and business, 659–62; and depression, 662–66; early career of, 637–38; and employment service, 664; and farmers, 659–60; and Japanese aggression, 668–69; and moratorium on war debts, 667; and public works, 671
Hopkins, Harry L., 472, 686, 697, 726, 746, 762
Hopkins, Samuel, 67
Horseshoe Bend, Battle of, 184
House, Edward M., 574, 575, 586, 601, 603, 604, 610, 705
House of Burgesses, 56, 74, 91, 94
House of Commons, 17, 63, 70, 85
House of Lords, 63, 71, 85
House of Representatives, 42; structure and powers of, 135, 136
House Un-American Activities Committee, 698
Housing and Development Act (*1965*), 824
Houston, Sam, 275
Howe, Elias, 314
Howe, Richard, 111
Howe, William, 103, 111, 112, 116
Howells, William Dean, 468, 470, 481, 482–83, 533
Hudson, Henry, 8
Hudson's Bay Company, 75, 276
Huerta, Victoriano, 580, 581
Hughes, Charles Evans, 562, 588, 619, 621, 624, 625, 629, 638, 645, 647, 648, 691, 694
Huguenots, French, 38
Hull, Cordell, 681, 706, 707, 710, 714, 718, 727, 728, 748, 749
Hull, William, 182
Hull House, 472
Humanitarianism. *See* Reform movement
Humphrey, George, 790, 799
Humphrey, Hubert H., 824
Hungary, 618, 623, 751, 764, 799
Hunter, Robert, 543
Huntington, Collis P., 439, 440
Hurley, Patrick, 768
Hutchinson, Anne, 24–25
Hutchinson, Thomas, 96, 99, 100, 101
Huxley, Thomas, 478
Huygens, Christian, 34
Hyde, Arthur M., 659, 672
Hyde, Edward, 38

ICC. *See* Interstate Commerce Commission
IWW (Industrial Workers of the World), 600
Iceland, 3, 726, 773
Ickes, Harold L., 681, 684, 726, 770
Idaho, statehood of, **421**, 508
Idaho Power Company, 802
Ikeda, Hayato, 815
Illinois, statehood of, 193, **194**, 203
Illinois Central Railroad, 310
Immigration, 19, 25, 35, 60, 203–04, 294, 303, 305–08, 429, 540, 541, 700; and cities, 466–67, 471, 472, 539, 540; and labor, 203, 305, 307, 456–57, 540; in mid-20th century, 828; and nativist reaction, 307–08, 323, 492, 560, 568, 578, 587, 618, 619, 620, 639; restriction of, 492, 601, 620, 639, 783*n*, 824. *See also* Frontier
Immigration and Nationality Act (*1952*), 783
Imperialism, American: early expansionist aims of, 299, 519; and Cuba, 299–301, 519; and Far East, 520, 534–35, 560–62; and Hawaii, 302, 524–25, 531; humanitarian elements in, 521, 531; jingoist, 522–23, 527–28; and Latin America, 301–02, 558, 646; and Open Door policy, 534, 535, 559, 562; and Philippines, 532–44. *See also* Frontier; Manifest Destiny; Mexican War; Spanish-American War
Imperialism, European: in American colonial period, 31, 42–50, 81, 84–85, 87–88; in Asia and Africa, 522, 524, 557, 558, 668–69, 712, 715; in Latin America, 557; and Second World War, 727–28, 735, 742–43, 745–46, 751–52
Incas, 5, 6
Income tax, 347, 387, 510, 571, 575, 601, 626; declared unconstitutional, 511; negative, 831
Independence, American, 106, 109–20. *See also* Declaration of Independence; Revolutionary War
Independent party, 403
Independent Treasury Act (*1840*), 243, 244
India, 4, 84, 558, 743, 797, 815
Indiana, statehood of, 193, **194,** 203
Indians, American, 321, 413–18; and Albany Congress plan, 81, 82, 93, 100, 104, 124; collapse of confederation of, 188; and colonialist wars, 72–74; Eastern tribes, **73;** and Europeans, 5–7; government and organization of, 3; in Northwest territory, 128, 183, 416; and Proclamation of *1763*, 88, 97, **98;** and removal policy of Jackson, 232; in Revolution, 114; in War of *1812*, 184; wars of, 150, 152, 416–18. *See also* individual tribes

Indochina, 522, 728, 794–95, 796, 797. *See also* Laos; Vietnam War
Indonesia, 797
Industrial League, 501
Industrial Revolution, 213–14, 217, 257, 315. *See also* Agriculture; Business; Industry; Technology
Industrial Workers of the World (IWW), 600
Industry, 437–60, 539, 615, 684–85, 690; consolidation of, 445; and factory system, 214–19, 313–15, 456, 550; and labor, 214, 455–56, 695–96; mass production techniques in, 456, 634–37, 829, 833; and natural resources, 437; regulation of, 442–44, 550, 552, 574, 577, 627. *See also* Business; Trusts
Ingersoll, Robert G., 836
Inland Waterways Commission, 553
Inquisition, Spanish, 9
Insular cases, 556
Intellectuals: and analysis of society, 837; and New Deal, 701; political role of, 533; protest of, 544–45. *See also* Art; Literature
Inter-American Conference (*1961*), 717, 817
Intermediate Credit Banks, 629
Internal Security Act (*1950*), 783
International Atomic Development Authority, 766
International Bank for Reconstruction and Development, 750, 765
International Conference of American States: *7th*, 707; *8th*, 707; *9th*, 717
International Information Administration, 800
International Labor Organization, 765
International Military Tribunal, 763
International Monetary Fund, 750, 765
International Red Cross, 749
International Trade Organization, 765
International War Crimes Tribunal, 764
Internationalism, 558–62, 580–82, 621, 623–25, 647–49, 706, 711, 721, 731, 744
Interstate Commerce Act (*1887*), 443, 444, 449, 498
Interstate Commerce Commission (ICC), 443, 444, 552, 567, 615–16
Intolerable Acts (*1774*), 98–100, 101, 102, 114
Ionesco, Eugène, 840
Iowa, statehood of, **281**
Iran, 767
Iraq, 798
Ireland, 35, 60, 97, 305–06, 429, 607
Irish Pioneer Emigration Fund, 306
Iron Curtain, 767, 770

Iroquois Indians, **73,** 76, 81, 97
Irving, Washington, 299
Isabella (queen of Spain), 4, 9
Ishii, Kikujiro, 609
Isolationism, 519–20, 531–36, 648, 770; demise of, 725; post-First World War, 621, 649, 705; pre-Second World War, 709, 711, 715, 717, 719, 721, 725, 731
Israel, 798–99
Italy, 534, 557, 628, 660; in First World War, 594, 604, 606, 609, 719; and invasion of Ethiopia, 712–13; in Second World War, 731, 739, 749, 764, 773; and Washington Conference, 623–25

Jackson, Andrew, 223, 225, 226, 228; Administration of, 229–43, 244, 246; and annexation of Texas, 275; and Bank of United States, 237–41; career of, 229; censure of, 240; and civil service, 225, 229, 230; and constitutional interpretation, 229; and Democratic party, 231; fiscal policy of, 233, 242–43; and Florida, 188–89; force bill of, 236; Indian policy of, 232; and Indian wars, 184; and internal improvements, 232, 242; and nullification, 234, 235–36; and tariff, 233; and War of *1812*, 180, 184, 186
Jackson, Clairborne, 342–43
Jackson, Ed, 640
Jackson, Patrick Tracy, 216
Jackson, Robert H., 695, 842
Jackson, Thomas J., 355, 356, 359, 361
Jacksonian democracy, 223–25, 229–31, 260, 281
Jacobs, Paul, 843
Jamaica, 32
James I (king of England), 14, 16, 18, 19, 21, 27
James II (king of England), 32, 34, 35, 36, 39, 41, 42, 43, 46, 48, 90
James, Henry, 481, 483
James, Marquis, 701
James, William, 533, 544
Jamestown, 14–15, 53
Japan, 522, 533, 534, 559, 561–62, 569, 579, 589, 666, 668, 714–15, 745, 750, 752, 756, 757, 770, 815; in First World War, 604, 605, 609; invasion of Manchuria by, 668–69; occupation of Korea by, 558, 560; and Russo-Japanese War, 560; in Second World War, 705, 735, 745, 763, 764, 767, 791, 808; and U.S. trade, 303–04, 562, 569; and Washington Conference, 623–25, 648
Jay, John, 120, 127, 130, 134, 138, 151, 152, 492
Jay's Treaty (*1795*), 152, 155, 159, 160, 176
Jazz Age, 651–53
Jefferson, Thomas, 94, 101, 120, 126, 127, 128, 132, 133, 134, 141,

New Haven, colony of, 25
New Haven Railroad, 549
New Jersey, colony of, 36–37, 62, 125; in Dominion of New England, 46–48
New Mexico, 285, 288, 289, 293, 321, **323;** statehood of, 567
New Nationalism, 568, 570, 574, 681
New Orleans, Battle of, 184, **185**
New York: colony of, **30,** 35–36; in *1888,* **462;** in Dominion of New England, 46–48
New York Central Railroad, 310, 441, 444
New York Stock Exchange, 451, 508, **632,** 650; and market crash of *1929,* 660–61
New Zealand, 605, 797
Newfoundland, 8, 11, 12, 27, 188; naval bases in, 722
Newlands Act (*1902*), 553
Newspapers, 67, 154, 163, 261, 477, 526, 644, 645, 835. *See also* Press
Newton, Sir Isaac, 68–69, 70
Newton, R. Huber, 475
Nez Percé Indians, 418
Niagara movement, 542
Nicaragua, 302, 558, 569, 579, 646
Nicholls, Francis R. T., 399
Nicholson, Francis, 48
Nicolls, Richard, 35, 36
Niebuhr, Reinhold, 531, 840–41
Nimitz, Chester, 744, 745, 751
Nine Power Treaty, 624, 668, 714, 715
Nisei, 734
Nixon, Richard, 785–86, 797, 799, 800, 801, 807, 808, 810, 811
Nkrumah, Kwame, 815
Nobel Prize: for literature, 637; for peace, 560
Nomura, Kichisaburo, 728
Nonintercourse Act (*1809*), 177–78
Non-Resistance Society, 262
Normandy, D-Day in, **730**
Norris, Frank, 543
Norris, George W., 566, 626, 627, 638, 654, 687, 725
Norsemen, 3, 7
North, Lord, 96–97, 98–99, 101, 102, 104
North Africa, 749, **797**
North African Front, 737, 738–39
North Atlantic Treaty Organization (NATO), 773, 781, 789, 795, 797
North Carolina, colony of, 12, 27, 37–39, 43, 97, 105
North Dakota, statehood of, **421,** 505
Northern Pacific Railroad, 386, 429, 439, 440, 444, 445, 549
Northern Securities Company, 549
Northwest Ordinance (*1787*), 129, 134
Northwest Territory, 127–29, 287
Norway, 429, 597, 719, 773
Nova Scotia, 3, 7–8, 27, 75, 76, 83
Nuclear weapons, 778, 795, 815; challenge of, 766; end of U.S.

monopoly of, 777–78; debate on use in Second World War, 756–57; testing of, **766,** 807, 818, 819–20
Nullification, 162, 234–37, 295
Nürnberg trials, 763–64
Nye, Gerald P., 711, 717

OAS (Organization of American States), 825
OEEC (Organization for European Economic Cooperation), 772
OPA. *See* Office of Price Administration
OPM. *See* Office of Production Management
Oberlin College, 260
Ocala Demands, 505
Odría, Manuel, **809,** 810
Office of Economic Opportunity, 830
Office of Economic Stabilization, 733
Office of Price Administration (OPA), 733, 734, 735, 769
Office of Production Management (OPM), 724, 731
Office of Scientific Research and Development, 732
Office of War Information, 734
Office of War Mobilization, 733
Oglethorpe, James, 76–77
Ohio, statehood of, 170, 203
Ohio Company, 82, 97, 125, 128
"Okies," 700
Oklahoma, statehood of, 430, **567**
Old State House, **140**
Olin-Mathieson Corporation, 92
Oliver, Andrew, 92
Oliver, James, 432
Olmsted, Frederick L., 480
Olney, Richard, 459, 510, 524
Ong, Walter J., 844
Onís, Luis de, 189
Open Door policy, 534–35, 559, 560, 579, 609, 624
Opium War, 303
Oppenheimer, J. Robert, 756, 800
Order of the Star Spangled Banner, 308
Order of United Americans, 308
Ordinance of *1787,* 287
Oregon, acquisition of, 247, 281–83, 287; settlement of, 276–78; statehood of, 335
Oregon Trail, 277, 278
Organization of American States (OAS), 825
Organization for European Economic Cooperation (OEEC), 772
O'Riley, Peter, 420
Orlando, Vittorio, 604
Osceola, Chief, 232
Ostend Manifesto (*1854*), 301, 325
Ostrogorski, M. I., 437
Oswald, Lee Harvey, 823
Otis, Harrison Gray, 186
Otis, James, 93, 94

Ottawa Indians, 88
Overman, Lee S., 598
Owen, Robert, 262

PWA. *See* Public Works Administration
Pacific Fur Company, 276
Packard, Vance, 837
Packers and Stockyards Act (*1921*), 629
Paine, Thomas, 105, 132, 153, 252, 800
Pakenham, Sir Edward, 184
Pakenham, Richard, 282
Pakistan, 797
Palmer, A. Mitchell, 616, 618, 619, 622
Palmer, Potter, 470
Palmer raids, 618–19
Palmerston, Lord, 358
Pamunkey Indians, 74
Panama, 301, 302, 558, 623, 824
Panama Canal, 558, 579, 824
Panama Treaties (*1936*), 707
Pan-American Conference (*1928*), 646
Pan-American pact, 580
Pan-American Union, 523
Panay, 716
Panic: of *1819,* 203, 218–19; of *1833,* 241; of *1837,* 241, 243; of *1857,* 327–28, 444; of *1873,* 388–89, 429, 438, 444, 499; of *1893,* 441, 444, 508; of *1901,* 549; of *1907,* 554, 576; of *1929,* 660–61, 665; of *1931* (European), 665, 667. *See also* Depression
"Paragon," **206**
Paraguay, 808, **809**
Paris Conference, 604–12
Parker, Alton B., 551–52
Parker, Peter, 110
Parker, Theodore, 251, 253, 266, 299
Parties, political, origin of, 153–54, 487–88
Paterson, William, 134
Pathet Lao, 815
Patrons of Husbandry, 404
Patten, Simon, 545
Patton, George, 673, 741
"Paxton Boys," 88
Payne, Sereno, 566
Peabody, Elizabeth, 253
Peace Corps, 816, 842
Peace Democrats, 347, 361
Peace movement, 262
Peace of Paris, 86
Peace of Ryswick (*1697*), 76
Peacock, Alexander R., 446
Peale, Norman Vincent, 836, 841
Pearl Harbor, **704,** 728, 731, 734, 735, 743
Peek, George N., 681
Pemberton, John C., 361, 362
Pendergast machine, 761
Pendleton, George H., 495
Pendleton Act. *See* Civil Service Reform Act
Penn, William: holy experiment

593, 602, 603; foreign policy of, 557–62; and Monroe Doctrine, 558; "new nationalism" of, 568, 570, 574; and Old Guard, 549, 551, 552, 553; and Progressive party, 571–72, 588; revolt of, from Taft, 569–70; on rights of labor, 554; and Spanish-American War, 526, 528, 530, 531; Square Deal of, 550

Root, Elihu, 548, 550, 555, 604, 621, 711

Root, John Wellborn, 480

Root-Takahira Agreement (1908), 562

Rosecrams, William S., 361, 364

"Rough Riders," 530, 547

Rovere, Richard, 783

Roxbury settlement, 22

Ruffin, Edmund, 331

Rumania, 751, 753, 764

Rural Electrification Administration, 700

Rush, Richard, 188, 200

Rush-Bagot Agreement (1817), 188

Rusk, Dean, 815

Russell, Lord John, 357

Russell, Jonathan, 187

Russell, W. Green, 420

Russell, William Howard, 348

Russia, 187, 276, 534, 559, 618, 619, 623, 668; alliance of, with China, 533; and Bolshevik Revolution, 594, 602, 604; and First World War, 582, 589, 594, 596, 604; and Menshevik revolution, 589–90; purchase of Alaska from, 519; war between Japan and, 560. See also Soviet Union

Russo-Japanese War, 560, 735

Ruth, Babe, 644

Rutledge, Edward, 111

Ryan, John A., 543, 672

Ryder, Albert Pinkham, 481

SAC (Strategic Air Command), 777

SEATO. See Southeast Asia Treaty Organization

SDS. See Students for a Democratic Society

SEC (Securities and Exchange Commission), 815

Sabotage Act (1918), 600

Sac Indians, 232

Sacco, Nicola, 620–21

Sagadahoc settlement, 15, 19

St. Augustine, 7

St. Clair, Arthur, 150, 152

Saint-Gaudens, Augustus, 481

Salem colony, 24

Salinger, J. D., 837

Salisbury, Lord, 524

Salt Lake City, 279, 280

Salvation Army, 474

Samoan incident, 519, 520, 523

Sampson, William T., 530, 531

San Jacinto, Battle of, 275

San Juan Hill, Battle of, 530

Sandburg, Carl, 543, 701

Sandys, Sir Edwin, 17, 18

Sankey, Ira D., 474

Santa Anna, Antonio Lopez de, 274–75, 276, 285, 302

Santa Fe Mission, 272

Santa Fe Railway, 439, 440

Santa Fe Trail, 275–76, 277

Santo Domingo, 558, 579; naval bases in, 519, 522. See also Dominican Republic

Saratoga, Battle of, 113, 114, 116

Sargeant, John, 240

Satellite countries. See Soviet bloc

Satellites, space, 795

Savannah, 52

Scalawags, 384, 390

Schine, G. David, 800, 801

Schofield, Arthur, 215

Schofield, John, 215

Schools, 129, 260–61; desegregation of, 803–05, 831; and land grants, 129, 347; and libraries, 476; parochial, 476; public, 475–79, 821, 824, 830; universities, 68, 347, 477–79, 834

Schurz, Carl, 387, 398, 491, 496, 498, 533

Schwab, Charles M., 446, 447

Scopes trial, 642

Scotland, 35, 49, 597

Scott, Dred, case, 326–27, 328, 331

Scott, Thomas A., 396, 439, 446

Scott, Winfield, 181, 183, 285, 294, 338, 350, 351, 352

"Sea Dogs," 9, 74

Seattle Central Labor Council, 618

Secession, Southern, 293, 332, 334–38; and attempts at compromise, 336; and border states, 335–36, 341, 342, 343, 358; and Civil War, 337. See also Confederacy; Nullification; State rights

Second World War, 718–21, 815; aggressions leading to, 718; allied victory of, 753–57; Asian front during, 727–28, 735, 742–46; casualties of, 731, 757; conferences of, 748–53, 756; European front during, 719–22, 724–25, 745, 739, 740, 741, 751; home front during, 733–34; national awakening toward, 715–16; North African front during, 738–39; peace treaties, 763–64; and Pearl Harbor, 704, 728, 731, 734, 735, 743; planning after, 750–51; price controls during, 733, 734, 735; supply lines during, 736–37

Securities Act (1933), 690

Securities and Exchange Commission (SEC), 815

Securities Exchange Act, 690

Sedition Act: of 1798, 162, 168; of 1918, 600

Segregation, 397–98, 399, 416, 476, 541, 556, 560, 578, 734, 776, 803–05, 821. See also Civil rights; Negroes

Seldes, Gilbert, 835, 837

Selective Service Act: of 1917, 593–94, 600, 601; of 1940, 723

Seminole Indians, 188, 232

Senate, U.S., 42; direct election to, 571, 571n; structure and powers of, 135, 136

Separation of powers, 134, 135

Separatists, 20, 24

Servicemen's Readjustment Act (1944), 769

Seven Days' Battle, 356

Sevier, John, 130

Sewall, Arthur, 513

Sewall, Samuel, 47

Seward, William H., 292, 322, 333, 338, 359, 382, 519, 522, 524

Seymour, Horatio, 348, 382

Shafter, William R., 530

Shakers, 262

Shakespeare, William, 838

Shannon, Wilson, 324

Sharecropping, 405–06, 697, 699

Shaw, George Bernard, 482

Shay's Rebellion, 133

Sheen, Fulton J., 836

Shelly v. Kraemer, 803

Shenandoah Valley, Battle of, 367

Sheridan, Philip H., 346, 367, 382, 416, 417

Sherman, John, 389, 437, 449, 489, 493, 494, 525, 533

Sherman, William T., 346, 361, 364, 367, 368, 369, 416, 417, 437

Sherman Antitrust Act (1890), 449, 459, 501, 569, 577, 683

Sherman Silver Purchase Act (1890), 501, 508; repeal of, 512

Sherman's march, 367, 368, 374

Shiloh, Battle of, 353

Shirley, William, 83

Sholes, Christopher L., 450

Short, William, 123

Shotwell, James T., 648

Shreve, Henry M., 215

Siberia, 560, 604, 624

Sicily, 739

Sidney, Algernon, 90

Siegfried line, 751, 753

Sierras, 436

Silesia, 607–08

Silliman, Benjamin, 217

Silver issue, 493, 501, 507–09, 512–13; and election of 1900, 536

Silverites, 511, 536

Simon, John, 710

Simpson, Jerry, 506

Sims, William S., 556, 597

Sinclair, Harry F., 621, 630

Sinclair, Upton, 543, 553, 636

Singer, Isaac, 314

Single-Taxers, 505, 514

Sino-Japanese War, 714–15

Sino-Soviet Pact (1945), 767

Sioux Indians, 415

Sioux War: of 1865–67, 416; of 1876, 417

Sipuel v. University of Oklahoma, 803

Sitting Bull, Chief, 417–18

Slater, Samuel, 215, 216

Slavery: and abolitionism, 263–66; and Civil War, 358–59; and

E 1
F 2
G 3
H 4
I 5
J 6
7